THEY CAME FROM BURGUNDY

THEY CAME FROM BURGUNDY

A study of the Bourgogne escape line

KEITH JANES

Matador
9 Priory Business Park,
Wistow Road, Kibworth Beauchamp,
Leicestershire. LE8 0RX
Tel: 0116 279 2299
Email: books@troubador.co.uk
Web: www.troubador.co.uk/matador
Twitter: @matadorbooks

ISBN 978 1788036 474

British Library Cataloguing in Publication Data.
A catalogue record for this book is available from the British Library.

Printed and bound in the UK by TJ International, Padstow, Cornwall
Typeset in 11pt Aldine401 BT by Troubador Publishing Ltd, Leicester, UK

Matador is an imprint of Troubador Publishing Ltd

For Patches – who watched over every word

Contents

Of the three major escape lines running through France during the Second World War – the Pat O'Leary line, which covered most of the country, the Comete line, which ran from Holland and Belgium through France to the Pyrenees, and Bourgogne – Bourgogne is the least well known.

"It would not be superfluous here to state that the organisation was remarkably successful and responsible for the safe evacuation of two or three hundred Allied evaders. It was at the same time brilliantly conceived and minutely organised, so that it achieved splendid results whilst protecting in a remarkable way the security of its agents. Its story is in a broad sense the story of any successful evasion line."[1]

---

1   NARA Bourgogne

Introduction

Escape lines – which should more properly be called evasion lines – can be described as organisations which helped stranded servicemen make their way from enemy occupied territories back to friendly territory – in this case, generally the UK. People who worked on the escape lines are simply known as helpers. Escape lines varied a lot – some comprised of small groups of local people who worked together to help any stranded serviceman who came their way, while others were sufficiently organised to have contacts over a wider area who could bring (say) downed airmen from much further afield. The ultimate escape lines of course were those that not only gathered and sheltered the servicemen but were also able to pass them, mostly via neutral territories, back to England. The servicemen themselves may have been escapers – men who had been captured but subsequently escaped – or (the vast majority) evaders, those who had never been captured – the difference being of purely academic interest to the helpers at the time. By the summer of 1944, the various escape lines in western Europe had helped some 1,800 Allied servicemen return safely to England, including about 700 American aircrew.

Escape lines are a largely unrecognised, or at least often overlooked, episode of the Second World War. For those who were involved, the helpers (mostly French, Belgian and Dutch civilians) or benefitted from them (mostly British, Commonwealth and American servicemen) this was a personal war, and it was, and remains, almost unknown to the outside world, despite the tragic loss of so many of those concerned. To the families of the servicemen saved, it must have seemed like a miracle to have their loved ones returned safely to them. For the helpers and their families who were caught, it often meant death.

The combination of circumstances necessary for such organisations to be created was a result of the unusual situation of the Second World War in Europe. Countries occupied by an oppressive enemy (in this case, Nazi Germany) but with a sympathetic and increasingly active resistance, together with a friendly nation (Great Britain) within reach, provided the possibilities – and the existence of numerous escapers and evaders –

augmented by ever increasing numbers of downed aircrew – provided the inspiration and motivation.

It should be noted that similar circumstances also existed in the Balkans and Greece, and later in Denmark (where Allied aircrew were taken to neutral Sweden) and other areas but this study will concentrate on France. The first escape line of the War – the organisation which evolved to become the Pat O'Leary line – was originally created by the men left behind in France and Belgium after Dunkirk – and more especially, the surrender of the Highland 51st Division at St Valery-en-Caux – in June 1940. Literally hundreds of British soldiers were helped by local French and Belgian sympathisers, first to evade capture (or recapture) and then to make their way to the relative safety of unoccupied France. The idea was that from southern France, particularly from France's second city, Marseille, they would be able to make their way back to the UK via boat to North Africa or across the Pyrenees to neutral (technically, non-belligerent) Spain and Gibraltar. This turned out to be harder than first anticipated but eventually a system was established, later with direct assistance from the UK, and from as early as July 1940, men began to return in ever larger numbers.

The Comete line was the result of a group of Belgian friends who also wanted to help, firstly stranded soldiers and then the increasing numbers of downed airmen landing in their country. Comete took evaders from Belgium, through France to the Spanish border near St Jean de Luz from September 1941 onwards.

Bourgogne was different. While the Pat line and Comete were created in occupied Europe and later supported by the British MI9, Bourgogne was one of a number of networks established by the French BCRA in London. Each prospective BCRA line was to be headed by an agent especially trained in England before being sent into France. These were intended to be professional organisations, run on a semi-military system with all the associated security that implics. Of all the BCRA escape lines, Bourgogne was by far the most successful. To put Bourgogne's contribution into some sort of context, in the period September 1941 to June 1944, Comete helped some 290 military evaders to cross the Pyrenees – Bourgogne helped a similar number of Allied servicemen escape to Spain in just fifteen months.

As already mentioned, the Pat line can trace its origins back to the summer of 1940, and Comete to 1941. By the time Bourgogne began in early 1943, the situation in France had changed radically. The Germans had taken over southern France (previously unoccupied, Vichy France) following the Allied landings in North Africa in November 1942, resistance to the occupiers generally had become more active – and ever increasing numbers of downed aircrew were arriving.

In the summer of 1942, while most evaders were having to walk across the Pyrenees, the Pat line had also arranged for a number of men to be collected by boat from the French Mediterranean coast and delivered directly to Gibraltar. Those sea evacuations, together with a number of fishing vessels arriving in England from Brittany (some with military evaders on board, some not) inspired MI9 in London to look at ways to bring more men back from France by sea, using Royal Navy gunboats to make the return trip across the Channel in a single night. Two agents, Val Williams, who had been picked up from the beach at Canet Plage himself, and Ray Labrosse, a young French-Canadian army radio-operator, were despatched to France to set up the Oaktree escape line.

The Oaktree mission was intended to build on contacts established in Brittany by Louis Nouveau of the Pat line but events conspired against its success. Firstly, the delayed arrival in France of Williams and Labrosse. They were meant to arrive in January 1943 but bad weather prevented them from landing by Lysander and it wasn't until 20 March that they were finally dropped by parachute over the Foret de Rambouillet. Meanwhile, the Pat line in Paris, where Nouveau was then based, had been penetrated by the French traitor and German infiltration agent Roger Leveneu, resulting in the arrest of Nouveau at Tours in February – news of which failed to reach London in time. Bad luck continued to dog the two Oaktree agents with one of their bicycles and both radios being damaged beyond repair in the drop but by the end of April they were ready to evacuate their first group of evaders. However, a lack of reliable radio communication (they used another circuit's radio-operator to contact London) and the rapidly shortening nights, meant that on 29 May, they received a radio message from London postponing the proposed cross-Channel MGB trips indefinitely. The evaders collected by Oaktree would have to be despatched to the Pyrenees after all.

Twelve days after Georges Broussine landed in France to establish Bourgogne, the Pat line was virtually destroyed following the capture of Pat O'Leary (and others) in Toulouse at the hands of Roger Leneveu. Two days after that, the heads of the Pat line operation in Paris were arrested. The Comete line was also under attack – Andree De Jongh had been captured at Urrugne in January and while Antoine d'Ursel and Fernando Radelet were rebuilding the organisation, Jacques Desoubrie (see later) was just one of the enemy agents working to dismantle it.

Author's Note

Bourgogne (or Burgundy) is the administration region in east-central France where the wine, for which the organisation is named, comes from. It should not to be confused with the commune of Bourgogne (Marne) in the Champagne-Ardenne region.

I should warn the reader now that this study is heavy on information but light on the narrative necessary to make for easy reading – and if this sounds like an apology in advance, then I suppose it is. Although I have produced one book before (*Conscript Heroes*) that was more an exercise in editing rather than any original input on my part – my creative writing being limited to the articles that appear on my website, generally a few thousand words at most. In this case, a narrative would be useful to explain the context of the various situations in which the helpers and evaders found themselves but since I wasn't there, nor even born in that era, I don't feel it appropriate to overlay my opinions on the storyline and would rather leave it to the reader to try and imagine the often harsh reality behind each event. The involvement of so many other organisations (as well as the inevitable vagaries of escape and evasion in an occupied country) makes an easily comprehensible storyline almost impossible to write, so the individual evader stories – which make up the bulk of the content – are grouped roughly in the order they left Paris for the Pyrenees. Generally, once in the hands of Bourgogne, the evaders were moved out of the French capital fairly quickly, although many of them may have evaded for weeks, or even months, before beginning the final stages of their return to the UK.

This story should primarily be about the helpers who made the line possible but because of a relative lack of available information about the helpers, I have based it around an updated version of the list of evaders found at the back of Georges Broussine's 2000 book '*L'evade de la France libre*' and used their MI9 and MIS-X escape reports, together with additional details from various other sources. Although I have had some difficulty with 'crediting' some evaders with the various escape lines, it should become clear from the text that in many cases, more than one organisation was involved.

There are some advantages in basing the story around the evaders as their reports were written on return to the UK and tend to be more accurate as far as dates are concerned – helper reports (whilst often containing more intimate detail) were compiled after the war ended, when memories may have faded.

There is doubt concerning the spelling of some of the helpers' names and/or addresses. I have tried to be consistent in the spellings – using the IS9 (Awards Bureau) Register of Helpers as a guide wherever possible – and welcome any corrections. Names with (query) or not found (nf) after them are unconfirmed from other sources. It should be noted that the IS9 Register has the helpers' post-war addresses and that some of the street names have changed. Note also that some of the *departements* have also changed – for example, Cotes-du-Nord is now Cotes-d'Amor, and the departement of Seine (which included Paris) was divided into four separate departements in 1968. I have retained many (although not all) of the older names.

The guides who took the evaders around the country should more accurately be described as convoyeurs (or convoyeuses) but for the sake of simplicity (and there being no equivalent English word) I will generally be referring to them as guides in the text and perhaps specifying mountain guides (although they should really be called passeurs) for the men who took evaders across the Pyrenees. Identifying many of these convoyeurs and passeurs is very difficult, and sometimes impossible, as they rarely gave names – and of course their addresses were generally unknown to the evaders.

MI9 and MIS-X reports are divided into several sections, with the finer details of escape and evasion being given only in the Appendix C. For some MI9 reports, these Appendix Cs are not available (or at least not yet found) although when they are, they are typed and often very detailed. Many of the American MIS-X reports have the Appendix C only as an interviewer's scribbled pencil notes, which can be almost illegible.

MI9 reports (as well as IS9 and Liberation reports) are available from the National Archives at Kew, London and may be found in the WO208 series of folders. MIS-X reports are available from the US National Archives and Records Administration (NARA) at College Park, Maryland – they are also posted on the NARA website and (unlike the British reports) can be downloaded free of charge. There are also a limited number of RAMP (Returned Allied Military Personnel) files for American evaders who were captured. Unfortunately, the only numbering system for RAMP files is the Folder (eg Folder 5) where they are stored (in Box 601) at NARA, and the page numbers.

Printed books tend to be accepted as being more authentically factual than websites, which by their very nature, are seen as ephemeral, and therefore not to be trusted as reliable sources. However, whilst websites vary tremendously, it is equally obvious that some books are better researched than others. I have used as many contemporary sources as I could find to write this study, together with contributions from numerous others (including some French researchers who specialise in their local areas) however further information is regularly being discovered, some of which may shed new light on the people and events covered here.

CHAPTER 1

Georges Broussine

Before the war began, Georges Broussine (a small, dark featured man of Jewish descent) was a medical student but in October 1939, he and fellow student Henri Boileau were mobilised as military nurses before both opted to be transferred to the infantry.

On 1 November 1940, Broussine was a twenty-two-year-old French army reserve officer cadet stationed at Cigogne, about 20 kms south-east of Tours. Next day, he resigned his position and with his friend Henri Boileau, began the long journey to London where they intended to join an almost unknown French general named de Gaulle. Their journey, which was interrupted by several months spent in various French prisons before the Pat O'Leary organisation took them across the Pyrenees to the British Consulate in Barcelona in March 1942, and further delayed when they were arrested in Madrid and sent to the Spanish *campo de concentracion* at Miranda-del-Ebro, took two and a half years.

Georges Broussine and Henri Boileau finally reached London in July 1942 and after two weeks of being interviewed at the Patriotic School in Wandsworth, reported to the FFL offices in Carlton Gardens.

Broussine and Boileau officially joined the FFL (*Forces francais libres*) on 10 September 1942 – although their engagement dates were shown as 4 March 1942, the day they left France and crossed the Pyrenees into Spain. Boileau was sent to America where he received more army training while Broussine was soon working with the evasion department of BCRA (*Bureau central de renseignement et d'action* – the Free French intelligence service) under Captain Roger Mitchell, a French army officer of Scottish descent with personal experience of the subject having been in and out of France by parachute and Lysander the previous year. Mitchell told Broussine that he would need between four and six months of training before he could be sent into the field and that he should have a code name chosen from a list of wines and spirits. Mitchell suggested 'Bourgogne' and Broussine accepted.

Most of Broussine's training was carried out at the Hans School, at Hans Place in London and included the use of radios, operating the sets as

1

well as coding and decoding messages. He was also trained in parachuting, which was carried out at Ringway near Manchester. During his time in London, Broussine inevitably came into contact with numerous other agents, including Jean-Claude Camors (see later) who took many of the same classes at the Hans School and lived in the same building as Broussine at 50 Queen's Gate.

Georges Broussine returned to France in February 1943 to establish the Bourgogne (aka Burgundy) escape line. Although obviously working with the full knowledge and co-operation of MI9, this was a purely Free French BCRA operation. Bourgogne was based in Paris but had connections with other groups throughout France. The first routes that Bourgogne used to take men across the Pyrenees to Spain were via Foix and Andorra but the extreme bad weather in October 1943 forced a change to the lower mountains south of Perpignan. When that more obvious route became too dangerous, in December 1943 (although it was used again in March 1944) men were mostly sent out through Pau. Broussine was also involved in other ventures, such as the sea evacuations from Brittany by fishing vessels, as will be mentioned later in the text.

Broussine's landing in France got off to a somewhat inauspicious start. He was supposed to have been parachuted to a field near Lyon from 138 SD Halifax W1012 but poor visibility made accurate navigation impossible and the bomber was shot down in the early hours of 20 February 1943 by light flak from Tours. After jettisoning the containers intended for other groups, pilot F/ Lt Peter Kingsford-Smith crash-landed his aircraft a few miles south-east of the city. Broussine led the crew of eight to the small village of Larcay where he knocked on the first door he came to, gave the airmen 20,000 French francs and left them with farmer Roger Bodineau and his wife Marcelle, saying that he would be back within forty-eight hours. When Broussine failed to return, the crew (who were given civilian clothes by the Bodineau family) split into pairs to evade but all eight men were eventually captured.

When they first met, and not knowing the circumstances, Roger Bodineau assumed that Broussine was a member of the local resistance who had rounded up the eight British aircrew within a couple of hours of their landing and led them to his door. On Broussine's return a few days later, when the situation was explained, he volunteered to help the new network in any way he could – see later.

The idea of Broussine returning to Larcay within two days seems unrealistic as he didn't know anyone in Tours who could help him. What

Broussine didn't tell the airmen was that he had to go to Paris and on to Lyon first, to meet Maurice Montet of the BCRA Brandy line. He did return to Larcay but that was several days later and by then the Halifax crew had decided to try and make their own way back.

Broussine, who had lost all his personal luggage in the crash, walked into Tours, where he says 'the affair of the plane' was all over town. After taking coffee in the first cafe he came to, and visiting a barber for a shave, he managed to catch the Bordeaux express train to Paris and reached the capital in the afternoon of 20 February.

Broussine decided to visit the parents of his medical student friend Henri Boileau (who was by then in Algiers). They received him willingly enough but Broussine didn't want to risk their further involvement and so asked where he might spend the night. They suggested he went to see Dr Jacques Cahen-Delabre, who Broussine also knew, and Cahen not only offered his own home on rue Gazan as shelter but also suggested other contacts, including Dr Jean Camp, father of another of Broussine's friends, Andre Camp. Jean Camp's son-in-law, Dr Francois Hauser, had moved to Narbonne where Jean Camp had numerous contacts, and Jean promised to try and find someone there who could help with passages to Spain via Perpignan.

On arrival in Lyon on 22 February, Broussine visited the chemist who was his 'letter box' and a rendezvous was agreed. Unfortunately Broussine strongly suspected that he was being followed from the chemist's shop and had to use some of his secret agent training to shake his possible 'tail' before he could meet Maurice Montet, chief of the Brandy network. Montet quickly agreed to help the stranded Halifax crew and sent one of his men, Hugues de Lestang-Parade, with Broussine back to the Bodineau farm at Larcay but by then, the airmen had gone and the two agents returned to Lyon.[1]

The original plan formulated by BCRA had been for Broussine to join the Brandy escape network, taking over while Maurice Montet went to London. Brandy was set up in May 1942 by Maurice's brother Lucien (aka Christian Martell) and passed to Maurice (aka Simon Martell) when he returned to England to fly 341 Sqn (Free French) Spitfires. However, another Brandy agent had already gone to England where BCRA appointed

1   Hugues de Lestang-Parade (of 5 Ave Matignon, Paris VIII) was later involved with supplying two radios for Bourgogne – and when he left France, it was Yves Allain who took him with a group of airmen evaders to the Spanish border. (NARA Allain & *Rapport par Yves Allain* dd May 1945 – French National Archives (FNA) File 72AJ/37/V)

him to a permanent position in London and Maurice decided he would rather stay in Lyon and run his escape line. This suited Broussine very well as he also wanted to run his own network and after another day in Lyon, the two men parted as friends to go their separate ways.[2]

After a detour to Grenoble, where Broussine paid rent in advance for an apartment that was never used, he returned to Paris.

He knew that he couldn't stay long in Dr Cahen's cluttered dental workshop so one of Broussine's first tasks was to find a place to live. He describes Rene Lalou, his son Etienne and Etienne's wife Suze, as three of the pillars of his support network and it was Etienne's widowed mother-in-law, Mme Marie Flament, who gave Broussine a room in her fifth-floor apartment at 14 rue de Castiglione, just 200 metres from the Jardin des Tuileries.[3] Another problem was the newly instigated STO (*Service du travail obligatoire*) which meant that every young man had to have a work certificate if he were to avoid being sent to Germany. Jacques Cahen introduced Broussine to one of his cousins, Rene Tourriol, who was an administrator in his father-in-law's factory. He organised a meeting with M Chauvelot who worked at the *Secretariat d'Etat à l'Artisanat* and Broussine (under an assumed name) was soon employed as an editor in the Vichy administration.

At the beginning of March, Broussine took a train via Toulouse to Narbonne where he visited Jean Camp's son-in-law, Francois Hauser and wife Linette. They gave Broussine the opportunity to visit Jean Olibo, secretary-general at the mairie in Perpignan who Broussine had met two years earlier in his first attempt to leave France. Broussine explained his plans to Olibo for paying local smugglers to take evaders across the mountains and while nothing was confirmed, the two men agreed to meet again. Broussine returned to Toulouse where he took a train to Foix and the address of a hotel that had been suggested by Francois Hauser.[4] The hotel

---

2   Maurice Montet (born October 1918) was arrested on 22 June 1943 (along with Jean Louis Merand) and deported to Germany. After surviving the camps of Neugamme and Fallersleben, he was liberated at Wobbelin in May 1945 and repatriated to France the following month. Maurice Montet was recommended for an MBE. (WO208/5459) Please note that I am not always able to confirm if the IS9 recommendations resulted in individuals receiving those actual awards.

3   Mme Vve Marie Eloire Flament (born March 1881) of 14 rue de Castiglione, Paris 1 was awarded the BEM. (WO208/5451)

4   Dr Francois Houser (born September 1912 in Paris) allowed his house in Narbonne to be used as a permanent retreat and resting place for agents. As well as putting Broussine in touch with an escape route through Foix to Andorra, in March 1944 he contacted a Dr Bernard in Quillan, who was already providing medical services to the maquis, to extend those services to Allied evaders. Dr Houser was recommended for a Kings Medal for Courage. (WO208/5456)

belonged to a M Audient and was used by local passeurs smuggling people to Andorra and their organisation impressed Broussine enough for him to decide to try it out.

On his return to Paris, Broussine found that his friends had been busy. Jean Camp had been discretely spreading the word amongst his associates at the Lycee Henri IV, Jean (sic) Lacroix and M Pastor, the director general of the Lycee, that an agent from London was looking to recruit young people for dangerous missions. Yves Allain immediately volunteered, soon followed by Claude Leclercq (born July 1924), Georges Baledent (born June 1921) and Jacques Niepceron (born September 1922).

Yves Allain (born June 1922 near Tregourez, Finistere) was a student at the Lycee who had been involved in resistance activities since 1941. First with the 'Front-National' he soon joined 'Volontaires de le Liberte' (VL) distributing clandestine pamphlets and journals. Other members of the VL 'Section Henri IV' included Pierre Cochery (born February 1922), Georges Guillemin (born February 1921), Jean-Louis Kervevant (born October 1922), Pierre Jacob (born December 1922) and Pierre Le Berre (born August 1921).

Allain really wanted to get to London but after failing to join Xavier Trellu – one of his old teachers in Quimper who left for England on board the Dalc'h Mad (along with RAF evader Gordon Carter) on 6 April 1943 – Maurice Lacroix (a professeur at the Lycee and honorary member of VL) suggested that Allain might be interested in helping an evasion line. Another VL member, M Boucher at Saint-Cloud (assume Jacques Boucher at 29 rue de Solferino) had already helped one airman and he introduced Allain to Leon Paster who in turn, introduced him to Georges Broussine.

When he first began working with Bourgogne, Allain was living with M et Mme Julien Cochery, parents of his friend Pierre Cochery, at 16 rue Damremont, Paris XVIII but towards the end of July, he moved to 4 rue du Lyonnais and lodged with M et Mme Derique. After about a fortnight he moved again, this time to stay with his Lycee Spanish teacher Jean Camp at 7 Place Paul Painleve where he shared with radio-operator Edmond Mallet. When Mallet was arrested at the end of August, Allain stayed for a few days with Mme Lucienne Delhaye at 4 rue Barbette, and then when Georges Broussine left for England in September 1943, took over Broussine's apartment (where Genevieve Soulie also lived) at 3 rue de l'Aude, Paris XIV. Allain stayed at rue de l'Aude until his marriage to Mimi (Marie Francoise Madec) on 12 April 1944.[5]

5   NARA Allain.

5

In his book, Broussine says that his first contact with downed aircrew came from Mme le docteur Bertrand-Fontaine, a professor of medicine at the Beaujon hospital in Clichy. She knew that Robert Ayle of Comete was having problems getting some of their evaders to Spain and she told one of her colleagues who knew Dr Georges Boileau who in turn told Broussine. Broussine went to meet Dr Bertrand in her surgery and she put him in touch with Ayle and so less than two months after arriving in Paris, Bourgogne handled its first three airmen. Broussine also says that over the following few weeks, Bourgogne took on another sixteen airmen from Comete and delivered them safely to Andorra.

Bourgogne's links with Comete continued until one day in early June 1943 when Broussine telephoned Robert Ayle's apartment on rue Babylone only to be answered by what he describes as a 'guttural' voice.

April 1943 was when Bourgogne started to become a 'real' escape organisation. Maurice Montet of Brandy had sent a radio message to London telling them about Broussine and the Halifax crash and as a result, two radio sets were delivered to Broussine in Paris. One set was installed in a factory run by Rene Tourriol and Broussine sent his first ever radio message to England from there. Soon after that, Broussine was walking along the Champs-Elysees when he bumped into Andre Minne, a radio-operator that Broussine had known at the Hans School in London. The network that Minne had been sent to join had failed but Minne wanted to stay in France, so after checking with London, he joined Bourgogne. Broussine also recruited an assistant for Minne named Edmond Mallet and the two men were soon installed on Roger Bodineau's farm at Larcay with the second set.[6]

In Paris, the core of the organisation began to take shape, notably after Gabrielle Wiame and her friend Madeleine Melot joined. They also worked with Comete (and Oaktree) until the arrest of Robert Ayle and had an extensive network of helpers already prepared to help evading airmen with clothes, food and shelter.

Gabrielle Wiame (aka Marie Wiame) (sister of Emile Debouche) was a 33 year-old (born May 1910) blonde haired Belgian woman married (in 1927) to Frenchman Charles Wiame and with a 16 year-old son named

---

6   Andre Minne (born December 1910) – who had been a guide for the organisation in Marseille before escaping to Spain himself in April 1941 – and Edmond Mallet (born April 1923) were captured whilst transmitting from Louis Bour's house in Meaux (north-east of Paris) on 20 August 1943 and deported to Germany. They were liberated by Russian forces in May 1945. Both men were recommended for Kings Medals for Courage. (WO208/5452)

Robert. She was introduced to Robert Ayle and recruited into Comete in 1942. She worked briefly with Val Williams and Ray Labrosse (and seems to have assumed them to be part of Comete) before joining Bourgogne where she continued guiding, sheltering and feeding evaders until the end of the year when her position was taken over by Genevieve Soulie. I suspect that Gabrielle Wiame, who was awarded the BEM, was a particularly tough and uncompromising lady who took very little nonsense from anybody.[7]

Madeleine Anna Perrine Melot (born January 1883) was the widow of Lt-Colonel Henri Melot who died in 1942. Early the following year, one of her friends, Mlle Giselle Chaintre, asked if she would shelter an American airman while his onward journey to Spain was arranged. Mme Melot agreed and soon she was involved with Elisabeth Barbier and groupe Vaneau. Following Elisabeth's arrest in June, it was again Giselle Chaintre who introduced Mme Melot to Georges Broussine.[8]

Madeleine Melot's apartment at 11 bis rue Larrey, Paris V is just a block away from the *Grande Mosquee de Paris* at 2 bis Place du Puits de l'Emile, two blocks from the Jardin des Plantes and less than half a kilometre from her friend Gabrielle Wiame at 46 rue Poliveau. Mme Melot's apartment became a centre for the organisation where helpers met, mail was received and where evaders were sheltered or collected before being housed at other safe lodgings in the vicinity.

7   Information from TNA folder WO208/5457 and Wiame NARA file.

8   Temoignage de Mme Melot recueilli par Mlle Patrimonio 15 Avril 1946. (FNA)

CHAPTER 2

The First Airmen

Georges Broussine says in his book that the first airmen to be helped by Bourgogne were three men passed to him by Robert Ayle of Comete. They were taken to Foix in April by Claude Leclercq who then handed them over to passeurs who took them to Andorra. He also recounts Leclercq telling him about a problem he had with two evaders on the train to Toulouse when German inspectors examined everyone's ID cards at Vierzon.

Claude Alfred Lucien Leclercq was just a teenager (born July 1924) when he became a regular guide between Paris and Foix as well as liaison with wireless operators, sometimes taking their sets across the country. In July (query) 1943, Georges Broussine sent him to Barcelona and so he accompanied a group of evaders all the way into Spain. After consultation with the British MI9 agent there, he returned to France, continuing his work with Bourgogne until December (query) when a series of arrests compromised his position and he crossed the Pyrenees again, going on to England where he joined MI9. Claude Leclercq was awarded a BEM.[1]

There is some confusion of events in Broussine's version but I think the two men in the incident at Vierzon were RAF Sgts Stanley Moore and Donald Ferguson. It should be noted however that neither name is included in Broussine's list and that their reports do not identify, nor even describe their guide.

Sgt Stanley J Moore and Sgt Donald Ferguson were the navigator and flight engineer of 7 Sqn Stirling BK760 (Chesterman) which was returning from Frankfurt in the early hours of 11 April 1943. Already damaged by flak, they were near the Dutch-Belgian border when they were attacked by night-fighters. The aircraft was set on fire and at very low altitude when the bale-out order was given. Moore and Ferguson were blown clear when the aircraft exploded shortly afterwards and were the only survivors.[2]

---

1   TNA folder WO208/5451.

2   Some details for this and other RAF bomber aircraft and their crews, are taken from W R Chorley's excellent 'Bomber Command Losses' series of books, published by Midland Publishing.

Both men landed near Bree (Limburg) close to the Maastricht Canal, were soon helped and two days later, brought together in Brussels where their subsequent journey was arranged.

They were sheltered by Mme Isabelle Pauli and her twenty-five-year-old daughter Dominique[3] at 30 rue de Naples in Ixelles until 29 April when Fernando Radelet took them, F/Lt Wilfred Murphy and W/O Archibald Cowe to Paris. They arrived at about eight o'clock the following morning where Fernando passed them on to M Paul (Frederic De Jongh). While Murphy and Cowe went elsewhere,[4] M Paul took Moore and Ferguson to Avenue du Colonel Bonnet where they stayed with Mlle de Bizien (aka the Marquise) – who told them she was not a member of Paul's organisation – and took their meals with Mme Benach at nearby rue Alfred Brunneau.

Mlle Leslie de Bizien (born Sept 1899) (aka Mlle Marie de Bizien, Christine de Bizien or Henri de Bizien) of 15 Avenue du Colonel Bonnet, Paris XVI was a liaison agent with both Comete and Bourgogne. She and her friend Mme Henriette Benech of 7 rue Alfred Bruneau (which adjoins the Ave du Colonel Bonnet) worked primarily with an intelligence organisation but they also guided and sheltered numerous evaders – including P/O John David and 2/Lt Johan Raeder – before having to leave the country themselves – they crossed the Pyrenees to Spain with Comete on 25 July 1943. Mlle de Bizien was recommended for a Kings Medal for Service.[5]

On 7 May, Moore and Ferguson were taken to stay with Maurice and Marguerite Mehudin at 41 Avenue Paul Doumer, Paris XVI until 15 May when M Paul gave them new ID cards, some French and Spanish money and led them to a park. They met a French air force lieutenant named Geugan (later in Gibraltar) and a man called Lefort whose real name they thought was Degoutte. That afternoon they were taken to the Gare d'Austerlitz and passed on to a guide who took them by train to Toulouse.

---

3   Mme Isabelle Louise Pauli (née Anspach March 1886) was arrested in January 1944 and deported to Germany, where she died. Her daughter Dominque was not caught. (WO208/5452) Note that while the IS9 Belgian Helper List agrees their address as 30 rue de Naples, the IS9 files say 81 rue de Bruxelles, Namur.

4   F/Lt Wilfred Murphy and W/O Archibald Cowe were passed to a different organisation which took them to Lyon, Toulouse and Perpignan. They were joined by more evading airmen – including Sgt Ronald Limage and Sgt Roland Hale – and two soldiers – Dvr George Newton and Pte John Grant, who had escaped from Poland. They were all captured at the end of May after their guide from Perpignan got lost on his first attempt to walk to Spain and when he returned with a lorry next day, they were stopped at a German road-block near Elne.

5   TNA folder WO208/5460.

When the train was stopped at Vierzon, on the old demarcation line, two German officers boarded the train while German soldiers patrolled the platform. One of the officers wasn't satisfied with the airmen's papers, which he retained, and said they should go to the end of the train. When they failed to report, an announcement was made saying that Robert Garray and Jacques Maure (the names on the airmens' ID cards) should go immediately to the German Control Office. When this order was repeated, their guide suggested the two airmen get off the train and try to board again as it was leaving the station. Moore and Ferguson duly got off and walked past the engine to wait in a railway worker's tool-shed. When the train eventually left (after the Germans had searched it twice and even checked underneath) the engine driver saw what they were trying to do and obligingly slowed enough to allow them to jump back on and return to their compartment.

Moore and Ferguson reached Toulouse at eight o'clock the following morning and after breakfast at the station cafe, went on by train to Pau. They were met at Pau where the plan was to take them by car to Oloron-Sainte-Marie but their lack of suitable papers to get through the known check-points resulted in them staying until 18 May when they were taken on a military ration lorry, driven to Oloron by a Spaniard. They set off walking that night, finally crossing the border near Pic de Lacoura (south of Sainte-Engrace) at six o'clock on the morning of 20 May 1943. They were arrested shortly afterwards and taken first to Isaba and then Pamplona where they were held until 5 June when they were transferred to Betelu (Navarra). Michael Cresswell (aka Monday of MI9) came to interview them and five days later they were driven to the British Embassy in Madrid.

The first name on Georges Broussine's list of evaders is a Sgt Allen and the most likely candidate is F/Sgt William Allen – but if that's correct then his crewmate F/Sgt David Bradley (with whom he evaded) should also be included, although there is no obvious involvement with anyone directly connected to Bourgogne.

F/Sgt William G Allen and F/Sgt David R Bradley were the flight engineer and wireless operator of 35 Sqn Halifax W7873 (Owen) which was on the way to Pilsen (Plzen, Czechoslovakia) on 16 April 1943 when they were shot down by flak about 30 kilometres west of Reims. Allen and Bradley were the only successful evaders.

Both men baled out and they landed close to one another in an open field near Villers-devant-le-Thour (Ardennes) about 30 kms south-east of Laon. They made their way to the village but finding the church locked overnight, waited until people began arriving in the morning. They hid in the priest's changing room and while waiting for the priest, cut the badges from their uniforms. The priest and a local woman gave them some food and directions and they carried on walking, heading for Reims. In the early hours of the following morning, they reached the outskirts of La Malmaison (Aisne) where they were recognised as evading airmen and taken into the village. Very early the following morning, two of their helpers, Robert and Eugene, took them to Amifontaine station but on finding no trains for Reims were stopping there, took them to another station (Saint-Erme-Outre-et-Ramecourt – query). However, on the way, they met a woman who took over from Robert and Eugene and she led them to a seed merchant's shop in St Erme (query) where they met a man named Constance, aged about fifty, and their journey was arranged …

On 20 April, a forestry official took Allen to Laon on his motorcycle while Constance took Bradley there by bus. They met at a cafe where they were joined by Mme Benech and the Marquise de Bezien (aka Leslie). The two women took Allen and Bradley on the 15.30 train to Paris and on to Mme Benach's apartment near the Trocodero, at 7 rue Alfred Bruneau. The airmen were sheltered at rue Alfred Bruneau until 3 May, during which time Leslie told them that she was a member of an organisation concerned with agents arriving by parachute and that she no longer dealt with evaders. However, she would put them in touch with an organisation which could help them. A few days later they were visited by a M Paul (Frederic De Jongh) who questioned them and on 1 May, they were taken to have their photographs taken.

At about nine-thirty in the evening of 3 May, Mme Benach took them to a Metro station where they were handed over to M Paul. He took them to Aimable Fouquerel's apartment at 10 rue Oudinot[6] where they joined Group Captain John R Whitley, Sgt Maurice A T Davies and Sgt Malcolm B Strange.[7] On 6 May, a girl took Allen and Bradley to a park where M Paul and Leslie met them with a car and drove them to stay with Dr Jules Tinel at 245 Blvd Saint-Germain. They stayed with Dr Tinel until 17 May, sharing with an unnamed RCAF sergeant.

---

6   This is the same address as Mme Lucienne Laurentie – see later.

7   Whitley, Davies and Strange crossed the Pyrenees later that month with Comete.

On 17 May, a woman helper took Allen and Bradley to the grounds of the University of Paris where they met M Paul and Dr Tinel's son Jacques. Jacques gave them 1,000 French francs and took them to the Gare d'Austerlitz. They were joined on the way by a Frenchman called Jean but when his identity card was found not to be in order, he was left behind. Jacques took them and two other Frenchmen by overnight train to Toulouse.[8]

They arrived at Toulouse at eight o'clock in the morning of 18 May and that afternoon, took the three o'clock train to Foix. They stayed overnight in what the airmen describe as a 'very poor kind of hotel' and next morning, were joined by the Frenchman, Jean. That evening, Jacques Tinel handed them over to a Spanish guide who led them across the Pyrenees to Andorra, reaching the capital, Andorra la Vieja, on the evening of 22 May.

They stayed at the Hotel des Pyrenees where the owner, Francisco Perez, looked after them and changed their French money for Spanish. On 24 May, Snr Perez drove them close to the Spanish border from where they walked through the night to a farm where a new guide, Antonio, took over. After three days rest, they walked for another three days to a small (unnamed) town where they met a Frenchman (another Jacques) and he and Antonio took the airmen by train to Barcelona. They arrived in the Catalan capital on 1 June and took a taxi to the British Consulate.

---

8   Jacques Louis Andre Tinel (born November 1920) was arrested on 20 May 1943 and six months later, deported to Germany – where it is believed he died. (WO208/5456)

CHAPTER 3

Some Comete, Chauny-Dromas and John Carter Connections

The Chauny line, headed by Captain Etienne Dromas (born December 1921) was founded in late 1942. It was centred on Chauny (Aisne) as a temporary refuge for evaders until they could be passed on to other lines – notably Comete and Bourgogne, and later Shelburn. After D-Day, Chauny-Dromas evolved to shelter men in the local area until Allied forces advancing from the Normandy beach-heads could liberate them. The Chauny organisation is credited with helping at least eighty-seven Allied evaders and Dromas was recommended for a KMS.[1]

John Carter (aka Jules/Julien) was born 1891 in Gouvieux near Chantilly (Oise) of English parents, and had dual nationality. Carter was put in contact with the PAO in August 1942 when George Whittinghill at the American Consulate in Lyon asked him to deliver the five-man crew from 138 SD Whitley Z9232 (Outram) which had crashed near Vierzon, to Dr Georges Rodocanachi in Marseille. Following Pat O'Leary's arrest in February 1943, Carter went to Switzerland where he contacted Victor Farrell (SIS station chief) who asked him to start taking evaders along the SOE Vic line route to Spain through Perpignan, or via Lavelanet to Andorra. Carter, who soon based himself in Lyon (where I believe he lived in an apartment on rue Vendome) made many useful contacts through his assistant, Annie Sabourault.[2] He also had good contacts in Paris where he says that Madeleine Grador represented him, while Jean Calmet (of 12 rue de Marseille, Lyon) helped as his conductor. Carter continued passing evaders on (including Operation Frankton survivors Herbert Hasler and William Sparks) until his arrest with three American airmen (see later) at the Hotel de France in Pamiers in January 1944. John Carter was deported and survived Mauthausen.[3]

---

1   TNA folder WO208/5453.

2   Mlle Anne Marie Emilienne Sabourault (born December 1906) of 284 rue Vendome, Lyon – who is credited with sheltering and guiding some forty Allied evaders – was recommended for a KMC. (WO208/5454)

3   This information (and more) from a post-war statement by John Carter found in Wiame NARA file.

2/Lt Homer Contopidis and Sgt Walter R Minor were the navigator and tail-gunner of B-17 42-29627 Midnight (94BG/410BS) (Spevak) which was returning from Lorient on 17 May 1943 when it was shot down by fighters. The crew baled out and the aircraft crashed at Le Cloitre-Saint-Thegonnec, about 15 kms south of Morlaix in Brittany. Two other members of the Midnight crew also evaded successfully, pilot Edward Spevak and co-pilot Donald Nichols, both with Oaktree and then Bourgogne – see later.

Contopidis and Minor were fairly typical of the American airmen landing in France at that time – Contopidis, from New York City, was twenty-three years old and had served with the USAAF for eighteen months. Minor, from Halifax, Massachusetts was a little older at twenty-five but had only served for thirteen months. Neither man spoke French and the only escape and evasion advice they had been given was during a half-hour lecture earlier that month. Later, more detailed E&E lectures were given to US aircrew, sometimes by men who had successfully evaded themselves.

Contopidis and Minor were both helped immediately on landing and brought together that afternoon. Two days later they were visited by a pair of Frenchmen who gave them civilian clothes and took them by bicycle to a house in Morlaix where their journey was arranged. They were taken by train to Brest and had supper with a baker named Lacroix (nf). That evening they were joined by a doctor's daughter who was apparently the link between Brest and an organisation in Paris. A few days later, on Monday 24 May, they were taken to Paris where they stayed for a week with the 'Countess B' (Genevieve de Poulpiquet). The following Sunday, a man came to give them new ID cards and take them by train to Lyon. They arrived in Lyon at eleven-thirty the following morning (31 May) and saw Sgt Gordon Murray and Sgt Ronald Goddard getting off the same train.

Sgt Ronald G Goddard was the navigator of 78 Sqn Halifax JB873 (Dane) which was returning from Bochum in the early hours of 14 May 1943 when it was shot down by a night-fighter and the aircraft abandoned to crash near Haasrod (Brabant) in Belgium. Both pilots were killed and five crew captured – Goddard was the only successful evader.

Twenty-one-year-old Goddard landed near Hamme-Mille where he was soon helped, sheltered and passed on to the Comete escape line. On about 24 May, Comete convoyeur Jean Masson brought Goddard and Sgt Gordon Murray, plus two US evaders (Capt Elmer McTaggart and S/Sgt Raymond Walls – query) to Paris. Goddard and Murray stayed with Drs

Andre and Marguerite Bohn at 116 Boulevard Raspail until Sunday 30 May.[4]

Sgt Gordon H Murray was the twenty-nine-year-old air bomber (bomb-aimer) of 429 Sqn Wellington MS487 (Fox) which was shot down on the night of 26-27 March 1943 and crashed near Wassenar in Holland. The pilot and two other crew were killed and one was captured – Murray was the only successful evader.

Murray landed in Holland and was sheltered at various addresses until 19 May when he was taken to Hasselt in Belgium – and next day on to Brussels and the Comete organisation. He stayed with Mme Isabelle Pauli at 30 rue de Naples in Ixelles for four days before being taken by train to Paris with Ronald Goddard and two Americans by Comete convoyeur Jean Masson.[5]

Sgt Alvin C Turner was the flight engineer of 419 Sqn Halifax DT646 (Bakewell) which was returning from Essen in the early hours of 6 March 1943 when it was attacked by night-fighters and abandoned over Holland. One crewman was killed and five captured – Turner was the only successful evader.

Turner landed just north of Amsterdam and made his way, over several days, to Liege in Belgium where he was helped with food, shelter and medical attention to his injured back. He was moved to Brussels (date uncertain) to stay with Mme Isabelle Pauli at 30 rue de Naples. On 14 May, Turner joined Sgt Joseph Sankey at the station and they took a train to Paris …

Sgt Joseph Sankey was the rear gunner of 10 Sqn Halifax DT788 (Illingworth) which was on the way to Cologne on the evening of 14 February 1943 when it was attacked by three Junkers 88s. Despite shooting down at least one of the fighters, the Halifax caught fire and was abandoned near the Dutch-German border. One crewman was killed and five captured – Sankey was the only successful evader.

Twenty-two-year-old Sankey was probably the last man out of his doomed aircraft and he landed somewhere between the German towns of

---

4   Dr Andre Bohn and his wife Dr Marguerite Bohn-Nageotte were arrested on 20 June 1943. They are credited with sheltering eleven evading airmen in their home at 116 Boulevard Raspail, Paris VII. The last two – Donald Parks and Marcus Davis (see later) – were, along with Francois Meunier of the same address, captured with them. Andre Bohn was held at Fresnes until deported to Dachau at the end of April 1944 – he was repatriated back to France in May 1945. Marguerite Bohn was held at Fresnes and freed with the liberation of Paris. Both were awarded the King's Medal for Service. (WO208/5453) Pierre Ducamp at this address is also acknowledged on the IS9 Helper List.

5   Jean Masson was an alias used by the Belgian-born traitor and infiltration agent Jacques Desoubrie – here making the second of three such trips before trapping Frederic De Jongh and Robert Ayle.

Kempen and Crefeld. After burying his parachute, Sankey set off walking through the night, firstly heading north-west and then following a canal until he was intercepted by a young Dutch boy who had been sent to work on a German farm and who already knew that Sgt J S King, Sankey's engineer, was being sheltered nearby.[6] The boy took Sankey back to the farm where he worked before guiding Sankey over the border to his home at Velden, just north of Venlo. The local priest was brought to the house and he gave Sankey civilian clothes and shoes in exchange for his uniform and flying boots before taking him across the river Maas by boat to Grubbenvorst. Sankey was hidden in the loft of the church at Grubbenvorst for the next two days.

On 17 February, Father van Burgh (query) took Sankey by bicycle to another village nearby and from there, the local police chief drove Sankey to a village some forty miles away. Sankey's new helpers then arranged for Sankey to be taken across the border into Belgium and a windmill somewhere north-east of Hasselt. On 22 February, Lambert Spanoghe took Sankey by bicycle to his home in Hasselt at 72 Chaussee de Liege, where he joined F/Lt Moire Pierre. Two days later Sankey was moved to another house where he stayed with Mme Simone Lamquin at 60 Chaussee de Liege.

On 6 March, Sankey joined F/Lt Pierre to take a train to Brussels, getting off just before the city and completing their journey by tram. They were met by members of an organisation and Sankey was taken on to Antwerp. On 22 March, Sankey was brought back to Brussels where he stayed with schoolteacher Henriette Smets at 122 rue Moortebeck for the next eight weeks. On 13 May, Sankey joined Sgt Alvin Turner at the station but they were unable to take the Paris train that evening and so spent the night in an apartment belonging to an English-speaking girl and her brother.

On 14 May, Turner and Sankey were taken to Paris where they stayed in an apartment near rue de Babylone, owned by a woman who said her husband was a French official in North Africa (Mme Lucienne Laurentie (née Serres) at 10 rue Oudinot) where they briefly met Paul (Frederic De Jongh) and had their photographs taken. On 16 May, they were taken to stay with an elderly woman in her apartment on Avenue de Clichy (Mme Vve Marie Dupille – query) until 30 May, when they were taken to the Gare d'Austerlitz where they joined Stanley Everiss and John Ford and took the train to Lyon.

---

6   Sgt J S King was subsequently captured (details unknown) and sent to Stalag VIIIB (Lamsdorf) – see 'Footprints on the Sands of Time' by Oliver Clutton-Brock published in 2003 by Grub Street.

Homer Contopidis, Walter Minor, Ronald Goddard and Gordon Murray found their contact in Lyon where they met Alvin Turner and Joseph Sankey – and F/O Stanley Everiss and Sgt John Ford from Stirling BK725.

Contopidis and Minor were taken to stay with Odette Zbyszynska, believed to be the French widow of a Polish fighter pilot, at 93 rue Servient for four days before being moved back to stay with the English airmen.[7] On the following Sunday (6 June) two new French guides took the eight evaders by train to Carcassonne and then on to Lavelanet where they caught a bus to Foix. That evening they started walking towards the mountains, collecting a new guide and a large group of Frenchmen along the way, and crossed into Andorra on 10 June 1943. They stayed three nights in a hotel before setting off again on Sunday to walk to Manresa in Spain, arriving on 20 June and from where they took a train to Barcelona and the British Consulate.

90 Sqn Stirling BK725 was returning from Mannheim in the early hours of 17 April 1943 when it was shot down by a night-fighter and crash-landed near Commenchon (Aisne). The eight-man crew were sheltered locally by the Chauny-Dromas organisation and although pilot P/O Peter D White was apparently denounced and soon captured, the other seven men were taken to Paris the following month.

According to second pilot Sgt W Edward Phillips, it was 'the Marquise' (Mlle Leslie de Bizien) and two men who brought him and fellow BK725 crewmen Sgt Andrew Smith and Sgt William J Fitzgerald by train from Chauny to Paris on 13 May. From the Gare du Nord, Smith and Fitzgerald were taken to be sheltered by a married couple (he spoke English and had been an army engineer captain in the last war) in their apartment at 35 Boulevard St Cyr (Rene Baruch-Levy at 45 Blvd Gouvion-Saint-Cyr, Paris XVII – query) until 22 May when they were taken to stay with a lady doctor on Avenue Victor (assume Avenue Victor Hugo) off the Champs-Elysees. I'm not sure where Phillips stayed (he says in a house near the Wagram Metro station) but Drs Andre and Marguerite Bohn are recorded as having supplied him with civilian clothing and an ID card.

---

7   Mme Odette Leonie Bidault Zbyszynska (born December 1914) was understood to be the French widow of a Polish fighter pilot who was killed in 1940 whilst serving with the RAF. Mme Zbyszynska was arrested in June 1943 and deported to Germany, surviving Ravenbruck and Neubrandenbourg (query) before being repatriated to France in May 1945. (WO208/5460) Note that I have not found any RAF airman named Zbyszynska being lost – the nearest is F/O Janus Zbyszynski, an Intelligence Officer with 308 (Polish) Sqn.

On 17 May, Leslie de Bizien and Henriette Benech brought the other four crew from BK725 – P/O Donald G Ross, Sgt Reginald G Gaisford, F/O Stanley F Everiss and Sgt John B Ford – and Sgt Hugh N Mackinnon from Wellington HE550 – to Paris. Ross and Gaisford were sheltered at 116 Boulevard Raspail by Drs Andre and Marguerite Bohn who contacted Frederic De Jongh and he arranged to have their ID photographs taken in a Bon Marche store. Everiss, Ford and MacKinnon (later captured – no further details) stayed with Henriette Benech at 7 rue Alfred Bruneau but two days later, the two BK725 men were moved to 28 rue Scheffer, Paris XVI where they stayed with Noemi Deon and were joined by 2/Lt Joseph Wemheuer.[8]

Wemheuer stayed with Mme Deon until 29 May when he was taken by train to Bordeaux and Dax, crossing the Pyrenees from Saint-Jean-de-Luz with Comete on 31 May 1943.

On about 25 May, Smith and Fitzgerald were taken to the Jardin des Plantes where they rejoined Phillips, Ross and Gaisford. The five BK725 evaders were taken by overnight train from the Gare d'Austerlitz to Toulouse by two guides, one of whom they called Jacques (Jacques Niepceron – query) and who was on only his third such trip. They took another train to Foix and Jacques took them to Saint-Paul-de-Jarret for the night. They returned to Foix next day where they met the Spanish mountain guides who took them across the Pyrenees, reaching El Serrat in Andorra on the morning of 28 May 1943. They continued on to the Andorran capital, Andorra la Vieja, where they stayed overnight at the Hotel des Pyrenees. The following night, a different guide walked them to the Spanish border and then on to Anserall where they were hidden on the mountainside. At about two in the afternoon of 2 June, a car arrived from the British Consulate but there was only room for three and it was Ross, Gaisford and Phillips who were driven to Barcelona that afternoon.

Smith and Fitzgerald stayed at Anserall for another five days before being moved to a farm nearer to Barcelona where they waited while their guide returned to Andorra to collect Edward Gimbel, Frederick Weight, Douglas Nolan and their party – see later.

On 26 May, Stanley Everiss and John Ford – along with Alvin Turner and Joseph Sankey – were taken by train from Paris to Lyon where they

8   Mme Noemi Deon, better known after her divorce as Noemi Hany-Lefebvre (born October 1913) of 28 rue Scheffer, was arrested on 19 June 1943 and interned for several months, but eventually released due to ill health. (WO208/5459) She is the author of the 1946 book 'Six Mois a Fresnes'. The IS9 Helper List also has Mme Jean Francois Chabrun at this address, with the note 'see Mme Hany Lefebvre'.

were later joined by Gordon Murray, Ronald Goddard, Homer Contopidis and Walter Minor.

Donald Ross states at the end of his report that he understood the organisation which helped his group was called Burgundy but the five BK725 crew also had help from Comete in Paris through Frederic De Jongh and so it seems likely that Smith, Fitzgerald, Phillips, Ross and Gaisford were among the sixteen men that Broussine says were passed to Bourgogne from Comete. However, in the case of Everiss and Ford, I think it more likely that they (along with Turner, Sankey, Murray, Goddard, Contopidis and Minor) were actually helped by the John Carter organisation for their passage across the Pyrenees.

The reader may be wondering why Frederic De Jongh seemed to be handing evaders over to other organisations rather than passing them down the Comete line to the Pyrenees. The fifty-four-year-old schoolmaster from Brussels had been forced by the attentions of the Abwehr and GFP-Luft (*Luftwaffe Geheime Feldpolizie*) to move to Paris the previous year (where the hunt for him was continued by the SD (*Sicherheitsdienst*) at rue des Saussaies) but in January 1943, was staying with the Dassie family in Bayonne. He had travelled from Paris by train with his daughter Andree and three RAF evaders, intending to cross the Pyrenees himself. After Andree De Jongh was captured with the three airmen at Bidegain Berri, Urrugne, he returned to Paris and had spent much of the time since, desperately trying to find some way of getting Andree released, even making a trip to Switzerland to raise funds for an exchange attempt. This last this may seem to have been a hopeless cause but such arrangements were not entirely without precedent, however previous exchanges had been for refugees rather than captured escape line agents, and even these slender hopes were further reduced on 25 March when Andree was transferred from Biarritz to the notorious Fresnes prison, south-east of Paris at Val-de-Marne. Hence, with Frederic De Jongh's distractions over his daughter, coupled with further (justified) concerns of the line having been infiltrated by German agents, in the first half of 1943, Robert Ayle and the Comete organisation in Paris handed many of their evaders on to other networks – including Bourgogne.[9]

---

9   For more information about the Comete line see 'Comete, le reseau derriere la ligne DD' by Philippe Le Blanc (pen name of Philippe Connart) published by Memogrames in 2015.

CHAPTER 4

Bourgogne's First Fighter Pilot

On 1 June 1943, P/O Edward Gimbel, Sgt Frederic Weight and F/Sgt Douglas Nolan left Paris by train for Toulouse and Foix.

P/O Edward L Gimbel was a twenty-four-year-old American from Chicago who had enlisted in the RCAF in October 1940. He gives his peacetime profession as 'independent means' so it seems reasonable to assume he volunteered early in the war (more than a year before America became officially involved) either from a sense of duty or for the excitement of flying. Either way, he almost lost his life on 4 April 1943 when he was flying 403 Sqn Spitfire BS110 to rendezvous with some bombers over Rouen – he was attacked by enemy fighters and shot down just north of Pavilly.

Gimbel spent the next week working his way south, getting occasional help as he went along, through Beaubray (Eure) and La Ferte Vidane (Centre) until reaching the Foret de Senonches. After being sheltered by a farmer, Gimbel walked through the Foret de Senonches and on 11 April, met Major Bush, an American who was married to a Frenchwoman and virtually interned in their home. Each week, Major Bush was visited by a Frenchman who worked as an interpreter for the German army at La Loup (Eure-et-Loir) and Bush hoped his friend would be able to assist Gimbel. Unfortunately his friend was not able to help and on 12 April, Gimbel was taken to stay overnight with another friend, a farmer. Next day, Gimbel carried on walking and by that afternoon had reached Fretigny where, since his feet and injured leg were troubling him, he declared himself to a farm labourer. Gimbel was taken to a nearby farmhouse where he was given food and some trousers and visited by the farmer's cousin, a schoolmistress named Jeanette Morvan. Jeanette told Gimbel that her brother, Jean Francois Morvan, lived in Paris and was in contact with an organisation and that Gimbel was to wait while her brother was contacted.

On 17 April, Jeanette Morvan took Gimbel by bus to La Loup then train to Sevres (south-west Paris) and her brother's house at 2 Place Gallardon. Jean Morvan worked at the Renault factory where he knew another employee, named Frazille (Pierre Leonard Fazille – query) who belonged to an organisation and this organisation provided Jean with money to help cover the expense of keeping Gimbel for the next five weeks. On 25 May, Gimbel was taken to Billancourt where he stayed with Frazille for a week, visited there by a man called Bouche (Jacques Boucher of 29 rue Solferino – query) who owned a large silk company. Through Bouche, Gimbel was put in contact with an organisation called 'Volunteers for Liberty' which produced pro-ally propaganda which was sent to Belgium, and received arms and ammunition. On 28 May, Bouche told Gimbel he would be back in the UK within eight days (presumably by aircraft) but this plan was soon cancelled and four days later, on 1 June, Gimbel was given an ID card with one of his own RAF photographs attached. He was then taken to the Jardins des Plantes where he joined Frederic Weight, Douglas Nolan and a parachutist (sic) called Raymond Kingsley ...

Georges Broussine explains in his book that having grown up on nearby rue Linne, and knowing the area well, he used the Jardin des Plantes as a rendezvous because of its clear approaches and multiple exits. It was also conveniently close to the Gare d'Austerlitz from where so many evaders were taken by overnight train to Toulouse. Since he regularly attended these meetings himself, he also decided to adopt a tactic gleaned from a seventeenth century text that said 'the habit makes the monk' – in other words, to the watcher, clothing (which can be easily discarded) may define a character to the exclusion of other details. Consequently, Broussine purchased and often wore a most outlandish yellow jacket to these meetings. Many evaders subsequently commented on the coat, which Broussine describes as 'canary yellow' but which his great friend and admirer Paul Campinchi later recalled to his daughter Jeanne as being nearer to the colour of goose excrement.

Sgt Frederic G A Weight and F/Sgt Douglas K Nolan RCAF were gunners on board 7 Sqn Stirling R9278 (Taylor) which was returning from Stuttgart in the early hours of 15 April 1943 when they were attacked by fighters and the aircraft abandoned to crash near Saint-Souplet-sur-Py (Marne).[1]

Weight, Nolan and their navigator, S/Ldr R H Lunney, landed close to one another in a ploughed field about twenty miles east of Chalons-sur-

1   Pilot F/Lt James T R Taylor evaded for six days, getting as far as Lugagnan (south of Lourdes) before he was picked up by Vichy police on 21 April 1943. He was held for two months in prison at Castres with SD pilots Peter Kingsford-Smith and Robert Hogg before being sent to Fresnes and then Stalag Luft III (Sagan) in October.

Marne. Lunney had dislocated his shoulder and insisted that he be left to seek medical attention by himself. After walking until late morning, and at the second time of trying, Weight and Nolan approached a labourer in a field who called another man over. The two airmen were taken to a hut where they were told to wait while food and clothes were brought for them.

The man who returned from Saint-Souplet-sur-Py with their original two helpers was an agriculturalist named August Leroux who took Weight and Nolan to stay at his house. While they were sheltered there, a friend of M Leroux's called Andre, went to Reims to try and contact a man he thought might help them. They were then visited by the man from Reims who asked them to fill in a form with their details. On 3 May, they were driven to Reims, where they stayed at the back of an undertaker's shop with a man they only knew as Pierre. Two days later, Henri Perceval (an ex-cadet from St Stanislas College in Paris) took them by train to Paris, arriving at about nine o'clock that evening. Henri first led them to an address near Luftwaffe headquarters but as there was no-one there, took them to a hotel where several cadet friends of his were staying. Next day, Henri took them to the Hotel Glasgow (query) and then to Stanislas College where Father Georges Murillo (nf) arranged for them to stay in a disused apartment belonging to one of the house-keepers. On 16 May, Raymond Patenotte took them to his unoccupied apartment at 8 Place de Breutil (near the statue of Louis Pasteur) while Father Murillo arranged to have food sent to them.

On 23 May, Henri Percival took Weight and Nolan to the Champs-Elysees where he passed them over to another man who took them to 51 rue de Miromesnil, Paris VIII where they stayed with Jean and Laura De Traz for a week, during which time they had their photographs taken for ID cards.

Jean Francois Edouard De Traz (born May 1895) and his wife Laure (born June 1881) sheltered some twenty evaders in their sixth-floor apartment at 51 rue Miromesnil as well as acting as guides around Paris. They also allowed their apartment to be used for radio transmissions and as a place to hide large amounts of organisation funds. Both were awarded KMCs for their escape line work.[2]

On 1 June, Weight and Nolan were taken to the Jardin des Plantes where they joined American Spitfire pilot Edward Gimbel.

A guide led the three airmen to the Gare d'Austerlitz where they took

2   TNA folder WO208/5451.

22

the eight-thirty, overnight train to Toulouse (arriving at nine o'clock next morning) where they changed for Foix, arriving there at three-thirty in the afternoon. At Foix they were taken to a park where they waited for an hour until a small lorry picked them up and took them a few miles outside town where they met their mountain guides.[3]

They set off in the pouring rain at eight o'clock that evening, finally reaching Ordino in Andorra at about ten o'clock on the morning of 4 June. They stayed at the Hotel Kine (Casa Quim – query) until the morning of 6 June when they were taken to stay the night with a smuggler guide before setting off again, crossing the border into Spain that evening. They walked for a week to Gironella, arriving at about two o'clock in the morning of 14 June, where they were supposed to catch a workman's train but the man sent to buy their tickets failed to return before the train left. They had by this time, been joined by Sgts Andrew Smith and William Fitzgerald from Stirling BK725. Whilst waiting for the afternoon train, the whole group – Gimbel, Weight, Nolan, Smith, Fitzgerald and Kingsley – were arrested and taken to Barca where they spent the next 26 days in gaol.

Note that evaders who weren't fortunate enough to be taken directly to the safety of the British Consulate in Barcelona, were almost inevitably arrested by the Spanish Guardia Civil and interned. Generally they would be repatriated to Allied control within a few weeks.

---

3   It should be noted that the majority of mountain guides (passeurs) did not work for any particular escape line. Although there were some exceptions, many passeurs were smugglers who would work for whoever could pay for their services at the time.

CHAPTER 5

The First Two Special Duties Crewmen

On 2 July 1943, P/O John Hutchinson and Sgt William Marshall left Paris by train for Toulouse and Foix.

News of the Bourgogne organisation was soon spreading to various resistance networks around the country. It was a group in the Centre region, some ninety miles south of the capital, which sheltered Hutchinson and Marshall for six weeks until they made contact with Bourgogne and arranged for the two airmen to be collected and taken to rue de Miromesnil in Paris.

P/O John T Hutchinson and Sgt William H Marshall were the air gunner and flight engineer of 138 Sqn SD Halifax BB313 (Robinson) which was returning from an SOE mission to France in the early hours of 13 May 1943 when it was hit by flak about twenty miles west of Troyes and abandoned. Second pilot Sgt John C Tweed also evaded successfully – he spent four months in France before being collected by 161 SD Lysander (along with SOE agent Ben Cowburn) from a field near Vandrimare (south-east of Rouen) the night of 17-18 September 1943.

Hutchinson and Marshall both landed in fields near Dierrey-Saint-Pierre (Aube) and soon joined up. They say they used the compasses from their escape kits to head south but they actually went west, reaching Faux-Villecerf at about six that morning. They rested in a barn for a couple of hours until spotted by a farmhand, who gave them a bottle of milk. They then carried on walking, passing through Courgenay (still going west) where they were given food and some blue overalls to wear over their uniforms – and allowed to rest for a few more hours. Later that afternoon, they met a farm labourer who hid them overnight in another barn. Next morning they did head south but because of the number of people about, spent most of the day in a field and only walked as far as Lailly (Yonne).

Hutchinson and Marshall were soon sheltered on a farm near Lailly (family Boivin at Toucheboeuf farm – query) where they were visited by Mlle Francoise Lapotre, daughter of Jean Lapotre, a schoolteacher at Thorigny-sur-Oreuse. Next day (14 May) Francoise took them back to her home on Route du Sens where they were visited by an English ex-army officer (aged about 50) who said he would help by getting them bicycles so they could cycle to Spain. Early on the morning of 16 May, one of Francoise' brothers took the two airmen to a cave near the village and that evening, Francoise brought a priest by the name of Barbier (Abbe Jules Barbier – query) and a former French aviator to see them. The aviator drove them to his home in Sens where they had a meal before going on to the priest's house, a fairly large chateau just outside the village of Chatillon-Coligny (Loiret) about 15 miles south-east of Montargis. Hutchinson and Marshall comment that Barbier seemed to be a very unorthodox priest who carried a revolver and told them that he was a member of an organisation engaged in sabotage and distributing arms and materiel brought by air from England.

On 18 May, a forty-four-year-old carpenter named Bannery took them by car to his home at Nogent-sur-Verisson. He said that he was a member of M Barbier's organisation and Hutchinson and Marshall stayed with him until 23 May when they were taken to stay with gamekeeper Andre Suplisson, also in Nogent. They only stayed a few days before moving back to M Bannery's and then on about 15 June, were moved again, this time to a farm near Pressigny-les-Pins. On 19 June, M Barbier visited to say he had contacted an escape organisation who would take charge of them and that same day, M Bannery took them back to Nogent once more. M Barbier told the airmen he had to collect some materiel that was to be dropped that night and later they saw a Halifax fly low over the house that seemed to confirm the story.[1]

Next day (20 June) M Bannery drove them to a garage in Montargis where they were given two suits of civilian clothes before a young man took them to the station. They joined a woman doctor (who said her husband was an American fighter pilot) and the two evaders were taken by train to Paris. They stayed with Dr Alice Willm at 51 rue de Miromesnil – having their photographs taken at a Bon Marche store and visited by a member of the organisation who they believed had been parachuted into France from one of their own SD aircraft.

Doctor Alice Willm (born June 1904) was a pediatrician who lived on the fifth floor at 51 rue de Miromesnil. Like her neighbours Jean and Laure De Traz on the floor above, she also sheltered numerous evaders in her

---

1   'Agents by Moonlight' (1999) by Freddie Clark, published by Tempus, says that F/O Afleck of 161 SD Sqn flew a sortie to France that night.

apartment and housed several escape line agents – she also guided two parties of evaders from Paris to Pau. Dr Willm was recommended for an MBE for her escape line work and received a KMC.[2] She is described by American evader John Wagner as tall, with dark hair and a dark complexion. Mlle Jeanne Gueremy, another one of Gabrielle Wiame's contacts and also listed by Broussine as a Bourgogne helper, also lived at 51 rue de Miromesnil.

On 2 July, Georges Broussine came and introduced Hutchinson and Marshall to a young Frenchman called Peter who spoke perfect English.[3] They also met another young Frenchman – referred to as 'Chief' – who had been with the French navy at Dakar. That evening the two young Frenchmen took them to the Gare d'Austerlitz where they boarded the eight o'clock overnight train to Toulouse. From Toulouse they took an electric train to Foix, arriving at three that afternoon. The two airmen and Peter were taken to the outskirts of Foix where they were picked up by car and driven to some woods to join two more Frenchmen and two Spanish guides and at ten o'clock that evening (3 July) they set off to cross the Pyrenees.[4]

Hutchinson and Marshall reached Ordino in Andorra at about eleven-thirty on the morning of 6 July. They stayed for two days in Ordino before being driven through the capital, Andorra la Vieja, to Sant Julia de Loria where they stayed another three days in a hotel. On 11 July, they set off with two Spanish guides and a local tobacco smuggler, walking through the night across the border into Spain and on to Manresa. The journey (some 135 kms) took seven days, their guides getting them food and shelter from farms along the way. On 18 July, they caught the seven o'clock morning train from Manresa to Barcelona and the British Consulate.[5]

---

2   TNA folder WO208/5451.

3   I think that Peter was Pierre Maroger (born January 1924 in Nimes). His IS9 recommendation for an award says that he trained in England before returning to France where he worked with an escape organisation. (WO208/5452). Broussine says that Maroger made several journeys between Paris and Madrid.

4   In the 1953 book '70 True Stories of the Second World War' published by Odihams Press, Marshall describes in extravagant detail the trial he endured on the rail journey to Toulouse, including having to hide under the train during a German check at the demarcation line for young men trying to evade the STO. However their combined Appx C (in TNA folder WO208/5582) says it was twenty-two-year-old Hutchinson who hid under the train while thirty-three-year-old Marshall remained in the compartment and 'was not visited by the German control' …

5   The location of the British Consulate in Barcelona changed throughout the war. In 1925, the Consulate was at 276 Consell de Cents, on the corner of Cents and Balmes but in 1942, it was located at the Casa Lleó Morera, further along Consell de Cents on the corner of the Passeig de Gracia. The third WWII location is the first floor of the building on the corner of Caller de les Jonqueras and Carrer de Trafalgar, near the Urquinova metro station. My grateful thanks to Geoff Cowling, former Consul-General at Barcelona, for researching these details.

CHAPTER 6

Some Pat Line and Oaktree Connections

The Oaktree escape line, set up by MI9 agents Val Williams (Vladimir Bouryschine) and Ray Labrosse in early 1943 with the intention of sending men out from Brittany by Royal Navy MGBs, was closely associated with Elisabeth Barbier and groupe Vaneau in Paris. Following the cancellation of the proposed sea evacuations at the end of May, Oaktree began sending men south to cross the Pyrenees from Pau but the arrest of Williams a few days later – and of Elisabeth Barbier later that same month – left many men trapped in the capital.

S/Sgt Frank W Greene was assistant radio-operator of B-17 41-24603 Green Hornet (303BG/359BS) (Sanderson) which was returning from Lorient on 23 January 1943 when it was damaged by flak and shot down by fighters. The crew baled out and the aircraft crashed near Plouray in Brittany. Three other Green Hornet crewmen also evaded successfully: navigator 2/Lt John W Spence and engineer Sgt Sidney Devers were taken across the Pyrenees by the Comete line in February, and radio-operator T/Sgt Miles B Jones by the PAO at the end of March.

Greene landed close to a village near the crash-site and was met on the ground by a crowd of Frenchmen. He ran to a nearby farmhouse where the farmer's wife hid his parachute and tended to his numerous facial injuries. Greene was moved to another house the following day where he stayed with a schoolteacher until 24 February when a man came to see him and arrange his subsequent journey. Greene was taken to Paris that night and sheltered by Simone Levavasseur. Mlle Levavasseur lived at 6 rue Mouton-Duvernet, Paris XIV and owned a chocolate shop called 'La Petite Chocolatiere', around the corner at 19 Avenue d'Orleans (renamed as Avenue du General Leclerc in 1948), the same building complex (*Villa Adrienne*) as Pat Line logeur Armand Leveque. Greene stayed in a room above the shop, just across a garden from the Leveque's first-floor apartment where Sgt Daniel Young was being sheltered.[1]

Simone Levavasseur (born December 1895) is credited with sheltering numerous evaders, often several at a time, either in her apartment or above her shop, La Petite Chocolatiere. Mlle Levavasseur had been recruited by Armand Leveque the previous November when he asked her to shelter Norwegian Spitfire pilot Thor Waerner. She is described by Robert Giles and Carroll Haarup, who stayed five weeks with her in late 1943 (see later) as a well dressed, attractive woman, about 35 (sic) years old, 5 ft 4 inches tall, with grey-streaked dark hair. Simone Levavasseur was awarded a BEM.[2]

Greene would visit Young and play cards with him, and Armand's daughter Andree had Greene's photograph taken for a new ID card. On the morning of 4 March, Armand Leveque telephoned to warn them to be extra careful and shortly afterwards, Greene saw five men in plain-clothes come and arrest Mme Marcelle Leveque, her sister Mme Julienne Lassouquere and Sgt Young.[3]

Mme Reine Merovitz (a Swiss woman who was hiding with Mlle Levavasseur) moved Greene to stay with Paul and Olga Christol in their sixth-floor apartment at 4 rue Edouard Quenu until 9 April when Andree Leveque took him to Elisabeth Barbier's apartment at 72 rue Vaneau.

---

1   Sgt Daniel C Young was the flight engineer of 35 Sqn Halifax W7885 (Thomas) which was hit by flak over Lorient on the evening of 13 February 1943 and abandoned to crash near Carhaix (Finistere). Young had been brought to Paris on 20 February – seeing his pilot and radio-operator at the station with another guide – and lodged at the Leveque apartment (while George Hallett prepared false papers) until 4 March …

With the exception of tail-gunner F/O William J Freeman, who died twenty minutes after landing, the other five crewmen from W7885 evaded successfully. Pilot Sgt James C Thomas was helped by the Pat O'Leary organisation in Brittany and taken to Paris by Georges Jouanjean. He was sheltered by Julienne Lassouquere at 20 rue St Ferdinand until 4 March when her niece Andree Leveque telephoned and told him to leave the house immediately. Thomas made his way to Switzerland, where he remained until September 1944. (Thomas interview with MMLB in Toronto 1997) Navigator F/O Gordon H F Carter and mid-upper gunner Sgt John Napoleon Barry were taken to Paris by Georges Jouanjean on 20 March but when he found the Leveque apartment on Avenue d'Orleans had been raided, Jouanjean took the two men back to Brittany and the Oaktree organisation. Carter was evacuated from Treboul on board the sardine boat Dalc'h Mad on 6 April and Barry taken across the Pyrenees in June, along with wireless operator Sgt Edward R Turenne and engineer Sgt Richard Martin.

2   TNA folder WO208/5451.

3   Armand Leveque escaped to Belgium (query) and was later betrayed by a Belgian known as M Metz and arrested at the Gare du Nord in Paris on 9 July 1943 – he died in Germany in January 1945. Andree Leveque (born June 1921) was also arrested on 9 July 1943 when she went to the Hotel Cyrano at 14 rue Papillon looking for her father. Andree and her mother Marcelle (born June 1889) survived deportation (Andree at least to Ravensbruck) and were repatriated from Buchenwald in May 1945. (WO208/5452)

Mme Marcelle Leveque says in a post-war interview that she believed her family were denounced by PAO courier Roger Leneveu. (Leveque NARA file) Pat O'Leary and Paul Ulmann had been arrested two days earlier at a meeting with Leneveu in Toulouse and Jean de la Olla, Alex Wattebled and Norbert Fillerin (all PAO and also betrayed by Leneveu) were arrested in Paris the following day.

Mme Julienne Renee Lassouquere (born September 1896) of 20 rue Saint Ferdinand, Paris XVII, was deported to Ravensbruck where she remained until liberated on 5 April 1945. (WO208/5452)

Greene was introduced to Frederic De Jongh of Comete who took him to be sheltered elsewhere. On 27 April, Frederic De Jongh turned Greene over to Oaktree boss Val Williams who gave him new ID papers and took him to the station where Genevieve de Poulpiquet, known as the countess, accompanied him, along with F/Sgt Gordon Spencer and other Oaktree evaders, on the train to St Brieuc where they changed for Etables.

Paul Jean Christol (born September 1892) – who worked as an engineer with Lever Bros in Paris – and his wife Marcelle Olga Christol (born August 1897) sheltered numerous evaders in their tiny apartment at 4 rue Edouard Quenu, Paris V as well guiding some of them to other locations. Both were recommended for awards and Olga received an MBE.[4] Drue Tartiere – in her 1946 book 'The House Near Paris' – describes Paul Christol as a short, grey-haired man of about fifty and his wife Olga as a small, kindly woman of about the same age.

Mme la comtesse Genevieve de Poulpiquet de Brescanvel (aka Gilberte) (born February 1905) and her husband le comte Cesaire sheltered numerous evaders in their home at the Chateau de Trefy near Quemeneven, Finistere. Following Cesaire's arrest in March 1943 – he was deported to Germany where he died – Genevieve, who was fortunate to avoid the same fate, was put in contact with Georges Jouanjean and Job le Bec of Oaktree.[5] She also had the address of Paul Campinchi in Paris and later moved to the capital where she continued with her escape line work, first with Oaktree and later with reseau Francois. Genevieve de Poulpiquet was recommended for a KMC.[6]

I mentioned earlier that this story could get confusing with so many other organisations being involved. As an example, it is perhaps worth noting that men sheltered at the Chateau de Trefy included five evaders from the B-17 41-24584 SUSFU, which was shot down over Brittany on 23 January 1943. All five were later captured at Tours with Louis Nouveau and Suzanne Gerard of the Pat line. The other two evaders from the crew were evacuated on board the Breton fishing vessel Yvonne along with Sgt Reginald Smith RAF, the first evader to be helped by Paul Campinchi. It

---

4   TNA folder WO208/5451.

5   Georges Jouanjean (born May 1917) of Carhaix worked with the PAO and then Oaktree, guiding and sheltering evaders in Brittany. He was arrested in Paris in June (see later) and deported to Germany. Georges Jouanjean was repatriated back to France in 1945 and recommended for a BEM. (WO208/5452) Jean (aka Job) le Bec (born June 1895) and his wife Anna (born October 1894) of the Moulin de la Pie, near Paule in Brittany, are credited with sheltering some thirty Allied evaders. Both were recommended for KMCs. (WO208/5458)

6   TNA folder WO208/5456.

was Mme de Poulpiquet who later introduced Paul Campinchi to Olga L'Hoir-Sivry, the lady who sheltered Campinchi and his wife Therese at her home at 6 rue Nicolet after they were forced to leave their apartment on rue des Ursines following the demise of Oaktree in June, and where Lucien Dumais and Ray Labrosse stayed when they came to Paris in November to set up the Shelburn escape line.[7]

Paul Francois Campinchi (born Oct 1903) first became involved with helping Allied evaders in January 1943 when he sheltered Sgt Reginald Smith RAF for three weeks in his Paris home before taking him to Quimper, Finistere. Smith was handed over to two men (known as Ronnie and Roger) who arranged his evacuation to England on board the Breton fishing vessel Yvonne (along with two SUSFU crewmen) which sailed from the north Brittany port of Carantec on 5 February. Campinchi's name was passed to MI9 in London and he became a contact for Val Williams and Ray Labrosse when they arrived in Paris the following month to set up the Oaktree mission. With the demise of Oaktree, Campinchi came under suspicion, forcing him and his wife Therese to leave their apartment on rue des Ursines but when Labrosse returned in November with Lucien Dumais to set up the Shelburn escape line, Campinchi was persuaded to help them. He created reseau Francois, the ultra secure organisation in Paris that collected and sheltered most of the evaders taken back to England by Shelburn on the five Bonaparte operations.

F/Sgt Gordon L Spencer RCAF was the air bomber (bomb-aimer) of 405 Sqn Halifax BB250 (Dennison) which was returning from Stuttgart in the early hours of 12 March 1943 when they were attacked by fighters and the aircraft abandoned to crash near Mondrepuis (Aisne).[8]

Twenty-one-year-old Spencer landed in a wood near Mondrepuis. His escape and evasion lecturers had advised against staying in heavily wooded areas as these were liable to be searched and on leaving the wood, he found some scattered paper fragments with writing that Spencer, a passable but not fluent French speaker, recognised as French – his first indication that he had actually landed in France. Spencer had prepared for the possibility

---

7   Mme Olga L'Hoir-Sivry (born September 1907) was recommended for a KMC. (WO208/5452)

8   Two crew were killed and rear-gunner F/Sgt Kennett RCAF was injured and later betrayed by the people he had sought help from but the other four men from BB250 also evaded successfully: second pilot S/Ldr Emerson L Logan RCAF and wireless operator F/Sgt Harold J Jennings RCAF crossed the Pyrenees in March 1943 – and pilot P/O Borden C Dennison RCAF and navigator F/Sgt Elmer L Bulman RCAF crossed the Pyrenees with Oaktree in June.

of being shot down and in addition to his aids box, carried a basic wash kit and some first-aid items. At daybreak he made his way to an isolated farmhouse but while he was studying it, was surprised by a customs officer armed with a pistol. Before Spencer could make his escape, the man came to attention and saluted, asking if he was an English parachutist. Spencer explained he was in fact Canadian and the Frenchman used Spencer's escape map to show him where he was. He also told Spencer that the people in the farmhouse could be trusted but he should wait until nightfall before approaching them. Spencer followed this advice and was sheltered in a hayloft on the farm for two nights before being taken into the house. He was visited by the maire of Mondrepuis, Georges Clement, who gave him civilian clothes and news of some of his crew. Next day (16 March) a doctor from Mondrepuis drove Spencer about ten miles south-east to the village of Aubenton where he joined his pilot P/O Borden Dennison and their journeys were arranged.

On 23 March, Emile Fontaine (one of Dennison's helpers from Aubenton) drove Spencer and Dennison to Any-Martin-Rieux where they caught a train to Charleville-Mezieres. A woman from the mairie took them back to her flat and they met a man named Stefan Brice (the IS9 Helper file has Etienne Brice of Charleville, Ardennes). Brice, who spoke some English and said he had earlier worked for an organisation in Lille, had a list of the crew from another aircraft (Halifax R9149) which included Sgts Douglas Cox and George Howard. Brice wanted Spencer and Dennison to confirm their identities (he seemed suspicious of Howard) but unfortunately they didn't know either of the 7 Squadron men.

A few days later, M Brice took Spencer and Dennison to stay with Andre Fainot (query) – they also met George Howard who was staying nearby with Robert Quespigne – until 7 April when Brice took them, Howard, Mme Fainot and a woman friend of hers, by train to Paris. They went to Paul's apartment (on the third floor at 28 rue Vaneau) where they stayed for about a month. They also met F/Lt Moire Pierre and learned that Paul (Fredric De Jongh) had paid all of Brice's expenses. On 6 May, Paul handed them over to Val's organisation (Oaktree) and they left Paris for St Brieuc in Brittany – the group being Spencer, Dennison, Howard and S/Sgt Frank Greene USAAF – with their guide, Genevieve de Poulpiquet. From St Brieuc they went on to Etables and then to a farm near St-Quay-Portrieux. On 1 May, they were taken to stay with Mme Emilie Cellarier at the villa Lein-au-Lan in Treveneuc, near Plouha.

Cox and Howard (and others) returned to Paris on 20 May and crossed the Pyrenees from Pau to Isaba with Dennison at the beginning of June – see note later.

On 3 June (query), Andree Leveque (who had left Paris following the arrest of her mother and was living in St-Quay-Portrieux) took Spencer, Greene, Sgt Henry Riley and a Russian evader named Abram Kononenko back to Paris to meet Val Williams who was supposed to give them new ID papers and take them to Pau. They got as far as St Brieuc but couldn't get tickets for the Paris train and so stayed overnight and didn't reach Paris until the following day. Andree took them to Elisabeth Barbier's apartment at 72 rue Vaneau before they were moved elsewhere – Spencer to stay with Albert Calonne[9] at 42 bis rue Poliveau until 15 June, and Riley and Kononenko with Madeleine Melot – whilst waiting for their tickets. On 6 June, they were told that Williams had gone to Bordeaux with two Polish evaders[10] and been arrested and a blonde lady called Marie (Gabrielle Wiame) took Greene to stay with a doctor from Paimpol. On 18 June, Elisabeth Barbier's apartment was raided and Elisabeth was arrested.[11]

Greene and Spencer remained in Paris, taken to be sheltered by two English ladies, Maud Couve and Alice Brouard in their third-floor apartment at 25 rue de Madrid, until Ray Labrosse (either through Paul Campinchi or Gabrielle Wiame – both of whom knew Georges Broussine personally) made contact with the Bourgogne organisation. On 8 July, Ray Labrosse took Greene and Spencer to meet Broussine at a Presbyterian church.

Maud Couve was French by birth (in 1905) but British by marriage to Edward Couve, who was in England at this time. They had two children – Jimmy aged ten and Betty, aged about three, who was physically handicapped.

9   Albert Calonne had only recently become involved with helping evaders. In May, his friend Emile Debouche had brought F/Sgt Elmer Bulmer from Chateau Thierry and delivered him to his (Emile's) sister Gabrielle Wiame, who lived just a few doors away from Albert. (undated *renseignement* from Albert Calonne in FNA files)

10   The two Polish evaders arrested with Val Williams were Sgts Leszek Zaborowski and Rech Urbanski from 138 SD Halifax BB340 (Jensen) which was shot down by flak near Caen on an SOE mission to France the night of 12-13 April 1943. Urbanski says there were three evaders and two guides – one of whom (Williams) was caught, leaving them with a locked case containing several million francs – but I've no idea who the second guide – or the third evader – might have been …

11   Elisabeth Barbier (born January 1912) and her mother Camille (born June 1889) were arrested in their apartment at 72 rue Vaneau on 18 June 1943. After being held at Fresnes, both women were deported to Ravensbruck – they were repatriated back to France in April 1945. Elisabeth Barbier was awarded the King's Medal for Courage and Mme Camille Barbier, the King's Medal for Service in the Cause of Freedom. (WO208/5455) Elisabeth Barbier and her mother are believed to have been betrayed by Belgian traitor and infiltration agent Jacques Desoubrie.

Alice Brouard was British (born 1904 on Jersey) and married to a Frenchman from Guernsey, John Brouard, who was interned at *La Grande Caserne*, just north of Paris at Saint Denis. They also had two children – Christine, aged thirteen, who was staying with her grandparents in Normandy, and fifteen-year-old Marguerite. The two-bedroom apartment at 25 rue de Madrid belonged to Maud Couve but Alice and Marguerite Brouard joined her there after both families were released from the internment camp at Besancon in March 1941. The following year, Maud Couve was asked by her dentist if she would consider sheltering downed airmen in her apartment and after discussion with Alice, she agreed. They were visited by M Robert (Robert Guillet) and Mme Marie (Gabrielle Wiame) but were never told which organisation they were working with. Both women were bilingual in French and English and Maud had a library with many books in English – a real luxury for evaders with time on their hands (they weren't allowed to leave the apartment) and little or no knowledge of French. Evaders stayed in the larger of the two bedrooms while Maud, Alice and their children slept in the living-room. Pseudonyms were not used and many evaders mention the two middle-aged ladies by name.

25 rue de Madrid was (and still is) a fairly up-market building that had been converted to have two apartments on each of four floors plus a fifth floor that had housed the maids. There was a lift and a service entrance with rear stairs that could be used by the evaders if necessary. Being British, the two women had to report to the police each day and neither was allowed to work. With so many visitors however (there was no telephone) their concierge began to wonder if they were prostitutes – a not unknown side-line for women in those desperate times. Their only friends were a select group of fellow helpers and resistance contacts. Maud and Alice sheltered numerous evaders in their tiny apartment, the last being F/Lt James L Kennedy RCAF who left on 28 November 1943 (see later) as well as guiding others around the city.[12]

Unlike Gordon Spencer and Frank Greene, who evaded for several months with Oaktree and group Vaneau before being passed on to Bourgogne, Lester Brown and John Houghton were on their way to the Pyrenees within twelve days of baling out – and safe in the neutral principality of Andorra two days later.

---

12   Following an email exchange in 2013, Marguerite Miller kindly sent me a copy of her 2002 book 'The World War II Years of Marguerite' by Marguerite Fraser née Brouard, printed at Regis University, Denver, Colorado, from which some of these (and other) details are taken.

S/Sgt Lester Brown and S/Sgt John H Houghton were the radio-operator and ball-turret gunner of B-17 42-30058 (384BG/546BS) (Rosio) which was shot down by fighters returning from Villacoublay aerodrome on 26 June 1943. The bale-out order was given and the aircraft abandoned to crash near Dourdan (Ile de France).

Six other crew also evaded successfully, five more with Bourgogne (see later) and bombardier 2/Lt Sidney Casden who was sheltered for four months in the suburbs of Paris before being passed on to the Francois-Shelburn organisation at the end of November and brought back to England by RN MGB 503 in January 1944 on the first Bonaparte operation.

Brown and Houghton were helped immediately on landing and soon joined fellow crewmen 1/Lt Joseph Rosio, 1/Lt George Evans, S/Sgt John Kuberski and S/Sgt Anthony Cucinotta. They were driven to Saint Cyr-sous-Dourdan and on 28 June, Brown and Houghton were taken to Paris where they were passed on to Georges Morin, the caretaker at Napoleon's Tomb (Les Invalides). They were visited that evening by two English-speaking Frenchmen and moved next day to the home of a Marquis on nearby rue de Varenne where the butler, Albert Rault (of 34 rue Saint-Dominique) sheltered them.[13] During their stay they had their photographs taken and were supplied with ID cards and work permits. Eight days later (on 8 July) they were taken to a Presbyterian church where they met Burgundy (Georges Broussine) who stamped their cards and gave them new clothing. They were passed to a guide known as Jacques (Jacques Niepceron) who took them and a French airman called Jean Bataille – and Oaktree evaders Gordon Spencer and Frank Greene – to the Gare d'Austerlitz and the overnight train to Toulouse where they changed for Foix.

From Foix they walked south until collected by a small Renault pick-up (at which point Jacques left them and was replaced by two Spanish mountain guides) and driven further south before starting their walk across the Pyrenees. They reached Andorra the following day (10 July) where they stayed for three days at the Hotel Coma in Ordino before being driven to the Spanish border. They crossed into Spain in the late evening of 14 July and then continued on foot to Manresa, arriving at about three in the morning of 21 July, where they took a train to Barcelona. They reached the British Consulate that same morning.

---

13   Marquise Elie Anne de Lubersac lived at number 60 rue de Varenne – and comte Alphonse de la Bourdonnaye at number 55. (IS9 Helper List)

CHAPTER 7

Another Four Oaktree Evaders

Frederic De Jongh and Robert Ayle were arrested on 7 June 1943 and the Paris operation of Comete was effectively – if temporarily – broken. Gabrielle Wiame says (in her NARA file) that she was abandoned with seventeen evaders and Ray Labrosse for three weeks until she was able to make contact with Georges Broussine.[1]

On 13 July 1943, Ray Labrosse took Sgt Henry Riley, Abram Kononenko, 2/Lt Frank Perrica and S/Sgt Salvadore Tafoya by train from Paris to Toulouse and Foix.

As already mentioned, evaders could be moved from one organisation to another – in this case, as for so many of the early Bourgogne evaders, from the ill-fated Oaktree line. Riley, an English airman who landed in eastern France in April 1943, was brought to Paris where he was passed on to Oaktree and taken to Brittany in the hope that he would be evacuated by sea. When that plan was aborted, he was joined by a Russian evader named Kononenko, and returned to Paris to be sheltered by group Vaneau. Following Elizabeth Barbier's arrest, the two men were taken on by Madeleine Melot and sheltered until she could pass them over to Bourgogne. On leaving Paris, they were joined by Perrica and Tafoya, two American airmen who had been shot down over Brittany six weeks earlier and brought to Elizabeth Barbier shortly before her arrest. They were then sheltered elsewhere in the capital until contact was made with Bourgogne via Oaktree radio-operator, Ray Labrosse.

Sgt Henry Riley was the twenty-four-year-old navigator of 51 Sqn Halifax DT670 (Inch) which was returning from Pilsen (Czechoslovakia) in the early hours of 17 April 1943. They had already been hit by flak near Mannheim on the way out that had stopped their port-inner engine and on the return leg, near Chalons-sur-Marne, there was a series of explosions, probably from a night-fighter attack, and the pilot gave the order to bale

---

1   Frederic De Jongh and Robert Ayle were shot at Mont-Valerien, Paris on 28 March 1944.

out. Five crew were killed and one captured – Riley was the only successful evader.

Riley landed close to his burning aircraft, in open country just east of Chaintrix-Bierges (west of Chalons-sur-Marne) (now Chalons-en-Champagne) and after hiding his parachute, headed west. Riley walked to the tiny village of Trecon and approached the first farm he came to, declaring himself to the farmer who gave him food and some wine. The farmer then contacted someone in a neighbouring village (presumably Epernay) and Riley's journey was arranged.

On 22 April, a man called Francois took Riley from Epernay to Paris, arriving at about eight o'clock in the evening, then by Metro to Denfert-Rochereau (Paris XIV). Riley was sheltered near the Metro station by an elderly businessman (who had four or five daughters) for five days,[2] during which time Riley met American evader Frank Greene. On 27 April, Riley was taken to stay with one of the daughters and her husband who lived nearby and on 30 April, taken into Paris where he met Val Williams and Andree Leveque. Williams gave Riley a new ID card and then took him, a Canadian pilot (query) and an American airman (query) to Montparnasse station where they took a train to St Brieuc. That afternoon they went to Etables and the home of maire, Jerome Camard on rue de la Gare where they met Sqn/Ldr Peter Lefevre. Later that same afternoon, Riley, the Canadian, the American and a British Flight Lieutenant (query) were taken to stay with Jean and Virginia Lanlo in St-Quay-Portrieux, where they joined Sgt Allen Fitzgerald USAAF.

On 3 May, the evaders were taken to Mme Cellarier at Lein-au-Lan near Plouha where they met F/Sgt Gordon Spencer and joined 14 (sic) others – including Sgt Charles McDonald, P/O Borden Dennison, F/Sgt Elmer Bulman, Sgt Douglas Cox and T/Sgt Jack Leuhrs USAAF. Riley stayed ten days with Mme Cellarier, during which time, most of the others were taken to Paris.[3] On 13 May, Riley, Spencer, the American and Abram Kononenko were moved to a house on rue d'Olive at St-Quay-Portrieux

2   It seems likely that the family in Denfert-Rochereau were Joseph and Antoinette Carmoin and their daughters Marie, Louise and Therese of 20 rue Giodano Bruno, Paris XIV.

3   The airmen who were taken to Paris earlier – F/Lt Brian D Barker, F/Sgt John N Barry RCAF, S/Ldr Peter W Lefevre, F/Sgt Edward R Turenne RCAF, Sgt Richard Martin, Sgt Charles E McDonald RCAF, F/Sgt David E James RCAF, Sgt William G Grove, Sgt James A Smith, Sgt James Hall, Sgt Reginald W Adams, P/O Borden C Dennison RCAF, F/Sgt Elmer L Bulman RCAF, Sgt Douglas M Cox RCAF and Sgt George R Howard – left the capital on 28 May (with a guide called Jacques) by train for Dax and Pau to be taken across the Pyrenees by the Oaktree organisation, crossing into Spain near the Pic de la Coura on 3 June and walking down to Isaba – where they were arrested …

where they stayed for another week. On 20 May, they moved to a house near the Lanlo's where they joined Frank Greene and met a French Canadian, Ray Labrosse, and were generally looked after by Andree Leveque, who was posing as Labrosse's wife.

On about 27 May, Andree Leveque took Riley and Kononenko by overnight train from St Brieuc to Paris. They went to Elisabeth Barbier's apartment for about an hour before Madeleine Melot took the two evaders to her home at 11 bis rue Larrey. Kononenko left the next day but Riley stayed until 11 June when Mme Melot took him to a friend's house in the commune of Vanves for a week before moving him again, this time to the Denfert-Rochereau district to stay with Simone Levavasseur. Riley was sheltered above Mlle Levavasseur's shop, La Petite Chocolatiere at 19 Avenue d'Orleans where Frank Greene had stayed previously. On 3 July, Mme Melot took Riley back to her apartment where he stayed for another ten days until "she handed him over to an organisation". Riley was taken that afternoon (13 July) to the Jardins des Plantes where he joined Abram Kononenko, Frank Perrica and Salvadore Tafoya – plus four or five Frenchmen.

Abram S Kononenko was either a sergeant or a private. He claimed to be serving in the Russian air force but attached to an army unit retreating from the Germans when he was captured in September 1941 near Peryateno, near Kiev.

Kononenko says he was sent to a POW camp at Proskurov, near the Polish border, from where he escaped on 17 December 1941. Kononenko made his way to the village near Kiev where his mother lived and where he was recaptured in May 1942. For some reason, he was then sent through Poland, Germany and Belgium to a work camp in France near Valenciennes. On 15 October 1942, Kononenko and another Russian (first name Gregory) escaped and made their way into Belgium where they made contact with an organisation in a village near Mons. Kononenko stayed four months near Mons before being put in contact with the organisation that arranged his journey.

2/Lt Frank R Perrica and S/Sgt Salvadore Tafoya were the bombardier and tail-gunner of B-17 42-29531 (305BG/422BS) (Peterson) which was hit by flak over St Nazaire on 29 May 1943 and abandoned. Two other crew also evaded successfully – co-pilot 2/Lt Harold E Bentz evaded to Switzerland in July and ball-turret gunner S/Sgt Peter P Milasius with Bourgogne – see later.

Perrica, Tafoya and most of the rest of the crew landed a few miles south of Quintin in Brittany. A crowd of Frenchmen came to help them and Perrica and Tafoya paired off together. On 2 June, they were near the village of Guignen (south-west of Rennes) where they approached a farmer named Raymond Yrvon who invited them into his farmhouse. A few days later he took them to his home in Paris at 52 Ave d'Italie, Paris XIII and called in two of his neighbours, M Desire of 52 (or 54) Place d'Italie and Andre Douette of 147 Avenue de Choisy, and it was decided that they should stay with M Douette until contact was made with an organisation. They slept at Avenue de Choisy – and took their meals at Raymond Yrvon's home – being taken around the city where they "saw all the sights". They had "a good time" for just over a week until Elisabeth Barbier and her mother Camille came to interview them before taking the two Americans back to their apartment at 72 rue Vaneau. They were only in the apartment for about an hour before a large blonde lady called Helene (Helene de Suzannet – query) took them to stay overnight with an actor named Maurice Laporte at 32 rue Poliveau. Next day Kitty (Mme Hina Zipine) took Perrica and Tafoyato to 68 Boulevard Auguste-Blanqui where they were sheltered by Suzanne Guelat for a month and a half during which time they were told that Elisabeth had been arrested.[4] On 13 July, Ray Labrosse brought new ID papers and took them to the Jardin des Plantes.

The four evaders – Henry Riley, Abram Kononenko, Frank Perrica and Salvadore Tafoya – were given tickets and sandwiches and taken to the Gare d'Austerlitz where they caught the eight o'clock evening train to Toulouse, arriving next morning, and then another train to Foix, arriving at about two o'clock that afternoon. Labrosse left them at Foix and one of the Frenchmen arranged for a car to take the party to a rendezvous a few miles outside the town where they met a Belgian member of the organisation and two mountain guides. They set off at six o'clock that evening and reached Andorra three days later, in the afternoon of 17 July. They stayed in a hotel until 20 July, being joined there by four more evaders – Joseph Milne, Edward Spevak, Allen Fitzgerald and Anthony Cucinotta (see later) – when they set off for Manresa. After leaving Cucinotta at Solsona, they reached

---

4   Mme Suzanne Guelat (born November 1912 in Lille) was a supervisor at l'Hospital Sainte Anne in Paris. Her recommendation for an award says that after the capitulation of France, she took an active part in resistance activities and in early 1943, joined an evasion group. She (and husband Olivier) sheltered about twenty Allied evaders at her home and found safe lodgings for many others. (WO208/5456) Paul Campinchi (Francois of Francois-Shelburn) also confirms that Mme Guelat (aka Aline) worked with his organisation for sixteen months as chef d'equipe de logeur groupe Porc'her. (Campinchi family files)

Manresa on 26 July where they caught a train to Barcelona, arriving at two o'clock that afternoon, and were taken to the British Consulate.[5]

It is sometimes difficult to know when an evader was actually in touch with the Bourgogne line rather than an individual helper or member of another organisation. In the case of Perrica and Tafoya, Suzanne Guerlat was sheltering them on behalf of Oaktree but with the arrest of Val Williams, had no-one to pass them on to. It would presumably have been Ray Labrosse and/or Paul Campinchi who arranged to have them handed over to Bourgogne for their journey across the Pyrenees.

---

5   From the British Embassy in Madrid, rather than being taken Gibraltar like the other evaders, Abram Kononenko was given a Spanish passport and a Spanish guide who took him to Portugal. After about six weeks in a pension at Paco de Argos, Kononenko was flown to England where he was interviewed by IS9 on 7 October 1943. (WO208/5582 1455)

CHAPTER 8

15 July 1943

On 15 July 1943, Sgt Joseph Milne, 1/Lt Edward Spevak, Sgt Allen Fitzgerald and S/Sgt Anthony Cucinotta left Paris by train for Toulouse and Foix – their guide was Yves Allain.

Between 15 July and 1 September 1943, Yves Allain and Georges Baledent took over from Claude Leclercq (who left for Barcelona on a mission for Bourgogne at about this time) and Jacques Niepceron, alternating as guides taking parties of evaders to Foix. They often included few Frenchmen wanting to escape as their presence was thought to make the group seem more plausible at the various railway stations.

Georges Victor Marcel Baledent (born June 1921) (aka Petit Georges) worked as a guide with Bourgogne until November 1943 when various arrests (see later) forced him to leave France for England himself.[1]

Jacques Niepceron (born September 1922) of 30 Avenue Theophile Gautier, Paris XVI (his father Auguste lived at 84 rue de Turenne) is credited with guiding some thirty Allied evaders as well as helping many more. He was arrested on 21 August 1943 (caught on a train at Bordeaux) and deported to Germany that December. Jacques Niepceron was repatriated to France in April 1945 and recommended for a KMC.[2]

Following his recruitment by Georges Broussine in June, Allain had returned to his father's house in Tregourez and acquired suitable papers that would allow him to travel more freely. His uncle, Joseph Allain (of 28 rue Kercon, Quimper) arranged for Doctor Pirou (of rue Aristide Briand) to issue Yves with a medical certificate that showed him unsuitable for STO, and through M Corbier (an Alsation who worked as an interpreter at the German Kommandantur at Quimper) a *carte de travail* from the Kommandantur – all these documents being issued in Yves Allain's own name.[3]

Sgt Joseph R Milne was the second pilot of 429 Sqn Wellington BK162 (Holmes) which was returning from Mannheim in the early hours of 17

---

1 TNA folder WO208/5451.

2 NARA Niepceron & TNA folder WO208/5453.

3 NARA Allain.

April 1943. Already damaged by flak, they were attacked by a night-fighter near Soissons and the bomber was immediately set on fire. Although the pilot gave the order to bale out, twenty-six-year-old Milne was the only man to leave the doomed aircraft.

I've mentioned numerous airmen baling out from their aircraft but I wonder if the reader can imagine what that was like – the sudden fear they must have felt, especially the British bomber crews jumping at night, probably for the first time, not even knowing if their parachute would work.[4]

Milne landed in a potato field somewhere south of Soissons and after burying his parachute, set off walking north. That night (17 April) Milne met Theodore Mansart who took him back to his house in Acy (Aisne) and the following morning, the wife of the local maire came to visit. She told Milne that he should give himself up to the Germans and when he refused, said she would not inform on him if he left immediately. M Mansart took Milne to stay overnight with an electrician friend who also gave Milne a jacket, a pair of trousers and some shoes. Next morning he took Milne by bicycle to a hospital in Soissons where the surgeon was a member of an organisation. On 22 April, Mlle Jeanne Jauquet (who owned a dispensary) took Milne back to her house at 2 rue Gustave Alliaume where he stayed for the next five weeks, followed by another week with a friend of hers. During this time, Mlle Jauquet made several journeys to Laon to try and get help for Milne and on one of those visits, obtained an ID card for him. She also provided more civilian clothes for Milne and returned those he had been wearing to the electrician. On 4 June, a man took Milne by car to Laon where he stayed overnight with a French pilot (name unknown) and next day, he was driven to see a surgeon at the hospital in Hirson who took Milne to stay with his parents. On 8 June, Milne was taken by car to stay with Mme Cornelia Vant'Westeinde on her farm at Auge, near Aubenton – Sgt William Laws RAF had also been sheltered there in April. On 1 July, Dr Alain Josso from Aubenton took Milne to a farm at Liart where he stayed overnight with Emile Fontaine (apparently their eighteenth evader) and next day, a railway-worker took him to Charleville where Milne was met by several people and taken to the house of another electrician.

---

4   The situation was slightly different for fighter pilots and American bomber crews as they flew in daylight, would probably have known roughly where they were and at what altitude. They also had the advantge of being more easily spotted from the ground and so more likely to be found by their prospective helpers, many of whom had made plans for that eventuality. There was still no guarantee the parachute would work of course (there was only one way to find that out) and some Americans – like 2/Lt William J Cook (see later) – even seemed to accept baling out as part of the adventure.

On 8 July, a young girl from Paris took Milne by train back to the capital and the Trocodero district to stay in the same house on rue Greuze where Allen Fitzgerald (see below) had been sheltered for three days in April. That evening, Milne was taken to stay with a French ex-officer at 6 Square la Fontaine, Paris XVI for two nights. Then he spent two days at a house opposite the Oxford and Cambridge Hotel (query) belonging to a dressmaker, and the following night in a scout's hut. On 13 July, Milne was taken to stay with Madeleine Melot at 11 bis rue Larray for two nights before he was taken to the Jardin des Plantes near the Gare d'Austerlitz where he joined three American airmen – Edward Spevak, Allen Fitzgerald and Anthony Cucinotta – and a French aviator.

1/Lt Edward J Spevak was the twenty-three-year-old pilot of B-17 42-29627 Midnight (94BG/410BS) which was returning from Lorient on 17 May 1943 when it was attacked by fighters. The crew baled out and the aircraft crashed at Le Cloitre-Saint-Thegonnec, about 15 kms south of Morlaix in Brittany.

Spevak landed in the street of a small village near Morlaix and was helped immediately. He was taken to a nearby house where he was joined by his co-pilot 2/Lt Donald L Nichols and waist-gunner S/Sgt Donald C Parks, who had serious shrapnel wounds. The three men started walking, passing through Callac during the third night and later stopped in Plourin-les-Morlaix where their journey was arranged with the Oaktree escape line. Their helper was the maire of Plourin-les-Morlaix who sheltered them for three days while he contacted Job le Bec at the Moulin de la Pie who in turn contacted Georges Jouanjean. On 30 May, Georges Jouanjean took them to stay with Betty de Mauduit at the Chateau du Bourblanc near Plourivo where they met – amongst many others – Allen Fitzgerald, Allen Robinson and Marcus Davis.

Sgt Allen M Fitzgerald was a waist-gunner on B-17 42-5232 Available Jones (305BG/364BS) (Jones) which was returning from Billancourt on 4 April 1943 when it was attacked by fighters. The aircraft was abandoned south of Rouen and crashed near Le Vaudreuil.

Fitzgerald was helped immediately on landing and soon sheltered by the Raoul-Duvals (parents of evader Lt Claude Raoul-Duval – see later) in their chateau just outside Le Vaudreuil. Within a couple of days Fitzgerald was taken to the station where he joined his pilot 1/Lt Morris M Jones and they and their helpers took a train to Paris. Fitzgerald and Jones were taken to the Raoul-Duval's apartment at 43 rue du Faubourg Saint-Honore until two women came to collect them – Fitzgerald being taken to an apartment on rue Greuze. After having his photograph taken at a Bon Marche store, Fitzgerald was visited by Robert Ayle (head of Comete in Paris) who interrogated him. Three days later, Fitzgerald was taken to 20 rue Greuze where he was sheltered by comtesse Helene de Suzannet[5] along with F/Sgt Elmer Bulman RCAF and joined on the third day by his own radio-operator, T/Sgt Jack Leuhrs. They were visited by Val Williams and also by an American girl from Charlotte, South Carolina named Elisabeth Carmalt, of 28 rue Vaneau. About three weeks later, Elisabeth Barbier and Ray Labrosse took Fitzgerald and Bulman to the station where they took a train to Brittany. They stayed with Jean and Virginie Lanlo[6] at their Villa Soleil in St-Quay-Portrieux for three days before moving to St Brieuc with fourteen others, including Jack Leuhrs. A week later, Fitgerald was taken to stay with Betty de Mauduit at the Chateau du Bourblanc.

Betty de Mauduit was Mme la comtesse Roberta de Mauduit. Betty (as she was always known) was born in Polwarth, Scotland in September 1920 but her father was American and Betty, who grew up in America, retained her American citizenship. She was married to a Frenchman, le comte Henry de Mauduit, who was serving with the Free French in England at this time, while Betty lived in the beautiful Chateau du Bourblanc at Plourivo. Betty was arrested on 12 June 1943 (see later) and eventually deported to Ravensbruck, later transferred to hard labour in a munitions factory at Leipzig until being liberated in April 1945.

On 29 May, news was received from England that the planned sea evacuations from Brittany had been abandoned and on 5 June, Georges Jouanjean and Oaktree radio-operator Ray Labrosse took Spevak, Nichols, Fitzgerald, Robinson, Parks and Davis to Paris. They were met by Elisabeth Barbier who told them that Val Williams had been arrested whilst on his way to Pau. Spevak and Fitzgerald were taken to stay with a lady from the Red Cross, Tiphaine Macdonald Lucas (la comtesse de Boisbussel) at 4 Avenue de Nancy, Saint-Cloud[7] where they were sheltered for a week

---

5   Helene de Suzannet was Mme la comtesse Helene de Suzannet (née Mareuil in Paris 1901 and widow of le comte Jean de Suzannet). She was arrested on 23 June 1943 and spent six months in prison before being released because of ill health. (WO208/5452) Her elderly maid, Mme Marguerite Cardor, is also listed as a helper.

6   Jean Marie Lanlo (born Pontrieux January 1878) – not to be confused with his son Jean Francois Lanlo (born January 1909) – was arrested on 11 September 1943 and deported to Neuengamme in Germany where he died on 25 December 1944. (WO208/5459)

7   Mlle Suzanne Legrand (born May 1913) also at this address is credited with sheltering at least eight Allied service personnel. She was arrested on 1 November 1943 and deported to Germany. (WO208/5452)

before Spevak was moved to 4 rue Nicolas Roret where he stayed with Hina Zipine (aka Kitty). Fitzgerald was briefly returned to Elisabeth's apartment before Gabrielle Wiame took him to stay with a man called Louis at 101 Avenue Philippe Auguste.[8]

S/Sgt Donald C Parks and S/Sgt Marcus K Davis (from B-17 41-24609) stayed on at Elisabeth Barbier's apartment until 11 June when they were taken to stay with Drs Andre and Marguerite Bohn at 116 Boulevard Raspail – and were captured with them on 20 June 1943. Marcus Davis (RAMP Folder 5, pages 80/81) only mentions Mme Pfahl of 85 rue de la Convention, Paris XV as sheltering him for two weeks – other names forgotten.

On 15 July, Gabrielle Wiame took Spevak and Fitzgerald to the Jardin des Plantes where they met Joseph Milne, Anthony Cucinotta, two French guides and two other young Frenchmen.

S/Sgt Anthony F Cucinotta was with fellow B-17 42-30058 (Rosio) waist-gunner John Kuberski for much of his time in Paris but because of his injuries, stayed behind with a Doctor Cohen (sic – I think this was Drs Bohn at Blvd Raspail) after the others left on 8 July, joining Joseph Milne and Oaktree evaders Edward Spevak and Allen Fitzgerald at the Jardin des Plantes a week later.

Milne, Spevak, Fitzgerald and Cucinotta left the Gare d'Austerlitz with a man said to work for the Cook's agency, on the overnight train to Toulouse where they changed for Foix. Each evader was given two sandwiches which they thought was for the rail journey but later found were intended for the mountains. They reached Foix at about two o'clock in the afternoon and were taken by truck to a rendezvous outside town where they hid in a wood. They were joined by their mountain guides and at nine o'clock that evening, set off for the mountains, reaching Andorra on 18 July. After two days resting in Andorra, they joined another group of evaders – Henry Riley, Abram Kononenko, Frank Perrica and Salvadore Tafoya (see earlier) – for the long walk to Manresa.

Cucinotta walked with them as far as the Catalan town of Solsona where he was left behind and had to pay a local man to get him to the British Consulate in Barcelona, finally arriving there on 9 August.

---

8   101 Ave Phillipe Auguste, Paris XI is also the address for Dr Nestor and Mme Armadine Firpi. (IS9 Helper List)

CHAPTER 9

20 July 1943

On 20 July 1943, 1/Lt Theodore Peterson, T/Sgt John Scott, S/Sgt Roy Martin, Sgt William Hughes and Sgt Alfred Mansford left Paris by train for Toulouse and Foix. The evaders don't give any details of their guide but it was probably Georges Baledent (see earlier).

The reader may have noticed that in the majority of cases, airmen – especially the fighter pilots and American bomber crews, who generally flew their missions in daylight – were helped by local people soon after landing. By the middle of 1943, the French had experienced the harsh realities of German occupation for three long years. Even those who had despised, or at least distrusted, the British – and there were many of those at the beginning of the war – were finding out first-hand just how unpleasant life under German rule was and realising that their only hope for a free and independent France lay with victory for the Allies. There were still some exceptions, people who genuinely preferred the idea of an organised German government – and some who simply wanted the cash rewards offered for information leading to the capture of Allied airmen – but these became rarer as the war continued and it became more and more obvious that it was only a question of time before the inevitable *debarquement* took place and the Germans were evicted.

On 29 May 1943, the B-17 42-29878 Lady Godiva (379BG/526BS) was returning from the first USAAF operation to St Nazaire when it was attacked by fighters and abandoned to crash into the sea near St-Quay-Portrieux in Brittany. All ten crew baled out safely but only the pilot 1/Lt Theodore M Peterson and radio-operator T/Sgt John M Scott evaded successfully – both with Oaktree then Bourgogne.

Peterson and Scott were both helped on landing and soon brought together. Peterson was collected by Ray Labrosse on the first night and taken to stay with him and Andree Leveque at St Quay where he joined Jack Leuhrs, Frank Greene, Gordon Spencer, Henry Riley and Russian evader Abram Kononenko. The following night, Scott and their waist-gunner Sgt William T Ayres were brought in. On Wednesday 2 June, Peterson and

Scott were moved to Mme Charneau's where they shared with Claude Raoul-Duval until the following Saturday when Jean Camard (son of Jerome Camard, the maire at Etables) took them to Paris.[1] They were met by Ray Labrosse and Elisabeth Barbier and taken back to Elisabeth's apartment at 72 rue Vaneau before spending the night in a hotel where they were joined by Edward Spevak. Next morning, Andree Leveque returned them to Elisabeth's apartment for the day before taking them out to a restaurant where they met Henri Figuamont. M Figuamont took them to his country house at Draveil where they stayed for two weeks in the care of Lucien Dalicieux. On 20 June, Andree tried to telephone Elisabeth and learned that she had been arrested so Lucien drove them to a sanatorium (*Preventorium Minoret*) at nearby Champrosay – an address not connected with the organisation. On 4 July, Ayres left without telling anyone and so Lucien moved the airmen out that evening in case Ayres was arrested – which I believe he was. Lucien took them to a deserted chateau for the night and then on to a nearby house for another three nights before taking them to Juvisy-sur-Orge (possibly to stay with Maurice Bidaud). On 12 July, Suzanne Guelat collected them from Juvisy and took them back to her apartment at 68 Boulevard Auguste-Blanqui, Paris XIII where they met Frank Perrica and Salvadore Tafoya who left the next day.[2]

Peterson and Scott left Paris on Tuesday 20 July with a French guide who took them by train to Toulouse and Foix in a group that included Roy Martin USAAF and RAF Sgts William Hughes and Alfred Mansford.

S/Sgt Roy A Martin was the ball-turret gunner of B-17 42-29767 Boot Hill (96BG/338BS) (Haltom) which was damaged by flak over Lorient on 17 May 1943 and attacked by fighters. The bale-out order was given and the aircraft abandoned a few miles north-west of Carhaix-Plouguer, Brittany. Martin was one of the six crew who evaded successfully, first with Oaktree and then with Bourgogne.

Martin had discovered a problem with the oxygen supply in his turret as they crossed the French coast and since the walk-about bottles wouldn't

---

1   Jean Jerome Marie Camard (born Oct 1923) was arrested on 20 June 1943 at 72 rue Vaneau, imprisoned at Rennes, Fresnes and Angouleme and sentenced to death in December. This sentence was later commuted to deportation and forced labour but on 6 March 1944, he escaped at Compeigne from a convoy bound for Germany and joined the FFI at St-Quay-Portrieux. (WO208/5456) Camard was caught (as were Georges Jouanjean and Jacques Bonneron) in the German *souricière* (mouse-trap) set up in Elisabeth Barbier's apartment following her arrest the day before.

2   I think this was an example of Gabrielle Wiame using her extensive contacts (which included Maurice Bidaud and Suzanne Guelat) to find safe houses for the men stranded by the demise of Oaktree – which she seemed to assume was a part of the Comete organisation.

have lasted long enough to be much use to him, was sitting over his turret, rotating it purely for the benefit of any enemy fighters, when they were attacked. S/Sgt William C Martin (apparently no relation although they both came from Arkansas) was wounded and Roy took his place at the waist-gun while William turned the ball-turret. As the aircraft went into its final dive, the survivors in the rear of the plane (the two Martins and S/Sgt Niles G Loudenslager – it's thought that tail-gunner S/Sgt Andrew L Jorinscay had already been killed) were trapped and it was only after the tail broke away that they managed to get out.

All six evaders were soon gathered together, taken to a nearby town and their journeys arranged – see later for more details.

Sgt William Hughes was the flight engineer and Sgt Alfred R Mansford the bomb-aimer of 102 Sqn Halifax JB840 (Hibben) which was on the way to Nuremburg on 8 March 1943 and about twenty miles west of Verdun when it was attacked by a night-fighter. The aircraft was set on fire and the captain ordered his crew to bale out. Hughes and Mansford were the only ones to evade successfully.[3]

Hughes landed in a tree in the Foret d'Argonne, about five miles south-east of Sainte-Menehould (Marne). Leaving his parachute entangled in the tree but after burying his Mae West, Hughes used the compass from his escape box and headed south-west until he reached the outskirts of Villers-en-Argonne. He saw some German troops questioning a farmer and so withdrew into the woods until daybreak. Once it was light, Hughes made his way into the village and asked a man where he was. The man's wife took Hughes to the house of miller Gerard Dot and his wife and later that morning a M Lautier (aged about 50, lived in Ante) came to see him, gave him food and sent for a girl who spoke some English. Once they were satisfied as to Hughes' identity, he was given some civilian clothes, a pair of shoes and 1,000 francs. At about four o'clock that afternoon, M Lautier took Hughes by bicycle to Voilemont, where he was introduced to the Burgomaster (name unknown) and stayed the night. Early next morning, M Lautier and the Burgomaster took Hughes by bicycle to Valmy where he sat in a cafe while M Lautier bought them both train tickets for Paris. While Hughes was waiting, he was approached by a man in overalls who turned out to be his navigator, Sgt F R Slocombe who was being helped by another Frenchman. Hughes, Slocombe and their respective helpers

---

3   Mid-upper gunner W/O Raymond Atkinson was caught on the overnight train from Dijon to Lyon when he was picked up in the early hours of 12 March in a police check at Chalons.

took the eight o'clock morning train for Chalons-sur-Marne where they went to another cafe while Slocombe's helper went to get more clothes for him. Slocombe was apparently headed for Switzerland and Hughes later heard that he was captured near the Swiss border. At about four o'clock that afternoon, Hughes and his helper took the train for Paris, arriving in the capital at eight o'clock that evening (10 March) where his journey was arranged.

In Paris, M Lautier took Hughes to a hotel kept by a Mme Friech (query) where Hughes stayed until the next day when M Lautier brought a man and a woman to see him. These people took Hughes to stay with a Mme Marion (query) (about 33 years old) at 26 rue de Constantinople.[4] Although Mme Marion spoke no English, she managed to tell Hughes that she was a member of a de Gaullist organisation, primarily concerned with helping French evaders but that they also had many English and Canadian airmen in hiding all over Paris. On 17 March, Hughes' bomb-aimer Alfred Mansford was brought to join him, probably by M Lautier.

Mansford landed in a grass field near the village of Brizeaux (Lorraine) on the southern edge of the Foret d'Argonne, south-west of Verdun-sur-Meuse. After exploring the local area for a while, Mansford returned to his landing spot, wrapped himself in his parachute and went to sleep. He was woken at six o'clock by the sound of church bells and spotted the church in the distance. After hiding his parachute, Mae West and other flying gear, he walked into the village and introduced himself to a man who was sweeping out a cowshed. The man immediately took Mansford into his house, gave him a meal and the offer of a bed. After lunch, one of the farmer's friends who spoke a little English came to see him and Mansford explained that he wanted to evade capture. That evening, the man and his son walked with Mansford through the night to another (unnamed) village where he was hidden in the loft of a mill and visited by an English-speaking woman who said she had a friend in Paris who would help him. That evening (10 March) the miller and the local station master took Mansford by bicycle to Voilemont for two nights and then, because the Germans were searching the area, to another (unnamed) village for another night.

Mansford was due to leave for Paris on 13 March but only got as far as returning to Voilemont where he was told that a German control at Sainte-Menehould station made his intended journey impossible. He spent the next three days sheltered in the little village of Valmy until finally leaving

---

4   A Mme Germaine Becue is listed at this address. (IS9 Helper List)

for Paris on 17 March along with a young Frenchman who also wanted to get to England. Their guide, who they had been told to follow, was also on the train. In Paris, Mansford was taken to a flat where he joined his flight engineer William Hughes.

Hughes and Mansford were sheltered for more than three months at rue de Constantinople, until the end of June when they were told that the Gestapo were looking for Mme Marion and a young girl moved them to another house for the night. Next morning an English-speaking Frenchman took Hughes and Mansford to stay with Mme Pauline Cornu-Thenard at 6 Place Saint-Sulpice, Paris VI – where great care had to be exercised because the servant girl was married to a German soldier. Mme Thenard said she could contact a French Intelligence Service and later brought an American woman to see them. The American woman questioned them and two days later, brought an unnamed Englishman to see them.

In mid-July, Mme Thenard took Hughes and Mansford to 51 rue de Miromesnil, Paris VIII where they stayed with Doctor Alice Willm on the fifth floor, and with electrical engineer Jean De Traz and his wife Laure, on the sixth floor. On 17 July, Jean De Traz brought two American sergeants, Joseph Woodstock and George Blackwell, who also stayed for a while with Dr Willm.

On 20 July, an unidentified French helper took Hughes and Mansford to the Jardin des Plantes where they met Oaktree evaders Theodore Peterson and John Scott from the Lady Godiva, and Roy Martin from Boot Hill. The five airmen were taken on the eight o'clock evening train from the Gare d'Austerlitz to Toulouse, arriving there at eight o'clock the following morning where they changed for Foix. They arrived in Foix at three in the afternoon and were met at the station before being taken to a field where they were picked up by car and driven to a wood to meet their mountain guide.

They set off at about five o'clock that afternoon but after two nights of walking, Mansford found his leg muscles were hurting and early on the morning of 23 July, said he couldn't continue. The guide told Hughes that they should carry on and that he would return for Mansford later so Hughes gave Mansford what little food he had before leaving him close to the Andorran border. The rest of the group reached Ordino in Andorra at about five o'clock that afternoon, where they had a meal (which Peterson paid for in French francs) before continuing to Andorra la Vieja where they stayed in a hotel. Mansford notes that they were not required to pay their hotel bill but were asked to sign it instead. On 25 July, they moved to another hotel and the following day, walked with a new guide and two Frenchmen to Sant Julia de Loria. After another meal, they began the long cross-country walk to Manresa. They reached Manresa on the morning of 30 July where they caught a train to Barcelona and then took a taxi to the British Consulate.

It's not clear whether their first guide did return for Mansford but he was driven down into Ordino by Julian (Julià) Reig, a local cigarette manufacturer (and smuggler) who lived near Andorra la Vieja. He put Mansford into a hotel – where he stayed in bed for the first four days – and sent for a doctor, telling Mansford not to be concerned about money. Mansford left Ordino by car for Sant Julia two weeks later, along with a Frenchman, three Poles and a man called Luis.[5] They stayed overnight in an apartment at Sant Julia with a man who provided their papers and next day were taken by car across the frontier into Spain. They stayed at a hotel in La Seo d'Urgell until collected by a Spaniard who drove them to Barcelona and the British Consulate.

<hr />

5   Luis was one of the many aliases used by a man who was otherwise known as Carlos, the contact in Barcelona for a Polish organisation. (Claude Benet 'Passeurs, Fugitifs et Espions' translated from Catalan into French and published by Le Pas d'oiseau in 2010.)

CHAPTER 10

22 July 1943

On 22 July 1943, four American airmen – S/Sgt Peter Milasius, 2/Lt Donald Nichols, S/Sgt Herman Marshall and T/Sgt Glen Wells – left Paris by train for Toulouse and Foix.

S/Sgt Peter P Milasius was the ball-turret gunner of B-17 42-29531 (305BG/422BS) (Peterson) which was damaged by flak over St Nazaire on 29 May 1943 and abandoned.

Milasius landed by the church in Le Vieux-Bourg, a few kilometres west of Quintin (about 20 kms SW of St Brieuc). Local people took his parachute and equipment before he ran out of the village and found his radio-operator T/Sgt Joseph P Freeborn in a field with multiple injuries, including a broken leg. Freeborn was later taken to a hospital where he was captured. Milasius spent the first night in a ditch and then the next few days in a barn. On 5 June, he was taken to St Brieuc where he stayed with a man called Marcel Bretagne (query) who had a resistance contact in Guingamp with an apartment in St Brieuc. Milasius stayed at St Brieuc until 28 June when three men came with bicycles to take him to St-Quay-Portrieux. He was passed on to Jean Lanlo who took him to stay with widow Pauline Bringuet at la Ville d'en Haut, 25 rue des Trois Freres Salaun.[1] On the first day, he was visited by French pilot evader Lt Claude Raoul-Duval. On 13 July, a blonde woman took Milasius – along with Boot Hill crewmen T/Sgt Herman Marshall and T/Sgt Glen Wells – by train back to St Brieuc and on to Paris where they met Ray Labrosse in a park. Milasius was taken to the home of another blonde woman, this one called Rosie (presumably Suzanne Guelat) where his bombardier 2/Lt Frank Perrica and tail-gunner S/Sgt Salvadore Tafoya were staying with Theodore Peterson and John Scott from the Lady Godiva, before moving next day to join Boot Hill waist-gunner William Martin at the home of a nurse.

---

1   Didier Moreau emailed me in April 2014 to say that his grandmother Pauline Bringuet had been very worried by Peter Milasius' lack of security – probably not helped by thirty-two-year-old Milasius claiming to be a Chicago gangster ... Didier also says it was his father, Pierre Moreau, who took Milasius to St Brieuc where Milasius caused yet more concern by openly staring at German soldiers.

51

2/Lt Donald L Nichols was the co-pilot of B-17 42-29627 Midnight (Spevak) – see earlier. After being separated from Spevak and Parks in Paris on 5 June, Nichols was sheltered by Dominique and Odette Carabelli at 45 rue Poliveau. On 20 June, he was taken to stay with a blind masseur named Felix Jolivot at 17 Avenue de la Concorde, La Varenne-St-Hilaire (Saint-Maur-des-Fosses) until 22 July when he was returned to Mme Carabelli who took him to Gare d'Austerlitz.

S/Sgt Herman L Marshall was top-turret gunner and T/Sgt Glen Wells the radio-operator of B-17 42-29767 Boot Hill (96BG/338BS) (Haltom) which was damaged by flak over Lorient on 17 May 1943 and attacked by fighters. The bale-out order was given and the aircraft abandoned a few miles north-west of Carhaix-Plouguer, Brittany. Marshall and Wells were two of the six crew who evaded successfully, first with Oaktree and then with Bourgogne.

All six evaders were soon gathered together, taken to a nearby town and their journeys arranged. Marshall, Wells and ball-turret gunner Sgt Roy Martin were taken to the Chateau du Bourblanc at Plourivo where the comtesse Betty de Mauduit sheltered so many evaders, and were later joined by their pilot 1/Lt Louis Haltom and waist-gunners S/Sgt William Martin and S/Sgt Niles Loudenslager. On 12 June, two Germans came to the chateau and arrested Betty. The airmen were safely hidden in prearranged places between the ceiling and floor and the following night they slipped out of the chateau and made their way to St-Quay-Portrieux where some of them had been sheltered before. The following morning, Marshall and Wells were moved to the Hotel de la Plage where they stayed for a month with an elderly couple named Ligeron, and met Peter Milasius. On 13 July, a blonde woman took all three of them to Paris for a rendezvous with Ray Labrosse before going on to stay with Maud Couve and Alice Brouard at 25 rue de Madrid for a week, during which time Labrosse visited and they met Kitty (Hina Zapine). On 22 July, Alice and Maud took them to the Gare d'Austerlitz where they joined Milasius.

On 22 July, Milasius, Marshall, Nichols and Wells were taken, along with three Frenchmen, by train via Toulouse to Foix. Their guides from Paris led them to some woods where their Spanish mountain guides met them that evening. They crossed the border to Andorra on 27 July where they stayed in a hotel – and (briefly) met Theodore Peterson, John Scott and Roy Martin – before walking across the Spanish border to La Seu d'Urgell where they were met and driven to the British Consulate in Barcelona, arriving there on Saturday 31 July.

CHAPTER 11

The Last of the Oaktree Evaders

The radio message 'Denise est morte' received from London on 29 May 1943 announcing the cancellation of any MGB pick-ups from Brittany in the foreseeable future, prompted the sending of a group of Oaktree evaders back to Paris. Ray Labrosse would probably have gone with them but the crashing of B-17 Lady Godiva in the sea off St-Quay-Portrieux that same day (see earlier) delayed him from leaving St Quay as he stayed to help the crew.

On 31 May, Jean Camard (and others) took F/Sgt David E James RCAF, Sgt William G Grove, Sgt James A Smith, Sgt James Hall, Sgt Reginald W Adams (all five from Stirling BK653), T/Sgt Jack O Leuhrs, 1/Lt Robert E Biggs, 2/Lt Robert E Kylius and T/Sgt Claiborne W Wilson in groups, and by various routes, to Paris where they were met by Val Williams and a young Frenchman called Yannec.[1] The next day, Yannec and a tall, dark French guide named Jacques Bonneron[2] took the evaders to the Gare d'Austerlitz where they caught a train to Bordeaux, Dax and Pau for the last of the Oaktree Pyrenean crossings. The group crossed safely into Spain on 5 June 1943 and were arrested near Uztarroz before being taken to Isaba.

Following the arrest of Betty de Mauduit on 12 June, the other four evaders from Boot Hill – pilot 1/Lt Louis L Haltom, ball-turret gunner Sgt Roy Martin and waist-gunners S/Sgt William Martin and S/Sgt Niles Loudenslager – joined Claude and Josette Raoul-Duval in St-Quay-Portrieux.

Spitfire pilot Lt Claude Raoul-Duval was shot down on 17 April 1943 and during his evasion had been passed to Elisabeth Barbier at rue Vaneau.

---

1   Yannec was Jean Tromelin (born June 1924), son of Jean Tromelin, the fanatically pro-Ally maire of Plouguin, Finistere. Yannec (the diminutive, familiar form for Yann, the Breton form of Jean) and his parents sheltered, clothed and assisted some twenty-five to thirty Allied evaders (including S/Ldr Peter Lefevre in April 43) as well as making frequent convoy journeys between Paris, Finistere and the Spanish frontier. (WO208-5457)

2   Jacques Paul Robert Bonneron (born Dec 1923) was captured on 20 June 1943 with Jean Camard (see earlier) in the *souricière* at 72 rue Vaneau – they had just returned from Pau where they had gone to investigate the arrest of Val Williams. Bonneron was deported to Germany but survived to be repatriated to France in April 1945. (WO208/5452)

Whilst being sheltered in Paris, Claude had contacted his fiance Josette in Bordeaux and they were married in Paris on 27 May. Elisabeth Barbier passed Claude on to Val Williams who sent him to Brittany on 29 May where the couple stayed with Mme Marie Louise Charneau, who had looked after Claude when he was a child, at St-Quay-Portrieux.

On 15 July, Josette Raoul-Duval took Roy and William Martin to Paris where they were met by Ray Labrosse who took Roy Martin to stay with Madeleine Melot at 11 bis rue Larrey, Paris V while a blonde girl took William Martin to join Peter Milasius at the home of a nurse. Roy Martin left Paris on 22 July (see earlier) with Theodore Peterson, John Scott, William Hughes and Alfred Mansford by train to Toulouse and Foix.

Shortly after that (date uncertain) a man and woman drove Haltom and Loudenslager to St Brieuc where they took the train to Paris. They stayed with Suzanne, a married nurse (Suzanne Bosniere at Rueil-Malmaison), for ten days before meeting Georges Broussine (aka Burgundy) on 28 July in the Jardin des Plantes. They were taken to the Gare d'Austerlitz where they joined their other waist-gunner, William Martin, and three RAF crew from Lancaster ED480 – Sgts Gerard Bartley, Sidney Hughes and John Duncan.

9 Sqn Lancaster ED480 (Duncan) was on the way to Gelsenkirchen in the early hours of 10 July 1943 when they were hit by flak and the aircraft abandoned near Cambrai. Sgt Gerard Bartley, Sgt Sidney Hughes and Sgt John D Duncan RCAF were all helped by the Chauny-Dromas organisation before being brought to Paris and passed on to Bourgogne. Two other ED480 crew also evaded successfully: navigator F/Sgt Henry Brown and tail-gunner Sgt David McMillan who were also passed to Bourgogne – see later.

Bartley landed just east of Cambrai and began making his way south. He had almost reached St Quentin on 13 July when he was approached by a roadman who hid him by the side of the road until early evening when two more men arrived to take him by motor van to Tugny. Bartley was sheltered in Tugny for two nights until being handed over to the organisation in Chauny.

Hughes landed a few miles north of Cambrai and spent the rest of the night in a farmer's woodshed. In the morning, he approached the farmer who gave him some milk and showed him where he was on his escape map. Hughes decided to head for the Swiss border and duly set off but at about eight o'clock that evening, a young Frenchman on a bicycle stopped and took him back to his house in Guise. He was driven to another nearby village for three nights before being returned to Guise where a local tailor measured him for a suit. He was then taken to another village for a further three days before being taken to Chauny where he joined Bartley.

Duncan also landed just east of Cambrai, and after hiding his parachute and Mae West, set off towards the south-east, walking until daylight when he hid himself in a haystack and slept until late morning. At about noon the next day, he stopped at a farmhouse where he declared himself. He was moved to another house for the night and the following day (12 July) taken to Chauny.

On 20 July, a guide from Paris collected the three airmen from Chauny and took them to the capital where he (or she) delivered them to a doctor's flat. Bartley stayed with the unnamed doctor until they all left Paris while Duncan only stayed overnight before being moved to a nurse's flat (Suzanne Bosniere) where he joined American evaders Louis Haltom, William Martin and Niles Loudenslager. Hughes spent four or five days in a nearby flat with the widow of a French army captain where he met P/O George Dickson RNZAF and S/Sgt Philip Fink USAAF just before he left.[3]

On 28 July, a young French guide took Bartley, Hughes, Duncan, Haltom, Martin and Loudenslager by train to Toulouse and on to Foix where they were handed over to two Spanish mountain guides who led them on a three-day walk to Andorra. They stayed three nights in a hotel before leaving for a seven-day trek to Manresa in Spain.

After five nights of hard walking, Hughes' ankle was giving him so much trouble that he was forced to drop out, and Bartley and Martin stayed with him. The rest of the party reached Manresa safely where they took a train to Barcelona, arriving at the British Consulate on the morning of 10 August 1943.

Hughes, Bartley and Martin found two guides at a farmhouse who took them the rest of the way to Manresa, although at least one of the guides must have regretted the arrangement as he was arrested there by the Guardia Civil. The other guide, after hiding them in a cornfield, disappeared. The three airmen spent the night in the cornfield and next morning went to a house where they were given food and shelter while the owner sent someone to Barcelona. That evening, a consular car collected them and delivered them to the British Consulate in Barcelona just twelve hours after the rest of their party.

---

3   Philip Fink says he was sheltered by a woman doctor named Mme Verow/Veroux (Mme Albertine Veron of 5 rue Stephen Pichon, Paris XV – query) from 3 August until he left Paris on 31 August. George Dickson says he stayed with Madeleine Melot and Georgette Perseval at 11 bis rue Larrey from 26 July until he left Paris.

CHAPTER 12

Barber and Lawrence

The NARA Bourgogne list includes a Sgt Barber RAF and Broussine has a Sgt Barrer and a Sgt Lawrence – the only evaders that seem to fit are Sgt Wilfred J Barber and Sgt James W E Lawrence from 158 Sqn Halifax HR779 who evaded with fellow crewman F/Sgt E Durant until he was shot and captured in the Pyrenees. I have included the following account, taken and lightly edited from the 2009 book 'RAF Evaders' by Oliver Clutton-Brock, for its own interest but am not convinced they should be 'credited' to Bourgogne.

> *"Raoul" was otherwise Jean-Claude Camors. He had begun his clandestine work as "Bordeaux" in mid-April 1943, when he was parachuted into France near Loches to set up the reseau Bordeaux-Loupiac. Before the end of the month he was on his way back to England, escorting three RAF evaders to Spain. Flight Sergeant E. Durant (later POW) Sergeant W.J. Barber and Sergeant J.W.E. Lawrence all same crew, shot down on 16/17 April 1943 (Pilsen) in eastern France, had been taken from Bar-le-Duc (Meuse) to Paris on 26 April by Rene Gerard (who was born in Bar-le-Duc) and by Roger Leneveu. Placed in a flat in Montmartre 'occupied by an elderly hairdresser whose wife had been killed by German bombing earlier in the war', they understood that they 'were now in the hands of the "Bordeaux" organisation.'*
>
> *On the afternoon of 27 April, Rene Gerard and Leneveu escorted them to Tours, and then to Gerard's house in Loches. Here they 'met Lieutenant Camors and a friend of his. Camors said that he was from the French HQ in London.' After staying for several days in the area of Loches everyone gathered again at Gerard's house on 10 May, when Camors told the airmen that arrangements had been made to take them to Spain. 'That night we were photographed and our identity cards were prepared. We were each given a special wallet containing about 1500 francs and a number of letters, French stamps, and various small papers, purporting to be additional proof of our identity as Frenchmen.' On 11 May the three airmen and the three*

56

Frenchmen took the train to Châteauroux, where Rene Gerard and Roger Leneveu left them. Alone with the airmen Camors told them 'that Roger's loyalty was suspect, and that some day it might be necessary to kill him.' Camors and Leneveu were to meet again.[1]

Making their way to Toulouse after a night in a railway carriage – too dangerous to stay in a hotel – Durant, Barber and Lawrence reached Perpignan on the morning of 12 May, and 'were met by a very old woman, who took us to a hotel where we met two other members of the organisation. Later we moved to the Hotel Notre Dame, where we had a meal.' Rather than risk the night in the hotel, a friend of Camors found them shelter in a garage. On 13 May, they were rolled up in a large piece of canvas in the back of a lorry and driven off towards the Pyrenees. Waiting for nightfall in a vineyard, they began the crossing that night with their guide. Fording the River Tech near Ceret at around 4.30 a.m. on 14 May, they 'stayed in a small farmhouse known to Camors. Here our guide was joined by another.'

Again waiting for the cover of darkness, they continued over the Pyrenees. Even though the two guides knew that the road from le Boulou to le Perthus (on the border) was patrolled by Germans, they decided to make use of it, and went on ahead to reconnoiter. While the others stayed hidden by the roadside, two German soldiers walked by heading in the same direction as the guides, who suddenly ran back and told them to disperse. When all was quiet again they resumed their walk along the road, in single file with the two guides out in front: 'Barber was leading the rest of the party and coming round a bend he saw the two guides talking to two German soldiers.' Unfortunately, the Germans saw the airmen and Camors, and shouted to them to halt: 'We immediately ran away from them, and they opened fire. We saw Durant fall heavily, and we think he may have been hit and captured. We saw no more of our guides.'

Camors, Barber and Lawrence made the decision to abandon the road, and with the help of an army-pattern compass that Camors had brought along, crossed into Spain. Later that morning, 15 May, on the road from le Perthus to Figueras, they were stopped by members of the Guardia Civil. Taken to Figueras, all three claimed to be RAF and were put in prison, where they met 'a Belgian flight lieutenant named Le Grand, T/Sgt Arthur B Cox

---

1   Ironic to note that it was the French traitor and German infiltration agent Roger Leneveu (or Le Neveu – aka *Roger le Legionnaire*) who had been directly responsible for the capture of Rene Gerard's wife Suzanne in February 1943 when she was arrested with Louis Nouveau and a group of American evaders on a train at Tours. Suzanne was deported and Rene (captured later but I don't have the details) was shot. (IS9 Helper files)

and an individual calling himself "Arthur George" [Georges Zarifi] who maintained that he was an Australian Private soldier who had escaped from France.' On 26 May, Camors and his two companions were transferred to Gerona, and three days later taken by a Spanish Air Force officer, via the Barcelona Consulate, to Alhama de Aragon, where they arrived on 30 May. Wing Commander Vincent took them to the Madrid embassy on 2 June, and twelve days later they were driven via Seville to Gibraltar, where they arrived on 16 June. Camors flew back to England on 20 June, two days before Barber and Lawrence, and was in London next day.

CHAPTER 13

Another Crossing from Pau

Broussine's list includes Gloudeman and Normile but since neither of them went to Paris, the only possible link to Bourgogne would seem to be at Pau.

F/O George H Gloudeman and 2/Lt Joseph Normile were the co-pilot and navigator of B-17 42-29847 High Ball (351BG/511BS) (Adams) which was on the way to St Nazaire on 23 June 1943 when it was shot down by fighters and crashed near Muzillac. Gloudeman and Normile were the only successful evaders from High Ball.

Gloudeman made a delayed jump (he waited before opening his parachute in order to reduce the time spent in the air) and landed in a field about thirty miles north-east of St Nazaire where he was helped by two young French boys who hid his flying equipment. Later that same day, Gloudeman approached a farmer who put him in a barn for the night and gave him breakfast the next morning. Another French family helped Gloudeman to locate himself on his escape map and bought him a train ticket to Tours. After changing trains a couple of times, Gloudeman finally reached Tours at midday on 30 June. He identified himself to a Frenchman in a cafe and was taken to a house where he was interrogated to confirm his identity before being taken to a house in the country where his journey was arranged.

Normile, who spoke a little French, was also helped soon after landing and by various other people as he made his way to Tours. From Tours he took an early morning train to Vierzon, where a friendly cafe proprietor showed him how to cross the demarcation line. After walking to the nearest town, he found that he had missed the last train for Chateauroux and so spent the night in a hayloft. Next morning he bought a ticket for Toulouse, changing trains at Chateauroux. At Chateauroux station, he saw his co-pilot Gloudeman boarding the same train and joined him.

Gloudeman and Normile arrived in Toulouse on 3 July where they changed for a late-night train to Tarbes and then an early morning train to Pau. They don't mention anyone else so presumably they travelled without a guide. Details in Pau are sketchy but they note Louis Mantien (and his mother-in-law) at 5 rue des Trois Freres Bernadac who sheltered them for a week. Gloudeman and Normile left Pau on 11 July and took a train to Izeste (due south of Pau) with a number of young Frenchmen carrying knapsacks, and were joined by Joseph Rosio, George Evans and John Kuberski.

1/Lt Joseph Rosio, 1/Lt George W Evans and S/Sgt John H Kuberski were the pilot, co-pilot and waist-gunner of B-17 42-30058 (384BG/546BS) which was shot down by fighters while returning from Villacoublay aerodrome on 26 June 1943 – see Brown and Houghton earlier.

Rosio, Evans and Kuberski were helped immediately on landing and soon joined fellow crewmen, S/Sgts Lester Brown, John Houghton and Anthony Cucinotta. Rosio, Evans and Kuberski were driven to Saint Cyr-sous-Dourdan and then next day Rosio and Evans were taken by train to Paris where Evans stayed with an English-speaking woman who had worked for Du Pont in New York, while Rosio stayed at a lawyer's house. Kuberski was taken to Paris on 30 June and sheltered by forty-six-year-old ex-POW, Rene Marcel Le Templier at 31 rue de Varenne (Paris VII) along with fellow waist-gunner Anthony Cucinotta. He also visited Lester Brown and John Houghton who were being sheltered nearby, on the same street. On 3 July, Evans joined Kuberski and they were moved to Rueil-Malmaison where they stayed with Susanne Bosniere at 56 rue de Bois (now rue Pierre Brossolette). On the evening of 9 July, Mme Bosniere took Evans and Kuberski back into Paris where they joined their pilot Rosio at the Gare d'Austerlitz, and a nurse and a young French boy called Jacques Philippe who took them by overnight train to Toulouse.

Rosio, Evans and Kuberski went on to Pau next day and spent the night in a hotel. The nurse left them in the morning and was replaced by a man. They joined a party of about forty – including George Gloudeman and Joseph Normile from B-17 42-29847 High Ball.

Rosio, Evans, Kuberski, Gloudeman and Normile began walking south from Bielle on Monday 12 July, crossing the border into Spain in the early hours of 15 July 1943 and continuing on to Canfranc – where they were arrested by a Spanish border patrol.

It's not clear why Rosio, Evans and Kuberski didn't leave Paris with their crew-mates Brown and Houghton although it seems likely there was a lack of suitable guides – one guide for a maximum of four evaders would seem to be the general rule at this time. It should also be noted that Susanne Bosniere, although associated with several of the Bourgogne evaders, was not part of the Bourgogne organisation – see later.

CHAPTER 14

Ray Labrosse leaves for England

Former Oaktree radio-operator Ray Labrosse left Paris for England on 17 August 1943 when Yves Allain took him, New Zealander P/O George Dickson and Americans Capt Kee Harrison, 1/Lt Floyd Watts, S/Sgt Joseph Woodstock and Sgt George Blackwell by train to Toulouse where they changed for Foix.

P/O George R Dickson RNZAF was returning from an early-morning Ramrod sortie on 14 July 1943 in 129 Sqn Spitfire MA596 when engine failure forced him to bale out just west of Rouen.

Dickson landed in a clearing in the Foret du Duclair where he was met by a Frenchman who gestured that he should escape to the south-east. Dickson buried his parachute and then ran to hide in some thick ferns about 500 yards away where he stayed until the early afternoon, when he began walking south. On reaching a river, he hid up again until nightfall when he set off once more. He had injured his knee on landing so progress was slow and on reaching a barn at about four in the morning, rested for the next several hours. At about one o'clock he declared himself to a Frenchwoman who he thought (rightly) must be the wife of the barn owner and she called her husband. He was told to stay overnight in the barn and next day an English-speaking Frenchman was brought to see him. Although clothing, money and an ID card were promised, before they could be delivered, the farmer came that evening to tell him there were Germans in his house and that Dickson should leave at once. Dickson continued heading south and reached St Pierre-de-Manneville in the early hours of 16 July where he was intercepted by two men with a dog. They took Dickson to a house where there was a young woman who spoke English.

Next day, the young woman from St Pierre-de-Manneville brought a Mme de Gaulle, understood by Dickson to be the sister-in-law of General Charles,[1] who questioned Dickson to confirm his identity. On 19 July, a man took Dickson across the Seine in a dinghy and then cycled with him

---

1   This was Madeleine Marie de Gaulle – wife of Charles' brother Pierre – and a friend of Madeleine Melot.

towards Rouen, meeting Mme de Gaulle along the way, and the three of them rode into Rouen together. The Frenchman took them to an apartment where they stayed for a few hours until Dickson was taken to be sheltered by an unnamed French girl. On 22 July, Mme de Gaulle passed Dickson on to another French girl, this one called Jacqueline. Dickson stayed overnight in an attic over a garage at Jacqueline's home and next day she took him by train to Paris. They stayed with a friend of Jacqueline's while Mme de Gaulle's father made further arrangements. On 26 July, Dickson was taken to stay with Madeleine Melot and Georgette Perseval at 11 bis rue Larrey[2] – and while he was there, met Sgt Sidney Hughes from Lancaster ED480.

On 17 August, Mme Melot took Dickson to the nearby Jardin des Plantes where he joined Kee Harrison, Floyd Watts, Joseph Woodstock, George Blackwell, Ray Labrosse and several Frenchmen.

Capt Kee H Harrison was the pilot of B-17 42-3190 (94BG/333BS) which was on the way to Le Bourget on 14 July 1943 when it was attacked head-on by fighters. The order was given to abandon the aircraft and 2/Lt Robert T Conroy and 2/Lt Roscoe F Greene jumped but the engineer's parachute was burned so Harrison crash-landed the aircraft near Berengeville-la-Campagne (north-west of Evreux) in Normandy and the remaining crew scattered.[3]

Harrison was sheltered at Feugerolles, a couple of kilometres north of the crash-site, for six days until a doctor who was connected to a Paris organisation took him by motorcycle to his home in Serquigny. On 20 July, a young man took Harrison to Paris where he stayed with Jean De Traz (a sixty-eight-year-old electrical engineer) and his wife Laure at 51 rue de Miromesnil, a week of which was shared with his co-pilot David Turner, while Joseph Woodstock and George Blackwell were staying in the apartment below with Dr Alice Willm. On 2 August, Harrison was moved to 11 rue du 29 Juillet where he joined Francis Green, who was being sheltered by Dora Rospape.[4] On 17 August, a blonde woman (probably

2   Madeleine Melot, Mme Georgette Perseval and Mlle Roberte Pagnier (all on Broussine Helper List) all lived at 11 bis rue Larrey, Paris V – Mme Perseval was the concierge and Mlle Pagnier, Mme Melot's domestique.

3   Five other crew from 42-3190 also evaded successfully, all crossing the Pyrenees to Spain in August – navigator 2/Lt Thomas R Conway with Comete, bombardier 2/Lt Roscoe F Greene from Peyrehorade – and co-pilot 2/Lt David H Turner, ball-turret gunner S/Sgt Jefferson D Polk and radio-operator T/Sgt Charles H McNemar who were helped by Bourgogne …

4   Mme Dora May Rospape (née Fife) was British by birth (born in London on 26 December 1901) but French by marriage. (WO208/5451) She is described by Eugene Mulholland (see later) as being very thin, with blonde hair that she dyed auburn when the Gestapo started to watch her.

Gabrielle Wiame) took Harrison to the Jardin des Plantes where he met Georges Broussine.

1/Lt Floyd B Watts was the pilot of B-17 42-3071 (94BG/331BS) which was on the way to Le Bourget on 14 July 1943 when it was attacked by fighters and abandoned.[5]

Watts landed near Louvres (Ile de France) and walked into a bicycle shop where the owner contacted Jacqueline Baron (the daughter of Pierre Baron, believed to be the maire of Louvres) who spoke English. Watts was sheltered with Louis Timbert in La Chapelle-en-Serval (Oise) for three weeks before being taken to the station and put on a train to Paris with a guide who already had two of his crewmen, John Carpenter and Samuel Potvin, with him.

They were met at the station by Ray Labrosse (known to the evaders as Paul) and Watts was told to follow a woman in a green dress who took him to stay with Mme Marie Francoise Guillaume at 29 rue Dareau. Whilst there, S/Sgt Philip Fink came and stayed for two days and at some stage, Mme Guillaume took Watts to a museum where he met fellow B-17 pilot Kee Harrison and Watts made the rest of the journey to Spain with him.

S/Sgt Joseph S Woodstock and Sgt George F Blackwell were gunners on B-17 42-3330 (384BG/544BS) (Munday) which was attacked by fighters as they turned away from Villacoublay aerodrome on 14 July 1943 and abandoned to crash near Les Essarts-le-Roi (Yvelines). Pilot 1/Lt James Munday, waist-gunner T/Sgt Francis Green and radio-operator T/Sgt Edward Ruby also evaded successfully with Bourgogne – see later.

Woodstock and Blackwell were both helped immediately on landing near Rambouillet (about twenty-five miles south-west of central Paris) and brought together that evening. On 17 July, an elderly couple took them to the station (where they saw their co-pilot 2/Lt Frederick T Marston with a Frenchmen) to catch a train to Paris where they were sheltered for a month with Dr Alice Willm at 51 rue de Miromesnil. On 17 August, Georges Broussine (using his alias of Jean-Pierre) took them to the Jardin des

---

5   Five other crew from 42-3071 also evaded successfully: co-pilot 2/Lt John W Bieger was evacuated from Brittany on board the Breton fishing boat Suzanne-Renee in October (see later), top-turret gunner T/Sgt John F Buise with Comete, tail-gunner S/Sgt Joseph E Manos, who was helped by the Francoise Dissard organisation to cross the Pyrenees at the end of October – and S/Sgt John L Carpenter and T/Sgt Samuel E Potvin with Bourgogne.

Marie-Louise 'Francoise' Dissard (born November 1881) was the lady in Toulouse who took over what was left of the Pat line after her great friend O'Leary was captured at the beginning of March 1943. Mlle Dissard was awarded the George Medal. (WO208/5453)

Plantes where they joined Ray Labrosse, George Dickson, Kee Harrison, Floyd Watts and two French officers, a major and a colonel.

Yves Allain took the evaders and Labrosse on the eight o'clock, overnight train for Toulouse (arriving just before eight next morning) and then the nine o'clock morning train to Foix, at which point Allain returned to Paris. Allain comments that the only problem during the train journey was when Labrosse's *carte d'identite* was queried at Vierzon and that while Labrosse's French was perfectly adequate, his French-Canadian accent was 'caracterise'. Fortunately, it was a German official who questioned him.

Labrosse and the evaders climbed a small hill to some woods on the outskirts of town where they waited two hours for their mountain guides and a truck to take them a few kilometres south. They began their walk that evening (18 August) walking across the Pyrenees to Andorra and arriving at Ordino during the night of 22 August, where their mountain guides from Foix left them. After resting for three days, they set off again on 25 August for the long walk to Manresa in Spain, which they reached in the early morning of 30 August. They stayed hidden in a cornfield until lunchtime when they were put on a train for Barcelona and taken to the British Consulate.[6]

Hardly any of the helpers in Foix are named by the evaders but Michel Alvarez (born May 1905 in Cueca, Spain) of 3 Place Lazenia, was the chief guide for the Foix region from August 1943 until his arrest on 28 February 1944 whilst on his way to the Hotel Leblanc. He was deported to Germany, surviving the men's camp at Ravensbruck (a much smaller camp, adjacent to but isolated from, the main women's camp) before being repatriated to France on 3 July 1945. Hotel Leblanc owners Jean Gilbert Leblanc and his wife Marie Louis were also arrested on 28 February 1944 and deported to Germany – they were repatriated in May 1945 and both recommended for a KMS.[7]

---

6   On his return to England, Raymond Joseph Marcel Labrosse (born 10 November 1920 in Ottawa) " ... was given a course of training and returned to France on 16 November 1943 as W/T operator with our agent Yukon [Lucien Dumais] of the Shelburn organisation ... Labrosse was promoted from Signalman to the rank of Acting Sergeant with effect from 10 March 1944 ... and recommended for the award of the Military Cross." (Labrosse NARA file)

7   TNA folder WO208/5458.

CHAPTER 15

22 August 1943

On 22 August 1943, four guides (one of them a young Russian Jewish girl called Tamara) took P/O Robert Stockburn, Sgt David McMillan, 2/Lt David Turner, T/Sgt Francis Green, T/Sgt Edward Ruby, S/Sgt Jefferson Polk, T/Sgt Charles McNemar, S/Sgt Donald Harding and S/Sgt Harry Eastman by train from Paris to Toulouse and Foix.

Readers may have noticed that groups crossing from Foix to Andorra were taking different amounts of time – some, four days (or more) and others overnight. There are numerous ways of going and the routes used would have depended on the local guide's experience and knowledge of both terrain and German activity. The routes vary between hard and very hard, with the lowest of the cols they might have used, the Port de Siguer at 2,396 metres above sea level. Bad weather could make even the easier routes quite impassable, even for experienced, well equipped mountain walkers – which the evaders certainly weren't.

P/O Robert C Stockburn was flying 501 Sqn Spitfire AA917 on a Rhubarb sortie to the Hazebrouck area on 11 July 1943. He had just carried out a successful attack on a train when his aircraft developed a glycol leak – probably as a result of flying through debris from the exploding locomotive. Knowing that he would not be able to make it back to England, Stockburn belly-landed his aircraft in a field just south of the Colme Canal.

Using the compass from his aids box, Stockburn made his way south-west until about nine o'clock that evening when he hid in a barn next to a farmhouse just east of the Forest of Clairmarais (east of St Omer). When the farmer came into his barn that evening, Stockburn declared himself to him and was taken into the house, given a meal and some civilian clothes and spent the night in the loft. Next day, Stockburn was told that German patrols were out – he was sold a bicycle and taken five miles to a signpost for Cassel then left to ride on alone. A short while later he decided to leave the road and slept in a barn (his bicycle hidden behind a hedge) for the rest of the day and following night. He was awoken early next morning by some German soldiers who came to the barn but didn't search it. Stockburn then cycled on through Hazebrouck and Bethune and on to Aix-Noullet where he stopped at a cafe. On asking for a beer, he was challenged by the woman who was serving and declared himself to her. She took him into a back room, gave him a meal and a bed for the night. Stockburn stayed at the cafe until 16 July when he set off again cycling south. He got as far as Biefvillers-les-Bapaume where he got a puncture, abandoned the bicycle and walked into Bapaume – where his journey was arranged.

Stockburn was helped in Bapaume by Edmond Delattre, proprietor of the Cafe Promenade (on the main street, adjoining the Gendarmerie HQ) and his brother Jean. M Martin, the local schoolmaster, and the local photographer (name not known) helped in the arrangement of his papers and Stockburn was sheltered on a farm outside Bapaume by Mme Estelle Perus (sister-in-law of the maire Abel Guidet who had a British MM from the First War). Stockburn says he was with David McMillan from Bapaume to Foix although McMillan says they first met at Achiet on the way to get the train for Paris.

Sgt David B McMillan RCAF was the tail-gunner of 9 Sqn Lancaster ED480 (Duncan) which was damaged by flak over Gelsenkirchen in the early hours of 10 July 1943 causing them to lose so much fuel that the pilot decided to head for France before the aircraft was abandoned.

Twenty-one-year-old McMillan was probably the last man to leave the aircraft and he landed in a field about a mile south-east of Le Cateau-Cambresis (Nord-Pas-de-Calais) spraining both ankles. On hearing church bells, McMillan went towards the village where he was promptly captured by a young German soldier. McMillan was taken to a guard house where he was searched and some items confiscated before being led off by the young soldier. They didn't get very far (it was still very early in the morning) before McMillan stopped to sit on a low wall because of his injured ankles and take off his boots. Finding a rock by the wall, McMillan was able to overpower his young guard and recover some of his confiscated belongings before making off along the main road.[1] McMillan reached Busigny by nine o'clock that morning and went to the station where he bought a train ticket for Paris. As the next train wasn't due until late that afternoon, McMillan left the station and was soon accosted by three Frenchmen who recognised him as British and hid him in a shed.

---

1   "It is imperative to remember that once an Evader has begun [his evasion], all arms and weapons must be discarded and force may no longer be employed. This does not rule out the rare occurrence where an Evader may have to dispose of an enemy; but, this method will only be used if and when the lives of helpers are not thereby jeopardized and there are no eye-witnesses." (MI9 Bulletin TNA file WO208-3268)

That evening, Raymond Gransard (nf) collected McMillan in his van and drove him to a dairy in Catillon-sur-Sambre owned by Albert Sents of rue de la Groise (M Sents had sheltered S/Ldr Henry Bufton (also 9 Squadron) in August 1941 before he was passed on to the Pat Line). Next day Lucie Bates[2] called at the dairy – she had come from seeing his navigator Henry Brown at Le Cateau. On 23 July, McMillan joined Brown who was being sheltered by Maurice and Yvonne Thuru at 8 (or 6) rue de la Republique.[3]

ED480 navigator F/Sgt Henry T Brown had been collected in the evening of 10 July by Mme Bates and driven to 17 rue de la Gare in Le Cateau-Cambresis where he was sheltered overnight by Edouard and Laure Richez.[4] Early the following day, Edouard Richez took Brown by train to Paris where he had an office (address forgotten) with a firm called Tisca Ltd. M Richez left Brown in the office while he tried to find someone who could help Brown but on failing that, they both returned to Le Cateau that evening. On 12 July, Mme Bates came to reassure Brown that M Richez would continue to try and find help for Brown but meanwhile, he was to be moved and that afternoon, electrician Maurice Thuru drove Brown to Montay, just north of Le Cateau, where he stayed with the maire, Alfred Delporte. On 20 July, Brown was sent back to Le Cateau where he stayed with Maurice and Yvonne Thuru at 8 (or 6) rue de la Republique and two days later, was joined there by his tail-gunner, David McMillan.

Next day Maurice Thuru and Edward Richez drove McMillan and Brown to Arras, collecting Sgt Frederick Smooker along the way before handing them over to Mme Henriette Balesi.[5] Mme Balesi introduced them to Mlle Lobbedez of 104 rue de Bapaume (daughter of the ex-maire of Arras) and through her, Mme Marie Louise Medlicott of 135 (or 195)

2   Mme Lucie Bates (born November 1895) is credited with helpe nine Allied evaders – acting as interpreter and contacting other helpers on their behalf – between July 1943 and her arrest in March 1944 when she was denounced by a German masquerading as an evader. Mme Bates was deported to Belzig (a sub-camp of Ravensbruck) and repatriated to France in May 1945. (WO208/5452) Her recommendation for an award gives her address as 131 rue Brancas, Sevres (Seine et Oise) but the IS9 Helper List (which says she was recommended for a Kings Commission) says she lived at Le Cateau.

3   Maurice and Yvonne Thuru were arrested (no date) and deported – and M Thuru was shot at Dienst. (NARA Bodin)

4   Edouard and Laure Richez were arrested and deported to Germany where Edouard died – IS9 Helper List only – no further details …

5   Henriette Anne Balesi (born June 1879 in Bonnefacio, Corsica) had worked for Edith Cavell helping Allied prisoners to escape during the First War. During the Second War, she sheltered at least twenty-seven evaders in her home at 1 rue Felix Faure, Bapaume as well as guiding men to Paris or Valenciennes. Mme Balesi – who is described by Georges Guillemin as *"un vrai demon"* – was recommended for a BEM. (WO208/5452) (aka la Trottinette according to Allain)

rue de Bapaume and her two daughters, with whom the three airmen stayed for a week.

On 31 July, Mme Balesi took McMillan, Brown and Smooker to walk through the night to the village of Bapaume where they stayed at the home of Mr George Bailey (War Graves Commission, interned) with their cooking done by a woman called Madeleine whose husband was serving in England.[6] A few days later Maurice Thuru took them to Achiet (either Achiet-le-Petit or Achiet-le-Grand) where they collected Robert Stockburn and were taken by train to Paris.

They were met at the station by Edward Richez and taken to the flat of electrician Rene Marcel Le Templier at 31 rue de Varenne, Paris VII. Brown and Smooker were sheltered at rue de Varenne (see later) while McMillan and Stockburn were taken to stay with Mme Simonie de Corment at 74 rue de Rocher. A week later, McMillan and Stockburn were moved to an empty apartment on the top floor of a building at 74 rue de Cherche Midi for a few days before being taken to Fontenay-sous-Bois where they stayed with 53-year-old Georges Masse, an ironmonger at 97 rue des Moulins, until leaving Paris on 22 August.

2/Lt David H Turner was the co-pilot of B-17 42-3190 (94BG/333BS) (Harrison) which was on the way to Le Bourget on 14 July 1943 when it was attacked fighters. The bale-out order was given and 2/Lt Robert T Conroy and 2/Lt Roscoe F Greene jumped but (as mentioned earlier) the engineer's parachute was burned so the aircraft was crash-landed near Berengeville-la-Campagne (north-west of Evreux) in Normandy and the remaining crew scattered.

Turner was soon given a coat, food and directions to travel. Next day he approached a farmhouse where he was sheltered (by Henriette Nantier at La Vacherie – query), questioned and taken to Arnieres-sur-Iton, near Evreux. A few days later he was joined by Richard Davitt and Harry Eastman from Good Time Cholly II.

S/Sgt Richard S Davitt and S/Sgt Harry L Eastman were the ball-turret gunner and tail-gunner of B-17 42-30243 Good Time Cholly II (94BG/331BS) (Saltsman) which was lost on an operation to Le Bourget on 14 July 1943. As soon as their Spitfire escort turned back they were

---

6   The woman called Madeleine was Mme Madeleine Declercq (born September 1900 in Seneffe, Belgium) who lived at 17 rue Felix Faure, Bapaume. Shortly after this, Mme Declercq became suspect and she was forced to go into hiding until the end of the war. (WO208/5456) Several evaders say that her husband was George Bailey of the War Graves Commission – McMillan says that he was interned but others understood that he was serving in England.

attacked by enemy fighters and with the controls shot away, the aircraft was abandoned to crash near Houlbec-Cocherel (Eure) about 15 kms north-east of Evreux.

Davitt and Eastman were both helped soon after landing and brought together the next day. After being hidden in a wood for three days, they were taken to a house near Evreux where they joined David Turner from B-17 42-3190 who was being sheltered with Hubert and Renee Renaudin at Arnieres-sur-Iton.[7] On 21 July, Andre Schoegel arrived from Paris and he, Hubert and Renee took Davitt, Eastman and Turner – along with S/Sgt Joseph Cornwall who had also been sheltered in Evreux – to the capital.[8]

David Turner and Richard Davitt were sheltered by their guide Andre Schoegel at his Orly home on rue Jenner where Davitt stayed on after Turner was moved across the city to join his pilot Kee Harrison at 51 rue de Miromesnil. After about a fortnight, Turner was moved again, this time to stay with Felix Jolivot at 17 Avenue de la Concorde, La Varenne-St-Hilaire (Saint-Maur-des-Fosses). On 22 August, Georges Broussine (using the name Jean-Pierre) gave Turner a new ID card and took him to the Jardin des Plantes near Gare d'Austerlitz while Gabrielle Wiame collected Eastman.

Harry Eastman and Joseph Cornwall (waist-gunner of B-17 42-3331 Salty's Naturals, which was also lost on the 14 July operation to Le Bourget) were taken by a woman called Andree (probably Mme Vandevoorde) to Napoleon's Tomb (Les Invalides) where caretaker Georges Morin and his wife Denise (of 8 Avenue de Tourville) sheltered them in one of the ward-houses at Les Invalides for eight days while an organisation that could take them to Spain was contacted. Eight days later, Marie (Gabrielle Wiame) took Eastman and Cornwall for a meal at Madeleine Melot's apartment on rue Larrey where they joined Davitt – and met New Zealand pilot George Dickson who was being sheltered there. After the meal, Marie took Eastman and Cornwall to stay with Maud Couve and Alice Brouard at 25 rue de Madrid. However, there were too many evaders for the tiny apartment (Davitt was already living there, having been moved from Andre

---

7   Hubert and Renee Renaudin lived at Les Tuilleries, Arnieres-sur-Iton, which is a small village just outside Evreux. Mme Renaudin (born May 1907) was arrested on 4 May 1944 and held at Fresnes. She was condemned to death on 8 June but freed two months later due to the efforts of the Swedish Legation. Mme Renee Renaudin was recommended for a KMC. (WO208/5453)

8   Andre Auguste Schoegel (born Nov 1902) began working for an escape organisation in 1943, assembling groups of evaders from the areas surrounding Paris and guiding them to the capital. He sheltered some evaders in his own home at 2 rue Jenner in Orly (Seine) or led them to other safe houses as well as taking them to rendezvous points for their onward journeys. (WO208/5452)

Schoegel's apartment a few days after Turner left) so Cornwall was moved elsewhere, his report says to the house at which Captain Harrison later stayed. Eight days later, Cornwall returned to the Morin household.

Mme Denise Morin (born Dec 1898) and her daughter Mlle Yvette Morin (born October 1921) were arrested on 5 July 1944 and deported to Germany – they survived Ravensbruck, Torgau, Buchenwald and Marckleberg to be repatriated to France in the summer of 1945. Denise Morin was recommended for an MBE and Yvette for a KMC. Georges Julien Morin (born Aug 1898) was also arrested on 5 July and deported to Germany – where he died.[9]

T/Sgt Francis M Green and T/Sgt Edward C Ruby were the left waist-gunner and radio-operator of B-17 42-3330 (384BG/544BS) (Munday) which was damaged by flak and shot down by fighters on an operation to Villacoublay on 14 July 1943. The aircraft was abandoned south-west of Paris and crashed near Les Essarts-le-Roi. Five of the crew evaded successfully – all with Bourgogne.

Green, Ruby and their pilot James Munday landed close to one another and decided to head for Paris together. They set off walking but Munday's injured hip and knee soon persuaded them to ask for help. They met a Frenchman who had been looking for them – he said that he had already helped one of their crewmates by giving him civilian clothes – and he took them back to his house where their journeys were arranged.

In Paris, Green, Ruby and Munday were sheltered by nurse Germaine Royannez in her apartment at 9 Avenue Niel until 9 August when Green was taken to stay with British-born Dora Rospape at 11 rue du 29 Juillet (opposite the Jardin des Tuileries), where Kee Harrison joined him for a week. On 22 August, Mme Rospape and a Russian girl called Tamara took Green to the Jardin des Plantes where he saw Gabrielle Wiame (again) and was put on a train to Foix.

Ruby and Munday were taken by a young boy to the Jardin des Plantes where they met Gabrielle Wiame who took them to the eastern Paris suburb of Montreuil. They stayed with WW1 veteran Jacques Liandier and his wife Francine at 30 rue de Vincennes – where Mme Guillaume and Floyd Watts joined them for dinner one evening – until 22 August, when Mme Liandier took Ruby to the station.

S/Sgt Jefferson D Polk and T/Sgt Charles H McNemar were the ball-turret gunner and radio-operator of B-17 42-3190 (94BG/333BS)

---

9   TNA folder WO208/5453.

(Harrison) which was on the way to Le Bourget on 14 July 1943 when it was attacked fighters – see Turner above.

Polk and McNemar evaded together, running into a wood where they were soon helped by a farmer. A man from the local organisation moved them about for a while until they were taken to Evreux, where they met Andre Schoegel – and S/Sgt Donald Harding – and Andre took them all to Paris.

S/Sgt Donald E Harding was the top-turret gunner of B-17 42-30105 Slightly Dangerous (95BG/412BS) (Sarchet) which was on the way to Villacoublay on 10 July 1943 when it was attacked by fighters. The aircraft was abandoned south of Rouen and crashed near Saint-Didier-des-Bois. 2/Lt Robert M McCowen was the co-pilot and only other evader from Slightly Dangerous – he was helped by John Carter and crossed into Spain on the SOE Vic line route from Perpignan on 22 December 1943.

Harding landed in an orchard and was helped immediately by an elderly woman who hid him in a house and brought him civilian clothing. He was moved to a nearby wood and visited next day by a man from an organisation who took him on foot to Elbeuf. Four days later he was moved into the country to stay with a Belgian woman. On 24 July, a man from Elbeuf brought him ID papers and Harding was taken by bicycle to Evreux where he met Andre Schoegel. Harding spent the night with a barber before being taken to the station where he joined Andre – who had Jefferson Polk and Charles McNemar with him – and Andre took them all to Paris.

Polk, McNemar and Harding were met at Gare St Lazaire and taken to be sheltered separately – Polk for five days with Georges Raut and Helene Renault at 12 Place Dauphine[10] and Harding in a wine dealer's house at 122 Boulevard Saint-Michel – until the following Monday evening when they were introduced to Mme Marie (Gabrielle Wiame). Mme Wiame took them by train to Juvisy-sur-Orge where Polk and McNemar were sheltered by wine merchant Andre Lefevre and his family at 29 rue Hoche, and Harding with garage owner Maurice Bidaud. They stayed in Juvisy for almost four weeks (until 22 August) before Gabrielle Wiame took them back to Paris and the Gare d'Austerlitz.

Andre Clement Lefevre (born September 1897) is described by evader Tim Marean (see later) as being about 5 ft 6 inches tall with brown hair and

---

10   There is a strange MIS-X Memo dated 24 November 1944 in the Wiame NARA file concerning an accusation from Georges Raut that airmen in Gabrielle Wiame's care were disappearing. He cites the apparent non-arrival of Jefferson Polk on the basis that no radio message concerning his safe arrival in England had been heard on the BBC. The memo makes a point of noting that Raut is an intimate friend of Jacqueline Legueu (query) …

brown eyes – an old French soldier who had been an interpreter for the Americans in 1918. Andre was married to Pauline Helene (born January 1897) and they had a daughter Pauline Madeleine (aka Paulette) (born September 1922). Andre and Paulette were recommended for KMCs and Pauline for an MBE.[11] Juvisy-sur-Orge is a commune about 18 kms south-east of Paris and easily reached by train from the capital. Maurice Bidaud (born April 1913) and his wife Marie have a home address of 4 Avenue Hotel de la Ville, Juvisy-sur-Orge although most evaders only mention his Garage du Parc, also in Juvisy.

The nine evaders and their guides took the eight o'clock evening train to Toulouse where they changed for Foix the following morning. Shortly after setting off from Foix on foot that evening there was 'an alarm' and David McMillan, Francis Green and Donald Harding were left behind.

The rest of the group followed a man on a bike for about a mile and a half before spending the night hiding in bushes. Next afternoon they were driven south for half an hour and met their mountain guide that evening. They walked by night and rested by day until reaching Andorra on the fifth night. They stayed one night in a hotel in Andorra – where they were joined by several others – before walking through the night and crossing the Spanish border at about noon. They were arrested on 2 September and taken to La Seu d'Urgell. Turner and one of the Frenchmen were released to contact the British Consul in Barcelona while the others spent five nights in jail before being taken to Lerida.

Harding says that a party of fourteen started off from Foix but that he, Green, McMillan and a Frenchman were separated when a man on a bike came down the road – they all jumped into a ditch but then failed to notice when the rest of the group went on. After spending the night in a barn, the Frenchman returned to Foix to try and find their guides. On the fifth night they went back to Foix where they joined Philip Fink, Joseph Matthews, David O'Brart, Jack Lee and Sidney USAAF who had left Paris a week after them – see later.

11   TNA folder WO208/5451.

CHAPTER 16

Henry Brown and Allen Robinson – plus two more who almost made it ...

ED480 navigator Henry Brown and Sgt Frederick Smooker stayed on with Rene Le Templier after Robert Stockburn and David McMillan left, Brown being taken next day by Mme Anne Aweng to her flat at 17 (or 26) rue de l'Universite, Paris VII. On 14 August, Smooker joined him there for three days until Olivier Richet (of 15 rue de l'Universite) moved them to two different addresses (neither remembered). On 22 August, M Richet took them by Metro to Barbes (assume Barbes-Rochechouart) where they stayed at a hotel on Boulevard de la Republique (query) for two days. On 24 August, M Richet took them to a hairdresser's shop at 6 rue Capucines, Paris II belonging to Mme Christiane Lucienne (aka Marie-Christine) Bodin where they spent the day before briefly going to her flat at nearby 38 rue des Petit Champs and meeting a Belgian, a Frenchman and S/Sgt Allen Robinson. That evening, Brown, Robinson, the Belgian and the Frenchman were taken to the station where they took the nine-thirty train for Lourdes – leaving Smooker behind because his ID card wasn't in order.

Sgt Frederick H Smooker was the sole survivor of 106 Sqn Lancaster ED720 (Rosner) which was shot down on the night of 8-9 July 1943 and crashed near Cambrai (Nord-Pas-de-Calais). Smooker landed near Bethencourt where a M Chamberlain (nf) sheltered him for two days before taking him to Caudry where he stayed with Lucien and Yvonne Janssoone at 12 rue Zola. Nine days later, Yvonne Janssoone's friend, Henriette Balesi (aka *la souris* – the mouse) took him to Arras and Bapaume where she looked after him and two other RAF sergeants (McMillan and Brown) for week ... In Paris, Smooker and Henry Brown stayed with Rene Marcel Le Templier at 31 rue de Varenne for two days. After Brown left Paris with Allen Robinson, Smooker was sheltered at 26 rue de l'Universite by Mme Aweng, and various other addresses (he also lists Mlle Elsa Janine McCarthy – a 55-year-old English teacher from Cork – of rue Sainte Anne) until being taken back to Marie-Christine Bodin's apartment at 38 rue des

73

Petit Champs. Mme Bodin was away at the time, taking another party (which included Brown and Robinson) south – Smooker would probably have gone with them but as already mentioned, his papers weren't ready. On her return, Mme Bodin and another woman (Suzanne Bosniere) took Smooker in a party of five – the others being F/Lt Geoffrey Ball and three unnamed Americans (Higdon, Ritt and Cronin – query – mentioned later) – by train for Lourdes but on 12 September 1943, the five airmen and were captured in a ticket-check on the train between Bordeaux and Dax.

F/Lt Geoffrey F Ball was flying a Sweep sortie on 19 August 1943 in 182 Sqn Typhoon JP400 when he was hit by flak and force-landed at Blangy-sur-Bresle, about 20 kms south-east of Le Treport (Seine-Maritime). He was hidden and helped by David Mathieu of Bouillancourt-en-Sery (Somme) and sheltered in nearby Boutencourt with M et Mme Leon Lallot (and helped by Mme Pierre Courmontagne – née Odette Sellier) until 31 August when M Geniaux took him back to his home at 12 rue des Voules in Rouen with the promise of a Lysander flight home. On 4 September, Ball was moved to a farm outside Conches-en-Ouche (about 15 kms west of Evreux) where a local schoolmaster (name not given) explained that arrangements had fallen through and the following afternoon, the schoolmaster's wife took Ball to Paris. He stayed with the schoolmaster's sister-in-law until 9 September when he was moved to rue des Petits Champs, where he joined Frederick Smooker.

S/Sgt Allen N Robinson was the engineer of B-17 42-5175 (306BG/367BS) (Downing) which was hit by flak over St Nazaire on 16 February 1943 and attacked by fighters. Losing altitude rapidly, and after turning inland from St Brieuc, the bale-out order was given. Once the rest of the crew had jumped, the two pilots turned the aircraft back out to sea before baling out themselves.[1]

Twenty-five-year-old Robinson landed somewhere between Lannion and Guingamp and walked south for five days until reaching the village of Josselin. He declared himself to the landlady of a hotel who sheltered him while she made contact with an organisation. Three days later Robinson was collected and moved around before being taken by train from Pontivy to Paris. He stayed three days with Maurice Janet (nf) superintendant of a school, then two nights with Marie Therese Gentille (nf) at 13 rue de

---

1   42-5175 co-pilot 2/Lt Howard W Kelly also evaded successfully. After landing near Quintin (south-west of Saint-Brieuc) and being helped by numerous people – but no really organised group – Kelly crossed the central Pyrenees to Montgarri (Lleida) Spain in early March.

Citeaux and two nights with Peter (later arrested for black-market activities) where he was questioned by a M Isley (query spelling) who then took him to stay with Elisabeth Barbier at 72 rue Vaneau. Whilst there, he was visited by Ray Labrosse (who gave him new papers), Val Williams, Elsa Janine McCarthy, Olga Pontremoli and Elisabeth Carmalt. After seven weeks with Elisabeth Barbier, Jean Camard took Robinson back to Brittany where he stayed with Jean's father Jerome Camard, a builder and the maire of Etables.[2] A week later Jean moved him to join a group of eighteen Oaktree evaders being sheltered by Betty de Mauduit at the Chateau du Bourblanc. A few days later Ray Labrosse took Robinson – along with Robert Biggs, Edward Spevak, Donald Nicols, Roy Martin, Marcus Davis and William Ayres – back to Paris. Elisabeth Barbier met them at the station with the news that Val Williams had been captured and Robinson was taken to stay with Lucien Demongogin at 18 rue Victor Hugo, Asnieres-sur-Seine.

Following the raid at 72 rue Vaneau on 18 June, when Elisabeth Barbier and her mother Camille were arrested, Helene de Suzannet took Robinson in a Red Cross truck back to her apartment at 20 rue Greuze before he was moved to various addresses – including a hotel owner's son, an English lady who lived in the suburbs, a lawyer named Gouttenois (query) at 2 Carrefour de l'Odeon (Paris VI) and a Mme Solange – until Mme Gouttenois took him to stay with Marie Betbeder-Matibet at 7 Square de Port-Royal, Paris XIII. He was visited there by Marie-Rose Zerling (aka Claudette) who contacted Ray Labrosse, who also came to stay.[3]

On 24 August 1943, Christiane Bodin took Allen Robinson, Henry Brown and four others (including a Belgian and a Frenchman) by train via Bordeaux to Tarbes and Lourdes, returned to Tarbes and then on to Bagneres-de-Bigorre (arriving 29 August) where they were passed over to their mountain guides. They started walking across the Pyrenees that night and after two days their guides left them in the mountains overlooking the border. The others in the party headed west but Brown, Robinson and another Englishman (who had joined them at Bagneres) went south – and were arrested by Spanish police. They were taken to Barbastro for a week

---

2   Jerome Paul Marie Camard (born Etables in August 1888) was arrested on 29 September 1943 but released on 25 June 1944 due to lack of evidence. His house on rue de la Gare, Etables was visited again in July 1944 but by then Jerome and his wife Josephine (born March 1894 at Plouha) had escaped to a safer area. Both were recommended for a KMS. (WO208/5459)

3   Mlle Marie-Rose Zerling (born February 1908 in Paris) – later with the Francois-Shelburn organisation where she was responsible for their safe houses in Paris – was arrested on 5 February 1944, sentenced to death and deported to Germany. She was repatriated to France in August 1945. (WO208/5454) Marie-Rose Zerling was awarded an MBE.

until a Spanish air force officer took them to Alhama de Aragon for another week before they were repatriated to Madrid.[4]

Allen Robinson spent six months evading in France, and although included on Georges Broussine's list, was first helped by the PAO in Brittany before being moved to Oaktree. With the arrest of Val Williams, he stayed on with group Vaneau but following the arrest of Elizabeth Barbier a few days later, Helene de Suzannet passed him on to Marie Betbeder-Matibet and the Samson network.

Henry Brown would probably have continued with Bourgogne had he not stayed behind when his tail-gunner David McMillan left Rene Templier's apartment with Robert Stockburn. As it was, Anne Aweng took him back to her apartment to stay overnight before Olivier Richiet moved him and Frederick Smooker to Mme Bodin, where he joined Allen Robinson.

---

4   Alhama de Aragon is a spa town near Saragossa (Zaragoza) Aragon where, from late 1942, many Allied airmen were interned at various hotels as guests of the Spanish air force. American journalist Alice-Leone Moats, who visited there in May 1943, describes it as a sleepy little village tucked into the hills. Despite the comfortable conditions the internees found themselves in (proper hotel bedrooms, plentiful food and access to the local hot-springs) boredom seemed to be real problem. See 'No Passport for Paris' by Alice-Leone Moats (1945) Putnam's Sons, New York.

CHAPTER 17

24 August 1943

On 24 August 1943, F/O Peter Ablett, S/Sgt Richard Davitt, S/Sgt John Carpenter, T/Sgt Samuel Potvin, 1/Lt James Munday and five Frenchmen – including RAF evader Claude Raoul-Duval (with his wife Josette) – left Paris by train for Toulouse and Foix.

F/O Peter D Ablett was the flight engineer of 78 Sqn Halifax DT768 (Marshall) which was returning from Montbeliard at just after midnight on 16 July 1943 when it lost flying speed (cause unknown) went into a dive and the pilot gave orders for the crew to bale out.[1]

Twenty-two-year-old Ablett landed near Nogent-le-Rotrou (Eure-et-Loir) and was soon helped by a local farmer, whose friend contacted Mlle Paule Levillain. Mlle Levillain collected Ablett from Nogent and took him back to her home at 17 Grande Avenue, Le Pre-Saint-Gervais where he stayed for a week before being moved into Paris. He was sheltered and helped by numerous friends of Mlle Levillain, including Mme Germaine Gimpel of 2 rue Louis Codet, M Albert Guillaume of 18 rue Cler (nf), Mme Marthe Boursain, a dressmaker of 348 rue St Honore – and Mme Vve Lily Asselanidis of 75 rue Fondary who passed him on the organisation (Bourgogne) which arranged his journey – Ablett joining a group of evaders leaving Paris for Foix on 24 August.

S/Sgt Richard Davitt, the ball-turret gunner of Good Time Cholly II, stayed on with Andre Schoegel at his home on rue Jenner after David Turner left (see earlier) and then with Maud Couve and Alice Brouard at rue de Madrid. On 22 August, he was moved to 46 rue Poliveau where he stayed with Gabrielle Wiame for two days until being taken to the Jardins des Plantes.

S/Sgt John L Carpenter and T/Sgt Samuel E Potvin were the ball-turret gunner and radio-operator of B-17 42-3071 (94BG/331BS) (Watts) which was on the way to Le Bourget on 14 July 1943 when it was attacked by fighters and abandoned. Carpenter and Potvin were both helped immediately on

---

1   DT768 wireless operator Sgt Ivor J Sansum (mentioned later) was the only successful evader from this aircraft, crossing the Pyrenees from Perpignan at the end of October with the John Carter and Vic organisations.

landing near Chennevieres-les-Louvres (just north of present-day Charles de Gaulle airport) brought together a few days later and their journey arranged.

Potvin was met on landing by Andrew Danieux (nf) and taken on the cross-bar of his bicycle to a restaurant where a man and woman gave him some civilian clothes. M Danieux then took Potvin back to his house and Potvin was hidden in nearby woods for three nights. On 17 July, an unnamed (but apparently wealthy) farmer took Potvin by motorcycle to the railway station at nearby Louvres where he was passed on schoolteacher Jean Lucien Denaux who took Potvin north by train to the little town of Chantilly (Oise). From the station at Chantilly, Jean Denaux took Potvin by bicycle to his home in Gouvieux where he stayed with Jean and his wife Diana for the next two weeks.

Carpenter was met by the constable of Chennevieres-les-Louvres, given some food and later that day, taken to be hidden in a church attic. Three days later, Carpenter was taken to the local maire who told him that he would be leaving by train in a few days time but meanwhile he was hidden, firstly in a field, then a wine cellar for four days before being taken back to the maire's house. On 22 July, the same wealthy farmer who had taken Potvin, took Carpenter by motorcycle to the railway station at Louvres. Carpenter was also passed on to Jean Denaux who took him (by the same route) back to his home in Gouvieux where Carpenter joined Potvin. On 30 July, Carpenter and Potvin were taken back to Chantilly and sheltered separately for the next few days.[2]

On 5 August, Carpenter and Potvin were taken by train to Paris – joined on the way by their pilot Floyd Watts (see earlier) – where they were met Ray Labrosse. They also met (briefly) a blonde woman (probably Gabrielle Wiame) before Hina Zipine (aka Kitty) introduced Carpenter and Potvin to Andree Vandevoorde who took them to the eastern suburbs of Paris and the commune of Fontenay-sous-Bois.[3] They stayed with the Vandevoorde family (Maurice, Andree and their twenty-four-year-old son Bernard) at 167 Avenue de la Republique until 24 August when Mme Vandevoorde took them back to Paris where they met the blonde woman again. She took them to the Jardin des Plantes where they joined Peter Ablett, Richard Davitt,

---

2   In Chantilly, Potvin and Carpenter were helped by Mme Yvonne Fournier (owner of the clothing store "La Belle Jardiniere" at 2 rue de Paris), by Mons Hugonnier (manager of the store "Le Comptoir Français" on rue de Creil) and by Jean Lacour (of rue du Marechal Joffre) who was also a guide. (research by Dominique Lecomte)

3   Mme Francoise Andree Vandevoorde (née Woittequand December 1905) was awarded a BEM. (WO208/5451)

James Munday, Claude Raoul-Duval and his wife Josette, and two French officers.

1/Lt James S Munday was the pilot of B-17 42-3330 (384BG/544BS) and had just turned away from Villacoublay on 14 July 1943 when they were damaged by flak and shot down by fighters. The aircraft was abandoned south-west of Paris and crashed near Les Essarts-le-Roi.

Munday was helped immediately on landing in a tree (damaging his hip and knee) and soon joined by his waist-gunner Francis Green and radio-operator Edward Ruby. The three airmen made their way to a farmhouse where they were sheltered – they also met their bombardier 2/Lt Robert L Olson who took a train to Paris and an address that he had been given. A few days later, Red Cross nurse Germaine Royannez drove Munday, Green and Ruby by ambulance to her apartment at 9 Avenue Niel, Paris XVII. A Doctor Soulier (Raymond Soulie of 23 Blvd Barbes, Paris XVIII – query) came to see Munday and took him back to his own house where Munday stayed for ten days before returning to Avenue Niel for another two weeks when they were all turned over to an organisation.

On 9 August, a young boy took the three Americans to the Jardin des Plantes where they met Gabrielle Wiame and she took Munday and Ruby to stay with WW1 veteran Jacques Liandier at 30 rue de Vincennes, Montreuil – where Mme Guillaume and Floyd Watts joined them for dinner one evening.[4] Ten days later Ruby was told that he would be going by aircraft (he didn't – see above) and so left with Mme Francine Liandier. Next day (query) Mme Guillaume took Munday to the Jardin des Plantes where Gabrielle Wiame gave him a railway ticket and he joined Richard Davitt, John Carpenter and Samuel Potvin on the train to Toulouse.

The party took an overnight train to Toulouse where they changed for Foix and after a ten-mile ride in a truck to Auzat, began their walk in a party of thirteen. They soon found that Munday (who was still suffering with his injured knee) had to be left behind but the others reached Andorra (via the Port de l'Albelle) on 28 August.[5]

---

4   Both Jacques Charles Liandier and Marie Francoise Guillaume (née Corson) – a forty-five-year-old (born July 1896) widowed nurse – were later logeurs for Paul Campinchi and reseau Francois-Shelburn.

5   Claude Raoul-Duval says in his report (WO208/5582-1471) that the guides told him the route they used from Auzat was an unusual one but safer than the ordinary route – which was presumably patrolled more frequently. They followed a north-south ridge parallel to a river to cross the border about three-quarters of a kilometre east of the Pic de Tristagne. I can tell the reader from personal experience that this route, past the Etang d'Izourt and across to the Port de l'Albelle (at 2,601 mtrs) where there is a steep descent before reaching the (present day) road at l'Estany Primer, is a tough enough walk even in daylight.

It's not clear how Peter Ablett came to be captured – the American reports say that he was left in Andorra but Ablett says he was taken ill after two days walking and had to drop out of the party, lost his way and was picked up by a German patrol (presumably still in France) on 29 August. The remainder of the group rested in Andorra for two days before crossing into Spain on 1 September and walking to Manresa where they caught a train to Barcelona and the British Consulate, arriving there on 7 September 1943.

Munday rested in the tiny commune of Genat until 4 September when (having presumably recovered sufficiently from his injuries) he joined a party of 23 Frenchmen on a four-day walk to Andorra. After a night at the Hotel Coma in Ordino, he carried on to Manresa in Spain and the British Consulate in Barcelona, arriving there on 13 September 1943.

CHAPTER 18

The Loss of Sidney USAAF

On 31 August 1943, Sgt David O'Brart, Sgt Jack Lee, S/Sgt Philip Fink, 1/ Lt Joseph Matthews and Sidney USAAF were taken by train from Paris to Toulouse and Foix.

Sgt David F R O'Brart and Sgt Jack Lee were the mid-upper gunner and flight engineer of 620 Sqn Stirling BK690 (Rogers) which was returning from laying mines off Bordeaux on the night of 6-7 August 1943. They were flying along the coast at about 3,000 feet and over Nantes when they were hit by flak which set light to a fuel tank and the aircraft burst into flames. The bale-order was given at about 02.30 and the bomber crashed shortly afterwards.

O'Brart landed just outside Nantes, on the Nantes-Carquefou road. He followed the road towards Carquefou for a few miles before turning off to a field where he buried his flying kit and waited for dawn. As it got light, he started walking south, heading towards Spain and knowing that he had to cross the river Loire. He was soon intercepted by some local people, including a cyclist who could speak a little English. He was then helped by a baker selling his wares from a large box attached to a bicycle who asked O'Brart to wait, presumably while he finished his transactions, and then got O'Brart to climb into the box. The baker then pedalled into Nantes. O'Brart was sheltered with the baker and his wife, receiving a note next day saying that a lady would come to meet him the following day. Sure enough, on 8 August a woman came with some civilian clothes and she took O'Brart to an apartment at the top of the building where she lived in the centre of Nantes – O'Brart's presence being a secret from her husband. Next day, O'Brart was questioned by a young man claiming to be from an 'Intelligence Service' and he told O'Brart that the bodies of his pilot and bomb-aimer had been found in their crashed aircraft. The young man then took O'Brart back to his own house where he made him a new ID card. Next day (10 August) his flight engineer Jack Lee arrived and they were told that their fellow crewmen Sgts Smith and Rashley were also being sheltered in Nantes

81

and expected to join them shortly. However, after waiting until the evening of 12 August, O'Brart and Lee left without them.[1]

Jack Lee landed in a field near Carquefou and used the compass from his aids box to head south-west for an hour before hiding in some scrub near the main Nantes-Angers road. At about six-thirty, Lee was spotted by an elderly Frenchman who told him to stay hidden as there were Germans about. The man came back at about eleven o'clock with two boiled eggs and some wine and promised to return again that evening. When the man failed to appear, Lee set off towards the river Loire – where he was challenged by a young German soldier who failed to realise he was an airman and let him go – and through Nantes to the village of Saint-Herblain. Lee went into a cafe where he was quickly recognised as English and taken into a back room. One of the customers, a plumber named Andre Boran (nf) then took Lee to the garden that he cultivated and stayed there with him overnight. Next day Lee was visited by an English-speaking Frenchman who said he was from 'French Intelligence' in Paris who took his details. Next day, Andre Boran took Lee back to his home in Nantes and the following afternoon, Lee was handed a note from his mid-upper gunner David O'Brart and that evening, Lee was taken to the house in Nantes where O'Brart was being sheltered by Jacques and his wife Frances.

O'Brart and Lee were taken by overnight train (with the help of the engine driver) to Le Mans (arriving early in the morning of 13 August) with five helpers, four of whom then left and it was sixteen-year-old Bernard Stockhousen who took them to his parents home just outside Le Mans at Les Grands Fougeray, La Chapelle-Saint-Aubin. Apparently there were delays in organising their onward travel to Paris and it wasn't until 28 August that Bernard and another young man took them to the capital. They stayed with two elderly ladies, one of whom spoke fluent English, until the evening of 31 August when they were taken to the Jardin des Plantes and Gare d'Austerlitz where they joined a group of three Americans and two Frenchmen.

S/Sgt Philip J Fink was the radio-operator of B-17 42-3188 Flak Alley Lil (384BG/544BS) (Cudderback) which was on the way to Villacoublay on 26 June 1943 when it was hit by flak over Le Havre and finished off by fighters. The bale-out order was given and the aircraft crashed near La Chapelle-Hareng in Normandy. Fink was the only successful evader.

Fink was helped immediately on landing in a field and sheltered locally for a month on a farm near Courtonne-le-Ville (now Courtonne-les-

---

1   Whilst BK690 rear gunner Sgt J R Smith is reported as captured, the other four crew of BK690, including wireless operator Sgt Colin E Rashley, were killed.

Deux-Eglises) until his journey was arranged. On 26 July, the farmer's wife took Fink to Paris and Neuilly-sur-Seine where he stayed with the French film actress Jeanne Helbling for three days at 9 bis rue Casimir Pinel and then four days with a young French artist called Michel. On 3 August, he was taken to stay with a woman doctor called Mme Verow/Veroux (Mme Albertine Veron of 5 rue Stephen Pichon, Paris XV – query) where he was sheltered until the end of the month when he left for Foix.

1/Lt Joseph G Matthews was escorting B-17s to Le Bourget in P-47 42-7949 (4FG/336FS) on 16 August 1943 when he was shot down by enemy fighters. Matthews baled out and landed in a tree in the Foret de l'Isle Adam, about 10 miles north-west of Paris.

Matthews was helped by a group of cyclists soon after landing and a few days later taken into Paris to stay overnight with a Mlle Delforge (nf) at 41 rue Francoeur, Paris XVIII before moving to the fire station at 47 rue Saint-Fargeau, Paris XX where he stayed with Lt Paul Poitier. Eight days later Matthews was taken to the Boulevard de Strasbourg, Paris X where he met an American evader called Sidney and they were turned over to a blonde woman (probably Gabrielle Wiame) who took them to north-east Paris and an apartment over a hardware shop near Le Bourget. On 31 August, a small brunette lady took Matthews and Sidney to meet the blonde woman who had Sgt Philip Fink and their guide to Foix with her. They went to the Gare d'Austerlitz where they joined Marcel (Marcel Canal – query)[2] and RAF sergeants David O'Brart and Jack Lee and took the train to Foix.

The five evaders stayed in the basement of a half-completed post office in Foix for three nights before setting off on 3 September with Francis Green, Donald Harding and David McMillan (see earlier). Sidney was lost when he fell off a cliff at about two o'clock in the morning of 5 September.

Philip Fink says that Sidney (from 384 BG) was aged about 35, married and from Denver, Colorado. He was exhausted and Fink had just passed him when he fell. Jack Lee says they were on a very narrow path around the top of a high peak – it was very dark and very slippery and they were all exhausted. Sidney was 35 year-old T/Sgt Sidney C Grinstein (born April 1908) from Denver, Colorado – the engineer/TTG of 384BG/546 BS B-17 42-5797 (Magowan) which was shot down on 16 August 1943 returning from Le Bourget. 39240604 Sidney Grinstein certainly didn't die in the Pyrenees – he was a POW at Stalag

2   Marcel Pierre Louis Canal (born April 1912) of 66 rue de la Republique, Toulouse, worked with two different escape organisations from September 1943 – not only procuring guides but sometimes leading parties to Andorra himself – until his chief was denounced and arrested in January 1944. (WO208/5452) His chief was Andre Pollac (Sherry).

Luft III (Sagan) and died in Denver in 1983. Grinstein's RAMP report (Folder 5 page 206) says that after being sheltered in Rambouillet (no names) he was brought to Paris and sheltered with Mme Ellen Walker at 83 rue Mederic, La Garenne-Colombes. Two weeks later, he was put on a train with a Frenchman and taken to Foix. He says that whilst crossing the Pyrenees, he lost contact with his party, walked into a German position and was captured.

The rest of the group reached Andorra in the early hours of Sunday 6 September. In Andorra, Green says that he and O'Brart drew the lucky cards in an arrangement with Andre Pollac and they were driven to the frontier with five Poles, crossing into Spain on 8 September and reaching the British Consulate in Barcelona two days later.

Andre Pollac (aka Sherry) had direct links to Bourgogne. After time spent with various underground organisations, Pollac had left France for Andorra in early 1943 with the help of M Bonafos of Place de la Republique in Rivesaltes. He made his way to the British Consulate in Barcelona where he volunteered to return to France and set up an escape line. He built his line with the aid of a Polish organisation and between August and the end of September 1943 – in addition to other activities – they passed convoys between Andorra and Spain. Funded by the British, they paid off the relevant Spanish officials and were able to deliver evaders direct to the British Consulate in Barcelona. Andre Pollac was later betrayed by a man called Louis Bordes and arrested in Perpignan on 23 January 1944. (Sherry NARA file) Andre Bertrand Pollac (born October 1920) was deported to Germany but survived to be repatriated to France – he was awarded an MBE.[3]

The rest of the group stayed another two days before being driven to the Spanish frontier (10 September) and started walking again. After a couple of days, Matthews borrowed a compass from Fink and went off on his own. He was soon arrested by Spanish border police who searched him (but took nothing) before turning him back to the border. At the border he was arrested again and sent to La Seu d'Urgell for the night before being transferred to Lerida. He was housed at the Hotel Palascio where he joined Robert Stockburn, Edward Ruby, Jefferson Polk, Charles McNemar and Harry Eastman – and two days later, by Fink and the party he had crossed with.

The rest of the group had walked to Ponts (having apparently missed the turning for Manresa) where they were arrested by two Guardia Civil on 12 September. After two days in jail, they were taken by bus to Lerida where they joined Matthews and the others.

---

3   TNA folder WO208/5452.

CHAPTER 19

Perhaps not with Bourgogne but …

There are several names included on the list of evaders in Georges Broussine's book that seem questionable – I am including details of some of them here.

F/O Joseph Lambert

Jean Coatelan, although French, was born in England in May 1916. While flying with the RAF he used the name Joseph Lambert in order to protect his family who were still living in France. Broussine lists a F/O Lambert and Jean Coatelan seems to be the only likely candidate – but links to Bourgogne are tenuous.

P/O Joseph Lambert was flying 340 (FF) Sqn Spitfire AR363 escorting Hurri-bombers (the fighter-bomber version of the Hawker Hurricane) on an early evening operation to St Omer aerodrome on 30 July 1942, when he was shot down by a Fw190 and baled out about five kilometres north of St Omer.

Lambert landed in an area of irrigation ditches, close to the Calais-St Omer railway line, and after hiding his parachute and Mae West, was shown a path by a group of railway workers that led him to the village of Serques. He was approached by some local people who gave him civilian clothes and food and directed him to an isolated cow-shed where he went to sleep. At about midnight, some more people took him by boat along the canal to a farm where he was sheltered all next day until the son of the household reported a German search and Lambert was returned to the cow-shed. Next day he began walking, making his way to an address he had been given in Berguette (where the occupant was too frightened to help him) before taking an evening train to Paris.

Lambert arrived in Paris at about ten o'clock, and assuming there was an eleven o'clock curfew, went to the apartment of one of his relatives. The relative (Louis Coatalen of 7 rue le Sueur – query) was away but the concierge let him spend the night there anyway and telephoned the relative, who arrived next day. After two days in Paris, Lambert and another of his relatives, took a train to Angouleme. Lambert had collected his old *Livret Militaire* while in Paris and was hoping that would be sufficient ID for travel. His companion soon proved that not to be the case and Lambert was fortunate to be able to leave Angouleme station through a temporarily unguarded exit. They had gone to Angouleme with the intention of crossing the demarcation line to unoccupied France but quickly found that wasn't going to be so easy. After being stopped by gendarmes and questioned – and Lambert having to show his *Livret Militaire* (which was of course in his real name) – they returned to Paris.

After another aborted attempt via Poitiers, Lambert contacted his father-in-law who was director of several industrial firms and allowed to cross the demarcation line. On (about) 15 August, Lambert and his brother-in-law took a train to Pougues-les-Eaux (just north of Nevers) and then walked to Guerigny where they were to meet Lambert's father-in-law. Unfortunately, they were stopped on the way by a gendarme who took down Lambert and his brother-in-law's details.

Lambert's father-in-law arranged to have one of his friends, who was a maire, to procure an identity card for Lambert in the name of another of Lambert's brothers-in-law, complete with a photograph supplied by Lambert's wife. Using the new card, he then applied to the German authorities for an *Ausweis* for Lambert to cross the demarcation line and Lambert duly crossed into the relative safety of Vichy France at Digoin (Saone-et-Loire) in his father-in-law's car a few days later. Lambert was taken to his father-in-law's house in Saint-Chamond, south-west of Lyon, where he joined his wife and children.

Lambert describes his position as "somewhat difficult" as the maire who had supplied his identity card had reported Lambert's presence to Pierre Laval, head of the Vichy Government. Since the Germans would undoubtedly also be aware of Lambert's presence, and because he feared his father might be taken hostage, Lambert decided his only option was to give his parole and stay with his family. This agreement was cancelled when the Germans took over the whole of France in November 1942.

Lambert reports that in November 1942, contact was made through Georges Salomon of the NGK Spark Plug company, with a man in Grenoble who said he could arrange for Lambert to be taken back to England by air – but this plan failed to materialise. He also says that he contacted an organisation that put him in touch with a man in Lyon but Lambert received no help from him either and it apparently took another nine months before Lambert finally found a man who would arrange his onward journey.

At the end of April 1943, Lambert met Georges Villiers, then maire of Lyon, and various schemes were discussed but it wasn't until Mme Sabine Berritz, who was working for 'Paris Soir' in Lyon, put Lambert in touch with M Aime of 65 Cours de la Liberte in Lyon, that his journey to Spain was arranged.

On (about) 20 August 1943, Lambert left Lyon with the Baron De Sevin (query). They took a train via Toulouse to Pamiers – Lambert using ID documents (including a *Certificate de Travail*) in his real name (Jean Coatelan) but with his place of birth altered from London to Lourdes. After waiting in Pamiers for three days for their next contact, a man named Cazeneuve (Jean Maurice Cazeneuve of Toulouse – query) directed them to a cafe in Mercus-Garrabet, Ariege (Louis and Lucienne Canal – query) just north of the restricted area that ran all along the northern approaches to the Pyrenees. They were taken by lorry to a house in Aston (south-west of Les Cabannes) and began walking at eleven-thirty that night. They reached El Serrat in Andorra some twenty-four hours later and next day, went on to Ordino where their mountain guide pointed out the way to Escaldes.

After two days in a hotel at Escaldes, guides were found to take them to Barcelona, crossing the border into Spain and walking to Manresa where they took a train to Barcelona. At the British Consulate, Lambert assumed British nationality by virtue of his place of birth and was soon sent on to Madrid – along with James Munday and Francis Green – see earlier.

Thomas Simpson and Robert Conroy

F/O Thomas W Simpson RCAF was the mid-upper gunner of 405 Sqn Halifax HR854 (Foy) which was returning from Montbeliard in the early hours of 16 July 1943 and heading towards Orleans, when they were attacked by two night-fighters. With both starboard engines hit, the aircraft was abandoned to crash near Tonnerre (Yonne).[1]

---

1   Five other crew from HR854 also evaded successfully: flight engineer Sgt John B McDougall crossed the Pyrenees in August from Perpignan, wireless operator Sgt Gregor MacGregor crossed the Pyrenees in August from Lourdes (see both later), bomb aimer S/Ldr Albert Lambert and navigator F/O Hugh T Huston crossed the Pyrenees from Quillan with Bourgogne in November, and pilot F/Lt James H Foy crossed the Pyrenees to Bielsa with a party of American evaders in March 1944.

Simpson landed in a small clearing in a forest, buried his parachute and Mae West and began walking south. He was helped by various people along the way, including a farmer and his English wife who sheltered him for three days before their two sons took him across the river (and the old demarcation line) to Saint-Florent-sur-Cher. Well supplied with food from the generous farmer, Simpson walked for another four days without meeting anyone until reaching Chateaumeillant (Centre) on the evening of 23 July where he was taken in for the night and helped with a train ticket for Toulouse.

Simpson reached Toulouse, apparently without incident, and began walking south-west, heading for the Spanish border. He had only been walking for a couple of hours when he was approached by a young man trailing a bicycle with a punctured front tyre, who asked him for a match. The young Frenchman obviously realised that Simpson was evading and offered to take him back to his house for the night. They returned to Toulouse and the next day, an English-speaking friend appeared who knew someone who could help Simpson.

Next evening (25 July) Simpson was taken to another house in Toulouse where he stayed with a midwife and her husband. Two days later, a M Biscuit (query spelling) came and told Simpson he would be taking him to Foix. For some unexplained reason, their first attempt at taking a train failed and M Biscuit disappeared for a week but on 4 August they finally left for Foix. M Biscuit took Simpson to a bicycle shop where the owner was in contact with some mountain guides and Simpson stayed for three days with a French marine officer called Jacques who was also going to Spain. They set off on 8 August in a party of eleven, with two guides. Included in the party was F/O Robert Conroy.

F/Sgt Robert F Conroy – a twenty-two-year-old Canadian serving with the RAF – was the pilot and only survivor of 429 Sqn Wellington HE593 which was on the way to Dusseldorf in the early hours 12 June 1943 when they were hit by flak and the aircraft abandoned to crash south-east of Eindhoven in Holland.

Conroy landed in a muddy field and after discarding his parachute and Mae West, began walking north-west, away from his burning aircraft. At dawn he hid in the middle of a wheat-field where he stayed for the rest of the day. He carried on walking that night and the following day until evening when he approached an isolated farmhouse where he was given a meal and a man from the neighbouring village of Oirschot (between

Eindhoven and Tilburg) was brought to see him. Conroy was taken to another house in the same village to stay the night in the family's barn. Next day, the man from Oirschot brought Conroy some civilian clothes and took him back to his house for the afternoon. That evening, he drove Conroy to Esbeek, near the Belgian border, and left him in a restaurant where Conroy stayed the night. Next morning, a Dutch policeman took Conroy to a nearby forest where he joined four Dutch students who were hiding from German forced labour service. On 18 June, another Dutch policeman took Conroy to the Belgian border where the first policeman was on duty. Conroy was given a Belgian ID card and handed over to a smuggler and his son who took him across the border and on to Turnhout, Antwerp and Brussels where he was given over to an organisation and his journey arranged.

Conroy's MI9 report stops at this point (and no Appendix C has been found) and only continues with a brief description of his crossing from Andorra to Spain on 13 August with F/O Thomas Simpson.

"We began travelling by night and resting by day, but were making slow progress. F/O Simpson and I thought the party was rather large and broke away from it on 15 Aug. That day we walked to a town, which was probably Berga, and continued south. At the outskirts of a village we stopped a man and asked him for cigarettes. We also asked for directions to Barcelona and enquired if there were police in the next village. The man preceded us and when we arrived there the police were waiting for us. They took us to the police station, where they were quite friendly. After lunch, an escort took us to the Police Headquarters in Barcelona, where we remained in a cell until 19 August. We were then moved to a gaol in Barcelona where the Consul visited us. On 8 Sep we were escorted from the gaol by a Spanish Air Force officer to the Consulate-General. That day we were taken to Alhama de Aragon. We were interned in a hotel here for about a week. On release, I was sent to Madrid (arrived 17 Sep) and left for Gibraltar on 19 Sep." (TNA File WO208/3315-1429)

Halifax HR854 – John McDougall and Gregor MacGregor

Sgt John B McDougall RCAF was the flight engineer of 405 Sqn Halifax HR854 (Foy) – see above. Whilst there no evidence from his report that McDougall was helped by anyone in the Bourgogne organisation, it is more than possible that the ID papers and mountain guides were arranged by Jean Olibo, Broussine's contact in Perpignan. Either way, I have included details of McDougall's evasion as an example of the trials and tribulations that faced the lone evader in 1943 occupied France.

McDougall landed in a clearing in a wood west of Bellegarde-du-Loiret (Centre) knocking himself out as he did so. After tearing off strips from his parachute to bandage his bleeding forehead, he buried the chute and Mae West and set off to the south. He says that he saw a white object in the distance (which he decided to avoid) which he thought later was probably his wireless operator MacGregor (see below) whose parachute had caught in a tree.

McDougall found a road that was sign-posted for Bourges and followed that until daybreak when he stopped at a farm where he was given Schnapps and water to bathe his wound. The farmer brought a Belgian who could speak some English and that evening, the Belgian returned with civilian clothes and a satchel that McDougall used to carry his uniform. McDougall set off again that night, reaching the little town of Sully-sur-Loire by daybreak (17 July) where he approached another farmer and was given food and shelter in a hayloft for the rest of the day. He set off again that evening, walking through the night to another farm just north of Argent-sur-Sauldre where again, he was given food and spent the day in a barn. McDougall carried on in similar fashion until he approached Bourges where he understood there were a number of Germans. Hailing a passing lorry, McDougall persuaded the driver (who hadn't intended to go that way) to take him through Bourges and drop him on the southern outskirts of the town. McDougall then followed the western bank of the river Cher through Saint-Thorette and Villeneuve to Saint-Florent-sur-Cher where, being very tired and having badly blistered his feet from walking in flying boots, he went into a hotel and ordered a beer.

It turned out to be a good choice of venue. The owner obviously recognised McDougall as an evader and after taking McDougall into a back room for a meal, brought a friend who not only spoke English but also had a spare pair of shoes that would fit McDougall. Next day, the hotel owner took McDougall to Chateauneuf-sur-Cher where he was introduced to a man who promised to make arrangements to get him to Perpignan. McDougall stayed on at Florent for the next six days while these arrangements were made and on 26 July, took the train for Perpignan with the man from Chateauneuf. They actually stayed in the little village of Tautavel, some ten miles north-west of Perpignan, while ID papers were made for McDougall and it wasn't until the late evening of 2 August that McDougall set off across the mountains with two guides and two young Frenchmen.

They crossed the border that night and McDougall and the two Frenchmen were soon arrested by the Guardia Civil. After a night at Espola police station, they were taken to Figueras from where McDougall was able to contact the British Consulate in Barcelona. After a couple of weeks in hospital with a fever, McDougall was transferred to a hotel at Alhama de Aragon for a further three weeks before being sent to Madrid and Gibraltar.

Sgt Gregor MacGregor was the wireless operator of 405 Sqn Halifax HR854 (Foy) and although on Broussine's list, I think it more accurate to credit MacGregor's successful evasion to Lucienne Bodin, Susanne Bosniere and the Samson network.

MacGregor landed in a pine tree just south of Bellegarde-du-Loiret. Not knowing how far he was from the ground, he waited until daylight before releasing his parachute harness and climbing down. He then hid in the wood until it got dark again before heading south, following the bank of a canal for several hours before settling down for his first full night in France. Next morning he carried on walking and that evening, approached a farm to ask for some water. The elderly couple at the farm gave MacGregor wine, bread and cheese but they had no spare clothing and he carried on walking through the night, reaching Ouzouer-sur-Loire early next morning (18 July). He crossed the Loire by swimming, his clothes tied in a bundle, and then approached a farm, where he was given some food. The farmers were nervous of MacGregor staying so he soon set off once more but hadn't gone far when a young man from another farm ran after him and offered him a coat. The young man took MacGregor back to his home where MacGregor had a much-needed shave and was given trousers and a shirt, for which he gave the young man 300 francs from his escape kit. About an hour later, a car arrived with a visitor for the family and he volunteered to take MacGregor back to his house in Sully-sur-Loire where MacGregor had a bath and a sleep while the man went to try and find some someone who could help. That evening, a young English-speaking Frenchman arrived and said that he knew someone who could help and that they would call the following morning.

On the morning of 19 July, Renee Owen came to visit MacGregor. Mme Owen, whose husband had been a Royal Navy captain in the First

War, took McGregor's details and that evening, MacGregor was taken to stay overnight with a Dr Doord. Next morning, the doctor drove McGregor to Mrs Owen's house in the nearby village of Saint-Florent-le-Jeune. Mme Owen had to report to the German authorities each week and was subject to random visits by them but she still managed to contact an organisation in Paris.

On 27 July, Mme Owen and Dr Doord drove MacGregor to Sully-sur-Loire station where they were met by Lucienne Bodin. She took MacGregor by bus to Pithviers where they caught a train to Paris, arriving at the Gare d'Austerlitz at ten-forty that evening. They took the Metro to Palais Royale where they joined Suzanne Bosniere before walking to Mme Bodin's house at 39 rue des Petits Champs. MacGregor was given more clothes and next day, Mme Bodin took MacGregor to have his photograph taken. MacGregor stayed with Mme Bodin for the next fourteen days – the delay apparently being due to one of the organisation's chiefs, a man called Paul, being captured on a visit to the Belgian frontier to rescue four Allied airmen. MacGregor was also visited by Paul Gaillard. On 11 August, Mme Bodin and Suzanne took MacGregor by train to Toulouse – arriving there at five-thirty in the afternoon – where they met Paul Gaillard who had brought a French Moroccan called Ali Ben Ahmed who joined them. They stayed overnight in Toulouse with a contact of Suzanne's called Michael. Early next morning (12 August) they left Toulouse for Lourdes and were led to a restaurant where they joined other members of the organisation, including one of the mountain guides, to whom Mme Bodin paid 5,000 francs for MacGregor's crossing.

They stayed overnight at Lourdes in a hotel and next evening, the mountain guide took MacGregor by train to Boo-Silhen and then walked the four kilometres to Prechac. They set off from Prechac that night (13 August) in a party of twenty-five, crossing the frontier near Mt Perdino at half past seven in the morning of 17 August. About 10 kilometres into Spain, they were stopped by Spanish police.

F/O Stanislaw Swida

F/O Stanislaw Swida was the navigator of 301 Sqn Wellington Z1491 which was on an operation to Saarbrucken in the early hours of 29 August 1943 when it was attacked by a night-fighter and abandoned to crash near Rummen (Belgium). Three crew were captured but the last three men to bale out all evaded successfully – the other two being wireless operator Sgt Anton Wasiak, who evaded with Comete, and pilot P/O Joseph Tyszko who crossed the Pyrenees in September. It is not clear why Swida's name is included on Broussine's list of Bourgogne evaders but I have included this account from 'RAF Evaders' for its own interest.

"*Swida, whose left cheek had been grazed by a bullet, 'came down in an orchard beside a small farm'. Believing that he was too close to the scene of the crash he 'decided to get away at once'.[2] Meeting a woman from the farm as he walked down a lane, she showed him the route to follow to avoid the Germans. Then a number of Belgians 'all advised me to go to the nearest village and give myself up to the police.' This was not what he wanted to hear, 'and after going along the road for a bit went across country again', ignoring the earlier advice.*"

He was making his way through another orchard at around 4 a.m. (29 August) when a gamekeeper, alerted by his barking dogs, came out to investigate. As the gamekeeper could speak only Flemish, and neither could understand the other, Swida was taken to his employer, with whom he 'talked for about an hour in French.' This man, as the other Belgians had done earlier, suggested that, as two others of his crew had already been captured in the neighbourhood, he should also give himself up. Still not convinced as to the merits of such a course of action, Swida told the man that he would try to get away, and was shown a wood near the house where it would be safe for him to spend the rest of the day. He set off again in the evening and walked all night (29/30 August), 'getting bread, water and cigarettes from peasants in the small villages I passed.'

In the morning, having bought a jacket to put over his battledress, Stanislaw Swida caught a train to Brussels, some 60 kms to the south-west. Despite the jacket, he was obviously an airman, and one of his fellow passengers 'whispered to me to follow him when we arrived in Brussels, and took me to his house there.' Trying unsuccessfully to make contact with a "British organisation" during the day, his benefactor advised him to go to Dour and cross the frontier into France, only 5 kms or so away. Unable at first to find anyone to help, he got into conversation with a woman who appeared to be very anti-German. Swida took a chance and told her who he was: 'She arranged for her husband to take me to a village (no name) near the frontier, whence the husband and a friend took me across the frontier to another small village, where they found me shelter for the night.'

---

2   Swida's report M.I.9/S/P.G. (-) 1584 in TNA file WO 208/3316. (original note)

Early on the morning of 31 August his French host advised him to head for Switzerland 'rather than for Spain, in view of the difficulty in getting across the Line of Demarcation into Unoccupied France.' For once taking the advice offered, Swida walked to le Quesnoy [Quesnoy-sur-Deule] 'intending to get the train to Nancy. I missed the only train of the day, and spent the night in an orchard.' On the train to Nancy on the following day two French plain-clothes detectives asked him for his papers, but 'when I said that I had no papers they began to search my pockets and found my R.A.F. identity card. They taxed me with being English, and, when I agreed, warned me that there were many Germans in Nancy, wished me good luck, and went off.' Four Frenchmen who had witnessed this incident 'got very excited'. Questioning Swida as to his intentions, they confirmed that it was too dangerous for him to go to Nancy, as there were too many German troops stationed there, and decided that he should go with them to Pont-à-Mousson.

There, one of the four men took him to 'an officer of the gendarmerie, who gave me a French identity card, for which I supplied one of the two photographs of myself in civilian clothes which I had had taken privately in England.' After Swida had spent the night (1/2 September) at his home, the man took Swida to Nancy. Buying him a ticket for Belfort, the man advised him to go from there to Montbeliard and on by bus to the Swiss frontier. At Montbeliard, while waiting for the bus, Swida 'went into a cafe and got into conversation with the proprietor.' She advised him not to catch the bus as planned but to go to St Hippolyte (Doubs) (not to be confused with St Hippolyte-du-Fort), about 25 winding kms by road to the south, and walk to Chamesol, some 3 kms north of St Hippolyte, where he would find help at a certain cafe only three or four kms from the Swiss frontier.

Unable to find the woman who was supposed to have helped him in the cafe at Chamesol, he spent the night in the woods out of harm's way. Returning to the cafe next day (3 September), he failed yet again to meet the woman. Too dangerous to remain any longer in such a small place, he struck out on his own for the Swiss frontier, and crossed unhindered into Switzerland during the afternoon of 3 September having been 'directed through the forests by peasants.' Of German guards there was no sign, but no sooner had he crossed the border than he was arrested by the Swiss and taken to a frontier post for questioning. Having no identity card – he had left his RAF one at Pont-à-Mousson and had destroyed the French one while still in France – he was put in the prison at Porrentruy for seven days and then taken to Berne, where he saw the Polish consular authorities and the British air attache.

Several weeks later, with the Swiss police believing him to be a spy, Swida was interned at Henniez (Canton Vaud) with a number of officers of the Polish Army's 2nd Infantry Fusiliers Division (2 Dywizja Strzelców Pieszych), who had crossed to Switzerland with their arms on 20–21 June 1940.[3] In August 1943, long fed up with the attitude of the Swiss, he 'decided to try to get away alone. I had no money, having received none from the British authorities since my internment.'[4] Even the Polish Consulate in Berne, to whom he had gone for help, said that it was impossible for him to get away alone, and suggested he went back to Henniez to await a signal from them, which came at the end of September. Making his way to Geneva, on 1 October he 'met a Pole (Stanislaw Piela) who often crosses the frontier. I crossed the frontier the same day with Piela and another Pole (Perzanowski) who acts with him on Intelligence work for the Poles and possibly for the British. We walked across the frontier to St Didier-en-Chaulais, where we got a train for Aix-les-Bains.'

After three days in Aix he was sent to Toulouse to meet a Pole named Barzycki, who was organising a party to cross the mountains to Spain. It was fortunate for Swida that he failed to rendezvous with Barzycki, 'for the party which he sent off that day was seized by the Gestapo in Andorra and taken back to France.' Swida returned to Aix, and a fortnight or so later met Barzycki there. Meeting as arranged at Toulouse on 29 October they travelled together by train to Boussens (Haute-Garonne) and by bus to Salies-du-Salat, 'where there is a large Polish community living in a camp. In the camp there is an apartment reserved for men escaping to Spain.'

On 2 November Swida, nine other Poles and a guide took the bus to St Girons and to Massat (Ariege), where they were joined by two Frenchmen. Setting off next day, it took three days to get to Andorra. After one night in the town of Andorra la Vieja, where Sgt Witold Raginis joined them, they crossed into Spain by bus, and went to La Seu d'Urgell. Swida and some of the party (not Raginis) were in Barcelona on 9 November. Spending the night at the Polish Red Cross, it was suggested that they should turn themselves in to

3   This division, operating with French troops in the Belfort area of eastern France, was engaged in heavy fighting from 17–19 June 1940. When the French retreated, the Poles, though virtually surrounded by the Germans, were able to break through to Switzerland. The 15,830 men of this division were, as of 15 June 1940, part of the 84,461 Polish soldiers in France, some 45,000 of whom had escaped from Poland. (original note)

4   Appendix C, Swida's report M.I.9/S/P.G. (-) 1584 in TNA file WO 208/5582. (original note)

the Spanish police next day, but Swida would have none of it, and reported instead to the British Consulate. Two days later, with two Americans and a Frenchman, he was at the British Embassy in Madrid. Eight days later he was on his way to Gibraltar, and flew back to England on the night of 23/24 November 1943."

CHAPTER 20

Georges Broussine leaves for London

At the end of September 1943, Georges Broussine left Yves Allain in charge of the organisation while he crossed the Pyrenees to Barcelona. From the British Consulate, Broussine was driven to Madrid before taking a train to Gibraltar, where he met the British agent Donald Darling – Darling interrogated each evader as they arrived and had built up an encyclopaedic knowledge of the various escape lines. A few days later, Broussine was flown to London where, in addition to reporting to BCRA, he also described to Airey Neave and James Langley of MI9 how Bourgogne was progressing. Neave was particularly enthusiastic about the idea of using RN gunboats to pick up evaders from Brittany and although it (Operation Charlemagne) was never fully developed, Broussine was sent to confer with the Royal Navy. It doesn't seem likely that Broussine would have been told about the imminent departure of MI9 agents Lucien Dumais and Ray Labrosse to set up the Shelburn line. After learning that he had been awarded a Military Cross by the British, Broussine returned to France by Lysander (Op Tommy Gun to pick up Yeo-Thomas) landing in a field near Arras on the night of 15-16 November 1943.

In August 1943, at Broussine's request, Yves Allain had recruited two new members to Bourgogne – Genevieve Crosson and Georges Guillemin – and while Broussine was away, Allain (with Claude Leclercq as his deputy) reorganised some aspects of the Bourgogne network.[1]

Genevieve Crosson (aka Jacqueline) was a twenty-two-year-old (born January 1921 in Paris) nursery nurse recruited into Bourgogne by Yves Allain. They met through a cousin of Genevieve's mother and in June 1943 he suggested she join him in his resistance work. On 31 August 1943, Genevieve met Georges Broussine and joined the Bourgogne organisation – her first assignment being to take a group of Allied evaders to Rivesaltes (see later).[2]

Georges Guillemin (aka Gilles) (born February 1921) was a student at the Lycee Henri IV who had been involved with resistance activities (distributing

---

1   Most details for this section are taken from the NARA Allain file and French National Archives (FNA) File 72AJ/37/V – *Rapport par Yves Allain dd May 1945.*

2   See "*Convoyeuse du reseau d'evasion Bourgogne*" by Genevieve and Pierre Le Berre (2009).

clandestine newspapers) since April 1941. He was recruited into Bourgogne by Yves Allain in August 1943 and took eight groups of evaders from Paris to Toulouse, Perpignan or Pamiers as well as collecting evaders from Normandy and Brittany, sometimes lodging them in his own home at 69 rue Victor Hugo in Colombes. He is described by Michele Agniel (see later) as being a distinguished looking boy, between 1.75 and 1.80 meters tall with blond hair – he was always well dressed and spoke good English.

Allain had been helping Broussine organise the groups leaving Paris – as well as taking some himself – buying train tickets via Eugene Desbois[3] and making the other arrangements as well as liaising with Madeleine Melot and Gabrielle Wiame who took care of lodging the evaders. He also explored alternate sources for bringing downed airmen to Paris, travelling to Loiret, Finistere and the Cotes du Nord. Although few of these trips paid off, they did at least allow Allain to establish a Breton sub-network with his family and friends in Finistere (including his old school friends Yves Boutefeu (nf) and Jean Borossi) that was used later – and meeting Maturin Branchoux in Guingamp who was to play such an important role in the Shelburn evacuations. He also made a trip to Issoudun where Hugues de Lestang-Parade (see earlier) supplied him with two radios to replace those lost when Andre Minne and Edmond Mallet were arrested on 20 August.

To keep in touch with London, as well as supply them with funds, Broussine had introduced Allain to an agent only identified as 'Michel' – contactable via Mme Lucienne Delhaye of 4 rue Barbette.

After the arrest of Jacques Niepceron (on 21 August) and Mlle Marguerite (Dr Marguerite Coltel – aka la doctoresse), Allain says it was Yvette Gouineau, a member of the *Volontaires de le Liberte* group, who provided a set of stamps and identity cards at a time when Bourgogne was completely out of them.

Claude Leclercq went to Perpignan to organise an escape route similar to the one he used when returning to France from his meeting with MI9 agents in Barcelona, and which Broussine used on his way to London. Their representative in Perpignan was Jean Olibo but the only other person Allain knew personally was the woman known as 'la Panthere'.[4] Although

---

3   Genevieve Soulie gives the address of M Desbois as 4 rue Barbette, Paris III – the same as Lucienne Delhaye (neither found in IS9 Helper files) – and Genevieve Le Berre (who lived on rue Barbette) gives his first name as Eugene.

4   Mme Vve Alice Pezieres (*aka la Panthere*) (born December 1898) of 1 rue de Prague, Perpignan, was recommended for a KMC. (WO208/5456) According to Genevieve Le Berre, she was given the nickname Panthere because of the fur coat she habitually wore.

rather expensive at 30,000 francs per evader, they started using the route in November with Genevieve Crosson taking over from Claude Leclercq as their regular guide and contact with Jean Olibo.[5]

Following a visit by Andre Page (aka Antonio) – sent by Mr Beaumont (assume British Vice-Consul and MI9 agent Rupert Henry Beaumont) in Barcelona – Allain and Page travelled down to the Pyrenees. They contacted M Bonafos at Rivesaltes and set up two routes, one directly to Spain and the other to Andorra. Both routes however were only tried once each before being abandoned – Allain says that two airmen were captured trying the first route, and the second only used to evacuate Georges Baledent, who was compromised following the arrest of Jacques Niepceron.

Another route went from Perpignan via Pamiers to Lavelanet (Elie Toulza). After Allain had returned to Paris, Andre Page also organised a third route through Boussens and an 'occasional' route through Quillan. The Quillan route was judged to be too complicated and risky although the one time it was used, was a complete success.

The one successful trip via Quillan was led by Jean-Louis Kervevant in November 1943 while other attempted crossings (also mentioned later) in November and December, were not organised by Bourgogne.

Given the increase in activities, Allain had to find more personnel for the network. He also had to replace Jacques Niepceron and Georges Baledent. As before, he recruited them from amongst his friends, adding Pierre Jacob, Jean-Louis Kervevant – both from the Lycee Henri VI and long-term members of 'Volontaires de le Liberte' – Charles Ploncard, who he'd met through Mme Lucienne Delaye, Jean Carbonnet, who was a friend of Georges Baledent, and the young girl in the house where Carbonnet was living, Michele Moet (who already knew Yvette Gouineau). He replaced

---

5   Jean Louis Cyprien Olibo (born Oct 1909) of 28 Route Lassus, Perpignan was secretary at the mairie in Perpignan. He worked from 1940 onwards with various escape lines, organising, sheltering and at times accompanying evaders to the Spanish border, until March 1944 when he was obliged to escape to Spain himself. Jean Olibo was recommended for an MBE and (I think) awarded an OBE. (WO208/5460)

Jacques Cornudella (born April 1915 in Lerida) of 15 Avenue Ribere, Perpignan was Jean Olibo's contact with Barcelona. In addition to being head of a Catalan separatist movement, he also sheltered some dozen evaders in his home. Various Bourgogne guides mention him in their reports and Jean Olibo credits M Cornudella with helping practically all of the groups passing through Perpignan. (WO208/5456)

Jenner Wagner Dalmau (born August 1915 in Zaragossa) of 20 rue des Augustines, Perpignan was head of a band of guides who were responsible for passing evaders across the Pyrenees. He worked with two major organisations (Oboe and Bourgogne) until April 1944 when he was arrested in Spain. He is credited with helping and guiding some twenty to thirty Allied evaders – as well as several agents – and was recommended for a KMS. (WO208/5456)

Georges Baledent with Robert Alouis (a young man introduced to him by the Abbe Jean Courcel) and in Brittany, recruited Jean Barossi (in October 1943) and Paul Le Baron (in December). Each agent was paid about 10,000 francs per month.

Pierre Jacob (aka Daniel) of 6 bis rue Collas, Sevres (Seine et Oise) is hardly mentioned in this study but he worked tirelessly for Bourgogne from October 1943 until the liberation. Basing himself in Paris and acting primarily a guide, Pierre Jacob brought many evaders from the provinces to be sheltered in Paris as well as taking several groups south to the Pyrenees or to Brittany for evacuation by sea. Married to Madeleine and with a young child, he also allowed his home in Sevres to be used for radio transmissions. Pierre Jacob (born December 1922) was recommended for a BEM.[6]

Jean-Louis Kervevant (aka Johnny) of 4 rue Boffrand, Cachan (Seine) was recruited into Bourgogne at the same time as Pierre Jacob. Like Yves Allain, Kervevant was a Breton, and like Pierre Jacob, he worked primarily as a guide until finally leaving France for England with Yves Allain in June 1944 – see later. Jean-Louis Kervevant (born October 1922) does not seem to have been recognised by IS9 and no recommendation for an award has been found.[7]

Guides to Perpignan were Genevieve Crosson and Charles Ploncard (alternating or together) and once, a friend of Andre Page called Carlos Mistler (nf). For Rivesaltes it was Genevieve Crosson and Georges Baledent (one party each) and for the one journey via Quillan, Jean-Louis Kervevant. For the Lavelanet and Boussens routes, Georges Guillemin and Robert Alouis, either alternating or together, depending on the size of the party.

Allain reports that the Lavelanet and Boussens routes were the most successful but they came to an ignoble end following the arrest of Georges Guillemin (see later) at the end of October – just when they were about to be abandoned for the winter anyway. He also established contacts with other organisations not mentioned by Broussine.

"Apart from the usual contacts of the network and thanks to my personal relations, I found airmen to evacuate – in Paris from Mlle Yvette Gouineau and from Belfort, M Rassinier (a teacher of 15 rue Papillon), including two Englishmen [Frederick Long and Roy Bridgman-Evans – see later] being taken to Germany and picked up by M Rassinier in France and then evacuated by Bourgogne.

---

6   NARA Jacob and TNA folder WO208/5451.

7   NARA Kervevant.

Through Mme MELOT, I made contact with a certain "GEO" [Georges Kahn] belonging to an organisation in Pantin. I made Jean CARBONNET responsible for this "GEO" and his colleague "LE MANCHOT". Several airmen were thus delivered to us, about fifteen of them, but I was soon to cut all contact with Pantin, after an arrest [see later] which took place within this organisation."

With Yves Allain taking on all this responsibility, it seems obvious that he had to reduce his field-work to concentrate on the overall running of Bourgogne. While Genevieve Soulie looked after the apartment (Broussine had specifically said she should not be involved in network activities, although he changed his mind soon after returning in November) Allain delegated the operational work. He explains how Bourgogne extended its interests in Broussine's absence:

"Another area exploited during this period was that of Brittany (Ille et Vilaine and Morbihan). We had to pick up airmen abandoned by another network (Bordeaux-Loupiac) after the death of its chief (RAOUL). It was again Jean CARBONNET who took care of this with Michele MOET. Other sources of airmen were the same as during the first period. In first place, M. Joseph BALFE, from near Amiens, an organisation with which Mme MELOT was in touch – an organisation from Creil and another from Chelles, contacted by Georges BALEDENT, then by Jean CARBONNET and Michele MOET. These organisations from the North were those who gave us the most airmen. Sometimes they sent them to us in Paris themselves, and sometimes with our guides. I never had personal contacts with these organisations, having enough to do elsewhere. I contented myself with staying at work and sending money to help with the expenses of these organisations. For more precise details of this we have to consult Mme MELOT and Mme WIAME, Georges BALEDENT, Robert ALOUIS, Jean CARBONNET and Michele MOET.

Another source for "BOURGOGNE" I have to mention are the people in Paris or the suburbs who lodged airmen and were often in contact with organisations from the provinces ... For this, one should contact Mme WILLM (Rue Miromesnil), Mme LEFEVRE (Juvisy), Mme CHRISTOL, Mme FLAMANT, Mme WIAME and Jean GUILLAUME etc. I also increased the lodging network for Bourgogne by supplying a few addresses given to me by Yvette GOUINEAU."

101

CHAPTER 21

13 September 1943

On 13 September 1943, Sgt James Trusty, WO2 Roderick Scott, Sgt Timothy Hay and a French airman (sic) called Claude were taken from Paris by train to Toulouse and Perpignan.[1]

Sgt James G A Trusty was the thirty-year-old mid-upper gunner, and WO2 Roderick A Scott the twenty-five-year-old pilot, of 138 SD Halifax BB334 on SOE Operation Spruce 20/21 to Dijon when, in the early hours of 13 August 1943 and flying at just above tree-top level, they were hit by flak. The port-inner engine caught fire and there was no time to even take up crash stations before they crash-landed in open fields near La Chapelle-Viel (Orne). Two crew were killed and five men escaped the burning aircraft, although two (Sgt Harries and F/Sgt Masson) were badly injured. Trusty and Scott were the only ones to evade successfully.

I don't know what happened to Sgt D H Owen (apart from him being captured) but Trusty, Scott, Harries and Masson took off their parachute harnesses and hid them in a ditch before making their way through woods to another field. While they were discussing what action to take next, two young Frenchmen arrived, one of whom spoke some English. After asking directions for Paris, Trusty and Scott set off, leaving the young Frenchmen to take their two badly burned crewmen to a hospital.

Trusty and Scott headed west to Auguaise then south, arriving just north of Bonsmoulins by dawn. They were looking for an isolated farmhouse they could approach when they were intercepted by a large black Alsatian dog, soon followed by its owner. Having only sign-language in common, they were taken to a nearby farm and given some milk. Unfortunately one of the farmer's elderly neighbours seems to have taken exception to this and contacted the local authorities – fortunately the farmer (Louis Berthou at La Moisiere – query) heard about it and moved the two airmen to a nearby wood before French gendarmes and German police arrived. Trusty and Scott stayed hidden in the wood all the next day and night, visited by

---

1   I suspect that 'Claude' was Claude Leclercq making his way to Barcelona (again).

an English-speaking man and fed by the farmer (who also provided overalls and a sack to put their uniforms in) before being moved back to the farm once more. Their helpers managed to contact an organisation and on 22 August, the two airmen were handed over and their journey arranged.

On 22 August, Trusty and Scott were taken by a man called Andre (Andre Schoegel) along with four other armed men, by car to a house at Arnieres-sur-Iton, just outside Evreux, where the weapons were handed over to the man at the house, Hubert Renaudin. Next morning their hostess, Renee Renaudin, took them to the station at Arnieres where her husband gave them a ticket each. Hubert and Renee went with them to Evreux where they were passed back to Andre who travelled with them to Paris.

They arrived in Paris at about midday and Andre took them to Orly and his apartment on rue Jenner where he took their particulars and wrote a letter to be handed to the Intelligence Services when Scott (who had it sewn into the shoulder of his jacket) reached England. Andre then took them by Metro to Les Invalides and M et Mme Morin where they met an American – Joe Cornwall – who had been there for about a month. Andre was angry that Cornwall had not left earlier.[2]

Trusty and Scott stayed with the Morins in their house in the courtyard of Napoleon's Tomb until 6 September, during which time there was much discussion about getting them away, firstly with the colonel's organisation (see footnote) and then with Richard's organisation. On 6 September, a fair-haired (and good looking, according to Scott) woman, said to be a countess, came to take Trusty, Scott and Cornwall but then Cornwall was left behind as his ID card was still not in order. The countess took them by Metro to the home of two elderly ladies (one of whom spoke good English) (Madeleine Melot at rue Larrey) and after a meal, the elderly ladies took them on foot to stay with Simone Levavasseur at La Petite Chocolatiere at 19 Avenue d'Orleans.[3]

---

2   According to Cornwall, the Morin family had become suspicious of Gabrielle Wiame and rather than have him go with her and Hina Zipine, got in touch with a Polish colonel (6 feet 2 inches tall, sparce grey hair, small moustache, no English). The colonel got new papers for Cornwall before taking him, Andrew Lindsay and Vic Matthews to Maurice Cottereau at Drancy – mentioned later. However, Maurice then investigated the Polish colonel and decided he couldn't be trusted either so Mme Morin came and collected Cornwall and took him back to Les Invalides. On 16 October, the Morin family took Cornwall to the Gare d'Austerlitz where he was passed on to an intermediary of BCRA agent Pierre Hentic (Trellu/Maho) and Cornwall was flown back to England by SD Lysander (Op Primrose) the night of 18-19 October 1943. (MIS-X #125 Cornwall)

3   Scott says they went by Metro (which seems more likely) to a Mme Marie who lived above a confectionary store about five miles away – the IS9 Helper List has a Mme Marie Chicot at 19 rue (sic) d'Orleans – she was the concierge there.

103

On 13 September, Simone Levavasseur took Trusty and Scott to a small zoological park where they met the elderly lady who spoke such good English and Sgt Tim Hay. The elderly lady took the three airmen to a Metro station where a man gave them railway tickets and they followed another man (who went all the way to Perpignan with them) to the Gare d'Austerlitz. On the same train was a French airman called Claude who was also trying to get to the UK.

Sgt Timothy M Hay was the twenty-four-year-old bomb-aimer of 61 Sqn Lancaster ED722 (Miller) which was on the way to Milan on the evening of 15 August 1943 when they were attacked by a night-fighter and shot down near Chartres (Centre). Five crew were killed and two were captured. Hay was the only successful evader although W/O Norman J Shergold almost made it – he was sheltered for four months at Saint-Escobille (Essonne) until he and his helper, Dr Roger Bonnet, were denounced and he was captured on 15 January 1944.

Hay baled out and landed on some railway lines. After hiding his parachute and Mae West, he walked for the rest of the night. He continued hiding during the day and walking through the night until the morning of 18 August when he declared himself to some farm workers near Bercheres-le-Pierre, about 6 kms south of Chartres. Hay was sheltered in a nearby house while his journey was arranged.

Hay was visited by an English-speaking man who went to Paris on his behalf and after about a week with his first helpers (no names) Hay was taken by bicycle into Chartres. He was sheltered in a house opposite the station by a pharmacist named Raymond Picourt[4] until a man known as Jean took him to Paris. Hay stayed in the Paris suburb of Joinville-le-Pont with a man called Henri (and his wife) where he was joined by 2/Lt Leonard Fink. About a week later, Jean and Henri took Hay and Fink into Paris where they were passed over to a lady (said to be a countess) who took them to stay with Madeleine Melot at 11 bis rue Larray. Fink was soon moved on to Fontenay-sous-Bois (see later) and on 13 September, Mme Melot took Hay to the Jardin des Plantes where he joined James Trusty and Roderick Scott.

---

4   Raymond Alfred Edouard Picourt (born October 1900) and his wife Elzevir Severine Leopholdine Picourt (born November 1895) are credited with sheltering more than fifty-one Allied evaders in their home at 15 Avenue Jehan de Beauce, Chartres as well as collecting numerous evaders from the surrounding area. Raymond Picourt was awarded the KMC. (WO208/5454) Unfortunately, their group was infiltrated in May 1944 after Colette Orsini introduced them to a man called Jean-Jacques. This was Jacques Desoubrie ... (research by John Hill)

Trusty, Scott and Hay arrived in Perpignan on 14 September and were met by two men, one of whom took them by tram to a cafe on the edge of town. They left the cafe (with a pack of sandwiches each) at about eight-thirty that evening and followed a man on a bicycle to a vineyard where they met their Spanish mountain guide. He led them through vineyards all the way to the foothills – the party consisting of Trusty, Scott, Hay, Claude and two more Frenchmen – Elie Vidreguin and Charles Boneau, both from Tours. They crossed the border into Spain during the night of 15 September and continued walking south, picking up a new guide outside of Figueras the following night.

Their guide advised them to follow the railway line to the next station but Scott (whose leg was troubling him), Hay and Claude (who had some Spanish money) decided to make their own way to Barcelona. This was a mistake. They eventually caught a train but were almost immediately picked up by the Guardia Civil who accompanied them to Barcelona where, rather than the Consulate, they were taken to the Model Prison. They were held there until 8 October when they were moved to a hotel in Saragossa for the night and then on to Alhama, where they remained until being driven to the British Embassy in Madrid on 16 October.

Meanwhile, Trusty, the guide and the two Frenchmen from Tours carried on along the railway line until about midday on 17 September when their guide turned off and took them to his house nearby. Next day, the guide took Trusty and one of the Frenchmen by train to Gerona where they jumped a goods train bound for Barcelona. They left the train again at the next stop after Gerona and walked across country to a house where they stayed the night and following day – the other Frenchman joining them there. On 20 September, the owner of the house took Trusty by train to Barcelona and the British Consulate – the two Frenchmen being delivered by car.

CHAPTER 22

The Winters and Ransom Groups

The Winters Group

On 23 September 1943, Sgt John McCallum, Sgt William Scott, 1/Lt August Winters, Sgt Norman Wagner, Sgt Joseph Cagle, 2/Lt William Harnly and 2/Lt Arthur Steinmetz were taken by train from Paris to Pamiers and Lavelanet (Ariege). One of their guides from Paris to Lavelanet was Georges Guillemin.

Sgt John McCallum was the flight engineer of 10 Sqn Halifax JD368 (Baker) which was returning from Nuremburg in the early hours of 28 August 1943 when it was shot down over Belgium by a night-fighter.[1]

McCallum landed in a field south of Mons (Belgium). He rolled up his parachute and began walking south on the main road towards Beaumont before turning west towards the French border, reaching the village of Equelinnes at lunch-time. Finding no help there, McCallum mingled with some local people and walked across the border to Jeumont. He continued walking, heading out into the French countryside until stopped by two French boys who warned him of Germans ahead. They led him across some fields, gave him civilian clothes and advised that he took a train from Jeumont to Paris. McCallum (who had no ticket) boarded a local train as far as Aulnoye where he swapped to the Berlin-Paris express which was waiting at an adjacent platform. On arrival in Paris, McCallum crossed the rails to another platform where there was only one ticket collector before waiting for the chance to jump the barrier and 'casually' leave the station. As it was fast approaching the midnight curfew, McCallum started looking for a hotel with an English sign and finally chose one that advertised 'de-luxe' and 'confort'. He waited until there was just one elderly lady in the foyer before going in, attempting to get a room and admitting to her that

---

1   Nineteen-year-old JD368 tail-gunner F/Sgt George R M Warren was killed in the attack but the other seven crew baled out safely and all but Sgt George Darvill evaded successfully, four – P/O Frederick N Lawrence, Sgt George Baker, Sgt Reginald W Cornelius and Sgt Vic Davies – with Comete and two with Bourgogne.

he was English. He was allowed to stay the night – a maid filled in his registration form – and early next morning was charged forty francs.

Next day McCallum walked out of Paris, following signs for Rouen, and got as far as Antony (Ile-de-France) where he declared himself to some people in a garden. An elderly man persuaded McCallum to accompany him to the local police station where he was assured of help so long as he could prove his identity.

That same day (29 August) a young man (Victor Delattre of 4 rue des Champs – query) came to the police station in Antony and questioned McCallum about his squadron, aircraft and target. McCallum refused to answer on the grounds that he might be handed over to the Germans but a policeman assured him that he would not and they were obviously doubtful about his identity. The Chief of Police came in and the policeman spoke to him and the young man then told McCallum that the police would take him to an organisation. One of the police officers put on a civilian jacket and took him by bicycle to Bourg-la-Reine to stay with M et Mme Charles Lesec at 5 rue Jean Mermoz. McCallum later learned that M Lesec worked in some sort of food control office in Paris and that he was the first evader they had helped. On 31 August, a tall slim doctor from the organisation came to see him and Mme Lesec explained that her husband was away getting an identity card for McCallum – which he brought the next day – and it was therefore decided to leave McCallum where he was. When M Lesec returned, he said that he had been talking to the British Secret Service, and that McCallum was to remain with him. The doctor returned on 4 September and told them that McCallum should meet him in Paris the next day.[2]

On 5 September, Mme Lesec took McCallum to Paris where they were met at the station by the doctor. They went to where M Lesec worked and then the doctor took McCallum to a priest's house where he stayed overnight. That evening, two young Frenchmen came and told McCallum there would be a delay in his leaving because of a tightening of controls by the Germans. Next day, McCallum was moved to Fontenay-sous-Bois where he and an unnamed American airman (Leonard Fink – query) were sheltered by Mme Andree Vandevoorde at Avenue de la Republique. F/O James McDonald was being sheltered nearby in a hardware shop by

---

2   John McCallum survived the war and died in 1999, after serving a full career with the Glasgow Police Service. His son Daniel was given the middle name 'Lesec' in honour of his helpers in Bourg-la-Reine. (My thanks to the late Geoff Warren, who sadly died in 2014, for this extra piece of information)

George Masse and his wife on rue des Moulins. Two nights later, a second American (Pasquale Delvento – query) came to stay with Mme Andree and McCallum was moved to share with McDonald.[3]

After one false start, Andree Vandevoorde took McCallum and McDonald back to Paris on 25 September where they were met by a tall, slim young man, who seemed to be the chief of the organisation (assume Yves Allain). They went to the Jardin des Plantes where it was found that McDonald's identity card was for 1942 and invalid. There were several Americans in the park and they were all given railway tickets before three members of the organisation took three of the Americans and McCallum to the Gare d'Austerlitz where they took an overnight train for Toulouse. They travelled with two guides and there were three more Americans on the train with another guide.

Sgt William E Scott Jnr was a waist-gunner and 1/Lt August Winters the bombardier of B-17 42-30163 (306BG/368BS) (Peterson) which was returning from Stuttgart on 6 September 1943 when it ran out of fuel and was abandoned to crash south of Dieppe.[4]

The 6 September 1943 attack on Stuttgart was a mass attack by the USAAF against Germany's heartland industrial area, with more than 400 heavy bombers being sent. Following on from the terrible losses suffered on the Regensburg-Schweinfurt raid of 17 August, the Americans had a point to prove but the target was uncomfortably close to their maximum fuel range, so even if events had gone to plan – which they didn't – it was always going to be a risky mission. The main problem was the weather, with heavy cloud breaking up the formations and covering the target, making anything like accurate bombing impossible. There were also mass attacks by German fighters which forced the bombers to take constant evasive action, further depleting their precious fuel reserves. As a result, some diverted to Switzerland while many more aircraft simply ran out of fuel

3   P/O James McDonald was the wireless operator of 78 Sqn Halifax JD108 which was lost the night of 13-14 July 1943 over Belgium. McDonald was helped for some time in Belgium before being taken to France where he was sheltered for two weeks at Chauny by Rene Felix and his wife at 26 rue du Brouage. On 11 September, he was taken to Fontenay-sous-Bois where he stayed with Georges Masse and his wife at 97 rue des Moulins, who also arranged his journey to the Spanish border. McDonald was captured on 30 September, along with a F/Lt Farmer (F/O C D Farmer, pilot of 149 Sqn Stirling BF477 – query) trying to cross the border on a train from Rivesaltes – see later.

4   Six of the 42-30163 crew evaded successfully, five with Bourgogne and tail-gunner S/Sgt Douglas G Wright who was sheltered in Blacourt before being passed on to Comete in Paris by Gilbert Thibault of reseau Alsace. Radio-operator T/Sgt William B Plasket Jnr also evaded with Bourgogne but he died in the Pyrenees on the approach to Andorra in October – see later. Ball-turret gunner Sgt Frederick E Huntizinger was captured on 21 November 1943 along with Marie-Christine Bodin, Suzanne Bosniere, Marie Betbeder-Matibet – and B-17 42-29789 pilot 2/Lt Benjamin J Zum.

before they could reach England, either ditching in the English Channel or landing in, or being abandoned over, France.

Scott landed about eight miles south of Beauvais (Oise) where he was soon joined by his tail-gunner, S/Sgt George Monser – and about a week later, by their bombardier August Winters and they (and their radio-operator T/Sgt William B Plasket Jnr) travelled together to Paris.

Winters[5] landed just east of Gournay-en-Bray (Seine-Maritime). He was concentrating so hard on avoiding a barbed wire fence that he hit an apple tree instead and knocked himself out. When he came around, he found the local French had already taken off his heavy flying gear and they helped him along to a lane where he was soon joined by his co-pilot, 2/Lt Edward Maslanka. Shortly after that, some barking dogs caused their helpers to scatter and then the two airmen separated as Winters had injured his leg and was unable to walk properly. Later that evening Winters approached three French women who hid him in their cart while one of them went for her brother who spoke a little English. This man hid Winters in a barn for five nights until he could be moved into a school house at Blacourt while his helper went to Beauvais to find organised help.

A French officer came with a picture of his tail-gunner, S/Sgt George Monser and next day took Winters to join Monser, waist-gunner Sgt William E Scott Jnr and radio-operator T/Sgt William B Plasket Jnr in Marseille-en-Beauvaisis, where they were being sheltered by Joseph and Albert Lesueur.

Henri Maigret, in his 1994 book '*Un reseau* d'evasion *dans l'Oise a Auneuil*' (which doesn't always agree with Winters' MIS-X report) says there were two women, his sister Fernande Hucleux and her Polish maid, and that he was the one they called to come and help Winters. Maigret hid Winters (his first airman) overnight in a barn before taking him back to the school in Blacourt where he was a teacher. A few days later, it was Gilbert Thibaut who came and questioned Winters before Fernand Dupetit (a locksmith of 15 rue de Clement in Beauvais) collected him in his lorry.[6]

The four evaders were taken to Paris the following day where they were met by Georges Guillemin (described as 19 (sic) years old, 5 ft 9 inches tall,

---

5   His family name is actually Winter but 'Winters' was put down on his original induction form and so that's how his name appears in all the records. By sheer coincidence, when Winters returned to the UK in November, he met his younger brother, T/Sgt Leroy R Winter, who had been shot down over Italy in August, escaped from PG78 (Sulmona) and was being interviewed by MIS-X that same day.

6   Henri Fernand Maigret (born February 1923) of l'Heraule par Beauvais, Oise (a schoolteacher at Blacourt) was recommended for an MBE – and received a KMC. (WO208/5452)

very thin with dark brown hair, spoke English) who took them for a meal with Mme Vve Jeanne Magnas at 3 rue du Guesclin, Paris XV, just south of the Eiffel Tower. After the meal, Monser and Winters were taken to stay with Dr Alice Willm at 51 rue de Miromesnil. On 23 September, a young girl took Winters to the Jardin des Plantes – while Monser was moved upstairs to stay with a book-binder for another week.

While Monser and Winters were moved to rue de Miromesnil, Scott and Plasket stayed on with Mme Magnas for a few more days until Madeleine Melot took them to the Jardin des Plantes. Apparently there was an unexpected delay before they could leave Paris so Mme Melot took them to her own apartment at 11 bis rue Larrey. Plasket was soon moved elsewhere and on 23 September, Mme Melot took Scott back to the park.

On 6 September 1943, the B-17 42-5890 (92BG/327BS) (Christenson) was returning from Stuttgart. Already damaged by flak and down to three engines, like so many other aircraft that day, they were running out of fuel. When a second engine stopped, the aircraft was landed (wheels down) in a field north-west of Paris, a few miles north-west of Poissy. All ten crew survived the landing and they paired off for their evasions.[7]

Waist-gunners Sgt Norman R Wagner and Sgt Joseph W Cagle headed south-west from the crash site. They were soon helped by a young man named Robert Gaultier who took them to a brick tool-shed and brought his father, Georges Gaultier (of 9 rue de Fougeres, Orgeval). They were given clothes and food and next day Georges Gaultier took them by train to Paris. They went to the Cafe Tartare, opposite the Fontaine des Innocents on Place Joachim-du-Bellay, where they stayed with Felix Werck (nf) (45 years old, 5 ft 7 inches tall, wore horn-rimmed glasses, said he was a factory manager) in an apartment above the cafe. They were interrogated by a young man (5 ft 11 inches tall, dark complexion, spoke some English) and on 10 September, were moved on. Wagner was taken to stay with Georges Rabache, a French professor of English, at 4 rue de l'Amerique while Georges Guillemin took Cagle to the Moet family home at 22 rue Sacrot, Saint-Mande.[8]

---

7   Eight of the 42-5890 evaded successfully: top-turret gunner S/Sgt James T Cimini and radio-operator S/Sgt Michael G Zelanak were evacuated from Douarnenez in Brittany at the beginning of October on board the cutter La-Perouse in an operation organised by Yves le Henaff's reseau Dahlia. Tail-gunner Sgt Kenneth R Moore crossed the Pyrenees to Andorra in October, pilot 1/Lt Richard A Christenson crossed the Pyrenees to Orbacieta in Spain in December and four – Wagner, Harnly, Cagle and Steinmetz – with Bourgogne. Co-pilot 2/Lt Lee Dunn Crabtree was one of four airmen captured on a train to Perpignan whilst traveling with Francoise Dissard.

8   Michele Agniel (née Moet) said later that she came home that day to find herself facing a huge man, who at 6 feet 3 inches tall, had the look and bearing of a cowboy – Cagle (from Mississippi) was their first American ...

On 23 September, Jean Carbonnet gave Cagle his ID papers (while a young girl collected Wagner) and Georges Guillemin took them both to the Jardin des Plantes where they joined their bombardier William Harnley, navigator Arthur Steinmetz, William Scott, August Winters and John McCallum.[9]

"It was at this time that Jean Carbonnet, who had managed to escape at Vierzon after being arrested by the French police, joined us. He could not return home because the police had his address. It happened one night, very late, after curfew, and he asked my parents to shelter him for the night! He stayed with us until he was arrested with us on 28 April 1944. He brought home everything needed to manufacture false identification cards, which had been previously hidden with Father Courcel at l'eglise St Roch. From then on, the false papers for airmen were made in the apartment. Blank cards could be purchased freely in all newsagents, the tax stamps in tobacconists. We took our boys to have their passport photos taken at the photomaton at the "Grands Magasins du Louvre". It was M Carel, a friendly printer at rue Jeanne d'Arc in Saint-Mande, who at the request of my mother, found special paper for the cartes de travail and printed them. Every man, who did not leave for the STO (labour service) had to have this card and collect them from the mairies. Every member of our family, even my younger brother, who was 12 years old, participated in the production of false documents." (Michele Agniel 2013)

2/Lt William E Harnly and 2/Lt Arthur Steinmetz were the bombardier and navigator of 42-5890 and they ran south for three hours before hiding up for the night. The following morning Steinmetz, who spoke good French, approached two girls who took them to a farm where they were given clothes and food – both men already had suitable shoes. They were directed to the Flambertin farm at Orgeval where they were taken in and their journey arranged after the local maire contacted an organisation in Paris. That evening a man (an ex-French military captain) collected Harnly and Steinmetz and took them back to his house in Poissy.[10] Next morning he took them by train to Paris where they were passed on to another man who took them to the Kocera-Massenet apartment at 10 rue Ernest Renan, Paris XV. They stayed with Mme Jeanne Kocera-Massenet until 23 September when they were

9   Jean Carbonnet (born December 1920 in Paris) was not only a regular guide, bringing evaders from various districts – Creil (Oise) Chauny (Aisne) Amiens (Somme) and Brittany – he was also responsible for supplying false papers for the servicemen. (WO208/5453) Jean Carbonnet took over from Georges Guillemin following his arrest at St Girons on 29 October.

10   I suspect this was Henri Bois of 104 rue de Paris, Poissy – recommended for a KMC.

taken to the station to join crewmates Norman Wagner and Joseph Cagle plus William Scott, August Winters, John McCallum and guides.

From Toulouse, the seven airmen took a train for Pamiers where there was a bus waiting to take them to Lavelanet where they had a meal. From Lavelanet they went to Montferrier and stayed with Jean Erpelding and his wife Marie.[11] They also met Elie Toulza, who was head of the organisation in Lavelanet. They walked to a barn in the mountains which was the rendezvous point to meet their mountain guides but they failed to appear. The evaders stayed three nights in the mountains before going back to Lavelanet, where they stayed two nights in a garage until a German came asking for a chauffeur – their helpers decided it was too dangerous for them to stay at the garage any longer so they were returned to the barn in the mountains. Next day, they were joined by Sgt Merlin Pearce, 2/Lt Glen Ransom and six others who had left from Paris a week after them. On 5 October, they were all taken by bus to meet their mountain guides near Saint-Paul-de-Jarrat and began their walk across the Pyrenees.

The Ransom Group

On 30 September 1943, three young guides (two of them linguists and one an escaper from Germany) took Sgt Merlin Pearce, 2/Lt Glen Ransom, S/Sgt Pasquale Delvento, S/Sgt Ralph Houser, S/Sgt George Monser, 1/Lt Russell Faulkiner, 2/Lt Leonard Fink and S/Sgt Norman Kreitenstein by train from Paris to Pamiers and then by bus to Montferrier.

Sgt Merlin Pearce was the bomb-aimer of 10 Sqn Halifax JD368 (Baker) which was returning from Nuremburg in the early hours of 28 August 1943 when it was shot down over Belgium by a night-fighter – see John McCallum earlier.

Pearce came down near Mons, hurting his feet in the landing, and after hiding his parachute, set off away from his fiercely burning aircraft. By morning, he was laying up near a farmhouse, waiting until almost everyone had left before approaching a woman and declaring himself to her. She said she would call a gendarme, assured Pearce that he was pro-British and in the meantime, bathed Pearce's feet. The gendarme arrived at lunch-time and brought Pearce some shoes – he also gave Pearce instructions on how to cross the frontier. Pearce crossed into France that afternoon and approached a

11   Jean Erpelding (born March 1908) and Marie Erpelding (born April 1908) – and their six children – of 6 Avenue de Foix, Lavelanet. (WO208/5452)

Frenchman in a field who took Pearce back to his farmhouse where he stayed the night. Next day, the farmer took Pearce to Maubeuge where he stayed overnight with the farmer's brother. On 30 August, Pearce took a train from Maubeuge to Paris and on the train, was befriended by a French butcher named (appropriately) Gaston Boucher to whom he declared himself. At the Gare du Nord, Pearce followed his new friend back to his home at 27 Avenue Secretan, Paris XIX where he stayed while an organisation was contacted.

Pearce says that he never knew how contact was established with the organisation but on 31 August, he was visited by two students from Paris University. One was Roland Girard of 2 rue du Pont de Lodi, near the Pont Neuf, whose father was in Rennes prison awaiting trial for having helped a British army officer. The father, who had been a few months in prison, was a colonial administrator and Roland asked Pearce to give a message to a Mr Schilling at the *Radio Agence de Londres*, and tell him about his father August. The other student was Numa Foures of 2 rue de Nesle, Paris VI. They questioned Pearce, asking if he had any password and for proof that he was English. Pearce gave them the number of his squadron. They brought another friend, Andre Toss (nf), a law student, and Toss took Pearce to his house on rue de Flandre (now Avenue de Flandre) where he stayed overnight. Next day Pearce went to Numa Foures' house in the university quarter while they tried to contact the 'transit' side of the organisation.

About ten days later, Pearce was moved to Anteuil (assume west of Paris at Yvelines) to a flat belonging to a sister of a Colonel Ouzilleau, an army doctor. Pearce saw the colonel's son and two daughters, but not the colonel. Numa Foures and the colonel's son stayed with him and the two daughters did the cooking. One day there was an air-raid and Pearce wanted the two sisters to go to a shelter. They insisted on him going with them – fortunately as it turned out as the house was hit by a bomb.

The following morning, Pearce returned to Foures' house for the day and a man from the organisation took him to be photographed and then to the Jardin de Tuileries where he met Gabrielle Wiame. She took Pearce across the river to the Jardin des Plantes where she collected three American evaders (Ransom, Delvento and Houser) and took the four men to Juvisy-sur-Orge. Pearce and Glen Ransom stayed with Maurice Bidaud (who they believed was the local chief of the organisation) at his Garage du Parc while Delvento and Houser stayed with a Mme Pierre (query). Pearce says that Maurice Bidaud was very imprudent and used to speak English to them in the streets at night. Pearce and Ransom were there for 13 days until

Gabrielle Wiame took them back to Paris, the Jardin des Plantes and Gare d'Austerlitz.

2/Lt Glen F Ransom, S/Sgt Pasquale J Delvento and S/Sgt Ralph E Houser were the pilot and waist-gunners of B-17 42-30271 Bomb Boogie (95BG/335BS) which lost power in two engines whilst approaching Stuttgart on 6 September 1943. Falling out of formation, the aircraft was attacked by fighters and after losing a wing-tip, the bale-out order was given. The bombardier says that they were surrounded by fighters and their pilot lowered the undercarriage as a sign of surrender but the crew was not properly notified so when a German fighter flew alongside them, the right waist-gunner (Houser) shot him down – and all hell broke loose! The ten-man crew abandoned the aircraft to crash near Pancy-Courtecon (Picardy), south of Laon. Five of them evaded successfully – all with Bourgogne.[12]

Ransom was the last man out of the aircraft and he made a delayed jump, opening his parachute just before landing in a field next to the village of Colligis-Crandelain. He was met on the ground – he says by the entire population – and quickly led away to be hidden in a wood. That evening he was taken to a barn where he joined his top-turret gunner, T/Sgt Harold R Knotts. The following night Ransom and Knotts were taken to stay with Marie, the daughter of a tax collector, who lived a couple of miles away. Next day the two Americans were driven in a bakers truck to stay with fifty-year-old seed merchant Julien Chapelet in his home at Place de la Gare, opposite the railway station at Saint-Erme-Outre-et-Ramecourt, where they found fellow crewmen Pasquale Delvento, Ralph Houser, Vincent Cox and Charles Peacock.

Delvento landed near Bouconville-Vauclair, south of Laon, and was quickly sheltered before being taken to a forester's house in the nearby village of Saint-Erme-Outre-et-Ramecourt where he was joined by his tail-gunner Vincent Cox and radio-operator Charles Peacock. Next morning the three evaders were taken to a wood where the forester brought their second waist-gunner, Ralph Houser, to join them before Julien Chapelet and his eighteen-year-old son Daniel took the four Americans back to their house in Saint-Erme-Outre-et-Ramecourt. Next day, Cox and Peacock were taken to stay with M et Mme Mueler (nf) at nearby Amifontaine and the following morning, their pilot Glen Ransom and top-turret gunner Harold Knotts were brought to the Chapelet home.

---

12   Bomb Boogie ball-turret gunner S/Sgt John W Beachan was one of four evaders captured on a train to Perpignan whilst traveling with Francoise Dissard. Radio-operator T/Sgt Charles B Peacock also evaded with Bourgogne but died in the Pyrenees on the approach to the Andorran border in October – see later.

On 16 September, Daniel Chapelet took Ransom, Delvento and Houser to Paris where they were met by Julien Chapelet and a veiled Frenchwoman who guided them to the English-speaking widow of a French colonel (Madeleine Melot) where they met Sgt William Scott. Next day, Gabrielle Wiame took Houser to her home at 46 rue Poliveau and the following day she returned to take Ransom and Delvento to the Jardin des Plantes where they met her son Robert who was with Houser and Merlin Pearce. The whole party went by Metro to Juvisy-sur-Orge and a garage where they met Maurice Bidaud. Ransom and Pearce were sheltered in the back room of a cafe (and ate at the garage) while Delvento and Houser stayed with Mme Pierre – described by Delvento as a fifty-year-old woman who had worked at a French Consulate in America many years earlier and had one son. They also visited two more American evaders, 2/Lt Howard Harris and S/Sgt Alfred Zeoli, who were staying nearby with the Lefevre family. On 30 September, Mme Marie Bidaud took Ransom, Delvento, Houser and Pearce back to Paris where they were met by Maurice Bidaud and Gabrielle Wiame who took them to the Jardin des Plantes.

S/Sgt George S Monser was the tail-gunner of B-17 42-30163 (306BG/368BS) (Peterson) which was returning from Stuttgart on 6 September1943 when it ran out of fuel and was abandoned to crash south of Dieppe – see earlier.

Monser landed a few miles south of Marseille-en-Beauvaisis (Oise) and was helped immediately. Three boys and a girl took him into a wood where they found waist-gunner Sgt William Scott. Clothes were brought and the two airmen were taken to a barn on a deserted farm where were joined that evening by their top-turret gunner T/Sgt William Plasket. Next day they were visited by Belveau (query) and Felix (query) who drove them to Marseille-en-Beauvaisis where they stayed with Joseph and Albert Lesueur for six days until two men (one 5 ft 7 inches, 27 years old, 140 lbs, slick black hair, spoke English – the other about the same height and weight, black moustache, greying hair, about 40 years old) interrogated them and they were joined by their bombardier August Winters – see earlier.

As already mentioned, Monser and Winters stayed with Dr Alice Willm at rue de Miromesnil until 23 September when a young girl took Winters to the Jardin des Plantes – and Monser was moved upstairs to stay with a book-binder for another week. Georges Guillemin (one of their previous helpers) brought papers for Monser and on 30 September, a young girl took him to the Jardin des Plantes where he joined Ransom and the other airmen, a French intelligence officer and three guides.

1/Lt Russell R Faulkiner was the pilot of B-17 42-3455 Lucky Thirteen (384BG/546BS) which was returning from Stuttgart on 6 September 1943 and like so many others, running out of fuel. They had already sustained flak damage before being attacked by fighters and the aircraft was abandoned south of Beauvais.[13] Faulkiner – along with his top-turret gunner T/Sgt Oscar K Hamblin and bombardier 2/Lt Harry H Hawes – was sheltered in and around Clermont, Creil and Chauny before being taken to Paris and the Bourgogne organisation.

Faulkiner landed near Beauvais and a local woodcutter took him back to his house where his wounds were treated and he was given some civilian clothing. However, a neighbour took exception to an Allied airman being sheltered there and threatened to denounce the family, so Faulkiner moved on. He made his way to somewhere between Bresles and Noailles and declared himself to an elderly man who took him home where the man's wife and daughter took care of Faulkiner and gave him more civilian clothing. On the second day, two men arrived on motorcycles and one of them, Gaston Legrand, took Faulkiner back to Clermont and his house on rue du Chatellier where he joined his TTG Oscar Hamblin and bombardier Harry Hawes. The following day, Black Ghost BTG Willard McLain arrived. On 10 September, Roland Delnaf[14] and Marcel Gerardot (an engineer in a boiler factory) took Faulkiner, Hamblin and Hawes back to M Gerardot's home on rue Henri Pauquet in Creil where McLain later joined them. On 15 September, Alfred Logeon took the four Americans back to his Garage St Charles at 24 rue de Brouage in Chauny where Faulkiner and Hawes stayed while Hamblin and McLain were taken to stay with Etienne Dromas at the mairie in Ugny-le-Gay.[15]

---

13   Marcel Mavre identifies the crash-site as Le Bois-des-Moines, next to the Ferme de Sebastopol at Airion, just north of Clermont – see 'La Guerre 39-45 Dans le Ciel de l'Oise' published in 2009 by Delattre.

14   Faulkiner says Joseph and Dominique Lecomte identifies Joseph as Roland Delnaf, BOA (Bureau des Operations Aeriennes) chief for l'Oise. Roland Delnaf (born November 1909) of 41 Faubourg de Senlis, Creil was arrested (in the cafe Le Drecher, Place du Chalet, Paris X) on 20 January 1944. He was deported to Germany, surviving Neuengamme and Gros Rosen to be liberated on 15 May 1945. Joseph Delnaf was recommended for a KMC. (WO208/5460)

15   Alfred Logeon (born June 1890) is credited with helping some fifty or sixty Allied evaders, sheltering some and guiding several groups to and from Paris – he was recommended for a KMC. (WO208/5455)

      Although Etienne Dromas (and his schoolteacher wife Renee) lived at the mairie – where according to P/O Donald Ross there was a secret room where he kept arms and ammunition – he should not be confused with the maire of Ugny-le-Gay, a man who was believed to collaborate with the Germans and detested locally.

On 29 September, Faulkiner, Oscar Hamblin and Harry Hawes were brought from Chauny to Paris by a young Frenchman (about 20 years old, 5 feet 7 inches tall, 120 lbs, black hair). He took them to the Jardin des Plantes where they were handed over to an elderly lady (known as the Lady in Black) who took Faulkiner to her apartment where he stayed overnight. The following morning, the elderly lady (Madeleine Melot) took Faulkiner back to the Jardin des Plantes and passed him on to a young blond Frenchman who spoke a little English and had his rail ticket.

2/Lt Leonard J Fink was the navigator of B-17 42-30058 (384BG/546BS) (Rosio) which was shot down by fighters returning from Villacoublay aerodrome on 26 June 1943 – see earlier.

Fink landed in a wood at Rambouillet, some miles north-west of the rest of his crew. He received some help after landing but generally made his own way to Ymonville (between Chartres and Orleans) where Mme Luna de San Pedro sheltered him and called a doctor. The house belonged to Rene Pierrot of Allee de la Gare who paid all Fink's expenses while Mme San Pedro contacted an organisation through the local maire. Fink stayed at Ymonville for eleven weeks until Colette Orsini took him to Paris where four burly men led him to a telephone booth and another man stamped Fink's identity papers.[16] Mme Orsini then took Fink to a house in Joinville-le-Pont where he joined Sgt Tim Hay RAF for three days before they were both moved to 11 bis rue Larrey to stay with Madeleine Melot. Hay remained with Mme Melot when Fink was taken to Andree Vandevoorde at Fontenay-sous-Bois, being joined on the second day by Norman Kreitenstein and Pasquale Delvento. Three weeks later, on 30 September, the three Americans were taken to the Jardin des Plantes.

S/Sgt Norman D Kreitenstein was the ball-turret gunner of B-17 42-5865 Janie (100BG/351BS) (Fienup) which was returning from Romilly-sur-Seine in the early morning of 3 September 1943 when it was attacked by fighters, hit by flak and abandoned to explode in mid-air, the wreckage landing near Chavigny-Bailleul (Eure). Three of the Janie crew evaded successfully – all with Bourgogne.

Kreitenstein says that he landed some thirty-five miles east of Paris and soon declared himself to a local man who hid him in a chicken coop. He was found next day by two Italian workers who gave him food and

---

16   Colette Orsini (of 7 rue des Batignolles, Paris XVII) is linked to Belgian traitor and German infiltration agent Jacques Desoubrie – who later shot and wounded her during a quarrel. She was still recovering in hospital when Paris was liberated ... (John Hill from a draft of his proposed book 'Hopeful Monster' about the traitor Guy Marcheret)

clothing and that evening took him to a house on the outskirts of Paris where an English-speaking woman interviewed him.[17] He was moved to the home of a cafe owner where he was visited by a gendarme called Pierre and a week later, Pierre took Kreitenstein into Paris and passed him on to Gabrielle Wiame. She had his photograph taken and papers arranged before taking him to stay with Mme Vandevoorde in Fontenay-sous-Bois where he was sheltered for three weeks, sharing with Leonard Fink and Pasquale Delvento until 30 September.

The eight airmen were taken by train to Toulouse and Pamiers. Their Paris guides left them at Pamiers after giving a big packet of money to the driver of the bus who drove them to Montferrier near Lavelanet. They walked for two hours to a barn where they found another party of seven evaders (including John McCallum and August Winters) who had been waiting there for a week. The two British and thirteen Americans stayed in the barn for another four days before being taken by bus to meet their guides near Saint-Paul-de-Jarrat.

Five miles after setting off on foot, Delvento fell as they were crossing a railway line – Cagle stopped to help him and they and Fink, Kreitenstein, Harnly, Houser and Steinmetz were left behind by the rest of the group. The seven Americans hid in a pig-pen in Mercus-Garrabet for three days until a guide found them and took them in a group of twenty-seven (including 2/Lt James G McMath and S/Sgt Louis F Weatherford from B-17 42-5720 who joined them during the first night) on a three-day walk via Auzat to El Serrat in Andorra, arriving on 10 October.

They stayed at the Hotel Coma in Ordino where they were joined by a group that included P/O George T Graham and Sgt Arthur F Charman and where Cagle, whose feet were in a bad condition, stayed on with the similarly stricken Charman – all expenses paid by the British.

After resting in Andorra for two days, Fink and the rest of the group (including McMath and Weatherford) – and joined by Graham and others – including Spitfire pilot F/Lt Frederick Gaze, F/O Ronald Isherwood and Sgt Bernard C Reeves – crossed into Spain and walked for another six days to Manresa (where Steimetz was arrested at the station) and took a train to Barcelona and the British Consulate, arriving there on 21 October.

On 25 October, the chief of the Andorran police took Cagle and

---

17   Kreitenstein fits the description of an American airman (named as Norman Alexander Ridge – not found) sheltered by a M Durot at 8 rue Camille Desmoulins, Bezons (Seine et Oise) that Albert Calonne arranged to have passed on to Gabrielle Wiame. (*Albert Calonne renseignement*) Thank you Michael and Edouard for making that connection.

Charman to Andorra la Vieja. Next day a man claiming to be the British representative in Andorra (probably Andre Pollac) drove them to La Seu d'Urgell where he got a safe conduct pass from the local police chief which allowed them to go on to Barcelona, where they duly arrived on 28 October.

After losing Fink and other six Americans at Mercus-Garrabet, Ransom, Winters and the remaining six evaders were taken over the Pyrenees (walking at night and resting during the day) and crossed into Andorra on 7 October. After two days rest at the Hotel Coma in Ordino, they made the long walk on to Manresa in Spain where they took a train to Barcelona and the British Consulate, arriving there in the morning of 15 October.

CHAPTER 23

Vic Davies and Walter House

Sgt Victor W Davies was the navigator of Halifax JD368 (the same aircraft as McCallum and Pearce – see earlier) shot down over Belgium on 28 August 1943. Although not helped directly by Bourgogne, he was helped by people associated with (although not members of) the line in Paris before being passed on to the Belgian Comete organisation.

Davies was sheltered in and around Le Cateau-Cambresis (Nord-Pas-de-Calais) until 14 September when he was taken to stay with M Morelle on rue de Crecy in Laon.[1] On 26 September, Susanne Bosniere collected Davies from Laon and took him back to Paris where he was sheltered for five and a half weeks with her friend Christiane Bodin (aka Marie-Christine) at 38 rue de Petit Champs, Paris XIX. He was joined ten days later by T/ Sgt Walter L House, the radio-operator of B-17 41-24507 Yankee Raider – another one of the many aircraft lost on the 6 September raid to Stuttgart.

Christiane Bodin (and Susanne Bosniere) already had contacts in Laon. Local man Paul Berthe (of Bruyeres-et-Montberault) had brought Mme Bosniere from Paris in July 1943 to collect Sgt John E McCrea (51 Sqn Halifax DT690) and two days later, Mme Bodin collected P/O J S Gasecki (305 Sqn Wellington HE347). The two airmen spent a day together in Mme Bodin's apartment on rue des Petits Champs before joining a small group of Frenchmen to be taken by train to Toulouse and Pau where they were passed on to John Carter, who was living at Jurancon, just outside Pau, at the time. Carter sheltered them with garagiste Robert Casenave at 24 rue des Anglais for three days until 25 July when Mrs Carter took them by bicycle to the bus station at Nay. They joined a Mme Bousque (query) and a party of Frenchmen to be taken south by bus to Arrens-Marsous before walking across the border on 29 July to Sallent de Gallego – where they were arrested .

Christiane Bodin and Suzanne Bosniere worked primarily with an intelligence gathering organisation known as Samson and only seem to

---

1   M et Mme Morelle are named as contacts in Laon by Suzanne Bosniere but not found in IS9 files. (NARA Bosniere)

have had a brief association with Bourgogne. However, they had been associated with Oaktree and groupe Vaneau (amongst others) and are personally credited with sheltering some thirty Allied servicemen, as well as convoying many more. They must have been well regarded in London as they were also the initial contacts for Lucien Dumais and Ray Labrosse when they arrived in Paris on 19 November 1943 to set up the Shelburn escape line – the two men were staying in Mme Bosnier's apartment when she and Mme Bodin were arrested two days later.[2]

Following the receipt of a blackmail note to Mme Bodin (100,000 francs or she would be reported to the Gestapo), she and Suzanne Bosniere moved Davies and House to stay with Marie Bebeder-Matibet at 7 Square de Port-Royal. Two weeks later, Mme Bebeder-Matibet failed to return from a meeting and that evening Mlle Helene Pezard moved them to stay overnight in her home at 9 Square de Port-Royal. Next day they were moved to another neighbour, Mlle Antoinette Six at number 3 and the day after that they were taken to stay with Mme Suzanne and Mlle Ghislaine de Mirbeck (a Red Cross nurse) at 2 Avenue du Nord, Saint-Maur-des-Fosses where they joined Sgt Clarence H Witheridge from Lancaster LM337. On 15 December Davies, House and Witheridge left Paris for Bordeaux, Dax and the Pyrenees.

Georges Broussine lists a T/Sgt House – and T/Sgt Walter L House is the only likely candidate – but he (like Davies and Witheridge) was handled by Comete from Paris and crossed the Pyrenees with them on 20 December 1943. However, House's comments in his January 1944 MIS-X interview concerning some other evaders are worth including here.

'At one place where I was staying with some French helpers, another evader there complained about the food he was receiving. Our French hosts were extremely annoyed at his complaints and at his lack of understanding of the difficulties which they face in helping Allied airmen at all. Still another

---

2   TNA Folder WO208/5459. Christiane Bodin, Suzanne Bosniere and Marie Betbeder-Matibet were denounced by a collaborator named Renard (suspect Marcel Renard of Nesles-la-Vallee). Mlle Betbeder-Matibet was arrested with two airmen (Frederick Huntzinger and Benjamin Zum) at the *cafe du Pied de Mouton* in Paris on 21 November 1943, and Mme Bodin and Mme Bosniere arrested at home that same day. Mme Bodin's husband, Jean Bodin, and Paul and Georgette Gaillard were also arrested. (NARA Bodin & NARA Bosniere)

Mme Christiane Lucienne Bodin (born Nov 1908) was deported to Ravensbruck – she was repatriated to France on 24 May 1945 and recommended for a KMC. (WO208/5459) Mme Suzanne Bosniere (born Oct 1906) was also deported to Ravensbruck – she was repatriated to France in the summer of 1945 and recommended for a KMS. (WO208/5453) Mlle Marie Betbeder-Matibet (born Dec 1899) died at Ravensbruck on 17 June 1944. (WO208/5456)

American [Huntzinger] who was staying with me became impatient because our French helpers were not moving us on quickly enough. It seems to me that aircrews should be made to realise that Frenchmen are staking their lives when they aid Allied airmen and that a man should be grateful for anything which he receives from these people – and make clear his gratitude. He should be told to ask no questions whatsoever once he is in the hands of real helpers, and he should also be told to be satisfied with whatever he receives. If he is getting poor food, he is receiving the best which can be secured for him. If he is not moving, there is good reason for the delay – it may be that some of his helpers have been shot. It seems to me that it is just as important for the evader to create a good impression with the French as it is for him to get back."

House doesn't name the evader who complained about the food (and neither will I) but the situation wasn't unique. Although most evaders were deeply appreciative of the help they were given, Drue Leyton recounts in her book '*The House Near Paris*' a story of visiting her friend Olga Christol one day to find her in tears because of the two airmen she was sheltering at the time. One was an officer and he apparently thought that not only Olga but also the sergeant evader he was sharing with, should serve his meals and do all the washing-up, making the sergeant polish his shoes and not even offering thanks for the cigarettes that Paul Christol bought especially for him on the black-market. Drue Leyton says that it took a real 'a bawling out' to explain the facts of life in occupied Paris to him before he faced up to the dangerous reality of the situation they were all in. She also recounts two more American aircrew who were apparently resentful about their bad luck in being shot down (as compared with having been killed – query) and when their hosts were unable to supply sufficient alcohol to satisfy them, befriended and were taken out one evening by an over-enthusiastic local cafe owner and got drunk. The final straw was broken after Ms Leyton remonstrated with them over their behaviour and they accused her of only taking care of them because of the money she was (allegedly) being paid for the privilege. Both men were moved on next day.

CHAPTER 24

Another Sherry Connection

S/Sgt Edward F Chonskie, S/Sgt John Zioance and S/Sgt Albert V H Carroll were gunners on B-17 42-5792 The Mugger (303BG/358BS) (O'Connor) which was attacked by fighters on 4 July 1943 whilst on the way to Le Mans and abandoned south-west of the city. They evaded more or less together – and I have included a summary of their story for its interest – but despite their names being included on Broussine's list, there is no obvious link to Bourgogne apart from the contact with Sherry in Andorra.

Shortly after landing, Chonskie approached two Frenchmen who hid him and then brought a friend who took Chonskie to his father's mill. He was given civilian clothes before a Doctor Noyer (nf) took him back to his own house and then to a farmhouse where Chonskie spent the night. Next morning M Georget (nf), the postmaster of Vion (Sarthe), took Chonskie back to his house where he joined Zioance and Carroll. (M George (sic) the postmaster at Vion, had previously helped British army evader Dvr John Shenton in June 1940)

Zioance had been collected by two elderly women and an elderly man who took him to a house and called an English-speaking countess. The countess arrived with a miller's wife and her son Albert and Zioance was taken to the miller's house, where Albert brought Carroll to join him that night.

Carroll had spent his first night walking and then hidden himself during the day until entering a farmhouse where the family gave him a meal and called the countess. While the countess was still there, Albert arrived to take Carroll to join Zioance. Next day Zioance and Carroll were taken to a farm where they were visited by Doctor Noyer and that night M Georget took them back to his house in Vion, where they joined Chonskie.

Chonskie, Zioance and Carroll stayed with M Georget for three weeks until a local woman threatened to denounce them and on 29 July, they were moved – Chonskie to a priest's house in Le Mans for a week then to stay with a butcher, while Zioance and Carroll spent a night in a barn before being moved to a cabin in the woods for two days and then taken by bicycle to a small town about forty kilometres away where they stayed with the mother of one of M Georget's neighbours. Here they met a balding, grey-bearded man, with a prominent nose and gold tooth – who claimed to an American working for British Intelligence – who took them to stay for two nights with a brick-mason in Le Mans.

Chonskie, Zioance and Carroll were reunited at the home of Alfred Auduc at 3 rue du Tourniquet, Le Mans and next day Mme Auduc took Zioance and Carroll by train to Poitiers while Alfred drove Chonskie to Tours where they got on the same train. At Poitiers they had dinner at the home of Mme Blau (see notes) before spending the night with Mme Tritz, who had served with the Red Cross in WW1. Next day, Chonskie and Zioance were taken to spend two nights with an elderly woman and then two more with Mme Marthe Blondeau (wife of garage owner Felix Blondeau) where Carroll joined them and Abel Blary took all three Americans by bicycle to his house in Chauvigny. Next day he took them to Mme Burdeau, wife of the maire of the small village where they lived – Chonskie and Zioance stayed with Mme Burdeau while Carroll stayed elsewhere. Two weeks later, M Blary, M Burdeau and Jean Ferchteau (the postman at Chauvigny) took the three Americans to a farm. Ten days after that, Mme Blau arrived in a car with a young, blond Frenchman who gave them 3,000 francs each for their mountain guide before Mme Blau drove them to a small town where they took a bus to Limoges and then a train to Pamiers.[1]

They met their Spanish guide at Foix on 24 September and paid him the money they had been given by the blond Frenchman. He walked them to a small town (probably Tarascon) where he tried to pass them on to two young boys, who wanted more money. When that failed, they were tagged

1   Felix Blondeau (born May 1886) and his wife Marthe (of 118 Faubourg du Pont Neuf, Poitiers) were arrested on 6 January 1944 and deported to Germany. Felix Blondeau died at Buchenwald on 29 March 1945. (WO208/5453).
     I suspect that Mme Blau was actually Clothilde Blanc, the blond Frenchman was Joseph Fradet and that Mme Tritz was Gabrielle Tritz of 22 rue Riffault, Poitiers.
     Mme Clothilde Blanc (born August 1889) of 32 rue de la Marne (and *La Clinique Moderne* at 3 rue de la Marne) was head of the local organisation. She and her husband Jean were arrested on 22 December 1943 and deported – Clothilde to Ravensbruck, where she died in August of the following year. M Joseph Fradet (born April 1905) a chauffeur of 19 Chemin Haut des Sables, was arrested on 7 January 1944 and deported to Buchenwald, where he died. Mme Gabrielle Tritz (born Thionville, Moselle in December 1898) was arrested on 6 January 1944 and deported to Ravensbruck – she was repatriated to France on 26 June 1945. (WO208/5453)
     Abel Blary (born September 1903) of La Varenne, Chauvigny sheltered, convoyed and generally assisted some twenty-two Allied evaders. He worked in close liaison with Mme Blanc from February 1943 but following her arrest, left the area to join a maquis and his evasion activity is presumed to have ceased. He was recommended for a KMC (WO208/5456) and I think received a KMS.

along with another group but when passing through a small village, found that Carroll had fallen behind. First Zioance and then the guide went back to find him but without success so they continued after the larger group. Eventually their guide slipped away and Chonskie and Zioance turned back, meeting Carroll a short while later and they all returned to Foix.

The three Americans decided to make the trip by themselves, simply heading south using a compass and the stars. They were about to give up on the fifth day, having run out of food and being soaked through after three days of rain, when they met an old man on a mule *(un âne des Pyrenees peut-être)* who gave them some bread and shelter in his hut for the night before pointing them in the right direction. After another eight hours of walking, they finally reached Andorra on 4 October. They were picked up by a Frenchman who let they stay in his haystack for twenty-four hours before going on to a small village where they stayed for two days. Here they met a policeman who contacted Sherry (Andre Pollac) who took them to a hotel in Escaldes run by an American woman. Sherry arranged a guide to take them into Spain the following day (7 October) and on to Barcelona.

CHAPTER 25

Trial by Goose

T/Sgt William LeRoy Utley was the engineer of B-17 42-30163 (306BG/368BS) (Peterson) which was returning from Stuttgart on 6 September 1943 when it ran out of fuel and was abandoned to crash south of Dieppe – see earlier.

Utley landed about half a mile from a small village near Beauvais and was helped almost immediately by a man called Pierre Freteaud and an unnamed Belgian who took Utley to an empty house where he spent the night. Next day, Pierre Freteaud took Utley to Paris where he was hidden in Pierre's father's apartment at 5 rue Boacot (query) for four days before his new friend decided to take him further. On 11 September, Pierre Freteaud took Utley by train to Blois where they took an evening bus to Saint-Aignan and crossed the demarcation line and Utley stayed for a month with some of Pierre's family while arrangements were made for his subsequent journey.

On 11 October, Pierre took Utley by overnight train from Chateauroux to Tarbes. Utley, who still had no ID papers, was supposed to be deaf and dumb – and there was a goose on the luggage rack above his head. The goose would honk at odd intervals through the night making everyone jump and Utley says that not jumping each time the goose honked was one of the hardest things he had to do throughout his evasion.

From Tarbes they went on to Pau and took a local train to Nay before walking several miles to Lys. Utley was sheltered by Cyprienne Sucra and her husband Michel at their cafe in Lys for thirty-seven days while the people there contacted what Utley was first told was an organisation but found later that he was their first evader. Their first guides declined to take Utley but an American woman named Rosemary Maeght (née Wright) and an Englishwoman named Joan Moy-Thomas visited him and said they knew of guides who had taken Americans before. On 16 November, Utley was collected by a car with three Frenchmen (one of whom spoke English) and their leader, a Pole known as M Georges.

They drove for about three hours into the mountains and stayed in a cafe at Mauleon (probably the Cafe des Sports with Dominique and

Germaine Montalibet) where Utley was joined by Spitfire pilot F/O Czeslaw Sniec and others, while a blizzard prevented their immediate crossing. After several days of rain – sometimes lost because their guides had not used this particular route for several years, and also having to spend days sheltering from the foul weather – Utley, Sniec and the rest of the group finally reached Spain on 22 November.

The following day, they were arrested at Orbaiceta by Spanish police and taken to stay overnight in a hotel in Pamplona before going on to Lecumberri (Navarra) for eleven days. For some reason, Utley and Sniec were then sent to the notorious Spanish concentration camp of Miranda de Ebro where they were held for another month before being repatriated – along with Sgt Len F Martin (Halifax LW240) and W/O George A Gauley (Whitley AD675) who had arrived by other routes – to Madrid on 7 January 1944.

M Georges was the Count Andre de Boka – Andre de Wyssogota-Zakrzewski (born May 1905 at Kalisz, Poland).[1] Wyssogota (who was awarded the KMC) was head of the Visgotha line and arrested later that month at Lecumberry (Aquitane) France. Note that although arranged by Rosemary Maeght and Joan Moy-Thomas (who were later to play such a prominent role with Bourgogne) Utley was actually taken across the mountains, free of charge, by the Wyssogota (Visgotha) organisation. Sniec, who had been brought down from Paris by Georges, who he had known in Poland before the war, confirms his name as Andzeg Zakrzewski.[2]

1   TNA folder WO208/5456.
2   TNA file WO208/5582-1703 Sniec.

CHAPTER 26

Journey via Rivesaltes, Axat and Rouze to Andorra

On 26 September 1943, S/Sgts Charles Fisher and James Wagner left Paris by train for Rivesaltes, just north of Perpignan. They were accompanied by Charles Ploncard and a small, brown-haired girl named Genevieve Crosson, who was making her first trip as a guide.

Charles Ploncard (aka Michel Lefevre) was described to me by Michele Agniel as being a very thin young man who often wore a 'drole' hat. He was what was known as a 'zazou' – which doesn't really translate into English but was a war-time Parisian fashion among some of the young, characterised by a love of swing music and the wearing of eccentric clothing – large, loud (often chequered) jackets and thick-soled shoes for the men – partly as a protest to government clothing restrictions – together with longer than usual hair, often slicked back. Georges would come to the Moet apartment with his fiancee Georgette before taking a group of evaders in order to prepare their ID papers.

S/Sgt Charles A Fisher was a twenty-one-year-old waist-gunner and S/Sgt James L Wagner the twenty-two-year-old ball-turret gunner of B-17 42-5720 (384BG/544BS) (Aufmuth) which was returning from Stuttgart on 6 September 1943 when they began to run out of fuel. Like other aircraft in the same formation, they started throwing excess equipment overboard and the pilot (Lester Aufmuth) gave his crew the choice of baling out or remaining with the aircraft. They opted to stay and were in sight of Paris when number three engine stopped. The crew changed into their GI shoes before the aircraft was landed in a hay-field near Pontoise (Ile-de-France) and six of them evaded successfully.[1]

GI shoes were US Army issue, ankle-high, brown leather boots which proved to be near ideal for crossing the mountains and were highly recommended by escape and evasion lecturers. Unfortunately,

---

1   42-5720 co-pilot 2/Lt James G McMath, radio-operator S/Sgt Louis F Weatherford, navigator 2/Lt Charles O Downe and waist-gunner S/Sgt Carl E Bachmann all crossed the Pyrenees with various groups over the next few months. Pilot 2/Lt Lester H Aufmuth was captured – along with Sgt Hugh F Snyder (tail-gunner of B-26 41-31684 Double Trouble) and F/Sgt George F Thomas (103 Sqn Lancaster ED751) – near the Spanish border on about 29 October.

with decent leather footwear almost unobtainable in war-time France, the wearing of early version GI shoes in public could be a giveaway. Later issue boots however, made with the leather rough side out, had the additional advantage of looking (according to at least one evader) or could be made to look, just like French peasant shoes. S/Sgt Hobart Trigg (see later) also recommended dying them black at the first opportunity.

Fisher stayed with pilot Lester Aufmuth and co-pilot James McMath to set fire to the aircraft before they made off to the nearby woods where they buried their flying gear. They soon met their navigator, Charles Downe, tail-gunner Carl Bachmann and ball-turret gunner James Wagner. After a quick conference during which Downe decided they were about 100 kms north-west of Paris, Fisher teamed up with Wagner and they set off heading north. That evening they declared themselves to an elderly Frenchman who took them back to his home and contacted some friends.[2] They were moved to various addresses over the next few days until being driven into Paris to stay with a man called DeGuillio (nf). They stayed at his house for three days before he moved them to his office on rue Saint-Georges, Paris IX. They stayed for two days and were visited by Andre and Raoul who interrogated them before taking them to stay with Maud Couve and Alice Brouard at 25 rue de Madrid. They stayed with Maud and Alice for twelve days during which time they were visited by Marie (30 years old, blonde, wore thick glasses) (Gabrielle Wiame) who brought them ID papers. On 27 September, Mme Brouard took them to the Gare d'Austerlitz where they were passed on to Claude Pinchart-Deny (sic) who took them by train to Rivesaltes in a party which included a French lieutenant, two RAF evaders (McDonald and Farmer – query), a French boy (Charles Ploncard) and a girl guide (Genevieve Crosson).

Andre was Andre Blateyron of 35 rue Berzelius, Paris XVII and Raoul – Pierre Berteaux of 64 rue Lemercier, Paris XVII – was his brother-in-law. Andre (Andre Blateyron) is described by evader Charles Fisher as being 5 ft 10 inches tall, with a dark complexion and a black moustache – and Raoul (Pierre Berteaux) as being 5 ft 8 inches tall, 155 lbs, with brown hair and moustache. 2/Lt Arthur Swap describes Raoul as about 27 years old, small and blond.

At Rivesaltes (where they met Vic Louis and Lt Lecrivain (sic) who accompanied them to Barcelona), the girl took Fisher and Wagner to a cafe

---

2   Included amongst their helpers were Andre and Madeleine Bollelandt of rue Nationale in Bornel (Oise). (Research by Dominique Lecomte)

where they stayed for two days (28 & 29 September) and met the local organisation chief (55 years old, crippled and with a glass eye) who fed them and arranged for guides to take them to Palau-del-Vidre. In Palau they collected two RAF evaders and six young Frenchmen and walked to a small town (possibly Sorede) where two guides started leading them over the mountains. After three hours, the guides disappeared and the walkers made their own way back to Palau where they stayed for the rest of the night before walking to Elne and taking a train to Perpignan. Fisher says that their tickets were examined by French inspectors in their carriage and Germans in the others and reports that the two RAF boys and six French boys were picked up.

In Perpignan, Claude was warned that the party was suspected by the police and so took Fisher, Wagner, Lecrivain and Vic Louis by bus to Axat (near Gorge de Saint-Georges) and walked to Rouze where they stayed four days with an elderly friend of Vic's called Martinez. On 3 October, two French Jewish couples and seven young Frenchmen arrived and Martinez and his son led the whole party of sixteen into the mountains and across to Andorra. Next day they were driven to La Seu d'Urgell and telephoned the American Consul. On 11 October they were driven to the British Consulate in Barcelona.

The two RAF evaders mentioned by Fisher were F/Lt James McDonald and F/O C D Farmer. F/Lt James McDonald (wireless operator of 78 Sqn Halifax JD108) was helped by the Chauny-Dromas organisation until being sent to Paris on 11 September and sheltered at Fontenay-sous-Bois by M et Mme Georges Masse at 97 rue des Moulins. On 27 September, they arranged his journey to Rivesaltes where he stayed with an unnamed family for three days while further arrangements were made for him to cross the frontier. F/O C D Farmer was the pilot of 149 Sqn Stirling BF477 which was lost the night of 5-6 September 1943 on an operation to Mannheim.

"On the train from Paris I had met F/Lt Farmer (a pilot) and on 30 Sep we set off to cross the frontier by train with a guide. At the station a suspicious looking dago kept staring at us. In the train he sat next to us and after a satisfactory inspection of our identity cards etc he followed the German inspector out and at the next station we were arrested by the same German."[3]

---

3   LIB/658 McDonald in TNA folder WO208/3331.

CHAPTER 27

17 October 1943

On 17 October 1943, Capt Roy Bridgman-Evans and F/O George Lents – and five other Frenchmen – left Paris by train for Perpignan with a young man and a girl as their guides – I suspect their guides were (again) Charles Ploncard and Genevieve Crosson.

Capt Roy H Bridgman-Evans and a party of 2 SAS had been dropped by parachute near Capizzi in Italy on 13 July 1943. Unfortunately the containers with their weapons failed to arrive and they were captured by Italian troops that same day. They were sent to Nicosia then by truck to Messina and boat to Gioja Tauro. After escaping from Gioja on 22 July and being recaptured on the beach, Bridgman-Evans was sent to Capua and then on 30 August, to PG19 at Bologna.

Following the Italian Armistice, the camp was taken over by German troops and on 11 September 1943, the inmates were sent by rail to Germany, arriving at the ORs (other ranks) camp of Moosburg on 13 September. A few days later the officers were moved to Fort Bismarck near Strasbourg (Alsace).

On 1 October 1943, Bridgman-Evans and Capt Frederick H Long escaped from the camp, covered by brother officers as they cut their way through the wire. They walked to Epinal in Lorraine where they found shelter for a couple of nights then on to Aillevillers-et-Lyaumont where they were sheltered by a man named Nicholas Vogelsang. Their photographs were taken and on 12 October, Emil Horn (of 7 Faubourg de Montbeliard) came from Belfort with ID cards for them. On 16 October, Emil Horn took them both by train to Belfort where they spent the day with Albert Zangelen at 16 Faubourg de Lyons and met Paul Rassiniers (of 15 rue de Papillon) head of the de Gaulle section.[1] Later that day, a guide took them overnight from Belfort to Paris where, outside the Place de l'Opera, they were handed over to the Bourgogne organisation.

---

1 Although several of these names and addresses are included on the IS9 Helper List, they also have notes like 'no trace' ... Paul Rassiniers however is also listed by Yves Allain as Bourgogne's 'intermediaire' in Belfort, Allain having met M Rassiniers during his time travelling the country for *Volontaires de la Liberte*. (NARA Allain)

131

Bridgman-Evans and Long were taken to Georges Guillemin's home at 69 rue Victor Hugo in Colombes where the two men parted and Bridgman-Evans left for Perpignan that evening.

F/O Georges Rene Lents, a twenty-three-year-old Frenchman from Rodez, was returning from a bomber escort sortie (Ramrod 258) to Paris on 3 October 1943 and flying at low altitude when he was hit by flak which stopped his engine. Being too low to bale out, Lents crash-landed his 341 (Free French) Sqn Spitfire JL347 in a field about 20 kms south-west of Abbeville.

After failing to set light to his aircraft, Lents ran across the fields until meeting some farm labourers who directed him to a house in Feuquieurs-en-Vimiue (Somme). His injured shoulder was dressed and he was hidden in a shed nearby when a German search party approached before being taken that evening to another house in Feuquieurs where he spent the night. Next day his host brought a schoolteacher friend who took Lents about ten kilometres by bicycle to a house in Friaucourt. On 6 October, he was moved a couple of kilometres to Ault where he was sheltered by (the hopefully inappropriately named) Dr Pierre Coffin until he was handed over to an organisation which arranged his journey. On 12 October, a man who Lents later discovered was a saboteur, drove him to Hornoy (Somme) where he was handed over to Joe Balfe at the Hotel de France.

Joseph Balfe (of Irish descent but born 1897 in Manchester) served with the Irish Guards during the Great War, attained rank of sergeant and was awarded the Military Medal. After he was demobbed, Joe stayed on in France, married Madeleine Gaudiere and took French nationality. They lived in Dunkirk and raised a family of two boys, John Paul and Joseph Patrick (Joe Jnr) and two girls, Madeleine and Marie-Therese. Between the wars, Joe worked on the cross-Channel ferries and became Chief Steward. Joe is described as a large burly man, about six feet tall, with a big belly and very strong. With his commanding personality, genial expression and remarkable resemblence to Winston Churchill, it seems no-one who met Joe Snr would easily forget him.

With the coming of the war, and with both sons serving in the French military, Joe took his wife and two girls away from the action and headed south. They got as far as Bordeaux but then decided to return, this time to Hornoy-le-Bourg in the Somme where Madeleine's mother ran the Hotel de France on rue de Molliens. At some point Joe blanked off part of the top floor corridor so that at least one room was only accessible from the rear of the hotel. Shortly after the family's arrival, the village was occupied by the Germans who made their headquarters opposite the hotel and billetted their officers in the hotel itself.[2]

Lents only stayed three days at Hornoy before a guide came to take him to Paris where he was lodged with Madeleine Melot at rue Larrey – leaving the apartment only once, to have his photograph taken – until he was taken to the Gare d'Austerlitz.

Bridgman-Evans and Lents arrived in Perpignan at about ten-thirty on the morning of 18 October and were taken by tram to a small hotel near a park on the outskirts of town. They left the hotel again at seven-thirty that evening, changing guides in the town and walking through the night until six the following morning. They slept through the next day before setting off again that night, continuing until the evening of 21 October when they reached Figueras where they spent the night in a field. Next day, they were taken to a farm where they should have been collected by car. However, something went wrong so in the evening of 23 October, their guide took Lents and Bridgeman-Evans on a series of trains to Barcelona.

2   Joe Balfe (Snr) – who with 'his gallant band of helpers' is credited with helping 'at least one hundred Allied Service personnel' – was recommended for an OBE. (WO208/5451)

CHAPTER 28

The Loss of Sgt Peacock

On 22 October 1943, Capt Frederick Long, Sgt Alfred Jaworowski, S/Sgt Anthony Marandola, T/Sgt Oscar Hamblin, 2/Lt Harry Hawes, 2/Lt Allan Johnston, S/Sgt Vincent Cox and T/Sgt Charles Peacock were taken by train from Paris via Toulouse to Pamiers and Lavelanet.[1]

Capt Frederick H Long was captured with his Commando unit at Lentini (Sicily) on 14 July 1943. He was held at Campo 66 (Capua) until mid-August when he was moved to PG19 at Bologna.

Following the Italian Armistice, the camp was taken over by German troops and on 11 September 1943, the inmates were sent by rail to Germany, arriving at the ORs camp of Moosburg on 13 September. A few days later the officers were moved to Fort Bismarck near Strasbourg (Alsace). On 1 October 1943, Long and Captain Roy H Bridgman-Evans escaped from the camp – see Bridgman-Evans earlier.

On arrival in Paris on 17 October, Long and Bridgman-Evans were taken to Georges Guillemin's home at 69 rue Victor Hugo in Colombes where the two men parted, Bridgman-Evans leaving for Perpignan that evening while Long was taken by Marie (Gabrielle Wiame) first to Maud Couve at rue de Madrid and then to stay overnight with Andree Vandevoorde at Fontenay-sous-Bois. Next day he was taken to a Mme Woittequand (assume Andree Vandevoorde's mother) at Vincennes where he met Major William Boren USAAF. On 21 October, Long was put in touch with Capitaine Level of the French army and four other Frenchmen with whom he was to travel – and Mme Marie provided Long with a new ID card. Next evening, Long was taken to the Gare d'Austerlitz where he joined the five Frenchmen, two American officers and five American ORs.

---

1   Long says there were also five Frenchmen in the party – Capitaine Level (French army) Capitaine Tanguy (French navy) Midshipman Poiret (Michel Pinet/Pinot – see below) Adjutant Dupuid and another French sergeant – and that their guide was a young Frenchman from Toulouse. (Long 1545 Appx C in TNA folder WO208/5582)

I have a copy of a letter (courtesy of Terry duSoleil) dated 29 April 1945 from Michel Pinet/Pinot thanking Louis Soum of Lavelanet for his and his wife's overnight hospitality to the group shortly before they set off for the mountains, and apologising for the loss of M Soum's coat during the crossing.

Sgt Alfred A Jaworowski and S/Sgt Anthony Marandola were the waist-gunners of B-17 41-24591 Rigor Mortis (305BG/366BS) (Halliday) which was returning from Stuttgart on 6 September 1943 and just short of Beauvais when they found, like so many others that day, they were running out of fuel. As they left formation they were attacked by fighters and the aircraft was abandoned to crash near Neufchatel-en-Bray (Seine-Maritime).[2]

Jaworowski was helped immediately on landing near Gournay-en-Bray and soon joined by the injured Marandola. They were hidden in a barn for two days until their journey was arranged. They were visited by Maurice Kolman, a herbalist at Gournay-en-Bray, who brought a young schoolteacher who was on holiday from her job in Paris. The two airmen were helped by various local people, given clothes and ID papers, until 11 September when they were taken by train to Paris. Jaworowski comments that while nothing happened on the train, everyone seemed to realise who they were. At Gare Saint-Lazaire, they were passed on to another French woman who took them to the luxurious home of an elderly woman in the Etoile area. They were visited by a Scottish nurse (widow of a Frenchman) from the American Hospital who tended to Marandola's injuries, and by a rich American woman called Elizabeth, wife of a movie director. They also met Andre Blateyron (who smoked a big pipe, like Sherlock Homes) and his brother-in-law Raoul (Pierre Berteaux), who supplied them with papers. Raoul was very dark, always wore a black hat and apparently had ambitions to become a Chicago gangster after the war.

On 18 September, Francois (about 19 years old) took them to his home near the Eiffel Tower where they stayed with his mother Germaine – and heard that the American woman Elizabeth and several other members of the organisation had been arrested. On 1 October, a short, blonde woman called Marie (Gabrielle Wiame) took them to stay with Maud Couve, Alice Brouard and Alice's daughter Marguerite (Maggie) at 25 rue de Madrid. Marandola was able to indulge in his love of cooking by preparing vegetable soup (there being very little food of any kind available without resorting to the black-market) while Marie would bring them cigarettes. They were also visited there by Andre and Raoul – and Maurice, a police inspector who took them out for drinks and got a new ID card for Marandola. On 22 October, Maud and Maggie took Jaworowski and Marandola to the

---

2   Three other members of the Rigor Mortis crew also evaded successfully: co-pilot 2/Lt Russell M Brooke and tail-gunner S/Sgt Duane J Lawhead were picked up by RN MGB 318 from Ile Tariec on the SIS operation Envious IIb at the beginning of December, and top-turret gunner T/Sgt Thomas C Shaver who crossed the Pyrenees with Comete in November.

station and passed them on to Marie who turned them over to their guide, described by Jaworowski as "a good-looking big-shot with an odd hat".

T/Sgt Oscar K Hamblin and 2/Lt Harry H Hawes were the top-turret gunner and bombardier of B-17 42-3455 Lucky Thirteen (384BG/546BS) (Faulkiner) which was returning from Stuttgart on 6 September 1943 and running out of fuel. They had already sustained flak damage before being attacked by fighters and the aircraft was abandoned south of Beauvais. Hamblin and Hawes – along with their pilot 1/Lt Russell R Faulkiner – were sheltered in and around Clermont, Creil and Chauny before being taken to Paris and the Bourgogne organisation – see Faulkiner earlier.

Hamblin was lucky to get that far, having first landed in a lake (presumably l'etang de Breuil-le-Sec) and almost drowning when he became entangled in the shrouds of his parachute. Fortunately he was carrying a hunting knife in his coveralls and was able to cut himself free and just as he released himself from the parachute, a French couple came with a boat to rescue him and row him ashore. However, according to Roland Luccesi writing in his 1984 book *'De l'interieur vers la force'*, that wasn't quite the end of the story. The French couple were Louis Faulon and his wife and when Louis asked Hamblin if he were American, Hamblin's Germanic sounding 'yeah' resulted in Mme Faulon trying to knock him overboard again with an oar and it was only her husband's intervention that prevented her. Hamblin was finally brought safely ashore and taken back to the Faulon home in Breuil-le-Sec to dry out. They contacted local resistance man (and village maire) Andre Pommery and two days later, Gaston Legrand collected Hamblin and took him by motorcycle back to his house in nearby Clermont.

On 29 September, Hamblin, Hawes and Faulkiner were brought from Chauny to Paris and the Jardin des Plantes where they were handed over to an elderly woman, known as the Lady in Black (Madeleine Melot). After taking Faulkiner back to her apartment, Mme Melot returned to deliver Hamblin and Hawes to Simone Levavasseur who sheltered them in a room above her sweet shop, La Petite Chocolatiere at 19 Avenue d'Orleans. They were visited regularly by the Lady in Black until the evening of Friday 22 October when she took them to the station.

2/Lt Allan G Johnston was the navigator of B-17 42-5057 (305BG/422BS) (Dahly) which was also returning from Stuttgart on 6 September 1943 and into a strong head-wind. Like so many aircraft that day, they were running low on fuel and eventually fell out of formation.

After half an hour of evasive manoeuvres against fighter attacks, the aircraft was abandoned over Picardy.[3]

Johnston landed south-west of Abbeville, near Blangy-sur-Bresle. He was helped by a young brother and sister named Fauget (nf) and sheltered for the next month with both the Fauget and Crept families (Honore Crept at Ferme Romesnil) in Nesle-Normandeuse. On 4 October, Johnston was moved, firstly to Blangy-sur-Bresle then to Eu, where he stayed with M Beauvisage at 60 Boulevard Victor Hugo and joined his radio-operator Grant Carter. On 8 October, Johnston and Carter were driven to Hornoy le Bourg where they stayed with Joe Balfe. After two days at Hornoy, they were taken to stay with Rene (aka Jean) and Odette Lemattre in Amiens for a week.[4]

On 15 October, a man in knickers (sic) and horn-rimmed glasses took Johnston and Carter to Paris and turned them over to the Lady in Black, a tall, red haired woman – wife of a French colonel – who lived on the fourth-floor of an apartment building in Paris XV (Madeleine Melot). They were sheltered there for a few days before Johnston was moved to 3 rue du Guesclin where he stayed with Peter Magnas until 22 October, when the Lady in Black took Johnston to the station.

S/Sgt Vincent J Cox and T/Sgt Charles B Peacock were the tail-gunner and radio-operator of B-17 42-30271 Bomb Boogie (95BG/335BS) (Ransom) which was abandoned over Picardy on 6 September 1943.

Cox landed near Saint-Erme-Oute-et-Ramecourt where a young boy called Henri hid him and returned later with food. That evening Cox was passed on to two men (one blond) who had his radio-operator Charles Peacock with them and taken to a house where they were joined by waist-gunner Pasquale Delvento. Next day, Cox and Peacock were moved to nearby Amifontaine where they stayed with M et Mme Mueler/Muller (query). On 16 September, Cox and Peacock were taken to stay overnight with the blond men who first had helped Peacock and where they joined their top-turret gunner T/Sgt Harold R Knotts. Next day, a Red Cross nurse from Paris took Cox, Peacock and Knotts to Paris by train. Cox and Peacock stayed three days with Simone Levavasseur in her apartment at 6 rue Mouton-Duvernet until Mme Blondie and the Lady in Black took

---

3   Two other men from 42-5057 also evaded successfully, tail-gunner S/Sgt William J Koger Jnr crossed the Pyrenees with a group of civilians in October, and T/Sgt Grant Carter with Bourgogne – see later.

4   Rene Lemattre (born November 1912) and his wife Odette (born September 1912) were both recommended for KMCs. (WO208/5452)

them to Asnieres-sur-Seine where they stayed with Pauline Hagues at 7 Avenue Marianne Rouston. On 22 October, a young man named Lucien Demongogin (of 18 rue Victor Hugo, Asnieres-sur-Seine) took Cox and Peacock to the station where Mme Blondie (Gabriele Wiame) turned them over to a guide who was leading 2/Lt Allan Johnston.

The eight evaders were taken by overnight train to Toulouse (where they changed guides to a short French officer who was on his way to Algiers to join the Free French) and then the three-thirty afternoon train for Foix but got off at Pamiers. They were joined by a man known as Antonio (Antonio Mandico/Antonis Manolico – query) and took a regular bus to Lavelanet where they ate a delicious (sic) meal courtesy of Louis Soum and his wife of rue de l'Hirondelle, and slept in a closed-down textile mill. Antonio and their French guide from Toulouse handed them over to mountain guide Georges Miquel of Les Cabannes and they were joined by more Frenchmen. The party left at nine the following evening and walked until 3 am next morning, getting lost in the process. They found a house (somewhere short of Les Cabannes, according to Long) where they were allowed to sleep in a barn and a boy from the house put them back on the right trail – they had apparently climbed the wrong mountain. They set off again the following morning, having by then fallen out with the French who were (allegedly) experienced mountaineers while the Americans, many of whom had had no exercise for weeks, were suffering, to a village. They stayed in the village all the following day before leaving at four in the morning of 27 October. They were supposed to walk 30 kilometres but four of the Americans got lost in the fog and snow and only caught up again by luck. They built a fire in a cabin before deep snow forced them to retrace their steps back to a valley and another house. Some of the Americans lagged behind again after one of them fell in a stream but caught up once more. The French stayed in the house with a fire and changed their clothes while the Long and the Americans were put in a wooden shed where they built a fire of their own, regardless of the lack of chimney. They stayed for the rest of the day at the house and after a row between the evaders and the French, set off once more on the morning of 29 October – this time in bright sunshine and at a very slow pace and taking a five minute rest every hour – until climbing one last mountain at 6 o'clock that evening. By that time, almost everyone except thirty-four-year-old commando Frederick Long was sick and vomiting (including some of the French walkers) and Cox and Peacock were left behind after the French officer from Toulouse insisted that the guides take them on as it was getting dark. They went to a hotel (the restaurant Calbo) in Soldeu, Andorra where the French had rooms and the evaders slept in a barn. Next day a taxi took the evaders to a small town, passing an exhausted Cox along the way – they didn't dare pick him up as the taxi driver wasn't part of the organisation but the French arranged for Cox to join them later that day. The seven remaining evaders were taken by bus across the border into Spain and La Seu d'Urgell – where they picked up Sgt Kenneth Moore – and were met by a Spaniard who gave them a meal and Spanish travel documents and they spent the night in a hotel. Moore hadn't been expected and so didn't have Spanish papers but the rest of the party left by car the following morning for Barcelona and the British Consulate, arriving there at five o'clock on the morning of 1 November.[5]

Marandola is particularly critical of this group of Frenchmen, saying the trip across the Pyrenees was unnecessarily disagreeable, with them treating the Americans 'like dogs' and saying it was a miracle there wasn't murder done.

Sgt Kenneth R Moore, tail-gunner of B-17 42-5890 (Christenson), had made his own way to Tarbes before joining a group of French and crossing into Andorra. It was another two days before suitable documents were supplied and he reached the British Consulate on 2 November.

While crossing the mountains, Cox was usually at the front but he dropped back to walk with Peacock who was exhausted. Peacock collapsed just after crossing into Andorra and Cox stayed with him until they lost touch with the rest of the party. The two men stayed overnight in the mountains and Peacock was unconscious when Cox left him to go down into Soldeu. On finding the guides, Cox told them where he'd last seen Peacock and they said they would go and find him. Cox waited another day but heard nothing more about Peacock – or the guides. At the time of writing this, and in spite of an extensive investigation in 1950 by the US Graves Registration Detachment – and further enquiries by Claude Benet in 2013 – 32385488 T/Sgt Charles B Peacock USAAF is still officially MIA.

---

5   Some additional details are taken from US 7887 Graves Registration Detachment Case 9938 file, the 1950 investigation into the fate of Sgt Peacock, kindly sent to me by Terry duSoleil of 95BG MIA Research.

CHAPTER 29

Three More Deaths in the Pyrenees

On 21 October 1943, P/O Yves Lucchesi, Major William Boren, 2/Lt Keith Murray, 2/Lt Charles Hoover, 1/Lt Olaf Ballinger, Sgt Francis Owens, 2/Lt Harold Bailey and T/Sgt William Plasket were taken by train to Toulouse. Their guides included a blonde girl with thick-lensed glasses.

P/O Yves Lucchesi was the pilot of 342 (Lorraine) Sqn Boston BZ388 on a daylight operation to Palaiseau Power Station, near Paris, on 3 October 1943. They were hit by flak over the target which stopped the port engine. Twenty minutes later, the starboard engine also failed and the aircraft was crash-landed at Jonquieres (Oise) south-west of Compiegne. Navigator P/O Barabier (who was badly injured) and rear gunner Sgt Godin (see below) were captured but wireless operator Sgt Guy Marulli de Barletta also evaded successfully – see later.

Lucchesi lost consciousness on landing and when he came around, found he was being helped by his rear gunner, Sgt Godin. They went to a nearby farm, where they were given civilian clothes before two Frenchmen took them to hide in some woods. A short time later, a car pulled up and someone called to them – Lucchesi refused to answer but Sgt Godin went to the vehicle, only to be captured by a German officer. Lucchesi heard Godin tell the German that he was alone and that his pilot had been killed in the crash. After the car had left, Lucchesi set off in the opposite direction and at about seven o'clock that evening, approached a father and his two sons who were working in a field. He was taken back to their home, an organisation was contacted and his journey arranged.[1]

Major William T Boren was the pilot of B-26 (Marauder) 41-31721 Cactus Jack (387BG/559BS) which was damaged by flak over Beauvais-Tille aerodrome on 21 September 1943 and abandoned soon afterwards.[2]

---

1   No Appendix C has been found but Lucchesi says at the end of his MI9 report (WO208/3316-1552) that his crossing of the Pyrenees was with a party of Americans and French and that his story is the same as Major Warren, an American who came back with him. I am confident that 'Warren' is William Boren and that Lucchesi is one of the otherwise anonymous Frenchmen mentioned by the American evaders.

2   Two others from the seven-man crew of Cactus Jack also evaded successfully: T/Sgt John L Connell with Comete and S/Sgt Francis W Anderson with Bourgogne – see later.

Boren landed in a field somewhere north-east of Beauvais. He was helped almost immediately, hidden in a barn within an hour of landing and then taken to a farmhouse where his journey was arranged. On 24 September, Boren was moved to a village where he met his tail-gunner S/Sgt Francis W Anderson. That afternoon, three men took Boren and Anderson to Georges Fleury at 25 rue de Mouy in Clermont where they met eight evaders from B-17 42-3452 – John Wagner, Arthur Vetter, Edward Fontaine, Warren Lush, James Bormuth, Edward Daly, Hobart Trigg and Wendell McConnaha.[3] Boren, Wagner, Vetter and Lush were then taken to stay with Gaston Legrand, Odette Sauvage and her son Edmond at their home on rue du Chatelier. On 5 October, Boren and Anderson were taken back to Georges Fleury where they met a blond man who spoke some English and he and George Fleury's son Alain took them by train to Creil, where Alain and the blond man got off and were replaced by a man and woman who took Boren and Anderson on to Paris.

Boren and Anderson were met in Paris by a young girl who took them to the Jardin des Plantes where they were passed on to a man wearing horn-rimmed glasses. He took them to an apartment with a collection of Indian relics where they had tea and were joined by two women – who were given 1,500 francs by each of the evaders. Boren and Anderson were separated at this point and Mme Marie (assume Gabrielle Wiame) took Boren to a French Red Cross nurse's apartment where another woman took him on to stay with Madeleine Linster at 32 rue du Cotentin, Paris XV. Two days later (8 October) Boren was moved to Fontenay-sous-Bois where he stayed with Maurice and Andree Vandevoorde and their twenty-four-year-old son Jacques at 167 Avenue de la Republique. On (about) 18 October, he was joined by Frederick Long and on 19 October, Boren and Long were taken to stay with Lulu (query) for two nights until Andree Vandevoorde took Boren to the station.

2/Lt Keith W Murray was the bombardier of B-17 42-30271 Bomb Boogie (95BG/335BS) (Ransom) which was abandoned to crash near Pancy-Courtecon (Picardy) south of Laon on 6 September 1943.

Murray evaded with ball-turret gunner S/Sgt John W Beachan more or less on their own until 12 September when they separated.[4] Murray then continued alone as far as Provins where he was sheltered and helped and

3   M George Charles Adrien Fleury (born January 1890) and Mme Rachel Clothilde Fleury (born July 1893) (WO208/5452)

4   S/Sgt John W Beachan was one of four evaders captured on a train to Perpignan whilst traveling with Francoise Dissard.

on 17 September, taken by bicycle to join 2/Lt Charles H Hoover and their journey arranged.

2/Lt Charles H Hoover was the co-pilot of B-17 42-29789 Big Time Operator (381BG/535BS) (Zum) which had already experienced trouble with one engine and lost two guns on 3 September 1943 before being damaged by flak over Romilly-sur-Seine aerodrome and attacked by fighters. The aircraft was abandoned to crash near Provins (Seine-et-Marne) south-east of Paris.

Hoover landed a few miles east of Saint-Just-en-Brie (Seine-et-Marne) and was soon helped. Charles Foras (nf) came and took him back to his house at St Just for three days before moving him to a blacksmith at La Croix–en-Brie for the day before he was moved again, this time to stay with Pierre Soueleme (nf) at Fontains, just south of Nangis. After a week with M Soueleme, Hoover was moved three houses down to stay with another blacksmith, Laurent Francois, where he was joined by Keith Murray from B-17 42-30271 Bomb Boogie. On 21 September, Andre and Raoul came from Paris to collect them and take them to stay with Elli Mignon at 66 rue Pouchet, Paris XVII where they joined Harold Bailey from B-17 42-5827 Lakanuki. Next day, Hoover was moved downstairs to stay in the concierge's apartment where he was visited by an Englishwoman (large-boned, straight black hair tied in a bun). On 24 September, Andre and Raoul took Hoover and Murray (and Bailey – query) to meet Dora Rospape whose husband took them to stay with his cousin Jeanette (Jeanne Rospape), a widow who ran a restaurant at 21 rue de Faubourg-Saint-Martin, Paris X. Hoover met several people from the organisation including Guido (a wealthy man who owned the Palace Hotel), Charles (a short man who tried to arrange an aircraft for them) and Andree (Lebegue) (a handsome woman of 23 (sic) who had an English (sic) aviator called Bob staying with her and was captured along with him). Meanwhile Raoul fell under suspicion of the organisation and was shot.[5] On about 16 October, they were joined by S/Sgts Edward Daly and Hobart Trigg from B-17 42-3452. When Andree was arrested (on 17 October) eight evaders – including Olof Ballinger, Harold Bailey and Francis Owens, who had been sheltered with Dora Rospape at 11 rue du 29 Juillet – were moved to Jeanette's hotel and restaurant at 21 rue Faubourg-Saint-Martin.

---

5   Raoul (Pierre Berteaux) was shot through the lung – but I don't know who by. After first being brought to the Couve apartment, Maud Couve arranged, through another contact, for Raoul to be admitted to Laennec hospital (Hopital Laennec, Paris VII) under a false identity where he stayed for six months recovering. (Marguerite Brouard)

On 21 October, Dora Rospape, Jeanette (Jeanne Rospape) and Jeanette's waitress (Simone Molin) took Hoover, Ballinger, Murray, Bailey, Owens and Plasket to a meeting with a colonel's wife (5 ft 6 inches tall, quiet, spoke English) (the Lady in Black) (Madeleine Melot). The colonel's wife took them to Marie (a short, blonde, Belgian woman who had already given them their papers) (Gabrielle Wiame) and six young Frenchmen who took them by train to Toulouse.

1/Lt Olof M Ballinger was the pilot and Sgt Francis E Owens a waist-gunner of B-17 42-29928 (381BG/533BS) which was on the way to Le Mans on 4 July 1943 when it was hit by flak over Laval which took out one engine and the oxygen supply. They dropped out of formation and were heading back north when the aircraft was attacked by fighters and abandoned to crash near La Coulonche (Orne).[6]

Ballinger landed about two kilometres south-east of La Coulonche and was helped almost immediately. Ballinger's written report is very hard to read and I'm not sure exactly what happened to him and Owens during their first eleven weeks in France. However, Andre Rougeyron wrote about his involvement with the two airmen and I have used his book to help fill in some of the details.[7]

Having finally seen S/Sgt William Howell and 2/Lt Paul McConnell on their way (see later), Rougeyron set out from his home in Domfront to find the rest of their crew. He had been told that two airmen were being sheltered by Andre Mazeline on a farm (La Troudiere) owned by Andre Geslin at Sainte-Opportune and it was arranged that Mlle Simone Viel (of 11 rue Gustave Lebon, Paris XIV) would meet Rougeyron and his friend Georges Gilard (of rue Georges Clemenceau, Domfront) at Le Ferte-Mace on 28 August and take them to the airmen. That evening, Gilard and Rougeyron drove the evaders (in what Ballinger describes as a delapidated car) to the village of Champsecret, a few kilometres north-east of Domfront, where they were sheltered with the postmistress. After three days at Champsecret, Rougeyron and Emmanuel Bourgoin (caretaker at the Chateau de l'Ermitage, just outside Champsecret) walked with Ballinger and Owens to the railway station at Saint-Bomer-les-Forges where they took a train to Flers. They

---

6   Three of the 42-29928 crew were killed in the aircraft, two were taken prisoner and four evaded successfully: co-pilot 2/Lt John M Carah to Switzerland, navigator 2/Lt Paul H McConnell with Comete and two with Bourgogne, Ballinger and Sgt William C Howell.

7   Andre Rougeyron wrote a book called 'Agents d'Evasion' which was published in 1947. It was later translated into English by Marie-Antoinette McConnell – wife of US evader Paul McConnell (also mentioned later) – and republished in 1996 by the Louisianana State University Press as 'Agents for Escape'.

arrived in Flers quite early in the morning and because the train for Paris wouldn't be leaving until late that evening, Rougeyron decided to store (sic) the two Americans with Mme Boschet at the Notre-Dame Institute. A guide (Rougeyron says his name was Petrel (alias Schoegel) and Ballinger says his name was Andre) arrived from Paris and that evening, he took the two airmen back to the capital – arriving there at 0500 according to Ballinger.

On arrival in Paris, Andre Schoegel took the two Americans back to his home in Orly and that afternoon, Andre and Raoul (Andre Blateyron and Pierre Berteaux) arrived to take them to Le Vesinet (Seine et Oise) where they stayed with Mme Lucienne Lamort at 28 rue du Marche.

On 25 September, Andre and Raoul took Ballinger and Owens back into Paris to be sheltered by Mme Lamort's sister and brother-in-law, M et Mme Lucien Normand at 26 (or 30) Blvd Bessieres[8] – where they joined Harold Bailey. On 3 October, Ballinger and Owens were moved to Dora Rospape's apartment where they were joined by William Plasket and met Bailey again. They also met Charles Hoover and Keith Murray who were staying with Mme Rospape's cousin Jeanette (Jeanne Rospape) along with two others (Edward Daly and Hobart Trigg – see later). Ballinger also reports Andree Lebegue's arrest (on 17 October) with an American evader called Bob, who had a scar on side of his face from ditching in the Channel.[9] That night, warned of Mlle Lebegue's arrest, Ballinger and Owens (and others) were moved to Jeanette's hotel, Chapon Fin at 21 rue du Faubourg-Saint-Martin, and next day to the home of Jeanette's waitress, Simone Molin at 86 rue d'Aboukir, where they were sheltered until leaving Paris for the Pyrenees.

2/Lt Harold B Bailey was the navigator of B-17 42-5827 Lakanuki (526BG/379BS) which was damaged on an operation to Le Bourget on 16 August 1943. Bailey baled out near Paris before pilot 1/Lt Sam P Satariano regained control of the aircraft and returned to the UK.

T/Sgt William B Plasket Jnr was the top-turret gunner of B-17 42-

---

8   Ballinger gives the Normand's address as Blvd Bessieres while the IS9 Helper List has M et Mme Lucien Normand at 29 rue Bezilius. Ballinger mentions being visited by an elderly English nurse who lived on Blvd (sic) Berzilius.

9   My thanks to Michael Moores Leblanc for identifying Andree as Mlle Andree Lebegue (born September 1908) of 205 rue Saint Honore, Paris Ier. Mlle Lebegue was one of Gabrielle Wiame's many contacts and had been sheltering Bob for about a month until she was denounced by two of her neighbours. Mlle Lebegue was deported to Germany in February 1944 but liberated from Belsen on 16 April 1945 and returned to France the following month. (NARA Lebegue)

Hobart Trigg, who was being sheltered across the road at the time, says that Bob was a top-turret gunner and that when his aircraft ditched, he was on last flight of his tour and quite crazy. Bob was T/Sgt Harold Robert Knotts, TTG of B-17 42-30271 Bomb Boogie (Ransom) – mentioned earlier. Knotts acquired the scar on his face when his (then) aircraft ditched in the North Sea on 30 July 1943.

30163 (306BG/368BS) (Peterson) which was returning from Stuttgart on 6 September 1943 when it ran out of fuel and was abandoned to crash south of Dieppe. Plasket was with 42-30163 waist-gunner Sgt William E Scott Jnr (see earlier) until he was moved from Madeleine Melot's apartment at 11 bis rue Larrey shortly before Scott left Paris on 23 September.

In Toulouse, a French captain took charge of the party and Boren says that a man called Antonio (also mentioned by Frederick Long – see earlier) arranged for the evaders to have supper in a cafe and some of them to spend the night in a hotel – Boren (at least) got a room over a hardware store. Next day they were taken by train to Montsaunes (near Saint-Martory) and then by bus to St Girons where they stayed overnight in a hotel. Next day, the party of seven Americans and four Frenchmen (one army captain and three naval officers) – plus two (sic) French guides – went by bus to Massat and then walked to Suc-et-Sentenac – where Ballinger dropped out with exhaustion and was left in a farmhouse to recover. The rest of the party continued over the Pyrenees but on the approach to the Andorran border, 2/Lt Harold B Bailey, T/Sgt William B Plasket and S/Sgt Francis Owens collapsed and had to be left in the snow – where it is believed they died from exposure.

The remainder of the party reached Andorra on 25 October and walked to a hotel from where Boren, Hoover, Murray and Lucchesi were collected by taxi and driven to the Spanish frontier. That night they were taken by car to Barcelona and the British Consulate, arriving there on 28 October 1943.

Ballinger rested at Suc-et-Sentenac until setting off by himself. He says in the written version of his escape report that he left Suc-et-Sentenac on 30 October and walked to Andorra the next day and then crossed into Spain on 4 November with six Spaniards and walked to Manresa – finally reaching Barcelona on 11 November 1943.

I originally thought that Harold Bailey, William Plasket and Francis Owens died at or near Port del Rat, and organised a small ceremony there in 2008 to remember them, but more recent information from Andorran researcher and historian Claude Benet (using a 1978/79 interview with guide Emile Delpy) suggests they were left at nearby Port d'Arinsal.

In answer to the question "Have you ever lost people in the mountains?" Emile Delpy replied : "Yes, it unfortunately happened. I had three dead in my group. As a guide It was very tough as I was in charge of the group. I had got lost in the snowstorm. I didn't know where I was. I thought I was in Port de Rat and I was actually further away, near Port d'Arinsal. The head of the group was a French captain. There were some aviators, English or Americans. Three English (sic) collapsed exhausted and frozen. I gathered the group and asked them to help me save the three men. They all refused and I understand them, they weren't much better off and I couldn't carry or drag them on my own. The captain told me, and I still remember it vividly: We must walk along as fast as possible or we will all die". He was right and so we did. These three men died near the Port d'Arinsal. A hundred metres later the captain collapsed. I didn't want to leave him. I put his arms round my shoulders and dragged him in the snow for kilometres. At nightfall I found an Andorran hut and broke the door open. I could light a fire as I carried a little petrol in a flask. I undressed him and rubbed his body with snow until he came round. He was saved."[10]

Further investigation by Claude Benet in 2015 found that "Three unindentified persons were found at "l'Estany" (Pla de l'Estany, just south of the Port d'Arinsal) and after having got the official authorization, they were buried in the cemetery in Arinsal on the 12th September 1944."

Using unpublished documents (including a local police report) from the Andorran National Archives, Andres Luengo, a journalist with the Andorran newspaper Bondia, confirms that the three bodies were found at Montmartell, just south of the Port d'Arinsal, in June 1944. On 8 November 1944, their remains were exhumed and buried in the US military cemetery near Liege, Belgium.

Summer visitors to the area today will find Port d'Arinsal at 2,734 metres (or Port del Rat at 2,450 metres) to be a fairly accessible climb from the car-park at the southern end of the Etang de Soulcem. However, it should be remembered that war-time evaders would not have had the luxury of being driven so far into the mountains. In this case, they had already walked some 17 kms (that's measured in a straight line) from Massat (probably via the Port de Lers at 1,517 metres) to reach Suc-et-Sentenac, where Ballinger dropped out, and Auzat at 725 metres, just outside Vicdessos. Then it's another 15 kms – and a 900 metre climb – to the car-park at 1,617 metres. Today you can drive there from Tarascon in about forty minutes but the evaders would have followed narrow tracks, in total darkness, over several nights just to reach this point. Add in the snow that is almost inevitable at that time of year and you might just be able to imagine what a trial

---

10   Temoignage recueilli par Olivier et Suzel Nadouce, et Jacky Souquet.

these routes to Andorra would have been. Considering the poor physical condition of many of the evaders, and their lack of suitable shoes, clothing or equipment, the wonder is not that men died in these mountains, but that more did not.

CHAPTER 30

22 October 1943

On 22 (or 23) October 1943, 2/Lt Merle Johnson, T/Sgt Asbury Perkins and 2/Lt Edward Maslanka left Paris by train for Pau.

2/Lt Merle Johnson and T/Sgt Asbury L Perkins were the co-pilot and radio-operator of B-17 42-5843 Black Ghost (384BG/547BS) (Pulcipher) which was returning from Stuttgart on 6 September 1943 when it was attacked by fighters and shot down near Beauvais.[1]

Johnson, Perkins and top-turret gunner S/Sgt Thomas E Furrey landed close to one another, about ten miles south of Beauvais. They made their way to Chauvry (north of Montmorency) where an elderly man took them in. He fetched two men, Jean and Paul, who took the evaders to the home of Jean's sister Yvonne in Bethemont-la-Foret where they stayed for eight days. They were interrogated by English-speaking Mederic Jost (of 35 rue du Boissy, Saint-Leu-la-Foret) and a Belgian woodcutter called Maurice. On 16 September, Johnson and Perkins were taken to Andilly where they stayed three days with a paperhanger named Edouard Pilard at 6 Place de la Liberation. On 20 September, Maurice drove all three Americans about 10 kms to meet a lorry where they joined Edward Manslanka from B-17 42-30163 and two men (Sgt Jim and Lt Charley) from the same 379 BG crew.

Sgt Jim and Lt Charley were 2/Lt Charles R Bigler and S/Sgt James A Dyson, the pilot and right waist-gunner from B-17 42-29866 Judy B (379BG/524BS) which was hit by flak over Le Bourget on 16 August 1943 and abandoned. Two of four crewmen to evade successfully from that aircraft, they crossed the Pyrenees together in February 1944.

2/Lt Edward L Maslanka was the co-pilot of B-17 42-30163 (306BG/368BS) (Peterson) which was returning from Stuttgart on 6 September 1943 when it ran out of fuel and was abandoned just before noon to crash south of Dieppe – see earlier. Maslanka reports that they encountered head-winds on the way to the target and then because of

---

1   Two other Black Ghost crewmen evaded successfully: pilot 1/Lt Ralph K Pulcipher made his own way to the Pyrenees and crossed to Figueras in Spain within a few days of baling out – and S/Sgt Willard D McLain with Bourgogne – see later.

148

heavy cloud, made three attempts before finally dropping their bombs on a secondary target that he describes as 'some tiny town in the hills'. He also comments that they had the 'heaviest gas-consuming plane on the field' and that by the time they had released their bombs, they realised they only had just enough fuel to reach the English Channel, where they planned to ditch. They were in sight of the Alps and could see other aircraft diverting to Switzerland.

Twenty-two-year-old Maslanka landed in an orchard (he says about 10 kms south-west of Amiens but Winters (see earlier) says near Gournay-en-Bray, which is about 25 kms WNW of Beauvais, although neither seem quite right) hitting a dead tree, breaking a rib and knocking himself out. When he came round, he was on his back with his parachute draped over him. A crowd gathered around but were reluctant to help so Maslanka set off across the fields. On reaching a road, he met another group of people, some of whom were smoking American cigarettes. Maslanka guessed they had come from one of his crew and after using his phrase-card (Maslanka didn't speak any French) was taken to join his bombardier August Winters. The two airmen were led to a haystack where they were hidden and brought civilian clothes – when the Americans advised the French to burn their uniforms (presumably with sign language as Winters didn't speak French either) they were laughed at and told the clothes would be dyed and reused – and moved that afternoon to some woods. Maslanka had injured his back and right side, and Winters had injured his leg and when Winters decided to stay where he was, Maslanka went on alone. He soon met a family with whom he had a long conversation via his phrase-card and was taken to stay overnight in a deserted barn. Next day, Maslanka set off walking towards Paris – some 90 kms away – passing Beauvais that afternoon and reaching the outskirts of another town that evening. On approaching a farmer and asking if he could spend the night in his barn, he was told no – but he could sleep in their spare bedroom. Next morning he was awoken for a breakfast of goose eggs before setting off again, latching on behind another farmer and imitating his shuffle as if going to work – and later joining a group of farm workers coming back from work. That evening (9 September – query) he approached a man in his garden to ask for a drink. When Maslanka declared himself as an American, the man took him into his house where his wife insisted that he stay the night. Unfortunately the state of Maslanka's feet and legs stopped him from walking on next day. The local people became suspicious of him (Maslanka thinks because he answered with a Germanic sounding 'yeah' to some of their questions) but one of the locals was Polish and Maslanka (who I'm guessing was of either Polish or Czech descent) was able to talk freely to him and satisfy him that he was genuine. Maslanka stayed at this unnamed place (just north of Pontoise) until his journey was arranged.

On about 20 September, Maslanka was taken through Pontoise by bicycle to Saint-Leu-la-Foret and a cafe which a woman was running after her husband had been taken in for questioning. She called Mederic Jost to question him and Maslanka was taken back to Jost's house – next door to Gestapo HQ – where he stayed for ten days (Friday to Monday). Maslanka met Prof (query) (an elderly man of about 70) – who had S/ Sgt James Dyson from Texas (Maslanka says Sgt Jim Brut) – staying with him, and Maurice the woodcutter who had a pick-up truck. On the Monday, Maslanka joined Dyson and Black Ghost crewmen, Merle Johnson, Asbury Perkins and Thomas Furrey. They were taken on the truck, collecting Dyson's pilot, 2/Lt Charles Bigler on the way, and driven to Meru (Oise) where – after dropping Bigler and Dyson off – they met the doctor who was running the organisation in Meru, waiting outside the town on a bike.

The scribbled pencil notes of Maslanka's report are very difficult to decipher at this point but after an encounter with some Germans, they were driven on 'a few more miles' to Soilly (Soilly, Marne – query) where they stayed the rest of the day at a bakery. They were visited by a butcher from Meru before being taken to the estate of 'high government official in Paris' where they stayed in the caretaker's house for the next five weeks.[2]

Manslanka's main report, which is typed, includes the encounter partly, he says, because it was amusing (although presumably only afterwards) but also because it shows what a man can "get away with if he can just stick it out".

"I was riding along in the back of a truck with a couple of other evaders and a large number of French. While we were stopped at the side of the road eating a sort of picnic lunch, a German sergeant on a bicycle passed us. I heard afterwards that he was a linguist and I figured he probably heard us speaking English too loudly. When we started off again, two German officers passed us in a car going in the other direction and looked at us curiously. A little while

---

2   It is about 100 miles from Meru, Oise to Soilly, Marne but the family Mellun (with a son in a German prison camp) are mentioned in Maslanka's MIS-X report (page 13) and the IS9 Helper List has a M et Mme Mellon in Soilly, Marne.

later the sergeant bicycled up to us, gave us long searching looks and went to the town ahead of us. In the town, we went around a curve in the street and found ourselves near a German headquarters with Germans blocking the street. Two of the Frenchmen in the back of the truck jumped off and starting running away at top speed but the Germans called them back. I could see myself sitting in the Dulag Luft already.

The Germans ordered everyone out of the truck. The Frenchmen lined up across the street but we evaders sat in the back of the truck, not knowing anything else to do. I figured they might as well come after us. The Germans lined the Frenchmen up against the wall and checked their identity papers, the Frenchmen protesting vociferously all the time. When the Germans checked the Frenchmen's papers, two officers yelled at us, apparently to get out of the truck. We had no identity papers, so we just sat there, waiting for the worst. All this time the Frenchmen were protesting about the outrage: their papers were in order, why were we stopped and so on, endlessly. The two German officers shouted at us angrily and when we still sat there, one came over to take care of us. The officer screwed up his monocle in the best movie picture fashion and looked us up and down. While we looked at him as coolly as we could, one of the Frenchmen came back, waving his papers and protesting about this outrage, stopping good Frenchmen and so on. He had a permit to go from one place to another with a working party and he waved it at the officer, gradually leading him up to the front of the truck all the time. Then both officers came back and gave us another going over and the Frenchman came back and lured them up to the front of the truck again. Finally, the Frenchman seemed to argue so loud and so long that the Germans got fed up and ordered them to get out of there as fast as they possibly could. When we pulled out without a German guard leading us away to prison, I thought that absolutely anything could happen. The paper, which had been one of the strongest points of argument for the French, was for a working party. The man in charge of this working party was dressed in his Sunday best, most of us were in pretty good clothes and one of the evaders (presumably Furrey in his pin-striped suit) was so well dressed as almost to be taken for a dandy. The only tools we had in the truck were for an entirely different kind of work from that the permit described. But the Germans let us go. I was clean-shaven, dressed in regular civilian clothes and wearing a beret." (MIS-X #222 Maslanka)

Maslanka says (and Johnson confirms) that Furrey got fed up and left after four weeks and so the others got in touch with Mederic Jost and asked

151

for their photographs to be taken for ID cards. On Friday 22 October, they were driven by truck back to Meru station where they were met by two men from an organisation and put on a train to Paris. On the train, they met three boys who said they worked for the Cognac organisation but their leader was on the run from the Gestapo and they were short of money. They took Maslanka, Johnson and Perkins to the fourth-floor of an apartment building where they stayed the afternoon before two different boys (at least one of whom was later in Miranda so assume he went to Spain with them) took them to the Gare d'Austerlitz.

They were taken by overnight train to Toulouse, the three evaders obviously travelling separately as Maslanka recounts in his report that:

"A German came through to check identity papers. I was warned of the German's approach so I walked to the other end of the car and found an old woman sitting with what looked like two of her children opposite her. I sat down next to her and moved up close to look like one of the family. They all gave me a sort of dirty look but I figured I could stand that easily enough. The German came along and asked for my pass first. I was hoping to be looked at in a hurry after he had carefully scrutinised the others. I fumbled for my pass, pulled it out and gave it to him. He looked at it for about half a minute and handed it back. Then he took the old woman's and studied it for a couple of minutes. I was afraid he was going to pick up the whole party and take me in too now that I looked like one of the family but after more study, he gave her papers back. I left the compartment practically on his heels."

They reached Toulouse at eleven the following morning, three hours later than scheduled and so missed their intended connection to Pau. They had to wait for a five o'clock train to Pau and arrived there at ten that evening. Next day, they were taken by train to Melun (assume Mauleon) where they waited until evening in the storeroom of a cafe. Their guide was a local postman and they started off at seven-thirty and walked in the rain until eleven, rested in a barn then carried on until two o'clock the following morning when they reached another barn and their postman-guide left them. A second guide arrived next evening and they set off in howling wind and rain, walking from nine o'clock until two in the morning then resting. Three hours later, another guide arrived and took them to a house where they stayed in a barn until five that afternoon when yet another guide took them to yet another barn (arriving at ten o'clock that evening)

152

for half an hour's rest before another guide walked them for a further two and half hours until they reached a house and had fried eggs. They were told that the Spanish border was only a few hours away.

Johnson, Perkins and Maslanka reached the Spanish border at six o'clock (dawn) on 29 October, having been taken through snow over the highest point visible, and down into a valley where, at about ten o'clock, they rested. A mile and a half later two Guardia Civil stopped and searched them before they were walked into Isaba.

Note that while Johnson, Perkins and Maslanka describe the harsh weather they had to contend with on their crossing from Pau, this was just four days after three other American airmen (mentioned earlier) and separately, Dvr Frederick G Williamson, a New Zealand soldier captured on Crete who had escaped from Stalag VIIIB (Lamsdorf) the previous month, lost their lives in the snow on the approaches to Andorra.

CHAPTER 31

Jean-Claude Camors and the Suzanne-Renée

On 18 October 1943, twenty-three Allied aircrew evaders were taken to the Breton fishing port of Camaret-sur-Mer, just south of Brest. The plan was to smuggle them on board a fishing boat called *Suzanne-Renée* the following morning in an operation organised by Jean-Claude Camors, head of the Bordeaux-Loupiac organisation.

F/O Arthur Riseley, F/Sgt Thomas Hedley, 2/Lt Walter Hargrove, S/Ldr John Checketts, F/Sgt Terence Kearins, S/Sgt James Wilson and S/Sgt William Rice had all been helped by Rene Guittard and the Bordeaux-Loupiac organisation in Frevent (Pas-de-Calais) before being brought to Paris.

F/O Arthur H Riseley and F/Sgt Thomas J Hedley were the pilot and wireless operator of 88 Sqn Boston BZ359 which was returning from Albert (Picardy) on 16 August 1943 when they were attacked by fighters. With both engines damaged, the aircraft was force-landed north of Auxi-le-Chateau, where it burnt out.

Riseley and Hedley were sheltered separately in Auxi and nearby Gueschart but brought together at Auxi-le-Chateau shortly before 24 September when Joseph Becker drove them and Walter Hargrove to Amiens.

2/Lt Walter Hargrove was the bombardier of B-17 42-29635 Augerhead (303BG/358BS) (Monahan) which was recalled from a visit to Romilly on 31 August 1943 and diverted to Amiens. An engine failure dropped them out of formation and a fighter attack forced them to abandon the aircraft. Hargrove landed just north of Abbeville and set off walking north-east. He evaded alone for four days before he found help near Willencourt, staying there for two days until 6 September when he was collected by a Gestapo agent named Becker and driven to Auxi-le-Chateau.

S/Ldr John M Checketts RNZAF was flying 485 Sqn Spitfire EN572 on a Ramrod (bomber escort) sortie to Cambrai on 6 September 1943 when he was shot down near Le Treport by enemy fighters and baled out. Checketts was helped almost immediately after landing in a field near

154

Tours-en-Vimeu (south-west of Abbeville) and taken to Visme-au-Val where he joined 181 Sqn Typhoon pilot P/O Edwin Haddock who was being sheltered by Marcel and Charlotte Lecointe. On 22 September, Checketts was moved to Boufflers where he stayed overnight with Mme Vve Marguerite Tellier at the Manoir de Gourlay on rue Principale before going on to Auxi-le-Chateau where he joined a group of evaders.

F/Sgt Terence S F Kearins RNZAF was flying 485 Sqn Spitfire EN573 on a Ramrod sortie to Amiens on 15 July 1943 when he was shot down by fighters and baled out. Kearins landed about five miles west of Hesdin (Nord-Pas-de-Calais) and was helped almost immediately, sheltered for eight weeks by M et Mme Theophile Forgez on their farm near Le Quesnoy-en-Artois. On 23 September, M Forgez drove Kearins to Auxi-le-Chateau and passed him over to the Bordeaux-Loupiac organisation. After being taken to buy shoes and a cap, he met an American pilot who spoke German and French and at about four o'clock that afternoon, joined fellow Kiwi Checketts and two Americans (Wilson and Rice) to be driven to Amiens by a man named Becker, who worked for the Gestapo.

Joseph Becker (born November 1910) was an Alsatian and naturalised German with his own transport company and a Gestapo permit to drive his German registered car – he was also one of the five local Bordeaux-Loupiac section heads! Becker was arrested on 15 December 1943 and condemned to death but escaped from prison in Lille the following month. Joseph Becker was awarded the KMC.[1]

The American pilot was actually 175 Sqn Typhoon pilot evader 700710 Sgt Harold Merlin – shot down on 16 August 1943 on the same Ramrod sortie as Soren Liby (see later). His parents were British but he was born in Greece and after emigrating to America for eight years, the family moved to Paris. Harold was educated in Switzerland and at the beginning of the war, as a fluent French and German speaker, was working for an American magazine in Paris.

S/Sgt James G Wilson was a waist-gunner and S/Sgt William W Rice the ball-turret gunner of B-17 42-30010 (92BG/407BS) (Asher) which was on the way to Stuttgart on 6 September 1943. They had just crossed the French coast when something happened (it's not clear from either of their reports exactly what) that caused the crew to abandon the aircraft. Rice was helped immediately on landing and Wilson within a few hours. Unfortunately neither of their Appendix Cs are very legible so I'm not sure

---

1   TNA folder WO208/5455.

how they wound up with Bordeaux-Loupiac at Auxi-le-Chateau before being taken to Paris.

In the afternoon of 23 September, Joseph Becker drove Checketts, Kearins, Wilson and Rice to Amiens station where they were put on a train to Paris. They were met at the Gare du Nord by a man known as Raoul (Jean-Claude Camors) and taken by Metro to an apartment in the Porte de Versailles area at 3 rue Claude Matrat. The following morning, Becker drove Riseley, Hedley and Hargrove to Amiens where Antoine (from Lille) and a young girl took them by train to Paris. They were also met at the Gare du Nord by Raoul and taken by Metro to the Porte de Versailles apartment, where a party of evaders was assembled.

After two (or three) nights in the apartment at the Porte de Versailles, Jean-Claude Camors, Pierre Charnier[2] and a girl (Paulette Depesme) took the group from Auxi-le-Chateau – Riseley, Hedley, Hargrove, Checketts, Kearins, Wilson and Rice – plus 2/Lt Russell M Brooke – by train to Cezy, near Joigny, Yonne (about 50 miles south-west of Troyes).

2/Lt Russell M Brooke and S/Sgt Duane J Lawhead were the co-pilot and tail-gunner of B-17 41-24591 Rigor Mortis (305BG/366BS) (Halliday) which was returning from Stuttgart on 6 September 1943 and just short of Beauvais when they found, like so many others that day, they were running out of fuel. As they left formation they were attacked by fighters and the aircraft was abandoned to crash near Neufchatel-en-Bray (Seine-Maritime).

Both men landed near Saint-Martin l'Hortier (Seine Maritime) were soon helped and as of 13 September, their journey together arranged. They were visited by Jeanette (Paulette Depesme) who took their names and ASN numbers. Two days later, on (about) 26 September, they were taken to Neufchatel station and joined Jeanette who took them to Paris, arriving at two o'clock the following morning. They were met by a man who took them to an apartment building where they joined the group of seven airmen from Auxi-le-Chateau. Lawhead stayed on in the Porte de Versailles apartment while the other eight were taken to Joigny.

2/Lt John W Bieger was the co-pilot of B-17 42-3071 (94BG/331BS) (Watts) which was on the way to Le Bourget on 14 July 1943 when it was attacked by fighters and abandoned. Bieger landed just north-east of Paris, near Mitry-Mory (Seine-et-Marne) and over the next eight days, made his

2   Pierre Charnier (born August 1917) of 42 rue d'Hauteville, Paris X was recommended for KMC. (WO208/5459)

way south some two hundred miles to Varennes-sur-Allier (Auvergne). After leaving the farm where he spent the night of 22-23 July, four men on bicycles caught up with him, one of whom had seen him at the farm and reported it to the local resistance chief. Bieger was taken to the home of one of the men, an Algerian with the code-name of Mesin, who spoke some English. He stayed with Mesin until 23 August, when he was moved to a resistance camp in the mountains. Mesin contacted a group in Lyon and on (about) 20 September, Bieger was taken to Lyon where he met Raoul (Jean-Claude Camors). Camors took Bieger to Joigny (Yonne) and he was sheltered with M Brun and his English wife at their home in Chassy par Aillant-sur-Tholon, south-west of Joigny, where he was joined by Soren Liby.

Lt Soren K Liby RNAF was flying 118 Sqn Spitfire EP126 on a Ramrod sortie on 16 August 1943 when he was shot down by enemy fighters. Liby was sheltered in and around Cabourg and Trouville (on the Normandy coast, east of Caen) until 6 September when he was taken to Paris and handed over to Jean-Claude Camors and another man at the Gare du Nord. They took him to stay with Mme Clothilde Derheimer at 150 rue Ordener, Paris XVIII until (about) 20 September, when Jean-Claude and a French barrister (query) collected him and took him to Joigny. He stayed one night in a German officer's club before being moved to Chassy par Aillant-sur-Tholon where he stayed with an Englishwoman named Mme Brun and joined John Bieger. On Thursday 30 September, Liby and Bieger were returned to Joigny where they met John Checketts et al.

On Friday 1 October, a young French boy took all ten airmen (the eight from Paris plus Bieger and Liby) back to Paris, where they were met by Jean-Claude Camors. After a meal at the Porte de Versailles apartment, they (and Lawhead) joined a group of nine more airmen brought from Troyes, and Camors and Pierre Charnier took all twenty evaders by overnight train to Vannes, on the Brittany coast, arriving 2 October 1943.

2/Lt Arthur M Swap was the pilot of B-17 42-30222 Lone Wolf (563BS/388BG) which was returning from Stuttgart on 6 September 1943 and north-east of Troyes when they were shot down by fighters. Swap landed about fifteen miles from Troyes and was soon helped, being sheltered by Joseph Foimici (nf) at Pel-et-Der (Aube) for three weeks. On about 20 September, Swap was driven into Troyes (his cover story being that he was a Polish thief being taken into custody by his driver's gendarme friend, Andre) where he was taken to the driver's brother's house and joined his co-pilot Alfred Kramer. A few days later the gendarme's wife Marie took Swap and Kramer to have their photographs taken before going on to a bakery where they joined one of their waist-gunners, William Vickless, top-turret gunner Merl Martin, radio-operator Allen Priebe, Richard Cunningham, Marius Brohard, Hershall Richardson and Floyd Carl. They were all given ID cards and on 29 September, put on a train to Paris with their guide Pierre Charnier.

1/Lt Alfred Kramer was also helped soon after landing although his helpers were suspicious at first, only being convinced of his identity after he answered a written question sent by his bombardier, 2/Lt Robert G Burnett, who was being sheltered nearby. On 9 September, Kramer was taken to a road where a car was waiting. The driver was a gendarme named Andre and he had Burnett with him. A few minutes later, they were joined by their gunner William Vickless and Andre drove the three Americans into Troyes. Kramer and Burnett stayed at Andre's house where they remained indoors until about 20 September, when Kramer was moved to Andre's brother's house and joined his pilot Arthur Swap.

S/Sgt William H Vickless was also helped soon after landing, taken home by a farmer who called two other men, one of whom took Vickless back to his home. Vickless was told that his fellow waist-gunner Walter Soukup had just left and that his radio-operator Allen Priebe had stayed overnight in the house that Vickless was going to. Next morning the farmer went into Troyes and in the afternoon, returned with a gendarme in a police wagon with his co-pilot Alfred Kramer and bombardier Robert Burnett already inside. They were driven into Troyes where Vickless stayed at the home of a gendarme (another one – query) and on the third day, a woman named Marie took him to stay with Rene Buitne (nf) where he remained until joining Swap, Kramer, Martin, Priebe, Cunningham and Brohard.

2/Lt Richard N Cunningham was the pilot of B-17 42-3425 In God We Trust (388BG/563BS) which was returning from Stuttgart on 6 September 1943 when they were attacked by fighters and the aircraft abandoned. He landed near Troyes and was soon intercepted by a French boy. The boy had apparently been looking for downed airmen because he had a bundle of civilian clothes with him that he gave Cunningham to wear before taking him on the handlebars of his bicycle, back to his home in Troyes. The boy's parents were too frightened to keep Cunningham so the boy arranged to have him taken to Rouilly-Saint-Loup and turned over to a saboteur named Louis Trepogny (nf). On 18 September, Cunningham was moved to St Parres (3 kms east of Troyes) to stay with the Mortrey family where the son was a local leader of saboteurs – his group collecting containers dropped by the RAF while Cunningham was there. At the end of the month, a girl came from Paris (Paulette Depesme) to interview Cunningham before Louis Trepogny drove him and a Belgian named Albert Kaiser, to a house in Troyes where Cunningham met Pierre Charnier – and joined Marius Brohard, Arthur Swap, Alfred Kramer, William Vickless and Hershall Richardson.

S/Sgt Marius L Brohard was a waist-gunner on B-17 42-3425 In God We Trust (Cunningham) (see above) and on landing near Sainte-Maure (just north of Troyes) was immediately hidden in a thicket by a farmer who brought him food and clothing and that night, took him to his father's house in Sainte-Maure. Later that night, three men came with bicycles to take Brohard into Troyes where he stayed with the same gendarme (Andre) who later sheltered Alfred Kramer. Brohard was interviewed by the English wife of one of the men who had collected him and on 10 September, was taken to stay with Raymond Wagner (head of the Troyes organisation) at 41 rue du Faubourg Croncels. He joined Allen Priebe, who had been collected by Wagner earlier, and Wagner brought a message from his pilot Richard Cunningham. On about 20 September, a girl (small, pretty, brunette) came from Paris to get their names and take their photographs, and she stayed the night at Wagner's house. On 29 September, Pierre came from Paris and had a meeting with the evaders in a bakery where they were divided into groups, each with their own guide – Brohard and Cunningham being taken by 'the mademoiselle' who lived in the flat above the Wagner family.

S/Sgt Herschell L Richardson was the right waist-gunner of B-17 42-30000 (92BG/327BS) (Bogard) which was returning from Stuttgart on 6 September 1943 when it was attacked by fighters and abandoned west of Troyes. Richardson landed about a quarter of a mile south of Estissac, some twenty kms west of Troyes, and a few moments later, was joined by his ball-turret gunner S/Sgt Floyd M Carl. The two men walked to Chennegy where they approached a farmer who hid them in his barn, gave them food and civilian clothes and sheltered them for the next four days. On 10 September, a man called Jacques arrived to take Richardson and Carl by lorry to a chateau at Chamoy where they stayed for fifteen days until a threatened German search had them moved to a barn. Jacques received supplies of guns, ammunition and explosives and told the Americans he could do with more 30 calibre machine-guns, Thompsons, smaller than

.45 automatic pistols, stout shoes and raincoats. Shortly after that their pilot 1/Lt Wayne C Bogard, radio-operator T/Sgt Max Gibbs and tail-gunner S/Sgt Cloe R Crutchfield were brought in and Jacques drove all five airmen to Troyes. After three days in Troyes, they were taken to a bakery where ID papers were being made and joined sixteen more Americans.

On 29 September, Pierre Charnier took a group of nine evaders – Arthur Swap, Alfred Kramer, William Vickless, Richard Cunningham, Marius Brohard, Hershall Richardson, Floyd Carl, Merl Martin and Allen Priebe – to Paris, where they were met by Jean-Claude Camors and taken to the Porte de Versailles apartment.[3]

The twenty airmen from Joigny and Troyes that Camors and Pierre Charnier had brought from Paris, arrived in Vannes (50 kms south-east of Lorient) at about eight o'clock on the morning of Friday 1 October and were quickly dispersed to various locations: Soren Liby, John Checketts and Terence Kearins were taken by Agnes de la Barre de Nanteuil to stay with a farmer named Levanant (nf) about six kilometres inland from Vannes. Arthur Riseley, Thomas Hedley and two Americans (assume Bieger and Rice) stayed at a house on the outskirts of Vannes, owned by a family named Filleul (nf).

Richard Cunningham and Russell Brooke stayed in Vannes with Dr Joseph Marie Audic at 12 Place Gambetta. Arthur Swap and William Vickless were sheltered near the centre of Vannes by Mme Guy Wilthew at 16 rue des Chanoines while Floyd Carl, Merl Martin and Allen Priebe were taken to stay the weekend with Mme De La Rey of 1 rue Allain Legrand. John Bieger and William Rice say they were sheltered in Vannes with a widow (no name given).

Alfred Kramer and Hershall Richardson were taken to Arradon (south-west of Vannes) to stay the weekend with a clergyman named Jean Allaniou while Marius Brohard and Duane Lawhead were sheltered on a farm by a M Maynard (nf).

James Wilson and Walter Hargrove were taken by bicycle to Larmor-Baden. Their guide was a dark haired, eighteen-year-old girl named Catherine de la Barre de Nanteuil who then took them by boat to the small island of Ile de la Jument. They were sheltered with her aunt (query) Solange Defforges and her husband Eugene Defforges (a sixty-four-year-

---

3   The other fifteen Americans left Troyes for Paris in two more groups shortly afterwards – one of which included Wayne Bogard, Max Gibbs and Cloe Crutchfield who were later taken to Rennes by Pierre Charnier.

old former naval officer – and active resistant) and his brother-in-law (query), brother of the Belgian Consul in London.[4]

Another group of evaders were assembled in Paris at the home of Henri Marechaux on rue de la Chapelle – only going briefly to the apartment at Porte de Versailles before being taken by train to Quimper in Brittany (about half way between Brest and Lorient) on Monday 4 October.[5]

1/Lt Demetrios Karnezis was the pilot of B-17 42-3293 Slightly Dangerous (388BG/560BS) which was shot down returning from Stuttgart on 6 September 1943. He was sheltered at La Chapitre (Yonne) until 10 September when he was taken to Paris. He was sheltered by Henri Marechaux, wife Emilienne and son Jacques at 19 rue de la Chapelle, Paris XVIII, being joined there by Warren Graff, Frank Kimotek, Edwin Myers and Andre Poirier.

F/O Warren E Graff was returning from a bomber escort sortie to Germany on 30 July 1943 in P-47 41-6391 (78FG/82FS) when he was shot down by enemy fighters. Graff landed near Dunkirk and after evading alone for six days, finally approached a farmhouse. Through a series of helpers, Graff was eventually taken to Wicquinghem (Pas-de-Calais) where the maire, Gaston Peroy, sheltered him for a week before taking him to the Fillerin farm at Renty. After two and half weeks with Mme Marguerite Fillerin and her three children (husband Norbert had been arrested on 5 March 1943), he and French pilot evader Andre Poirier were driven to Anvin (on about 28 August), taken by train to Paris by M Peroy's son Lucien and delivered to the Marechaux apartment on rue de la Chapelle. After a few days, Poirier left with his father, Georges.[6] Graff was visited by Raoul and Pierre and on 6 September, joined by Demetrios Karnezis and Frank Kimotek.

S/Sgt Frank Kimotek was the radio-operator of B-17 42-29635 Augerhead (303BG/358BS) (Monahan) which was over Amiens on 31 August 1943 when they were attacked by fighters and the aircraft abandoned. Kimotek

4   Agnes de la Barre de Nanteuil (born September 1922), her sister Catherine and the Defforges, were arrested in March 1944 and deported. Agnes was in the last convoy of prisoners from Rennes in August when their train was attacked by Allied aircraft and she was fatally injured. Her mother Sabine was la vicomtesse Gabriel de la Barre de Nanteuil (born January 1899) of 35 rue Jeanne d'Arc, Vannes. (WO208-5459)

5   Henri Alfred Marechaux (born April 1896) wife Emilienne Augustine (born February 1900) and son Jacques Raymond Marechaux (born September 1926) of 19 rue de la Chappelle, were arrested at Rugles (Eure) on 4 January 1944 and deported. Henri and Jacques were sent to Flossenberg where Henri died on 25 October 1944 and Jacques disappeared – only Emilienne, who was recommended for a KMC, returned. (WO208-5452 & 5454)

6   Georges Poirier was arrested on 18 November 1943 and deported to Charleville – where he died on 4 June 1944. (IS9(AB)/F/4336)

came down just south-west of Dieppe, landing in a tree where he stayed for some time because he could hear people below. When he did finally climb down, he was spotted immediately by a group of Frenchmen who had been searching for him. They took his parachute and flying gear but then scattered at the approach of some German soldiers. After hiding overnight, Kimotek met an elderly man who gave him some food and civilian clothing and the following afternoon, Kimotek approached a large farm where he was taken in and given a meal. After two more farmers were called, one of whom spoke English, Kimotek to taken to another farm to stay overnight. When Kimotek told them he wanted to go to Paris, one of the farmers arranged to have him taken to the railway station at Senoport and for a young woman schoolteacher to go with him to the capital. They met the woman's cousin, a young girl called Therese, who took Kimotek back to her apartment where first Pierre (an ex-officer in the French army, about forty-five years old, short and stocky with thin, light coloured hair) and then a man called Maurice came and interrogated him. Next day, Maurice and Therese took him to an apartment next to the German hospital near the Gare du Nord where Kimotek stayed until French pilot evader Andre Poirier took him to the Marechaux apartment at 19 rue de la Chapelle where he joined Warren Graff.

T/Sgt Edwin R Myers was the radio-operator of B-17 42-29789 Big Time Operator (381BG/535BS) (Zum) which was over Romilly on 3 September 1943 when they were attacked by fighters. After losing two engines, the aircraft was abandoned. Myers made a deliberately delayed jump, aiming for a wood (which he missed completely) and landing in an open field near Chalmaison (Seine-et-Marne). After walking to nearby Famboin, Myers was helped by various people until being taken to the home of a clergyman in Chalmaison. Nine girls from Paris (aged between fourteen and twenty-three) were staying there and after about six days, two of the girls and their mother, took Myers to their apartment in Paris. On about 15 October, he was moved to a hotel opposite the Saint-Philippe du Roule Metro station (presumably on Avenue Victor Emmanuelle III – now Avenue Franklin D Roosevelt) where the owner took care of him. A week later, Myers was taken to stay with Mme Suzanne Sykes at 27 rue Brezin, Garches, Seine-et-Oise for another week before he was returned to Paris and taken to the Marechaux apartment at 19 rue de la Chapelle.

On Monday 4 October, Paulette Depesme (aka Jeanette) came to collect the four Americans and they joined Camors and Pierre Charnier who were taking Jack Ryan and Wayne Rader by train to Quimper in Brittany.

2/Lt Jack E Ryan and 2/Lt Wayne S Rader were the co-pilot and bombardier of B-17 42-30001 Mary Ann (379BG/526BS) (Bedwell) which was over Le Bourget on the morning of 16 August 1943 when they were attacked by fighters. With only two functioning engines and the inter-phone, electrical systems and tail-guns knocked out, the aircraft was abandoned.

Ryan landed near Morsang-sur-Seine (Ile-de-France, south-east of Paris) and that evening, met a woodcutter who brought Eugene Isadore Fauze (Ryan says Foss), owner of a hotel at Morsang-sur-Seine. The following evening, M Fauze and his son took Ryan to the river Seine where two teenage brothers, Roland (19) and Claude (16) rowed him across and took him to their home where he stayed with their parents, father (name not given), a retired salesman, and Suzanne Papoint, a mid-wife of 18 rue de l'Avenir, Corbeil-Essonnes. Mme Papoint owned a maternity home (employing one nurse and a maid) and Ryan had been there for two nights when a local resistance leader, M Houdet (nf) came to Ryan and told him that his bombardier Wayne Rader was being sheltered by a one-armed and (allegedly) rather psychopathic young Frenchman who was refusing to let him go unless he was promised an American decoration. M Houdet, Jacques Houdet, Roland and Claude took Ryan to the house where they persuaded the Frenchman to let Rader go. Ryan and Rader then returned to the nursing home where they stayed for the next six weeks.

Rader was thrown from the aircraft when it exploded and he landed near Corbeil-Essonnes, close to his navigator 2/Lt Mario W Delke Jnr. Delke had a broken leg and insisted on Rader leaving him but he didn't get far before a crowd of Frenchmen appeared. Rader decided to avoid them and ran across some swamp-land to a road where he used another group of Frenchmen as camouflage to leave the immediate area. He soon met another man who called some friends to bring clothes and food. They also brought a doctor and that night, one of them stayed with Rader in a deserted hut. The following night, a one-armed man of about twenty-three arrived and took Rader back to his house in Corbeil-Essonnes.

On 30 September, M Houdet brought a 'beautiful twenty-one-year-old girl' who took Ryan and Rader by train into Paris and an apartment in Issy-les-Moulineaux (or Port de Versailles) where Raoul (Camors) took them to have their photographs taken and false papers were made for them. They also met Pierre Charnier, who was supposed to meet a party of eleven men from Troyes at the Gare de Lyon that evening and bring them to the nearby

Gare de Montparnasse where they would join Ryan and Rader. The plan was then for Jeanette (Paulette Depesme) to take them to Vannes but when Pierre's group failed to arrive, Jeanette took Ryan and Rader to Vannes anyway. Unfortunately, Raoul was the only one who knew how to contact the group in Vannes and he was with Pierre at the Gare de Lyon. When Raoul failed to arrive in Vannes, Jeanette took Ryan and Rader back to Paris where they found a note saying that Raoul had already left for Vannes with the evaders from Troyes, plus another group of airmen that Pierre had brought from Joigny. Rather than go back to Vannes immediately, Jeanette decided they should stay in the Issy-les-Moulineaux apartment until after the weekend. Before they left Paris, Jeanette went to another house (19 rue de la Chapelle) where she collected Demetrios Karnezis, Warren Graff, Frank Kimotek and Edwin Myers, and Raoul and Pierre took all six Americans by train to Quimper, arriving late (after curfew) on Monday 4 October.

From Quimper, the airmen were taken in groups by Mlle Joe (Mme Ghislaine Niox), Pierre Philippon and another Frenchman (Jean de la Pateliere – query), to various homes to wait the six hours for an early morning train to Brest. Mme Niox and Pierre Philippon then took the airmen to Brest where they were met by Paul Le Baron before Mme Niox took them to stay with her parents, Colonel and Jeanne Scheidhauer at rue Neptune.[7]

Meanwhile, Camors visited Marguerite Vourc'h at Plomodiern before he and Yves Vourc'h went to make final arrangements for the operation with local organiser Pierre Merrien at Camaret.

On Tuesday morning (5 October) seven of the evaders brought to Vannes from Paris the previous Friday – Arthur Riseley, Thomas Hedley, Richard Cunningham, Russell Brooke, Floyd Carl, Merl Martin and Allen Priebe – were returned to Vannes station where they met four more evading airmen.

Donald McGourlick, Harold Nielsen, Thomas Adams and Lionel Drew arrived by train from Nantes and while McGourlick stayed in

---

7   Paul Jean Le Baron (born August 1924) of 2 rue Traverse de l'Eglise, Brest was awarded a KMC. (WO208/5453)

Colonel Scheidhauer's wife Jeanne was later killed in the bombardment of Brest. Their son, Sous-Lt Bernard W M Scheidhauer, also died. He ran out of fuel in his 131 Sqn Spitfire on 18 November 1942 and landed on Jersey where he was captured. Sent to Stalag Luft III (Sagan) he escaped on 25 March 1944 and was one of the fifty men who were murdered after their recapture. Despite these personal tragedies, Colonel Michel William Scheidhauer (born March 1877) continued his "magnificent work for the Allied cause" and was awarded an OBE. (WO208/5451)

Vannes, Nielson, Adams and Drew joined the other seven airmen to take the train for Brest.

F/O Donald F McGourlick RCAF was the tail-gunner of 106 Sqn Lancaster DV196 (Wodehouse) which was returning from Milan the night of 7-8 August 1943 and approaching Dijon when some incendiaries which had hung-up in the bomb bay, ignited and set the aircraft on fire.

McGourlick landed near Bligny-sur-Ourche (Cote d'Or, Burgundy) and was sheltered, along with two of his crew, wireless operator Sgt Harold L Nielsen and flight engineer Sgt Thomas H Adams, by Georges Baudoin at Notre Dame, Semur-en-Auxois. On 16 August, the three airmen were taken by train to Joigny by a man named Alain Lascombes and that same night, driven to Aillant-sur-Tholon where they stayed with veterinary surgeon Pierre Argoud, his wife and daughter. Here they met Lionel Drew and on 18 August, McGourlick and Drew were moved to Saint-Aubin-Chateau-Neuf where they stayed with the maire Maxine Carre while Nielsen and Adams went to Bleury (Poilly-sur-Tholon) where they stayed with *cultivateur* Lucien Boudot. On 6 September, Nielson and Adams joined them at St Aubin and all four were immediately taken back to Joigny and on to Paris by two men – Raoul (Camors) (tall and dark) and Pierre (short and fair). Raoul and Pierre (Charnier) took them to an apartment where they stayed until 8 September when they were moved to the Hotel de Paris (or Grand Hotel de France) at 27 rue de Provence, Paris IX. On 12 September, they were moved to an apartment in the Mairie d'Issy district (or Port de Versailles). On 23 September, Raoul and Pierre took them by train to Nantes, where Nielsen and Adams stayed in a small village about 6 kms south of Nantes while McGourlick and Drew went on to Sainte-Pazanne (about 20 kms SW of Nantes) to stay with painter and decorator Robert Garand and his wife Renee on rue de la Cure. On 4 October, they were taken back to Nantes, collecting Nielsen and Adams at the station on the way. At Nantes they were supposed to join Raoul and Pierre who were coming from Paris with twenty Americans. They stayed with a man called Jacques Dubois (which I'm guessing is a pseudonym) until ten that evening before going to the house of a French ex-officer until five the following morning when the train from Paris was due. They joined the train and proceeded to Vannes, arriving there at about eight-thirty in the morning of 5 October. McGourlick then left the others to be sheltered with Marcel Charles (head of a sabotage organisation) at rue Marechal Foch.

1/Lt Lionel E Drew Jnr had baled out on 25 June 1943 from a 423 BS B-17 (so far unidentified) which then returned to England. He landed about four miles north-east of Pont l'Eveque (Calvados) and that evening, found shelter at La Raconciere with Hubert Caillaux and family. Four days later, Hubert took Drew into town and passed him on to Georges Castelaine (only Rene Castelaine found in IS9 list) and Drew stayed on the second floor of his restaurant. Some time later, Drew was taken to stay on a farm near Ouilly-du-Houley with Edouard and Clara Lanos. While he was there, Drew met a red-haired man of about twenty-seven called Andre who came from Lisieux and rode a motorcycle. After five weeks at the Lanos farm, Andre took Drew by bicycle to Lisieux and Pierre Cornet (an ex-aviator) took Drew by train to Paris.

They were met by two boys – one of them Adrien, a friend of Raoul's and the other "a chap with fair hair and a moustache, who spoke good English and did not look French" and the fair-haired chap took Drew to an apartment near the Convention Metro station (Paris XV). Next day, Pierre Cornet took Drew to his apartment at 51 rue Vauvenargues, Paris XVII where Drew met Pierre's wife Francine and their three children before Adrien returned him to the first apartment. On the third day, Pierre Cornet took Drew to the Gare de Lyon and gave him a ticket for Joigny (Yonne).

After dinner at a hotel with some people called Allient (nf), Drew was taken to stay with veterinary Pierre Argoud at his home in Aillant-sur-Tholon – where he was joined by Donald McGourlick, Harold Nielsen and Thomas Adams.

The ten evaders who left Vannes that Monday morning on the train for Brest were (again) split into groups: Russell Brooke, Floyd Carl, Merl Martin, and Allen Priebe got off at Quimper where Pierre Phillipon took them to stay overnight with Mme Selan (Mme Celton of Ergue-Armel – query). Next day, Pierre took them on an afternoon train to Douarnenez where they stayed with Marcel Laurent and Mlle Marguerite Seznec at 3 rue Emile Zola until 30 October.[8]

Harold Nielsen, Thomas Adams and Lionel Drew got off at Chateaulin where they were met by Mme Vve Christine Aimee Magne who took them back to her house in the tiny village of Saint-Nic. On 21 October, they were moved from Saint-Nic because the Gestapo were looking for Mme Magne's sister, Ghislaine Niox – Ghislaine and Paul Le Baron took them to Brest

---

8   Russell Brooke and Floyd Carl were later evacuated by MGB on Operation Envious IIb – and Merle Martin and Allen Priebe on Operation Felicitate II.

where they stayed overnight with Mme Magne's parents, Colonel and Mme Scheidhauer at rue Neptune and then with Mme Yvonne de la Marniere at 17 rue Voltaire. Two weeks later they left for Landerneau and on to Ile Guennoc – all three airmen were later evacuated by RN MGB on Operation Felicitate II.

Arthur Riseley, Thomas Hedley and Richard Cunningham stayed with their guide Yves Vourc'h all the way to Brest where they were sheltered by Colonel Scheidhauer (chief of the local Civil Defence) at 1 rue Neptune, and where they were joined by Jack Ryan's group of six from Paris. Ryan's group had been taken to Quimper by Camors and Pierre Charnier on Monday evening before being brought to Colonel Scheidhauer's house the following morning by his eldest daughter Ghislaine Niox. Note that it is not certain from the conflicting reports which group arrived first or exactly when.

On 11 October 1943, Jean-Claude Camors, Remy Roure and other members of the Bordeaux-Loupiac organisation were in Rennes and that evening, they gathered at the tiny, back-street cafe de l'Epoque at 16 rue Pre Botte. They were waiting to collect a group of evaders (including Wayne Bogard, Max Gibbs and Cloe Crutchfield who had been brought from Paris by Pierre Charnier the previous day) and take them to the coast. Tragically, Camors recognised (and was recognised by) the French traitor Roger Leneveu and in the ensuing confrontation, Leneveu shot both Camors and Roure. Although Roure survived to be deported to Buchenwald (which he also survived) Jean-Claude Francois Camors died of his wounds later that night – just eight days before his twenty-fourth birthday.[9]

Soren Liby, John Checketts and Terence Kearins stayed in Vannes until (about) 12 October when they were taken to Quimper. They were sheltered overnight with the wife of a garage proprietor, before being taken on to Chateaulin and a church some 10 kms away at Menez-Hom.[10] They stayed one day and night, sharing with three Americans – Swap, Vickless and Rice – who had been brought there by Pierre Philippon, before walking

---

9   Roger Eugene Victor Leneveu (born February 1919 in Calvados) – also known as Roger la Legionnaire, having served five years with the Foreign Legion – was arrested in July 1942 trying to smuggle Jewish refugees into Spain. After three months in prison, he was recruited as a German agent that October. On 27 May 1944, Roger Leneveu and fellow V-Mann Robert Demay were caught trying to infiltrate a maquis group at Mont Mouchet (Auvergne). Demay was killed in the ensuing gun-fight and Leneveu wounded. After interrogation, Leneveu was executed the following morning.

10   Laurence Christu contacted me in March 2014 to confirm that it was his grand-parents, Armand and Fernande Nargeot who sheltered Liby, Checketts and Kearins overnight in their home at 3 rue du Pont l'Abbe in Quimper. He says that he had heard the story from childhood of the airmen staying and how the Germans had come to the door that evening. Fernande kept them talking while her daughter Jeanne, Laurence's mother, took the three airmen and hid them in the *soldatenkino* (a cinema for German soldiers) which opened into their garden, until the Germans left.

to Crozon and then Morgat where all six stayed with Mons E Gouriou, proprietor of the Hotel Sainte-Marine. The hotel, close to the beach at Morgat, had been requisitioned by the Germans and the evaders actually stayed in M Gouriou's house next door. On 18 October, the six airmen were taken to Camaret-sur-Mer where a party of twenty-three were assembled in M Bathany's bakery before being taken to board a fishing boat.

Arthur Swap and William Vickless stayed with Mme Guy Wilthew at 16 rue des Chanoines in Vannes for about eight days until a young friend of Raoul's (Jean de la Patelliere – query), who lived in Vannes, took Swap, Vickless and six others (Kramer and Richardson, Brohard and Lawhead, Wilson and Hargrove) to Quimper. Swap and Vickless stayed overnight in a radio repair shop and next day, were taken on to Plomodiern. They walked to the church at Menez-Hom where they stayed for a day and night before going on by train to Morgat to stay with M Gouriou, owner of the Hotel Sainte-Marine, along with Liby, Checketts, Kearins and Rice. After five days at Morgat, Swap and Vickless walked the seven or so kilometres to Camaret while the other four were driven by a doctor. At Camaret, they went to M Bathany's bakery where twenty-one other evaders and four Frenchmen were gathered.

William Rice seems to have shared with John Bieger in Vannes, staying on after Bieger left until about 13 October, when he was taken to Chateaulin, where he changed trains for Crozon then walked to Morgat. He stayed next to the Hotel Sainte-Marine with Swap, Vickless, Liby, Checketts and Kearins for five or six days before a doctor drove him, Liby, Checketts and Kearins to Camaret.

Arthur Riseley, Thomas Hedley and Richard Cunningham joined Jack Ryan's group of six – Ryan, Rader, Demetrios Karnezis, Warren Graff, Frank Kimotek and Edwin Myers – and all nine were provided with passes, certifying they were working in the prohibited zone.

On 16 October, Paul Le Baron took the nine airmen by train from Brest to Chateaulin (where I think they may have changed trains anyway) but were told the weather was too bad to let them go on to Camaret and so got off at Plomodiern instead. They walked to the stone church at Menez-Hom where they joined eight others (McGourlick, Kramer, Richardson, Brohard, Lawhead, Bieger, Wilson and Hargrove) and spent the night.[11]

11   Many of the evaders refer to a stone church near Plomodiern which Roger Huguen identifies as la Chapelle Sainte Marie du Menez-Hom. It can be found today on the D887, just north of Plomodiern and almost due east of Saint-Nic.

Donald McGourlick stayed in Vannes until 10 October, when Jacques Dubois took him to Quimper. On 15 October, he was taken to Plomodiern and the church at Menez-Hom where he met Riseley, Jack Ryan et al.

Alfred Kramer and Hershall Richardson stayed in Arradon until (about) 10 October when one of M Allaniou's sons took them to Quimper and passed them over to Pierre Philippon. Pierre delivered them to a bakery for one night then moved them to stay with lawyer Albert Forget at 5 rue Valentine. A few days later, Pierre (and another Frenchman) took them to the church at Menez-Hom where, on the second night, they were joined by Jack Ryan et al.

Marius Brohard and Duane Lawhead were sheltered for about a week in a farmhouse near Vannes until Pierre Philippon took them to his house in Quimper. They were joined by John Bieger (also brought from Vannes by Pierre) and on 16 October, by another five evaders (McGourlick, Kramer, Richardson, Wilson and Hargrove) to be taken by train to Chateaulin. The eight men then walked to the stone church at Menez-Hom where they stayed four days, being joined on the second night by Cunningham, Jack Ryan et al.

James Wilson and Walter Hargrove spent about ten days on the island off Larmor-Baden before Catherine de la Barre de Nanteuil brought them back to Vannes and took them by train to Quimper, where they joined Brohard and Lawhead.

On 18 October, the seventeen evaders at Menez-Hom were divided into two groups – Ryan's group went back to Plomodiern and the others went slightly further west, to Saint-Nic before both groups caught the same train to Camaret. They were met by French guides who led them to a baker's home on the water-front where the evaders from Morgat were already waiting (making twenty-three airmen plus three young Frenchmen). Early next morning, they were rowed out into the harbour in small groups to board an eleven-metre fishing boat called *Suzanne-Renée*. Unfortunately the boat was so crowded that four of the airmen – Duane Lawhead, James Wilson, Walter Hargrove and William Rice – had to be left behind.[12]

The *Suzanne-Renée* stayed another four days in harbour waiting for the weather to improve before her crew – Jean Marie Francois Balcon,

12   Duane Lawhead was later collected by MGB 318 (Mason) on Operation Envious IIb from Ile Tariec (Aber-Benoit) at the beginning of December – and James Wilson, Walter Hargrove and William Rice on Operation Felicitate II from the neighbouring Ile Guennoc on Christmas Day – both operations were organised by Pierre Hentic (Trellu/Maho) of the SIS Jade-Fitzroy intelligence network.

Joseph Morvan and Alain Marchand – were able to set out from Camaret-sur-Mer on the morning of Saturday 23 October. They remained with the fishing fleet until nightfall when they headed first west and then north, finally reaching Penzance in Cornwall at about five o'clock the following afternoon.[13]

13   More details on Jean-Claude Camors and the Suzanne-Renee episode can be found in 'Par les nuits les plus longues' (1976) by Roger Huguen, published by Les Presses Bretonnes, Saint-Brieuc, page 129 onwards. My thanks also to Anne Ploux Vourc'h for some of the information used in this chapter.

CHAPTER 32

Motheral and Dumsday – Pas-de-Calais to the Pyrenees

On 31 October 1943, P/O Clarence Motheral, P/O William Dumsday, T/
Sgt Grant Carter, 2/Lt Franklin Resseguie and T/Sgt John Wagner – plus
two Dutchmen, four Belgians and three Frenchmen – were taken by train
to Toulouse and Perpignan.

P/O Clarence O Motheral RCAF and P/O William J Dumsday RCAF
were the pilot and navigator of 180 Sqn TAF Mitchell FL190 which was
returning from St Omer on the evening of 30 August 1943 when they were
hit by flak and the aircraft abandoned.[1]

Motheral landed near Steenvoorde (Nord-Pas-de-Calais) and Dumsday
at nearby Eecke. They were brought together by their helpers that evening
and their journey arranged.

A man known locally as de Gaulle took them to a farm near Eecke
belonging to Paul Vanoudendycke (of Saint-Pol-de-Mer) – de Gaulle was
a member of an organisation and he provided Motheral and Dumsday
with a set of good quality clothes that they wore throughout their journey.
After breakfast on 1 September, Motheral and Dumsday were taken by
Paul Vanoudendycke and two members of the organisation by train to
Hazebrouck and Armentieres. They were met by the wife of one of the
guides, Jules Houcke (the maire of Pont-de-Nieppe) and his brother
Marcel. Motheral went with Marcel to his house at 325 Route Nationale
whilst Dumsday went with the maire to his house at 216 Route Nationale.
That evening the two evaders were taken to stay with Mme Stephanie
Planquart (who kept a herbalist shop) at 302 Route Nationale. On 7
September, following the arrest of one of the guides who had taken them
to Armentieres, Motheral and Dumsday were moved to spend the day with
the maire's sister (address unknown). That evening they were taken by
bicycle to La Creche, Bailleul, where they had a meal with Jean Sonneville,
before being taken (at midnight) to stay with a French customs official
named Lucien Regeaux (nf) who dealt in contraband and lived in a house

---

1   The other two FL190 crewmen, wireless operator F/Sgt Victor E Scuse and air gunner Sgt Efion
Lewis, were killed.

belonging to Jean Sonneville. On about 28 September, they moved back to Jean Sonneville's home and then on about 21 October, returned to stay with Stephanie Planquart.

On 23 October, a woman member of the organisation visited, took their personal details and said she was going to Paris to make arrangements for them. About four days later, Jean Sonneville and his cousin (another Marcel) took Motheral and Dumsday by bicycle back to Jean Sonneville's house in Bailleul and the following day, cousin Marcel took them by bus to Lille to meet a British captain (Michael Trotobas) who was head of the organisation there. That evening they were taken to Arras where they stayed the night (address unknown) and the following afternoon (26 October) went to a cafe where they met the maire of Bapaume, Abel Guidet.[2] The maire drove them to Bapaume where they stayed with Madeleine Duclercq at 17 rue Felix Faure and met American fighter pilot, Franklin Resseguie. Next day, the maire drove Motheral, Dumsday and Resseguie a few miles south to a house in Peronne. On 28 October, an elderly lady (known as Mme Blanche) (Henriette Balesi) took them on the ten o'clock train to Paris. They followed her to a cathedral (probably l'Eglise Saint-Laurent on Boulevard de Magenta, near the Gare du Nord) where they were handed over to two women, one of whom took them to stay with Simone Levavasseur at 19 Avenue d'Orleans.

On 31 October, Mlle Levavasseur and her friend Mme Audette (nf) (who had a wine shop nearby) took Motheral, Dumsday and Resseguie to the Gare d'Austerlitz where they joined a group of Frenchmen in the charge of one of the women they had met at the cathedral. The group were split into twos and threes, each with a French guide, and boarded the nine o'clock overnight train to Toulouse, arriving at ten o'clock the following morning.

T/Sgt Grant Carter was the radio-operator of B-17 42-5057 (305BG/422BS) (Dahly) which was returning from Stuttgart on 6 September 1943 and into a strong head-wind. Running low on fuel, they eventually fell out of formation and after half an hour of evasive manoeuvres against fighter attacks, the aircraft was abandoned over Picardy.

Carter was sheltered with a variety of people in and around Blangy-sur-Bresle until meeting up with his navigator Allan Johnston – see earlier. After they were separated in Paris, a girl (Jeanne Gueremy – query) took

2   Abel Guidet (born November 1890) of 44 rue Faubourg de Peronne, Bapaume was arrested on 27 November 1943 and deported to Gross-Strelitz, a lime quarry work camp attached to Lamsdorf. He was later transferred to Gross-Rosen concentration camp where he died in November the following year. (WO208/5456)

Carter to 51 rue de Miromesnil and a sixth-floor apartment, upstairs from her own, where he stayed with engineer Jean De Traz and his wife Laure. He was joined by John Wagner and they were there for two weeks until Dr Alice Willm (Sigmund Sandvik says he met Wagner and Carter at Dr Willm's before a Mlle Francoise took them elsewhere) took them to meet a blonde lady (aged about 30) who took them to Montreuil (Seine) where they stayed overnight in a small grocery shop (probably with Mme Jeanne Delapraye at 71 rue Beaumarchais). Next morning a girl (aged about 23) took them by Metro to the Gare d'Austerlitz where they met the Lady in Black with a group of evaders and their guides – including Jean de Gennes (nf) (born in Indiana).

2/Lt Franklin B Resseguie was flying P-47 41-6240 (78FG/84FD) to relieve a Spitfire escort of B-17s on 18 October 1943 when engine trouble forced him to drop out of formation. As he lost altitude, he was hit by flak which stopped the engine and he baled out near Arras.

Resseguie was helped immediately on landing and taken to a house on the edge of St Leger (Nord-Pas-de-Calais) where an Englishman (stocky, with a moustache) from the resistance organised his evasion. Next morning, Resseguie was taken to the maire of St Leger who gave him clothes and an ID card and then the Englishman took him by bicycle to the maire of Bapaume, Abel Guidet, where he was sheltered in an apartment above the mairie for the rest of the afternoon. A white-haired lady known as Mme Blanche (Henriette Balesi) took him to the house of a French-speaking Belgian woman (wife of an Englishman now in the UK) (Madeleine Duclercq) where Resseguie joined two Canadian airmen, Clarence Motheral and William Dumsday – S/Sgt Orville Greene and T/Sgt Bertil Erickson also report meeting Resseguie here. On 27 October, Resseguie, Motheral and Dumsday were taken to Paris by the short, white-haired lady. She took them to a church and passed them over to a tall woman (about fifty years old) and a younger woman (nice looking, about 38 or 40) (Simone Levavasseur – who refers to Motheral and Dumsday as Curly and Bill) who owned a perfumery (sic) at 14 Avenue d'Orleans where they stayed until the end of the month. On 31 October, a young girl took Resseguie, Motheral and Dumsday to the Gare d'Austerlitz where they joined Grant Carter, John Wagner, two Dutchmen, four Belgians and three Frenchmen.

T/Sgt John M Wagner was the radio-operator of B-17 42-3452 (100BG/350BS) (Vetter) which was damaged by flak over Paris on 15

September 1943 and attacked by fighters. With two engines out and the instrument panel shot away, the aircraft was abandoned at low altitude to crash north of Beauvais.[3]

Wagner landed in a field (damaging his ankle in the process) where local people were waiting to help him. He was taken to a farmhouse where he met his pilot Arthur Vetter and tail-gunner Warren Lush. Next day, the three airmen were moved to another farm and the following day taken to Clermont where they stayed with Gaston Legrand and Odette Sauvage on rue du Chatelier for twenty-five days, being joined there by William Boren and Francis Anderson from B-26 41-31721 Cactus Jack.[4]

Boren and Anderson left for Paris on 5 October and a week later, Wagner, Vetter and Lush were also taken by train to the capital. Wagner stayed with Madeleine Melot at 11 bis rue Larrey and Vetter with the Moet family at Saint-Mande (where he joined Joe Balfe's elder son John Paul) while Lush was taken to rue Montmartre where he joined Francis Anderson (see later). About two weeks later, Wagner was moved to rue de Miromesnil where he joined Grant Carter who was being sheltered by Jean and Laure De Traz.

One of their guides from Paris is described as an English-looking man (whatever that means) of medium height, dark complexion and a moustache and he took them by overnight train to Toulouse. They had a meal at the station restaurant before catching the three o'clock afternoon train to Perpignan – arriving after nightfall at about six that evening. They were met by two girls and taken by bicycle to meet their Spanish mountain guides who gave them a meal of bread and sardines, along with some soft-soled shoes – presumably local traditional espadrilles. They spent the rest of the night and all next day hiding under some bushes until setting off the following evening.

It was pouring with rain and it continued to rain throughout their journey. They walked through the night then lay up until the following evening when they again walked through the night (and crossed the frontier) and through the early morning of 4 November. Resseguie, Carter and one of the Belgians lost their guide and the rest of the party but they

3   Seven of the 42-3452 crew evaded successfully – four with Bourgogne. Ball-turret gunner S/Sgt Edward W Fontaine crossed the Pyrenees with a group of Frenchmen in November. Waist-gunners S/Sgt Edward M Daly and S/Sgt Hobart C Trigg travelled to Paris with fellow crewmen Bormuth and McConnaha and then had their own adventures before making their way to Pau where they joined a party of Bourgogne evaders and crossed the Pyrenees in March 1944 – see later. Navigator 2/Lt Wendell K McConnaha died crossing the Pyrenees in December 1943.

4   Wagner was helped by Jacques Buquet at Laneuvilleroy (Oise) and the Herve and Violet families also sheltered him, Vetter and Lush in their homes at nearby Pronleroy. Vetter and Lush were also helped by Georges and Rachel Fleury in Clermont. (research by Dominique Lecomte)

made their own way on foot and by train to the British Consulate in Barcelona, arriving there on 8 November.

Motheral, Dumsday and Wagner were also separated from the group and just after crossing a river on 6 November, were captured by some Spanish soldiers. They were taken to Figueras where they spent six days in prison before being transferred to Gerona, Saragossa and finally Alhama de Aragon for three days until they were released and sent to Madrid.

CHAPTER 33

Two Pairs to Perpignan

On 14 November 1943, Sgt Guy Marulli de Barletta, Sgt France Delorie, F/O David Prosser and S/Sgt Willard McLain left Paris by train for Toulouse, Narbonne and Perpignan.[1]

Sgt Guy Marulli de Barletta was the radio-operator of 342 (Lorraine) Sqn Boston BZ388 (Lucchesi) on a daylight operation to a power station outside Paris on 3 October 1943. They were hit by flak over the target which stopped the port engine. Twenty minutes later, the starboard engine also failed and the aircraft was crash-landed at Jonquieres (Oise) south-west of Compiegne. Navigator P/O Barabier (who was badly injured) and rear gunner Sgt Godin were captured but pilot Yves Lucchesi (see earlier) also evaded successfully with Bourgogne.

After the crash-landing, Lucchesi and Godin went off to try and find help while Marulli stayed with the injured P/O Baralier but when German troops arrived to search the area, Baralier ordered Marulli to leave him. Next morning, Marulli set off in a westerly direction, reaching Sacy-le-Grand and asking a farm worker for help. Marulli then went on to a small hotel near Liancourt where he stayed while the owner contacted a man in Compiegne who contacted an organisation. On 2 November, Marulli was taken to Compiegne where he stayed overnight with M et Mme Louis at 4 Impasse Puiscernea (IS9 has Mme Eugenie Louis at 4 Impasse Dupuy Correard). The following day, two women took him to Paris where he stayed with Madeleine Melot at 11 bis rue Larrey until 13 (sic) November – just six days before she was arrested.

Sgt France B G Delorie was the bomb-aimer of 101 Sqn Lancaster W4275 (Ager) which was returning from Cologne in the early hours of 9 July 1943 when they were attacked by fighters. The controls were shot away and the aircraft abandoned to crash near Guise (Aisne) – Delorie was the only successful evader.

---

1   In their reports, the two Frenchmen say they left Paris on 13 November and the Americans say 14 November, but neither date is guaranteed. However, they all travelled on the same train and I think that Sunday 14 November is the most likely day of their departure.

Delorie (who was from the Seychelles) landed in a field near the hamlet of Feronval. After hiding his flying gear and parachute, Delorie spent the rest of the night hiding in some woods. Next day he declared himself to a farmer who brought him food and then led him to a barn where Delorie spent the rest of the day. That night, Dr Maurice Sablon collected Delorie and took him to the Hotel du Commerce in Etreaupont (Aisne) where he stayed for two nights. On 12 July, Dr Sablon drove Delorie to a farm at Auge owned by a M Vant'Westeinde, where Delorie stayed for ten and a half weeks, looked after by Dr Alain Josso from nearby Aubenton.

On 21 September, Dr Josso took Delorie to a farm at Liart for the night and the following morning, a M Fournesse (nf) took him to the railway station at Charleville. That evening, a guide arrived from Paris and on 23 September, Delorie was taken to Fontenay-sous-Bois where he stayed with Georges Masse at 97 rue des Moulins. He was visited there by Marie (Gabrielle Wiame) and also by Robert Guillet (alias Max) (head of the organisation) of 81 rue du Bac, Paris VII. M Robert told Delorie that he was very short of money and had many evaders on his hands. Robert took Delorie to meet an Englishman (said to be known as Dede at the War Office) to help explain Robert's cash problems and it was arranged that Dede would travel with Delorie. After returning to Fontenay-sous-Bois and waiting a week for Dede, Delorie was moved to 15 rue Jean-Jacques Rousseau (just off rue Saint-Honore), Paris I where he stayed with Mme Albert Kemsnviz for two nights before moving again to stay with Mme (sic) Boury at 14 rue Montmartre.[2]

On 17 October, Delorie met Dede at the Gare d'Austerlitz and they travelled together to Rosporden (Finistere) where they were met by Dr Chapelle who took them to his home in nearby Scaer. From there they went to Quimper where Delorie was told there was a plan to evacuate them by submarine but that plan (a Dahlia operation organised by Yves Le Henaff (Fanfan) see later) fell through and on about 6 November, they returned to Paris where Delorie stayed until 13 (sic) November.

Delorie was probably returned to Georges Masse at Fontenay-sous-Bois – David Prosser, who was also sheltered at Fontenay mentions travelling into Paris with him on the Metro the day they left for Toulouse.

---

2   Mlles Yvonne Renee (born June 1894) and Solange (born June 1897) Boury are credited with sheltering seven Allied evaders, some for as long as two months. Both sisters were recommended for awards. (WO208/5451)

Delorie says that although he didn't know it at the time, he travelled on the same train as Guy Marulli de Barletta and two other Frenchmen to Toulouse, where they changed for Perpignan. At Perpignan, they joined four Americans – James Wilschke, Robert Neil, David Prosser and Willard McLain – and nine more Frenchmen.

F/O David G Prosser was the navigator of B-17 42-29725 Hi-Lo Jack (92BG/407BS) (Bruce) which was on the way to Romilly-sur-Seine on 3 September 1943 when it was attacked by fighters and abandoned to crash near Aulnoy (Seine et Marne).[3]

Prosser baled out at about 20,000 feet but delayed opening his parachute until about 10,000 feet. He landed in a field (spraining his ankle) and was met by a large group of people. Prosser spoke enough French to ask them to take his flying equipment but finding no other help, set off by himself. Eventually he was challenged by two workmen who, when he told them he was an American, offered to hide him. Prosser was taken to a nearby house where his AGO card convinced his helpers that he was genuine and they asked what was wrong with his ankle.

Twenty-two-year-old David Prosser had trained with the RCAF before transferring to the US Army Air Force as a Flight Officer six months earlier and he had obviously considered the possibility of having to evade in Occupied France – in addition to wearing civilian shoes in the aircraft (which may have contributed to his badly sprained ankle) and although he already spoke some French, Prosser also had an English-French dictionary with him.

The family helping Prosser had no contacts with any escape organisation. They were also very poor so after ten days of inactivity, Prosser decided to make his own way south. The family gave him food tickets and on 16 September, Prosser was taken into Paris and put on a train for Nevers (Burgundy) where his evasion lecturers had told him that help could be found. Unfortunately Prosser found Nevers to be full of German troops and it was only by chance that he met a Czech worker who was able to put him in contact with a man who arranged his journey.

Prosser was sheltered in Nevers by Roland Blondeau at 4 Boulevard de la Republique for eight days until 25 September when he was taken by

---

3   Three of the Hi-Lo Jack crew were captured but the other six also evaded successfully: pilot 2/Lt Ralph Bruce to Switzerland, radio-operator T/Sgt Mike Flenszar and waist-gunner S/Sgt Robert D Muir with Comete, bombardier 2/Lt Bertram R Theiss crossed the Pyrenees in October, and co-pilot 2/Lt Sabron A McQueen and engineer T/Sgt Hedley E Cassidy crossed the Pyrenees from Pau in November with the Visgotha organisation.

truck about seven kilometres out of Nevers to stay with a wealthy farmer called Morac (query). Four days later, he was driven back to Nevers and the furniture shop where he had spent his first night in the town.

Prosser's basic report is excellent – and the intelligence section is written clearly in his own hand – but the Appx C is a faded, pencilled scribble by his interviewer (Donald Emerson – query) and almost illegible. Fortunately, David Prosser wrote a book called "Journey Underground" about his adventures in France and I've used that to decipher some of the notes in Prosser's report.[4]

On 29 September, two men (called Johnny and Alphonse in Prosser's book) came from Paris to collect Prosser and take him back to the capital. They arrived in Paris too late to meet their contact so went to Johnny's flat, 'on the top of a new apartment house', somewhere near Boulevard Victor Hugo. Next day, Gabrielle Wiame and her son Robert came to collect Prosser and take him to the Latin Quarter, home of the Woman in Black (11 bis rue Larrey) where he met Willard McLain and Russell Faulkiner. Mme Wiame then took Prosser and McLain to a Metro station where she passed them over to Andree Vandevoorde. Mme Vandevoorde took them by Metro to Port de Vincennes, then by bus to Fontenay-sous-Bois where they were sheltered by First World War veteran Ulysse Grassot and his wife Germaine at 159 rue du Plateau for the next six weeks. In his book, Prosser says that Mme Andree delivered them to a hardware shop with a home at the back. The owner M Pelerin (Georges Masse at 97 rue des Moulins) then drove them about ten blocks to a 'small, typically suburban bungalow' where they stayed with M Maurice, a wine merchant who was partially disabled from the First War, and his family.

Prosser uses pseudonyms for everyone in his book and Johnny is described as being American in appearance while Alphonse definitely looked Latin with his dark complexion and toothbrush moustache. Johnny told Prosser that his father was an American soldier who had married a French girl that he met during the First War. Johnny was (of course) Pierre Berteaux, and Alphonse, his brother-in-law, Andre Blateyron.

Prosser says they were 'taken about a bit' and in his book, includes a visit from M Pelerin with an RAF boy they had met in the hardware shop – the two Americans (query) with him had left that day. Frank (France Delorie) was a British subject born of French parents and brought up in Kenya. Prosser also mentions an incident on Sunday 31 October when

4   Published in 1945 by E P Dutton & Company, Inc. New York.

Mme Andree took him and McLain into Paris. They found Mme Marie (Gabrielle Wiame) waiting with two more American evaders (assume Carter and Wagner – see earlier) but their intended journey south was abandoned (later explained as there only being room for one more airman in the party and their helpers thought (erroniously) that Prosser and McLain wanted to stay together) and Andree Vandevoorde returned them once more to Fontenay-sous-Bois.

S/Sgt Willard D McLain was the ball-turret gunner of B-17 42-5843 Black Ghost (384BG/547BS) (Pulcipher) which was returning from Stuttgart on 6 September 1943 when the already flak-damaged aircraft was attacked by fighters and abandoned near Beauvais (Oise).[5]

McLain landed in a ploughed field north-west of Beauvais at about twelve-thirty in the afternoon, buried his parachute and ran to some nearby woods. Later that afternoon he approached a wood-cutter who indicated there were Germans to the north-east so McLain set off in the opposite direction. After spending the night in an isolated barn, McLain continued his walk until coming to a large clearing where he decided to wait until dark before crossing. While he was waiting he saw a Frenchman hauling hay and approached him. He was given some food and later other men came with more food and some civilian clothing. That evening he was given a pitchfork to carry and led some twenty kilometres to a house in Anderville where he was given better trousers and a note saying he would be back in England in ten days. The following afternoon, two men drove him to Clermont where he was sheltered by Gaston Legrand and Odette Sauvage at their home on rue du Chatelier and joined Russell Faulkiner, Oscar Hamblin and Harry Hawes from B-17 Lucky Thirteen who assured him (quite rightly) that he was in good hands.[6]

Faulkiner, Hamblin and Hawes left (on either Friday or Saturday) and McLain was told that he would leave following Monday (13 September). Early on Monday morning, McLain was taken by train to Creil where he stayed overnight with Marcel and Renee Gerardot at 107 rue Henri Pauquet. Next day he was taken by train to Chauny where he met Faulkiner,

---

5   Three other Black Ghost crewmen also evaded successfully: pilot 1/Lt Ralph K Pulcipher made his own way to the Pyrenees and crossed to Figueras in Spain within a few days of baling out – and Merle Johnson and Asbury Perkins with Bourgogne – see earlier.

6   In addition to the Bourgogne evaders already mentioned, Gaston Legrand and Odette Sauvage also sheltered numerous others, including many who were passed on to Paul Campinchi's reseau Francois.

Hamblin and Hawes again and he and Hamblin went to stay with Etienne Dromas at the mairie in Ugny-le-Gay. Two weeks later (McLain says on 31 September but Faulkiner etc say 29 September) McLain and Hamblin were taken back to Chauny station where they, Faulkiner and Hawes took the train to Paris. At the Jardin des Plantes they met a woman dressed in black (Madeleine Melot) who took Faulkiner back to her apartment on rue Larray. One of their guides from Chauny took McLain to the same apartment, where he saw Faulkiner and met David Prosser. Andree Vandevoorde then took McLain and Prosser to Fontenay-sous-Bois where they stayed with Ulysse Grassot and his wife Germaine at 159 rue du Plateau for the next six weeks.

On 14 November, Andree Vandevoorde took Prosser, McLain and Delorie into Paris, getting off the Metro one stop before Gare d'Austerlitz. Prosser and McLain shared a bench while Delorie and Mme Vandevoorde sat on another nearby until it was time to go to the station. Despite this pause, they still arrived at Gare d'Austerlitz some time before the train was due to leave. They were introduced to their guide, a young girl of about nineteen, and she and two of the Frenchmen who were also in the party sat with Prosser and McLain in a carriage together – Delorie having gone off with three of the other Frenchmen.

They arrived in Toulouse at about ten o'clock the following morning, where they had a disappointing meal before taking an afternoon train for Narbonne and Perpignan. They reached Perpignan at eight o'clock that evening and set off straight away for the mountains, being passed on to their Spanish mountain guide a few miles out of the town.

Delorie, Marulli, Prosser and McLain were joined on the walk across the mountains by 2/Lt James S Wilschke and S/Sgt Robert G Neil. Wilschke and Neil were the bombardier and radio-operator of B-17 42-5219 (Indiere) which was shot down by fighters near Lorient on 17 May 1943. They were helped and sheltered by numerous people and groups (none of whom seem to have had contact with any escape organisation) for several months, during which time they were moved to central France. However, seeing no further progress in sight, they finally decided made their own way south and after some days of walking, took a train to Narbonne. From Narbonne, they set off on foot once more and couple of days later, reached Rivesaltes, where they were put in touch with Jean Villaroux. On 15 November, they were taken by horse and buggy to Perpignan before setting off that evening for the mountains. They comment that although:

"the hike to Spain was pretty rough, it was much easier for us than the other [two] Americans. We had been walking thirty kilometres a day for some time whereas the others had been cooped up for weeks".

The six airmen and a group of unidentified Frenchmen set off with their three guides at about nine o'clock in the evening of 15 November. They walked through the night, reaching the foothills the following morning and climbing for another two hours before stopping about two kilometres from the frontier. They spent the rest of the day in hiding before continuing the following evening, crossing the border at about three o'clock next morning. They stopped a little later and hid up for the day before walking all the following night to Vilajuiga where they intended to get the train but were instead, arrested by the Guardia Civil and taken to Gerona.

In their MIS-X reports, the Americans don't seem to recognise the two French airmen as being Allied aircrew evaders (although Prosser acknowledges them in his book) – and the two Frenchmen apparently elected not to enlighten them.

CHAPTER 34

Journey via Carcassonne and Quillan

On 14 November 1943, S/Ldr Albert Lambert, F/O Hugh Huston, 2/Lt Howard Harris, S/Sgt Alfred Zeoli and 2/Lt Arthur Vetter left Paris by train for Toulouse and Carcassonne. There were six Frenchman in the party, including their guide, Jean-Louis Kervevant, who is described by Harris as a very short, English-speaking man with curly hair and a round, chinless face. In fact, one of the other Frenchman had been born in England but brought up in France and was married to a Frenchwoman.

S/Ldr Albert Lambert and F/O Hugh T Huston were the bomb-aimer and navigator of 405 Sqn Halifax HR854 (Foy) which was returning from Montbeliard in the early hours of 16 July 1943 when it was attacked by a night-fighter and abandoned near Bellegarde-du-Loiret (Centre). All seven crew are believed to have landed safely – and all but rear-gunner Sgt A O Prior evaded successfully – see earlier.

Lambert and Huston landed close to one another near the village of Bellegarde-du-Loiret (Centre) and quickly joined forces. They moved south, reaching a canal and then, as it started to get light, hid in a small wood for the rest of the day. Next evening, they continued along the canal until they found a way across then carried on south to hide overnight in another wood. They reached the village of Les Bordes in the early hours of 18 July and after watching for a while, approached a farmhouse where they were taken in, given a meal and some civilian clothes. They left again that evening to cross the river at Sully-sur-Loire before the German guards arrived at eleven and went on to Argent-sur-Saudre. Reaching Argent in the morning of 20 July, they were accosted by a gendarme to whom they were forced to declare themselves and he advised them to avoid the next town south, Aubigny-sur-Nere. After another night sleeping out, they approached a farmhouse near Mahun-sur-Yevre where they were taken in and sheltered for the night. Next morning, the brother-in-law of their host drove them across the old demarcation line. They walked on past Charost, Touchay (where they were given another meal), Beddes (where a farmer gave them tobacco and his lunch) and on towards Chateaumeillant. They skirted the town of Chateaumeillant and after another night in the woods, were just outside Chatelus-Malvaleix (Limousin) when they encountered a woman and a girl who asked if they were airmen.

Lambert and Huston were taken to a quarry and the woman (Mme Denis Martin) (IS9 has Marie Clothilde Martin) fetched local lawyer Roger Bertran. They were taken back to Mme Martin's house in Chatelus-Malvaleix where they stayed until 29 July when they were moved to nearby Genouillat to be sheltered with Raymond Shilling while Mme Martin tried to contact an organisation. On 10 September, they were taken back to Mme Martin's home where they stayed until 28 October when Jean-Louis Kervevant came from Paris and took them that night by train back to the capital. They went first to the home of a lady doctor and then to a house near a mosque, owned by a colonel's wife (Madeleine Melot). They were collected from there by a girl who handed them over to Maud Couve and Alice Brouard who took them to Asnieres-sur-Seine to stay with Lucien Demongogin at 18 rue Victor Hugo. On 14 November, Alice and Maud brought them back into Paris and Gabrielle Wiame's home on rue Poliveau and then on to the Gare d'Austerlitz where they joined a party of Frenchmen and Americans and were put on a train for Toulouse and Carcassonne. On the train they found the same guide who had brought them to Paris from Chatelus-Malvaleix.

2/Lt Howard M Harris and S/Sgt Alfred J Zeoli were the navigator and one of the waist-gunners of B-17 42-30035 Torchy (100BG/351BS) (Winkleman) which was on the way to Romilly-sur-Seine on 3 September 1943 when it was hit by flak, setting fire to the left wing. As they fell out of formation, fighters attacked, the bale-out order was given and the aircraft abandoned to crash (still with a full bomb-load) on a farm belonging to the Billarand family, near La Ferte-Alais (Essonne).[1]

Harris landed near Melun and ran into a wood where he hid until evening when a Frenchman who had seen him land, took him to a house in a nearby village. He was given a coat and some food and then went on his way, spending the rest of the night in a haystack. Next day, after walking for several hours, Harris was picked up by another Frenchman who took him to join waist-gunner S/Sgt Michael Darcy and the following day, the two

---

1   Three of the Torchy crew are believed to have been captured but the other five also evaded successfully: 2/Lt Ralph D Smith, 2/Lt William H Booth and T/Sgt Thomas E Combs with Comete, 2/Lt Charles B Winkelman with Francois-Shelburn – and S/Sgt Michael F Darcy who left Harris and Zeoli in Paris and crossed the Pyrenees from Bagneres-de-Bigorre in October with RAF evaders Denis Cowell and Royston Falcus – see later.

men were taken to a chateau at La Ferte-Alais which was used to house the children of theatrical families. The superintendant, Andre Raquin (a shot-put and hammer thrower) and his wife Madeleine put Darcy and Harris into a room in the chateau – and that night they were joined by their other waist-gunner Alfred Zeoli who had landed near D'Huison-Longueville. The following morning (6 September) they were driven to the station at La Ferte-Alais where they caught a train to Paris and were taken to the city home of Andre and Madeleine Raquin, their apartment on Boulevard Brune.[2]

On 9 September, Maurice Bidaud (who was already sheltering Merlin Pearce and Glen Ransom – see earlier) took Harris and Zeoli to Juvisy-sur-Orge where they stayed with his neighbours, wine merchant Andre Lefevre and family at 29 rue Hoche, for the next two months.

> *"They very quickly integrated into our family life. My father became 'Andy', as courageous as he was modest, he beamed happiness and pride at his contact with his 'boys'. He rediscovered his English and around the family table it was all questions about our different ways of life and customs. My mother was immediately 'Mama', treated with respect and attentiveness. She replaced their 'real' Mums who were a long way away, on the other side of the Atlantic. There was also my grandmother, experiencing her third war, who tried hard to spoil them. Our dog Samy started learning English and obeyed commands such as 'stupid dog' or 'dead dog'. As for me 'Paulette' as they called me, I was their sister, the one they followed blindly when it was time to leave, onto our suburban train into Paris, to the unknown rendezvous round about the Gare d'Austerlitz." (Translation from an interview with Paulette Pavan-Lefevre published in the 2004 Juvisy Info, no 147.)*

On 14 November, Andre Lefevre took Harris and Zeoli back into Paris and handed them over to Gabrielle Wiame who took them to the station.

2/Lt Arthur M Vetter was the pilot of B-17 42-3452 (100BG/350BS) which was damaged by flak over Paris on 15 September 1943 and attacked by fighters. With two engines out and the instrument panel shot away, the aircraft was abandoned at low altitude to crash north of Beauvais. Seven of the crew evaded successfully – four with Bourgogne.

---

2   Andre Raquin (a professor of physical culture – born March 1913) of 77 Boulevard Brune, Paris XIV was arrested in May 1944 and deported to Germany – he was liberated and repatriated to France in 1945. (WO208/5452)

Vetter landed in a yard where several French people were waiting for him. They took his parachute and Mae West and told Vetter to hide in a nearby wood. That evening, a man took Vetter to a house where he was soon joined by his radio-operator John Wagner (who had broken his ankle) and tail-gunner Warren Lush. On 17 September, Wagner was taken to Clermont where he stayed with Gaston Legrand, Odette Sauvage and her seventeen-year-old son Edmond, and next day Vetter and Lush were brought by motorcycle to join him. A week later, Vetter was taken to visit four other members of his crew – James Bormuth, Edward Daly, Hobart Trigg and Wendell McConnaha. On about 27 September, Vetter, Wagner and Lush were joined by William Boren and Francis Anderson from B-26 Cactus Jack and they were all provided with ID papers by Georges Fleury.

On 12 October, Vetter, Wagner and Lush were taken by train to Paris where Vetter stayed with Gerard and Genevieve Moet and their seventeen-year-old daughter Michele – Michele Moet being Vetter's guide around Paris. A French evader from Germany (sic) called Jean (Jean Carbonnet) who was 'high up in the organisation', also lived there. On 14 November, Michele Moet took Vetter – and John Paul Balfe – to the Jardins des Plantes where she passed them over to their guide for the rail journey south. Vetter reports meeting Howard Harris and Alfred Zeoli on the train.

John Paul Balfe was the elder son of Joe Balfe (of the Hotel de France in Hornoy, Somme) and he had been staying at the Moet apartment, waiting to join a group leaving for Spain. Although born in England, he had French nationality – his mother Madeleine was French, his English-born father a naturalised Frenchman and his wife Jacqueline (née Sauts) was French – and so John is included as one of the six Frenchman in the group. John (better known as Jack) joined his brother Joe Jnr in England (brought out by Comete the previous September) where they both trained as agents with MI9.[3]

The five airmen evaders and six Frenchmen went by train to Toulouse and Carcassonne where Jean-Louis Kervevant handed them over to a local man. They were taken to Quillan (Languedoc-Roussilon) where they spent three hours in a cafe waiting for their mountain guide. Leaving the other five French to walk, the airmen and their guide were driven several kilometres into the mountains before walking another three kilometres to a farmhouse where they slept for four hours, during which time the other

---

3   Joe Balfe Jnr telecon Feb 2014.

Frenchmen from the train joined them. They continued their walk the following evening (16 November) and carried on through the night before resting briefly in a barn and then walking again all the next day. Late in the evening of 19 November they reached a point in the mountains where they were picked up by truck and driven through the night to Barcelona – arriving there at four o'clock in the morning of 20 November 1943.

CHAPTER 35

Michael Darcy

Michael Darcy was probably not helped by Bourgogne but he evaded as far as Paris with fellow crewmen Howard Harris and Alfred Zeoli who were (see earlier) and his version of events and subsequent story are well worth relating.

S/Sgt Michael F Darcy was a waist-gunner on B-17 42-30035 Torchy (100BG/351BS) (Winkleman) which was on the way to Romilly-sur-Seine on 3 September 1943 when it was hit by flak and abandoned to crash near Saultz-les-Chartreux (Essonne).

Darcy landed near Ballancourt where he was met by a group of Frenchmen who took him to a deserted house where a man called Georges interrogated him. Later a French boy took Darcy to meet Rene who ran a cafe where Darcy stayed overnight and next morning, a woman brought his bombardier 2/Lt Howard Harris to join him. They were visited by the comte and comtesse de Sugny and went to their chateau at d'Huison-Longueville the following day. At the chateau, a wealthy farmer and ex-cross country running champion, brought them running outfits and ran with them to another chateau at La Ferte-Alais which was used for the children of theatrical families. The superintendant, Andre Raquin (a shot-put and hammer thrower) and his wife Madeleine put Darcy and Harris into a room in the chateau and that night they were joined by their other waist-gunner S/Sgt Alfred Zeoli. Darcy was told that their top-turret gunner T/Sgt Thomas E Combs had been helped but had left suddenly and their hosts were concerned that he might have been captured (he was not). Next day, the three Americans were driven by car to the railway station and taken by train to Paris with Andre's brother, Madeleine and the wealthy farmer as their individual guides. They were taken to the city home of Andre and Madeleine at 114 Boulevard Brune where they were visited by a Jewish woman (who lived at 24 rue Copernic) who told Darcy that she had a friend in an organisation. The following day (9 September) another woman collected Harris and Zeoli (and took them to Andre Lefevre at Juvisy), and that afternoon Darcy was interrogated by a Jewish man who claimed to be with British Intelligence.

The Jewish man took Darcy to visit a French detective called Marius (who provided ID cards) and Camille Lacroix (a short stocky man with black hair and moustache, who walked with a stoop and wore a golden 13 insignia on his waist-coat). Camille Lacroix took Darcy to his house at 3 Boulevard Edgar Quinet, Paris XIV where he stayed for a week and met Ronnie (a railway worker who spoke English) and Robert (about 32 years old, 5 ft 6 inches tall, thin, consumptive – a former POW who worked in the Bar Chalot at 6 rue du Texel (Erick d'Ornhjelm – query). Marius, Ronnie and Robert took Darcy to a cafe where he met the manager Charlot (42 years old and a well-known accordionist) and his wife Olga (40 years old, dyed blonde hair, pianist and singer) who sheltered Darcy for the next twelve days. He was visited by Constant, Alesia (a former music-hall dancer who had been a prisoner of the Germans but was now a prostitute), Charlot's mother, Charlot's wife Bubble and a violinist called Tito. Finally a young, stocky man from another cafe near to 6 rue du Texel came and made arrangements for Darcy.

F/Lt Kenneth E Cooper (Halifax LW273), who was sheltered at a cafe at 6 rue de Tesel (sic) for about four weeks from 20 November 1943, describes the cafe as a headquarters where he met a number of members of the underground movement as well as two other Allied airmen.

On 28 September, Georges (query) (scar under left eye, slender, small moustache, nervous) along with Camille and Robert, took Darcy to the railway station where they joined two British evaders, Sgts Denis Cowell and Royston Falcus, and two Frenchmen.

Sgt Denis W G Cowell and Sgt Royston Falcus were the second pilot and navigator of 78 Sqn Halifax JD108 (Toon) which was returning from Aachen in the early hours of 14 July 1943 when they were attacked by a night-fighter. The aircraft was abandoned to crash near Froidchapelle (Hainault) in Belgium and both men landed near Rance. Flight engineer Sgt Lawrence G Donaldson also evaded successfully – he was taken across the Pyrenees by Comete in August.

Cowell and Falcus were probably not helped by Bourgogne either. It was the Felix network that helped them cross from Belgium into France on 7 August, where they were passed to Fernand Vanaerde of Tourcoing. They were sheltered for ten days in Wattrelos with Georges Parant at 39 rue Alfred Delecourt before being moved back to Tourcoing to stay with Robert Deguisne at 11 rue de la Croix Rouge until 26 August, then with gendarme Gaston Vorreux at 123 rue Lamartine. They fail to identify their helpers in Paris – being taken by an unnamed woman to Paris on 14 September and staying overnight in her apartment. Next day, they were taken to another house where they met a M Georges (who said they would leave for Spain next day) and then to an ex-girls dormitory next to the Paris Execution Prison. They somehow missed a rendezvous at the Gare d'Austerlitz with M Georges and were returned to the dormitory until going to his headquarters on 27 September, where they were issued with deaf and dumb papers before being taken with some French boys to Toulouse and Lourdes next day.

Georges accompanied the three airmen to Lourdes where they stayed at the Hotel Regent (with hotelier Henri Borde) and joined two more Britishers (sic), two Dutchmen and five Frenchmen. Two days later they went on to Bagneres-de-Bigorre and then, following a warning that the Germans were on their way to Bagneres, Georges took them all to a barn in the mountains for the night of 2-3 October. Next day they began their walk across the Pyrenees, with French mountain guides, crossing into Spain on 8 October where their guides left them. The airmen were soon arrested by Spanish soldiers and taken next day to Bielsa. The British Military Attache visited them the following day before they were transferred to Barbesto and later to Alhama de Aragon. On 27 October, they were taken to Madrid and the following day, to Gibraltar.

The reader may have noticed that whilst some of the evaders who crossed from Perpignan or via Andorra were delivered to the safety of the British Consulate in Barcelona, others, including almost all of those crossing from Pau, were routinely left at or near the frontier by their guides and advised to surrender themselves to the first Spanish officials they encountered. It should be understood that whilst military evaders would be interned prior to repatriation, if their guides were caught, many of whom were Spanish Republicans, they would probably have been shot.

By 1943, the Spanish were, with a few exceptions, no longer detaining Allied servicemen in camps like Miranda del Ebro (where F/Sgt John Whyte says conditions were much better than the prison at Figueras) but instead, sending them to the relative comfort of hotels in the spa town of Alhama de Aragon.

CHAPTER 36

Arrests, Confusion, Intrigue and Murder

The complex links, intricacies and betrayals in 1943 Paris are far too complicated to try and explain here (even if I understood them all myself) but fortunately for readers of this story, despite multiple arrests in November, Bourgogne managed to survive relatively unscathed.

F/Lt James L Kennedy RCAF was the pilot of 24 OTU Whitley AD675 which was returning from dropping leaflets over Orleans on the night of 3-4 November 1943 when one engine failed and the aircraft was abandoned to crash near Courtalain (Eure-et-Loire).

Kennedy is included in Georges Broussine's list of evaders but whilst he was certainly helped by people associated with Bourgogne, many of them also worked with Comete, the organisation that took Kennedy from Paris and got him safely over the Pyrenees to Spain at the beginning of December 1943.

Kennedy landed in a field near Courtalain and ran for about an hour before spending the rest of the night in a tree. Next morning, he was found by a gendarme and a young girl, and after a couple of false starts, Kennedy was taken to a country house near Courtalain from where his journey was arranged. Next day, he was taken to Paris where he followed a man he had met in Courtalain to an apartment belonging to Mlle de Mollard (query) a nurse. On 7 November, Kennedy was questioned to establish his identity and on 10 November, taken for lunch with a tall dark woman known as 'the colonel's wife' (Madeleine Melot) who led him to the apartment of Mme Jeanne Magnas at 3 rue du Guesclin, Paris XV. On 17 November, the colonel's wife took Kennedy to have his photograph taken – she also took most of the money from his escape kit. Two days later, Mme Marie, wife of a gendarme (Gabrielle Wiame) came to Mme Magnas' apartment with news that the colonel's wife had been arrested – apparently after a French boy (Jean Woussen – see below) she had sheltered and supplied false papers to had been arrested in Toulouse (sic). Within a few minutes, Kennedy was moved to 25 rue de Madrid where he stayed with Maud Couve. Marie came to tell them about two more arrests and Maud told Kennedy that she didn't trust Marie. Maud also told him that Raoul (Pierre

191

Berteaux) had been shot and was in hospital and that Marie had told her that she was responsible. Germaine Bajpai (a friend of Maud's but member of another organisation) came to visit and arrange for Kennedy to be moved again.[1]

On 28 November, Mme Bajpai collected Kennedy from the rue de Madrid apartment and took him to stay with Elisabeth Buffet at 93 rue de Courselles, Paris XVII where he joined F/O Geoffrey Ward. On the way Kennedy was quizzed by 'the Chief' – Jacques le Grelle – who also gave Kennedy 500 francs and Kennedy told him about Marie. That evening (1 December) Germaine Bajpai took Kennedy and Ward to a Metro station where they met the Chief again and a small dark woman named Marcelle Douard, who was to be their guide. After a meal they took the ten o'clock overnight train to Bordeaux.[2]

Jean Edouard Gaston Woussen (born August 1925) was arrested at St Girons on 29 October along with Georges Guillemin, who seems to blame Woussen for their capture.[3] According to researcher Michael Moores LeBlanc, nineteen-year-old Woussen resisted his interrogators until being forced to watch his mother being tortured in front of him. Jean Woussen died at Terezin/ Theresienstadt concentration camp in Czechoslovakia in May 1945.

Woussen was (along with Alberic Volkaert – see later) the subject of a *Recherche* (Wanted) poster, complete with photographs. There was a 500,000 Belgian franc reward for their capture following an incident in Arras where a German soldier was shot (and may have died) when they were both working with SOE agent Michael Trotobas.[4] It was Trotobas who contacted Henriette Balesi who in turn contacted her friend Madeleine Melot with the request to shelter Woussen until he could be got out of the country. In

---

1   Marguerite Brouard says that, due to various arrests, and the suspicions of their concierge, Kennedy was the last evader to be sheltered by Alice and Maud at rue de Madrid. This must have eased the constant tensions and fears felt by the two ladies, both for themselves and their children. They were too well known by too many people to have ever felt secure, and as British subjects, were obviously known to the German authorities as well.
   Germaine Bajpai of 93 Boulevard Philippe August, Paris XI was French by birth (born October 1894) but a British subject by marriage to an Indian who was a magistrate in India at this time. She looked to be in her thirties and is described as tall, blonde and elegent. Mme Bajpai is credited with helping at least forty-eight Allied evaders. (WO208/5451) She and her friend Fernande Onimus were arrested in January 1944 and deported to Germany – both women died at Ravensbruck in 1945.

2   Count Jacques Alphonse Marie Ghislaine Le Grelle was arrested on 12 January 1944, condemned to death and deported to Germany. He was repatriated to Belgium on 6 June 1945. (WO208/5452)

3   Georges Jacques Hyacinth Guillemin (born February 1921 in Paris) was deported to Germany in April 1944 – he was liberated from Dachau on 29 April 1945 and recommended for a KMC. (WO208/5454)

4   According to various accounts, it seems that Woussen did give up the name of a man who had helped him in Lille. This led to the arrest of a second man who supplied an address where Captain Michael Alfred Raymond Trotobas (born May 1919) was found on 27 November 1943 and subsequently killed in the ensuing gun battle.

his book, Georges Broussine is scathing about Wousson (he says Woutters and calls him a traitor) but Broussine was working from post-war written accounts by Mme Melot and Georges Guillemin and I am not sure that he ever knew the whole story.

Broussine had just returned from England at this time – he was landed back by Lysander to a field near Arras on the morning of 16 November and says he reached the Gare du Nord that same afternoon. He quickly learned of Madeleine Melot's arrest (three days later) but says it was just two or three days after that of Guillemin.

Madeleine Melot was arrested on 19 November 1943, the same day that MI9 agents Lucien Dumais and Ray Labrosse arrived in Paris, and two days before the arrests of Lucienne Bodin, Suzanne Bosniere and Marie Betbeder-Matibet. These last three were denounced by a collaborator and although it is understandable that Mme Wiame might blame Woussen for her friend's capture, it seems too much of a coincidence to assume that Mme Melot's arrest might not be part of a larger German operation.

"The day that Mme Melot was arrested, we had a rendezvous in the late afternoon at her home to take in lodgers, airmen that Jean Carbonnet was bringing from the north. Fortunately, Mme Wiame, who lived close by at rue Poliveau had been advised of the descent of the Gestapo and kept watch. She ran after me when she saw me coming. Very quickly we needed to stop Carbonnet from going into the lion's den. I called our telephone relay, M et Mme Hauchecorne at 4 Villa Marces, Saint-Mande who warned my mother.[5] She joined us at the Gare du Nord where Carbonnet and his boys would arrive. With the three of us and a lot of luck we could save Carbonnet and the group of airmen. Mme Wiame took 2 or 3, mother and Carbonnet took the others to our home where they all spent the night. Me, I went to the Abbe Jean Courcel's home [at 24 rue Saint-Roch, Paris 1], but he was not there. I delivered a message to the priest who lived with him – but knew nothing about the clandestine activities of his colleague – and asked him to give him a message upon his return. The message said "Perrine highly contagious was taken urgently to hospital, impossible to see." So he was able to contact everyone he knew and warn them. The next morning, while I was already in high school, mother and Jean Carbonnet took our guests that night to other landlords. Unfortunately, we were not able to do anything for Mme Melot." (Michele Agniel Dec 2013)

---

5   The IS9 Helper List has M et Mme Auguste Jean Hauchecorne at 21 rue Sacrot. Villa Marces is a cul-de-sac just off rue Sacrot.

With the arrest of Madeleine Melot, it was assumed that her friend Gabrielle Wiame would also be at risk of imminent arrest and she was asked to turn over her contacts to Genevieve Soulie. In fact it seems that Mme Melot didn't give anyone away, admitting only that she had sheltered Woussen – which her interrogators already knew – which makes her an extremely brave woman.[6]

Shortly after the arrest of Georges Guillemin (but before that of Madeleine Melot) another episode took place that is still surrounded by mystery. Broussine says that Mme Melot reported Woussen as acting suspiciously and having a worrying attitude – which seems hardly surprising considering the circumstances, although Mme Melot may not have appreciated that at the time. Shortly before the arrest of Woussen and Guillemin, two more men had arrived with dubious references. According to Broussine, Rene Lalou contacted Yves Allain (who was in charge of the network while Broussine was away in London) through Mme Flament, asking him to contact Pierre Herbard, who was at that time living in Andre Gide's apartment on rue Vaneau. Herbard told Allain that he had picked up two English airmen who needed to be taken out of the country. Allain duly passed the two 'airmen' onto one of the organisation's logeurs – actually, a friend of one of the logeurs. Unfortunately, it was soon realised that the two men were neither English nor airmen but actually two young Dutchmen who simply wanted to get to England. It was however, their behaviour which apparently sealed their fate as they showed themselves to be very badly behaved and particularly indiscrete. With their behaviour continuing to raise suspicions, and following on from the arrest Georges Guillemin, the decision was made to eliminate them.

Broussine doesn't give her name but it was Gabrielle Wiame who recruited an executioner and it was she who led the two men from their shelter on Boulevard du Montparnasse to a dark street (Broussine gives the date as 13 November 1943) where they were shot in the back of the head.

Broussine says that the arrest of Guillemin and Woussen probably compromised the Foix to Andorra route, and that with the increasingly bad weather making the high mountain passes too dangerous anyway, he decided to concentrate on the easier routes south from Perpignan – although that didn't prevent another tragedy ...

---

6   Mme Madeleine Melot spent four months at Fresnes prison before being deported to Ravensbruck. She was repatriated to France in June 1945 and recommended for an MBE. (WO208/5454)

CHAPTER 37

Bourgogne is reorganised

Yves Allain sums up what happened in Broussine's absence by saying that Georges Guillemin and Madeleine Melot had been arrested and that Georges Baledent had been sent to Spain, with Claude Leclercq and Robert Alouis to follow as their safety had been compromised by the capture of Guillemin. Agents remaining included Genevieve Crosson, Charles Ploncard, Pierre Jacob, Jean-Louis Kervevant, Jean Carbonnet and Michele Moet – and Jean Borossi and Paul Le Baron in Brittany. Logeurs included Gabrielle Wiame (although she would need to be replaced following the arrest of Madeleine Melot) and Jean Carbonnet and Michele Moet – the latter two also being responsible for supplying false documentation for the evaders. The only route still being used was through Perpignan with the possibility having been explored of evacuating airmen through Brittany.

While Broussine was away, radio messages to London were sent through a source that Allain only identifies as 'Michel' or via an intelligence network in Lyon. It was also 'Michel' who supplied (minimal) funding for the organisation.

On Broussine's return, Robert Alouis was evacuated to Spain and Gabrielle Wiame replaced as chief logeur by Genevieve Soulie, to whom Mme Wiame was asked to pass over her list of helpers. When asked if Mme Wiame was offended to have been asked to leave the organisation, Mlle Soulie said that "she thought so, but did not think she was angry about it."

New contacts in Paris included Broussine's old friends Jacques Cahen, Andre Camp and Rene Lalou, and in April, 'a band of zazous' at rue de Bourgogne.[1] New guides recruited by Georges in January were Rene Lalou's son Etienne and his wife Suzanne,[2] and later, Yvette Gouineau (mentioned earlier) and Catherine David.

---

1   This was Mme Alice Goret (born March 1899 in Belgium) and her teenage son Francis Rene Goret at 28 rue de Bourgogne, Paris VII. They were recommended for a BEM and KMC respectively. (WO208/5451 & 5452)

2   Etienne Lalou of 95 Boulevard Raspail, Paris 6 was recommended for a KMC. (IS9 Helper List only)

Radio-operators Pierre Le Mogne and Henri Ruelland (neither found) were also recruited by Georges in January with Charles Ploncard (assisted by two policemen, Alain Barbecch and Gaston Lapouge) responsible for security and liaison. In March, this was taken on by Xavier Poincet until the arrival of Martin Mary and Michel Bourgeois (aka Maxime). Locations used by the radio-operators included the De Traz apartment on rue de Miromesnil, Jacques Ducaud's home at 28 rue de la Jonquiere and Roger Schwob's home at 56 rue des Francs-Bourgeois.[3] Georges Broussine adds a factory arranged by Rene Tourriol (mentioned earlier) to the list of radio transmission sites.

Note that Michel Bourgeois was a BCRA intelligence agent, sent to reconnoitre landing fields (presumably for both aircraft and parachute drops) and Martin Mary his radio-operator. Georges Broussine explains that in addition to their other activities, they agreed to send messages on Bourgogne's behalf.

Martin Antoine Mary (born January 1908 on Corsica) had been working for British Intelligence since 1941. He went to England in 1943 for training as a radio-operator before being returned to France (landed at Plage Bonaparte near Plouha with Michel Bourgeois) on 28 February 1944. In his IS9 recommendation for a BEM, Martin Mary is described as completely fearless ... and when faced with almost certain capture or death, his courage and resource saved him. (WO208/5451)

"On the 5th June [1944], Martin Mary was transmitting from an apartment in Montmartre while a look-out kept watch in the street and Xavier Poincet watched out of the window. A car full of German policemen burst noisily on the scene and with a piercing screech of tyres, stopped in front of the building where Poincet and Martin Mary were operating. The men entered the hall, dashed up the stairs and hammered on the door. Poincet just kept quiet, looking out of the window while Mary threw the quartz crystals and holiday plans [transmission times] into the kitchen dustbin and kept silent. Suddenly there was a cry, probably a request for reinforcements. The policemen who had stayed outside the apartment, entered the building to join their comrades, leaving the road deserted. Poincet and Mary rode their luck. There was a balcony around the apartment, separated from the adjoining balcony by a grill. This balcony made an angle between the street by which the enemy had arrived and another at right-angles. So our friends passed from one balcony

---

3   FNA File 72AJ/37/V – *Rapport par Yves Allain* dd May 1945.

to the other. It was a lovely day and a window was open. They went in. Two elderly ladies were sitting in the room. Poincet apologised, "We are just passing through". Without saying a word the ladies directed them to the door. They left the building without meeting a soul and went calmly to catch the Metro …" (Translated from 'L'evade de la France libre')

CHAPTER 38

Crossing from Perpignan – and another death ...

On 4 December 1943, 2/Lt Sigmund Sandvik, T/Sgt Arthur Beach, T/Sgt Joseph Schwartzkopf, S/Sgt Walter Soukup, S/Sgt Francis Anderson, S/Sgt Warren Lush, 2/Lt James Bormuth, 2/Lt Wendell McConnaha, S/Sgt Orville Greene and T/Sgt Bertil Erickson left Paris by train for Toulouse, Narbonne and Perpignan.

2/Lt Sigmund J M Sandvik RNAF was flying 332 Sqn Spitfire LZ898 on a Ramrod bomber escort sortie to France on 11 September 1943 when he left formation to attack an enemy fighter. The encounter didn't go well for Sandvik as his aircraft was hit and the twenty-one-year-old Norwegian was forced to bale out near Villers-Ecalles (Normandy).

Sandvik headed generally south, looking for a way to cross the river Seine. On 13 September, he stopped at a small farm just outside the little village of Pissy-Poville (a few kilometres north-west of Rouen) where he was given food and shelter while his helpers went to find some friends. Next day, Sandvik was taken to the house of a schoolteacher in Pissy-Poville (Suzanne Dujardin – query) where both the woman (Sandvic says Mme Coissy – phonetic) and her son (who was in hiding to avoid being sent to work in Germany) spoke a little English. On about 24 September, Sandvik was taken by bicycle to Crosville-la-Vieille (south-west of Rouen) where he stayed overnight. The following evening he was taken on to Louviers and a big house on the outskirts of the town belonging to an organisation chief called Drai (nf). Sandvik stayed with M Drai for about two weeks while Drai went twice to Paris to try and get help for him. On about 10 October, Sandvik was moved to Saint-Pierre-du-Vauvray where he stayed in a room by himself for twelve days, with his food brought to him, and then another house north of St Pierre for another three days until M Drai took him to Paris.

In Paris, Sandvik stayed with M et Mme Devalle (address unknown) where a Frenchman who claimed to be a pilot visited him. After three days chez Devalle, Sandvik was taken to stay with Dr Alice Willm at 51 rue de Miromesnil where he joined Grant Carter and John Wagner. Three days later, a Mlle Francoise (query) took the two Americans elsewhere then returned to take Sandvik to the Lycee Sophie Germaine at 9 rue de Jouy where he was sheltered by one of the teachers, Mme Marie Droin. Mme Francoise said she would come back at the end of the week but she never returned and Sandvik stayed at the school for about seven weeks until Genevieve Soulie came to tell him that he would be leaving Paris on 4 December.

Mlle Genevieve Germaine Soulie (born September 1922) had a French father and English mother, and was perfectly bilingual. Various evaders describe her as being about 5 ft 6 inches tall, with blue eyes, dark blonde hair (which she often wore in plaits) and glasses – she had a turned up nose, a round face, was slightly plump and always wore black. When Mme Flament left Paris at the end of July, Genevieve moved into her apartment on rue de Castiglione to look after Georges Broussine. A few weeks later, Broussine moved to an apartment that Mme Flament rented for him at 3 rue de l'Aude, Paris XIV and Genevieve went with him. She had been working at a library on rue Blanche but after a short holiday at the end of August, quit her job to work full-time for Broussine. When Broussine left Paris a few days later to go to England, Yves Allain joined her at the apartment, soon followed by Jean-Louis Kervevant (aka Johnny) and Pierre Jacob (aka Daniel). Following the arrest of Madeleine Melot in November, it was assumed that her friend Gabrielle Wiame was also *brûlé* and Mme Wiame was asked to pass over her list of contacts to Genevieve.[1]

On the evening of 4 December, Genevieve Soulie took Sandvik to the Gare d'Austerlitz where he met Francis Anderson, Warren Lush and the Frenchman who was to be their guide. They took the overnight train to Toulouse where they changed for Narbonne. After a four hour wait at Narbonne, they took a train to Perpignan where Sandvik, Anderson and Lush joined another five Americans, two Frenchmen and two Spanish guides.

T/Sgt Arthur R Beach was the engineer/TTG of B-17 42-30000 (92BG/327BS) (Bogard) which was returning from Stuttgart on 6 September 1943 when it was attacked by fighters and abandoned west of Troyes.[2]

---

1   NARA Soulie. Genevieve Soulie was recommended for an OBE. (WO208/5451)

2   All ten crew baled out and seven of them evaded successfully: co-pilot 2/Lt Robert D Larsen to Switzerland, waist gunner S/Sgt Hershell L Richardson was evacuated from Brittany in October on board the Suzanne-Renee, ball-turret gunner S/Sgt Floyd M Carl was picked up by RN MGB 318 from Ile Tariec (SIS operation Envious IIb) at the beginning of December, radio-operator T/Sgt Max Gibbs and tail-gunner S/Sgt Cloe R Crutchfield crossed the Pyrenees in January 1944 – and bombardier Sgt Taylor D Harrison who was also helped by Bourgogne. Pilot 1/Lt Wayne C Bogard was captured at Toulouse station in February 1944 – see later.

Beach was helped immediately on landing near Dierry-Saint-Julien and taken to a Polish family where his journey was arranged. Unfortunately, the details in his report are almost illegible from this point.

Beach was taken into Troyes at some stage (after a couple of weeks – query) where he met Joseph Schwartzkopf, Walter Soukup and Warren Laws – and later Max Gibbs and Cloe Crutchfield from his own aircraft – and Beach went to stay with Mary-Rose Gilbert at 1 rue de Molesme, Troyes. Mary-Rose is described by Laws as a good looking, twenty-two-year-old blonde girl who worked for the Red Cross.[3] About three weeks later, Beach went to Paris, meeting Gibbs and Crutchfield again on the way (and three other fellows – Laws, Schwartzkopf and Soukup – query) but any plans for moving them on fell through and they returned to Troyes. About a month later (at the end of October) things 'suddenly became hot' when an Allied airman who had been brought to Troyes was found to be a German agent and so Beach, Schwartzkopf, Soukup and Laws were taken to stay with Marcel Dore at Montieramey. Back to Paris again at some stage and on to Juvisy where Beach and Schwartzkopf were sheltered by wine merchant Andre Lefevre and his family at 29 rue Hoche.[4]

T/Sgt Joseph G Schwartzkopf was the radio-operator of B-17 42-30349 (388BG/563BS) (Wilken) which was returning from Stuttgart on 6 September 1943 and over France when it was attacked by fighters. Several of the crew were probably killed in the attacks before the aircraft was abandoned to crash near Montgueux, about seven kms west of Troyes, Champagne-Ardenne.

Schwartzkopf evaded with his co-pilot Warren Laws until they (and others) were brought from Sainte-Savine (Troyes) to Paris. Schwartzkopf and Arthur Beach were taken to Juvisy-sur-Orge where they stayed with Andre Lefevre while Laws and Walter Soukup stayed in Paris with Suzanne Guelat at 68 Boulevard Auguste-Blanqui – Soukup (at least) until 22 November.

On 22 November (query), Schwartzkopf was taken to stay for a week with jeweller Andre Francois in his Paris apartment over the Galerie de Montpensier before a blonde girl took him to Juvisy where he and Beach

---

3   Mary-Rose Gilbert is a mystery to me – she is named by several evaders but I have not found any further details.

4   The intention had been for Beach, Schwartzkopf, Soukup and Laws to go to Rennes and meet Bordeaux-Loupiac agents Jean-Claude Camors and Pierre Charnier who would take them to the coast for evacuation by sea. I believe that Charnier took them to Rennes but the shooting of Camors and Remy Roure in a Rennes cafe by Roger Leneveu on 11 October put a stop to that idea and they were returned to Troyes ...

stayed with the Lefevre family at 29 rue Hoche. On 4 December, Andre Lefevre and his twenty-one-year-old daughter Paulette took Schwartzkopf and Beach back into Paris and the Gare d'Austerlitz where they were put on a train for Toulouse and Perpignan, seeing Francis Anderson and Warren Lush on the train.

S/Sgt Walter R Soukup was the left waist-gunner of B-17 42-30222 Lone Wolf (388BG/563BS) (Kramer) which was returning from Stuttgart on 6 September 1943 when it was attacked by fighters. The hydraulic and electrical systems were knocked out and the aircraft was abandoned near Troyes.[5]

Soukup evaded alone for several days before hailing a passing cyclist. Stanislav Mhaeveski was Polish and since Soukup spoke fluent Czech, they were able to communicate easily. Soukup was hidden in a barn near Montieramey (Aube) getting his meals from a nearby restaurant for a week until another man was brought who arranged his journey. Soukup was taken to another barn for ten days then moved to Luyeres (about 10 kms north-east of Troyes) where he met Marcel Varf (query this name) (head of the local organisation) and stayed with Marcel and Carmen Dore at Montieramey. After another week, Soukup was taken into Troyes where he stayed with Mary-Rose Gilbert for two days before he and Arthur Beach were taken to a house near the railway station. That evening (about 1 October) the wife of a gendarme named Andre (who said that his pilot Alfred Kramer and fellow waist-gunner William Vickless had left Troyes three days earlier) took them to Paris, meeting Joseph Schwartzkopf and Warren Laws on the train. On (about) 22 November, Soukup was taken to Juvisy-sur-Orge where he was sheltered with chemists Leon and Amelie Meilleroux until leaving Paris on 4 December.

S/Sgt Francis W Anderson was the tail-gunner of B-26 41-31721 Cactus Jack (387BG/559BS) (Boren) which was damaged by flak over Beauvais-Tille aerodrome on 21 September 1943 and abandoned soon afterwards.

Anderson evaded with his pilot William Boren until 5 October when they were brought from Clermont (Oise) to Paris. They were taken to the Jardin des Plantes where they met Mme Francoise (Andree Vandevoorde) (who was in charge of them) and taken to an apartment where they were

---

5   Nine of the Lone Wolf crew are believed to have baled out safely and eight of them thought to have evaded successfully: pilot 1/Lt Alfred A Kramer, co-pilot 2/Lt Arthur M Swap and right waist-gunner S/Sgt William H Vickless returned to England on board the Breton fishing vessel Suzanne-Renee, top-turret gunner T/Sgt Merl E Martin and radio-operator T/Sgt Allan J Priebe by RN MGB 318 on Operation Felicitate II, bombardier 2/Lt Robert G Burnett was sheltered in France until liberated, tail-gunner S/Sgt William W Chapman who is thought to have evaded to Switzerland – and Soukup.

separated. Anderson was taken to 14 rue Montmartre (Les Halles) Paris – where he was joined a few days later by Warren Lush – and stayed with Mlles Solange and Yvonne Renee Boury (and Jean Bimbault) for seven and a half weeks until 4 December.

S/Sgt Warren G Lush was the tail-gunner of B-17 42-3452 (100BG/350BS) (Vetter) which was damaged by flak over Paris on 15 September 1943 and attacked by fighters. With two engines out and the instrument panel shot away, the aircraft was abandoned at low altitude to crash north of Beauvais – see John Wagner earlier.

Lush doesn't say where he landed but he was soon surrounded by about thirty French people who took his parachute and Mae West before leading him to a farmhouse where he was given civilian clothes. That evening, he was taken to join his pilot Arthur Vetter and radio-operator John Wagner and the following night, all three were taken to a place where their journeys were arranged.

Unfortunately, the interesting part of Lush's report is almost illegible so his story is mostly put together from other sources. He mentions Gaston (Legrand) taking him by motorcycle to his house in Clermont where Lush stayed from 18 September to 12 October, and meeting William Boren and Francis Anderson. On 12 October, Lush was taken to the Fleury home (also in Clermont) and he, Arthur Vetter and John Wagner caught an early afternoon train to Paris with M Fleury's son Alain. They were met by a tall lady in black and a Mme Francoise and while Vetter and Wagner were sheltered elsewhere (see earlier), Lush was taken to 14 rue Montmartre where he joined Francis Anderson and they stayed with the Mlles Boury for the next seven and a half weeks. During this time, Lush thought some members of the organisation were picked up after being betrayed by someone in Spain. He also mentions Mlle Genevieve being in charge.

2/Lt James G Bormuth and 2/Lt Wendell K McConnaha were the bombardier and navigator of B-17 42-3452 (100BG/350BS) (Vetter) – see above.

Bormuth landed in the grounds of the Chateau de Plainval (just north of Saint-Just-en-Chaussee) where Mme de Maissin and Anne-Marie de Jandin (stepmother and sister of owner Charles de Jandin) immediately helped take off his parachute before hiding him in the grounds. Later, Charles' brother Pierre (who spoke some English) arrived and asked Bormuth if he preferred to hide in the house but Bormuth opted to stay in the woods. Late that night, Charles and Pierre moved Bormuth to a shelter of straw bales and brought civilian clothes, food and some English reading matter. On 17 September, Dr Edmond Caillard (from Saint-Just-en-Chaussee) collected Bormuth and drove him to the Chateau de Wavignies where the caretakers, Henri and Yvonne Vincenot, were already sheltering his navigator, Wendell McConnaha. On 21 September, Bormuth and McConnaha were taken to stay with the Fleury family in Clermont where they joined their waist-gunners, Edward Daly and Hobart Trigg.[6]

After being sheltered in Clermont until 9 October, the four Americans were taken to Creil where they caught a train to Paris. Bormuth says they were met by Mme Moux and Lulu (query) and that they were taken to an elderly lady's apartment (her husband had been a French army colonel) (Madeleine Melot) where they met Mme Marie (Gabrielle Wiame) a tall blonde woman whose husband was said to be a police inspector. Daly and Trigg were taken to an Englishwoman who was married to a Frenchman (Dora Rospape) (see later) and next day, Mme Marie took Bormuth and McConnaha to Montreuil (Seine). They were sheltered with a man who had worked in the fur business and spent some time in New York, and later to other various addresses, including two weeks with Mlle Simone Besson at 8 rue Emile Allez, Paris XVII – and meeting her sister (query) Andree – before being moved to Gagny (Seine et Oise) where they stayed with Pierre Chanez at 28 Avenue Maurice for ten days. On a Wednesday, Pierre's son Rene took them back to Paris where the man who had taken them to Gagny returned them to Simone Besson once more.[7] On 3 December, they were visited by Genevieve Soulie and the following day she took them to the Gare d'Austerlitz.

S/Sgt Orville G Greene and T/Sgt Bertil E Erickson were the ball-turret gunner and bombardier of B-17 42-29716 The Venus (351BG/508BS) (Suit) which was on the way to a V1 rocket site at Watten (Nord-Pas-de-Calais) on 27 August 1943 when they were attacked by fighters and the aircraft abandoned to crash near Aubigney-en-Artois. Greene and Erickson were the only two from The Venus to evade successfully.[8]

---

6   Information from Dominique Lecomte. As well as being a friend for many years, Dominique is (as of March 2014) the chairman of the ASAA (*Association des Sauveteurs d'Aviators Allies*) and this is taken from their website.

7   Mlle Simone Besson (born September 1899) gives her occupation as chief bank clerk. (WO208/5451) Don Lasseter, in his 2002 book 'Their Deeds of Valour' (page 322) says that when she sheltered George Padgett and Wayne Bogard in January (see later), Mlle Besson was still mourning the death of Wendell McConnaha.

8   Note that although the first V1 flying bomb wasn't launched against England until 12 June 1944, details of the weapon were known to the Allies and many of the launch-sites had been identified much earlier.

Greene landed near Arras and was immediately helped by a young boy who hid his parachute and flying gear before taking him to his house. After spending the night in a haystack, Greene began walking but was soon picked up by a man in a truck who took him to Frevent where he joined his bombardier Erickson. The two men were sheltered by Rene Guittard's Bordeaux-Loupiac organisation until 20 September when Mme Blanche (Henriette Balesi) took them by taxi to Arras. They stayed overnight with Mme Cecile Dumontier at 102 bis rue de Saint-Quentin before going on to Valenciennes where they were sheltered with an electrician called Georges before moving to stay with Dr Claude Potty at 194 Avenue de Nain. After 24 days, the doctor received a message saying it was known that he was sheltering Americans so the two evaders were moved to a chemical engineer friend for the next four days until Mme Blanche took them by train to Bapaume where their host's mother (Madeleine Duclercq – query) spoke English and where they met Franklin Resseguie. They stayed at Bapaume for two days until Mme Blanche took them to Paris where they met Simone Molin and British-born Dora Rospape who took them to Mme Molin's apartment at 86 rue d'Aboukir.[9]

Whichever group was helping Greene and Erikson at this time (both women are listed by Gabrielle Wiame) seem to have been having problems of their own (including the arrest of Robert Guillet who had brought many of the evaders sheltered by Mme Molin). At some point Greene and Erikson were visited by Genevieve Soulie who told them they were now in another organisation (Bourgogne) and that they would be leaving soon.

On 4 December, Genevieve Soulie brought Greene and Erikson more clothes and told them they would be leaving that night. At about seven o'clock that evening, a heavy-set man (about 25 or 30 years old, 5 ft 8 inches tall, spoke good English) collected them, gave them rope-soled shoes and Metro and train tickets for Perpignan. He took them to the station where they joined a group of Americans that included S/Sgt Walter Soukup. At Toulouse station they changed platforms and for some reason lost contact when Soukup and the others left for Perpignan.

Greene and Erickson walked out of Toulouse station at about six o'clock that evening and slept out that night. Next day, they approached a woman in a farmhouse who took them next door where they were fed before a man

---

9   Mme Simone Molin (born August 1908) sheltered at least thirty-five evaders in her home at 86 rue d'Aboukir, Paris II. She also arranged to have many of them photographed for their ID cards before taking them on the next stage of their journeys. (WO208/5452) Simone Molin was awarded a KMC.

called Gaston Lejeune (with an English wife named Joan) took them to his house at 13 rue Helene Boucher in Montaudran. M Lejeune was able to contact a guide in Toulouse who had apparently been taking people across the mountains for two years. On 13 December, they took the nine o'clock morning train to St Gaudens where M Lejeune turned them over to a man who took them to Montrejeau where they were met by an unnamed American who had apparently been living in France for the last nine years. Three days later they joined a party of about twenty-six (they were the only Americans) and began their walk across the Pyrenees, reaching Spain on 17 December – where I suspect they were arrested.

After waiting several days for the weather to improve – and staying at various addresses in the town – the other eight evaders and their guides left Perpignan, setting off to walk across the Pyrenees through the night of 9 December and next day. The following evening, Wendell McConnaha was lost just after they crossed the frontier on the night of 11 December. Lush says that he believes McConnaha fell down the mountain because all they found was his scarf and beret.

Shortly after that, the rest of the party became split into two groups: Schwartzkopf and Laws were arrested by Spanish soldiers the following afternoon and taken to Figueras then Alhama de Aragon for five or six days before being repatriated to Madrid and Gibraltar. Sandvik, Beach, Anderson, Lush, Bormuth and the two Frenchmen carried on walking to Figueras where their guides left them and a Spanish boy took them to a farm south of the town. From there they took a train to Gerona, where they changed guides, then a taxi to Tordera where they stayed for two days before catching a train to Barcelona and the British Consulate.

CHAPTER 39

Paul Pascal

1/Lt Paul Pascal was the navigator of B-17 42-5865 Janie (100BG/351BS) (Fienup) which was returning from Romilly-sur-Seine in the early morning of 3 September 1943 when it was attacked by fighters, hit by flak and abandoned to explode in mid-air.[1]

Pascal lost his left shoe when his parachute opened and sprained his ankle when he landed near Thomer-la-Sogne (Eure), about 10 miles south of Evreux. He was helped immediately on landing and two men carried him to a small wood where he was hidden in some bushes. His helpers returned that evening and he was taken by bicycle to stay with Hubert and Renee Renaudin just outside Evreux at Arnieres-sur-Iton. Pascal met his bombardier 2/Lt Blanton G Barnes next day (4 September) when he stayed overnight with a grocer from Evreux but doesn't know where he went after that.[2] He also met 2/Lt Andrew G Lindsay and Sgt William M Callahan from B-26 41-34971 Pay Off who left on about 16 September. On 20 September, Sgt Clarence Witheridge from Lancaster LM337 arrived, made himself unpopular and on about 3 (or 5) October, was moved to another house nearby to stay with Charles and Yvette Madelaine at the Cafe d'Agriculture in Damville. On about 17 October, F/Lt Hugh L Parry arrived in very poor health (he had been hit in the shoulder and the wound had turned septic) and Renee, who was a nurse, looked after him – Parry was only just ready to get out of bed when Pascal left.[3]

---

1   Two others from the Janie crew also evaded successfully: S/Sgt Norman D Kreitenstein (see earlier) and 2/Lt Eugene V Muholland – both also with Bourgogne.

2   Barnes went on to Paris but was arrested 11 September 1943 on a train during a ticket check at the demarcation line. (RAMP Folder 5, 23/24)

3   F/Lt Hugh Laurence Parry was flying 41 Sqn Spitfire MB802 on a Ramrod sortie on 24 September 1943 when he was shot down just north-west of Beauvais (Picardy). Parry walked for four days before finding help with M et Mme R Baes on a farm at Mercey, south-west of Vernon. After questioning, he was driven into Vernon and sheltered with M et Mme Marcel Fournier at 40 bis Route de Rouen. A few days later he was taken ill and moved to a farm at Arnieres-sur-Iton where he was attended by Dr Suzanne Huet from Evreux and nursed by Hubert and Renee Renaudin for the next three months. On 11 January 1944, Helene Gill and Jean-Pierre de la Hutiere took Parry (who was still extremely ill) to Paris where he was sheltered by Mlle Paule Vastel at 39 rue Claude Bernard – see later.

On 25 October, Hubert Renaudin took Pascal to Paris where they were met by Captain Martin (liaison with the 'passage' organisation) who took Pascal to stay with Felix Eugene Gruz at 26 rue d'Hauteville, Paris X. Just before he left there, three Americans – 1/Lt Phillip E Higdon, 2/Lt Louis E Ritt and S/Sgt Willard J Cronin, all from B-17 42-3459 Jolly Roger – came to the house.[4] On 28 October, M Renaudin sent seventeen-year-old Jean Herment (of 4 rue de Metz, Le Ban-Saint-Martin, Metz) to take Pascal to the Gare d'Austerlitz where Jean bought them both tickets for Toulouse.

Pascal and Jean Herment arrived in Toulouse at eight o'clock the following morning but Jean had no contacts there so they wandered about until eventually they were advised by a M Poicignon (query) to go the Hotel Paris-Nice. Pascal was welcomed by M et Mme Milhorat (nf) and family as he was the first evader they had ever helped. Pascal and Jean and stayed at the hotel until 5 November when a *rafle* (a police round-up in the streets) so worried the family that Pascal and Jean went to stay the night with M Poicignon before catching the five o'clock morning train to Pamiers and then a bus to Lavelanet. Jean had an old password of 'Arthur' that he used to try and make contact with a group in Lavelanet and they wound up staying with a M De Fort (query) at the Hotel du Parc. Apparently M De Fort was a passage agent but had never helped an Allied airman before so he took them to see an English-speaking man called M Bougou (query). That evening, M De Fort took them about six kilometres to the Chateau Mondini where they stayed with Mme Loraine-Dereure – a young woman whose husband was away – until 13 November, during which time they made three long practice walks. On 13 November, Mme Loraine-Dereure took Pascal and Jean to Foix where they stayed with Mme Mena (who had apparently sheltered some thirty-seven people before but not an Allied airman). On 22 November, they were taken to the assurance office of Marcel Caralp (of 33 Allees de Vilotte, Foix) where M Caralp arranged a payment of 1,000 francs to the guides for Pascal (while everyone else paid 4,000 francs each) and Jean wrote to his uncle in Evreux to get the money sent.

The crossing was supposed to take three days but their guide got lost and it took eight days of walking through deep snow. The party of sixteen (Pascal being the only airman) ran out of food and on the fourth day, also

4   Thank you Edouard Reniere for identifying Higdon, Ritt and Cronin. According to Gabrielle Wiame, the three airmen were sheltered with Mme Chatagnat at 5 rue Jeanne d'Arc, Paris XIII. (NARA Wiame)

lost six of the party. Two more of the French gave up before the remaining walkers finally reached the Andorran border.

They walked down to La Continada (south of Llorts) before being taken to Escaldes and the Hotel Palacin. When the others went on to La Seu d'Urgell, Pascal stayed behind at the Hotel Pyrenees in Andorre-la-Vieille (Andorra la Vella) with Jean Herment and a Belgian. Next day, a man called Juan came from the British Consulate in Barcelona and took them by bus to La Seu d'Urgell where they stayed at a hotel and joined the other walkers who had come from France with them. On about 7 December, Pascal was driven to Barcelona and the British Consulate.

CHAPTER 40

Some Mlle Bourgeois, Bordeaux, Dahlia and Felix connections

The reader was warned at the start of this account that it would be heavy on detail but light on narrative. This chapter in particular is likely to confound the most ardent of students with the interaction of so many other characters and organisations, and references to other events which may (or may not) be covered in more detail elsewhere.

The lady known as Mlle Bourgeois apparently had her own organisation. She is described by Charles Bailey and William Quinn as being a homely woman with a heart of gold. She had ankles the size of a man's thigh and her two front teeth were buck. Her organisation had no money so she was using her own – she taught philosophy at the University of Paris. Further research into 'Mlle Bourgeois' has revealed nothing so far and I have no idea who she was or even if Bourgeois was her real name – she is not listed as such by IS9 or the French *Service Historique de la Defense*.

On (about) 14 December 1943, S/Sgt Floyd Terry, 2/Lt John Heald and Sgt William Quinn were taken from the Gare d'Austerlitz by train to Montauban, Toulouse, Narbonne and Perpignan.

On 19 December 1943, 2/Lt John Dougherty, S/Sgt Robert Sheets, S/Sgt Charles Bailey, 2/Lt John Herrick, 2/Lt Warren Laws, S/Sgt Herbert Dulburg and S/Sgt Thomas Mezynski were also taken by train from the Gare d'Austerlitz to Montauban, Toulouse, Narbonne and Perpignan.

S/Sgt Floyd H Terry was the twenty-two-year-old ball-turret gunner of B-17 42-29789 Big Time Operator (381BG/535BS) (Zum) which had already experienced trouble with one engine and lost two guns before being damaged by flak over Romilly-sur-Seine aerodrome on 3 September 1943 and attacked by fighters. The aircraft was abandoned to crash near Provins (Seine-et-Marne) south-east of Paris.[1]

---

1   Two other Big Time Operator crew evaded successfully: radio-operator T/Sgt Edwin R Myers was evacuated from Camaret in Brittany in October on the Suzanne-Renee – and 2/Lt Charles H Hoover also with Bourgogne. Pilot 2/Lt Benjamin J Zum was captured in Paris on 21 November 1943 along with Marie Betbeder-Matibet and 42-30163 ball-turret gunner Sgt Frederick E Huntzinger.

Terry landed in the Foret de Fontainebleau (south of Melun) and was helped almost immediately. He was taken to a nearby village and an organisation in Paris was contacted. Terry was taken to the north-eastern Parisian suburb of Drancy and the Cafe du Moulin Rouge at 42 Avenue Henry Barbusse where he met Maurice Berthe-Cottereau and three doctors. The following evening (about 8 September) he was taken to stay with Theodorine Quenot at 15 rue Alcide Veillard, Bobigny.[2] On about 10 September, he was joined by 61 Sqn Lancaster pilot, Sgt Vic Matthews and sometime between 15 and 20 September, they were joined by James Armstrong from Yankee Raider, and five days after that by Andrew Lindsay from B-26 41-34971 Pay Off. Mme Theo took the four airmen to Maurice's restaurant for the Quimper expedition at the end of October (see later) and afterwards, a girl called Allouette brought Terry back to Paris with John Heald.

It was Mlle Bourgeois who took Terry and Heald to a hotel opposite the College de Paris (sic). They stayed about two weeks at the hotel before a guide took them to Toulouse where they picked up two French naval officers. They made an abortive attempt to cross the Pyrenees from Quillan in bad weather but Terry collapsed and the whole party returned to Paris where they went to the apartment of one of the French officers, Pierre. At this point, a new lady (Mlle Davy aka Madeleine) took Terry and Heald to another rooming house where they stayed for a week until a boy took Terry and Heald to his brother's apartment – both boys were very young, one a medical student. The same boy also took them to a bar where they met Genevieve Soulie who took them to rue Montmartre where Terry and Heald stayed for about a week with the Mlles Boury.[3]

On (about) 14 December a tall, very blond young man took Terry and Heald to the Jardin des Plantes where they joined William Quinn and a man who asked them to tell the first US Consul they met that they had come from Burgundy.

---

2   Mme Theodrine Quenot (born February 1896) lived with her son Raymond at 15 rue Alcide Vellard, Bobigny (WO208/5452). Mme Quenot is described by Floyd Terry as a peroxide blonde, about 5 ft 2 inches tall, about 40 years old, with a pale complexion – she wore glasses and spoke good English – and by Vic Matthews as a woman with dyed blonde hair and whose sister Madeleine lived at 182 Putney Bridge Road, London. In addition to her work with Bourgogne, Mme Quenot had other connections – in April 1944, she sheltered F/Sgt Gerard Shaughnessy for two weeks, and 2/Lt Gilbert Stonebarger overnight before passing them on to the Dutch-Paris organisation. They joined a party which included Sagan escaper F/Lt Bram van de Stok to be taken across the Pyrenees to Canejan, Spain in June.

3   Heald and Terry are the first two of the 116 evaders listed by Genevieve Soulie as helped by her – taking them from Mlle Davy (aka Madeleine) and delivering them to the Mlles Boury. (NARA Soulie) Her IS9 recommendation for an award says that Mlle Mary Madeleine Davy (born September 1907) of 21 rue Racine, Paris 6, had to give up her work as a guide and 'flee to the provinces in order to evade arrest' in December 1943. (WO208/5459)

2/Lt John Heald, 2/Lt John Dougherty and S/Sgt Robert M Sheets were the bombardier, navigator and one of the waist-gunners of B-17 42-5797 (384BG/546BS) (Magowan) which was returning from Le Bourget on 16 August 1943 when one engine failed and had to be feathered. As they fell out of formation they were attacked by fighters and the aircraft was abandoned. Heald, Dougherty and Sheets were the only successful evaders from this aircraft, although top-turret gunner T/Sgt Sidney C Grinstein almost made it – see earlier.

Robert Sheets landed near Rambouillet and after two days alone, approached a girl who hid him and said she would find more help. A few days later, Sheets was taken to a farm where he joined his bombardier John Heald.

John Heald landed in the Foret de Rambouillet, where he stayed for the rest of the day and following night. Next morning, he approached a young girl who was tending some cows and while they were talking, her father arrived. He suggested that Heald hide in a ditch where later, a mother and her two daughters visited. He was taken to a house and two days later, two Frenchmen arrived – one an English-speaking student from Paris who took Heald's details. They had a note from a man known as 'Froggie' Familisterre (query) assuring Heald that he would be taken to Paris in the next few days. A couple of days later, Froggie himself arrived. He was an elderly man who spoke English, having gone to school in England and worked there, and now ran a *tabac* in Rambouillet. Two days after that, another Frenchman arrived with news that he had located another American who he said he would bring for Heald to identify. Then five more Frenchmen (three locals and two from Paris) arrived to say he would be leaving that afternoon by train for Paris but before that, he should verify the American's identity. They brought in Robert Sheets who immediately said that Heald was his bombardier. This turned out to be a good move since Heald, having only joined the crew at the last moment, didn't actually know the sergeant and they realised later that if Heald had not confirmed his identity, it's likely that Sheets would have been killed.[4]

Heald and Sheets were taken by cart into Rambouillet and the two men from Paris, Lionel (sic) (who spoke English and seemed very well

---

4   "It sometimes happens that two or more individual members of an aircrew are picked up by helpers in different places. In such an event it is important for each member to know and remember the names and descriptions of each member of his crew. When they can give these details to their respective helpers it enables the latter to check up, among each other, on the genuineness of each individual in their charge and help prevent the possibility of enemy agents masquerading as Allied airmen for the purpose of betraying helpers to the Gestapo. The betrayal of a helper invariably results in his death and in that of the whole of his family." (MI9 Bulletin TNA file WO208-3268)

educated) and Raoul (aka Pierre) (Pierre Berteaux) took them to the capital. They went to an apartment at 66 rue Pouchet, Paris XVII where they met Robert (a sickly looking anaemic man of about 27 with blond hair and a moustache) and stayed with a man, wife and their five-year-old daughter for a week (and visited there by a man who claimed to have helped Joseph Rosio and George Evans earlier). On 31 August, Raoul moved them to stay with his aunt, Mme Normand, and her husband Lucien at nearby 29 rue Berzelius.

Heald and Sheets were told they would be leaving soon for England or Spain and on (about) 9 September, they were visited by a woman called Marie Christine (possibly Madeleine Melot see Sidney Casden report) who brought them more clothes and said they would leave that Saturday (11 September). However, two days later another man came to say they wouldn't be leaving after all because the organisation didn't have enough money to pay for their onward journey.

Shortly after this (date uncertain), Maurice Cottereau took Heald and Sheets by truck to his bar, the Cafe du Moulin Rouge in Drancy, where they met Andrew Lindsay, Vic Matthews and a gunner named Joe – Joseph Cornwall. Heald and Sheets were taken to a grain-dealers' house for the night and on about 16 September, to stay with a butcher named Pierre Mangeolle and Mme Louise Faivre at 28 Allee du Chevalier de La Barre where they joined their navigator John Dougherty and met Sgt William Howell and 2/Lt Paul H McConnell.

John Dougherty landed near Poigny-la-Foret (north-west of Rambouillet) and was helped immediately by an Irish girl called Lilly Hannigan (Elisabeth Hannigan (born 1919 in Dublin) was a governess for the Le Bret family of Poigny-la-Foret) and some local women. He hid in some woods while his helpers contacted Paris and on the following Monday, Dougherty was taken by train to the capital where he met Maurice Cottereau (believed by Vic Matthews to be chief of the local organisation) at his bar, the Cafe du Moulin Rouge in Drancy. That night (23 August), Dougherty was taken to stay with an elderly couple, Gabriel Pons and his wife at 174 Avenue Jean Jaures in nearby Bobigny. On 26 August, he was joined by William Howell and Paul McConnell and Maurice told Dougherty that he had located his fellow crewmen, John Heald and Robert Sheets. On 28 August, Dougherty, Howell and McConnell were taken to Les Pavillons-sous-Bois where they stayed with Pierre Mangeolle and Louise Faivre at 28 Allee du Chevalier de La Barre, and on about 9 September, John Heald and

Robert Sheets joined them. On about 11 October, they were also joined by S/Sgt Gary L Hinote.

On 29 October, Heald, Dougherty, Sheets, McConnell, Howell and Hinote were taken to Quimper, Finistere where they joined James Armstrong, Floyd Terry, Andrew Lindsay, Vic Matthews, France Delorie, Royce Fidler, Leslie Woollard, Anthony Reynolds, Charles Bailey and William Quinn. They were to have been embarked by sea in a Dahlia operation organised by Yves Le Henaff (Fanfan) – the idea being to take the evaders from the harbour at Douarnenez by fishing boat and rendezvous at sea with a Royal Navy torpedo boat – but the plan fell through and evaders returned to Paris on (about) 6 November.[5]

Heald and Floyd Terry were brought back to Paris (where Heald saw Andrew Lindsay with Mlle Bourgeois) by a woman called Allouette. She handed them over to a girl who took them to a fifth-floor apartment at 2 Place de la Sorbonne where Heald also met Mme Baron, who lived on the second floor. Mlle Bourgeois told Heald that he and Terry were leaving for Spain and a small, curly-haired boy in his early twenties, took them to join T/Sgt Otto Bruzewski. The three Americans were taken by train to Toulouse where they joined two French naval officers (who Heald names as Pierre Lavissiere and Andre) both of whom spoke English. They were taken on to Carcassonne and Quillan where they met another organisation chief, a chubby man of medium height with a round face. They stayed overnight in a hotel and next day a guide called Martinez arrived and drove them to his house. While waiting in a barn for another group of Americans to join them, Heald picked up a cold and Terry got the grip (sic) (influenza). After three days they left, driving through the night in heavy rain. Their

---

5   Sgt Percival Victor Matthews (pilot of 61 Sqn Lancaster W5002) and two unnamed Americans (probably Davidson and Krueger – see later) were to have been taken to Spain in September but their guide failed to appear and so after meeting Maurice Cottereau at his bar at Drancy, had been sheltered with Floyd Terry by Theodorine Quenot at 15 rue Alcide Veillard, Bobigny for about a month. At the end of October, a Frenchman took them, James Armstrong and Andrew Lindsay to Quimper. Matthews met Fanfan (Yves Le Henaff) and after the planned sea evacuation was abandoned, returned to Paris with him. After a night at Le Henaff's apartment, Le Henaff took Matthews by train to Argenton and then by taxi to somewhere near Montmorrillon (Vienne). That evening, Matthews was taken by truck to a landing field near Haims where, after two day's delay because of bad weather, he was picked up by Lysander (Operation Oriel) and flown back to England the night of 11-12 November 1943.

    2/Lt James E Armstrong was evacuated from Brittany in January 1944 on the fishing boat Breiz-Izel – see later.

    2/Lt Andrew G Lindsay crossed the Pyrenees with Comete in February 1944.

    Sgt Royce Fidler and Sgt Leslie C Woollard were taken to Quimper by Gilbert Virmoux of the Bordeaux organisation – the same man who brought them down from Tourcoing to Paris on 24 October and sheltered them in his one-room flat at 41 rue Saint-Merri, Paris IV. They left France on board the Breizh-Izel in January 1944 – see later.

guide said it would be impossible to get through but the Americans insisted on trying it anyway, carrying on until Terry collapsed. They made their way back to a small village where they found rooms in a hotel and called a doctor for Terry before returning via Foix to Paris where Pierre Lavissiere (nf) took them to his house in the 'smart' section of the city.

The three Americans were visited by a very tall French aviator (described by Heald as having big teeth and a pinched face) before a girl took them to the Hotel de Mexique (query) where Mlle Bourgeois brought a man to measure them for coats. They also met a man called Henri (query) and his friend and were told there was another possible boat operation from Quimper. The Americans left the hotel about a week later after it was found that one of the maids had gone through Henri's bag – Heald and Terry to stay with Henri's brother (who was studying to be a doctor) and Bruzewski elsewhere (see later). Heald and Terry were then taken to a cafe where they met Genevieve Soulie who took them to be sheltered by Mlles Solange and Yvonne Boury at 14 rue Montmartre. They stayed eight days with the Boury sisters before they were taken to the Jardin des Plantes and joined William Quinn.

On their return to Paris from Quimper, Dougherty, Sheets, McConnell and Hinote were met at Montparnasse station by Mlle Bourgeois. McConnell says "they milled around in front of the station while Fanfan conferred with Mlle Bourgeois" before Mlle Bourgeois' companion Marguerite (aka Regina) took him and Dougherty to the Hotel Bienvenue (Mlle Myriem Ledoux) at 4 rue Saint-Sulpice, Paris VI where they were joined by Andrew Lindsay and William Howell. Sheets was sheltered by Gilbert Virmoux of Bordeaux-Loupiac along with James Armstrong, Royce Fidler and Leslie Woollard at 41 rue Saint-Merri, Paris IV. As Gilbert's one-room apartment was so small, Armstrong and Woollard slept in the flat below with M et Mme Le Callonec.

On 12 November, Sheets and Armstrong were taken to the Chateau de la Fortelle – about 12 kms from Marles-en-Brie (Seine-et-Marne) – where they joined Dougherty and others. Bailey and Quinn say the Chateau de la Fortelle was used as a training camp to get the evaders in shape for the Pyrenees – and that the owner (comtesse d'Eshtel (query) who didn't live there) thought it was being used by French students and didn't know what was really going on. Armstrong says they spent their time toughening up for the Pyrenees by hiking in the woods, chopping down trees and playing volley ball.

On 3 December, Dougherty and Sheets returned to Paris where they were met by Suzanne (query) and two others, and taken to the (third-rate) Hotel Bienvenu for the night. Next day, they went to meet the comte Noel de Villeneuve at 12 Avenue du General Mangin, Paris XVI who told them he had no faith in the organisation they were with, that Mlle Bourgeois was being hunted by the Gestapo and that he knew of another organisation who would to take them to Spain in sealed freight wagons. This plan did not materialize. On about 15 December, Sheets was visited by Genevieve Soulie and two days later she took him to stay with an older couple in their house. On 19 December, Sheets joined John Dougherty, Warren Laws, Thomas Mezynski, John Herrick, Charles Bailey and Herbert Dulburg to be taken to the Gare d'Austerlitz where they caught a train to Montauban, Narbonne and Perpignan.

Paul McConnell and Gary Hinote were passed on to Comete soon after they returned to Paris from the Chateau de la Fortelle.

S/Sgt Charles K Bailey was a waist-gunner and Sgt William N Quinn the radio-operator of B-17 42-5867 Alice from Dallas (100BG/350BS) (Claytor) which was on the way to Regensburg on 17 August 1943. Their group was flying too close to the one ahead and their plexiglass nose had already been smashed by discarded cartridge cases when they were hit by flak, setting the left wing on fire and badly damaging the right wing. The bale-out order was given and the aircraft abandoned over Belgium.[6]

Bailey and Quinn were helped by the newly established Felix organisation of Charles Gueulette who sheltered them with Florent Biernaux at 16 Boulevard Thonissen in Hasselt. At the end of October, they were taken to Paris and passed on to the Dahlia network of Yves Le Henaff (Fanfan) for an aborted attempt to evacuate a group of evaders by fishing boat from Douarnenez (Finistere). On returning to Paris they were taken on by Mlle Bourgeois who sent them to the Chateau de la Fortelle for three weeks before returning them to Paris on 10 December 1943 where they were passed on to Genevieve Soulie of Bourgogne.

Charles Bailey landed in someone's garden where fifty (sic) people were waiting for him. He was directed to hide in a ditch and a little while later, Jean Achten appeared with a bicycle and took him to his fiancee Marie Klinkers at her cafe in Diepenbeek (Limburg). Marie dressed his injuries and an RAF questionnaire was produced. William Quinn was

---

6   Alice from Dallas pilot 1/Lt Roy F Claytor, co-pilot 2/Lt Raymond J Nutting and top-turret gunner T/Sgt John W Burgin also evaded successfully – all with Comete.

met on landing near Diepenbeek by a countess whose husband was the governor of Limbourg and she took Quinn to hide in the nearby woods. The following morning Jean Achten visited him and that evening took him to join Bailey.

The following evening (19 August), Jean Achten took Bailey and Quinn by bicycle to Hasselt where they stayed with Florent and Olympe Biernaux at 16 Boulevard Thonissen. During their stay they were visited by a British agent called Felix (aka Victor) (Charles Gueulette) who was head of the newly established organisation, and J C de Coster (aka Criticouse). On 28 October, Olympe Biernaux took Bailey and Quinn to Brussels where they met Felix in a car-parts shop owned by a sixty-five-year-old Englishman. Felix and another man took them to the station and passed them on to another man who took them to Ghent where they stayed the night. Next day they were taken to Mouscron (where Bailey says they walked into the back end of a cafe and out through the front door and were around the Belgian border) and on into Tourcoing. After several hours at the house of a French captain (Fernand Vanaerde, who says they arrived in the morning of 23 October and left that evening), Mlle Simone Michaut collected them and took them to Paris. They arrived at midnight and were met by a priest (Michel Riquet – query) and a short, plump girl called Edwige Gillet who led them to an apartment at 32 Boulevard Henri IV, Paris IV where her parents, Pierre Gillet and his American wife Ann Bailry, apparently owned the whole block. On 21 October, they were taken to be sheltered with Simone Michaut for five days at an address near the Eiffel Tower (query) before being taken to Quimper.[7]

On their return to Paris from Quimper (about 5 November), Bailey and Quinn were met by Haralampos Laghos (an American-born Greek who had gone to school in Berlin) and his wife who took them, Jacob Dalinsky and Anthony Reynolds (both also previously with Felix) back to their home near the Cite Universitaire at 63 rue de l'Amiral Mouchez – they were now (they say) in the organisation of Mlle Bourgeois. They stayed with M et Mme Laghos for about eight days before being taken to the Chateau de la Fortelle where they spent three weeks with William Howell, James Armstrong, Paul McConnell, Gary Hinote, Andrew Lindsay and Robert Sheets getting fit for the mountains. They returned to Paris on 10 December where they stayed for another three or four days with M Laghos before they were separated.

---

7   Jean Achten, Edwige and Pierre Gillet, Ann Bailry and Simone Michaut from evasioncomete.org.

Bailey stayed at the Lycee Sophie Germaine (Institutrice, Mme Vermot) on rue de Jouy for six days until Genevieve Soulie took him to the Gare d'Austerlitz where he joined John Dougherty and was taken by train to Perpignan.

Quinn was taken by M Laghos to meet Genevieve Soulie at Mlle Bourgeois' headquarters opposite the University of Paris. Genevieve then took Quinn to stay with a forty-four-year-old woman who worked at the Banque de France, was 'built like Mae West' and lived on the other side of Paris – this was almost certainly Simone Besson at 8 rue Emile Allez, Paris XVII. Three days later, Genevieve took him to the Jardin des Plantes where he joined John Heald and Floyd Terry and was taken by train to Perpignan.

2/Lt John W Herrick was flying P-47 41-6188 (78FG/82FS) on a bomber escort mission over Paris on 26 November 1943 when he was shot down by an Me109 and baled out.

Herrick landed in a ploughed field near the northern Parisian suburb of Garges-les-Gonesse and was immediately surrounded by French people. He started running but was soon caught up by an elderly man on a bicycle who directed him to a nearby cafe. He was then picked up by a truck driven by a man called Rafe who took him to Leon Achille Alcouffe and his sixteen-year-old daughter Nicki (sic) at 89 rue Belliard, Paris XVIII who gave him a civilian coat. Later that evening, Herrick was taken to another apartment nearby where he met a man and two nurses who had helped evaders before. The younger woman (described as 5 ft 6 inches tall, good figure and hair pulled back in a bun, spoke good English) made Herrick an ID card before M Alcouffe moved him to another apartment twelve blocks away. Next morning, M Alcouffe brought civilian clothes and Herrick was moved back to the nurses apartment for the day. That evening he was taken to stay with M Renaud (query) in his apartment at 27 Avenue Gambetta, Paris XX. On 5 December, Herrick was moved again, this time to stay with M Chanfreau (assume Rene Chanfreau of 2 Avenue du General Maistre, Paris XIV) and his twenty-six-year-old daughter Marthe, both of whom worked at the Banque de France. On 19 December, a man (aged about 24) took Herrick to a rendezvous in front of a church where he joined John Dougherty, Robert Sheets, Charles Bailey, Warren Laws, Herbert Dulberg and Thomas Mezynski.

2/Lt Warren P Laws was the co-pilot of B-17 42-30349 (388BG/563BS) (Wilken) which was returning from Stuttgart on 6 September 1943 and over France when it was attacked by fighters. Several of the crew were probably killed in the attacks before the aircraft was abandoned to crash near Montgueux, about seven kilometres west of Troyes.

Laws was soon joined on the ground by his radio-operator T/Sgt Joseph Schwartzkopf and the two men walked south, reaching Torvilliers the following day where they were approached by Marcel Vergeot and a Polish man who told them the rest of their crew had been killed. It was Marcel Mullot who took them by bicycle to Marcel Vergeot's house in Torvilliers before they spent the night with M et Mme Leon Nelle at Cliquot (query). A man claiming to be an officer in British Intelligence visited them and said there was an organisation in Troyes for getting airmen out but that it was full, with 43 (sic) airmen in and around the town already. After four days, Laws and Schwartzkopf were taken to stay with Joachim Ledantec at his delicatessen at 27 Avenue General Gallieni, Sainte-Savine. Joachim had a daughter called Anne-Marie and they were visited by the abbe Jean Bonnard (from Clerey) while a baker in the same street supplied their food. After about a month they were moved again, this time to stay with the abbe Jean Bonnard and his sister Paulette at 17 rue Traversier where they were visited by Marcel Mullot, Marcel Dore and his wife Carmen – and Marie-Rose Gilbert, who was sheltering Arthur Beach and Walter Soukup. They made one abortive journey into Paris (see Beach report earlier) before returning to the Bonnards. Following a German search for evaders, Laws, Schwartzkopf, Beach and Soukup met at the abbe's seminary with Marie Louise Bonnard (another sister, she worked at the Banque de France in Paris), Marie-Rose, the abbe and Jacques (a Frenchmen who wanted to leave France) and they all went by train to Paris. They were met by a man and his wife who took Laws and Soukup to the apartment of a nurse, an operating room technician named Suzanne Guelat and her husband Olivier at 68 Boulevard Auguste-Blanqui, Paris XIII, while Schwartzkopf and Beach were taken to Juvisy-sur-Orge where they were sheltered by Andre and Pauline Lefevre.

Two days later, Laws was taken to jeweller Andre Francois at his apartment over the Galerie de Montpensier where he met a medical student called Guillaume before a girl took him to stay with Felix Gruz at 26 rue d'Hauteville, Paris X. The following day, a woman (about 36 years old with short dark hair) brought Herbert Dulberg from the B-17 Battlin' Bobbie to join him. On 19 December, Genevieve Soulie took Laws and Dulberg to a meeting place near the Pantheon – presumably the Jardin des Plantes – where they joined more American evaders and a Frenchman who spoke

English. The Frenchman took them by train to Montauban where they were joined by another Frenchman, understood to be a captain in French Intelligence, and on to Narbonne and Perpignan.

S/Sgt Herbert W Dulberg was the radio-operator of B-17 42-29876 Battlin' Bobbie (379BG/525BS) (Hoyt) which was on the way to Nantes on 16 September 1943 when it was attacked by fighters and the aircraft abandoned over Brittany.[8]

Dulberg was helped immediately on landing near Rennes, taken to a farmhouse and that evening, his journey was arranged. Dulberg's report is almost illegible from this point but we can get some clues from his waist-gunner, William Miller, who says he was soon taken to join Dulberg and their pilot Elton Hoyt and next day they were joined by their tail-gunner Edward Shaffer. The four men were together until being taken to a monastery at Saint-Helen near Dinan where Hoyt left them. Miller, Shaffer and Dulberg were only a few days at the monastery before Roger Pansart arranged for a truck to drive them to a cafe at Ploermel (on about 15 October) where they met a man in big tortoiseshell glasses (Emile Guimard) at which point, Dulberg went with Francois Lequitte (of Ploermel), Shaffer was taken by Henri Boulet to Taupont, Morbihan while Alex Joubaud took Miller to Villa Gohan, his house near Taupont. On 22 November, Miller rejoined Shaffer and Dulberg – and met T/Sgt Samuel Blatchford, S/Sgt Cyril Koval, S/Sgt Elmer Schroeder, S/Sgt Alfred Held (all from B-17 42-29901), S/Sgt Harry Boegaholz (from B-17 42-3042) and a French fighter pilot called Guillaume Bernard. Miller says that a guide named Emile (Emile Guimard) took him, Dulberg, Blatchford, Koval and Bernard to Paris the next day where they lost Dulberg on the Metro. Dulberg says they had two guides, the other slender, about 5 feet, 10 inches tall and that it was this slender guide who separated him from the others on the Metro.

Emile Guimard (born June 1915) played a significant part in helping several of the evaders in Brittany. As will be seen, he had contacts with

---

8   Seven other crew from the Battlin' Bobbie also evaded successfully: waist-gunner S/Sgt Harry L Minor was evacuated by RN MGB 503 from l'Anse-Cochat near Plouha in February 1944 (Op Bonaparte 2) with the Shelburn organisation, the other waist-gunner, T/Sgt William J Miller and tail-gunner Sgt Edward R Shaffer crossed the Pyrenees in March 1944 with the Dutch-Paris organisation – and pilot 1/Lt Elton Hoyt, co-pilot 1/Lt Norman C Schroeder, navigator 2/Lt William J Cook Jnr and bombardier 2/Lt Louis H Glickman with Bourgogne.

The 16 September raid to Nantes was a disaster for almost everyone, with the actual target, the German U-boat supply ship Kertosono, being missed completely. The majority of bombs dropped on Nantes that day landed in the town, killing over 1,000 French civilians.

Bourgogne, with Camille Nicolas at Livry-Gargan, the Bordeaux-Loupiac organisation and with SOE.[9]

While the others were taken to the Parisian suburb of Pantin (see later), Dulberg went to stay with Felix Gruz at 26 rue d'Hauteville, joining Warren Laws who had arrived there the day before. On 19 December, Genevieve Soulie turned him over to an English-speaking guide (5 ft 10 inches, dark hair, clean complexion, about 165 lbs, about 25 years old and married) who took them to Montauban, Narbonne and Perpignan.

S/Sgt Thomas R Mezynski was the right waist-gunner on B-17 42-30604 Badger's Beauty V (100BG/350BS) (Helstrom) which was returning from Frankfurt on 4 October 1943 when the navigator realised they were so far off course (although still in formation) that he didn't have maps to cover them. They were also about to run out of fuel and the aircraft was landed (wheels up) south of Caen in Normandy.

The ten-man crew split into small groups: pilot Capt Harold B Helstrom with navigator 1/Lt Harold H Cuttice – co-pilot F/O Hubert E Trent with bombardier 1/Lt Hilbert W Philippe – LWG S/Sgt Joseph Shandor with tail-gunner S/Sgt Charles E Crippen and top-turret-gunner S/Sgt William D Edwards – and radio-operator T/Sgt Robert C Giles and BTG T/Sgt Carroll F Haarup with Mezynski.[10]

Mezynski, Giles and Haarup headed south-east and after getting some food (and civilian clothes that only fitted Giles) they slept out the first night. They walked for five days until they found a man who took them back to his home. This same man helped them get train tickets for Vernay (Verneuil-sur-Avre – query) but after a delay at Argentan, Haarup became so ill that they had to get off the train at L'Aigle. Walking out of the town, they approached a farmhouse where they slept overnight before going on to a small village with a railway station. The railway line was abandoned but the station-master gave them some sandwiches and directions to Chartres. A little further on and it was clear that Haarup wasn't getting any better so they stopped in another small village, Saint-Maurice-les-Charencey. This

9   Huguen (page 406) says that Emile Guimard lived at Le Roc-Saint-Andre (Morbihan) although the IS9 Helper List has him at Parc a Forage, Vannes – Jean-Claude Bougeon says he lived at Lizio, near Le Roc-Saint-Andre.

10   Trent evaded to Switzerland but I have no information on Helstrom or Cuttice and presume they were captured. Philippe joined Shandor, Crippen and Edwards in Paris where they were helped by the John Carter organisation. The group were divided for the train journey from Lyon to Lavelanet – Annie (Mlle Sabourault) took 2/Lts Jean Pitner and Arno Plischke from B-17 42-31215 (Ford) – Jean Calmet (of 12 rue de Marseille) took Kenneth Skidmore and Shandor – and John Carter took Crippen, Edwards and Philippe. Carter and the three Americans were captured in Pamiers – see later. (John Carter statement found in Wiame NARA file).

turned out to be very fortunate as it was from Saint-Maurice that their journeys were arranged.

On 29 October, Mezynski, Giles and Haarup were taken to Paris where they stayed with Simone Levavasseur (who refers to them as Tom, Bob and Carol) at La Petite Chocolatiere, 19 Avenue d'Orleans – and Giles was told that he was the twenty-first evader to have stayed there. They were later told that their original contact (Mme Melot) had been arrested and they would be passed to a different organisation. They were visited by Genevieve Soulie, who took their details, and also met Olga Christol (and her husband Paul) who said that she would get them out on 5 December with her organisation – apparently called Organisation Todt because they used papers intended for labourers. On 9 December, Genevieve Soulie came and told them that Olga Christol was wanted by the Gestapo and they should be ready to leave in a hurry. Simone Levavasseur's friend Mme Boy (Mme Marthe Boy born July 1879) took Mezynski to her home at 9 rue Ernest Cresson, Paris XIV and a young girl (possibly Mme Boy's daughter Jane) took Giles and Haarup to the Christols apartment at 4 rue Edouard Quenu but there was no-one there so they went to stay with Mme Boy as well.

On 19 December, a French boy who had John Herrick with him, collected Mezynski from Mme Boy and took him to the station where he joined Warren Laws and travelled with him on the train to Montauban, Narbonne and Perpignan.

John Heald, Floyd Terry and William Quinn arrived in Perpignan on (about) 15 December where they were picked up two men and taken to the room of one of them. Five nights later they left with a guide and joined a group of seven more Americans that included John Dougherty.

John Dougherty, Robert Sheets, Charles Bailey, John Herrick, Warren Laws, Herbert Dulburg and Thomas Mezynski arrived in Perpignan on 20 December 1943 where they were met by a man on a bike and a girl on foot who led them for about two hours to a rendezvous where they joined Heald, Terry, Quinn and a group of Frenchmen who had been there for several days.

It took three days to cross the mountains and on the second night (during which they crossed the border) Laws was left in the mountains but caught up again three hours later. Their guides took them to Vilajuiga and left them to take a train to Barcelona. Having no tickets they went into town to get something to eat while Herrick hopped a goods train.

When it stopped at Figueras, Herrick got off and was unable to get back on again when it left. He was arrested and sent to prison in Espolla for the night of 23 December where he was joined by the rest of the group, who had been arrested at Vilajuiga. On 25 December, they were visited by the American Consul (Roberto Estrado) from Gerona before being taken on to Figueras, Gerona, Barcelona, Saragossa and Alhama de Aragon until being repatriated to Madrid and Gibraltar the following month.

CHAPTER 41

Crossing from Perpignan with Captain George Millar

On 18 (or 19) December 1943, T/Sgt Otto Bruzewski, Sgt William Howell, 1/Lt Norman Schroeder, 2/Lt Eugene Mulholland and S/Sgt Rosswell Miller left Paris by train for Montauban, Narbonne and Perpignan.[1]

T/Sgt Otto F Bruzewski was a waist-gunner on B-17 42-3225 (381BG/535BS) (Disbrow) which was returning from Schweinfurt on 17 August 1943 and still over Germany when it was attacked by fighters. After losing three engines, the aircraft was abandoned to crash near Liege in Belgium.[2]

Bruzewski landed in a tree, his feet just inches from the ground, somewhere near Liege. After avoiding the immediate search, he walked south through the night, rested the next day and walked again the following night before resting again. He awoke to find a man standing over him and when he declared himself to be an American the man told him to wait where he was. Shortly after that a woman approached with coffee, sandwiches and civilian clothing and told him to follow another woman – after which his journey was arranged. He was taken to a house where he slept for a while before being moved to a priest's house where he joined his ball-turret gunner Joseph Walters, radio-operator Thomas Moore and tail-gunner William Kiniklis. They had a meal together before being taken (on 20 August) to M et Mme Charles Kremer in Liege – where they met 2/Lt Raymond J Nutting (co-pilot of B-17 42-5867 Alice From Dallas) – and Bruzewski stayed for the next seven and a half weeks.[3]

---

1   Norman Schroeder Jnr emailed me in May 2013 to say (amongst other things) that one of his father's guides to Perpignan was Genevieve Crosson – although Mulholland only mentions a man as going with them ...

2   Three other crewmen from 42-3225 also evaded successfully: top-turret gunner S/Sgt Joseph J Walters with Comete, radio-operator T/Sgt Thomas R Moore was evacuated from Brittany in January 1944 on the Breiz-Izel, and tail-gunner S/Sgt William P Kiniklis crossed the Pyrenees with Bourgogne – see later.

3   Charles Jean Mathieu Kremer (born September 1905) and his wife Celestine Henriette Marie Kremer (born December 1909) of 3 rue des Premontres, Liege, were arrested on 11 December 1943. Charles was shot a month later but Celestine was released in May 1944. (WO208/5451 & 5452) Note that Nutting and the IS9 Belgian Helper List both give the Kremer address as 8 rue d'Amay – same as the IS9 address for the de Ruyters below ...

On about 10 October, Bruzewski was taken to stay with Marcel de Ruyter and his wife Mariette where he joined Alice From Dallas TTG T/ Sgt John W Burgin and bombardier 2/Lt Kenneth R Lorch.[4] On about 22 October, Charles Kremer took Bruzewski and Thomas Moore to Brussels, then Ghent and on to cross the frontier at Mouscron (using the same Felix route as Alice From Dallas crewmen Bailey and Quinn – see earlier). They walked from one cafe across the border to another and on to Tourcoing (where Fernand Vanaerde says they were sheltered overnight with Gaston Vorreux) and a new guide took them by train to Paris. They missed their Metro connection and had to spend the night of 24-25 October at the station but early next morning they were taken to an apartment near Odeon station (Paris VI) where they were sheltered by a student organisation.

Sgt Harold Bailey RAF describes how he and a group of American evaders (Frank Tank, Ernest Stock, Eric Kolc and Russell Gallo – mentioned later) were brought from Brussels and taken across the border in January 1944. Going first to the *Cafe des Sports* [204 rue de la Marliere] at Mouscron, they walked across the frontier to the *Cafe Sans Moustaches* [*Au Rendez Vous des Sans Moustaches* (Jean-Louis Barbe) at 390 rue des Trois Pierres] where they were met by the owner of the Cafe des Sports who had crossed the frontier elsewhere. He then took them into Tourcoing where they caught a train to Paris.

On 28 October, Bruzewski and Moore went with S/Sgt Harry Horten and S/Sgt Edward Sobolewski to Quimper, travelling overnight and arriving at ten o'clock the following morning. They stayed at various addresses before finding that the promised boat scheme from Douarnenez had fallen through and they were taken back to Paris.

Bruzewski, Moore, Horten and Sobolewski returned to Paris on 6 November and a blonde woman took Bruzewski to the home of a French professor of English who lived near the station. On 20 November, the blonde woman moved him to a girl's apartment where he met Floyd Terry and John Heald. They and two French boys (both called Pierre) took a train to Toulouse and Carcassonne then diesel truck to Quillan (Languedoc-Roussillon) where they stayed overnight in a hotel. Next day, they were driven to a little town near Rouze (Ariege) (at 1,000 metres

4   Monsieur le Baron Marcel August Charles Georges Gislain de Ruyter (born April 1910) and his wife Mariette Francoise (born October 1910) of 8 rue d'Amay, Liege were arrested in December 1943. Marcel was shot ten days later but the Baroness was released in May 1944. (WO208/5451 & 5452) Alice co-pilot Raymond Nutting who had moved there earlier from the Kremer apartment at rue d'Amay, says the de Ruyters were living at 52 Quai Orban.

elevation and about 8 kms from the Spanish border) where they waited three days for another group of Americans to join them – they never did so on 25 November, the three evaders set out with two guides to cross the mountains. They walked through deep snow until three o'clock the next morning when Terry collapsed and the attempt was abandoned. Note that John Heald's version of events (see earlier) is slightly different.

They returned to Paris on 28 November and Bruzewski (at least) stayed in a small hotel near the Odeon. On the morning of 5 December he was taken to a shop eight blocks away where he spent the night alone and in the morning, William Howell and Norman Schroeder arrived and they spent the night there.[5]

Sgt William C Howell was the tail-gunner of B-17 42-29928 (381BG/533BS) (Ballinger) which was on the way to Le Mans on 4 July 1943 when it was hit by flak over Laval which took out one engine and the oxygen supply. They dropped out of formation and were heading back north when the aircraft was attacked by fighters and abandoned to crash near the village of Le Val-de-Vee in Lower Normandy.

Howell doesn't specify a location in his report but he landed just north-east of the Foret d'Andain. His only footwear was his heavy flying boots so progress was slow. After avoiding several of the German troops that he saw searching the area, Howell finally met a Frenchman who took him back to his house where Howell was given some fish, which he couldn't eat, and cider, which made him sick. He spent the night there before setting off, using his escape kit compass to head south. It rained all day and Howell began to suffer from the metal fragments he'd picked up when his aircraft was attacked. Late that afternoon he found a barn and hid in the hayloft. That evening, a boy began working the hay and Howell was forced to reveal himself. Once Howell had persuaded the boy that he was an American, the family brought him some food and let him stay the night in their barn. Next morning, Howell set off again and that afternoon met a group of people, one of whom worked for M Challemel du Roziers (query) (owner of the Chateau du Petit-Jard) who took him home where Howell convinced them that he was American by producing an American penny from his pocket. He was given cognac (which really cheered him up) and his first hot meal since leaving England. That night he was taken to La Ferte-Mace where a doctor removed 'a lot of shrapnel' from his body – and Howell slept until

---

5   2/Lt Sidney Casden reports Bruzewski, Howell and Schroeder as leaving Andre Lefevre's home in Juvisy-sur-Orge together at about this time …

the following afternoon. That night M Challemel du Roziers set Howell up with a tent and sleeping bag in the woods – where he spent the next few days, disguised as a boy scout but not sleeping very much due to constant rain and the sound of wild boar – while his journey arranged.

On 19 July, Lucienne Bourgoin (she and her husband Emmanuel were caretakers at the nearby Chateau de l'Ermitage) took Howell by horse and buggy to Domfront where he joined his navigator Paul McConnell who was lodged with Andre Rougeyron at Le Chalet de la Rocque on rue Montgomery – they were alternated between Le Chalet and the nearby home of one of Andre's aunts.[6]

On 26 August, a friend of Andre Rougeyron called Havas arrived by car with two other men (one with the resistance pseudonym of Fiquet) and a woman. That evening, another friend of Rougeyron's, Georges Gilard, drove Rougeyron and the two Americans in a borrowed car and followed Havas to Flers where the Americans were put on a train to Paris.

Howell and McConnell were taken to meet Maurice Cottereau at his bar in Drancy before joining John Dougherty at 174 Avenue Jean Jaures in nearby Bobigny where he was being sheltered by Gabriel Pons and his wife.[7]

1/Lt Norman C Schroeder was the co-pilot of B-17 42-29876 Battlin' Bobbie (379BG/525BS) (Hoyt) which was on the way to Nantes on 16 September 1943 when it was attacked by fighters and the aircraft abandoned near Rennes, Brittany.[8]

Schroeder landed near the village of Saint-Ganton (Ille-et-Vilaine), about 6 kms south-west of Messac, and hid for the rest of the day until fourteen-year-old Robert Massiot took him back to his home where his parents, Albert and Clementine Massiot (nf) gave Schroeder a meal and civilian clothes. Schroeder then set off walking south, covering about 120 miles by the end of the month (and crossing the demarcation line) before finally declaring himself at a farmhouse just outside Poitiers, belonging to Auguste and Henriette Vergnaud (nf). On 1 October, Auguste took Schroeder by bicycle to Lussac-les-Chateau where he stayed with Auguste's mother-in-law, Mme Vayer, at the Hotel de la Gare while his journey was

---

6   Some additional details are taken from the 1947 book '*Agents d'Evasion*' by Andre Rougeyron as translated into English by Marie-Antoinette McConnell and republished in 1996 by the Louisianana State University Press as 'Agents for Escape'.

7   It's almost impossible to decipher the hand-written scrawl of the interviewer's notes from this point which cover a trip to Quimper for the aborted boat scheme at the end of October (see elsewhere) and staying at the Chateau de la Fortelle where they trained for the Pyrenees, to where he joined Eugene Mulholland and Rosswell Miller on the train to Perpignan …

8   Eight of the Battlin' Bobbie crew evaded successfully – see earlier.

arranged. Two days later, Pierre Martin and garagiste Roger Andrault (nf) drove Schroeder by truck to M Martin's home at 10 rue d'Ypres in Montmorrillon (Vienne) where he stayed overnight before Raoul Gaschard (of Saint-Savin) took him to Le Vigeant. Schroeder was sheltered in a German concentration camp (run by a French lieutenant) with twenty-five black Madagascan soldiers but lived in the officers' quarters with an organisation man called Joel.[9]

On 25 October, Schroeder was taken by car back to Montmorrillon, where he stayed with M Guibert and Ernest Neveu (of Haims), before being escorted by two gendarmes on bicycles to a field where he hoped to be picked up by aircraft. No aircraft appeared and Schroeder was returned to Montmorrillon and Le Vigeant for three more weeks until the next full moon.[10]

After returning once more from the landing field at La Nocelière, Raoul Gaschard and Robert Lajon[11] took Schroeder to be sheltered at the chateau de l'Epine. He stayed at the chateau until 27 November when he was moved to Saint-Savin (Vienne) and sheltered with watch-maker Roger Tiffineau and his wife. On 5 December, Schroeder left Saint-Savin by car for Poitiers with a Parisian girl called Anne-Marie who then took him back to the capital by train, arriving early next morning. Schroeder was taken to a young student's house (sic) for breakfast before Sgt William C Howell was brought there.[12]

2/Lt Eugene V Mulholland was the co-pilot of B-17 42-5865 Janie (100BG/351BS) (Fienup) which was returning from Romilly-sur-Seine in the early morning of 3 September 1943 when it was attacked by fighters, hit by flak and abandoned to explode in mid-air.[13]

---

9   Much of the additional information about Schroeder's evasion comes from Jean-Claude Bourgeon who retraced the route from Messac with Schroeder's son Norman Junior and his wife Barbara in 2015.

10   Schroeder seems to have been given the usual aircraft story but in this case it almost came true. After the first attempt for the night of 9-10 November was cancelled due to bad weather, three RAF SD Lysanders came back to Oriel landing field (3.5 kms NNW of Haims – Poitou-Charentes) for Operation Oriel – organised by Yves Le Henaff and intended to take him back to London on the night of 11-12 November. Only one Lysander landed – pilot Robin Hooper cancelled the other two because it was so muddy – and it was Vic Matthews and two French officers who were flown back to England.

11   Robert Leon Charles Lajon (born December 1911) of Saint-Germaine par Saint-Savin, who began his resistance and evasion activities in 1940, was arrested on 27 January 1944 and deported. His recommendation for a KMC says that his silence under torture was instrumental in saving the lives of many comrades. He was liberated from Flossenburg in April 1945. (WO208-5459)

12   Norman Schroeder Jnr told me (by email in 2013) that his father was sheltered with the Meilleroux family (at Juvisy-sur-Orge) and visited the Lefevre home to play cards with Bruzewski and Howell.

13   Mulholland was the third man of the Janie crew to evade successfully – all helped by Bourgogne.

Mulholland landed in a field and a crowd of people rushed to meet him but they could not understand one another so Mulholland ran into some woods to hide from approaching German troops. He walked for two days before declaring himself to a man who directed him to a house where he was helped by a woman (Mme Suzanne Charise – query) who was visiting from Courbevoie (north-west Paris) who took him back to her home that evening. Next day, a man from an organisation came to interview him and that night he was moved to nearby 3 rue de Visien, Courbevoie where he stayed with an old man and his two daughters Di Champ (query) and a coiffeur named Andre Kocher (of 62 rue du Strasbourg). Mulholland stayed three weeks in Courbevoie and understood that he was the first American they had helped. On 27 September, Raoul and Andre brought Mulholland ID papers – and removed all his US possessions – before taking him to 12 rue Sarrette, Paris XIV to stay with a machine-shop owner named Andre Verger.[14] Mulholland was there for three weeks, joined by Rosswell Miller from the B-17 Wee Bonnie II after a week and visited by Robert Guillet (about 40 years old, sandy hair, 5 ft 9 inches tall, very thin) (head of organisation) who said he was going to shoot Raoul because of money matters – M Robert's organisation was very short of funds.[15]

On 18 October, Mulholland and Miller were passed over to the organisation which had been providing money to M Robert. They were taken to a Metro entrance where they met Mme Marie (a short, blonde Belgian wife of a gendarme) (Gabrielle Wiame) and British commando Frederick Long and she took them to Maurice and Andree Vandevoorde at 167 rue de la Republique, Fontenay-sous-Bois where they met William Boren and a French spy who had a picture of Norman Kreitenstein who had left 18 days earlier. They only stayed one night because the best friend of their hostess was arrested (previously mentioned – Andree Lebegue who was arrested on 19 October with an evader called Bob) and so Mulholland and Miller were moved to the home of an elderly couple near Le Bourget. Their son had recently escaped from the Germans so again the two Americans only stayed overnight before being taken back into Paris. They were sheltered with a Mme Mary (coiffeuse) at 12 rue Clapeyron, Paris

---

14   The IS9 Helper List has a M Andre Verger at 262 Avenue Daumesnil, Paris XII.

15   Robert Guillet (born June 1904 in Quimper) of 81 rue du Bac, Paris VII, was arrested on 15 December 1943 and deported to Germany. He was last seen at the American Hospital in Ludwigslust in May 1945 by a French priest who administered the last Sacraments. (WO208/5459) Robert Guillet is believed to have worked with both Comete and Pernod as well as possibly heading an organisation of his own.

VIII until about 12 November when they were moved again when her concierge became suspicious of their presence.[16]

Dora Rospape (who they had met whilst with Mme Mary) took them to stay with Mme Nelly Autret (who worked at the Pasteur Institute) at 45 rue Dutot.[17] They were there for a week and Mulholland says that two Belgians visited them but acted suspiciously and so they were bumped off and Mulholland and Miller were promptly taken to stay with the Andureau sisters, Alice and Andree – one was a doctor at the Pasteur Institute – for five days. On 23 November, Dora Rospape took Mulholland and Rosswell back to rue Clapeyron but as Mme Mary was not there, they stayed the night at 25 rue de Madrid where they met Maud Couve, Alice Brouard, the children and Raoul's friend Andre (Andre Blateyron). Next day, Mme Rospape took them back to Mme Mary where they stayed until 4 December when Mme Rospape came to tell them that the organisation had been broken up, that the Colonel (head of the organisation and apparently a woman) (Madeleine Melot) had been arrested – although Marie, who worked under her was not caught – and she took them back to stay with Nelly Autret at rue Dutot. Genevieve Soulie – who had a list of men sheltered around Paris – came and took their details and on 18 December, a short, dark-haired girl and two men (one of whom went with them to Perpignan) took them to the railway station. The other man (middle-aged, about 5 ft 6 inches, stocky, dark hair, spoke some English) asked them to tell the Consul they had come from Burgundy. When they changed trains at Montauban, they saw that Otto Bruzewski, William Howell and Norman Schroeder were travelling with them to Perpignan.

S/Sgt Rosswell Miller was one of the waist-gunners of B-17 42-30362 Wee Bonnie II (388BG/561BS) (Porter) which was on the way to Beaumont-sur-Oise on 9 September 1943. They were about to start their bomb run when an Me109 attacked the aircraft with heavy-calibre cannon fire. The B-17 began to spin out of control and the pilot gave the bale-out order.

The five evaders from the eleven-man crew of Wee Bonnie II (which included cameraman S/Sgt Ralph Mallicote) are a good example of the vagaries of escaping and evading through occupied France. Co-pilot 2/Lt Harold E Thompson and navigator 2/Lt Henry C Rowland were returned

---

16   Mme Mary – or Marry/Meray – all as per Wiame NARA file but not found elsewhere.

17   Mme Nelly Autrot (born March 1900) laboratory assistant of 45 rue Dutot, Paris XV. (WO208/5452)

to England by MGB 318 from Brittany in the early hours of 2 December on Operation Envious IIb – tail-gunner Sgt Ivan L Schraeder crossed the Pyrenees from Perpignan in November with a party of civilians but the other waist-gunner, S/Sgt Clement Mezzanotte didn't cross into Spain until late April 1944.

Miller, a twenty-six-year-old steel worker from Ohio, baled out at about 20,000 feet but made a deliberately delayed jump, not opening his parachute until about 3,000 feet. He landed in a small town (probably Chatou) where local people advised him to run so he abandoned his parachute and ran 'several blocks' before hiding in a garden. Later some people came and hid him in a sun-flower patch and when it got dark, he was taken to a deserted house where he was given civilian clothes and spent the rest of the night. Next day, Miller was taken to a point north of Montesson and after crossing the Seine, made his way south to Noisy-le-Roi and Bailly where he spent the night in a barn on the edge of the village. He began walking south again the next day, following signs towards Versailles, until he was picked up by a man in a car who drove him back to Noisy-le-Roi. A week later, Miller was driven to Versailles where he was sheltered by a Mme Marie (5 feet 3 inches tall, dark complexion, blonde hair), her disabled father and a short, blonde, light-skinned English woman named Elizabeth. On 3 October, two young men (both about twenty years old – one tall, blond with light complexion and the other with dark hair and moustache) took Miller into Paris where he joined Eugene Mulholland from the B-17 Janie.

The five Americans were joined in Perpignan by Captain George Millar (1 Rifle Brigade) who had been captured whilst on patrol near Msus in Libya in January 1942, escaped from a POW train taking prisoners from Stalag VIIA (Moosburg) in October 1943 and had made his way to Perpignan where his helpers from Saint-Gervais-les-Bains (Rhone-Alpes) had a contact. Millar more or less took charge of the evaders, partly because as at thirty-three, he was the oldest, and partly because he spoke good French and so could act as interpreter between the Americans and their French helpers.

Following their take-over of southern France in November 1942, the Germans had declared a zone interdite (forbidden zone) along the foothills of the Pyrenees. Special permits were required to live or travel there. South of Perpignan, the zone interdite began at the river Tech, which runs into the sea between Elne and Argeles-sur-Mer. During the summer, the Tech isn't much of an obstacle but in the winter months, it can become lethally dangerous. I think the local passeurs probably liked to use the coastal route that Millar and the others were taken along because after passing Argeles-sur-Mer, it is only about 10 kms due south, to the Spanish border.

Howell thought they had an especially rough crossing with three separate and exhausting starts and George Millar describes the events in detail in his 1957 (revised) book 'Horned Pigeon'.[18] Their primary contact in Perpignan was a man named Pierre (or Louis) Cartelet and he organised their shelter and guides for the crossing. Their first attempt, led by an experienced guide, a Catalan who Millar names as Pedro, was hampered by the inclusion of an elderly and belligerent Belgian (Alberic Volkaert – see later) who seems not to have been fit enough to make the crossing even in ideal conditions. They were then defeated by the river Tech and had to return to Perpignan two nights later. They never saw Pedro again – Millar was told that his body was found in the river in suspicious circumstances and so a second guide was appointed at short notice.[19] This (unnamed) man turned out to be complete fraud, an arrogant Frenchman who fancied the idea of being a passeur but had never used the route and had no idea at all about navigation. Setting off once more in the evening of Monday 3 January, their third guide was a small, elderly Catalan who despaired at the lack of fitness among the Americans (Volkaert had returned to Paris by then) but persevered to lead them safely to the border – although Mulholland gave up just before that and Rosswell Miller elected to go back and help him – and arranged for the four remaining walkers to be delivered safely to the British Consulate in Barcelona.

Mulholland says that although their guide told them they were just half an hour from the frontier, he could not take another step. Eventually he persuaded the others to leave him behind and he slept all the next day in a barn. The owner of the barn went into Banyuls-sur-Mer to call the police (having assured Mulholland they were friendly) and later, two gendarmes drove up near the farm before walking across to the barn. At the same time, two Germans also arrived and all four men found Mulholland laying "in ragged trousers and bleeding profusely". One of the gendarmes went through Mulholland's pockets while explaining to the Germans that

18   Published by Pan Books. Millar doesn't use any real names for the five Americans in his book but readers should be able to identify Trapper, Fritz, Clark Gable, the Chauve Souris and Charlie easily enough.

19   The guide that Millar names in his book as 'Pedro' is mentioned by S/Ldr Fletcher Taylor as joining his party on 31 January 1944 and being recognised by one of his French companions (Marguerite Avons' son Serge from Frangy, who had travelled to Perpignan with Millar) as the man believed to have drowned whilst guiding Millar's party. Serge didn't challenge the guide for fear of his life.

Mulholland was an escaped inmate from a home for the deaf and dumb and that they were going to return him to the home. This seemed to satisfy the Germans who duly left, leaving the gendarmes to confirm Mulholland's real identity in whispers. When he agreed that he could manage to walk another kilometre, they took him back to the police station in Banyuls where Mulholland says he met the entire police force. He was fed and washed, given a new pair of trousers and taken to spend the night in a cosy tower. Next morning (9 January) Mulholland was taken back to the police station and turned over to a man who gave him a steak dinner in a cafe. The police gave him a knapsack filled with "food, wine, alcohol, cookies and sugar" and after his meal, drove Mulholland back to a spot near the farm. They collected the farmer and drove further into the mountains to a place where they could point out the way to Spain.

Mulholland set off once more at midday, finally crossing the border and reaching a Spanish village at about ten o'clock that evening. After spending the night in a barn, Mulholland made his way to the railway station where he telephoned Mr Forsyth at the consulate. He was advised to turn himself over to the police who would take him to Gerona where he would join other Americans. Not knowing how to contact the local police, Mulholland traded his watch for a train ticket to Barcelona and was arrested on the train.

Rosswell Miller says that both he and Mulholland were "awfully tired" and helped each other as much as they could until Mulholland gave out completely. Miller stayed with him for a while then went to get help. Not finding any, he then couldn't find Mulholland again so went on to Spain by himself where he was arrested by the Guardia Civil and spent some days in a prison at Figueras.

Having said that it's 'only' ten kilometres, I should point out that visitors to the region today will need, in the absence of a reliable passeur, a good map and compass if they intend to try and follow any of the myriad trails that run through the tangle of foothills from Argeles to the Spanish frontier. This might seem to have been a fairly straight forward hike (especially when compared to some of the crossings to Andorra) but it should be remembered that this was December, it was very cold and rained a lot, the airmen were not particularly fit and most of all, they were walking in almost total darkness. They were also poorly equipped and clothed, had no idea where they were going, nor how much further they would have to walk.

CHAPTER 42

The Trap at Eglise de Pantin

At five o'clock in the afternoon of 17 December 1943, a group of eighteen airmen evaders were captured in a German trap at Eglise de Pantin – actually the market behind the Eglise Saint-Germain l'Auxerrois at Place de l'Eglise, in the north-east Parisian suburb of Pantin, opposite the Eglise de Pantin Metro station.

The group was made up of men helped by Bordeaux-Loupiac, who were captured along with some of their helpers – and a much larger group helped by the CDLL (*Ceux de la Liberation*) organisation that had been sheltering them in the commune of Livry-Gargan prior to passing them on to Bordeaux-Loupiac for evacuation by sea. Georges Kahn (aka Geo) of CDLL was also arrested.[1]

It could have been even worse – the twenty-nine men sheltered by CDLL were taken to Pantin in two groups – the first group went by bus to Eglise de Pantin and the second were driven in a lorry. Fortunately, Camille Nicolas, who was sitting in the front of the lorry, sensed trouble ahead. He ordered the driver to park while he got out and walked towards the church. On seeing men that he was sure were German agents, he waved the lorry forward, jumped back in and had the thirteen airmen driven back to Livry-Gargan.[2]

The thirteen airmen who escaped with Camille Nicolas in the lorry were: F/Sgt Frederick Page, Sgt John Vass, F/Sgt Robert Ellis, 2/Lt Charles Downe, 2/Lt Karl Miller, 2/Lt Jack Horton, Sgt James Tracy, 2/Lt Chauncey

---

1   Georges Kahn (born February 1906) had been involved in resistance and evasion work since 1942. He collected numerous evaders from other organisations and sheltered several of them at his home in Garches. Following his arrest, he was taken to rue Saussaies and subjected to 'brutal torture'. Georges Kahn later died 'under tragic circumstances'. (WO208/5453)

2   Camille Raoul Nicolas (born September 1895) of 19 rue de Meaux, Livry-Gargan, began his evasion activities in September 1941, using his lorry to collect downed aircrew. He joined Georges Kahn, working with CDLL, in July 1943. Nicolas was arrested shortly after the trap at l'Eglise de Pantin, together with his wife and father-in-law but released on 26 January 1944 for lack of evidence. Nicolas, who took over from Georges Kahn as chief of CDLL and continued his evasion work until the liberation, was recommended for a KMC. (WO208/5458) There is now a rue Camille Nicolas in Livry-Gargan.

Hicks, 1/Lt Elwood Arp, 2/Lt Howard Sherman, S/Sgt Carl Bachmann, T/Sgt William Miller and Sgt Edward Shaffer.

The fourteen men from the bus who were captured that day were: F/O Zbigniew Frankiewcz, F/Sgt William Bennett, T/Sgt Samuel Blatchford, S/Sgt Elmer Schroeder, S/Sgt Alfred Held, S/Sgt Cyril Koval, F/O William Mildren, 2/Lt Stanley Bolesta, S/Sgt Henry Cunningham, Sgt Kenneth Rimer, 2/Lt Jacques Keshishian, Sgt Norman Stephens, 2/Lt Nathan Weltman and S/Sgt Harry J Boegaholz.

Sgt Andre Poirier, who was acting as a guide for Bordeaux-Loupiac, brought fellow Spitfire pilots W/O John Daly and F/Lt Leslie Prickett, along with Boston air-gunner F/Lt Graham Kelly to the rendezvous separately. They had only just joined the other airmen when they were also captured.

John Daly was being sheltered in the Marechaux apartment at 29 rue de la Chappelle with Kelly and Prickett when, on 17 December they had to leave in a hurry as:

> "a Gestapo raid was expected, two members of the organisation having been arrested the previous day. That afternoon, Sgt Poirier, who was one of the contacts with the organisation, escorted us to a rendezvous in a square in the Northern suburbs of the city where we joined a party of 14 Allied aircrew evaders ... About two minutes after our arrival, we were surrounded by 25 Gestapo and captured." (LIB/603 Daly)

Andre Poirier describes how on arrival at Pantin:

> they were "immediately surrounded by armed Germans. They obviously knew of the plan and after our arrest more Germans seemed to come from all directions." (LIB/1499 Poirier)

The Marechaux family had received a telephone call that day telling them they had been denounced to the Gestapo. They moved to Rugles (Eure) under an assumed name but were arrested there on 4 January 1944. All three were deported. Henri Alfred Marechaux and his son Jacques Raymond died in Germany and only Mme Emilienne Marechaux survived to return to France.[3]

F/Sgt William Bennett (who had been sheltered by gendarme Gabriel Bouyer at 87 rue Haxo before being passed to Georges Kahn and Louis

---

3   TNA folders WO208/5452 & 5454.

Jacquelin and joining John Vass and the others) was one of the airmen taken to Eglise de Pantin on the bus. They were waiting in a nearby cafe when the chief of the organisation (Georges Kahn) gave the women instructions.

Bennett says they were taken to the market place by the chief, two women and a girl.

"We waited until nearly 1700 hrs – all split up – I suddenly heard shouts and saw the chief and three of our men with their hands up. I tried to make a getaway but the Gestapo men cut me off. There were about 12 Gestapo men in civilan clothes for this round up. I don't know who to suspect for the betrayal. One of the women walked away from the scene after the round up, one was captured and the third – the girl – left in a car before we were captured." (LIB/1027 Bennett)

Spitfire pilot Sgt Jan Trnobranski and B-26 co-pilot F/O Ernest Grubb were the only two airmen who got away from the actual rendezvous point at Place de l'Eglise. They had travelled from Livry-Gargan to Pantin with William Bennett – Grubb saying they were a party of sixteen airmen – including Trnobranski and his squadron friend (Frankiewcz) plus his own crew (Mildren, Bolesta, Cunningham and Rimer) and some RAF – taken by autobus (sic) along with Jeannine (head guide) and Andre's wife.

Jeannine was Jeannine Jouve – the IS9 files have Jean Jouve (born May 1881) coal merchant of 22 rue de Meaux, Livry-Gargan. Jeannine is reported by some of the evaders as being the daughter of Camille Nicolas. Nicolas, who lived across the road at 19 rue de Meaux, was married to Marie-Louise (née Jouve, January 1910), daughter of Jean Jouve. Jeannine Jouve was Marie-Louise's younger sister, Camille's sister-in-law. Andre's wife was Mme Andree Paulet Mourot, wife of Andre Mourot (born September 1916) who had been sheltering Trnobranski and Grubb at 20 rue de Meaux.

The rendezvous with Georges Kahn was set for five o'clock and the party who came by bus were early. Jacques Keshishian says there was a miscalculation and they arrived about 45 minutes too early. The group was quite large, they all wore berets and looked more or less the same. They quickly realised that such a large group all together was very suspicious and they attempted to spread themselves out. Two or three went into a nearby cafe, two more joined them and then two more. Kahn came in and told them they had to disperse, that they had been sold out. They went behind the church where there was some kind of square or garden. While they were there, Keshishian suddenly saw Kahn and another man who was speaking to him, raise their hands. He and another aviator tried to escape but they were too late and the whole area was surrounded by Gestapo who captured them all.[4]

The first party may have been early but the second group, were late. Roger Spiller says that shortly before arriving at l'eglise de Pantin, the truck was involved in an accident with a cyclist who demanded a written report (*un constat d'agent*) before he would let them drive on. (NARA Spiller)

On arrival at the church, Trnobranski, Grubb, Frankiewcz and an unnamed Frenchwoman decided they didn't want to be seen with such a large group and so walked to a nearby cafe where they found about twenty other airmen already installed. While they were having coffee, Trnobranski says that he noticed 'an odd looking man' come into the cafe. He looked 'furtively' at them while drinking his coffee and making a pretence of reading a newspaper. The head of the organisation (Georges Kahn) came in and spoke to Jeannine and the rest of the evaders left. When Trnobranski, Grubb, Frankiewcz and the Frenchwoman finished their coffee, they went over to a bus queue and were told that the others had gone to the market place. Trnobranski told the Frenchwoman to try and stop the party from congregating by the church as there were 'Gestapo' about. Trnobranski and Grubb then moved to a street corner where they could watch both the bus queue and market place and five minutes later saw the rest of the party, including Frankiewcz, with their hands raised and surrounded by Gestapo. Trnobranski and Grubb stood while more Gestapo walked past them before making their way between the houses, entering one at random and asking if they could sit down and have some water. They then returned to the bus-stop and bought two tickets for Livry-Gargan, being joined on the bus by Jeannine. At Livry-Gargan, Jeannine took them first to Camille Nicolas' house and then across the road to Andre Mourot. That night, Trnobranski and Grubb were taken to Montfermeil (about three kilometres away) where they stayed with Andre's parents, Charles and Claire Mourot at 12 Avenue de Chelles.

Grubb says that they got out of the bus by the church, walked past the church and into a cafe. He was with Jan (Trnobranski), Andre's wife (Andree Mourot) and the other Polish boy (Frankiewcz) and that other

---

4   NARA Jacquelin – Visit of Capt Jacques Keshishian to the Officer's Club at West Palm Beach, Florida on 29 July 1946.

groups had tables together with the older ladies (Mmes Yvonne Renault and Alice Demeneix) who were their guides. He says that Frankiewcz saw men come in and order drinks and that they seemed nervous. They stared at Grubb's group and Frankiewcz told Andre's wife that he thought the men were Gestapo, and she told Jeannine. The man from Paris (who Grubb had met at Brosville earlier) came into the cafe and called Jeannine over to another table. Jeannine told him about Gestapo man but the Paris man (Georges Kahn) said no, he was a guide. They all left the cafe and Grubb, Trnobranski, William Mildren and Andre's wife walked by the church. There was a market place on one side selling vegetables and they saw all the Americans standing around in groups of three. Mildren walked over by the wall of the church and Grubb, Trnobranski and Andre's wife walked up the street for a block and then crossed and came back on the other side from church. They stopped on the corner and then crossed the street again where Grubb lit a cigarette. Jeannine and a young English boy came over and sat on bench about fifteen feet away. Grubb saw two men, one of them wearing a light cream trench-coat, walk into the church. Three or four minutes later, he saw a group of men come around from the church with their hands up. A Gestapo agent turned around and ran about 40 or 50 feet up the road, then turned and ran back into market. Grubb saw his pilot Mildren by the church with his hands up and others nearby, also with their hands up. When the Gestapo man turned back, Grubb, Trnobranski and Andre's wife crossed the street into alley and then ran and hid in a building. Grubb says that Andre's wife was scared and left. She told them to stay where they were but she didn't return. They asked a man to help them but he refused so they walked to the bus-stop and got on a bus to Livry-Gargan. Jeannine was also on the bus and she took them back to Andre Mourot's house. Grubb says:

> *"Nicolas thought that the wine merchant (who had helped them) [Andre Lassialle] was in the Gestapo deal."*

The 'young English boy' mentioned by Grubb is probably the same as the young 'Lancaster (sic) engineer' that Miller says Camille Nicolas told him had walked away. Nicolas could only have heard that from Jeannine and I'm guessing this was actually 21 year-old F/Sgt William Bennett.

Lt Andre R Van Nes of the Netherlands Security Service says in a report dated 20 November 1945 that two of the women guides were Mlle

Jeannine Jouve and Mme Renault. Mme Renault was arrested at Place de Pantin (later released after convincing the Germans she was only there for the market) while Mlle Jouve, who had all the airmen's papers in a sachel, went into a second-floor apartment and obtained permission to burn the papers in the occupants' kitchen.[5]

Sgt Jan Trnobranski was flying 308 Sqn Spitfire EN916 on 22 September 1943 and returning from a Ramrod (bomber escort) sortie when he was shot down by enemy fighters. Trnobranski baled out and landed in a field near Evreux. He was soon picked up by a man driving a horse and cart who took Trnobranski back to his house. The man gave Trnobranski a meal and let him stay overnight before taking him south-west to a house in the little village of Glisolles. Trnobranski had some difficulty in convincing his helpers he was genuine until a Polish woman was brought to interrogate him, at which point his journey was arranged.

On 25 September, Trnobranski was visited by Louis Maury who brought his wife Yvette, their baby and two Frenchmen with him.[6] One of the Frenchmen was Alphonse Pasco, a priest who spoke good English and was an active member of the organisation.[7] Trnobranski stayed at Glisolles (address unknown) for about a week, frequently visited there by M Pasco. At the end of the week, M Pasco took Trnobranski to his home, a chateau (Chateau des Angles – query) in the forest near Brosville, where some of Pasco's friends, also priests, would visit with cigarettes and books. During this time, Trnobranski's wrenched back, which he'd injured when baling out, prevented him from walking or moving his arms properly. After three weeks with M Pasco, Trnobranski was taken to stay with Pasco's brother and sister-in-law, in the same village. Towards the end of October, Mme Maury came to see Trnobranski and she and Alphonse Pasco took Trnobranski by bicycle to Mme Maury's house in Evreux (at 6 rue de la Rochette). Yvette Maury offered Trnobranski railway tickets for Brittany

---

5   NARA Nicolas.

6   Louis Prosper Maury (born July 1912 in Vancouver, Canada) – a teacher (at the *lycee technique d'Evreux*) – and his wife Yvette France Maury (born January 1915) of 7 rue de la Rochette, Evreux, are credited with sheltering and conveying about thirty Allied evaders. Their work continued until 19 May 1944 when Louis was arrested. He was deported (to Neuengamme) on 15 July and repatriated back to France in June 1945. Louis and Yvette Maury were both recommended for KMCs. (WO208/5453)

7   Alphonse Jean Marie Pasco (born April 1923) of Chatel la Louvre, Le Noyer-en-Ouche (sic) commenced his escape line activities in September 1943. He was primarily responsible for locating safe havens in his area and providing false papers but he also conveyed numerous evaders between Beaumesnil and Paris. (WO208/5459) His recommendation for a KMC gives his profession as gardener but John Vass says it was his father who was the gardener. The IS9 Helper List also has Mathurin and Jeanne Pasco at Le Noyer-en-Ouche, who I think were Alphonse' parents.

where he was told he could stay on a farm but Trnobranski refused and cycled back to Brosville with M Pasco that night. M Pasco was visiting on 3 November when they saw an aircraft shot down and five men bale out. Pasco ran for his bicycle and returned later with the five men, including Ernest Grubb and his pilot Bill (William Mildren). Grubb and Bill joined Trnobranski while the other three (Stanley Bolesta, Henry Cunningham and Kenneth Rimer) were taken to another house. Trnobranski adds that two RAF airmen were brought to the house – a Warrant Officer called Johnny (John Vass) and a Typhoon pilot called Henry (Robert Ellis) – shortly before Alphonse Pasco and five Frenchmen took them all to Paris.

In Paris they were taken to a large apartment over a shop at 21 rue Godot de Mauroy, where they met an American airman who spoke good French (2/Lt Jacques Mihran Keshishian, born November 1918 in Marseille, navigator of B-17 42-3185 Queen Bee, who had been sheltered by the Jacquelin family at Neuilly since 22 November), a British pilot (Halifax engineer F/Sgt William Bennett) and a man (tall, with a long face, dark hair and glasses, he spoke good English) (Georges Kahn) who they were told was head of the organisation.

Louis Ambroise Vincent Jacquelin (of 17 rue de Chartres, Neuilly-sur-Seine and a business address of 21 rue Godot de Mauroy, Paris IX) says that on about 5 December 1943,

"Cmdt MARTIN (pseudo) told me he had a dozen parachutists in his region (Evreux) whom he didn't know how to get out. I told him I could take charge of them. On 11 December, he brought 11 boys (2 Poles, 5 Americans, 4 English). In the afternoon I passed these boys to Mr GEO and Mr QUATRE."

He also says that he passed on another Pole (Frankiewcz) to Mr QUATRE of Livry-Gargan on Sunday 12 December.[8]

That night, Camille Nicolas and his daughter (sic) Jeannine took them back to his house at 19 rue de Meaux in Livry-Gargan where there were 'about 20 British and American airmen'. Trnobranski and Grubb were sent to stay at a house on the other side of the road (with Andre Mourot) where they were joined by F/O Zbigniew Frankiewcz from Trnobranski's squadron. Frankiewcz had crash-landed his Spitfire near Bernay on 19 November and been sheltered on a farm near Piseux (Eure) until being

---

8   NARA Nicolas, Jaquelin Declaration dated 2 November 1944

brought to Paris a few days earlier. About a week before Christmas, they were all collected and taken to a church.

F/O Ernest O Grubb was the co-pilot of B-26 41-34763 (449BS/322BG) (Mildren) which was hit by flak near Evreux (Eure) on 3 November 1943 and abandoned. Grubb landed in the grounds of a farm and seeing no-one, ran towards some trees. He was spotted by two young Frenchmen who took him back to their farm, gave him a meal and then hid Grubb in a hayloft. Later that same day, a boy brought civilian clothes and took Grubb by bicycle to a small village about three miles away, each cross-roads being guarded by men who warned Grubb's helper if the way wasn't safe. He was hidden in a farmhouse while his journey was arranged.

Grubb was taken first to the boy's house, where he met Jan Trnobranski and then to the boy's sister's house. They stayed three days with boy's sister, Mme Louise Peschrey (query) and Alphonse Pasco. Grubb's written report isn't clear but at some point he was joined by his pilot Mildren and whilst at Brosville, they met a Parisian resistance chief (Narcy/Narcies) (tall, slender, wore glasses – talked with a halt in his speech – spoke some English) (assume Georges Kahn) who told them that a man would come from Paris to take them to Brittany for a boat operation. Grubb was also told that three other members of his crew – Bolesta, Cunningham and Rimer – were being sheltered nearby and that his radio-operator S/Sgt William K Lahm had a broken leg and been captured. There was some moving about following various alarms but Grubb and Trnobranski stayed in the area, mainly with Mme Louise Peschrey, until 9 December. Sometime before leaving for Paris, Grubb learned that two RAF men – a Typhoon pilot (F/Sgt Robert Ellis) and a Polish boy (assume Frankiewcz) – were also in the area. On 9 December, the airmen were taken to Evreux by Alphonse Pasco, Louis Maury and two young guides. They stayed overnight in Evreux before taking an early morning train to Paris.

Grubb and the others were taken to a dress-making shop at 21 rue Godot de Mauroy where Grubb met Karl Miller and his pilot Jack Horton, and Camille Nicolas and his daughter (sic) Jeannine, who took them by Metro to Livry-Gargan (actually to the terminus at Eglise de Pantin where they would have caught a bus to Livry-Gargan). In the party was a French speaking American (Jacques Keshishian). At Livry-Gargan, the airmen were housed at various addresses – Grubb, Trnobranski and Frankiewcz staying with Andre Mourot, who although giving his profession as mechanic, is described by Grubb as "a black-market butcher who made forged ration tickets."

F/Sgt Frederick J Page was the twenty-three-year-old Australian rear-gunner of 27 OTU Wellington X3966 (Dowling) on a Nickel (leaflet dropping) raid to Orleans on 23 September 1943 when they were hit by flak over Paris. Having jettisoned the leaflets and realising they wouldn't make back to the UK, the pilot ordered his crew to bale out before he crash-landed the aircraft south of Amiens. Three of the other four crewmen also evaded successfully – pilot F/Sgt G K Dowling crossed the Pyrenees alone in early October, air-bomber Sgt Eric J Anderson crossed the Pyrenees with P/O Harold Hobday and F/Sgt Frederick Sutherland in November, and wireless operator Sgt William Todd with Comete, also in November.

Page landed near Rumaisnil (Somme) at about ten o'clock that evening, suffering injuries to his eye and right arm. He spent the night close to where he landed and set off the next morning towards a nearby church. Two women soon took Page back to a house where he was sheltered, given food and his arm dressed. Two days later, one of the women went to find a doctor, and also a man could speak some English. On understanding that Page wanted to make his way to Spain, the woman contacted her nephew who knew someone who might help.

On 1 October, Joe Balfe took Page to his home in Hornoy, gave him civilian clothes and contacted a Red Cross nurse named Marmousez. Next day, Mlle Marmousez took Page first to an eye specialist in Amiens, and then to her home in Roubaix (which she shared with her mother Eugenie) at 29 rue Saint-Herbert. The following day, she took Page to an eye specialist in Roubaix and on 7 October, he was operated on and his injured eye removed. On 1 November, Jean Carbonnet took him to Paris and the Moet family home at 22 rue Sacrot, Saint-Mande. Two days later, Mme Genevieve Moet took Page to a Metro station where she passed him on to Camille Nicolas.

Camille Nicolas drove Page, collecting four American evaders (Elwood Arp, Howard Sherman, Chauncey Hicks and Nathan Weltman) on the way, to the commune of Livry-Gargan where Page and Hicks were sheltered in "a sort of shop" – Hicks says with "some kind of merchant on rue de Meaux with a man named Andre". On about 11 December, John Vass joined them and on 17 December, Nicolas took them into Paris where "something went wrong and we were nearly caught by the Gestapo".

Sgt John R Vass was the wireless operator of 35 Sqn Halifax HR798 (Dallin) which was returning from Cannes when they were shot down near Lisieux (Calvados) in the early hours of 12 November 1943. Air-bomber P/O Henry B Hall also evaded succesfully – crossing the western Pyrenees in January 1944.

Vass baled out and landed in a field near Auquainville (Calvados). Before he could roll up his parachute, Vass was fired upon from the village and so headed in the opposite direction until he found a barn where he spent the rest of the night. Next day he encountered a farmer who took him back to his cottage. The family were suspicious of Vass until he offered to pay for his meal and produced English coins from his pocket, at which point he was invited to stay the night and learned that he was in the village of Cernay. Vass says that he had intended to move on next day but heavy rain delayed him and he stayed with the family in Cernay until 4 December, by which time his journey had been arranged.

Vass was collected from the cottage at Cernay by a priest and two other men who took Vass by car to a small village. On the way they picked up F/Sgt Robert Ellis – this was F/Sgt Robert Owen Ellis, who was flying 609 Sqn Typhoon JR147 when he was shot down on 17 November 1943 on the same Rhubarb sortie to Rouen as Sgt George Watelet – see later. Vass and Ellis stayed with a young priest called Alphonse Pasco – his father was a gardener at the Chateau des Angles. On 10 December, they were moved to Evreux and stayed overnight in a horticultural shop next to the Gestapo headquarters, where a young lad was preparing identity cards for the organisation. Early next morning, they were taken to Paris by the priest (Alphonse Pasco) and three others, one of them a woman. Vass and Ellis were taken to a room above a bird-shop (sic) where they were joined by others, including RAF flight engineer F/Sgt William Bennett. Later that same day, a tall man with thick-lensed glasses called and took their particulars. Then a man called Nicolas took six of them to a Metro station where they were joined by the remainder of the party. They went by Metro to another station (Eglise de Pantin) and then took a bus to Livry-Gargan where Vass met F/Sgt Page and their story is the same from this point.

2/Lt Charles O Downe and S/Sgt Carl Bachmann were the navigator and tail-gunner of B-17 42-5720 (384 BG/544BS) (Aufmuth) which was returning from Stuttgart on 6 September 1943. As they began to run out of fuel, the aircraft was crash-landed north-west of Paris, near Pontois (Ile-de-France). All ten crew left the aircraft safely and they divided into groups to evade. Downe and Bachmann were two of the six crewmen from this aircraft to evade successfully.

Downe and Bachmann headed south, crossing the Seine, and after four days of walking, met an English-speaking woman who knew a man who could take them to Montargis (Loiret) in his truck. They were duly driven to Montargis where they met a local resistance man and on 16 September, were taken to the little village of Migneres where they were sheltered by Albert Demoveaux for the next two months. They were visited by a local resistance chief called Georges and his brother-in-law Albert (a chief of resistance from Paris who had lived in Boston for 25 years) and on 16 November, Albert took Downe and Bachmann by train to Paris where he passed them on the Camille Nicolas.

1/Lt Jack Horton and 2/Lt Karl Miller were the pilot and co-pilot of B-17 42-3430 Carolina Boomerang (96BG/338BS) which was returning from Schweinfurt on 14 October 1943. They had lost two engines to flak and when the supercharger on a third engine failed, Horton told his crew to bale out.

Miller spent his first night in France trying to get some sleep in a wrecked trailer. Setting off early next morning into the fog, he soon approached a man he heard ploughing. Whilst explaining the situation, a man who spoke English approached and took over, hiding Miller in a wood for the rest of the day before returning that evening with two bicycles.

Miller was taken to a small village near Laon where he was sheltered by Mlle Suzanne Verchere at Foudrain par Crepy-en-Laonnois. Ten days later, a French policeman took Miller on his motorcycle to Chauny where Miller was handed over to Etienne Dromas. Miller was sheltered with M Chede at Frieres-Faillouel where he was joined by his pilot Jack Horton (who had been sheltered by Mme Paul at 4 rue Lakanal, Colombes) and on 9 November, they – along with George Glatthar and James Tracy – were taken to Paris.

T/Sgt James E Tracy was the top-turret gunner of B-17 42-30457 Jimmy Boy II (94BG/331BS) (Beal) which was returning from Schweinfurt on 14 October 1943 when they were attacked by enemy fighters and the aircraft abandoned. Tracy was one of eight crewmen from Jimmy Boy II to evade successfully. He landed (with a fractured skull) in some woods near the villlage of Crepy-en-Valois (Oise) and was soon helped by an elderly man who took Tracy back to his house. Tracy says that within half an hour, his journey was arranged.

Tracy and his navigator, 2/Lt George E Glatthar, were sheltered in Crepy-en-Valois for two days and then on 16 October, taken to Creil, where they stayed with Paul Toussaint (born February 1873) at 15 rue Charles Somasco. Glatthar reports that he later heard the head of the organistion (at Creil) was picked up by the Gestapo on 23 October. From Creil, Tracy and Glatthar were taken by train to Chauny where they were sheltered by the Chauny-Dromas organisation and stayed (20-25 October) with Jean Bruxelle at 40 rue Maurice Moceau, Flavy-le-Martel before returning to Chauny where they met Karl Miller and his pilot Jack Horton. On 9 November, the four Americans were taken to Paris by a man called Joseph (a short, good-looking fellow of about 20) arriving at the Gare du Nord at about five o'clock that afternoon. Tracy doesn't seem to mention it but after meeting Georges Kahn at the station, Glatthar was separated from the others and he went on to cross the western Pyrenees with WO2 George A Gauley RCAF in early December.

On arrival in Paris, Tracy, Miller and Horton were taken by Metro to a rendezvous point where a lady named Marthe Powell approached Miller and told him to follow her, alone. She took Miller back to her house at 84 Kleber Avenue (Paris XVI) where Miller stayed for the next thirty days, seeing only friends of Mrs Powell. Finally, she took Miller to a house where he met "about 25 other fellows". They were all taken by different guides to Livry-Gargan, Miller in a party of four.

James Tracy and Jack Horton were taken direct to Livry-Gargan where they stayed with Camille Nicolas and family at 19 rue de Meaux. Tracy says he was taken to see Andre (Andre Lassialle), a wine merchant who lived about two blocks up the street (he wore very thick glasses and looked short because he was very stocky) who Nicolas said was getting black-market goods for them but was a collaborator. Nicolas said that he going was going to kill Andre afterwards but for the time being, he needed him for money and supplies.

Albert Stegel (born April 1903) who says he was an "information agent and performed acts of sabotage" was, along with Roger Spiller, chief assistant to Camille Nicolas, who managed "evasion affairs" for the FFI at Livry-Gargan. M Stegel, who (in common with several other helpers mentioned in this story) had a very low opinion of Camille Nicolas, says this about Nicolas and Andre Lassialle:

"LASSIALLE is a wine merchant in Livry-Gargan and is commonly known to have been the first and greatest collaborationist of the town. Before the war, he did a moderate business and was known to have had numerous

debts, which he was unable to pay. During the war however, he was able to build a chateau with the profits of his relationships with the Germans, his wine business, and his black-market operations, in which he was protected by the occupying powers ... The only break in this harmonious NICOLAS-LASSIALLE relationship was immediately after the Pantin affair, when NICOLAS formerly accused LASSIALLE of being the person who informed the Germans of the forthcoming rendezvous at the church of Pantin, and when, at the time of his arrest, NICOLAS told everyone not to tell LASSIALLE where the aviators who had escaped the trap were hidden."[9]

Tracy also says that Nicolas had talked to Capt Dydy (sic – more usually Dede) of British Intelligence who told Nicolas that they were going to an "RAF organisation". However, on about 10 December, it seems that contact with this organisation was broken and Nicolas arranged a new plan for getting them out by boat. His new contact was "Le Grand monsieur de Metro" and they would be leaving Paris in trucks to go to "some place on the Brest peninsula".

1/Lt Elwood D Arp, 2/Lt Howard Sherman, 1/Lt Chauncey H Hicks and 2/Lt Nathan Weltman were the pilot, co-pilot, bombardier and navigator of B-17 42-5763 Bomb Boogie (91BG/401BS) which was on the way to Stuttgart on 6 September 1943 when they were attacked by fighters and the aircraft abandoned near Lille.

They were sheltered in the Pas-de-Calais-Nord for more than two months before finally leaving for Paris at the beginning of November. Their journey was delayed at Arras for ten days by the visit of Hermann Goering (who was doing a tour of northern French airfields) and it wasn't until 14 November that a woman – described by Hicks as "a burly lady, aged about 28-30, about 5 ft 3 inches tall, who spoke English" – from the organisation at Livry-Gargan came to collect them. They were met at the Gare du Nord by Camille Nicolas who took Arp, Sherman and Hicks to his home in Livry-Gargan. Hicks went to stay with a wine-merchant Andre Lassialle (who Nicolas warned Hicks not to trust) also on rue de Meaux, while Arp and Sherman stayed with Nicolas where they (and ten other evaders) lived "without incident" until 17 December. Hicks says that from the station, Nathan Weltmen went with the burly lady but I don't know who she was or where she took him.

---

9   NARA Nicolas, statement by Albert Stegel dd 11 August 1945.

Hicks reports that when they reached Camille Nicolas' house, 2/Lt Edward Burlay and three sergeants – Levoun Jawgochiam, Lawrence Sheck and Robert Hamrick – were there, along with Australian Fred Page.

2/Lt Edward R Burlay Jnr, S/Sgt Levoun J Jamgochiam, S/Sgt Lawrence B Sheck and S/Sgt Robert J Hamrick were the navigator and three of the gunners from B-17 Jimmy Boy II, the same aircraft as James Tracy. Like Tracy, they all landed near Crepy-en-Valois on 14 October 1943, meeting Tracy and their navigator George Glatthar briefly before Tracy and Glattar went on to Creil two days later. It's not clear exactly when they left Crepy but they were taken by a man called Paul, direct to Paris and the Jardin des Plantes where they were handed over to Madeleine Melot. They stayed with Mme Melot until she took them to Livry-Gargan and passed them over the Camille Nicolas on about 10 November.

Burlay and the three sergeants left Livray-Gargan on about 15 November and Hicks says that he and the others were supposed to follow them (to the Pyrenees) three days later but before that, Camille Nicolas took Arp and Sherman to meet "le Grand Chef de Metro" (Georges Kahn).

Hicks was taken to Andre Lassialle's home on rue de Meaux where Nicolas told him not trust the wine-merchant – "Use him, but don't trust him" – and he comments on the arrival of a group of eleven airmen (including Cyril Koval and Jacques Keshishian), and Miller and Shaffer being taken to stay with M Bernard. He also says that four men were taken to the "big fat woman who ran a cafe (not the one who had N) [his navigator Nathan Weltman] but Amy (query) who was picked out."

T/Sgt William J Miller was a waist-gunner and Sgt Edward R Shaffer the tail-gunner of the B-17 42-29876 Battlin' Bobbie (Hoyt) which was on the way to Nantes on 16 September 1943 when it was attacked by fighters and the aircraft abandoned over Brittany. They (and six other members of their crew) were soon sheltered at various addresses in Brittany.

Miller made a delayed drop and landed in an apple orchard near the village of Redon (Ille-et-Vilaine). Before he could even disentangle his parachute, he was surrounded by a group of Frenchmen who took his parachute and pointed in the direction they thought he should go. Miller had only walked about two kilometres when a man asked him where he was going and Miller was taken back to the man's house. That evening, Miller was taken to join his pilot 1/Lt Elton Hoyt and radio-operator S/Sgt Herbert Dulberg – and two days later, they were joined by their tail-gunner, Edward Shaffer.

Shaffer also landed in an apple orchard, this one about ten miles west of Redon. He had a broken foot and a woman (aged about 30, with a dark complexion) took him to her house where his foot was bandaged by an elderly woman. He was given civilian clothes and put into a hayloft. Two hours later, the woman brought her twenty-three-year-old son and spent the rest of the afternoon talking to Shaffer in French. That evening, they brought a girl named Lucienne (aged about 20, also with a dark complexion) who spoke English and told Shaffer that Hoyt, Dulberg and Miller were outside Redon in an empty house that had formerly been a German headquarters. Lucienne asked Shaffer if he wanted to join them and he said he did. Shaffer spent the night in the hayloft and next morning, a miller brought a truck-load of straw. Shaffer was hidden in the straw and driven to the man's house on the outskirts of Redon where Shaffer was carried upstairs and a doctor came to set his foot, asking Shaffer not to scream as he did so. That evening, the miller drove Shaffer (in his car this time) to join Hoyt. Shaffer stayed with Hoyt (whose report is almost unreadable) until they went to a monastery at Saint-Helen (Huguen says Chateau de la Guerche) about twenty miles south-west of Saint Malo. Two days after their arrival at the monastery, Shaffer and Cyril Koval (waist-gunner of B-17 42-29901) were taken to a doctor's house. The doctor (not named) was aged about 55 and spoke fluent English having lived in England with his English wife until she died some fourteen years earlier. They stayed with the doctor for eight days (by which time, Shaffer says too many people knew about them) before moving to stay with a wine merchant in Dinan. The wine merchant (an ex-cavalry lieutenant) was a rich man, aged about twenty-seven who lived with his mother and a maid in a house three blocks west of the Hotel d'Angleterre. That night, Shaffer and Koval were taken to the barn where Miller and Dulberg were staying – and Shaffer was with Miller and Dulberg (whose report is almost unreadable) until they reached a cafe at Ploermel (on about 15 October).

From the cafe at Ploermel, Shaffer went with a man named Raymond (Raymond Guillard – query) who took him to stay with Henri Boulet at the Villa Georgette in Taupont. Miller was sheltered with Alex Joubaud at the Villa Gohan, his house about four kilometres west of Taupont – he and Shaffer would meet two or three times each week. Dulberg went with Francois Lequitte (of Ploermel) and Shaffer says that Koval stayed with some people (unidentified) outside of Ploermel, on the main road. While at Taupont, Shaffer met Harry Boegaholz (waist-gunner of B-17 42-3042) and Guillaume Bernard (described by Shaffer as a French aviator from Africa who he was sure was American) who were being sheltered by Raymond, about twelve kilometres away. After five weeks, Shaffer rejoined Miller who says they were together until they got off the bus at Livry-Gargan on 23 November (although they travelled to Paris in separate groups).

On 22 November, Miller, Shaffer and Dulberg joined T/Sgt Samuel Blatchford, S/Sgt Cyril Koval, S/Sgt Elmer Schroeder and S/Sgt Alfred Held (all from B-17 42-29901), S/Sgt Harry Boegaholz and a French fighter pilot (query) called Guillaume Bernard.

Next day, Emile Guimard and another man (described by Dulberg as slender) took Miller, his radio-operator Herbert Dulberg, Samuel Blatchford, Cyril Koval and Guillaume Bernard to Paris. They managed to lose Dulberg in the Metro (taken by the slender guide, he joined a group that crossed the Pyrenees from Perpignan in December) but Emile got the rest of them safely to a bakery in the Paris suburb of Pantin. When it got dark, Emile took them to Eglise de Pantin where they rejoined Edward Shaffer, Elmer Schroeder, Alfred Held and Harry Boegaholz, and Emile handed them over to Camille Nicolas. M Nicolas then took them by bus to Livry-Gargan where Shaffer and Blatchford were passed on to another Frenchman while Nicolas took the rest to a cafe.

Shaffer reports that the man known as Guillaume Bernard had no identification whatever and the organisation would have nothing to do with him, and so he disappears from this story after meeting Camille Nicolas at Eglise de Pantin.

Shaffer says that when they got out of the bus, Nicolas told him and Sam Blatchford to follow another fellow who had been on the bus (5 ft 11 inches tall, dark moustache, foreman of a truck company at Livry-Gargan), who lived four blocks away from last bus stop at Livry-Gargan. They stayed at his house for three days but then the man had to go to a funeral in Bordeaux so Jeannine Nicolas (sic) took them to stay with Ernest and Blanche Bernard at 5 rue Emile Zola, where Shaffer rejoined Miller.

I think that Samuel Blatchford was actually taken to 40 rue de Meaux where Alice Demeneix (born July 1895 and described as a hotelier) was sheltering his crewmates, Cyril Koval, Elmer Schroeder and Alfred Held. Samuel Nathan Blatchford (1925-2005), who went on to serve in both Korea and Vietnam, is said to be "the most highly decorated American Indian to date" with numerous awards, including a Freedom Medal (sic) for his work with the French Resistance. I have no information on his contribution to the resistance nor whether any of his crewmates, with whom he evaded throughout his time in France, were similarly recognised.

Miller (at least) stayed overnight at the cafe with owner Pierre (aged about 50 with short dark hair, he had been an aviator in the last war). Next day, Nicolas took Miller back to his own house where Miller met Elwood Arp, Howard Sherman, Chauncey Hicks, Charles Downe, Carl Bachmann, James Tracy and an Australian F/Sgt named Fred Page. Ernest Bernard then came and took Miller back to his home at 5 rue Emile Zola, Livry-Gargan where he lived in a small house with his crippled wife. A few days later, Jeannine brought his tail-gunner, Edward Shaffer to join him.

17 December – Place de Pantin

"*Following the orders of G KAHN, the aviators lodged in the home of Mme RENAULT, Mme DEMENEIX, Mr BERNARD and M MOUROT were conducted 18 Dec to the Eglise de Pantin. 11 were arrested.*

The same day, I left with a small truck loaded with 15 parachutists, and following the orders of KAHN, I took them to the entrance of PANTIN, where they would embark in cars. I waited for 5 hours, until 6 o'clock, and not seeing anything come and after a telephone call to the home of G KAHN, I returned to Livry-Gargan, where I learned of the affair of PANTIN. I put my aviators in the home of my father-in-law, Mr JOUVE after passing one hour in the home of Mr RENARD. The next day, I placed these aviators : 4 in the home of Mr MOUROT in Montfermeil, Rue de Chelles; and the 10 others in the home of Mr SPILLER, Rue d'Orleans, Livry-Gargan. This same evening, some of the aviators in the home of Mr SPILLER, were turned over: 2 to Mr REMY, Pavillons-s-Bois and 2 others to Mr BOURGEOIS, Avenue de la Convention, Livry-Gargan. They were: Edouard SHAFFER and William J MILLER. 2 others in the home of Mr BERNARD, 3 Rue Emile Zola, 2 in the home of Mme GIRARD, 2 in the home of Mr STEGEL, finally, Mr SPILLER kept the following 2 aviators: Elwood D ARH (sic) and John WASS (sic). These last two stayed in the home of SPILLER until 10 Feb." (NARA Nicolas)

Note that Camille Nicolas' account of the events at Place de Pantin does not correspond with those of the evaders. Also note that Camille Juillard (see later) claims that he took "charge of lodging the 14 aviators who had escaped the clutches of the Gestapo."

William Miller says that on 17 December, he and Edward Shaffer were supposed to ride in a truck (which was driven by a butcher named Fayolle) with Carl Bachmann, James Tracy, Frederick Page, John Vass, Robert Ellis, Elwood Arp, Howard Sherman, Chauncey Hicks, Charles Downe and two other Americans (Karl Miller and Jack Horton), while another group of 16 went in a bus – Koval, Blatchford, Held, Schroeder, the Polish Spitfire pilot (Jan Trnobranski) and others, with four women escorts.

"We were supposed to all meet around the Eglise de Pantin, we were going to be met there by 2 German trucks. The original plan was for us to see a car in front of the church with a Nazi flag in the window. We saw the car but no flag. We went down a side street, parked and waited 15 minutes then we drove around once again and parked again. One man came to Monsieur Nicolas to ask him [about] a street and after receiving an answer, went to the wrong direction. Nicolas looked around, saw eleven men standing around the corner. He told the driver to drive away. Just as we were leaving, the man who asked the road, opened the curtain in the back of the truck and saw the 13 of us. He kept on standing and watched us drive away and then ran to the other men who were standing on the corner. They in turn ran for an automobile. We drove down a side-street, it was getting dark now and Nicolas and 2 other Frenchmen made a telephone call to his home, asked if his sister-in-law, who was escorting the bus party, had returned – they said no. We were supposed to go to Bordeaux with these trucks as recruits for the German army – we were to have joined 30 others and get on a boat near Bordeaux." (MISX #636 Miller)

"On 17 December, 13 of us were driven to a church in a truck. Nicolas, who was in the front, had the car park on a side-street while he walked toward the church. The whole scheme for this rendezvous sounded too easy to him and he had become suspicious. Nicolas, on nearing three men, realised that one was Gestapo. He asked directions as a ruse and then motioned for the truck to get underway. When the Gestapo agent saw this, he crossed toward the truck, which pulled out just as Nicolas jumped in the front and the agent started to raise the canvas under which we were hiding in the rear. I do not believe he had time to see us there in that light.

We stayed in a garden until dark and then started down the street. As we did so, two Gestapo agents started towards us with flash-lights. At this point, a truck not connected with us in any way, rounded the corner. The two men, thinking it to be our pick-up, went for it and we got away." (MIS-X #604 Arp)

250

William Miller also recounts what Camille Nicolas told him after the event.

> *"Nicolas told us about this. When they got out of the bus, the chief, Monsieur de Metro [Georges Kahn] was standing in front of a nearby church. They went up to him and as they reached him, a German civilian approached the chief and pulled out a revolver. Most of the group was captured because they raised their hands. But the Polish Spitfire pilot and one American [Grubb] walked away in the crowd, came to the same bus and went back to Mr Nicolas. The women escorting kept on walking too. One woman was picked up and cleared because she said she was going to the market. The Lancaster engineer walked away, he looked like a young guy. M Nicolas also told us that M de Metro was caught and that someone very high up in the organisation must have given away the plot." (MIS-X #636 Miller)*

17 December – Return to Livry-Gargan

Jan Trnobranski and Ernest Grubb – who returned to Livry-Gargan by bus with Jeannette – were taken to Montfermeil where they stayed with Andre Mourot's parents, Charles and Claire Mourot at 12 Avenue de Chelles. They were joined next day by Charles Downe and Chauncey Hicks.

Charles Downe, who was in the truck with Camille Nicolas, says that (on 17 December) Nicolas told him that all twenty-nine of them were going to Paris. They were to meet in front of a church where they would be met by trucks and taken to Brittany.

> *"16 left by truck – Grubb in party – 13 in car (Miller, Horton, Tracy, Hicks, self, 3 English boys, Sherman, Arp, Bachmann, Sgt Miller and Sgt Shaffer). We went to Paris then back to Livry and excitement because something bad had happened. Met Grubb and Jan Trnobranski (Polish Spitfire pilot). Hicks and I went with them to M Mourot at Montfermeil, 3 kms away. Ernie [Grubb] and John [Trnobranski] said they had gone to Paris and were in a large group in front of a church waiting for us. Then Gestapo came out of the church and all evaders taken – Ernie and John are the only two who escaped – they met Jeanne on auto-car." (MIS-X #411 Downe)*

On 16 January, the young woman took Charles Downe and Ernest Grubb to Paris – and a young man took Karl Miller and Jack Horton. The four

251

airmen were then passed on to a Dutch guide who took them by train to Toulouse where Downe and Hicks left Miller and Horton.

Downe and Grubb crossed the frontier to Les on 26 January 1944 with Sgt James C Hussong (tail-gunner of B-24 42-28599) and Sgt Leonard H Cassady (right waist-gunner of B-17 42-39759 Sarah Jane).[10]

Jan Trnobranski (who says that Grubb left a week before him) and Chauncey Hicks didn't stay at Montfermeil for long either, they were soon put in touch with the Dutch-Paris organisation and a couple of weeks later, taken by Metro to l'Eglise Pantheon. They walked to the home of a Swiss family, where they were joined by James Tracy. They were each given heavy boots, gloves and an overcoat and next day, taken by train to Toulouse. They went on to cross the central Pyrenees, arriving in Spain on 2 February 1944.

The evaders in the truck with Camille Nicolas were driven back to Livry-Gargan where many of them spent the night in what is described by Elwood Arp as a chicken-house (by others as a barn) belonging to Nicolas' father-in-law, Jean Jouve. Next day, Charles Downe and Chauncey Hicks were taken to Montfermeil while the rest were taken to Roger Spiller at 32 Avenue d'Orleans, Livry-Gargan and with the exceptions of Vass and Arp, dispersed to other addresses from there.

John Vass and Elwood Arp stayed with Roger Spiller at Avenue d'Orleans until leaving Livry-Gargan for Paris on 10 February 1944.

Frederick Page says that on his return to Livry-Gargan,

"We were taken to a cellar where we stayed for four hours before spending the rest of the night in a barn. Next day, M Nicolas took us to the home of Roger Spiller at 32 Avenue d'Orleans, Livry-Gargan where we stayed until 31 December. Then we [Page and Carl Bachmann] were moved to the house of M Albert Stegel, 19 Allee des Ormes, Livry-Gargan where we stayed until 13 February 1944. We heard that during this period, Nicolas had been arrested by the Germans but released after 29 days as they could prove nothing against him. In the absences of Nicolas, we were in the charge of M Louis Rene [Remy] of 85 rue Aristide Briand, Les Pavillons. On 14 Feb we were collected by a man and woman who, we were told, were of the Dutch-Paris organisation and taken to Paris for the day and on that night by train." (WO208/5583-1876 Page)

---

10   Their epic crossing with Dutch evaders Rudy Zeeman and Robert van Exeter, and guides Henri Marrot and Palo Treillet, is commemorated at the Musee de la Chemin de Liberte in Saint-Girons, Ariege.

Carl Bachmann confirms going with Page to the home of Albert Stegel on Allee des Ormes where they lived for about two months, adding that during this time, Roger Guard, who lived in the Allee Duferme (Roger Louis Girard of 15 Allee de la Ferme – now Alle Fernande Baudot) and his family were also helping them.

Albert Stegel (born April 1903) says that after returning from Place Pantin and spending two (sic) nights at M Jouve's home, the airmen were taken to Roger Spiller at 24 (sic) Avenue d'Orleans, where they stayed for three days. The group was then broken up and placed in different homes. Among the places where Bachmann stayed from December 21 to December 27 was the home of M Remy (Pavillons-sous-Bois). On December 27, Remy brought Bachmann and Page back to the home of M Roger Spiller. That same evening, M Stegel happened to be at Spiller's home to discuss some forthcoming acts of sabotage. Spiller and Remy were at a loss as to where to put Bachmann and Page. M Stegel then stepped forward and volunteered to take them to his house, to which proposal all parties agreed.[11]

Karl Miller says that on returning from Eglise de Pantin, he spent two hours in the backyard of a house before going to a hay-barn for the rest of the night. Next morning, he followed Nicolas to a house on the outskirts of Livry-Gargan where he, Jack Horton and James Tracy stayed with an ex-gendarme (Louis Remy) for three nights. The ex-gendarme – who contacted the organisation for them – took them to a cafe where they met a man (Camille Juillard) who took them to an empty house for the night. Next day, Camille Juillard took Miller and Horton to stay with an elderly couple two kilometres out of Livry-Gargan (Albert Delphien and his wife at 40 bis Avenue Etienne Dolet, Pavillons-sous-Bois). They spent five nights (including Christmas) chez Delphien before the same man (Camille Juillard) moved them to a house in the country where Miller, Horton and later Tracy stayed with Mme Jeanne Jones and her daughter Helen at 17 Avenue des Fauvettes, Montfermeil. On 21 January, the Dutch-Paris organisation took Miller, Horton and Tracy to Paris – they joined Grubb and Downe and were taken by train to Toulouse – where they lost Grubb and Downe.

Karl Miller and Jack Horton joined Sgt Harold W Bailey and four crewmen from B-17 42-39759 Sarah Jane – 2/Lts Frank Tank and Ernest Stock, and S/Sgts Eric Kolc and Russell Gallo. They were taken to Foix and set off across the mountains but after two days of walking, Horton had to

---

11   NARA Nicolas, interview with Albert Stegel dd 11 August 1945.

be left in a French farmhouse. Miller and the others carried on and crossed the Pyrenees to Andorra on 27 January 1944.

James Tracy was taken, along with Jack Horton and Karl Miller, by local resistance chief Camille Juillard to stay overnight in an empty house. Next day, while Miller and Horton went to stay with Albert Delphien at Pavillons-sous-Bois, Juillard took Tracey to his own home at 2 Boulevard Faust in Livry-Gargan. On about 5 January, a gendarme came to tell Juillard that the Gestapo were coming to get him and Tracy was then moved to join Miller and Horton at Montfermeil.

Camille Juillard was arrested on 31 January 1944 and deported. He explained that his deportation had nothing to do with the evaders – he was arrested as a "terrorist" and the Gestapo remained ignorant of his work for aviators.[12]

"We spent the night in the chicken-house belonging to Nicolas' father-in-law. The next day, Lt Downe and Sgt Hicks were taken to a farm. The rest of us were taken to the home of Roger Spiller and farmed out – I and John Vass of the RAF stayed with Roger Spiller until 10 February." (MIS-X #604 Arp)

"From 18 to 21 December I lived with an enthusiastic communist. He owns a radio shop and is a friend of Roger Spiller at Livry-Gargan. On 21 December, I went to Lucien [M Petillou at 2 bis Avenue Jean Jaures – query] until 31 December. He owns a delicatessan in Livry-Gargan. He is in the black market and his son shoots Germans. Sgt Bachmann (still in Spain), Fred Page RCAF, who has lost an eye, Sgt Robert Ellis, who could not make the Pyrenees because of a crippled foot, and is be sent to Switzerland, were also at Lucien's.

On 31 December, Ellis and I went to Marcel Nicot, 48 rue de Normandie, Gagny. We were there until 10 February. He is a poor man [born March 1901] with little food and lots of friends. He devoted all his time to the resistance movement and was very good to us. One of his friends, a wealthy baker, and another one who is a one-armed guard at an insane asylum, were very kind and helpful during this period. Rene [Rene Bourgeois], a retired policeman in Livry-Gargan, was good to all of us and was the one who finally contacted D-P." (MIS-X #608 Sherman)

William Miller and Edward Shaffer were returned to stay with Ernest and Blanche Bernard at 5 rue Emile Zola:

---

12   NARA Nicolas, report by Andre Van Nes.

"At Mme Bernard's house (where the Pole [Trnobranski] came and told us how he got away) we met Monsieur Nicolas, he explained the story to me. He told me also that M de Metro [Georges Kahn] was caught and that someone very high up in the organisation must have given the plot. Seven days later the Gestapo arrested M Nicolas, his wife and his mother and father-in-law living across the street, M and Mme Jouve. The day after Nicolas arrest, I was moved (with Shaffer) to Monsieur Bourgeois [Rene Bourgeois of 2 Avenue de la Convention] (42 years old, thin, worked as an electrician at Westinghouse, wife and three young children) in Livry-Gargan by Monsieur Reuin [Louis Remy of 85 rue Aristide Briand, Les Pavillons-sous-Bois] (6 feet tall, aged about 35, dark hair) a French policeman in civilian clothes. I stayed with them until about 10 February. That day I was taken with Shaffer to Arp's house." (MIS-X #636 Miller)

Up to 10 February 1944 – when the last group leave for Spain

"During this, Nicolas was arrested and held in Paris for 29 days. When he was released he came to see me immediately, although all the French were afraid that he was being trailed. It seems that he had contacted another organisation through his radio man in Paris. This organisation, into which the Gestapo had worked itself, was supposed to take us out of France." (MIS-X #604 Arp)

Note that Andre Poirier was certainly compromised, having "failed to take the usual precautions to hide himself as normal evader would have done." He stayed at his parents' address in Paris where he was recognised by neighbours who had known him before the war. One of them, Mlle Yvette Casenave, was the mistress of a superior officer of the Gestapo, and she told her lover, who immediately had Poirier senior watched, and eventually arrested.[13]

"Nicolas claimed that all the Gestapo was ever able to get against him was his telephone number, which had been found on the radio man. Between playing up his illness and faking ignorance, he obtained his release. When the Gestapo had come for him, he had been carrying our names and home addresses. He got rid of these in the latrine after feigning illness. While in

---

13   IS9 Memo dated 12 April 1946 concerning the recommendation for a pension for Mme Vve Yvonne Poirier.

prison he saw the radio man unconscious and beaten beyond recognition. He also saw a woman beaten with a chair. Three of the airmen were there too, doubt they were receiving good treatment. This prison [Fresnes] is I believe the biggest in Paris. It is on the western outskirts of the city and the Red Cross and Germans feed it alternatively in weekly periods.

I understood that Nicolas was the only person from Livry-Gargan involved. The radio man came from Paris – I saw him once at a day-long rendezvous which he and Nicolas held at a Metro station. He was a large, tall man, with a big nose and ★★★ face, he wore glasses." (MIS-X #604 Arp)

"That day [10 February] taken with Shaffer to Arp's house. There I met again Arp and John Vass. While we are there we met Sherman, Robert Ellis and Bachmann. Saw Nicolas, who had been released by the Germans because impersonating insanity (he would shudder and drag his foot etc). He said the Germans had showed him pictures of Sherman, Arp, Bachmann, Downe, Hicks, myself, Shaffer, Ellis and Tracy – he failed to recognise us. They also had a picture of Metro beaten up and out of shape – it was the chief terribly beaten. Then a friend of Nicolas came to Arp's and took us (Miller & Shaffer). From there on our journey is the same as Arp." (MIS-X #636 Miller)

On 10 February, Camille Nicolas, Roger Spiller, Rene Bourgeois and Andre Mourot took Frederick Page, John Vass, Elwood Arp, Howard Sherman, Carl Bachmann, William Miller and Edward Shaffer into Paris. They were passed on to a Dutch couple, Mike and Marie of Dutch-Paris and that night, Marie and a French girl took them to Toulouse.

They were in a group of more twenty evaders who crossed the Pyrenees to Bossost in Spain on 19 March 1944.

Robert Ellis was also taken into Paris on 10 February but his injured foot meant that he would not be able to walk across the Pyrenees and he was left in the capital. F/Sgt Robert O Ellis was captured on 26 February 1944 at 11 rue Jasmine, Paris XVI (home of Fernande Goetschel) along with a Swiss national named Jean Milleret. Both Goetschel and Milleret were members of the Dutch-Paris organisation.[14] Ellis was sent to Stalag Luft VI (Bankau) on 6 June 1944 where he worked in the camp's hospital before being transferred to Stalag 383 (Hohenfels).

All the airmen who escaped the trap at Place de l'Eglise were passed to the Dutch-Paris organisation and with the exceptions of Jack Horton and Robert Ellis, crossed the Pyrenees to Spain.

---

14   NARA Duchanel.

I don't know who was responsible for leaking the planned pick-up at Pantin but it was almost certainly someone connected to the Bordeaux organisation. However that, like CDDL and Dutch-Paris, is another story.[15]

15   My thanks to Michael Moores LeBlanc for his many contributions to this chapter in particular.

CHAPTER 43

The Breiz-Izel

There were many boats that left Brittany for England during the war, some of which included evading aircrew among their passengers. The two boats in this story are the *Jeanne* and the *Breiz-Izel*.

Sometime in late November (shortly after his return from London), Georges Broussine received a message from Paul Campinchi, asking for an urgent meeting. Broussine already knew Campinchi from the early days with Val Williams of Oaktree. After Williams' arrest, Campinchi had left his apartment at 19 rue des Ursins but not given up the business of recovering downed aircrew. They arranged to meet in a milliner's shop on rue Saint-Honore and Campinchi arrived accompanied by a young man. The young man wasn't introduced by name but Broussine was reminded of a Breton friend that he had trained with in London named Guy Vourc'h – and later questioning revealed this to be his brother Yves.

Yves Vourc'h, who was still living in Plomodiern with his family – all of whom were also active resistants – told Broussine a story about a BCRA agent who had been parachuted into France to organise an escape line from Brittany for downed aircrew. With the help of the agent's family, an operation was set up to take aircrew back to England from Treboul harbour (Douarnenez) on board a vessel called Jeanne. Tragedy struck when the agent recognised the French traitor Roger Leneveu in a Rennes cafe. In the ensuing confrontation, Leneveu shot the agent in the stomach – a wound from which he subsequently died. The loss of the agent and the money that he had promised to fund the operation, meant the whole plan would have to abandoned unless an alternative source of funds could be found.

Broussine had no doubt that the agent was his friend from London, Jean-Claude Camors (who had parachuted back into France in July) and Broussine says that he felt a moral obligation to him. He agreed to put up the necessary funds (300,000 francs) and made Yves Allain, himself a Breton, responsible for assessing the situation and coordinating the operation. Broussine also says that his one condition was that all the evaders that Bourgogne had at the time should be included and that Bourgogne would be responsible for getting them to the embarkation point. Note this was a completely separate operation to the *Suzanne-Renée* which sailed from Camaret-sur-Mer on 23 October, shortly after Camors' death.

With Yves Vourc'h making all the arrangements and a young man named Yves Le Guillou as captain, the operation was scheduled for the night of 24-25 December 1943, surely a time when German surveillance might be relaxed enough to allow a 'discrete' departure. In the days leading up to Christmas, Yves Allain and Pierre Le Berre duly brought a total of fourteen aircrew evaders to Douarnenez ready for the departure – but other events were also taking place.

In early December, Broussine had been visited by Manuel Vals de Gomez, a Spanish republican colleague of Jean Olibo in Perpignan. De Gomez brought a young French naval lieutenant who had come from London (in June), a Breton who said he was responsible for organising an escape route by sea for downed aircrew. Like Yves Vourc'h, he declined at first to give his name but again, Broussine made the connection, this time through a friend at the *faculte de medecine* named Maryvonne Le Henaff – she came from Quimper and this young man, another Yves, was her brother. Broussine met Yves Le Henaff again a few days later at Le Henaff's mother's apartment where Le Henaff, having learned about the proposed operation at Christmas, asked Broussine to cancel it on the grounds that it could compromise his own projects. What the young lieutenant probably didn't mention was that he worked jointly for the British MI9 and the French Algiers based DST (*Direction de la surveillance du territoire*). Broussine explained that he had made too many promises and commitments to cancel at that late stage and Le Henaff apparently accepted Broussine's reasoning.

Yves Le Henaff (along with Victor Salez) and his Dahlia organisation had already carried out three successful evacuations by fishing vessels from Douarnenez – the *Moise* on 23 August, whose passengers included Sgt Cecil Bell USAAF – the *Ar Voularc'h* on 17 September with RAF Sgts Sydney Horton and Robert Parkinson, and 2/Lt John George USAAF – and *La-Perouse* on 2 October with USAAF evaders S/Sgt James Cimini and Sgt Michael Zelenak Jnr – as well as Victor Salez himself – on board. Le Henaff (aka Fanfan) had also arranged the Lysander Operation Oriel that collected Sgt Vic Matthews RAF in November.

While Le Henaff may have accepted the situation, it seems quite possible that others did not.

*"On the morning of the day of departure, the situation, up to then favourable,
deteriorated drastically. Le Guillou received an anonymous letter threatening
to denounce him to the Germans if the Jeanne left port. Moreover, one of his
comrades told him that, according to one of his friends, the Germans already
knew about the operation. All this was very worrying. However, throughout
the day nothing happened to confirm this news and we learned later that it was
untrue. In any case this was the reason why, in spite of the reserves of the owner of
the vessel, it was decided, under the influence of the representatives of Bourgogne
who were there, to take no notice of these terrible suspicions. During the night,
the passengers for the Jeanne, including our airmen, embarked without mishap.
The Germans did not intervene. However, it was quickly seen that access to the
petrol reservoir on the dock was unusable, the feeder valve had been blocked.
Also the engine itself was not working, probably sabotaged. So we had to give
up the operation and the intended passengers had to disembark."*[1]

The reasons for this apparent sabotage have been investigated and debated
ever since – was it the result of disaffected fishermen at Douarnenez who
knew their livelihoods were at risk if another vessel were known to have
escaped from their harbour, or was it the action of the group surrounding
Yves Le Henaff who felt they had the exclusive right to operations from
the port? Perhaps we'll never know but the end result was the same – the
'Jeanne' operation was cancelled. However, rather than return the evaders
to Paris, they were sheltered in various homes in and around Douarnenez.

After the failure of the 'Jeanne' operation, a fisherman named Gabriel
Cloarec offered the use of his new boat, the *Breiz-Izel* (a twelve tonne,
flush-decked, single-masted pinnace, launched in 1931). This time it was
Yves Le Guillou (Noel Yves Marie Le Guillou – born Christmas Day 1910)
who organised the operation while Yves Vourc'h bought the boat, using the
same 300,000 francs that Broussine had provided for the Jeanne. The *Breiz-
Izel* duly sailed for England on the night of 22-23 January 1944, arriving at
Falmouth in Cornwall some thirty-six hours later, with about thirty people,
including the fourteen airman, on board.

In his book, Broussine describes the circumstances of the departure of
Breiz-Izel as *"truly acrobatic"* and says that

*"Luck was on our side on that night but it required the utmost coolness,
determination and skill of the captain, Gabriel Gloarec, to carry it out. His*

---

1   Translated from *'L'evade de la France libre'*.

The fourteen evaders were Sgt Royce Fidler, Sgt Leslie Woollard, WO2 Russell Jones, Sgt John Carleton, S/Sgt Harry Horton Jnr, S/Sgt Edward Sobolewski, T/Sgt Thomas Moore, T/Sgt Robert Giles, T/Sgt Carroll Haarup, Sgt Ardell Bollinger, S/Sgt Leonard Kelly, S/Sgt Joseph Kalas, 1/Lt Dwight Fisher and 1/Lt James Armstrong.

Sgt Royce Fidler was the rear gunner of 100 Sqn Lancaster LM333 (Preston) which was on the way to Berlin on the evening of 23 August 1943 and crossing the Dutch coast when they were hit by flak and the aircraft abandoned – Fidler was the only successful evader. Fidler landed in a field near Ossenzijl (Overijssel) and after hiding his parachute and flying gear, began walking south. The following day, Fidler met two men who recognised his uniform as that of a British airman and soon arranged to have it exchanged for a suit of overalls. After being given a meal, Fidler was taken by bicycle to an unnamed village where he stayed until 26 August when he was taken over by an organisation of young Dutchmen avoiding work in Germany and his journey arranged.

On 26 August, a Dutchman named Peter van der Hurke, who worked for the Germans as a black-market controller, took Fidler to the nearby village of Meppel where Fidler was sheltered by Protestant pastor Willem van Nooten and his family at Zuidende 53. Van Nooten had apparently sheltered a Canadian airman previously with the full knowledge of the local police chief who warned them whenever the Germans came to the village searching for Dutch youths. Fidler reports the arrival of F/O Herbert H Penny to the house on 2 September.

Sgt Leslie C Woollard was the mid-upper gunner of 617 Sqn Lancaster JB144 (Knight) which was damaged whilst attacking the Dortmund-Emms canal on the night of 15-16 September 1943 and abandoned over Holland.

The pilot was killed and two other crew captured but navigator P/O Harold S Hobday and front-gunner F/Sgt Frederick E Sutherland crossed the Pyrenees together in November while wireless operator P/O Robert G T Kellow and bomb-aimer F/O Edward C Johnson were helped by Comete, crossing into Spain in October and December respectively.

Woollard landed near Den Ham (Overijssel) and after hiding his parachute and Mae West, walked for two hours before hiding in a ditch near a farmhouse. Next morning, he approached the farmhouse where he was taken in and given food while a girl from the house fetched a local doctor who passed him on to an organisation. Two days later, Woollard was sent to Miss Frouke De Vries at 3a Prins Hendrikstraat in Meppel. On about 1 October, Woollard was moved to the Van Nooten home at Zuidende 53, where he joined Royce Fidler and Herbert Penny.

Early on the morning of 15 October, Peter van der Hurke and another Dutchman, took Fidler, Woollard and Penny by bicycle to Zwolle to catch a train to Baarle-Nassau where their Dutch guides left them. They were joined at Baarle-Nassau by an American airman (S/Sgt Paul F Shipe from B-17 42-3227) and the local chief of police led the four men across the frontier into Belgium. That afternoon, he took them by bus to Turnhout, tram to Antwerp and finally by train to Brussels. The police chief delivered them to a flat where a fat lady (name not given), her daughter and son-in-law lived. The son-in-law took them to a fish-shop where there was a store of clothes and shoes for evaders and they met one of the heads of the organisation – about 50 years old, 5 feet 5 inches tall, well built, clean shaven, with thin dark hair – possibly Felix (Charles Gueulette). They stayed in a house attached to the fish-shop where they were photographed for identity cards. Next day, Penny and Shipe left (both later helped by Comete) and Fidler and Woollard were moved to a flat (no address) for two days before moving back to the flat by the fish-shop. The following day, Fidler and Woollard were taken to a Brussels suburb where they stayed with Maurice and Yvonne Olders at 187 rue des Tanneurs. About a week later, they were taken to stay overnight with an elderly Englishwoman (no name) and on about 22 October, a Belgian guide took them to Ghent where they were sheltered overnight with a policeman. Next day, they were taken to Tournai from where an English-speaking guide led them across the frontier to Tourcoing in France and handed them over to French ex-army captain Fernand Vanaerde and his son Jean. They were collected by Gilbert Virmoux and a Frenchwoman called Denise (both identified as members of the Bordeaux organisation) and taken via Lille to Paris. They stayed in Virmoux's apartment at 41 rue Saint-Merri, Paris IV from 24 to 28 October when Virmoux took them and two or three Frenchmen to Quimper (Finistere).

At Quimper, Fidler and Woollard joined "about 30 Americans" who were then sorted out and sent to different houses to await a boat. Fidler and Woollard stayed with the head of the organisation, a Frenchman called Fanfan (Yves Le Henaff) who had been sent from England with a French-Canadian radio-operator. The intended departure date was between 4 and 6 November but on 6 November they heard that the boat would not be leaving after all. The evaders were returned to Paris in groups and it was Fanfan himself who delivered Fidler and Woollard back to Gilbert Virmoux's flat. They were told there would be a three-week delay before the organisation could arrange their departure for Spain and meanwhile, on 13 November, they were taken to the Chateau de la Fortelle where they "and fourteen or fifteen others" – all Americans except for one Englishman, Sgt Anthony A J Reynolds – stayed for three weeks, toughening up for the Pyrenees.

Fidler and Woollard returned to Paris on about 4 December, going back to Gilbert Virmoux's flat with 2/Lt James Armstrong and 2/Lt Andrew Lindsay – who they knew as Andre. As there was only one room, Woollard and Armstrong slept downstairs in a flat belonging to M et Mme Le Callonec. On about 11 December, Gilbert Virmoux and Denise (Mlle Denise Lenain of 12 Ave d'Orleans, Paris XIV – query) took the four airmen to Carcassonne along with W/O Russell Jones and S/Sgt Edward Sobolewski. At Carcassonne, Virmoux failed to find his next contact and knowing no-one else in the town, took the party on to Quillan (Aude) in the foothills of the Pyrenees, where he believed his contact lived. Still unable to find him, Gilbert and Denise booked the group into a hotel for the night and the next day, they all returned to Paris once more. After another week at Virmoux's flat, Fidler and Woollard were moved to another (unspecified) address to stay two nights with an unnamed elderly couple. On 24 December, they comment that they changed from Bordeaux to the Burgundy organisation and new French guides (Yves Allain and Pierre Jacob) took them to Quimper (again) and Douarnenez, where they arrived on Christmas Day. They say there were about forty people, including twelve (sic) Americans and two other British airmen (Russell Jones and John Carleton) and at eleven-thirty that night they all walked in stockinged feet down to Treboul harbour.

WO2 Russell A Jones RCAF was the navigator of 431 Sqn Halifax LK967 (Passant) which was returning from Frankfurt in the early hours of 26 November 1943 and somewhere near Arras when they were hit by flak and the aircraft abandoned. P/O Pierre Bauset RCAF (see below) and Sgt Raymond F Nelson also evaded successfully – Nelson crossing the Pyrenees from Bidarray in December.

Jones landed in a field near a town that he thought was called St Mesmin (Saint-Mesmin, Aube). His bomb-aimer, P/O Pierre Bauset landed close by and they hid their parachutes in a stream before setting off through what was left of the night. After resting in a wood, they saw a man with a cart and Bauset, who was from Montreal and spoke fluent French, approached him. The farmer immediately recognised Bauset as an Allied airman and told him that Germans were searching for his crew. He also pointed out that Bauset could catch a train for Paris from the station at the next village. Before reaching there, another man took them in for the night, fitted them out with civilian clothes and gave them train tickets. Early next morning, they took a train to Paris where Bauset was able approach various people until finally getting directions to the Red Cross. Officially no help was available there but a girl overheard their conversation and led them an address where their journey was arranged.

The address of 12 rue d'Arras, Paris V was that of a priest named Michel Louis Riquet.[2] After a meal, abbe Riquet brought two secretaries who gave the airmen identity cards but on deciding that their issued photographs weren't suitable, took the two men to a shop to have their photographs taken again. Later that day, they were taken to a building opposite the University of Paris where there was a lecture in progress. After about an hour, the two were separated, Bauset was taken to room upstairs while Jones joined newly arrived American evader Harry Horton (see below) in another, very small, upstairs room. Jones says that Bauset stayed with a lady whose name sounded something like Mme Barrage (Mme Baron of 2 Place de la Sorbonne) who told them they were in the hands of the Bordeaux organisation. She also said that the first woman they had met in the building – about 45 years old, well built, dark hair – was the chief of this organisation (other evaders refer to her as Mlle Bourgeois). She also spoke no English, which is presumably why Bauset was asked to stay with

---

2   Abbe Michel Louis Riquet (born September 1898) was a long-term helper with Comete in Paris. Arrested on 18 January 1944 and deported to Germany, the abbe was repatriated on 16 May 1945 and recommended for an MBE. (WO208/5454)

the organisation as an interpreter, which he did until 18 January 1944 when he left Paris for Switzerland.

On about 11 December, a girl called Denise took Jones and Edward Sobolewski by train to Carcassonne. On the train they joined Royce Fidler and Leslie Woollard and two Americans, James Armstrong and Andrew Lindsay – and their other guide Robert (sic) Virmoux. As already related, they failed to find their contact at Carcassonne or Quillan and returned to Paris.

On their early morning return to Paris, Denise took Jones and Sobolewski to her flat for the rest of the day before moving them to stay with Mlle Christiane Braillard (query). Four days later, a young girl (believed to be a student) moved them to another address and told them they were being transferred to the Burgundy organisation. Before leaving Paris (for the second time), Jones and Sobolewski were taken to a church where they joined Fidler, Woollard and other members of the party being taken by train to Quimper and Douarnenez.

Sgt John D H Carleton was mid-upper gunner of 620 Sqn Stirling EE905 (Frost) which was shot down on the way to Remscheid in the early hours of 31 July 1943 and crashed near Willerzie (Namur). Carleton was the only successful evader – W/O Frederick J Frost, bomb-aimer Sgt John L Snelling and engineer Sgt Ronald B Spencer-Fleet were captured (with others) in Paris on 18 September by the Belgian traitor and German infiltration agent Prosper Dezitter.

Carleton landed on an island in the river Meuse near Givet (Ardennes) close to the Belgian border. After burying his parachute, he used his Mae West to float down and across the river. He got out of the river near a graveyard and on finding he had sprained his ankle, spent the rest of the night in a vault. Next morning, after stripping off and drying his clothes in the sun, he crawled his way into an orchard where he was spotted by a young boy and his mother who told him that someone would come and fetch him. That evening, the same boy brought a man and together they walked to the Belgian village of Hastiere-Lavaux (Namur) from where Carleton's journey was arranged.

On 3 August, Carleton (who is referred to as Irish and known as Paddy to some of the Americans) was taken to Brussels where he met Sgt Anthony Reynolds. They stayed in Brussels for one day and night before being moved to Liege. They were taken to a food shop for two days until receiving news that the local organisation chief had been arrested. Carleton was then taken to stay with a police commissioner in the suburb of Beyne-Heusay while Reynolds was sheltered by Mme Anna-Marie Aelens on Boulevard de la Constitution. After about a month with the police commissioner, Carleton was moved to Ans where he stayed with garage-owner Joseph Alexander. Two weeks later, he was taken back to Liege where he joined several American evaders – including S/Sgt William P Kiniklis and his waist-gunner S/Sgt Ernest C King (who was later captured on his way to Switzerland) – being sheltered by baron Marcel de Ruyter and his pregnant wife Mariette at 52 Quai Orban.

On about 20 October, a man called Pierre took Carleton and Kiniklis by train to Brussels where they were interrogated by a member of the Felix organisation (perhaps Felix himself) and that night, a Belgian guide took the two airmen to Ghent where they stayed overnight with their guide. Next day, they were passed on to another man who led them across the frontier from Mouscron into France and walked them into Tourcoing where they stayed overnight with policeman Gaston Vorreux at 123 rue Lamartine. Next day, they were moved to 27 rue Gambetta where they were sheltered by insurance agent Fernand Vanaerde and his wife Celeste. Carleton and Kiniklis stayed with the Vanaerdes for about seven weeks (from 29 October to 15 December), being joined after about three weeks (on 15 November) by F/Lt Ian Covington and 2/Lt Stanley Alukonis.[3]

On 15 December, a young boy called Henri took all four airmen to Paris where they were met at the station by three women. The party was split and one of the women (described by Carleton as being very mannish looking, severely dressed and with short Eton-cropped hair) took Carleton and Kiniklis to the flat of a young girl. Next day, they were moved to the home of a policeman – his home seemed to be some sort of Customs House with an engine running all the time. Three days later, they were taken to a church where they were separated. Kiniklis went to Gilbert Virmoux's flat at 41 rue Saint-Merri, while Carleton was taken to 75 Avenue d'Italie, where he was sheltered with the Belleville family (Andre, Alice and sons Bernard, Daniel and Maxime). Four days later, Carleton was returned to the church where he rejoined Kiniklis and met Royce Fidler and Leslie Woollard.

For some reason, when the rest of the group were taken to Quimper and Douarnenez, Kiniklis was returned once more to Gilbert Virmoux's flat on rue Saint-Merri, where he was joined by Covington and Alukonis a

---

3   Dates in Tourcoing from NARA Vanaerde.

few days later. Kiniklis left Paris on about 19 January 1944 with Sgt Anthony Reynolds. They and Sgt Douglas J Farr went on to cross the Pyrenees from Pau later that month – see later. Covington (pilot of 97 Sqn Lancaster JA716) and Alukonis (co-pilot of B-17 42-37750 Mary T) were passed to Comete and they also crossed the Pyrenees to Spain in January.

S/Sgt Harry H Horton Jnr and S/Sgt Edward F Sobolewski were the waist-gunners of B-17 42-3227 (381BG/534BS) (Forkner) which was on the way to Schweinfurt on 17 August 1943 when they were attacked by fighters and the aircraft abandoned over Holland. Two other crew also evaded successfully: TTG S/Sgt Paul F Shipe (mentioned earlier) was brought back by Comete, and pilot 1/Lt Hamden L Forkner who was sheltered in Maastricht with Justine Pinkas at Brusselseweg 120 until liberated in September 1944.

Both men landed safely near Limburg, although Horton sprained his ankle quite badly when he came down in an orchard. Both were soon helped by local people who disposed of their parachutes and flying equipment and the following night, they were brought together and their journey arranged. Unfortunately Sobolewski's statement (which is in the jumbled pages of Horton's file – there doesn't seem to be one for Horton) is a set of scribbled notes by his interviewer (Donald Emerson) but I think they stayed in Holland for about two months before being taken through Belgium to Ghent with Otto Bruzewski and Thomas Moore, crossing the border to Tourcoing (following the Felix route and staying overnight with Gaston Virreux) and on to Paris.

They were met at the station by a tall woman with black hair, a dark complexion and prominent buck teeth (Mlle Bourgeois) who took Horton and Sobolewski to a room opposite a school, three blocks from the Boulevard Saint-Germain. Three days later, Horton and Sobolewski were separated and sheltered at different apartments.

Sobolewski was taken to No 2 Place de la Sorbonne where he met a "hefty" woman who spoke no English – he says that Moore was upstairs. Sobolewski stayed on the third floor with Mme Baron (who had been married to an Englishman) for four days.

On 28 October, Sobolewski was reunited with Horton and they joined Otto Bruzewski and Thomas Moore for the first trip to Quimper (see earlier), before returning to Paris on about 6 November.

Sobolewski says that when he returned to Place de la Sorbonne, he stayed for two weeks with Jones the Canadian and Pierre (Bauset) before a "beautiful girl from the Bordeaux organisation" came to tell them they were going to the Pyrenees. Sobolewski tells a very similar story to Jones of Denise taking him and Jones to the station where they joined Gilbert Virmoux, Armstrong, Lindsay, Fidler and Leslie, another Englishman (Woollard) and going to Carcassonne. Having failed to find their guide there, they had to wait for the little train to Quillan. Still failing to find their guide, they returned to Paris where Sobolewski and Jones stayed with Christiane Braillard (query) at 7 rue du Plaix (rue du Plat d'Etain – query) for four days. Apparently, Ms Braillard worked for the Germans and her mother was a collaborator. Ms Braillard seemed to think they were going to the Pyrenees and it was Denise's sister (query) who took Sobolewski and Jones to a church where they met Armstrong and some other Americans. Sobolewski and Jones then spent five days at another address where Genevieve Soulie visited and told them they were now in the Burgundy organisation.

I think that when Horton returned from Carcassonne and Quillan, Gabrielle Wiame took him and Thomas Moore to Montreuil to be sheltered by Jeanne Delapraye and her daughter at 71 rue Beaumarchais.[4] They stayed at Montreuil, waiting to go to the Pyrenees, until Genevieve Soulie came to see them just before Christmas.

T/Sgt Thomas R Moore was the radio-operator of B-17 42-3225 Chug-A-Lug Lulu (381BG/535BS) (Disbrow) which was returning from Schweinfurt on 17 August 1943 when they were attacked by fighters and the aircraft abandoned over Belgium. Three other crew also evaded successfully: top-turret gunner T/Sgt Otto F Bruzewski and tail-gunner S/Sgt William P Kiniklis (see earlier and below), and ball-turret gunner Sgt Joseph J Walters who was helped by Comete and crossed the Pyrenees in October.

"I hit in the middle of a sugar beet field and thought that I was in Germany. Some farmers came running at me with pitchforks in their hands. There was not time to hide any place, so I stayed where I was. They came and took my parachute. They talked French but at that time, I could not tell French from German. They kept repeating "Belgique, Belgique" so I decided that I must be in Belgium. A number of people came up and they all grabbed me and kissed me, a most embarrassing welcome. One man told me to go so I followed

---

4   Mme Jeanne Alice Delapraye (born December 1893), a grocer who lived at 71 rue Beaumarchais, Montreuil-sous-Bois, is credited with sheltering nineteen Allied personnel. (WO208/5451)

him to an apple orchard. There we came upon a man and my helper left quickly. This man had a dictionary and told me to surrender. I refused. I saw that he had no gun and that he was no bigger than I so I was quite prepared to fix him up in case he wanted to help me to surrender. When he did not interfere with me, I ran away and managed to find the man with whom I had first been. He took me to a gully to hide, and I found one of my crew members [Kiniklis] there already. That night, a girl brought us waffles and a boy brought us some other food. We were moved to a place where our journey was arranged." (MIS-X #332 Moore)

Moore and Kiniklis were taken to Liege and a priest's house where they joined their ball-turret gunner Joseph Walters and B-17 42-3435 tail-gunner S/Sgt Kenneth Fahncke. On about 20 August, the four evaders were taken to stay with Charles Kremer and his wife in Liege, and the following day, their top-turret gunner Otto Bruzewski and waist-gunner S/Sgt Ernest King arrived.

Bruzewski reports Charles Kremer taking him and Moore to Brussels and Ghent on about 22 October. They went on to Mouscron, following the route used by the Felix organisation, and across the frontier to Tourcoing. They were then passed onto a new guide who took them by a train to Paris where they were sheltered by a student organisation in an apartment near Odeon station (Paris VI). On 28 October, Bruzewski and Moore were taken to Quimper, along with Harry Horton and Edward Sobolewski and (as mentioned earlier) returned with them to Paris on 6 November. Moore's own report ends with him meeting Horton and Sobolewski, apparently in Brussels.

Following an aborted attempt to cross the Pyrenees from Quillan later that month with 2/Lt John Heald and S/Sgt Floyd Terry, Otto Bruzewski left Paris on about 18 December by train for Perpignan, crossing the Pyrenees with Captain George Millar in early January 1944 – see earlier.

T/Sgt Robert C Giles and T/Sgt Carroll F Haarup were the radio-operator and ball-turret gunner of B-17 42-30604 Badger's Beauty V (100BG/350BS) (Helstrom). They were returning from Frankfurt on 4 October 1943 when the navigator realised they were so far off course (although still in formation) that he didn't have maps to cover them. They were also about to run out of fuel and the aircraft was landed (wheels up) south of Caen in Normandy at about one-thirty in the afternoon.

As mentioned earlier, the ten-man crew split into small groups: pilot Capt Harold B Helstrom with navigator 1/Lt Harold H Cuttice – co-pilot

F/O Hubert E Trent with bombardier 1/Lt Hilbert W Philippe – LWG S/ Sgt Joseph Shandor with tail-gunner S/Sgt Charles E Crippen and top-turret gunner S/Sgt William D Edwards – and Giles and Haarup with waist-gunner S/Sgt Thomas R Mezynski.

"With heavy flak being poured up at us, we made three runs on the target. Two fighters were seen and called out but they did not attack our element. As far as we know, there was no damage to the aircraft when we left Frankfurt to return to base. We were back in France when the navigator said we were off course and that his maps did not cover the area which we were flying. Our fuel tanks were reading zero and we had to let down. Other ships were leaving formation as we dropped through clouds to find we were over water. There was land ahead of us. The navigator asked for a QDM but every station tried was busy. The pilot said it didn't matter because we were going to crash-land. We thought we were coming down in England until tracers from machine-gun fire were seen off the wing.

After the crew had taken crash positions in the radio room, the pilot made a beautiful belly-landing. Previous to this, all extra weight had been thrown out of the ship but the secret equipment had not been destroyed. Within a few seconds, Frenchmen appeared from all directions. The order was given immediately for all equipment to be destroyed. During the next fifteen minutes each man was busy with his own job. The bombardier could speak some French and it was he who learned we were a few kilometres south of Caen. There were no Germans in the immediate vicinity but they would be there before long, the French said. When we offered our heavy flying equipment to the Frenchmen they wouldn't take it. The bombardier opened several chutes and draped them over the engine nacelles but the plane would not catch fire. The Frenchmen were motioning us all this time to leave quickly and let them destroy the plane.

The pilot told us to split any way we wanted. We got everything we needed from the plane, changed into GI and low-cut shoes, drew straws to decide with whom we would travel, then held a last minute conference to orient ourselves before choosing the best direction for travel. A young boy had brought overall maps of France to the plane with him and after studying this, the navigator said we should go south-east. The pilot and navigator walked south across the field and then changed their direction so that they were walking north. The co-pilot and bombardier followed a minute later in a general south-east direction. Sgts Crippen, Shandor and Edwards were behind them but at the other end of the field when we started south-east with Sgt Mezynski. In the wooded and hilly countryside, our small groups quickly lost sight of each other.

We were dressed in light summer flying jackets, flying coveralls and green fatigues. For warmth, we had kept our blue heated suits beneath the coveralls.

We crossed some fences and ran through several fields with the other three sergeants not yet out of sight. To give them a chance so that we should not all be clustered together, we crawled into some bushes and got out our maps. While discussing the situation, the bombardier and co-pilot stumbled upon us. There was another hasty farewell and good luck spoken with them before they went on south-east. We stayed in the bushes a little longer making our plans. We decided to stay together as long as possible, walk south-east and look for help along the way. If necessary we would walk to Spain because we had heard at Group of that being done. Leaving the bushes, we filled our water bottles, checked our compasses and started walking." (MIS-X #333/334 Giles & Haarup)

After walking for several hours, the three evaders came to a small village where they approached a woman in an isolated farmhouse. They told her that they were American airmen and she gave them food and some clothes that had belonged to her young son and only fitted Giles. She refused their offer of payment and told them there were no Germans in the immediate area. They spent their first night in France in some stocks of fodder. After some days of walking and living off whatever they could find, they met a Frenchman who helped plan a route south via Alencon and Chartres to cross over the demarcation line. He guided them to the railway station at Bellou but would go no further and so it was Haarup (using mainly sign-language) who bought them a third-class family ticket for the two o'clock train to Vernay. It soon became obvious that local people recognised them as evaders – a woman at the station passed them a pack of sandwiches and a man managed to convey the message that they were to watch and follow him when he got off the train. Giles comments that the only person on the train who didn't seem to know who they were was the German soldier at the other end of their carriage. Soon after leaving Argentan, Haarup began to feel sick and in desperation, they left the train at L'Aigle. Not knowing what else to do, they started walking out of the town and after about five kilometres, approached an isolated house where they declared themselves to the owner. After a night sleeping in a shed, they set off on

271

their fifth day of walking and reached a village with a railway station. The line was abandoned but there was a still a station-master who gave them sandwiches, a map and directions to Chartres. That afternoon, they stopped at a farmhouse where they were taken inside and they had their first warm-water wash and shave since landing but were not allowed to stay the night. They got as far as Saint-Maurice-les-Charencey (Orne) later that evening by which time Haarup had become very ill indeed and so they looked for a Catholic church. They finally knocked on the door of the only house with a light on – and from there, their journey was arranged.

The house belonged to a shoemaker who seemed very happy to see them but his wife wouldn't let them stay there. Then an older man (who owned a garage which serviced German cars) took them to his house. He called a doctor for Haarup (not named but possibly Dr Pierre Heuze) who arrived with his nephew (who spoke some English) and after checking their identities, assured them they were in safe hands – this was late Saturday, 9 October 1943.

Giles, Haarup and Mezynski stayed for a week in Saint-Maurice-les-Charencey while the doctor's nephew went to Paris to try an contact an organisation. Meanwhile, the doctor's wife bought them new clothes and the shoemaker repaired their shoes. The following Saturday (16 October) they were taken by truck for a short drive to a chateau (assume Chateau de Champthierry) where they stayed for the next two weeks, spending much of their time in bed, being waited on by the family servant. While they were at the chateau, they were told that the doctor and two school-teachers had been arrested and that both the local priest and the next-door neighbour of the old man with the garage, were collaborators.

On 27 October, the same truck-driver came with three other men and drove them to the outskirts of Verneuil-sur-Avre where they stayed two nights in a house on the main road. On 29 October, a man claiming to be in French Intelligence told them they would be leaving that night and later that evening, a woman who spoke English took them to the station (where the three men from the truck acted as guards while tickets were acquired) and then by train to Paris.

Giles, Haarup and Mezynski followed their woman guide onto the Metro for two stops before walking to 19 rue d'Orleans where they were sheltered by Simone Levavasseur in the apartment above her chocolate shop, La Petite Chocolatiere. They were told they would only be there for a week but they actually stayed five weeks following the news that the head of the organisation (Madeleine Melot) had been arrested. Simone then told them that they would be passed to another organisation and they would leave on 5 December. Whilst they were there, they met Simone's daughter and Simone's fiance George (query) who came for dinner several times – he owned a shop where they had their photographs taken for new ID cards – and a dentist who supplied much of their food. At the end of the third week, they were visited by Genevieve Soulie who took their names and ASNs – and also by Olga Christol, the person who was supposed to take them out on 5 December with her Organisation Todt. On 9 December, Genevieve came and told them that the Germans were looking for Simone and they should all leave immediately. Simone refused to go because of her family but Simone's friend, Mme Boy took Mezynski to her apartment at 9 rue Ernest Cresson and a young girl took Giles and Haarup to Olga Christol's apartment at 4 rue Edouard Quenu. Unfortunately there was no-one there so they were taken to stay overnight at Mme Boy's as well. Next day, Olga Christol collected Giles and Haarup from Mme Boy – she took Giles to stay with theatre manager Germaine Hairaux at 5 Avenue d'Orleans, and Haarup back to her own apartment.

As mentioned earlier, Mezynski stayed on with Mme Boy until 19 December when he was taken to the station to join a group of evaders, including John Dougherty, Herbert Dulburg and Robert Sheets, who were on their way to Perpignan and the Pyrenees – which they crossed to Vilajuiga later that month.

While Giles was staying with Germaine Hairaux, he met American actress Dorothy Tartiere and was visited by the dentist (and his wife) who supplied food to Simone Levavasseur. On 21 December, Giles was moved back to join Haarup at rue Edouard Quenu. They were supposed to follow the same route as Mezynski but when Paul Christol took them to a rendezvous at a church, they couldn't find anyone. Finally they were approached by a man who, having ascertained their identities, took them to another church where they joined Irishman John Carleton before moving on to a park where they found Genevieve Soulie. She pointed out the man they were to follow and he took them, Russell Jones, Harry Horton and Thomas Moore by train to Quimper and Douarnenez.

Sgt Ardell H Bollinger, S/Sgt Leonard J Kelly and S/Sgt Joseph M Kalas were the radio-operator, left waist-gunner and ball-turret gunner of B-17 42-3459 Jolly Roger (384BG/546BS) (Higdon) which was on the way to Rennes on 23 September 1943.

"At 1730 hours we made landfall over France and picked up our escort two minutes later. Eight minutes later, four FW 190s attacked, setting our number 3 engine on fire and starting a fire in the radio room. We left formation and the order to bale out was given. The action had not taken more than twenty seconds.

The right waist-gunner was trying to salvo (sic) the waist door. I went to help him and together we got it away. Sgt Kelly had gone to help Sgt Kalas climb out of his ball-turret and put on his chute. The tail-gunner jumped first, followed by the right waist-gunner. I was next before Sgt Kelly and Sgt Kalas. We were out of the plane around 22,000 feet and each man opened his chute almost immediately. I counted seven chutes; looked around to find the plane and saw it once more, smoking but in level flight and while I watched, it exploded in mid-air.

I had about eighteen minutes in the air, most of which time was taken up with manoeuvring the chute and trying to remember how to land without breaking a leg. I recalled Sgt Brown (E&E No 52) of my Group who had returned after being shot down and remembered the first thing he had done was to join up with a crew member and go in hiding for a day.

I landed in a pasture and before I could release the chute, a girl ran up to me with her mother and father not far behind her. They motioned that I should run quickly and from their gestures, understood that they would take care of my chute. I left them and headed in the direction of Sgt Kelly who landed a few seconds before I was down. While I was hopping towards him on an injured leg, another girl ran up and gestured that an injured comrade had fallen nearby. I went with her and found our bombardier (2/Lt Lawrence E Johnston) unconscious and badly wounded. While I was trying to help him, Sgt Kelly and Sgt Kalas joined us. In ten minutes of hitting the ground we were all together." (MIS-X #335 Bollinger)

Their report doesn't specify but they landed somewhere close to Plouguenast, about 25 kilometres due south of Saint-Brieuc. They say that the French were so concerned about Lt Johnston that they sent him to hospital at Loudeac where, it was later reported, he died of his injuries.

Bollinger, Kelly and Kalas spent the next ten days wandering in a generally southerly direction via Langast, Plessala and Merdrignac until finally finding someone at the little village of Brignac who could help to arrange their journey.

On 5 October, Bollinger, Kelly and Kalas were taken in a fish-truck from Brignac to Rennes. They walked across town to a school-teacher's house where they stayed overnight. Next day, Kelly became ill and a doctor who had helped them earlier was called. After treating Kelly and leaving him there, the doctor took Bollinger and Kalas to another house where they spent the next five days in a room above a bar. On the second day they met Sgt William Bilton RAF, 1/Lt Wayne Bogard and two of his crew – Sgts Max Gibbs and Cloe Crutchfield – and 2/Lts George Padgett, Sidney Elskes and Arnold Wornson – nine in all for dinner. The organisation was broken up while they were there, a girl told them that Pierre (Charnier) and two friends had been at a bar (the Cafe de l'Epoque on 11 October) and a Frenchman in the Gestapo (Roger Leneveu) shot two of them. On fifth day, Martine (query) took them to a closed truck where they rejoined Kelly and met 2/Lt William Cook and 2/Lt Joe Burkowski (from B-17 42-9893 El Diablo) and were taken to the Chateau de Laille. They were sheltered by Mlle Andree Recipon (born 1885) who said they would leave by aircraft but then General Allard arrived to take Cook and Burkowski back to Messac. Bollinger, Kelly and Kalas stayed at the chateau for a further twenty days and mention Marie Therese (a nice looking, slightly chubby girl of about 22 who spoke English) visiting them. On 5 November, a truck came with Marie Therese and two men who took them to a farm at Lizio, near Vannes – they stayed at nearby Saint-Servant for the next twenty-six days with Louis Boulvais, his wife, two children and mother. They were visited by Simon (query) from Plouguenast who said that Louis Boulvais (who is described on the IS9 list as a *transporteur*) was going to take them to Paris to find an organisation. They understood that the boat deal was off and they would be crossing the Pyrenees instead – and that there were thirty-eight Americans in and around the Vannes neighbourhood.

On 1 December, Germain (query) moved them to the home of Jean Bernard (also in Saint-Servant) because of Louis Boulvais' plans. Germain said that he was going to take them to Paris in five or six days but they never saw him again. On 20 December, Louis Boulvais came to see them after contacting an organisation and told them that Simon had found a boat that was leaving on Christmas Day. On 23 December, they were taken to meet Jean Richard (of rue Valais) at Martigne-Ferchaud (Ille-et-Vilaine) – they also met Louis there. They say they walked 20 kms to Simon's house at Plouguenast (although this doesn't seem to make sense) where they stayed overnight before leaving early next morning to be driven by truck to Vannes with Louis Boulvais, Simon and Jean Richard. Everyone except the truck driver then took the train to Quimper where they changed for Douarnenez.

1/Lt Dwight A Fisher was the bombardier of B-17 42-3858 (95BG/336BS) (Clark) which was returning from Rennes on 29 May 1943 when they were shot down by fighters. Major Edgar B Cole who was flying as pilot observer, also evaded – he crossed the Pyrenees from Elne just two weeks after being shot down.

Fisher, whose head was badly burned, made a deliberately delayed jump from the blazing aircraft, twisting his back when his parachute opened at about 10,000 feet, and was unable to move after landing in the middle of a ploughed field about nine miles south of Parame. He was helped immediately on landing and taken into some woods where he stayed for the next ten days, with civilian clothes, food and blankets brought to him until he was taken to a house and his journey arranged.

Like so many others, Fisher's account is only available as a series of scribbled, almost illegible notes. He mentions Roger Pansart, his wife (Aimee) and their two daughters, Odette and Jeanne at Parame (just outside St Malo) and says that although not members of any group, they had guns and ammunition hidden on their farm (La Buzardiere) ready to help when the invasion came. Fisher stayed with the Pansart family for about two months, during which time Odette Pansart taught him French. He says that M Pansart collected a number of airmen and names Herbert Dulberg, Peter Hoyt, Harry Minor, John Beilstein, William Miller, Edward Shaffer, Steve Koval and Joe Burkowski. He mentions M Belleville (Andre Louis Belleville of La Rocca, Chemin de Rivasselou, Parame) and M Pansart taking him and Beilstein to Trigavou.

In early October, Roger Pansart came to tell Fisher that he was going leave by boat and Emile Guimard took him, Harry Minor and John Beilstein by truck to Malestroit. Fisher was sheltered with Norbert Letexier of rue St Julien, Malestroit for about two weeks until it became too hot (there was a lot of German military activity in the town) and he was taken to stay with a M Duval (assume Louis Duval at Serent, Morbihan) where he joined Beilstein, Joe Burkowski and George Padgett. The four airmen stayed with M Duval until the end of November when they left for Paris along with Elton Hoyt, William Cook and Wayne Bogard.

Fisher confirms Michelle Moet and Jean Carbonnet taking him and others by overnight train to Paris on 1 December and the Moet home at

Saint-Mande. There, the group were split up and Fisher was taken to stay with an elderly couple named Dunoyer on Avenue Alphand. When Jean Carbonnet collected him on 24 December, Fisher thought he was on his way to the Pyrenees but Carbonnet delivered him to a church opposite Montparnasse station. Fisher was handed him over to guides Yves Allain and Pierre Jacob who took him (and others) by train to Quimper and Dournanez, where he arrived at two o'clock in the afternoon of Christmas Day.

1/Lt James E Armstrong was the pilot of B-17 41-24507 Yankee Raider (384BG/546BS) which was returning from Stuttgart on 6 September 1943. Despite problems with #1 engine they had managed to stay in formation but then spent about half an hour circling the target. Shortly after setting off for home, they ran out of fuel pressure for #3 engine and the supercharger on #4 engine failed. As they lost height, they became easy prey to German fighters and at about mid-day, the aircraft was abandoned to crash south of Gisors (Eure). Yankee Raider radio-operator T/Sgt Walter L House and tail-gunner S/Sgt Clifford Hammock also evaded successfully: House with Comete (see earlier) and Hammock with the John Carter organisation.

Armstrong landed (badly) in a ploughed field near the little village of Gamaches-en-Vexin. He injured his ankle on hitting the ground but managed to hobble his way to outskirts of the village. Whilst trying to get around the village, he met a man who brought him some food and indicated that he should hide in the nearby woods. Armstrong stayed in the woods for nine days until he felt fit enough to set off walking towards Paris and another two days before he found someone who could help him and arrange his journey.

Armstrong was driven to Paris and soon introduced to Maurice Cottereau at his bar, the Cafe du Moulin Rouge in Drancy. Two days later (about 20 September), Armstrong was taken to 15 rue Alcide Veillard in nearby Bobigny where he joined Floyd Terry and Vic Matthews who were being sheltered by Theodrine Quenot. They were told that the frontier with Spain was closed but after about a month, they heard a story about a boat that was due to go to England. Armstrong says that he met "the boys from Pavillon" – William Howell, Paul McConnell, John Dougherty, John Heald, Robert Sheets and Gary Hinote who were being sheltered at Les Pavillons-sous-Bois. At the end of October, they were all taken by train to Quimper where I think that Armstrong, Vic Matthews and Andrew Lindsay stayed with Jacques Mourlet and his family at 9 rue Anastole Le Bas.

On 6 November, following the abandonment of the Dahlia (Fanfan) operation from Quimper, they were taken back to Paris where Armstrong, Royce Fidler, Leslie Woollard and Robert Sheets stayed in Gilbert Virmoux's apartment at 41 rue Saint-Merri. On 12 November, a girl called Denise took Armstrong and Sheets, and Gilbert Virmoux took the two Englishmen, to the Chateau de la Fortelle where they joined William Howell, Jacob Dalinski, John Dougherty, Paul McConnell, Gary Hinote, Charles Bailey, William Quinn, Andrew Lindsay and Anthony Reynolds for about twenty days of toughening for the mountains. On about 10 December, Armstrong, Fidler, Woollard and Andrew Lindsay returned to Paris and Gilbert Virmoux's flat.

As mentioned earlier, McConnell and Hinote seem to have been passed on to Comete at this point – they crossed the Pyrenees together in January 1944.

They were fitted out for mountains and on about 11 December, Gilbert Virmoux took Armstrong, Fidler, Woollard and Lindsay – and Denise took the Russell Jones and Edward Sobolewski – by train to Carcassonne. As already described, their attempt at crossing the Pyrenees from Quillan failed and they returned once more to Paris. At about this time, Armstrong reports someone saying that they were leaving Bordeaux for the Burgundy organisation.

Denise took Jones and Sobolewski back to her apartment while Armstrong, Fidler, Woollard and Lindsay returned once more to Gilbert Virmoux's flat. Lindsay was soon collected (by Madeleine Davy (query) – he later crossed the Pyrenees with Comete) and two days later, Gilbert took Armstrong, Fidler and Woollard to a church where they met a blonde girl with braided hair (Genevieve Soulie) who had Jones and Sobolewski with her. Armstrong was taken to 11 rue Valentin Hauy, Paris XV where he was sheltered by twenty-nine-year-old accountant Mlle Odette Drappier – she told him that he was her first American – and two days later, a young boy came to tell him that he would be leaving by boat. Armstrong was taken to a church near Montparnasse station where he joined Fidler, Woollard, Jones, Sobelewski, Dwight Fisher and John Carleton to be taken by train to Le Mans where they changed for Quimper and Douarnenez.

On their arrival at Douarnenez, several of the evaders mention meeting the head of the organisation (Yves Le Guillou) who was known to some of them as Noel. He is described as a good-looking, muscular man, about six feet tall with long black wavy hair. He was teaching German, having been a prisoner in Germany for two years, and some local people apparently thought he was a collaborator. He had a wife and two daughters, aged four and ten, and a sister who was working with him.

After abandoning the first operation (Jeanne) as already mentioned, the evaders were sheltered at various homes in and around Douarnenez. Royce Fidler, Leslie Woollard, John Carleton, Thomas Moore and Dwight Fisher stayed with Mme Josephine Telec (whose husband and son were in England) and her daughter, Mme Desiree Kervarec (whose husband was in Germany) at 16 rue Jean Bart until the evening of 21 January 1944.

Russell Jones and James Armstrong were taken by a M Guyer (query) who ran clothing shop, back to his home on rue Jean Bart. On New Year's Day, they were moved to a flat on the opposite corner of the street at No 2 rue Jean Bart where they stayed with Mme Malhomme until their departure.

Harry Horton and Edward Sobolewski were sheltered with Louis Ridel, a fish-merchant who had moved to Douarnenez from Dieppe, while Robert Giles and Carroll Haarup were sheltered with Mlle Marguerite Seznec at 3 rue Emile Zola for a few days before moving to stay with Mme Alberte Pensec at 21 rue Louis Midi.

Ardell Bollinger says that the organisation head (Yves Le Guillou) and Klacken (Pierre Claquin of 12 rue Saint Jean, Treboul) a short, heavy man who worked on the railways at Douarnenez, took seven (sic) of them – Bollinger, Kelly and Kalas plus S/Sgt Glenn Blakemore (from 306BG/367 BS B-17 42-5130 Sweet Pea) and three others – to a house in Treboul (at 38 rue Professeur Curie) where they stayed with Gabriel Cloarec. They report Blakemore leaving with a Frenchman and heard later that he had been captured, along with the family that helped him.

Bollinger also reports Claquin going to the port of Audierne to see about another boat but returning about four days before they left to tell Gabriel Cloarec that the owner of the boat at Audierne wanted 900,000 francs. According to Cloarec's mother Catherine, Gabriel had intended that his brother Pierre should sail the *Breiz-Izel* but having sheltered the evaders in his house, and on receiving notice to report for work in Germany, Gabriel decided to skipper her himself.

There is some confusion in the evader reports about which day the *Breiz-Izel* actually sailed from Treboul (the harbour for Douarnenez) because the evaders were gathered late in the evening of 21 January and departed in the early hours of the following morning. However, the crossing took about thirty-six hours and all the reports (with one exception) agree that they reached Falmouth in Cornwall at about lunch-time on 23 January 1944.

> *"On the night of 21 January, the chief of the organisation told us we were leaving. The party went to the quay at Treboul and boarded a boat at about 2145 hrs. We left at 0250 hrs. There was a German guard at the mouth of the harbour, and as the boat was going out, someone shouted "Halt". We heard a scream and were told afterwards that the German searchlight had been switched on and then went out suddenly, as a result of an attack on the Germans, arranged by the organisers. The boat was able to leave the harbour without mishap and the engine was started. We arrived at Falmouth about 1300 hrs on 24 (sic) January. The party on the boat consisted of 16 Frenchmen, 10 Americans and four British." (WO208/5582 1718/1719 Fidler & Woollard)*

Research by Pierre Tillet suggests that in addition to the fourteen evaders, and Gabriel Cloarec and his crew (Pierre CLOAREC, Pierre CELTON, Pierre DREVILLON, Yves PERON, Emile RALEC), Jean CELTON, Andre DELFOSSE, Theodore DOARE, Francois JAOUEN, Yves LE FOL, Jean de la PATELIERE, Yves PERON, Pierre PHILIPPON, Jacques REVERCHON, Jean RICHARD, Yves VOURCH and Jos LE BRIS were also taken to England on board the *Breiz-Izel* – a total of thirty-two people. Jean de la Pateliere and Pierre Philippon are both known to have been involved with Jean-Claude Camors and the Bordeaux organisation, guiding evaders prior to the departure of the *Suzanne-Renée* in October 1943 – see earlier.

CHAPTER 44

Fanfan and the Jouets-des-Flots

As already mentioned, Yves Le Henaff (Fanfan) and his Dahlia network organised several evacuations from Brittany by fishing boat. As was the way with such things, some were successful and others not. Tragically, his last operation, which should have returned Le Henaff to England as well, was a disaster.

By the end of January 1944, BCRA agents Pierre Brosselette and Emile Bollaert had been trying to get back to England for some months but bad weather had prevented any Lysander operations in January and so they turned (in despair, according to M R D Foot) to a Breton sea escape line.

Just over a week after the *Breiz-Izel* left for England, the requirement to get Brosselette and Bollaert out of France, had become urgent. They, along with Emile Laffon and Jacques Maillet, joined a group of Frenchmen and seven evaders to be taken from Douarnenez on board a fishing boat called *Jouet-des-Flots*.

Six of the evaders were airmen – John Watlington, John Pilkington, Roy Davidson, Fred Krueger, Lee Gordon and Ralph Hall. The seventh man was an Indian who had escaped from prison at Rennes – none of the airmen give his name but it was Buland Khan.

F/O John H Watlington was the pilot of 400 Sqn Mustang AG641 which was shot down near Neufchatel on 22 June 1943. Amongst his many adventures had been the failed attempt from Quimper at the end of October so this was his second trip to the Breton town. While he'd been sheltered in Paris with Charles and Jeanne Ramsey at 47 rue Dulong (Paris XVII) in January – and apparently frustrated by further delays – Watlington asked Mrs Ramsey if she could put him back in touch with Mme McDonnel (who had sheltered him at her home at 119 rue Exelmans the previous October) and 'the organisation on the coast'. Mme McDonnel contacted Charlotte Le Henaff (Yves's mother) at rue Michelet and it was arranged that she and Jeanne Ramsey would take Watlington to Montparnasse station where he was passed over to a Dahlia guide called Felix.

"On arrival at Quimper we were taken by truck to a cottage outside the town. In the truck I met Kreuger and Davidson again [they first met in Paris in November]. There was also another RAF man in the party – a Tempsford navigator whose name I do not know. Just before sunset two cars came for the party, which was under the direction of Fanfan and a French admiral. We were taken to a fisherman's cottage about 200 yards from the beach. As soon as a German patrol had passed we were taken to the beach itself. There were in the party six airmen, 28 to 30 Frenchmen, and about six French sailors who were to form the boat's crew. We were led through a minefield on the beach and along to a house in which we waited. It was a moonlit night.

After a time a boat showed up and we embarked in three small rowing boats and paddled out to the boat, a fishing smack about 60 feet long, equipped with engine and sail. We set off at 21.30 hrs from a point near Pen Morvan. Soon after we started the weather got very rough and the boat began to leak. We tried to keep the water down by bailing and by using an inadequate pump. As the water mounted the engine cut out and we had to rely on the sail. The rendezvous with the speed boat was to have been at 0800 hrs off the Chausee le Sein islands but at 0600 hrs we had to turn back. We reached the coast in a small bay near Pointe de Feunteun-Aod. We all got ashore and onto the highway, and split up.

I lost contact with my group and returned to the neighbourhood of the boat to look for Fanfan. By this time the boat had sunk and I am sure I saw some Germans in the vicinity. I saw one of the Americans who had lost his shoes in jumping overboard. When walking along the road we saw two French members of the party ahead of us being questioned by a German police patrol. The patrol saw us as we rounded a corner and both the French and I turned and ran back up the road. A German came after us on his bicycle and I branched off up a slip road, leaving the American … After a time, I met some members of a maquis group with the American. We stayed the night with the maquis group at a house in the bay at Primelin." (TNA file WO208/5583-1925 Watlington)

John Watlington returned to Paris alone a few days later. He stayed with the Ramsays until 19 February when he left for Toulouse and another of his previous helpers, Mme Collaine at 14 rue Temponieres who put him in touch with yet another organisation … Watlington was finally taken across the Pyrenees from Bagneres-de-Luchon by the Dutch-Paris organisation in March 1944.

The 'Tempsford navigator' was F/Lt John Graham Pilkington from 161 Sqn Halifax EB129 which was on an SOE mission to Lyon the night of 10-11 November 1943. Bad weather had prevented them from seeing any signal lights and they were returning to England with their containers still on board when the engines failed and the aircraft lost height. Pilot P/O M A Line RAAF gave the order to bale out but Pilkington was the only man able to do so before the aircraft crashed with the loss of all on board.

Pilkington landed in a field just outside Thiron-Gardais (Eure-et-Loir) and after burying his parachute and Mae West, set off walking. At about eight o'clock that morning, a passing cyclist recognised Pilkington as an airman and took him to M et Mme Germaine Merel who sheltered him on their farm at La Tuilerie, just outside Thiron-Gardais. He was visited there by two members of the resistance and after three weeks, a woman (either Mme Delaforge or her daughter Monique) came from Paris and took Pilkington back to her home on Route Nationale in La Chapelle-en-Serval (Oise). He was sheltered with Mme and Mlle Delaforge for a month before being taken to stay with Theodorine Quenot at 15 rue Alcide Veillard in Bobigny, where he joined two American airmen (Davidson and Krueger) for another month.

On about 30 January, a man and woman took Pilkington and the two Americans to a railway station where they joined another American (Lee Gordon) and guide. They were passed on to two more guides who took them by train to Quimper in Brittany and a house where they were joined by three (query) more Allied airmen. Early next morning, they were taken along the cliffs and put into small boats, together with about twenty Frenchmen, including a number of secret agents, who were waiting for them. They were rowed out to a fishing boat in the middle of the river which immediately set off. After about three hours sailing, they ran into heavy seas which stopped the engine, blew away the sails and started a leak. Despite their best efforts at bailing, the captain decided they had to head back to the coast. They managed to fasten the boat to a rock and scramble ashore where they split up into small parties – Pilkington went with three of the Americans. They had only been walking for half an hour when they were stopped by a German soldier. Being unable to answer any of his questions in either German or French, they were arrested.

2/Lt Roy G Davidson and S/Sgt Fred C Krueger were the pilot and top-turret gunner of B-17 42-30453 Thunderbird (94BG/333BS) which was returning from Schweinfurt on 14 October 1943 when they were attacked by fighters. Three crew baled out over Germany before Davidson crash-landed the aircraft in a field near Saverne (Alsace).

Roy Davidson (RAMP Folder 5, 82/83) lists Pierre (leader of an organisation) at Epernay making arrangements for his return in October 1943, Alfred Point (professer) at Epernay sheltering him for two weeks, Rene Charpentier of Fromentieres, Marne sheltering him for two weeks, M [Raymond] Montchausse of Orbais L'Abbaye, Marne sheltering him for six weeks and Mme Quenot as sheltering him for about two months at 15 rue Veillard, Bobigny.[1]

Sgt Lee Gordon was the ball-turret gunner of B-17 41-24623 (305BG/365BS) (Stallman) which was shot down off Wilhelmshaven on 26 February 1943. At least two crew were killed and Gordon and the rest captured but Gordon escaped from Stalag VIIA (Moosburg) on 13 October 1943. In contrast to one of his earlier attempts when Gordon rode a bicycle bought from a German guard and wore especially commissioned lederhosen to disguise himself as a member of the Hitler Youth, this time he simply changed into French civilian clothing and walked out of the camp as though on a work party. He made his way to Munich where he contacted a French *Arbeitskommando* who passed him on to other groups of French workers until he finally reached the relative safety of Strasbourg on 30 October. From there he went to St Nicolas-du-Port (Lorraine) where an organisation (Marie-Claire – query) became involved and sent him to Paris in November.

Gordon was the one who lost his shoes – he'd taken off all his clothes thinking he would probably have to swim ashore and then his shoes were washed overboard. He later bought replacements (actually just slippers) from an elderly farmer for 200 francs.

Lee Gordon joined up with John Watlington to be taken back to Quimper but the scribbled notes of his report make it hard to know exactly what happened after that. He certainly returned to Paris soon afterwards because the next news I have for him is when he left from Montparnasse station on about 23 February 1944 by train for Guingamp in Brittany with F/Sgt Leon Harmel. Both men were taken back to England by MGB on the second Shelburn operation from Plage Bonaparte the night of 26-27 February.

---

1   F/Sgt Hubert Salter reports meeting Davidson and Krueger at Epernay (Champagne-Ardenne, south of Reims) at the end of October and travelling with them to Paris and on to Quimper. They joined other evaders for a boat evacuation with Fanfan (Yves Le Henaff) that was aborted, before returning to Epernay. Salter left them there on 24 October when he joined Sgt Leonard Marsh and Sgt Harold Clark. (WO208/5583-1748 Salter)

Gordon ends his epic report by saying that he was a long time in France (four months) and became very impatient but his helpers reminded him – "patience, courage, confidence" – and says (on page 215) there is no better advice for an escaper.

T/Sgt Ralph Hall was the top-turret gunner of B-17 42-31212 (Johnson) which was returning from Bordeaux on 5 January 1944 with an already damaged tail from flak over the target. As they dropped out of formation, they were attacked by fighters and the aircraft abandoned to crash somewhere west of Pontivy in Brittany. Hall's report doesn't give many details apart from saying he contacted the French underground at Gourin on 7 January and was sent to Douarnenez. After getting ashore from the wreckage of the *Jouets-des-Flots*, Hall was sheltered by Mlle Marguerite Seznec at 3 rue Emile Zola in Douarnenez for nearly seven months. On 22 August, Hall was taken to Plouha where he was met by a Captain James Harrison who helped him get transport to Rennes where he rejoined American forces. Captain Harrison was Lucien Dumais, the French-Canadian MI9 agent responsible for returning six others from Hall's crew to England by MGB on various Shelburn operations in February and March.

Buland Khan was cook for the officers of 22 Animal Transport Company (Mules) RIASC. They had been stationed at Marseille when the German offensive began in May 1940 and were quickly moved up to a small village near Metz. They (along with other units) were forced to retire south and were captured at Gerardmer (Vosges) on 24 June. Khan was sent to Stalag VIIB (Lamsdorf) until September when he was transferred (presumably with his officers) to Oflag IV(E) (54) at Annaburg. In December 1942, he was moved to Rennes.

In February 1943, an Indian doctor (who had also been at Annaburg) asked Khan to take on the duties of a nursing orderly at the *Ecole Premiere Superieure* hospital, which was being used for Indians, Moroccans and Senegalese (and others) outside the camp and in the town of Rennes. The only security seems to have been a barbed wired fence, a wall and a German sentry at the front door. On 23 November 1943, Khan and his friend Sgt Shahzaman escaped from the hospital.

Khan and Shahzaman were helped by a French girl called Lise de Rider who took them back to her lodgings in Rennes where she gave them civilian clothing. The following night, she took them to her home in Paris at 17 rue d'Oleron (query) where they stayed for a month. On 24 December, Lise took the two men by train to Vannes, where they stayed at 13 rue Saint-

Gildas. On 30 December, Lise left and a man known as M Emil (Emile Guimard) took them to Saint-Aubin, where they stayed for a week, then on 7 January, to Gourin (the same date as given by Hall above). On 15 January, a French guide took them to Douarnenez, where Shahzaman was questioned by a gendarme and arrested.[2]

Khan makes no mention of the boating adventure, saying only that he returned to the same address (not given) in Gourin but it seems too much of a coincidence for him not to be the unidentified Indian mentioned by both Hall and Lee Gordon. Buland Khan left Gourin for Guingamp on 14 March and was evacuated by MGB 503 from the beach at Anse-Cochet near Plouha the night of 19-20 March 1944 on Operation Bonaparte 4.

The loss of the *Jouets-des-Flots* in the early hours of 4 February 1944 was a disaster for the French Resistance in general because, although Emile Laffon and Jacques Maillet escaped, amongst those who were subsequently captured were Pierre Brosselette and Emile Bollaert.

It was news of the capture of Brossolette and Bollaert (and the hope that Brossolette hadn't yet been identified) that sent his friend, SOE (RF Section) agent Forest Yeo-Thomas back to France to try and rescue him – a mission that also failed. Yeo-Thomas was betrayed and captured in Paris on 21 March – just one day before Pierre Brossolette, after extensive torture, managed to throw himself from a fifth-floor window – he died later that evening. Emile Bollaert was deported to Germany but survived Buchenwald and Bergen-Belsen to be repatriated to France in 1945.

Yves Le Henaff was also captured. He was held in prison at Rennes and after extensive interrogation, was deported to Germany. Lieutenant de Vaisseau Yves Henri Leon Le Henaff (born October 1914) died on the way to Dachau in July 1944.

---

2   Harry Minor, who was also sheltered at Saint-Aubin (along with John Semach and two 'Hindus' who had escaped from Rennes), reports being taken to a cafe in Gourin on about 8 January where they joined 2/Lt Ernest Hugonnet, S/Sgt Donald McLeod and Sgt Marion Hall – all later Bonaparte 2. He and the other Americans were then driven to Concarneau, leaving the two Hindus at the cafe.

CHAPTER 45

The Adventures of Lt Glickman

The reader will have realised by now that it's impossible to write about Bourgogne in isolation and that I have to mention some of the other organisations involved in helping the numerous evaders. Many of the men shot down over Brittany in late 1943, were passed to Bordeaux-Loupiac but that organisation ran into all sorts of problems of its own. I am guessing that Louis Glickman would also have been passed on to Bordeaux if the opportunity to try and send him out with SOE agent Paul Deman hadn't arisen. It then seems only logical that with the failure of the first Var line operation (and despite being listed by Broussine) he should have been passed to one of SOE's more usual Vic line (named for its creator, Vic Gerson) routes for evacuation across the Pyrenees.

2/Lt Louis H Glickman was the bombardier of B-17 42-29876 Battlin' Bobbie (379BG/525BS) (Hoyt) which was on the way to Nantes on 16 September 1943 when it was attacked by fighters and the aircraft abandoned over Brittany – see earlier.

Twenty-three-year-old Glickman delayed opening his parachute until entering heavy cloud at about 10,000 feet after which he landed in a farmyard, just yards from the farmhouse of la Ferme de Saint-Marc, near Guipry. The Bree family watched as Glickman gathered up his parachute but did nothing to help until he ran into their barn – they followed and Glickman, who spoke some French, explained that he was an American who needed help. The only word that farmer Henri Bree seemed to know was 'Allemand' and so Glickman, assuming the Germans might arrive at any time, took his parachute, crawled under a cider press and waved the family away. Glickman checked his maps (and ate his escape ration chocolate) until M Bree returned about three hours later and Glickman asked him if he could stay the night in his barn. Next morning, M Bree brought Glickman some breakfast – and later lunch and an evening meal – after which he gained sufficient confidence to bring a young man called Rene (locally recruited SOE agent Rene Bichelot of Francois Vallee's Parson circuit) who checked Glickman's identity. Rene then took Glickman to stay with the farmer's son-in-law, Georges Daniel of La Vallee en Messac, for two days until General Marcel Allard took Glickman to Les Hautes-Folies, his home at Messac. After lunch, the general arranged for Glickman to move into the village where (on 21 September) he joined El Diablo tail-gunner S/Sgt John Semach and stayed with M Gerard, who worked at the Prefecture in Rennes, at La Tertre.

Glickman and Semach stayed with M Gerard until 10 October, during which time Glickman heard that his pilot Elton Hoyt and three other Americans (his waist-gunner Harry Minor, John Beilstein and S/Sgt Cyril G Koval) had left for Saint Malo, when a local miller named Eugene Justeau (Eugene and his wife Maria had previously sheltered Elton Hoyt at Pipriac) took Glickman and Semach by truck to Ploermel.

Glickman and Semach were driven to St Jean, a large house near Ploermel and home of *cultivateur* Julien Moureau before taking a train with Glickman's navigator William Cook, El Diablo navigator 2/Lt Joseph Burkowski and two guides to Rennes, where they stayed with one of the guides. They were told there was a scheme to get them – and others, including Harry Minor – out by boat but the shooting of Jean-Claude Camors by Roger Leneveu at the cafe L'Epoque on 11 October, put a stop to that plan.

With no help in sight, Glickman and John Semach walked out of Rennes the following morning, intending to head north towards the coast but getting lost and eventually getting a lift, directions and a map to find their way back to Messac and General Allard's house. The gardener told them that the general had gone to Rennes to investigate the shooting and it was the General Allard's wife Marguerite who let them stay until the general returned and took them back to stay with Georges Daniel. Glickman also heard that Cook, Burkowski and two others had been brought back from Rennes – Cook and Burkowski (at least) being taken first to Andree Recipon at the Chateau de Laille before returning to Guipy where they were sheltered by the teenage Alphonse Vallais (and his family) at Le Bas Chemin.

On about 15 October, Henri Tanguy, Raymond Guillard and Emile Guimard used the Citroen camionnette (*Boulangere*) belonging to the Mallard sisters at Plumelec to drive Glickman, Semach, Cyril Koval and a French pilot (presumably Guillaume Bernard) to the cafe Cherel at Ploermel where they joined Harry Minor. Glickman was taken to stay with schoolteacher Mlle Madeleine Travers at 41 rue General Duberton while

Minor and Semach (and Koval – query) were taken to a farm near Josselin where they were sheltered with Mlle Guillo, an elderly cousin of Emile Guimard and whose brother, the maire of Guehenno, lived downstairs.

"Around the centre of Ploermel were men who had been shot down my date – now together were Hoyt, Cook, Beilstein, Shaffer, Burkowski, Miller, Fisher, Semach and a few others, including Harry Minor. Toward (query) 1 December, a group of eleven (sic) men were taken to Paris – EMs – and the second week another group – Hoyt, Fisher, Cook, Beilstein and Burkowski – and I learned all left were Minor, Semach and self. Think reason we left behind [is] because French thought we were happy – from time to time they asked how we were and I said all right because they [were] doing the best they could and I didn't want to bitch." (MIS-X #370 Glickman)

Glickman is referring to the group of (seven) American sergeants taken to Paris on 23 November, all of whom except Dulberg, were passed over to Camile Nicolas to shelter at Livry-Gargan prior to passing them on to Bordeaux-Loupiac at l'Eglise de Pantin (see earlier). The officers – Hoyt, Fisher, Cook, Beilstein and Burkowski (plus Bogard and Padgett) – were taken to Paris on 1 December. Note that while Michele Moet names Lizio (see below), most of the evaders refer to Ploermel as the nearest large town. Taupont, Guehenno and Saint-Servant are also nearby.

"At the end of November 1943, Jean Carbonnet went to Brittany, a pretty village called Lizio, near Vannes, where he had been told that several airmen were gathered and were waiting to be repatriated to England.
    At the very beginning of December, Jean Carbonnet and I left for Vannes where we expected a certain 'Mimile', whose real name Emile Guimard, who became a leader of the Maquis of Saint-Marcel [just outside Maelstroit]. In his gazogene car, without headlights because of the curfew, he took us to Lizio. The next morning, at dawn, he took us to a little dirty and dilapidated building. The interior was divided into two parts by wooden slats. On one side cows, on the other we were facing about fifteen young men who appeared to be in good physical condition, but with trousers too short for their long legs and jackets with sleeves too short for their long arms. They probably thought they would all leave. It was up to me, who only sputtered a poor school-girl English, to tell them that we could only take seven and gave instructions for the trip. It was too dangerous to take all these boys together, if identifiable.

What a disappointment on the faces of those who were not chosen. What would we have done if we had known that a few weeks after that, they were caught arriving in Paris? I do not know how and why they left. The same afternoon, we left Lizio for Paris, taking the train from Vannes with Fisher, Cook, Hoyt, Burkowski, Beilstein, Bogart and Padgett.

Bud Fisher was hosted by the couple Dunoyer at Avenue Alphand in Saint-Mande before being repatriated quickly before all others [on board the Breiz-Izel]. Peter Hoyt and William Cook were sheltered in Paris by Anita Lemonnier and her mother at 2 rue Ernest Renan, Paris 75015 until their departure for Spain. John Beilstein was hosted by the couple (Marcel) Soreau at 6 rue de la Republique, Saint-Mande. George Padgett was sheltered with Mme Castagnier at 1 rue Washington, Paris 75008 and then by Liliane Jameson (who was married to an American) and her mother at 2 rue Gervex, Paris 75017. Joe Burkowski and Wayne Bogart stayed with my parents at 22 rue Sacrot, Saint-Mande until 15 January when we moved them to stay with M Legros at 21 rue Gabrielle, Charenton 94220 – and then with the Besson sisters (Simone and Andree) at 8 rue Emile Allez, Paris 75017."
(Michele Agniel Dec 2013)

On 23 December, Henri Tanguy arrived in his truck, very excited because Glickman, Minor and Semach were going to be taken out that night. He drove them to Saint-Aubin, Malestroit but when Emile Guimard arrived, he told them there was only room for one more American in the party, and as Glickman was an officer (which Glickman dismisses as baloney) it was the two sergeants who were left behind when Glickman was taken to Bedee, about 20 kms north-west of Rennes.[1]

Glickman joined General Allard, who was now on the run from the Gestapo following the arrest of his wife and daughter (on 1 December) and five young French *resistants*. They were driven in a charcoal-burning (*gazogene*) lorry to Pleherel-Plage-Vieux-Bourg (a few kms west of St Malo) where Glickman met William Bilton and four Americans – Max Gibbs, Cloe Crutchfield, Sidney Elskes and Arnold Wornson. An English-speaking Frenchman called Paul (SOE agent Erwin Deman) (5 ft 7 inches

---

1   After Glickman left, Minor and Semach stayed on in Saint-Aubin (Saint-Aubin-en-Plumelec) with the Mlles Yvonne, Marie and Lucie Mallard in a flat above their shop ... In January, they were joined by Buland Khan and his friend Sgt Shahzaman, who had escaped from a hospital at Rennes and on 8 January, they were all driven to Pontivy, where they changed lorries (and organisations) to be taken to Gourin. Harry Minor and John Semach were later taken to Brest (where they stayed with Colonel Scheidhauer) before going on to Guingamp and the Shelburn organisation. They were both evacuated by MGB 503 (Marshall) in February on the MI9 Operation Bonaparte 2.

tall, stocky, medium, dark hair, aggressive attitude) was to arrange their evacuation by boat that evening and they got as far as climbing down the cliffs "three at a time, in a series of movie stunts" to the beach and seeing the boat off-shore when "flares were fired all over the sky" and shots were fired.

This was one of the first SOE Var line operations, organised by Erwin Deman and local recruit Aristide Sicot as an alternative to the SOE Vic line which ran across the Pyrenees. Var was intended for the exclusive use of SOE personnel but in addition to the six agents planned for the embarkation, General Allard was given a priority place and a number of evading airmen were also included.

SOE Operation Jealous III was planned to land and collect SOE agents from Pointe-de-Saint-Cast (about 20 kms west of St-Malo) but abandoned after MGB 502 (Williams) was spotted from shore and fired upon. A mixed party of agents and evaders were collected at the Sicot family villa of Les Feux Follets.

"MGB 502 anchored off the Pointe-du-Chatelet in the early hours of Christmas Eve and the surf-boats had just been lowered when a white flare burst overhead, turning night into day. The surf-boats were hoisted back in, the grass anchor warp cut with an axe and the gun-boat's engines restarted. Her stealthy approach meant that the ship was still lying facing the head of the bay but because she was so far into the bay, she was beyond the field of fire from the German cannon at the entrance. However she did receive machine-gun and small-arms fire as she turned at speed to make her exit, heading at full speed and with violent changes of course as she escaped back into the Channel, suffering only the loss of a signal halliard."[2]

Glickman and the others ran back up the cliff and Felix Jouan (a miller from Bedee) took them back to the house, Les Feux Follets at Saint-Cast-le-Guildo, where they were hidden in an underground shelter that had been dug under the dining-room floor. Next day, General Allard decided that he wanted to stay with the Jagu family at La Chapelle-Thouartault where he and Glickman were sheltered for a week until Paul Deman and Felix Jouan came with a tall 'mannish' Frenchwoman called Lucy (described by

---

2   Extract from 'Secret Flotillas' by Brooks Richards. The failure of Operation Jealous III meant the landing beach near St Cast couldn't be used again and subsequent Var line operations (Easement, Septimus and Scarf) were moved further west to the beach at Beg-an-Fry.

Wornson as Paul's chief lieutenant) and took Glickman to join the other evaders at Bedee.[3] That evening (3 January) Glickman and the others were taken to Redon where Glickman stayed with an unnamed family for a week until Wednesday 12 January, when Lucy took him, Arnold Worson and William Bilton to Paris.

In Paris, Glickman, Worson and Bilton stayed in a small apartment until the Friday evening when they were taken to a railway station and met a man that Glickman assumed was the head of the organisation – slight and suave, with spats, a cane and wearing a velvet collared coat – and they were instructed to follow a woman. She and a young Belgian called Charles then took them to Lyon. Glickman stayed overnight in the apartment of a young, pretty woman who said her husband was in England – and met two more Belgians, Jean and Francois – and the following evening (15 January) was taken by train to Perpignan.

Glickman stayed overnight in Perpignan at the home of a young (unnamed) couple then on 16 January, was taken to meet a man called Jacques and two mountain guides. They walked all that night, crossing into Spain, and the following night until reaching Figueras at about eight o'clock in the morning. Glickman and Jacques were driven to the house of a Frenchman where they stayed the night before taking a train to Barcelona and the British Consulate.

Glickman was obviously helped by the John Carter organisation in Lyon, despite Carter himself having been arrested shortly before Glickman arrived, and so it was presumably the SOE Vic line that took him across the Pyrenees.[4]

---

3   The IS9 Helper List has Antoine Jagu of 80 rue de Dinan, Rennes.

Felix Jouan was arrested (almost by chance and with Sicot lucky to escape the same fate) in Rennes on 13 January 1944, caught transporting SOE equiment in his gazogene truck which broke down at a particularly unfortunate moment. (Secret Flotillas 225/226) Felix Marie Jouan (born December 1892) was deported to Germany and died at Neuengamme in May 1945. (WO208/5456)

Jean-Claude Bougeon identifies 'Lucy' as Marie-Therese Stoeffler (IS9 Helper List says Stoffel – of 12 rue Bourg les Bourg, Quimper) – recruited by Erwin Deman at Quimper.

4   My thanks to Jean-Claude Bourgeon of Messac for much of the additional detail used in this chapter – any remaining mistakes are my own. See also Roger Huguen 'Par les nuits les plus longues' (1976), 'Secret Flotillas' (1996) by Brooks Richards and 'SOE in France' (1966) by M R D Foot.

Chapter 46

Another Bordeaux-Loupiac Diversion

Sgt William Bilton, T/Sgt Max Gibbs, S/Sgt Cloe Crutchfield, 2/Lt Sidney Elskes and 2/Lt Arnold Worson probably weren't helped by Bourgogne, but their stories are linked to men who were.

Sgt William H B Bilton was the wireless operator of 10 Sqn Halifax HR920 (Dunlop) which was on the way to Montlucon on the evening of 15 September 1943. They were about 30 miles south-west of Rouen when they were hit by flak and attacked by fighters which set the aircraft on fire and it was abandoned. Two crew were killed and four captured – Bilton was the only successful evader.

Bilton landed in a field at about ten-thirty that night and after burying his parachute and Mae West, set off to the north-west. He walked through the rest of the of the night until about four-thirty next morning when he hid himself in a hedge for the day. That evening, he approached a shepherd boy who was feeding some dogs in a field near a farmhouse. The boy told Bilton there were collaborators in the house and that it should be avoided. While they were talking, the boy's sister arrived with a meal (presumably intended for her brother) and insisted that Bilton share it. A short while later she returned with her father and two other men who took Bilton to a house in a village near Rugles – Bilton never knew the name of the actual village but his host, who was a cider manufacturer, seemed to be the maire. Later a man who spoke some English came and made an ID card and ration tickets for Bilton and on 22 September, sent him to Damville where his journey was arranged.

Bilton was taken to the police barracks where a gendarme checked his papers and arranged for a rendezvous in Rouen. At the rendezvous, Bilton was handed over to a young man who took him to stay in a room at a school. Next day, the young man took him to a cafe where he met 'the Chief' and a young girl who spoke excellent English. They told him they would get him to England in the next two or three days but this plan fell through and Bilton was moved to a florist's shop in the Place de Nantes (query) in Rouen with owner Germaine Cheron.[1] Bilton understood he would be there for a couple of days but he actually stayed until 9 October – apparently because the people he was to be sent to in Paris had been arrested.

Mme Cheron contacted another organisation (Bordeaux-Loupiac) and on 9 October, Bilton was taken by train to Paris where he was passed over to a young man named Pierre Charnier who took him on another train to Rennes. Bilton stayed in an apartment by the river, taking his meals in the cafe de l'Epoque at 16 rue Pre Botte. Bilton was due to leave for the coast on 11 October but that evening, some people in the cafe were shot and the organisation broke up.

Bilton was taken back to the apartment by a girl named Francoise Elie (of 3 Place du Colombier), a friend of the cafe owner Franz Nouet.[2] Two days later, Francoise moved Bilton to a room at the back of the Rex Bar, a black-market cafe on rue de Nantes, where Bilton stayed for the next four weeks – still hoping to be taken off either by boat or aircraft – and joined Max Gibbs and Cloe Crutchfield.

T/Sgt Max Gibbs and S/Sgt Cloe R Crutchfield were the radio-operator and tail-gunner of B-17 42-30000 (92BG/327BS) (Bogard) which was returning from Stuttgart on 6 September 1943 when it was attacked by fighters and abandoned west of Troyes.

After landing near Estissac and being brought together by their helpers, Gibbs and Crutchfield (and their pilot Wayne Board) were taken to Troyes on 28 September and sheltered at Saint-Savine by a butcher named Max Claren (nf). On 4 October, Crutchfield was taken to stay with Raymond Wagner at 41 rue du Faubourg Croncels while Gibbs stayed with Raymond's mother-in-law. On 8 October, they were visited by Pierre Charnier and next day, Pierre and Paulette Depesme (aka Jeanette) took them and Bogard to Paris – where they met another Pierre (a heavy-set fellow, 50-60 years old with a German haircut) (Remy Roure) – and on to Rennes next day.

When Gibbs, Crutchfield and Bogard arrived in Rennes on 9 October, they were taken to the Cafe de l'Epoche where they met William Bilton and French Spitfire pilot, Andre Poirier. Two evenings later, they were waiting in an office to be picked up by Pierre Charnier and taken 'to catch a boat'

1   Mme Germaine Cheron (born March 1906) of 21 rue de la Chaine, Rouen sheltered several evaders at her home until she was denounced and arrested. She was deported to Germany in June 1944, surviving camps at Sarrebruck, Ravensbruck and Neubradenburg until liberated in April 1945. (WO208/5452)

2   See 'Francoise Elie (1905-1968) Portrait d'une resistante rennaise' (Merci Beatrice)

when the shooting in the Cafe de l'Epoche took place, and Francoise Elie quickly moved them to the Rex Bar on rue de Nantes.[3]

2/Lt Sidney Elskes and 2/Lt Arnold Wornson were the navigator and co-pilot of B-17 42-29937 (379BG/525BS) (Breidenthal) which was on the way to their secondary target of an airfield near Rennes St Jacques on 23 September 1943 when a direct flak hit stopped their #3 engine, set the left wing on fire, damaged the controls and the aircraft was abandoned.[4]

Elskes and Wornson – along with their bombardier George Padgett – were also in Rennes at this time. In their almost illegible accounts, they mention hoping to be evacuated by fishing boat and describe Pierre (Remy Roure) as a tall, thin man with glasses, aged about 55 and thought to be a journalist. They also mention meeting Gibbs, Crutchfield and Bogard, three sergeants whose names they couldn't remember, and Sgt Bilton RAF in the Rex Bar.

Before this, Wornson says that he was taken to the Chateau de Laille for half a day where he met the owner (Andree Recipon) who was in the Intelligence Service. It was her Polish driver who took him to a rendezvous at a garage where he transferred to a truck which took him to Rennes and the home of M Le Fevre (assume either Eugene Lefeuvre of 31 rue des Trente or M Lefevre of 23 rue Francois Lanno). M Lefevre took him another house from which his bombardier and navigator (Padgett and Elskes) had just left – Worson's identity being confirmed by him knowing them. He was then returned to M Lefevre where he stayed until Francoise Mottay (Mlle Renee Jeanne Mottay, born November 1916, of 74 rue Paul Feval) took him to join Padgett and Elskes at the home of a woman called Therese.

Elskes also mentions meeting Francoise Mottay who took him and Padgett to the home of a girl who went by the name of Didulle (query) for two nights before returning to Mlle Mottay who then took them by bicycle

---

3   Sgt Andre Poirier was in the cafe de l'Epoque at the time, also hoping to be taken off by boat. He says that Roger Leneveu shot and killed a friend of de Gaulle and seriously wounded the chief of the organisation, Jean Coulaincourt (sic). Jean-Claude Camors was using the name Raoul Caulaincourt and he died of his wounds, aged twenty-four. Remy Roure (born October 1885, who first met de Gaulle when they were both prisoners in the First War) was the man who was wounded. He survived to be deported to Buchenwald – which he also survived.

In the chaos of the shooting, Poirier says he managed to run away and hide in an empty house for two days before returning to Paris. He continued working with the Bordeaux-Loupiac group until 17 December 1943 when he led F/O Graham Kelly and F/Lt Leslie Prickett to a rendezvous at l'Eglise de Pantin where they (with many others) were captured – see earlier.

4   All ten crew from 42-29937 baled out safely and eight were captured – including bombardier 2/Lt George C Padgett who was captured at Toulouse station in February 1944 – see later.

to stay in a house belonging to the father of a Mlle Huchett (query) about ten kilometres south of Rennes. Mlle Huchett lived with her family in Rennes and the house was empty apart from a caretaker. Later, they were returned to Rennes to stay in the servant's quarters of the Huchett house and Francoise brought their co-pilot Worson to join them.

A few days later, they were moved stay with Mlle Huchett's friend Anne (query). Some time after that (very difficult to decypher) they were taken to stay with Gaston (query) who ran a bar in Rennes. About two weeks later, Mlle Mottay came to tell them that a boat was supposed to be leaving on about 15 October from the Saint Malo area and they were driven in Gaston's car to a black-market cafe in Rennes called the Rex Bar. Elskes says that after the shooting, it was Mlle Mottay who sent Padgett and Bogard by tram to somewhere into the country – they were supposed to leave by plane.

On about 6 November, Bilton and four Americans – Sidney Elskes, Arnold Wornson, Max Gibbs and Cloe Crutchfield – were taken to the Chateau de la Bothelleraye near Pipriac (which was occupied by the comte Paul de Rosaz) and then three days later, to a house in Malestroit. On 12 November, they were moved to St Aubin where they stayed for a month in a general store with Mme Malard Moeul of St Aubin par Plomb, Manche who told them that another maritime 'take off' operation had been arranged for them. On 15 December, they were taken back to Rennes and the following day, a man who called himself Paul (Erwin Deman) took them to St Cast, on the north Brittany coast, just west of Saint Malo. They were due to be taken on board a torpedo boat on the night of 23-24 December and although Bilton never saw the boat, he was told that it came in too close to the shore and was fired upon by German guns (see earlier). Bilton and the Americans were rushed to another house in the village where they stayed for the rest of the night. Next morning, Bilton, the four Americans and four Frenchmen were taken by truck to a house outside Rennes, owned by a baker called Phoenix (sic – Felix Jouan), where they waited (in vain) for another boating operation. On 7 January, a girl called Lucy (Marie-Therese Stoeffler) took Bilton and the Americans back to Rennes where they took a train to Redon (about 50 kms east of Vannes).

It's not clear where Bilton or Worsen stayed in Redon but on 12 January, Lucy took them and Louis Glickman to Paris where they stayed with two 'old maids' (address unknown) for two nights and on 15 January, all three were taken by train to Lyon. Glickman was taken elsewhere (see earlier) while Bilton and Worsen stayed in an apartment owned by a postmaster.

On 23 January, a man known as Georges arranged for a girl called Louise to take Bilton and Wornson by train to Perpignan where they were handed over to guides who took them, Sidney Elskes, Max Gibbs and Cloe Crutchfield, across the Pyrenees to Figueras. They crossed the border on 26 January and walked to Figueras where they stayed until 1 February when they went by goods train to Barcelona and the British Consulate.

It's not clear where Elskes, Gibbs and Crutchfield stayed in Redon either – Elskes mentions staying with a potter who lived somewhere outside Redon – until the three of them were taken to Paris where they stayed with a woman called Germaine. Elskes says that he met the head of the organisation, a man who could fit the description of Georges Broussine but no name is given. It was the same Germaine who took him to the station (no date) where he rejoined Gibbs and Crutchfield to take a train to Lyon. From Lyon, a man called Georges arranged their journey via Narbonne and Carcassonne, a trolley to Quillan and then by bus to Perpignan where they rejoined Bilton and Wornson, who Elskes says, had travelled a different way.

CHAPTER 47

Some Chauny-Dromas, Gilbert Thibault and John Carter connections

S/Sgt John W Lowther was a waist-gunner on B-17 42-29571 Charlie Horse (303BG/358BS) (Hartigan) which was on the way to Duren on 20 October 1943 when it was attacked by fighters and abandoned to crash near the French-Belgian border between Valenciennes and Mons.[1]

Lowther is listed by Georges Broussine as being helped by Bourgogne but I think the connection is a tenuous one via Gilbert Thibault before Lowther was passed on the John Carter organisation.

Lowther landed near Valenciennes (Nord-Pas-de-Calais) and was sheltered by the Chauny-Dromas organisation until 30 November when he and two English airmen, RAF Sgts Norman Cufley and John Harvey, were taken to Creil. Lowther was handed over to dentist Georges Budin2 who took him to stay with a middle-aged Scottish woman (short, with red hair and freckles) whose father lived in London. Three days later the three airmen were taken by train to Beauvais where they were collected by Gilbert Thibault who took them and another English airman, Sgt Robert Griffith, back to his home in Auneuil.3

A week later (on 15 December), the four evaders and Gilbert Thibault were taken to Paris in a closed van driven by a Belgian. They went to an apartment at 87 rue Rochechouart where Marguerite Schmitz was sheltering Jean Pitner, Arno Plischke and Delton King but Lowther only stayed for a few hours before he and Griffith were taken to stay with a college student named Jean Jacques Piot (of 2 Square Alboni, Paris XVI).

---

1   Three other members of the Charlie Horse crew also evaded successfully: pilot 2/Lt William R Hartigan and navigator 1/Lt Lorin F Douthett with Comete, and radio-operator T/Sgt Robert L Ward who was taken to Switzerland within a few days of baling out.

2   Georges Budin (and his wife Marie) lived on rue Gambetta in Creil. (Dominique Lecomte)

3   Lieutenant Gilbert Jean Joseph Thibault (born July 1912) was a French cavalry officer on leave from Morocco in October 1942 when he began to explore the possiblities of creating an escape organisation. There was discussion after the war concerning an exceptional award of an OBE for Thibault rather than the more usual military award of an MBE because he was a soldier – see IS9 Awards Bureau files in TNA folder WO208/5452.

Two days later, Lowther and Delton King left for Lyon with a man called Jean (Jean Calmet) who stole personal belongings from some of the evaders. Lowther and King stayed the day with a blond Englishman and his (attractive) wife before being taken to stay with Emilus Moene (query spelling), a saw-mill owner at St Andre (Saint-Andre-la-Cote – query). Six weeks later they were taken back to Lyon where the attractive woman told them that her husband, John Carter, had been caught (on 6 January) while on a trip to the south of France. Shortly after that Lowther and King were taken to Switzerland, arriving there on 22 February 1944.

CHAPTER 48

The Final Days of the John Carter Organisation

In early January 1944, a letter arrived from John Carter in Lyon, telling his group in Paris to be prepared to leave the capital with all the airmen in their care. It was arranged that Madeleine Grador would leave in the morning (10 January) with two airmen – Sgt Robert Griffith (who was sheltered with Marguerite Schmitz) and S/Sgt Clifford Hammock (who was sheltered with Jeanne Huet) – and that Mme Huet would take Sgts Norman Cufley and John Harvey (who were also staying in her eight-room apartment on the seventh floor at 48 Avenue du President Wilson) in the evening. Madeleine Grador had already left with Griffith and Hammock when a letter was delivered from Julien's secretary (Annie Sabourault) asking them to stop sending parcels as Julien had had a very dangerous accident and a few parcels had been lost.[1]

Sgt Robert E Griffith was the navigator of 75 Sqn Stirling LJ442 (Parker) which was hit by flak over Cologne and later attacked by fighters and abandoned over southern Belgium at about eight-thirty in the evening of 18 November 1943. Griffith landed in a field near Masnuy-Saint-Pierre (Hainaut). Walking through the village, he knocked on the door of one of the last houses and was given civilian clothing (while they took his flying gear), bread and coffee, and a package of more bread to take with him. Griffith carried on walking and over the next few days, made his way across the frontier into France near Valenciennes, through Le Quesnoy to Rouvel (Somme), south-east of Amiens, from where his journey was arranged.

Griffith spent the night of 24-25 November with Marcel Grenier on his farm at Rouvrel. Neither Marcel nor his brother, who lived on the neighbouring farm, were members of any organisation but next day, Marcel took him to a general store in Guiscard (Oise) where the owner, Gabriel Hedin, was. M Hedin told Griffith that he would have to wait

---

1   NARA Gill – although her post-war personal account has some of the finer details slightly wrong. Mme Gill also says that the head of the organisation in Paris was Jacques Dupuis (born January 1897) of 5 rue d'Aumale, Paris IX.

while the organisation checked up on him and for the ten days this took, Griffith stayed at 5 rue Chauny with M Hedin who supplied him with civilian clothes. On 5 December, a young man took Griffith by bicycle to Noyon and caught a train to Creil where he was sheltered overnight by a man who worked at the Industrial Co-operative Society. The following evening, another young man took Griffith to Beauvais where he stayed with a local 'secret army' chief (named either Robert or Raoul and aged 35-40, ex-French air force officer) and the following night with a young Frenchman named Jean, who had also served in the French air force. On 8 December, Gilbert Thibault drove Griffith to his home in Auneuil where he met Norman Cuffley, John Harvey and John Lowther – see earlier.

Griffith says that the night after Lowther and King left Paris for Lyon, they were followed by 2/Lts Jean Pitner and Arno Plischke. Shortly afterwards, P/O Henry Hall arrived in Paris – after being sheltered with (amongst others) Marguerite Schmitz, Hall left for Bordeaux on about 6 January with Evelyne Vassius and a young Frenchman called Andre. On 10 January, Griffith was taken to the Gare d'Orleans where he joined Clifford Hammock and Madeleine Grador (aka Colette) who took the two airmen by train to Lavelanet. At the Hotel Gabon, they joined Pitner and Plischke and met Sgt Kenneth Skidmore and S/Sgt Joseph Shandor. They also heard that Jules had been captured along with three of the crew from Shandor's aircraft (Philippe, Edwards and Crippen). Jeanne Huet was due to bring Norman Cufley and John Harvey from Paris next day – and a man called Jean (Jean Calmet) was supposed to be coming from Lyon with two more (Lowther and King) but none turned up so it was just the six of them who left for the crossing to Canillo in Andorra three days later.

S/Sgt Clifford Hammock was the tail-gunner of B-17 41-24507 Yankee Raider (384BG/546BS) (Armstrong) which was returning from Stuttgart on 6 September 1943 and running out of fuel when they were attacked by fighters and the aircraft abandoned. Hammock landed near Beauvais and was helped almost immediately by an elderly woman who was herding sheep and that evening, a Frenchman took him to a barn. After a week in the barn, Hammock was moved to a house (no address) where he stayed for a month before moving to another house, where he spent another month until being collected by Gilbert Thibault. Thibault and another man drove Hammock to Paris where he was sheltered with M et Mme Payen (nf) at 20 rue Saint-Lazare. Whilst there, a blond Belgian (thought by Hammock's interviewer to be an agent known as Cashbox) visited and said that Hammock would be moved on about 16 December. However, Thibault (who visited frequently) told him that something had gone wrong and on about 14 December, Hammock met Madeleine Grador, two others and an Englishman (about 5 feet 6 inches tall, 135-140 lbs with brown hair and blue eyes) (John Carter) who told him that the Belgian organisation had been broken up. This last news may have been premature as the Belgian returned to collect Hammock but his hostess wouldn't let him go and promptly contacted a friend of Gilbert with the news. On about 28 December, Gilbert's friend contacted Madeleine's group and she and a Frenchman came to tell Hammock he would be leaving on 31 December. On that day, two people took Hammock to stay with Jeanne Huet in her apartment at 48 Avenue du President Wilson where he joined Norman Cufley and John Harvey. On 10 January, Paule Vastel, who visited her friend Mme Huet every day, took Hammock to stay overnight in her apartment at 39 rue Claude Bernard. Early next morning, Paule took him to the station where they met Madeleine Grador and Robert Griffith and Mme Grador took the two airmen by train and bus to Lavelanet where they joined Kenneth Skidmore, Joseph Shandor, Jean Pitner and Arno Plischke.

Sgt Kenneth Skidmore was the flight-engineer of 158 Sqn Halifax HR791 (Evans) which was returning from Cannes in the early morning of 12 November 1943 when they were hit by flak and the aircraft abandoned to crash near Surville (Calvados). Skidmore landed near Bonneville-la-Louvet and was sheltered in the Normandy area until 10 December when Helene Gill and Jean-Pierre de la Hutiere brought him to Paris. Mme Gill took him to stay with Jeanne Huet where he was visited by Jules (John Carter). On 14 December, Jules took him by train to Lyon where he was supposed to join a group of five other evaders to be taken to the Spanish border. However he was told that the guides would only take five so Skidmore stayed on in Jules' apartment (address not known) until 17 December, when he was moved to another house on the outskirts of Lyon (address not known) with a man, wife and their two children. On 4 January, Jules took him back to his apartment and 'kitted him out' for the Pyrenees and on 6 January, a man called Jean (Jean Calmet) took him and Joseph Shandor to Lavelanet. They were meant to be joined by Jules and three Americans but they failed to arrive and Skidmore stayed in a hotel in Lavelanet where he was joined by Robert Griffith.

S/Sgt Joseph Shandor was a waist-gunner on B-17 42-30604 Badger's Beauty V (100BG/350BS) (Helstrom) which was badly off-course returning from Frankfurt on 4 October 1943 and running out of fuel. The aircraft was belly-landed south of Caen and the crew split into groups to evade. Shandor went with fellow waist-gunner S/Sgt William Edwards and tail-gunner S/Sgt Charles Crippen. They had various adventures in Normandy (where their co-pilot F/O Hubert Trent and bombardier 1/Lt Hilbert Philippe were also being sheltered) before their helpers finally decided to take them south, via Paris by train to Culoz (Ain, Rhone-Alpes) and a nearby maquis camp. On about 12 December, they were joined by Trent, 2/Lt Clarence D Willingham (co-pilot of B-17 42-30837 Ole Bassar) and 627 Sqn Mosquito DZ479 crew F/Lt L R Simpson and Sgt Peter W Walker who had also been sheltered in Caen – these last four were taken to Lyon in January and the following month, to Switzerland.

On about 10 January 1944, Shandor says an order came for them to move and he, Edwards, Crippen and Philippe were taken by truck to a small village where they were turned over to a guide named Jean. Jean Calmet took them to Lyon where Jules (John Carter) met them and took them back to his apartment. They were outfitted with new clothing before Annie Sabourault took them back to Jean Calmet. Mme Annie took Pitner and Plischke while Shandor went with Jean to pick up Kenneth Skidmore. When they got to the train, Jules instructed them to sit in different compartments for the journey. Shandor, Skidmore and Jean got off at Bram to catch a train for Lavelanet while the others continued to Toulouse to take a connecting train from there. While they were waiting for Jules in a hotel in Lavelanet, Annie Sabourault arrived with Jean Pitner and Arno Plischke. After waiting two days for Jules, it was assumed he and the three Americans had been captured. Meanwhile, Colette (Madeleine Grador) had arrived from Paris with Robert Griffith and Clifford Hammock.

2/Lts Jean B Pitner and Arno E Plischke were the co-pilot and navigator of B-17 42-31215 (100BG/349BS) (Ford) which was shot down on 26 November 1943 and crashed south-west of Beauvais. They (and their waist-gunner Delton King) were helped by Gilbert Thibault and on 2 December, the three airmen and Thibault were driven into Paris where they took the Metro and then walked to an apartment house (which they describe as a rendezvous for helpers) where they met a chemist named Mme Vassius.[2] That same day, Marguerite Schmitz collected them – someone else took

2   Mme Evelyne Vassius (born January 1897) of 26 rue de Clichy, Paris IX was head of the Clichy sub-group of the Wyssogota-Lorraine (Visigotha) escape line and secretary to its chief, Andre de Wyssogota-Zakrzewski. Mme Vassius was arrested on 16 February 1944 and deported to Ravensbruck, where she died. (WO208/5458)

King – and took them to her apartment at 87 rue Rochechouart. Whilst there, they met Pierre Grador (a veterinarian with a practice in Brittany) and his wife Madeleine. On 17 December, Mme Grador took them to Lyon where they met Jules (John Carter) and went back to his apartment before being taken to stay with Roger and Marcelle Thomas (nf). They also report meeting Paul Bonnamour and his wife (daughter of Gordon Bowers (Herbert Hasler who stayed with the Bonnemours in January 1943, gives his name as Barr) of Barclays Bank in London). Jules supplied them with heavy clothing for the mountains and on 6 January, Annie Sabourault took them by train to Toulouse where they joined Hilbert Philippe, William Edwards and Charles Crippen from the B-17 Badger's Beauty V. Kenneth Skidmore and Joseph Shandor were also on the train with their guide Jean Calmet but they got off at Bram to take another train direct to Lavelanet. From Toulouse the five airmen were divided into groups to take separate trains to Pamiers with Annie taking Pitner and Plischke, and Carter taking Philippe, Edwards and Crippen. After waiting (in vain) for Carter to arrive at Pamiers, Annie took Pitner and Plischke by bus to Lavelanet where they rejoined Skidmore and Shandor. The following morning, Annie and Jean returned to Lyon, leaving the airmen in a hotel. Meanwhile (as already mentioned), Madeleine Grador had arrived from Paris with Robert Griffith and Clifford Hammock. Arrangements had already been made with their Spanish guides so while Jean and Annie returned to Lyon, the six airmen left on (about) 16 January for Andorra.[3]

The crossing to Andorra took three nights and they spent another night at Canillo before moving to the Hotel Coma in Ordino to recover. Two days later, they were driven to the Spanish border, which they crossed on foot to an unnamed village from where, after a slight delay, they were collected by truck and driven to Barcelona.

Sgts Norman B Cufley and John Harvey were the wireless operator and flight engineer of 77 Sqn Halifax JD247 (Charlesworth). The aircraft had already lost one engine on the way to Ludwigshaven on the evening of 18 November 1943 and when two more engines failed on the return, the aircraft was abandoned to crash south of Saint-Quentin, near Moy-de-l'Aisne.

Cufley and Harvey only spent one night with Mme Schmitz (see earlier) before being taken to stay with Robert Roques in his apartment at 7 rue

---

3   Following John Carter's arrest, Mlle Sabourault escaped to Switzerland for two months before returning to Paris where she re-established contact with the organisation and resumed her work as a convoyeuse. (WO208/5454)

Chaligny, Paris XII. On 17 December they moved back for another night with Mme Schmitz and next day, were taken to 48 Avenue du President Wilson where they stayed with Jeanne Huet. They say they enjoyed complete freedom for the month they were there and often went out. They also say that Mme Huet's husband was an American who apparently didn't know that she helped evaders, and that their son was serving in Algeria. On 19 January, they were visited by Captain Hamilton (MI9 agent Lucien Dumais) of the British Intelligence Services who passed them over to guides who took them by overnight train to St Brieuc and Plouha in Brittany where they joined thirteen Americans waiting to be taken off by RN MGB 503 on the first Operation Bonaparte.

CHAPTER 49

The Advice of Ivan Schraeder

Sgt Ivan L Schraeder was the tail-gunner of B-17 42-30362 Wee Bonnie II (388BG/561BS) (Porter) which was on the way to Beaumont-sur-Oise on 9 September 1943. They were about to start their bomb run when an Me109 attacked the aircraft with heavy calibre cannon fire. The B-17 began to spin out of control and the pilot gave the bale-out order.

Schraeder baled out at about 20,000 feet but (very sensibly) delayed opening his parachute until about 2,000 feet before landing near a river. His questionnaire says that he landed near the commune of Montesson (Yvelines) in the western suburbs of Paris and so presumably, this was the river Seine. He ran and hid in some reeds by the river but apparently not very well as some local people soon urged him to move further along the river bank where others were waiting to help him. He was taken to a factory where he had a shower and changed into some donated civilian clothes before being taken to a house where his journey was arranged.

Schraeder spent three days with Paul Provost (nf) before being taken into Paris where he met Mme Jeanne Duteurtre who took him to her home at 7 rue Bremontier, Paris XVII. Mlle Dupont (query) brought him some books and after two weeks, she and an elderly lady, Mlle La Buice/Buise/Bris (Mlle Le Bris of 1 Quai des Fleurs – query) took Schraeder to 75 Avenue d'Italie where he stayed with the Belleville family – M et Mme Andre Belleville and their sons, Bernard (20) Daniel (18) and Maxime – for the next two months.[1]

Unfortunately, the Appx C of Schraeder's evasion report is very hard to decipher and it's not clear exactly when he left Paris for Toulouse and Perpignan but Schraeder seems to have been the only military evader in the party. The crossing took three days and Schraeder arrived in Spain on 19 November 1943 but (again) it's not clear whether he was delivered

---

[1]   Bernard Belleville (born April 1923) of 75 Avenue d'Italie, Paris XIII was arrested in July 1944 while acting as a courier. He was deported but returned and awarded a KMS. (WO208/5452) Mlle (sic) Alice Belleville (born June 1897) at this address also acted as a guide and convoyer and was also recommended for an award. (WO208/5451)

direct to the British Consulate in Barcelona or whether he was arrested by the Spanish authorities. The fact that he didn't reach Gibraltar until 31 December would tend to suggest the latter.

Schraeder advises that aircrew should be told not to be discouraged or disillusioned by rumours that they will be returned to England in ten days, flying back or coming some other way, "Whatever version of this story you are given, you just walk over the Pyrenees anyway."

CHAPTER 50

Some individual Belgian initiative

Sgt George Louis Watelet was returning from a Rhubarb (freelance ground attack sortie) to France on 17 November 1943 in his 609 Sqn Typhoon JR191 when he was hit by flak near Beaumont-le-Roger (Upper Normandy) and then shot down by fighters five minutes later. Watelet is listed in Broussine's book but links to Bourgogne seem tenuous.

Watelet baled out and landed near Les Planches. Being Belgian by birth and speaking fluent French, Watelet had little difficulty in making his way to Heudreville-sur-Eure where he was sheltered by Gaston Roland (nf) and his mother Mme Drancier (nf) and contact made with an organisation. On 19 November, a M Coderce (phonetic) took Watelet in his lorry to Gravigny, just north of Evreux, where Watelet was sheltered at his home on the Gravigny-Evereux road. On 23 November, Watelet was moved to the other side of Evreux and the village of Arnieres-sur-Iton. He met F/Lt Hugh Parry (who was being sheltered by Hubert and Renee Renaudin) and that afternoon, was driven to another small village where a doctor drove him and a maquis member who was to be his guide, to a railway station north of Evreux where they caught a train to Paris. Watelet's guide had intended to take him to Haute Savoie that evening but when they found the trains weren't running, Watelet took the guide to stay the night with his cousin Marcel Brancart at 90 Boulevard Richard Lenoir, Paris XI. Next day, they took a train from the Gare de Lyon, arriving at Thonon-les-Bains (Rhones-Alpes) on the shore of Lake Geneva, at about one o'clock in the afternoon. The guide took Watelet to a girl known locally as Jeanette Croix de Lorraine where Watelet was left while his guide went to collect some more evaders. The reason given for bringing Watelet to this area was that aircraft were landing locally that could take him back to England but then the story was changed to say the aircraft were going to Switzerland, where Watelet knew he would be interned. After much activity but little result, Watelet made his own way to Marseille, arriving there on 17 December – where his efforts at leaving the country by various means were also frustrated. On 25 January,

308

he went to Cambo-les-Bains (Aquitaine) where he thought he might get help with crossing the Pyrenees and this time had better luck, crossing into Spain near Amaiur-Maya (Navarra) on about 31 January 1944 and giving himself up to the Guardia Civil.

CHAPTER 51

Some more Charles Kremer and Felix connections

On (about) 19 January 1944, Sgt Anthony Reynolds, S/Sgt William Kiniklis, Sgt Douglas Farr and their two guides, left Paris by train for Toulouse and Pau.

Sgt Anthony J A Reynolds was the navigator of 428 Sqn Halifax DK229 (Bowden) which was returning from Gelsenkirchen in the early hours of 10 July 1943 when they lost two engines (cause unknown) and the aircraft was abandoned to crash near Koln (Cologne) in Germany. Reynolds was the only member of the crew to evade successfully.

Reynolds landed in the middle of a small field, hid his parachute and flying gear in a haystack, donned a pair of RAF issue shoes and set off to leave the area. His initial efforts were thwarted by the barking of a local dog so he decided to hide in a small copse until daybreak before trying again. Reynolds walked through Germany for eight days, living off his aids box and whatever he could scrounge until finally finding a bicycle he could steal. Two days later he rode through the Seigfried Line and crossed into (what he thought was) Belgium unchallenged. From Saint-Vith he went north to Malmedy, actually still in the newly defined Germany, before turning west and reaching Stavelot on the afternoon of 22 July. By this time, Reynolds was extremely weak and hungry and so declared himself to a householder who took him in and introduced him to his wife. Later, a younger man (a gendarme) came and questioned Reynolds before taking him back to his own house where he was given a meal and put to bed.

Next day, Mme Victoria Vandeghen (née Louis) came and questioned him in perfect English. Reynolds refused some of the questions but apparently still managed to satisfy her because his photograph was taken and he was given civilian clothes and an ID card. On 24 July, two gendarmes took Reynolds to the station and put him on a train to Spa, another gendarme taking their place during the journey. He was taken to a chemists's shop – the *Pharmacie Vandeghen* at 1 Avenue Reine Astrid – where Reynolds was given more civilian clothes and stayed with the

310

Vandeghens – who said they had previously helped two other RAF evaders.[1]

On 27 July, Reynolds was moved to Brussels where he stayed overnight with M Vandeghen's brother. Next day, a man called Ronnie took him to Schaerbeek where Reynolds stayed with Ronnie's brother Alphonse and his wife. On 1 August, Ronnie took Reynolds back to his apartment in Brussels where he met several members of the organisation. On 3 August, he met a man called Victor who took him to another apartment where he met Pierre and Louisette (a small woman with dyed-blonde hair) and Sgt John D H Carleton, and Pierre and Louisette took the two airmen to Liege. Reynolds and Carleton spend the night in a shop and next day, Mme Anna-Marie Aelens (née Dexters) took Reynolds to her house at 153 (or 155) Boulevard de la Constitution where he stayed for the next three weeks – Carleton leaving at this point to stay with a police commissioner in the suburb of Beyne-Heusay.

After about a month (query) with the commissioner, Carleton was sheltered for two weeks in the village of Ans with a garage owner named Joseph Alexandre (of 101 rue de l'Yser) before being taken back to Liege where he joined William Kiniklis and others at the de Ruyter apartment – see later.

While Reynolds was in Liege, a member of the organisation was arrested, which delayed Reynolds' onward journey and it wasn't until about 23 August that Louisette collected him. Louisette took him to meet Pierre who led him to the headquarters of an espionage organisation where he met two American airmen – one of them Sgt Jacob Dalinsky. Next day, a woman called Mme Meunier/Meuller (query) (about 45 years old) took Reynolds and Dalinsky to 55 rue des Jardins in Huy (Liege) where they stayed with Georgette Romainville for seven weeks. In the middle of October, Mme Meunier's brother-in-law took them to Brussels where they met a dark, slightly bald, plump, middle-aged man named Charles Gueulette (aka Felix) at a church and he took all their money. They were taken on to Ghent by another guide and stayed overnight with a man called Charlie (aged about 28, dark, slim, wore spectacles). Next day they travelled

---

1   The IS9 Helper files have Mme Louis Vanderbeghen (sic) at this address and a phone call by Edourd Reniere in December 2013 to the present owners of the chemist's shop – now *Pharmacie Renard* – confirmed help given to evading airmen by the then owners of the pharmacie. A further telephone conversation with Patrick Vandeghen that same day confirmed his grandmother's name as Victoria Louis, wife of Albert Vandeghen. Edouard also identified Anna-Marie Aelens from the IS9 Belgian Helper List.

to the border where they walked into a cafe (assume the Cafe des Sports at Mouscron) and then through the barrier over the frontier without being questioned. They walked on to Tourcoing and the house of a carpet factory manager who took them to the house of a policeman named Gaston (tall, middle-aged, slightly bald) (Gaston Vorreux at 123 rue Lamartine) where they received new ID cards. On 21 October, Simone Michaut (a slightly built girl aged about 23, thin features, medium colouring) took them to Paris.

After staying overnight in her house (which Dalinsky says Simone shared with her parents and three brothers), Simone took Reynolds and Dalinsky by Metro to a church at Place de Madeleine where they met a fair-haired young man who walked with a limp and had served in the French air force – they were told later that he had been arrested by the Gestapo. Dalinsky was then taken to a doctor's house and Reynolds to stay with Celestin Simon Jean-Jean and family at 21 rue de la Chine, Paris XX. On about 28 October, the French ex-air force officer took Reynolds to the house of a priest called Pere Riquet (Abbe Michel Riquet) where he met Charles Bailey and William Quinn and was given another ID card. Next day, Simone took them all to Quimper where they joined a party of about thirty evaders, including Dalinsky, in a cafe. A man came in and took Reynolds, Royce Fidler, Leslie Woollard and three Americans (Bailey & Quinn + one) to a house where they stayed until 31 October when Yves Le Henaff (aka Fanfan) moved them to another house on the outskirts of the town.

The plan to evacuate the evaders by sea having failed, Reynolds and others left Quimper on about 5 November and returned to Paris. Reynolds, Dalinsky, Bailey and Quinn were met at the station by M et Mme Laghos and taken back to their home at 63 rue de l'Amiral Mouchez, Paris XIII. A few days later, two young guides (one of them a schoolteacher called Regina) took them to Rozay-en-Brie and the Chateau de la Fortelle where they joined other evaders, members of the organisation and some maquis. After about three weeks of training for the Pyrenees, Regina brought the four airmen back to Paris on about 25 November. She took them to a house near the university where they met Mme Bourgeois (a big woman, with dark curly hair and prominent teeth), apparently head of a Paris organisation, before returning them to stay with M et Mme Laghos. On about 2 December, they were taken to the Bourg-la-Reine district where they stayed with a Jewish family before returning to Paris once more, where the evaders were separated (Bailey and Quinn see earlier and Dalinsky to Comete, he crossed the Pyrenees to Spain in January). Reynolds stayed at several addresses – with the gardener at the Jardins de Luxembourg, with Gilbert Braquet at 48 Boulevard des Batignolles, Paris XVII, a lawyer who worked at the Palais de Justice, and other places until twenty-four-year-old Marie-France Geoffroy-Dechaume, who worked as a librarian in Paris and (query) lived on rue de Grenelle, took him, William Kiniklis and Douglas Farr to her father's house at Valmondois, north of Paris. They stayed for two weeks in Valmondois before Marie-France returned them once more to the capital.

S/Sgt William P Kiniklis was the tail gunner of B-17 42-3225 Chug-A-Lug Lulu (381BG/535BS) (Disbrow) which was returning from the Schweinfurt raid of 17 August 1943 and still over Germany when it was attacked by fighters. After losing three engines, the aircraft was abandoned to crash near Liege, Belgium.[2]

Kiniklis delayed his jump (perhaps too much) and was knocked out when he hit the ground. He regained consciousness to find some thirty or so Belgians standing around him. They took all his flying equipment away and a few minutes later, brought his radio-operator, Thomas Moore, to join him before they were both taken to another place where their journeys were arranged.

Kiniklis and Moore were joined by Joseph Walters and Otto Bruzewski – and S/Sgt Kenneth Fahncke, the tail-gunner of B-17 42-3435 – and they were all taken to stay with Charles Kremer in Liege – see Bruzewski earlier.

Kiniklis report is almost illegible but part of his story is told by Sgt John Carleton with additional information from 2/Lt Raymond J Nutting, the co-pilot of B-17 42-5867 Alice From Dallas, who was also sheltered by the Kremer family at rue d'Amay and later at the de Ruyter apartment with his top-turret gunner T/Sgt John W Burgin.

As mentioned earlier, John Carleton and Anthony Reynolds were moved back to Liege sometime in early October 1943 where they joined several Americans, including Kiniklis. They had been moved from the Kremer household – Nutting says on 29 September, following a domestic situation between Charles and his wife Celestine – and were being sheltered by the baron Marcel de Ruyter and his wife Mariette (who was

---

2   Three other Chug-A-Lug Lulu crew also evaded successfully: ball-turret gunner S/Sgt Joseph J Walters with Comete, radio-operator T/Sgt Thomas R Moore on board the Breiz-Izel in January and waist-gunner T/Sgt Otto F Bruzewski with Bourgogne – see earlier.

expecting a baby) in their first-floor apartment at 52 Quai Orban. On about 20 October, Carleton and Kiniklis were taken to Brussels by a man known as Petit Pierre. They went to a church where they were interrogated by a sturdily built man, about 5 ft 6 inches tall with thin, dark hair who was either Felix (Charles Gueulette) or one of his associates. Their interrogator apparently spoke no English and a second man acted as interpreter. That same night, Carleton and Kiniklis were taken by a guide to Ghent, where they stayed overnight before another man took them to cross the border, via a bar (assume the Cafe des Sports at Mouscron) into France near Tourcoing. They walked to the home of gendarme Gaston Vorreux at 123 rue Lamartine, before staying with Fernand and Celeste Vanaerde at 27 rue Gambetta. They stayed with the Vanaerdes for about seven weeks, being joined after about three weeks by Ian Covington and Stanley Alukonis.

Fernand Jean Vanaerde (born February 1892) and his wife Celeste Emilienne (born September 1899) were arrested at their home on 19 April 1944, along with their daughter Gisele Yolande (born August 1921) and son Jean Francois (born July 1924). Fernand Vanaerde was deported to Germany in September 1944 and liberated from Dachau on 29 July 1945. The family are credited with helping at least twenty Allied evaders and Fernand Vanaerde was recommended for a KMC.[3]

On about 7 December, the four airmen (Carleton, Kiniklis, Covington and Alukonis) were taken by train to Paris by a young boy of about eighteen called Henri and met at the station by a group of women. One of the women (described by Carleton as very masculine looking, severely dressed and with short, Eton-cropped hair) took Carleton and Kiniklis to the apartment of a young girl where they were sheltered overnight. Next day, they were taken to stay with a policeman and three days after that, Carleton and Kiniklis were temporarily parted – Kiniklis going to Gilbert Virmoux's flat at 41 rue Saint-Merri while Carleton stayed with the Belleville family at 75 Avenue d'Italie. Four days later, Kiniklis was taken to a church, where he rejoined Carleton – and met Royce Fidler and Leslie Woollard. Carleton, Fidler and Woollard left Paris for Quimper and Douarnenez at this point – see earlier – but for some reason, Kiniklis was returned to rue Saint-Merri.

Meanwhile, Covington and Alukonis had been taken to stay with an elderly lady and her daughter, both of whom were deaf, in a flat either on or near rue du Bac. A few days later, the masculine looking woman took them to a church where they were passed on to Gilbert Virmoux (about

3   NARA Vanaerde and TNA folder WO208/5452.

22 years old (born December 1919) with black, curly hair) who took them by Metro to his flat on rue Saint-Merri where they rejoined Kiniklis. The three airmen stayed over Christmas and about a week later, were joined by Anthony Reynolds and Andrew Lindsay.

Ian Covington, Stanley Alukonis and Andrew Lindsay were all passed on to Comete – they crossed the Pyrenees in January 1944 with 2/Lt Robert C Gilchrist.

We next pick up Kiniklis' story in the first week of January when he and Anthony Reynolds were taken to a railway station where they joined Douglas Farr and Marie-France Geoffroy-Dechaume who took the three airmen to stay at her father's house at Valmondois.

Sgt Douglas J Farr was a waist-gunner on B-17 42-29963 Judy (379BG/527BS) (Camp) which was on the way to Ludwigshaven on 30 December 1943 when they were hit by flak which damaged the #1 engine. Unable to stay in formation they turned back for England and were approaching Paris when they were attacked by fighters and the aircraft abandoned to crash south of Beauvais.[4]

Farr (who had been hit in the leg before baling out) was helped immediately after landing by a group of Frenchmen on bicycles, one of whom had the presence of mind to bring Farr his GI shoes which he'd left attached to his parachute harness.[5] Two men, a garage mechanic and a schoolteacher, then took Farr by bicycle to the home of Jean Muffat (a Frenchman born in America) in Orvillers-Sorel, Oise, about 50 kms north of Paris. After Jean Muffet had interrogated Farr (and given him first-aid and some clothes), the schoolteacher took Farr to Paris to stay with Jean's brother Roland at 15 rue de la Paix. Roland Muffat, who had connections to the Cartier company, arranged medical treatment for Farr and he was questioned by a tall, blond-haired Frenchman who wore glasses and got him an ID card. A week later, the tall man took Farr to the station and passed him over to Marie-France Geoffroy-Dechaume who took him, along with William Kiniklis and Anthony Reynolds to her father's home at Valmondois, about 25 kms north of Paris. Marie-France's father, Charles Geoffroy-Dechaume, had lost a leg in the 1914-18 war and was a painter,

---

4   Three other Judy crew also evaded successfully: bombardier 2/Lt Edward J Donaldson and waist-gunner Sgt Neelan B Parker were evacuated by MGB 503 from Plouha on the Francois-Shelburn Operation Bonaparte 3 – and radio-operator S/Sgt Milton J Mills Jnr who was helped by Bourgogne and crossed the Pyrenees from Pau in April 1944 – see later.

5   Because it got so cold in the rear of their aircraft, most American gunners wore electrically-heated suits, including footwear – the more experienced (or perhaps better advised) attaching GI shoes to their parachute harness ready for use in the event of baling out.

315

well known in England. About two weeks later, Marie-France returned the three evaders to Paris and an apartment near the Etoile where they stayed overnight with an elderly Jewish lady whose husband had been arrested the day before. The following evening, Marie-France, the tall man with glasses and another tall, dark Frenchman, took them to the railway station, joined on the way by a short French boy, who, with the tall dark Frenchman, took them by train to Toulouse.[6]

Reynolds, Farr, Kiniklis and their two guides arrived at Toulouse the following day and had lunch in a restaurant before catching the three o'clock, afternoon train to Pau. Reynolds, Farr and the short Frenchman ate at one hotel (where they were known) before staying at another (where they were not) for two days and nights. In the afternoon of the second day, Kiniklis rejoined them (he seems have got himself lost on the first evening and only rejoined by chance) and they were taken to the bus station.

They went by bus to Navarennx where they were joined by Jack Zeman and the short Frenchman who had brought them from Paris left after making arrangements with a taxi that was waiting for them. Bus conductor Robert Piton put the four airmen into the taxi which took them and another guide some 24 kilometres nearer the mountains before leaving them to walk the rest of the way to a farm.

2/Lt Jack R Zeman was the pilot of B-17 42-30676 Baby Dumpling (381BG/532BS) which was returning from Tours airfield on 5 January 1944 when they were hit by flak that blew a large hole in the right-hand side of the cockpit and stopped #3 and #4 engines.[7]

Zeman was probably the last man out of the doomed aircraft, blacking out as he left and only pulling his rip-cord seconds before he hit the ground. Still in a dazed condition, and suffering from an injured groin that was to trouble his walking for the next two weeks, Zeman was operating on instinct and training as he tried to hide his parachute in a stream, and succeeded in falling in himself. The soaking did at least help to make him think more clearly but that night the front of his uniform began to freeze and he was forced to seek help. Next morning, Zeman followed a path

---

6   Pierre Ducamp says that Marie-France Geoffroy-Dechaume was a member of reseau Vengeance and that it was one their guides, Robert (Bob) Alexandre who took the evaders to Pau. (*Termoignage de Pierre Ducamp*) Mlle Geoffroy-Deschaume also passed airmen on to reseau Francois-Shelburn, as in the case of 2/Lt Charles Winkleman.

7   Two other crew from the Baby Dumpling also evaded successfully, both more or less alone – waist-gunner Sgt Raymond F Chevraux crossed the Pyrenees from Hendaye the night of 18-19 January and ball-turret gunner Sgt Herve A Leroux who crossed near Saint-Jean-Pied-Port the night of 23-24 January.

which soon led him to a group of people to whom he asked "Parlez-vous francaise?". Their reply of "camarade" confused him for a moment until he realised they were French and not going to turn him over to the Germans.

After several days of wandering and getting occasional help, Zeman was eventually directed to Auguste Francois Herisse, a *cultivateur* at La Loyere, Chigne (Maine-et-Loire) north of Noyant and joined there by Albert, a young Frenchman who had been in the French navy and who spoke some English. Zeman stayed for a week at Chigne until 15 January when one of M Herisse's employees, a man named Roger, took Zeman by bicycle to Tours and the home of a postman who lived near the airfield – the same one that Zeman had bombed ten days earlier – for a few hours before he was sheltered with Robert and Marguerite Coupaisse (nf) on rue Loisserand. Two days later, Roger took Zeman by train to Bordeaux. Roger didn't have a contact there but he did manage to find a railway worker who could put them on a train to Dax. From Dax they took yet another train south but their good luck seemed to have run out when the train was soon stopped and a German soldier entered one end of the carriage and a German civilian the other – but maybe not, as Roger and Zeman were the only two people whose papers were not examined. They left the train at Habas and approached an elderly couple they had seen on the train who directed them through the town and onto the road for Puyoo, from where they took a train to Pau.

In Pau, Roger approached Julien Latouquette (another railway worker) and they were taken to his apartment just outside the town, on rue de la Mairie in Billere. Julien lived with his mother, married sister and her husband and it was Julien's sister's husband who contacted Maurice Meyer and his English-speaking son at Villa Marie Rene on the adjoining rue de Bayonne. After five days with the Latouquette family, Roger returned to Chigne and Zeman was taken to stay with Maurice Meyer where he was looked after by a Mme Beauchamp (nf) while Julien Latouquette contacted Georges Neville (nf) at Villa Bagatelle on Avenue Beaumont in Pau. George Neville's wife contacted her twenty-two-year-old cousin Giselle who was married to Robert Elclart (nf) and a week or so later, Robert Elclart collected Zeman in a potato truck and took him back to his apartment at 17 rue Castetnau for a week. Robert then contacted an organisation chief (aged about 50 with dark hair and pointed features) who came to see Zeman and next day, Andre Bonnard's sister took Zeman by taxi to her brother's house in Monein (about 20 kms west of Pau).

317

Zeman had only been at Andre Bonnard's house for an hour when a boy who worked on a bus rushed in to say that Zeman was going to Spain that night. Zeman took the bus to the end of the line at Navarennx where he joined Anthony Reynolds, William Kiniklis and Douglas Farr.

The two-day mountain crossing is described by Zeman as "stumbling in the dark and rain for endless hours". It began with them setting off at four-thirty in the morning and walking until ten o'clock for a rendezvous. Their journey was delayed by having to avoid German patrols and they should have been there two hours earlier but managed to join two new guides and a party of French and Poles (fifteen in total) anyway before setting off again at eleven o'clock. At the frontier (on 27 January 1944) the party was split into two groups, the group with Zeman and the other airmen followed a road next to a river – straight into some uniformed Spaniards.

"We were caught by the customs guards almost immediately. I demanded the American consul but they paid no attention and took us all off to jail. They were however most friendly and only asked our names, ranks and serial numbers. When we reached town we were searched and our razor blades and French money was confiscated. They then asked who we were, one of the party spoke Spanish. He said we had escaped from the Germans. The rest of us all said "Si" and we were asked (for) no further explanation. They then told us that if we had Spanish money we could stay at a hotel instead of in jail. One member of the party had changed some francs to pesetas, so we all went off to the hotel. The guards wore green uniforms with black hats and yellow belts and holsters." (MIS-X #417 Zeman)

CHAPTER 52

27 January 1944

On 27 January 1944, 1/Lt Charles Walters, 2/Lt J M Bickley, T/Sgt Louis Del Guidice, Sgt Carl Hite, 1/Lt Elton Hoyt, 2/Lt William Cook, 2/Lt Donald Hanslik and an elderly Belgian (understood to be a British spy sentenced to death by the Gestapo) left Paris by train for Toulouse and Pau.

B-24 42-40990 On The Ball (93BG/328BS) (Walters) was returning from Ludwigshaven on 7 January 1944 when it was attacked by fighters near Chartres and abandoned. Four of the crew – pilot 1/Lt Charles W Walters, co-pilot 2/Lt J M Bickley, radio-operator T/Sgt Louis B Del Guidice and top-turret gunner Sgt Carl E Hite – evaded successfully.[1]

Charles Walters was helped on landing near Brou (Eure-et-Loir) and taken to a farmhouse. Later that evening he was taken by bicycle into the village and a house where he joined his co-pilot J M Bickley. Later that night the two men were moved to another house where they joined their radio-operator Louis Del Guidice and top-turret gunner Carl Hite and their journey together was arranged.

The four men stayed overnight in Brou with gunsmith Maurice Vouzelaud (born October 1912) and were taken next day by truck a few kilometres south to Arreu where they took a train to Paris. Del Guidice and Hite were taken to 51 rue de Miromesnil where they met Dr Alice Willm and a French pilot called Ronnie, who had escaped from Germany. Del Guidice stayed on with Dr Willm while Hite was taken that evening to an apartment on the adjoining Avenue de Friesland to stay overnight before being moved to Juvisy-sur-Orge where he was sheltered by Andre Lefevre at 29 rue Hoche. He was visited several times by Genevieve Soulie and also met various other evaders. Del Guidice stayed three nights with Dr Willm before he was moved to Juvisy-sur-Orge to join Walters who was being sheltered with chemists Leon and Amelie Meilleroux at rue Pasteur, just around the corner from rue Hoche. It's not clear where Bickley stayed.

---

1   On The Ball navigator 2/Lt Harmon Smith Jnr and bombardier 2/Lt Jack D George almost made it – they got as far as Toulouse before being caught in a ticket check at the station on 3 February 1944 – see later.

On 27 January, Paulette Lefevre (Andre's daughter) and Amelie Meilleroux took Walters, Del Guidice and Hite into Paris and a cathedral near Notre Dame where they met the chief of the organisation (Georges Broussine) before rejoining their co-pilot Bickley and meeting some other Americans – Elton Hoyt, William Cook and Donald Hanslik – and an elderly Belgian named by Hanslik as Ernest Baille and claiming to have worked for British agent Captain Michel (Michael Trotobas).[2]

On 16 September 1943, B-17 42-29876 Battlin' Bobbie (379BG/525BS) (Hoyt) was on the way to Nantes when it was attacked by fighters and the aircraft abandoned near Rennes in Brittany. Eight of the crew evaded successfully – five with Bourgogne.

1/Lt Elton (aka Peter) Hoyt III was the pilot of Battlin' Bobbie and last man to leave the doomed aircraft. He baled out at about 20,000 feet, seeing two or three other parachutes in the air, watching his aircraft go down in flames and seeing three enemy fighters fly past. He was met on landing and quickly led to a house where his flying equipment was taken away. A short while later, his radio-operator, S/Sgt Herbert Dulberg, was brought in, already dressed in civilian clothing. Soon after that they were taken to a place where their journeys were arranged.

The Appendix C of Hoyt's report is an almost illegible pencil scrawl with the story petering out soon after meeting Emile Guimard.

Hoyt landed somewhere near Guipry (Ille-et-Vilaine) where his first helpers were a girl called Lucienne (who also helped Edward Shaffer – see earlier) and her father who asked Hoyt where he wanted to go. When he said Spain, they said that was impossible as there were too many Germans in the way. They arranged for him and Dulberg to be taken by truck to a mill about fifty minutes away to stay next door to where their waist-gunner William Miller and tail-gunner Edward Shaffer were living. Three or four days later, Hoyt (at least) was moved to a miller's house (assume Eugene Justeau at Pipriac) and saw Aime (query) who had Joe Burkowski with him. A week or so later (query) Roger Pansart and a couple of friends working with him – Albert and Pansart's brother (query) – brought a bus with John Beilstein, Harry Minor and Cyril Koval already on board and drove them all to Roger Pansart's house at Parame, near St Malo. They were told they should be leaving by boat almost immediately but that didn't work out

2   Ernest Baille was Alberic Volkaert, the fifty-seven-year-old Belgian who shared a Recherche (Wanted) poster with Jean Woussen with a 500,000 Belgian franc reward for their capture. This is the same man who caused so much trouble in an earlier attempt to cross the mountains from Perpignan when he joined George Millar's party.

and a week later, they were moved to a monastery at Saint-Helen, near Dinan. A few days later, the group was broken up – this being the last time that Hoyt saw Miller, Shaffer, Dulberg and Koval – leaving just Hoyt and Minor at Saint-Helen, with Dwight Fisher and John Beilstein "somewhere else". Two nights later, a priest took Hoyt and Minor to another mill near Dinan where they stayed overnight with the head salesman for a Renault garage and next day, the Renault salesman took them to a farm. They stayed on the farm for "one week exactly" before a very large man (aged about 30-40) from town visited them and he and the Renault salesman took them into Dinan and the home of the man who had come with the German-looking man (sic). Roger Pansart, Albert, the priest from monastery and the big fellow were already there with Fisher and Beilstein, and Harry Minor says they changed trucks – and organisations – at this point. After having their photographs taken, the four airmen were driven to meet Emile Guimard who was supposed to be organising a boat to take them to England – Hoyt thought from the Quimper area – and they were taken to a chateau where William Cook was staying with Jean Barthomeuf – the first time that Hoyt had seen his navigator since baling out. According to Cook, Jean Barthomeuf (of Saint-Servant) was wanted by the Gestapo and had been living under his wife's name at the unidentified chateau near Lizio for about a year.

Hoyt reports a boy coming from Brest (about 5 foot 8 inches tall, straight, good looking, black curly hair, carried a gun) with note from Francoise Elie of the "little black-market place in Rennes" but his report ends there apart from some miscellanous notes. He doesn't say anything else about his time in Brittany nor about being brought to Paris on 1 December.

2/Lt William J Cook Jnr who was on his eighteenth mission, was the navigator of Battlin' Bobbie and he describes his experience of baling out:

"When you bail out, for some unknown reason you remember the little things that you have been told. I was no more afraid of parachuting than lighting a cigarette. It was a lot worse coming back from Germany on fire or running out of gas returning from Frankfurt. After we were hit there was little time to think about anything. The fire was hot on my legs. I slid out of the escape hatch. I left at about 20,000 feet and knew that I should delay my jump. As it was I opened my parachute too soon, at about 19,000 feet. When I pulled the rip-cord, it did not work immediately. I had to take both hands and pull for all I was worth. When my parachute

opened, I was on my back and was almost knocked out. The straps were tight and I was badly caught in the crotch and in terrific pain. I was feeling pretty despondent, then I saw three Me109s flying at me. I remembered that Lt Peterson [1/Lt Theodore Peterson – see earlier] from my group had warned us about being shot. The planes passed within 100 yards of me, I could see the pilot's expression – I waved – they never altered course. It was so damned quiet and peaceful in the air that it was hard to realise what was happening. Suddenly I was all alone. Just below the low cumulus clouds I looked down to see what kind of terrain I was approaching. I saw three aircraft, apparently fighters, scattered on the ground. I heard a terrific explosion and saw our plane close to the ground. I landed about half a mile from it." (MIS-X #410 Cook)

Cook says that he made a beautiful landing about three or four kilometres north of Guipry and was met on the ground by about twenty-five people. When they saw him trying to set light to his parachute, they evidently realised that he was American. They assured Cook there was no immediate danger and after he had given away his flying boots and jacket, several of the men took off their trousers and offered them to him, embarrassing Cook and amusing the women in the group. Cook left his parachute, OD trousers and shirt and flying gear, keeping just his GI shoes. He was encouraged to hide in a nearby haystack but remembered Peterson's advice at an E&E lecture in England and hid instead in the undergrowth on the edge of a wood while several local men stood guard around him. Later that day he was told that he was with an organisation and next day his journey was arranged.

The faded pencil notes of Cook's Appendix C are just as hard to read as those of his pilot. Like Elton Hoyt, Cook has very nice hand-writing but unfortunately, these notes are scribbled by their interviewer. To paraphrase Snoopy – curse you Donald Emerson.

Cook mentions George Padgett, Wayne Bogard and Joseph Burkowski (see above) and lots of other evaders but about the only helper names in Brittany I've managed to decypher are Bernard [Bernard Bougeard of Guipry – query], Big Pierre (who took Bogard and TG – Cloe Crutchfield – to Rennes) [Remy Roure] and Little Pierre [Pierre Charnier] – 31 year-old Jean Barthomeuf [of Saint-Servant] who was wanted by the Gestapo and living under his wife's name – Gabby [Gabriel Mainguy] who sheltered him and Wayne Bogard at Le Roc-Saint-Andre – and Mme [Jeanne] Vallais and her children, Alphonse (19) Monique (18) and Jeanne (13) at Le Bas Chemin, on the extreme outskirts of Guipry.[3]

Cook says that when Jean Carbonnet and Michele Moet brought them to Paris on 1 December, some women took Padgett before the rest went on to Saint-Mande. Beilstein stayed across the street from the Moet home, while he went with Hoyt and Bogard to Clamart (Seine). Cook stayed with Henri Leboeuf (of 11 rue Martial Grandchamps) while Hoyt and Bogard went with a civilian inspector of police named Robert De Medicis and his family – Hoyt reports that Bogard took the opportunity to assess the bomb damage at nearby Villacoublay airfield. About a week later, Michele Moet brought Cook (and Jean Carbonnet brought Hoyt and Bogard) back to Saint-Mande. Cook was taken to the abbe Jean Courcel (of 24 rue Saint-Roch) and from there, another abbe sent him to 39 rue Victor Hugo to stay with Jack – who had an English mother – and Helene (Helene Laurencet – query). A Gestapo scare then had Michele Moet returning him to Saint-Mande once more before taking him to join Hoyt, who was being sheltered by Anita Lemonnier (at 2 rue Ernest Renan). Cook then says that just before Christmas, he was brought back from Anita's to Saint-Mande again and this time taken to to M Legros – the abbe Coursel knew him – at Charenton (Charles and Marthe Legros at 21 rue Gabrielle, Charenton-le-Pont) although Cook doesn't say how long he stayed there.

2/Lt Donald W Hanslik was the bombardier of B-24 42-64444 Consolidated Mess (448BG/715BS) (Foster) which was returning from Ludwigshaven on 30 December 1943 when it was shot down by fighters. Only two of the crew were able to bale out before the aircraft crashed near Crepy-en-Valois (Oise) – Hanslik and waist-gunner S/Sgt Chester W Janeczko, who was captured (no further details).

Hanslik was met on landing by Jackie Huyton (nf) who took his parachute and directed Hanslik to hide in some nearby woods. Hanslik stayed in the woods for next two nights until found by a woodchopper. He was brought an overcoat and rubber boots to replace the shoes he lost while parachuting and told that arrangements were already being made to help him. That evening, Jackie Huyton took him to Gondreville (a small village between Crepy-en-Valois and Vaumoise) where he was sheltered with a Mlle Denise overnight before moving to stay with Roger Mora in

3   Jean-Claude Bourgeon confirmed (by email in December 2009) that in Brittany, Cook and Joe Burkowski (from 42-9893 El Diablo) were sheltered for three weeks with Alphonse Vallais at Guipry near Messac, and that Alphonse was alive and well – as indeed he still was in August 2016.

a school house.[4] On 6 January, Roger Mora and his wife took Hanslik to Paris where they were met by a woman who had previously worked with French Intelligence. She took Hanslik back to her home in Vincennes (Mme Anna Henry of 18, rue Daumesnil – query) before he was moved that same day to a green-grocery shop. He stayed in the shop – visited by a gendarme called Marcel (Marcelin Villemont – query) and sharing with a fifty-year-old Belgian who was using the apparent alias of Ernest Baille (Alberic Volkaert) and who claimed to work for British Intelligence – until 28 January when Genevieve Soulie sent a guide to bring him and the Belgian to a church where they joined William Cook and others.

The faded notes of Cook's report are the only source I've found for information on their journey from Paris. They took a train to Montauban, where they waited in a park before going on to Toulouse. One of their two French guides was called Daniel (Pierre Jacob) and just before they left Paris, Genevieve Soulie had told them they were with Burgundy. They arrived at Toulouse at about two o'clock in the afternoon and caught a five o'clock train to Pau, arriving there at eight that evening. After a night in Pau, they were apparently given directions to Bielle, although they were actually taken there by a man called Leon (assume Leon van de Poele – see later) who led them to a barn where they joined a group of about sixteen 'maquis' … There seems to have been a lot of confusion after that (and a mixed group of civilians) but they had been told by Genevieve in Paris that when they got to Spain to go to the house of a *douanier* (customs officer) – which they did on 10 February 1944, although this didn't prevent them from being arrested.

---

4   Roger Mora (a teacher at nearby Vauciennes) also lived at Gondreville and although not found on the IS9 Helper List, is confirmed by Dominique Lecomte as sheltering Donald Hanslik.

CHAPTER 53

26 February 1944

On 26 February 1944, Sgt Thomas Banner, Sgt John Upton, 1/Lt Roland Marean and S/Sgt Willis Spellman left Paris on a late afternoon train for Toulouse with their guide Jean-Louis Kervevant – a short, dark, smartly dressed man, known to the evaders as Johnny.

Not stated but probably on the same train, 1/Lt James Shilliday, T/Sgt Halleck Hasson and Sgt Taylor Harrison – along with a Russian Jew linguist known as Jack – also left Paris by train for Toulouse. At Toulouse station the two groups joined up and took a train for Perpignan.

Sgt Thomas W Banner RCAF was the wireless operator of 428 Sqn Halifax LK739 (Reain) which was on the way to Berlin on the evening of 20 January 1944 when it was hit by flak. The bomb-load was jettisoned in an attempt to regain altitude but they continued to be hit and lost most of their fuel. Shortly after that a recall signal was received due to the weather conditions but since their fuel tanks were almost empty, they decided to head for France before abandoning the aircraft a few miles north-east of Châlons-sur-Marne (now Châlons-en-Champagne).[1]

> *"Banner was the last to leave the aircraft apart from the pilot – and the first to get back to England. Landing in pitch darkness in a tree near the village of L'Epine, half a dozen kms north-east of Châlons, but with no idea how far he was off the ground, he released his harness and dropped to the ground, knocking himself out for about five minutes. Having recovered his senses he ran and walked south until hiding in a hay barn. Watching the occupants of a nearby farmhouse, at dusk he 'approached the farmer with my phrases card and indicated that I was English, hungry and thirsty.' After he had been fed and watered Banner was advised to go to Châlons, but rather than go in to the town itself he skirted round it until he came to another farmhouse.*

---

1   Apart from tail-gunner Sgt W Wynveen RCAF, who was captured, the rest of the LK739 crew also evaded successfully: pilot F/Sgt Frederick F E Reain, bomb aimer F/O Yves Lavoie, navigator F/O Alvin R Fisher and engineer Sgt William E Fell crossing the Pyrenees in March with Bourgogne (see later) and mid-upper gunner Sgt L R Fryer, who evaded to Switzerland.

As before, he stayed hidden all day. Towards evening he asked a young woman for help but, scared by his sudden appearance, she ran off to fetch her husband. Having fed Banner the couple advised him to go south along minor roads, pointed out where the bridge was that he would have to cross over the River Coole at Nuisement-sur-Coole, and gave him two Michelin maps to help him on his way. When he got to Nuisement it was so dark that he was unable to find the bridge. Instead he went to a house that was showing lights, and was invited in by a man to whom Banner declared that he was an RAF wireless operator: 'The man immediately turned the wireless on to a station that was sending out morse signals and asked me to take it down. I told him the morse was German and he seemed satisfied.'

In the morning, having shown Banner where the bridge was on the map, the man gave him a cap and a satchel of food, for which Banner gave him the detachable tops of his flying boots. Walking all day, most of it in pouring rain, Banner passed a number of French people but, apart from a few curious glances, no one took the slightest bit of notice of him, and he saw no Germans. By the end of the day he had walked a good 35 kms and, with very sore feet, approached an isolated farmhouse (the recommended practice). He was again invited in by a woman and her husband. An English-speaking woman was summoned, who said that she would put him in touch with an organisation next day, 24 January. After spending the night at the farmhouse he was taken to the woman's house where he 'was visited by a middle-aged woman', who was a member of the organisation that took him down to Spain."[2]

Banner stayed with the English-speaking woman for nine days – her husband Marcel (about 32 years old, short, with dark wavy hair) was a novelist by profession and being made to work for the Germans – and visited there by a grey-haired woman (Jeanne Kocera-Massenet – query) who took two of Banner's photographs for an ID card and travel permit. A man was supposed to come from Paris to collect Banner but he didn't appear so on about 3 February, Banner cycled with Marcel and his wife to Sompuis where they caught a bus to Chalons. They waited in the station waiting room until the woman who had provided Banner's ID card appeared and she took him to Paris.[3]

---

2   Extract from the 2009 book 'RAF Evaders' by Oliver Clutton-Brock, published by Grub Street.

3   Conjecture on my part that this was Jeanne Kocera-Massenet but both she and her son Jean Yvan Kocera-Massenet (of 16 rue de Saint-Senoch, Paris XVII, born April 1908 in Italy, married to a Norwegian girl and with three small children) also worked with the Francois-Shelburn organisation, Jean as a courier while his mother sheltered evaders in her apartment at 10 rue Ernest Renan, Paris XV. On the other hand, Banner makes no mention of two other evaders – Louis Feingold and Warren Tarkington – who were staying with Mme Kocera-Massenet at about this time, and nor do they mention him ...

They went to the woman's apartment (10 rue Ernest Renan – query) where her son Jean (about 24 years old, dark skinned with blue eyes) arrived with a girl who spoke English. Jean took all of Banner's escape aids and foreign currency, leaving just his French money. On about 12 February, Banner was taken to rue d'Aboukir where he stayed with Simone Molin for two weeks, visited there by Dora Rospape, Maud Couve and Alice Brouard.[4] On 26 February, Genevieve Soulie (short, fair-haired, medium build) took him to the station where he met a young man called Johnny (Jean-Louis Kervevant) who had a Canadian, John Upton and two Americans – Tim Marean and Bill Spellman – with him. Johnny took them by train to Toulouse where they joined another party of Americans.

Sgt John H Upton RCAF was the navigator of 24 OTU Whitley AD675 (Kennedy) which was returning from dropping leaflets over Orleans the night of 3-4 November 1943 when one engine failed and the aircraft was abandoned to crash near Courtalain (Eure-et-Loir).[5]

Upton landed in the Foret de Vendome and walked south for about four hours before spending the rest of the night sleeping in the open. He carried on walking the next day and spent the night in a barn, passing through Vendome and Chateau-Renault next day and finding shelter on a farm near Tours the following night. After two days resting, Upton was advised to turn away from Tours and on 10 November, had reached Loches where he was arrested by a gendarme. He was taken to the gendarmerie where the chief (M Adelbert) and assistant chief of police questioned him. As Upton didn't speak any French, a professor of English was brought to interview him and fortunately for Upton, it turned out that all three men were members of an organisation. The professor took Upton back to his house and next day told him that three Americans – James Shilliday, Roland Marean and Halleck Hasson – had also turned up in Loches and that he had sent them to different houses in the town. On 13 November, Upton and the three Americans were taken to stay with Paul Bertrand on rue de la Porte Poitevine. On 26 November, all four were taken to Le Blanc, a small town some sixty kilometres south of Loches, where they were sheltered

4   Note that although Maud Couve and Alice Brouard no longer sheltered evaders at 25 rue de Madrid following the departure of Kennedy in November, that didn't stop the two ladies from continuing to help some of them.

5   Three other AD675 crew evaded successfully: pilot F/Lt James L Kennedy RCAF with Bourgogne until passed on to Comete (see earlier) WO2 George A Gauley RCAF was taken across the Pyrenees from Behasque-Lapiste (Aquitane) in December and Sgt Albert E Spencer RCAF who was with a group of maquisards until evacuated from Izernore (Rhone-Alpes) by USAAF C-47 on Operation Mixer in July 1944.

with Armand Delaune on rue de Chateauroux (query) – Shilliday and Hasson being moved four days later to stay just outside the town with Mme Alphonse (Marie-Louise) Lebeau at Place de l'Eglise, Concremiers. On 2 December, Upton and Marean were joined by Taylor Harrison and on 17 December, the three men were taken to a chateau belonging to a vicomtesse de Poix at Douadic, about ten kilometres north of Le Blanc. On 6 January 1944, Upton and Marean were returned to M Delaune at Le Blanc – and Harrison was taken to join Hasson and Shilliday.

On 31 January, Upton had his photograph taken and was given a new ID card by the professor and that evening, the professor and a guide from Paris, drove them all to Loches (Harrison says Tours but there is a rail link between the two) where the five airmen and their guide, Jean-Louis Kervevant (known as Johnny), took the eight-thirty train to Paris.

On 6 September 1943, B-17 42-30203 Shack Up (388BG/560BS) (Mohr) was returning from Stuttgart where flak had hit the #4 engine and blown a large hole in the left wing before it was attacked by fighters and lost #3 engine. As the bomber dropped out of formation, more fighters attacked, stopping any of the gun-turrets from operating and setting fire to the nose of the aircraft. Then #2 engine failed and the aircraft was abandoned south of Paris. Three of the crew evaded successfully – all with Bourgogne.

Shack Up navigator 1/Lt James G Shilliday begins this account of 203's final mission:

"In the chill, foggy pre-dawn at 05.37 on the sixth of September 1943, plane number 30203 was airborne with a full crew aboard. Old 203 was sulky under the heavy load. The Tokios [sic – extra fuel tanks] were full and in the bomb bays were ten dangerous looking 500 pounders labelled "Stuttgart, Germany – to be delivered by air – freight pre-paid". Finally, under the familiar caressing of pilot 1/Lt Ray H Mohr, the old girl settled down and the crew relaxed and prepared themselves for that monotonous two hours of aldis [signal lamps] and assembly which proceeds the electrifying moment when the wing turns east for keeps.

I'm 1/Lt Jim Shilliday, the navigator, and I share the nose with 1/Lt Tim Marean, the bombardier. Both of us are making our tenth mission – I mention this so you will know that we had no false illusions about where we were going or what might happen. If you're lucky, Jerry picks on somebody else, if you're not, you fight like hell, try to stay in formation, do a lot of praying and maybe you come home.

We crossed the English coast in good formation and right on schedule. I remember it was clear and cold at 21,000 feet and I pulled on my fur-lined gloves to warm my hands for a while. Tim turned and gave the OK signal which indicated that Ray and the co-pilot Elmer – he was 2/Lt Elmer A Schultz – were doing a swell flying job. We were tucked in nicely – lead ship, second element, lead squadron.

At mid-Channel I called the crew and gave them the okay for testing their guns. Off to the left we could see our initial fighter cover – Spitfires and Thunderbolts. They were in position above us as we crossed the French coast. All seemed peaceful below us and as far as we could see the sky was ours alone. After we had flown for about five minutes over the continent, little mushrooms of smoke began to appear around and about. Except for the instinctive action of putting on our steel helmets, Tim and I took little notice of the ground fire – it was obvious that we were now flying out of range of their guns. Another uneventful fifteen minutes and we bid good-bye to our guardian angels. Soon, we knew, the real trouble would begin and we steeled ourselves against the appearance of those little tormentors with the blinking lights. We had not long to wait before our interphone crackled and we heard our tail-gunner say "Here they come – low at seven o'clock." At the same time Tim and I could see another group of fighters circling in the sun preparing for an attack on the group in front of us. Then, as if out of nowhere, a Fw190 streaked through our formation, rolling his armoured belly into our forward guns and trailing that long streamer of exhaust smoke that indicates that the fighter pilot had reduced his throttle and was preparing to break the dive. For about ten minutes the FWs stayed with us, occasionally making a pass and giving us an opportunity to return their fire. This attack was not particularly persistent or intensive. I estimated about 50 fighters were in the air and they seemed to be playing that cagey game of lobbing long shots at us in an attempt to disable one or more Forts which then they could attack en masse and kill with less danger to themselves. The fighters soon spent their fuel supplies and the "Big Ones" were left to lick their wounds and continue the mission. I now searched the sky below and above in an effort to determine the extent of our damage. To the best of my knowledge, our group was still intact." (MIS-X #481 Shilliday)

Shack Up bombardier 1/Lt Roland (aka Tim) Marean takes up the story:

"We headed for Stuttgart with the undercast getting heavier as we hit Germany. Arriving at Stuttgart we met about ten FWs and some very

329

accurate flak. At the IP, number 4 engine was knocked out and a large hole (about two feet) shot in our left wing. Still holding formation, we continued the run. The target was completely obscured so we circled and made a run on an unknown town. Our #4 engine wouldn't feather so it was windmilling. After dropping our bombs we encountered a few more fighters and trouble developed in #3 engine. The formation began drawing away and in about ten minutes we met our first heavy wave of fighters at about 20,000 feet. They came in from 11 and 1 [o'clock], high and low, 7 and 5 high and low, in pairs – we estimated between 28 and 30 fighters were on us. At this time our tail-gunner Robert Ammerell was wounded by a 20mm thru the groin. Our ball-turret gunner Barney Becker got one enemy aircraft on the first attack. Then they shot out the hydraulic system in the ball turret and flooded the turret so Barney was forced to abandon it. The right hand oxygen system went out and the nose was set on fire by 20mm. Lt Shilliday and I got it out by stomping it out. The trouble developed in the top turret (cause unknown) so we had no protection from the tail, upper and lower turrets. The e/a [enemy aircraft] noted this and pressed much closer, one Fw came in level at twelve o'clock and it looked like he was bent on crashing us. I simply held the gun on him.[6] Seconds after this #2 propeller ran away and sounded like a siren. The ship began vibrating very badly. The cowling came off and we could see white-hot metal dripping from it. Finally the prop came off and went over the wing without touching the ship.

With one engine and both turrets and tail guns out, and a fire in the #2 engine, our situation was becoming hopeless. The pilot gave orders to abandon ship. The intercom was unharmed and the armorer gunner asked for a few seconds to toss the tail-gunner out. The assistant engineer helped him. They set his back to the door, put his hand on his 'chute and rolled him out. The assistant engineer followed immediately and both 'chutes opened.

Before jumping, I went up into the cockpit to check on injuries. Pilot and co-pilot were okay and ship was flying level on AFCE. The pilot asked me if we were on fire – yes – he said "Okay, we have everything under control and will be down in a minute". I yelled "Good luck" and went feet-first thru the nose hatch. The altitude was between 15,000 and 14,000 feet and as there were fighters still around, I had already decided on a delayed jump. The first sensation was of terrific speed as the slipstream hit me. Then it seemed as though I had stopped falling and was floating through the air.

---

6   On a B-17, the bombardier is also the nose gunner.

By doubling up I could somersault. I was astonished to find that by flexing different muscles, I could control my position completely. When I could clearly see a horse and a man plowing in a field, I pulled my rip-cord and the 'chute popped immediately. I was wearing low cut oxfords and as I landed, I cracked my right ankle. I recommend that all men wear high shoes to give all the protection possible." (MIS-X #482 Marean)

James Shilliday sprained his ankle as he landed in a ploughed field about six kilometres north-east of Puiseaux (Centre), where he was soon found by two young men (Pierre and Edouard) who were looking for him. They took Shilliday to a farm near Boulancourt where he stayed overnight with a young man and his wife. Next day Edouard took him to hide in some woods until the afternoon when a Doctor Michel May (nf) and the maire of Boulancourt came to visit. That evening Dr May drove Shilliday to Cmdt Pierre Charie's house in Egry (Loiret) where he met a Dr Francis and his wife Simone who had left their home in Paris after a Gestapo scare. Shilliday stayed for about a week with Pierre Charie, being joined on the sixth day by his bombardier Roland Marean. Note that Marean's account is slightly different.

Roland Marean and Shack Up radio-operator T/Sgt Halleck H Hasson landed about half a mile north of Coudray (Loiret) and the two men evaded together for much of the time. S/Sgt Robert Wallin (one of their waist-gunners) also landed nearby but his ankle was wounded by shrapnel and he couldn't walk, so after giving him first-aid, he was left behind. That afternoon, Marean and Hasson were approached by a woman who took them to her home. Next day, Michel Landry (about 32 years old, 5 feet 7 inches tall, with black hair and dark eyes – his wife Renee was about 27 years old, also with dark hair) came with a bicycle and took Hasson the nine kilometres to his house in Malesherbes before returning to collect Marean.[7] They were visited by a man called Andre who told them that his friend was looking after their navigator James Shilliday. On 13 September, Marean and Hasson were driven south to Egry (Loiret) where they stayed with wholesale wine merchant Pierre Charie. On 30 September, a man from Montereau and an elderly lady took them to stay with gamekeeper Andre Soupplisson at Adon where they were visited by a priest (tall, slender,

7   There is a Michel Landry with a Paris address of 20 Avenue Ledru-Rollin listed on the IS9 Helper List along with a note of 19,200 francs compensation being paid – presumably for expenses incurred whilst sheltering evaders.

wore glasses, rode a motorcycle) who was the liaison with an organisation in Paris. On 21 October, a truck from Montereau took them back to Pierre Charie in Egry where they joined Shilliday. On 30 October, the three Americans were sheltered with Doctor Michel May at Puiceaux until 12 November when Hasson and Shilliday were taken a few kilometres north to stay with the maire of Boulancourt – Marean joining them there a week later.

At this point Michel Landry decided to try and take Shilliday, Marean and Hasson to Spain himself and he got them as far as Loches before they were arrested at the Hotel de la Providence by French police. Fortunately for them, the chief of police decided to help them and he arranged for a local English schoolteacher (Upton refers to him as a professor) who claimed to have flown to and from England, to pass them on to a wood-worker named Paul Bertrand at rue de la Porte Poitevine who was already sheltering John Upton. Three weeks later Marean and Upton were collected by Roger Pesch (of rue de Ruffec, Le Blanc) and taken to stay with Armand Delaune at Le Blanc. On about 16 December, Marean and Upton were joined by Taylor Harrison and on 19 December, they were taken a few kilometres north-east to Douadic where they stayed at the chateau Les Piniers owned by the vicomtesse de Poix. M Pesch took Hasson and Shilliday in the opposite direction to Concremiers where they stayed with Mme Alphonse Lebeau and where Harrison joined them before they all moved back to Armand Delaume at Le Blanc on 4 January.

Sgt Taylor D Harrison was the bombardier of B-17 42-30000 (92BG/327BS) (Bogard) which was returning from Stuttgart on 6 September 1943 when it was attacked by fighters and abandoned west of Troyes. As mentioned earlier, all ten crew baled out and seven evaded successfully.

Harrison landed in woods north-east of Troyes where a Polish wood-cutter gave him a beret and smock and Harrison headed south towards Spain, establishing a regular routine of walking all day and asking for (and receiving) shelter each night. On the ninth day (15 September) he reached a village north-east of Aigurande (Champagne-Ardenne) where he was taken in and his journey arranged. After three days on a farm, Harrison was driven to Chateauroux where he stayed for another three days with a schoolmistress (and secretary of the local organisation) before being driven to Mezieres-en-Brenne where he was sheltered by Professor and Mme Rene Rigault of the *Lycee la Canal* in Paris. Three days later, Harrison was driven to Obterre (Indre) where he stayed with schoolteacher Jean Delalez (the local organisation chief) for seven weeks – his lieutenant was M Pesch, another schoolteacher. Harrison was then returned to Chateauroux and M Limoges (of Mezieres-en-Brenne) took him by train to Toulouse. They were unable to find their contact in Toulouse so M Limoges took Harrison back to Mezieres-en-Brenne where he stayed with a wealthy man on his estate, Le Tizanes. After a month, Harrison was moved to Le Blanc to stay with market-gardener Armand Delaune where he joined Tim Marean and John Upton. Two weeks later Harrison, Marean and Upton were taken to stay with the vicomtesse de Poix at her chateau Les Piniers at Douadic, north-east of Le Blanc. After a month at Les Piniers, Harrison was taken (in early January) to stay with the Dean of a high-school in Le Blanc (her son was an organisation radio-operator) while Upton and Marean returned to M Delaune – where they joined James Shilliday and Halleck Hasson. On 30 (or 31) January, Harrison, Upton and Marean were reunited and they, plus Shilliday and Hasson, were driven (query) to Tours where they were met by Jean-Louis Kervevant (aka Johnny), who took them by train to Paris.

Upton, Shilliday, Marean, Hasson and Harrison arrived at the Gare d'Orsay at seven o'clock in the morning of 1 February and Jean-Louis Kervevant took them to meet Genevieve Soulie. After breakfast in her (nice) apartment, the evaders were separated. Shilliday, Hasson and Harrison were taken to Juvisy-sur-Orge where Shilliday and Hasson stayed with Andre Lefevre and family at 29 rue Hoche for a month while Taylor Harrison stayed with their neighbours, chemists Leon Meilleroux and his wife Amelie (who Harrison describes as being 35 years old, 5 feet 7 inches tall with dark hair, blue eyes and an olive complexion) at 30 rue Pasteur. Upton and Marean were taken to Montreuil where they stayed with Jeanne Delapraye at 71 rue Beaumarchais.

S/Sgt Willis E Spellman was the radio-operator of B-24 42-7614 (93BG/328BS) (Carnahan) which was returning from Ludwigshaven on 7 January 1944 with one engine already damaged by flak over the target when a second engine stopped, the aircraft filled with petrol fumes and the radio exploded. The aircraft was finally abandoned to crash south of Paris.[8]

8   Two other 42-7614 crew evaded successfully: waist-gunner S/Sgt Robert K Fruth was evacuated by MGB 503 from the beach at l'Anse-Cochat in March on the Francois-Shelburn operation Bonaparte 3 and co-pilot 2/Lt Edward C Miller crossed the Pyrenees at the end of March.

Nineteen-year-old Spellman landed just north of Milly-la-Foret (Ile-de-France) where he was helped by a seventeen-year-old boy called Coco who took him to a farm run by two elderly Russian sisters. Next day, Coco brought Marcel Buisson who took Spellman back to his home at 30 bis Avenue Jean Jaures in Dammarie-les-Lys, just south of Melun, where a woman called Giselle, wife of a doctor, tended to his wounds. On 10 January, another Giselle (eighteen-year-old daughter of a shoemaker) came with Coco and questioned him and three days later returned with an ID card in the name of Jean Bouvet. On 22 January, the Hollywood actress Drue Leyton (Dorothy Tartiere) collected Spellman and took him by train to Paris.

Mme Dorothy Tartiere (aka Drue Leyton) (born June 1903 in Winsconsin) was the widow of French actor Jacques Tartier who was killed in Syria in June 1941. She was living in Barbizon (Seine-et-Marne, south-east of Paris) but had an apartment at 18 Quai d'Orsay, Paris VII. Dorothy Tartier was recommended for a KMC.[9] Her 1946 book 'The House Near Paris' (published by Simon and Schuster) mentions several of the evaders and their helpers and some of the details have been taken from there. Note that Spellman refers to a M Grue as his initial helper together with wife Maria and son Jannie but I am pretty sure this was actually Marcel Buisson.

Mme Tartiere took Spellman to stay overnight with an elderly American woman named Katherine Dudley at 13 rue de Seine. Next day Spellman visited Irving Schwayder and John Gilson (both from B-17 42-31179) who were living with Paul and Olga Christol on rue Edouard Quenu. The following day, Spellman was moved to 160 rue Jeanne d'Arc, Paris XIII where he stayed with Jacques Goux (26 years old, 5 ft 10 inches tall with blond curly hair, thin face, blue eyes, ex-French navy – he was a pastry cook at the Coq au Vin restaurant in the Halle aux Vins) and his wife Giselle (daughter of Londoner Alf Grand, proprietor of the American Bar in Barbizon, Giselle spoke perfect English). A few days later Spellman visited Robert Hauger and Revis Smith – he refers to them in his report as Henry and Harry – and Genevieve Soulie took Spellman to have his photograph taken for a new ID card.

On 26 February, Spellman left the Goux family to meet Genevieve Soulie at the carousel in the Tuileries Gardens where she passed him on to Jean-Louis Kervevant (23 years old, 5 ft 4 inches tall, curly black hair) who had Tim Marean and two RCAF airmen, Sgts William Banner and John

9   TNA folder WO208/5451.

Upton, with him and they walked across the river to the Gare d'Orsay (query) where they caught a late afternoon (17.35) train for Orleans and Toulouse.

William Banner, John Upton, Roland Marean and Willis Spellman arrived in Toulouse at one o'clock in the morning of 27 February and joined James Shilliday, Halleck Hasson, Taylor Harrison and Jack, the Russian linguist. They were passed onto another guide, referred to as Steve, and a red-haired woman called Toto, who took them by train to Narbonne and Perpignan – such a large party that (according to Banner) they passed themselves off as a football team.

On 1 March 1944, they were joined by Wesley Coss and Joseph Kinnane (see below) and at about nine o'clock that evening, set off with two Spanish mountain guides, walking through the night and losing Upton along the way. They crossed the river Tech and a railway line and by nine o'clock the following morning had reached the top of the first ridge of mountains. Jack (the Russian) rather slowed their pace and Banner wound up carrying him at some stages. They set off again that night and crossed the frontier at about three o'clock in the morning of 3 March, completely exhausted after crossing seven rivers on their journey. Hasson and Harrison were left behind near the frontier but they also crossed the border later that day. Two miles into Spain, the rest of the party stopped to light a fire and dry their clothes. They continued on to Figueras where the man who should have sheltered them failed to appear so they spent the night in the open. Next day, he showed up with food and they walked to a house on the outskirts of town where they slept in a stable. They stayed there for two nights and on the third night, Banner and one of the guides went on to Barcelona by goods train where the guide delivered Banner to the British Consulate. Shilliday, Marean, Spellman, Coss and Kinnane stayed at the farm until late on 7 March when they took a series of trains to Barcelona and reached the British Consulate the following morning.

John Upton had turned his ankle and he made his own way back to Perpignan and the Hotel Del Font de la Gay (query) where he had eaten one evening before and the proprietor took him to a private house in the town. Next day, some people from the organisation arranged for him to stay in an empty house for four days before he was taken by lorry to Ceret where he stayed with a Frenchman whose name Upton never knew. On 20 March, two French guides took Upton across the border to a Spanish farm just north of Massenet de Cabrenys where they had breakfast and his guides gave Upton general directions towards Gerona. Upton walked on that day, and after spending a night in a farmhouse a few kilometres north of Figueras, was arrested. On 24 March, Upton was taken to Gerona where he was turned over to a representative from the British Consulate and joined Hasson and Harrison.

Thirty-six-year-old Halleck Hassen dropped out in the mountains on the second night, just short of the Spanish border, telling the others to go on without him. After resting, he managed to follow their tracks by moonlight for a while but then rested again until dawn. He then walked on until about ten that morning when he met some woodcutters who confirmed that he was in Spain. After spending the night in a farmhouse, Hasson had almost reached Cantallops when he was arrested. Twenty-three-year-old Taylor Harrison stopped about 100 yards after Hasson. He only rested briefly before continuing in the tracks of the party but then stopped to rest again once across the frontier at about midnight and was arrested as he descended into Spain the following morning. He was taken to Figueras then Gerona – where Hasson arrived four days later.

1/Lt Wesley G Coss and S/Sgt Joseph M Kinnane were the pilot and one of the waist-gunners of B-17 42-5746 (99BG/347BS) which had made the long flight from Tortorella (Foggia) Italy to Salon de Provence aerodrome on 27 January 1944. They were approaching their target (about halfway between Marseille and Nimes) when they were attacked by fighters. With #1 and #2 engines hit, the aircraft dropped out of formation and the bale-out order was given.

Coss landed in a fairly deserted area and after walking for a few hours decided to spend the night in a haystack. Next morning he set off again and later that morning approached a man in a vineyard. He was told to hide himself while his new friend went to a nearby farm. He soon returned with another man who promised to come for him after dark. That evening two men arrived to take Coss to a farmhouse about four kilometres away where he was given civilian clothes. Later he was taken to another place where his journey was arranged and he was joined by his waist-gunner Jack Kinnane.

Unfortunately their combined Appx C is almost illegible ... They were sheltered with Rene Maroc (query) and wife ... taken to Marseille where they changed for Avignon then a train to Narbonne and Perpignan where they stayed in a hotel – they mention Simone Pasque – and eventually joined Marean and others at Perpignan.[10]

---

10   One of the few helper names found in their report is Simone Pasque, listed in Broussine's book and included on the IS9 French Helper List with her address as the Lycee de Strasbourg, Perpignan.

CHAPTER 54

Six Americans captured at Toulouse

On 2 February 1944, eight American evaders – 1/Lt John Beilstein, 2/Lt Irving Shwayder, 2/Lt Joseph Burkowski, 1/Lt Wayne Bogard, 2/Lt George Padgett, Sgt John Gilson Jnr, 2/Lt Harmon Smith and 2/Lt Jack George – left Paris with their three guides by overnight train to Toulouse.

1/Lt John N Beilstein was the bombardier of B-17 42-9893 El Diablo (379BG/524BS) (Jameson) which was on the way to Nantes on 16 September 1943 when it was shot down by fighters. El Diablo tail-gunner S/Sgt John Semach also evaded successfully – see earlier.

Michele Agniel says that Beilstein baled out and landed at Val Dreo, Plechâtel (Ile-et-Vilaine) where he was hosted by the Gautier family (Pierre Gautier of La Genaisse en Messac) then the Quentel family (Louis Quentel of Scaer) before being sent by the gendarmes of Grand-Fougeray first to Parame (just outside St Malo) and then to Lizio, Morbihan.

Beilstein simply says that he landed south-west of Bain-de-Bretagne and was too weak to move. Fortunately, he was soon helped and taken to stay overnight at a farmhouse where he was given an identity card and civilian clothes. Next day, a very good-looking Frenchman, about thirty years old, took him by bicycle to a small town (presumably Grand-Fougeray) where he was sheltered by two gendarmes (Leon Gravier and Jean Landron – query). Beilstein says it was a Saturday (16 October – query) when he was taken to Langon, collecting S/Sgt Cyril Koval on the way, to stay with the elderly Mlle Marie Moquet and her father at La Chaussee, Langon, Ille-et-Vilaine. While they were staying with Mlle Moquet, Beilstein met three members of Koval's crew (T/Sgt Samuel Blatchford, S/Sgt Elmer Schroeder and S/Sgt Alfred Held) who were "down by the river kept by some fishermen". They stayed for three days with the Moquets until two men in a truck drove Beilstein and Koval about ten kilometres west (collecting S/Sgt Harry Minor on the way) to a farmhouse. Unfortunately, a few days later, a French aviator (Guillaume Bernard – query) came asking about the three Americans and they were quickly moved to a nearby chateau where they were installed in the abandoned servants quarters.

"We were given an orientation talk in excellent English by an old count – he always wore a red beret. The chateau belonged to a very old marquess who did not know of our presence but the comte was a friend of the marquise and they were handling us. They had no trust in the servants and kept us hidden the whole time. They stole food for us from the pantry but it could only be cooked in the fireplace at night because of the smoke. We were there about a week."
(MIS-X #421 Minor)

Beilstein says they met M Guillonatt (assume Roger Guillouet of 15 rue le Pailleur, Saint-Servan-sur-Mer) who, with Roger Pansart, Albert (query) and another man, drove them to meet a bus where they joined Herbert Dulberg, Elton Hoyt, William Miller and Edward Shaffer. The Frenchman on the bus had a note from Dwight Fisher saying that he could be trusted and they were driven to a large house outside St Malo, the home of Roger Pansart at Parame. Harry Minor says that M Pansart was a supposed collaborator, a wealthy man in the transportation business, owning boats, trucks and busses, and that his wife drove a lovely Lincoln.

They had only been at Parame for a week when word was received that the chauffeur of the truck that was supposed to collect them was actually a member of the Gestapo and they were rushed to a monastery (Fisher describes it as a religious school) at Saint-Helen. After three days at Saint-Helen, one of the priests (and another man – M Silvio of St Malo – query) drove Beilstein, Koval, Fisher, Miller and Shaffer to Trigavou (Cotes-du-Nord) where they were sheltered by a French admiral (Fisher says elderly retired naval officer) that I haven't been able to identify. They were visited by Roger Pansart who told them he had contacted an organisation and that a man would come and take them to Paris.

Fisher says that in early October, Emile Guimard took him, Harry Minor and John Beilstein by truck to Malestroit (Morbihan). Fisher was sheltered with Norbert Letexier of rue St Julien, Malestroit for about two weeks before moving to join Beilstein, Joe Burkowski and George Padgett who were staying with a M Duval (Beilstein says Charles Duval – IS9 has Louis Duval at Serent, Morbihan). The four airmen stayed with M Duval until the end of November when they left for Paris along with Elton Hoyt, William Cook and Wayne Bogard.

On (about) 1 December, Michele Moet and Jean Carbonnet took Beilstein and the other six officers to Paris and Beilstein went on to Saint-Mande and around the corner from the Moet apartment on rue Sacrot to

6 rue de la Republique (now rue du General de Gaulle) where he stayed with M et Mme Marcel Soreau for the next two months. On 2 February 1944, Michele told him that he was leaving and she brought his navigator, Joseph Burkowski, and Wayne Bogard (from 42-30000) and she and Jean Carbonnet took all three, along with George Padgett (from 42-29937) and two others, to Montparnasse. As they were leaving for Toulouse, they were asked to say they came from Burgundy.

2/Lt Irving J Shwayder was the navigator of B-17 42-31179 (351BG/511BS) (Putman) which was returning from Bordeaux on 31 December 1943 when flak stopped one of the engines. After crossing the Brest peninsula they were attacked by fighters and the aircraft was abandoned. Shwayder was the only one of the ten-man crew to evade successfully.

Shwayder landed west of Lezardrieux (near Paimpol, Brittany) and was immediately taken home by a young farmer. Next morning, Shwayder was interrogated by a gendarme called Joe (who had spent five years in America and so spoke the language well) (Louis Toupin at the Gendarmerie – query) who took him to his home in Lezardrieux and arranged for Shwayder to stay with neighbours. On the fifth day, Shwayder was moved to Pontrieux where he saw his waist-gunner Sgt John J Gilson Jnr and stayed ten days at various addresses before going on to St Brieuc. He met the chief of the local organisation (a man with a bushy white moustache) in an apartment near the station and was joined there by Gilson later that day. The two airmen stayed in St Brieuc with a printer called Louis (Louis Le Bigaignon – query) and his wife Loulou (sic) for about a week (Gilson says he was sheltered by Joseph Forester (sic) in a farmhouse near Saint-Brieuc) until a young man who spoke English came and took them to Paris.

They were taken to an apartment (apparently the organisation HQ) where they met a small dark man (assume Georges Broussine) and Genevieve Soulie who took them to stay with Olga Christol and her husband Paul at 4 rue Edouard Quenu. Mme Christol knew Dorothy Tartier (aka Drue Leyton) and Mlle Beatrice (query) (two older American women) and an Englishman named Charles William Herring of 3 rue Ernest Cresson, Paris XIV – described by Drue Tartier as an elderly sports writer married to a Frenchwoman – and Mme Tartier brought Bill Spellman to meet them. They stayed with Olga Christol for about ten days until 2 February when the Christols (on instructions from Genevieve Soulie) took Shwayder and Gilson to the Tuileries where they joined two other Americans.

A girl took the four Americans (and others) by train to Toulouse, arriving early in the morning of 3 February. At the barrier, the three Americans in front of Shwayder (including Gilson) were stopped by a 'Gestapo' man. Shwayder walked straight through and waited outside the station to be joined by John Beilstein who was also the only one of his group of four Americans not to be picked up.

The three airmen with Beilstein were 1/Lt Wayne C Bogard, 2/Lt George C Padgett and 2/Lt Joseph Burkowski. The other two Americans with Shwayder were 2/Lt Harmon Smith and 2/Lt Jack D George, navigator and bombardier from B-24 42-40990 On The Ball (Walters).

There are only a few RAMP reports by Americans who were captured and so details of Bogard's, Padgett's and Burkowski's evasions come from various sources. Jack George says he was sheltered at Arrou (Eure et Loir) for two weeks until an organisation was contacted and the internet says that Jack George and Harmon Smith were sheltered in Paris by Pierre Bietrix at 2 bis rue de Monceau.[1]

1/Lt Wayne C Bogard was the pilot of B-17 42-30000 (92BG/327BS) which was returning from Stuttgart on 6 September 1943 when it was attacked by fighters and abandoned west of Troyes.

Bogart landed near Troyes and Michele Agniel says that when he was taken to Paris the first time, he was sheltered by M Leboeuf at Villacoublay (assume Henri Leboeuf of 11 rue Martial Grandchamp, Clamart), and police inspector Andre Maitre at 5 rue Louis Dupont, Clamart – although this doesn't seem to agree with Cook's account. In Brittany, where he was among the many airmen sheltered around Lizio, Bogard was hosted by Mme Barthomeuf at 7 Blvd Surcout in nearby Saint-Servant.

When he was brought back to Paris again (on 1 December), Bogart and Joseph Burkowski stayed with the Moet family at 22 rue Sacrot, Saint-Mande. On 15 January 1944, because of an alert in the system and as a precaution, they were moved, first to stay with Charles and Marthe Legros at 21 rue Gabrielle, Charenton-le-Pont and then with Simone Besson at 8 rue Emile Allez, Paris XVII.[2]

2/Lt George C Padgett was the bombardier of B-17 42-29937 (379BG/525BS) (Breidenthal) which was on the way to their secondary

---

1   Pierre Louis Bietrix, physician, born October 1907. (WO208/5452) The IS9 Helper List says that Dr Bietrix was awarded a King's Commission.

2   Information from Michele Agniel in 2013.

target of an airfield near Rennes St Jacques on 23 September 1943 when a direct flak hit stopped the #3 engine, set the left wing on fire, damaged the controls and the aircraft was abandoned.

"Padgett landed in a field behind the church at La Chapelle-Thouarault, Ille-et-Vilaine and was soon sheltered by Louis and Pierre Blanchard and hidden on their farm 'La Huardiere'. He also received help from Benard [Jean Bernard at Saint-Servant – query], Antoine Jagu [of 80 rue de Dinan, Rennes] and Madame de Solminihac, before being taken to Lizio where we found him." (Michele Agniel 2013)

2/Lt Morton Shapiro reports meeting George Padgett in Paris sometime in early January 1944 when a young girl brought him to 28 rue George Sand (Paris XVI) where Shapiro was being sheltered by Jacques Aude – Padgett told Shapiro that he was staying in another apartment (no address) along with Joe Burkowski. Shapiro was taken to Plouha on 19 January and evacuated on the first Shelburn Operation Bonaparte ten days later. Padgett says (in his RAMP report) that he was sheltered for two months by Mme Andree Castanie at 1 rue Lamennais, Paris VIII.

The same girl who had brought Shwayder from Paris took him and Beilstein to meet nineteen-year-old Jacques La Har (Jacques Larre-Brieux – query) who took them by train to Pau where they rejoined the girl and two men from Paris. They stayed with a painter and his brother.

After about a week they were taken back to the station where they were met by the guide who had brought Beilstein from Paris and he took them by train to Tarbes. Next day they were taken on another train to Nogaro, where they stayed overnight before going on by car to the little village of Luppe-Violles (a few kms to the south-west and about 60 kms north of Pau) where they stayed in a hotel. They stayed at Luppe-Violles for two weeks before being taken to a big farm on the other side of Nogaro. Next day, Jacques La Har collected them by car and drove them back to his home in Pau (Villa Marguerite, 28 Blvd Alsace Lorraine – query). On their second night in Pau, they met American-born Rosemary Maeght who took them by bicycle to meet a blonde Belgian woman named Isabelle who took them to stay with Leon van de Poele – S/Sgt Joseph L Kirkner (who was there in January) says he spoke good English. After four days, Rosemary took them back to her home at Villa Innisfail,

Chemin de Billere where she was living with an Englishman and where they met Frank Greenaway.[3]

Several evaders report staying with the Belgian wool (or cotton) broker. They describe him as being tall, slim and dark, in his early forties and a good English speaker. Leon van de Poele and his wife Henriette lived at Villa Chant des Oiseaux on rue Saint-Jammes with their four children – Mary (born 1927), Jacques (born 1929) and twins Pierre and Michel (born 1931). All four were still at school and despite having so many evaders periodically sheltered at their home, according to elder daughter Mary, none of them were aware of their parents' resistance activities at the time.[4]

F/O Francis H Greenaway was the navigator of 21 Sqn Mosquito HX961 which was the way to bomb a rocket installation near Abbeville on 4 January 1944 when a flock of birds caused his pilot, F/Lt F J Pearce, to clip the ground and force-land in the middle of the Somme estuary. Both men were captured but Greenaway managed to escape from a lorry in Paris. He made his own way to Saint-Martin-d'Auxigny (Cher – just north of Bourges) where he found shelter on 14 January with Mme Casson (query) and his journey was arranged.

That same day, Auguste Foret, the cure at Valencay, called around. He was told that Greenaway was there and that afternoon, Greenaway was taken to M Foret's house where he stayed for the next two weeks. Despite claiming to be in contact with an organisation, M Foret was unable to arrange any definite help so on 27 January, a Mme Aubrey (of Coust – query) accompanied Greenaway in a van to Issoudun and then by train to Chateauroux (accompanied part of the way by a gendarme) and had

---

3   Mme Rosemary Maeght (née Wright in May 1917 near Massachusetts) had an American father and English mother. Educated in England, she married Frenchman Pierre Maeght and went to live in Pau in 1939. (WO208/5456)

Isabelle was the comtesse Isabelle de Liedekerke (born December 1924). She and her mother (comtesse Anne de Liedekerke – born September 1896) are credited with helping some thirty Allied evaders – Isabelle was recommended for a KMC. (WO208/5452) From 1942, Isabelle had been associated with the Belgian reseau Ferdinabel – a contraction of Ferdinand and Isabelle, the pseudonyns of Rene de Chaineux and Isabelle's cousin, Odette de Bligniere. (see '*Basses Pyrenees Occupation Liberation 1940-1945*' by Louis Poullenot – extracts kindly sent to me by Bernard Baquie)

4   Leon van de Poele (born November 1903 at Ensival, Belgium) a wool merchant, and his wife Henriette (born July 1900 at Menin, Belgium) are credited with sheltering at least thirty-five Allied evaders at their home (no address given) in Pau. Both were recommended for KMCs. (WO208/5451 & 5459)

Details of the van de Poele family from Mary d'Hoop (née van de Poele) in Feb 2014. At the suggestion of Edouard Reniere, I contacted Leon and Henriette's grandson, former F1 racing driver Eric van de Poele, who put me in touch with his aunt Mary. Harry Fisher, who received a letter from Leon van de Poele in November 1944 (see Scottish Saltire Aircrew Association Library Ref: 148 'Addendum to Bailing Out' published in 2009) says his business address was c/o Ste Textile Wattine and Co, 1 rue Leon Daran, Pau.

'no difficulty' in crossing the demarcation line. That night they took an express train to Toulouse, arriving at eight o'clock on the morning of 28 January, and continued on to Lourdes. At Lourdes, Mme Aubrey took Greenaway to stay with M et Mme Clement Boussard at the Villa Igustian on Route de Pentacq (M Boussard was by then living under an assumed name). Greenaway was never sure if the Boussards were members of any organisation but he also spent two days with Mlle Carraz, who apparently was.[5]

There was a delay before Greenaway could be sent to Spain and the group intended to send him to a maquis in the Haute Savoire but while they were waiting for his taxi to arrive, the local commissioner of police telephoned to say that the maquis had been attacked that morning.

On 7 February, M Boussard took Greenaway by bicycle to Estialescq, near Oloron-Sainte-Marie, where he was sheltered by M et Mme Cyril Bur until 19 February when he was taken to stay with M et Mme Rene Fleury in Oloron itself. On 27 February, Greenaway was moved to the home of a police inspector named Louis Henron (nf) until 2 March when a Frenchwoman in the organisation took him by taxi to Pau where he was passed on to (what he understood to be) an 'American' organisation – Greenaway being the first Englishman they had handled. In Pau, Greenaway met the woman in charge, Miss Joan Moy-Thomas, who told him that his journey had been arranged by a French professor that Greenaway had never met and about whom, Moy-Thomas knew nothing more.[6] Greenaway stayed two days in Pau before leaving by bus for Navarennx with two Americans, Bud Shwayder and John Beilstein.

Rosemary Maeght took the three evaders to the station where they were turned over to their guide, an elderly man who took them by bus to Naverrenx with a small, dark woman named Jacqueline Cintrat.[7] From Navarennx, M Ternac (Pierre Ternynck from Lasseubetat – query) drove the evaders and guide to Mauleon-Licharre where their guide left them with Dominique and Germaine Montalibet at the Cafe des Sports. On the fourth night, their guide returned to take them into the foot-hills for about 10 kilometres, collecting a group of five Frenchmen on the way, before passing them on to a young Basque passeur who led them into the

---

5   The IS9 Helper List has Mlle Henriette Carraz of 15 rue Paul Painleve, Caluir-et-Cuire, which is a northern suburb of Lyon.

6   Miss Joan Caroline Moy-Thomas (born May 1907 in London) of 18 rue Louis Barthou, Pau. (WO208/5456)

7   Mme Jacqueline Cintrat (born July 1895) of 12 Route de Tarbes, Pau. (WO208/5456)

mountains. That night they walked to Lacarry-Arhan-Charritte-de-Haut where they stayed in a barn for the rest of the night and following day. They set off again the next night, the group scattering at one point to avoid a German patrol but regrouping at Larrau where they stayed all the following day. That evening they set off with the Basque passeur's brother who took them across the frontier into Spain where he left them to make their own way down to towards Orbaiceta. They spent their first night in Spain (11-12 March) sleeping in a forester's house before carrying on to Orbaiceta, where they were arrested. After a night in a hotel, they were taken by bus (with an escort) to Pamplona.

CHAPTER 55

The George Whitehead and James Clarendon groups

On 22 March 1944, P/O George Whitehead, Sgt Arthur Jones, S/Sgt Robert Hauger and F/O Revis Smith left Paris for Toulouse and Pau with a guide called Jean Michel. On 25 March 1944, 1/Lt James Clarendon, Pvt Webber Mason, S/Sgt George Bennett, S/Sgt Charles Atkinson and 2/Lt Philip Warner left Paris by train for Toulouse and Pau with a large man wearing a white scarf who had a Frenchman called Gaspard Flandres with him.

P/O Garnet George A Whitehead was the pilot of 76 Sqn Halifax LL116 which was returning from Berlin in the late evening of 20 January 1944. The aircraft had already been damaged by flak over the target which had blown out most of the nose, destroyed the navigation instruments and radio, and killed the bomb-aimer, F/O Harry Morris. Further flak at Brunswick injured their wireless operator, Sgt L Stokes, and they found the fill-cocks of the starboard wing tanks were out of action. Whitehead turned for France and gave the bale-out order, staying with the aircraft for a further five minutes before baling out himself.[1]

Whitehead landed in the back garden of a house in Lens (Nord-Pas-de-Calais), hitting the roof in the process and waking up the inhabitants. Despite their rude awakening, the family seemed quite pleased to meet an English airman and they gave Whitehead a meal and a large glass of brandy before putting him to bed in the attic. Next morning, Whitehead was given trousers and a cotton jacket to wear over his battle-dress, a Michelin map of France and some bread and butter. One of the sons showed him the way out of Lens and Whitehead set off walking along the main road past Arras. He reached Sailly (assume Sailly-au-Bois) that afternoon and at the third time of trying, found shelter for the night in a farmhouse. Next day, he was given bread and two boiled eggs before continuing his journey south towards Paris. At Ham (Picardy) he went to a large house on the outskirts of the town where a woman (wife of a veterinary surgeon in Ham) had already recognised him as a British airman (later confirmed by the blisters

---

1   LL116 navigator WO2 J McTrach, mid-upper gunner Sgt J M Fisher and rear-gunner Sgt Bernard Compton also evaded successfully, all sheltered in France until liberated.

on his heels – surely no German would have taken that amount of trouble) and she put him in her mother's bedroom where the maid (who she didn't trust) wouldn't see him. That evening he was taken to another house on the outskirts of town where two men and a woman (none of whom spoke English) managed to explain they were members of a resistance organisation.

At midnight, a doctor named Auguste Pouchet came from Ham and drove Whitehead to a cafe in Beaumont-en-Beine run by an Italian named Louis Zanni. M Zanni said that he provided the local resistance with flour, petrol and ration cards, although Whitehead soon decided it was his wife Germaine who was really the brains of the outfit. Whitehead was sheltered next door with Edouard Ponchon but had his meals in the cafe. M Zanni contacted a local organisation and a man called Le Noir (query) came from Chauny to get personal details from Whitehead and a few days later, returned with an ID card for him. Le Noir also gave Whitehead a pair of trousers while M Zanni contributed a jacket. Whitehead was also visited by Dr Pouchet and a man referred to as the 'Director' – probably of a local company. On 8 February, M Zanni took Whitehead by bicycle to Chauny – coincidently the same day that an American aircraft came down locally and one of the crew landed about two kilometres away. Zanni's nephew apparently found the airman, hid him in a barn and brought him civilian clothes but Whitehead didn't meet him or learn his name. Whitehead was taken to a garage opposite the German headquarters where he met 2/Lt Philip Warner. A short time later, the maire of Viry-Noureuil took the two airmen in a horse-drawn buggy to the home of the cure in Viry and then on to a farm (also in Viry) where they were sheltered by Lucien Doucet, being visited there several times by Le Noir.

On 15 March, Whitehead and Warner were taken back to Chauny where they joined James Clarendon, and the three airmen were taken by train to Noyon where five more American evaders – George Bennett, Charles Atkinson, Webber Mason, Lee Frakes and Arthur Jones – were put on the train by Le Noir, and their two guides, Michele Moet and Jean Carbonnet, took them all to Paris.

1/Lt James P Clarendon was the navigator and Pvt Webber L Mason the tail-gunner of B-17 42-3357 Immortal Lady (482BG/813BS) (Gold) which was headed for Frankfurt on 8 February 1944 but the formation was off course and they missed their rendezvous with fighter support. As they turned on course, they were attacked by enemy fighters who hit all four engines and Immortal Lady was abandoned at high altitude to crash near Chevincourt (Oise). Immortal Lady waist-gunner S/Sgt Elres D Dowden was also helped by Bourgogne – see below and later.

James Clarendon lost his gloves in the jump and froze his hands before landing near Dreslincourt (Oise). He was almost immediately taken to the local resistance leader, Maurice Varet, who checked his identity before taking him back to his house in Dreslincourt. That evening, Clarendon was moved to the mairie at Ribecourt-Dreslincourt where his frost-bitten hands were treated before going on to a house on the main Paris-Compiegne road (probably at Longueil-Annel) where he joined his radio-operator T/Sgt Stephen Rodowicz and waist-gunner S/Sgt Herbert Gebers. Clarendon reports Pistol Packin' Momma navigator 2/Lt John A Kupsick – also shot down on 8 February – as just leaving for medical treatment in Compiegne with a resistance chief from Ribecourt called Martine (nf). Kupsick was sheltered by the Chauny-Dromas organisation until the area was liberated in August 1944.

Next morning, the three Americans were moved to a concrete bunker normally used for storing fodder and that night they were joined by Immortal Lady waist-gunner Elres Dowden and two other Americans (query). All six airmen were then taken to the home of a man named Norbert – an organisation member in Elincourt-Sainte-Marguerite – before Clarendon, Rodowicz and Gebers were sheltered with Roger Veron at Vieux-Moulin (south-east of Compiegne). On 24 February, Norbert and Martine took Clarendon, Dowden, Rodowicz and Gebers – collecting Kupsick along the way – to Alfred Logeon in Chauny. Clarendon and Kupsick were then sheltered with Emile Alexandre Napoleon Gossart at 23 rue Camille Desmoulins.[2]

On 15 March, Alfred Logeon took Clarendon to Chauny station where he joined George Whitehead and Philip Warner and they took the train for Paris. When they got to Noyon, they were joined by George Bennett, Charles Atkinson, Lee Frakes, Arthur Jones and Clarendon's tail-gunner, Webber Mason.

Webber Mason landed near Choisy-au-Bac and after evading the initial search, was helped and taken that evening to Noyon where he stayed with Andre Brezillon and his son Max on rue du Monchel. Two days later he

---

2   Thank you Dominique Lecomte for the corrected names and address of helpers in Oise. Dominique also lists Marcel Merlier of Crisolles as helping Clarendon, Gebers, Rodowicz and Dowden – and Norbert and Simone Hilger of rue du Casquet, Chevincourt as more of Dowden's helpers.

was joined by George Bennett and the following night by Lee Frakes. The three evaders stayed fifteen days with the Brezillons before they were moved – Mason to stay with Jean Grecourt and his Scottish wife Frances at 26 rue du Monchel for another nineteen days.

On 15 March, a young girl came from Paris and took Mason to Noyon railway station where he joined George Bennett, Charles Atkinson, Lee Frakes and Arthur Jones.

S/Sgt George F Bennett and S/Sgt Charles E Atkinson were the radio-operator and engineer of B-17 42-39782 Pistol Packin' Momma (379BG/527BS) (Rossberg) which was on the way to Frankfurt on 8 February 1944 when it was attacked by fighters and crashed near Noyon (Oise).[3]

Bennett and Atkinson both baled out at high altitude as their aircraft was disintegrating about them. Bennett passed out during his long descent and by the time he regained consciousness, he was on the ground and two young Frenchmen were helping take off his flying equipment. Bennett had injured his leg in the aircraft and so he was carried to a barn where his helpers left him. He was visited that evening by an older man who brought him food and again the following morning. Next evening, his helpers returned to take him to Lagny where two friars washed and tended to his injuries until Rene Philippon and Max Brezillon came with a car to collect him. Bennett was taken to Max Brezillon's house on rue du Monchel in Noyon where he joined Lee Frakes and Webber Mason. On 26 February, word came that the house was compromised by an informer and that evening Frakes was taken away to join Arthur Jones who was being sheltered by William Walks, a French-Canadian veterinary on rue de Lille in Noyon. Mason was collected the next day and sheltered with Jean and Frances Grecourt on rue du Monchel where he was hidden first in a workshop and then in a caravan at the bottom of the garden. A warning system was installed that allowed a bell to be rung from the house in case of any German visitors and which five-year-old Gisele Grecourt delighted in ringing until being told in no uncertain terms that it wasn't a game. In the evening of the following day, Rene Philippon collected Bennett in his car and took him back to his house at 6 rue du Faubourg d'Amiens. On 3 March, Rene Marechal came with a horse and buggy and took Bennett to the Ecole Mairie at Sermaize (about 5 kms NW of Noyon) where he was

---

3   Some details are taken from the 1992 book 'Shot Down! Escape and Evasion' by Col (USAF retired) George Floyd Bennett – published by MediaWorks, West Virginia. A much treasured and personally dedicated copy was kindly lent to me by Dave Minett and his wife Gisele – daughter of Jean Grecourt.

sheltered by Mme Yvonne Meha.[4] Next day, Mme Meha took Bennett to visit Rene Marechal's farm (called Haudival) where Charlie Atkinson was being sheltered. Atkinson had been helped on landing and brought to the Marechal farm the same evening. On 15 March, Bennett and Atkinson were driven into Noyon where they joined Lee Frakes, Arthur Jones and Webber Mason at the station.

Sgt Lee R Frakes was the radio-operator and Sgt Arthur B Jones a waist-gunner on B-17 42-40020 Good Pickin (305BG/364BS) (Stuckey) which was on the way to Frankfurt on 8 February 1944 when it was attacked by a Fw190 which destroyed the controls and set two engines on fire. The aircraft went into a dive and was abandoned to crash near Hirson (Picardy).[5]

Frakes landed just outside Beaurains-les-Noyon (Oise) and the following morning an elderly Belgian took Frakes into his house in Beaurains where he was visited by Dr William Walks, the Canadian veterinary from Noyon.[6] That night, Max Brezillon took Frakes back to his home on rue du Monchel where he lived with his father Andre Brezillon, step-mother and sister. Webber Mason was already staying there and they were joined next day by George Bennett. About two weeks later, the three evaders were moved and Frakes spent the first night with Marcel and Marcelle Cauet on Boulevard Ernest Noel before moving to stay with Dr Walks and his French wife Henriette on rue de Lille where he joined his waist-gunner Arthur Jones.

Arthur Jones landed near Thiescourt (Oise) and was helped soon after landing ... That evening, the family sent for a schoolteacher from nearby Cannectancourt who came with a young man who took Jones back to his home. He was given civilian clothing before being taken to stay with an elderly couple in Ville. Several days later, Max Brezillon and William Walks collected him and took him back to Dr Walk's house on rue de Lille in Noyon where he was later joined by his radio-operator Lee Frakes.

While Frakes and Jones were in Noyon, Marcel Cauet and a local theatre owner called Roger went to Paris to make contact with an organisation and as a result, Jean Carbonnet (short, slender, grey eyes) and Michele Moet (small, about 20 years old, light hair, brown eyes, spoke some English)

---

4   Note Mme Yvonne Meha – not Mme Micat as per Bennett's book – research by Dominique Lecomte.

5   Two other Good Pickin crew also evaded successfully: tail-gunner Sgt Carl W Mielke was helped by the Francois-Shelburn organisation and evacuated on Operation Bonaparte 3 in March 1944, and waist-gunner Sgt Odis R Pickering who was sheltered by the Chauny-Dromas organisation until liberated.

6   In Beaurains-les-Noyon, Frakes stayed with market gardeners Jules and Marcelle Lecat. (Dominique Lecomte)

came from Paris to arrange their ID cards. On 15 March, Henriette Walks took Frakes and Jones to Noyon railway station where they joined George Bennett, Charles Atkinson and Webber Mason.

Jean Carbonnet and Michele Moet took all five evaders to Paris, along with the three from Chauny, George Whitehead, James Clarendon and Philip Warner. In Paris the party was met by Genevieve Soulie and a short dark man, also called Jean (probably Georges Broussine).

2/Lt Philip B Warner was the co-pilot of B-17 42-3545 (95BG/334BS) (Roznetinsky) which was returning from Frankfurt on 29 January 1944 when #2 engine failed. They already had a faulty fuel gauge and then after dropping their bombs, the bomb-bay doors refused to close electrically (and the hand-crank was missing) so they dropped out of formation. They were attacked by fighters which killed the enlisted men in the rear of the aircraft, stopped #4 engine and set the wings on fire. As the aircraft rapidly lost altitude, it was abandoned to crash near Roeslare in Belgium.[7]

Warner landed just north of Menin, near the Belgian-French border. He was helped immediately on landing by a man who gave him food and civilian clothes and directed him south. Warner walked for four days, being helped across the frontier near Menin by a gendarme. On the fifth day, Warner reached Roupy (Picardy) where a farmer directed him to M Touron (nf) the local maire. M Touron sheltered Warner for three days until two men – Guy and Marcel Nicolas – took him to Tergnier and the Chauny-Dromas organisation (aka the Cercle du Nord). Warner was sheltered in Viry with George Whitehead until the end of February when they were taken to Chauny station by a young couple from Paris and joined James Clarendon on the train to Noyon.

On arrival at the Gare du Nord, the eight airmen followed Genevieve Soulie and their guides to a church where they waited while other guides bought them Metro tickets and then the whole party went to the Moet family apartment at 22 rue Sacrot, Saint-Mande. During the afternoon, all the evaders were moved elsewhere except George Whitehead, who stayed overnight, and Arthur Jones.

James Clarendon and Charlie Atkinson were taken to stay with gendarme Gabriel Bouyer at 87 rue Haxo[8] while another gendarme,

---

7   Four other 42-3545 crew also evaded successfully: bombardier 2/Lt Omar M Patterson Jnr and navigator 2/Lt Jennings B Beck were taken across the Pyrenees in March 1944 by the Francoise Dissard organisation while pilot 1/Lt Andrew Roznetinsky and top-turret gunner T/Sgt Frank W Vandam were sheltered until liberated in September – Roznetinsky in Lille and Vandam in Heule, Belgium.

8   Gabriel Joseph Bouyer (born September 1909) of 87 rue Haxo, Paris XX was recommended for a BEM (WO208/5451)

called Felix, took George Bennett to stay with a student gendarme and his grandmother. Webber Mason was sheltered by Odette Drappier at 11 rue Valentin Hauy, a tall, multi-lingual, 26-year-old brunette who was a secretary at the Ministry of Agriculture, while Philip Warner was taken to stay with gendarme Marcelin Villemont and his wife Marie at 151 Boulevard Davout.[9] During his stay, Warner was visited by Jules Bernard (sixty years old, lived in an apartment two floors above with his wife), Georges (who worked for the French-American Export Company) and a short, bald bachelor who worked as a bank-teller and made pastry for a vocation. Lee Frakes was taken by Jean (query) to Juvisy-sur-Orge where he stayed with Leon and Amelie Meilleroux at 30 rue Pasteur until 28 March – see later.

After staying overnight at the Moet apartment, George Whitehead was taken to stay with a girl named Anita (aged about 27) and her mother, who had a millinery business in London. Whitehead understood that although they had sheltered two pairs of Americans previously, he was the first evader to come from this particular organisation.

This was Anita Lemonnier (sister of actress Meg Lemonnier) and her mother Marie Suzanne Lemonnier at their apartment at 2 rue Ernest Renan. Some of their previous guests had been supplied by Paul Campinchi's reseau Francois-Shelburn organisation and the last two, T/Sgt Harold R Vines and 2/Lt Robert K Fruth, had left just four days earlier. Whitehead reports that he was visited by the head of the sea-evacuation organisation (no name) who said he would include Whitehead in a party if he had approval from the organisation in whose hands he was in. Since Mlle Lemonnier was unable to contact anyone in Bourgogne, this opportunity was lost and on about 22 March, when he might have left for Brittany and the last of the Francois-Shelburn Bonaparte operations, Jean Carbonnet came to collect him.[10]

On 22 March, Michele Moet and Jean Carbonnet took George Whitehead and Arthur Jones to the Gare d'Austerlitz where they met Genevieve Soulie, who had brought Robert Hauger, Revis Smith and several Frenchmen.

S/Sgt Robert G Hauger and F/O Revis L Smith were the radio-operator and bombardier of B-24 42-7593 Blunder Bus (389BG/565BS) (Smith)

---

9   Mme Vve Mariette Lami (KMS) also gives 151 Boulevard Davout, Paris XX as her post-war address although she and her late husband Vassilli Lami (who died following deportation to Germany) actually sheltered evaders in their apartment at nearby 7 rue du Cher. (WO208/5456)

10   Both Mme Marie Suzanne Lemonnier (born February 1875) and her daughter Alice Suzanne Anita Lemonnier (born September 1908) were recommended for awards – Anita for a KMC. (WO208/5451)

which was returning from Ludwigshaven on 7 January 1944 and about 100 kms south of Paris when #4 engine failed and they dropped out of formation. They were attacked by fighters which took out #2 and #3 engines and the aircraft was abandoned to crash near Orgeres-en-Beauce (Loiret).[11]

Hauger and Smith landed close to one another in an open field northwest of Artenay (north of Orleans) and hid overnight in some woods. Next day, they were spotted by a man passing by who later brought them food and civilian clothes and took them back to his farmhouse on the outskirts of Artenay. They stayed at the farm for four days, during which time they were told that their co-pilot, 2/Lt Robert H Hirsch, was being sheltered nearby. On the fourth day, M Seville (nf) came from Orleans and took them back to his house for another four days before they were moved to the outskirts of Orleans. They stayed with a farmer named Maxime (query) for a couple of weeks before they were moved to other addresses in Orleans until an English-speaking girl called Marie took them back to her home in a village just east of Artenay (at Trinay – query). They stayed with Marie's family for fifteen days until Maxime drove them to Toury where they were sheltered by a butcher and his family. Eight days later, two plainclothes policemen from Paris took Hauger and Smith to the capital where they were passed on to Olga Christol. They stayed with Paul and Olga Christol at rue Edouard Quenu for seven weeks, during which time they met Dorothy Tartier (American actress Drue Leyton), Genevieve Soulie and an English-speaking Frenchman called Philippe (25 or 30 years old, 5 ft 9 inches tall, dark complexion) (Philip Keun – query). They also met Bill Spellman who was staying with Jacques and Giselle Goux on rue Jeanne d'Arc. Food and tobacco were sent to them by an elderly American woman named Sarah Watson although she never visited the apartment.

After seven weeks with the Christol family, Genevieve Soulie took Hauger and Smith to the Gare d'Austerlitz where she turned them over to a Frenchman called Jean (about 25 years old, 5 ft 8 inches tall with sleek, dark hair) who had George Whitehead and Arthur Jones with him – and that evening, Jean took them by train to Pau.

George Whitehead, Arthur Jones, Robert Hauger and Revis Smith arrived in Pau on the evening of 23 March but on failing to make their planned rendezvous, their guide Yves Allain put them into a hotel for

---

11   I believe that Blunder Bus navigator 2/Lt Duane C Strayer evaded until 26 March 1944 when he was captured in Biarritz.

the night. Next morning, he passed them on to a blonde-haired English (or American) girl in red stockings who took them to a house where two women, one French (Jacqueline Cintrat) and one English (Joan Moy-Thomas), fed them and gave them bus tickets for Navarennx. They were put on the bus with conductor Robert Piton and at Navarennx, were collected by car and taken to a house in the mountains.[12] They stayed in a barn for three days before being taken to a farmhouse where they joined James Clarendon, George Bennett, Charles Atkinson, Webber Mason and Philip Warner.[13]

Yves Allain says that he took the first Bourgogne airmen by what he refers to as the "Pau II" route – the first Pau route (query) having been abandoned. However, there was a problem.

> *"The address given me by Etienne LALOU, our representative in this town, was wrong. It was obvious that the owner of the hotel was not expecting us. I had to hide my five (sic) airmen in a park in the town until curfew. After that I had to get them one by one, unnoticed, into the room which I had reserved for myself. We passed the night as best we could but our noises and movements drew the attention of the owner and in the morning he threatened to go to the police. It was only by threatening him in turn, that he backed down. After that, remembering another address which I had from Etienne LALOU, I managed to get into contact again with the network and things returned to order.*
>
> *The people who looked after our Pau II route were known to LALOU and LE BERRE : Mme JEAN (Route de Tarbes) [Jacqueline Cintrat], Jacques [query], Louis [query] and Marie-Rose [Rosemary Maeght]. I must also mention the owners of the Hotel Chazal [M et Mme Chazal] and Hotel Bernadotte [Mlle Marcelle Berot] who lodged us and our evaders."*[14]

Louis Poullenot says in his 2008 book '*Basses Pyrenees Occupation Liberation 1940-1945*' that the Bourgogne representative in the Basses Pyrenees was Georges Claverie. M Claverie ran a cafe hotel (cafe Claverie) at 17 rue Mathieu Lalanne, Pau and was responsible for organising the guides and people to supply food and lodging for the evaders.

---

12   Robert Piton (born November 1921) of 4 rue Henri IV (or 4 rue Marechal Foch), Pau. (WO208/5452)

13   Hauger and Smith account.

14   Translated from '*Rapport par Yves Allain*' (FNA File 72AJ/37/V).

On 25 March, Genevieve Soulie collected Clarendon, Atkinson and Bennett from their gendarme hosts and took them to meet Georges Broussine near the Gare de Lyon, just across the river from the Gare d'Austerlitz, before going on to the Jardin des Plantes, where Philip Warner was brought to join them. That same afternoon, Odette Drappier brought Webber Mason by Metro to Jussieu, walked with him down rue Cuvier, past the Jardin des Plantes to Quai Saint-Bernard where she handed him over to Genevieve Soulie and Georges Broussine. The five airmen were led to the Gare d'Austerlitz and passed on to a large man wearing a white scarf who had a Frenchman called Gaspard Flandres (query) with him.

The five airmen, Gaspard Flandres and their guide left by overnight train from the Gare d'Austerlitz early that evening but delays meant that it wasn't until the following afternoon that they reached Toulouse and only just managed to catch the train for Pau. Bennett, Atkinson and Mason stayed the night with American-born Rosemary Maeght while Joan Moy-Thomas took Clarendon, Warner and Gaspard Flandres to the villa of Belgian textile merchant, Leon van de Poele.

Next morning, they were all taken by bus to Navarennx (where they had a meal) and then by car to the foothills near Tardets where they met their two Spanish mountain guides before walking to a farmhouse where they joined George Whitehead, Arthur Jones, Robert Hauger and Revis Smith.

That night their guides led the nine airmen and Flandres into the mountains. They walked for two nights, crossing the border at five o'clock in the afternoon of 29 March at the Pic d'Orhy where their guides gave them directions to Isaba before leaving them. They were told to follow a river-bed to town but found that wasn't so easy as it turned out to be a muddy cattle track, however they eventually reached Isaba, where they spent the night and were arrested by Guardia Civil the following morning. They were taken to Pamplona and then, because Flandres (who spoke Spanish) told their guards they were soldiers, they were all taken to Lecumberri.

CHAPTER 56

The Robert Charters Group

On 28 March 1944, P/O Robert Charters, F/Sgt Thomas Squance, W/O Bernard Edinborough, F/Sgt Percy Tansley, Sgt Harley Gammon and Sgt Lee Frakes left Paris by train for Montauban, Toulouse and Pau.

P/O Robert B Charters RCAF was the navigator of 199 Sqn Stirling EE957 (O'Connor) which was returning from an SOE mission late in the evening of 3 March 1944 when they were attacked by a night-fighter and aircraft abandoned to crash near Is-sur-Tille (Burgundy) about 25 kms north of Dijon. Charters was the only member of the seven-man crew to evade successfully.

Charters landed in a tree and after disentangling himself (but leaving his parachute caught up in the branches) set off walking to the south-east. He soon turned north-east in order to avoid a group of people he heard moving about, through the Foret de Velours and by-passing Orville until finding help from a man working in a railway-crossing control box. The man (no name) took Charters back to his house, where Charters had a meal, and then to the house of a Swiss family where one of the sons spoke English. Later that morning, another member of the family took Charters to a man in a resistance group who worked at another railway crossing. Charters stayed at this house, visited by the local resistance chief (who told Charters he would contact London on his behalf) until 7 March when the chief of the Dijon resistance took Charters to the outskirts of Selongey where a lady from the Red Cross in Dijon, Giselle Chaintre, was waiting with a car.[1] Charters was taken to a furniture shop (Derczier – query) just off the main square in Dijon where he was sheltered for the next six days. Charters reports that on 8 March, the local head of the resistance took him to have his photograph taken and gave him lunch at his house but after taking Charters back to the furniture shop, was arrested on returning home.

---

1   Mme Giselle Chaintre (born March 1912) of 100 bis Avenue Kleber, Paris 16 was a Red Cross ambulance driver who helped numerous Allied evaders in and around Paris and Dijon. (WO208/5454) Mentioned earlier, she was the friend of Madeleine Melot who introduced Mme Melot to Georges Broussine.

On 12 March, two men came to question Charters but as there was some doubt about their identities, Charters was moved to a nearby cafe in order to avoid them. It was by then considered unsafe to keep Charters at the furniture shop so on 13 March, Giselle Chaintre moved him to an apartment over a chemist's shop and library in Dijon, the owner of which was 'rather nervous' about having Charters stay. On the evening of 16 March, Charters was taken to the station where he joined Lucien from the furniture shop. In order to avoid the curfew, they stayed in the station waiting-room from ten-thirty until two-thirty in the morning when they took the train to Paris.

Giselle Chaintre met them in Paris and took Charters to another Red Cross friend who looked after him for the day until a young French lawyer took Charters to stay with an elderly professor at the University of Paris. Charters stayed for two nights with the professor until the lawyer moved him to the apartment of a college friend of his about five miles away. On 21 March, Charters was joined by Thomas Squance and they were both moved to their host's father's house. That evening, Genevieve Soulie took them across the city to an apartment where they were sheltered with an elderly couple until 28 March when Genevieve took them to the Jardins des Plantes.

F/Sgt Thomas C Squance was the navigator of 90 Sqn Stirling LJ509 (King) on an SOE mission to France in the late evening of 10 March 1944 when they were attacked by a night-fighter. The bomber was set on fire and the Squance was the only survivor.

Squance baled out and landed just south of Brazey-en-Plaine (Burgundy) and after burying his parachute, set off walking south-east. He reached the river Saone near Saint-Jean-de-Saone, which he dared not cross and so turned north-east to Tillemay where he knocked on the door of a farmhouse. He was given breakfast and rowed across the river by the farmer who directed him towards Dole. Squance spent most of the next day hiding up in a wood, continuing that evening to a cluster of houses near Saint-Seine-en-Bache where he was given food and shelter for the night. His host (Camille Marcaire – query) was apparently busy during the night because next morning (12 March), a man named Frederic Mayor (manager of a cheese warehouse) arrived with two bicycles and took Squance back to his house in Dole, Les Orphelins on Faubourg de Chalon.

On 20 March, M Mayor took Squance by overnight train to Paris and the Metro station at Gare de Lyon where they met Giselle Chaintre. She took Squance to a cafe where he was handed over to Genevieve Soulie who took him to an apartment where he joined Robert Charters.

W/O Bernard Edinborough and F/Sgt Percy A Tansley were the pilot and bomb-aimer of 90 Sqn Stirling EF147 which was returning from an SOE mission near Peronne (Somme) on the evening of 5 March 1944, when they were hit by tracer shells (source not stated) south-east of Abbeville and crash-landed 2 kms north of Pont-Remy. All seven crew left the aircraft safely and Edinborough and Tansley paired off to evade together.[2]

Edinborough and Tansley walked to the village of Long where they spent the rest of the night and all next day hiding in a barn. That evening (6 March), they declared themselves to the farmer who let them stay a second night in his barn. Next morning, they were given civilian clothes and taken to another house for a meal before the farmer's son took them across the Somme to Longpre where he used some of their escape-kit money to buy them tickets and put them on a train for Paris.

They arrived in Paris at about seven-thirty in the evening of 7 March and after getting away from the station area, declared themselves to a cafe owner. The owner called a man who could speak English who then offered the two airmen his bed for the night. Next morning, they set off early and walked out of Paris, through Villeneuve and Juvisy-sur-Orge, reaching Lisses (Essonne) that evening. Again they declared themselves to a cafe owner and again they were helped. After being taken into a back room – where they used their ID discs and escape kits as bona fides – they were taken to a house where they stayed overnight. Next morning, an English-speaking man brought a member of an organisation to see them and he led them a little way out of the village where they were collected by a garage break-down van which took them back to Maurice Bidaud's garage in Juvisy-sur-Orge. They were given refreshments in the garage office before being taken to stay with Andre Lefevre and family at 29 rue Hoche. On 28 March, Paulette Lefevre and Amelie Meilleroux took Edinborough, Tansley and American evader Lee Frakes – who had been sheltered nearby with the Meilleroux family – back into Paris and the Jardin des Plantes.

Sgt Harley E Gammon was the rear-gunner of 425 Sqn Halifax LW390 (Waite) which was returning from Stuttgart in the early morning

---

2   Two other pairs of crewmen from EF147 also evaded successfully: navigator F/Sgt Norman E Cartwright and flight engineer Sgt Richard L Wensley were sheltered at Flixecourt (Somme) until British troops arrived in September – and wireless operator F/Sgt Charles J Singer and mid-upper gunner F/Sgt C W Walmsley RCAF who were also sheltered in France until liberated – only tail-gunner F/Sgt L E Cox was captured.

of 21 February 1944 when they were attacked by a night-fighter near the German-French border. The bomber burst into flames and was abandoned to crash near Souastre (Nord-Pas-de-Calais).[3]

Gammon landed about a kilometre west of Saint-Amand.[4] After hiding his Mae West and parachute in some bushes, Gammon began walking east along the river to the outskirts of Coigneux where he turned south – flames from his burning aircraft being visible to his left. At about six-thirty, he met a man on a bicycle and declared himself to him. Gammon was taken to the southern outskirts of the tiny village of Bus (south-west of Cambrai) where he was given civilian clothes, shoes and shelter.

On the afternoon of 24 February, Gammon was taken to Paris by lorry and delivered to a garage where the daughter of his helper in Bus worked. Next day he was visited by a man called Boulcour (nf) and a French civilian pilot (name unknown). Gammon was taken to stay overnight with a man who worked on the trams and next day, the civilian pilot took him back to his home (address unknown). On 1 March, Gammon was moved again, this time to stay with M Boulcour's secretary (name and address unknown) until 6 March when Boulcour and the pilot drove him to meet a woman with a deformed right hand (name and address unknown) who was the local resistance chief. This woman took Gammon the stay the night with a lawyer and next day he in turn took Gammon to another (unnamed) lawyer for another night. On 8 March, a girl came to take some details from Gammon and that evening, a man took him into central Paris where a man called Jean took him to his apartment (address unknown) where he met a girl called Liliane Jameson (mentioned earlier as being married to an American and living with her mother) who took Gammon back to her home at 2 rue Gervex, Paris XVII. Gammon stayed for three weeks with the Jamesons until 28 March when Jean took him to the Jardin des Plantes.

At the Jardin des Plantes, the six evaders were given new ID cards before being taken to the Gare d'Austerlitz where they were handed over to their guides, a young woman and a small bespectacled young man (Genevieve Crosson and Pierre Le Berre). They travelled third-class to Montauban where they stayed in a park until one o'clock before taking

3 Two other crew from LW390 also evaded successfully – flight engineer Sgt William Johnstone and bomb aimer F/Sgt Edmund A Powell were both helped by the Joe Balfe organisation at Hornoy, Somme – Johnstone staying in Amiens with Mme Vignon until liberated and Powell being passed on to Bourgogne on 17 April. Navigator F/Sgt W R McDonald and wireless operator Sgt G T Gibson were both helped by Rene Guittard and the Bordeaux-Loupiac organisation before they were captured.

4 Gammon's report says that he landed west of Coigneux (Somme) but from the description, I think it more likely that the village was Saint-Amand.

another train to Toulouse where they spent another three hours, moving about the platforms in pairs, waiting for their connection to Pau. They finally reached Pau at 10 o'clock that night (29 March).

They were met by two girls – one of whom, Rosemary Maeght, took Charters and Squance to stay the night with a middle-aged woman (name not given) while Edinborough, Tansley, Gammon and Frakes were taken to a house of a tall Belgian (Leon van de Poele on rue Saint-Jammes) where they stayed overnight in his villa.

Next morning, the six airmen – Charters, Squance, Edinborough, Tansley, Gammon and Frakes – were taken to Navarennx and then driven down the RN618 south of Tardets (collecting a guide on the way) before hiding until nightfall. That evening, they walked for another two hours to a waiting vehicle where they joined S/Sgts Edward Daly and Hobart Trigg from B-17 42-3452, a Frenchman and another guide.

On the second night they reached a village in the hills where they were joined by Yves Lavoie, Alvin Fisher, Frederick Reaine and William Fell from Halifax LK739 – see later. The whole party walked across the mountains with two changes of guides and crossed the frontier somewhere west of Pic de Lacoura at six o'clock in the morning of 1 April (query) 1944. Their guides pointed out the way to Isaba where the evaders were arrested by the Guardia Civil and taken to Pamplona. Next day they were taken to Lecumberri – where they joined James Clarendon, George Bennett, Charles Atkinson, Webber Mason and Philip Warner.

S/Sgts Edward Daly and Hobart Trigg were the two waist-gunners of B-17 42-3452 (100BG/350BS) (Vetter) which was damaged by flak over Paris on 15 September 1943 and attacked by fighters. With two engines out and the instrument panel shot away, the aircraft was abandoned at low altitude to crash north of Beauvais – see earlier.

I almost didn't include details of Daly and Trigg's epic evasion despite them being mentioned several times by other evaders. This was mainly because their names don't appear on Broussine's (or anyone else's) list of men helped by Bourgogne. However, whilst following up on an investigation of their tail-gunner Warren Lush's adventures, I realised their story was as relevant to this study as any of the other airmen mentioned.

Daly and the rest of the crew had time to change into their GI shoes before jumping and he landed in an open field somewhere near Saint-Just-en-Chaussee. After hiding his parachute and Mae West under some hay, Daly set off walking into the evening. Some eight hours later, he reached the tiny village of Cernoy and after failing to get into the locked church, falling rain persuaded him to enter a storage loft on top of one of the nearby houses. Daly spent the second night and all next day hiding in the loft before letting himself down into the house itself that evening. His arrival (obviously) startled the woman of the house, who was in the process of cooking the evening meal and she called her husband. By showing his dog-tags and a packet of American cigarettes, Daly managed to convince the middle-aged couple that he really was an American airmen and later that evening, the husband contacted someone and Daly's journey was arranged.

On 18 December, a young man named Guy and another older man, took Daly by bicycle to Guy's house in nearby Remecourt where he was joined by fellow waist-gunner Hobart Trigg.

Trigg baled out at about 2,000 feet and landed in a tree near Montiers (Oise) only about 300 yards from his burning aircraft. He was still trying to pull his parachute free when some people came running towards him. Trigg ran in the opposite direction, throwing his Mae West into a bush and hiding in a field of alfalfa (sic). A little while later, someone came crawling through the crop to shake him by the hand. Trigg's new friend pointed to a haystack and after discarding his heated suit, Trigg went to the stack where he waited for the Frenchman to join him. However, remembering the advice from his E&E lectures, Trigg wanted to lay low for the first twenty-four hours and besides, he didn't want to risk the Frenchman being a collaborator, so after filling his pockets with vegetables, and his water bottle from a stream, Trigg went on his way.

Trigg spent all the next day hiding, only coming out at dusk when he approached a group of men cutting clover. One man was suspicious and threatened him with a sickle, only mollified when Trigg opened his coveralls to reveal a t-shirt marked 'US Army Air Force'. Several of the group donated food and cigarettes before leaving (presumably to go home after their day's work) and Trigg carried on walking.

The following morning, Trigg met a farmer (again showing his t-shirt as means of identification) and that night was taken back to the man's home. An elderly lady there spoke to Trigg in German but not understanding a word, Trigg noted but dismissed the incident. Next day however, a group of 'tough looking' men arrived – obviously, Trigg's blond hair, blue eyes and regular replies of (what sounded to them like) 'Ya' aroused their suspicions. Fortunately, one the Frenchman understood enough English for Trigg to be able to explain himself. Trigg was then asked to write down the names of his crew and the answers were compared with a piece of paper the men had brought with them. When the two lists agreed, Trigg was driven next morning to Remecourt (Oise) where he joined his crewmate Edward Daly.

Next day, Gaston Legrand collected Trigg on his motorcycle and took him back to Clermont and later brought Daly by car. They stayed at the Fleury home on rue de Mouy and on 22 September, were joined by their bombardier James Bormuth and navigator Wendell McConnaha. Their pilot Arthur Vetter, radio-operator John Wagner and tail-gunner Warren Lush were also being sheltered locally (with Legrand on rue du Chatelier) and a few days later, they were joined by B-26 Cactus Jack pilot William Boren and his tail-gunner Francis Anderson.

On 9 October, Daly, Trigg, Bormuth and McConnaha were driven to Creil where they took a train to Paris. They went to an apartment where they were split up – Trigg and Daly being taken to an Englishwoman (married to a Frenchman) (Dora Rospape at 11 rue de 29 Juillet) and her three children, and where four other Americans (Ballinger, Owens, Bailey and Plasket) were already being sheltered. Trigg makes a point of saying that she lived across the road from Andree (Andree Lebegue of 205 rue Saint-Honore) (sister of Simone Besson – query) who was sheltering an American top-turret gunner – referred to earlier as Bob. Mme Rospape took them to Jeanette (Jeanne Rospape) (a cousin of Dora Rospape's husband, she ran a restaurant at 21 rue de Faubourg-Saint-Martin) where they joined Charles Hoover and Keith Murray – and were later joined by the other four Americans. On 19 October, Andree was arrested, along with the American gunner, and Jeannette moved them all to one of her hotels (sic).

Trigg and Daly seem to have lost contact with anyone connected with Bourgogne at about this point because next day, they were taken to a railway station. They met Bonnard (query) and Voinbeck (query spelling) of the maquis who took them to Joigny (Yonne) where they stayed overnight in Bonnard's home near the river. Next day, they were moved next door and that night moved again, this time to stay with rheumatoid couple named Bonneret – and supplied with food by farmer Maurice Cameau (of rue d'Epizy). Three days later, they were taken to stay with a gardener named Joseph who worked for a Parisian manufacturer named Wetter (query) and then a week later to a Belgian who had been a band-leader before the war. They also met an elderly lady who had lived in Americe for forty-five years. From 25 November to 7 December they stayed with Mme Varrey and her son Roger, who was a mechanic on the railways and involved in sabotage, at 54 Faubourg Saint Florentin. While they staying with Mme Varrey, they also met the Marechal brothers (query) with whom they later crossed the Pyrenees.

On 7 December, a schoolteacher (unnamed) (Marcel Pillin – query) from Bonnard (about 10 kms south-east of Joigny) took charge of them. Trigg cycled to nearby Beaumont where he stayed for three days with a man who ran a factory making shoe-nails before returning to Bonnard. He rejoined Daly and the two of them were taken about three kilometres south of the village to be sheltered by the cure, abbe Roger de Ternay, at Chichery. On 29 December, the schoolteacher drove them back to his home in Bonnard, where they stayed the night, before returning them once more to Mme Varrey in Joigny. Over the following two months they had various adventures that have little bearing on this story.

On about 2 March, Daly and Trigg were taken to Paris by a woman and a man they called Curly who led them to the home of one of his cousins, a violin-playing gendarme. That night, Curly and his girl took them to a railway station (presumably the Gare d'Austerlitz) where they joined three Englishmen (query) – they also knew that two Americans, Frank Mitchell and Charles Bronako (query) were on the same train (see later). They reached Bordeaux on 4 March and went to the home of Robert and Andree Delbur at 68 Cours de la Martinique. The Englishmen went on to Pau that afternoon and while Trigg and Daly stayed with the Delburs, Andree Delbur sent Mitchell and Bronako to stay with her brother-in-law (assume Raymond Delbur of 8 Place de Relais, Bordeaux).

On 30 March, Daly and Trigg were driven (in separate cars) to Pau and started walking that night. The following evening, they met Charters, Frakes and their party.

CHAPTER 57

Bleu et Jonquille to Bourgogne ...

"Typical of many small lines, Bleu et Jonquille (Blue and Pale Yellow) operated within a small area in and around the town of Châlons-sur-Marne (today Châlons-en-Champagne) in eastern France. It was formed, with no military or political axe to grind, by Maurice Rehheiser, a policeman in Châlons-sur-Marne.[1] In 1942 he enlisted the help of a number of police inspectors – Emile Bourges, Rene Bronne, Henri Herry, Robert Kister, Andre Loisy and Joseph Menou – and in time was able to form two other units outside the town, one at Champigneul, to the west, led by Jules Rieu (of Champigneul) and his father Alexandre, and the other at Togny-aux-Boeufs, to the south, with Denis Hollender in charge. At its peak Bleu et Jonquille, whose speciality was the preparation of false papers, could call on some ninety members to help evaders of all sorts, including airmen and Frenchmen trying to avoid the STO, forced labour in Germany.

Three airmen known to have been helped by this organisation – Flying Officer A.R. Fisher RCAF ; Flying Officer J.G.Y. Lavoir RCAF ; and Sergeant W.E. Fell RCAF – were from Halifax LK739 which, when some twenty minutes short of the target on the night of 20/21 January 1944 (Berlin), was hit by flak in its fuel tanks. Another burst caused more leakage as they were heading for home. With only ten minutes or so of fuel left the pilot, Flight Sergeant F.F. Reain RCAF, gave the order to bale out. All seven of the crew managed to do so, landing in the area of Tilloy-et-Bellay (Marne), 10 to 15 kms north-east of Châlons-sur-Marne.

Flying Officers Fisher and Lavoie independently of each other, worked their way to the west of Châlons-sur-Marne, and at Ambonnay (Marne) came into the hands of Bleu et Jonquille's Champigneul section. Sergeant Fell had reached Châlons by the afternoon of 22 January, but just before entering the town he 'saw some German soldiers on parade. I therefore turned back and walked across some fields. A girl who was coming towards me, stopped me and spoke to me. She only spoke a few words of English, but she told me

---

1   Born in Reims on 18 July 1910. (original note)

her people were Welsh, and as she seemed to know who I was, I asked her if she could help me.' She agreed, and as they were walking along together they were overtaken by a man on a bicycle. She stopped him, told him who Fell was, and the man took him away.[2]

After they had been collected by Bleu et Jonquille, Marcel Vangeluwe, a garage proprietor (of 2 rue St Lazare) in Châlons, drove the three airmen, and Maurice Rehheiser, Henri Egly and Rene Ruttloff, two more members of Maurice's group, to Epernay railway station on 4 February 1944. The six men went to Paris and on to Toulouse. On the recommendation of Andre Clement, a former member of the Tritant group in Châlons which had been shut down by the Germans, they went to the house of M. Linzeau, a veterinary surgeon living in Salies-du-Salat (Haute-Garonne), a short distance from the Pyrenees. There the airmen and their escorts parted company.

Taken to Spain, and on to Gibraltar, Fisher and Lavoie were flown back on the night of 1/2 May, with Fell returning four nights later."[3]

F/O Yves Lavoie RCAF was the bomb-aimer, F/O Alvin R Fisher RCAF the navigator, F/Sgt Frederick F E Reain the pilot and Sgt William E Fell the engineer of 428 Sqn Halifax LK739 which was returning from an aborted sortie to Berlin on the night of 20-21 January 1944. Whilst still over Germany, the aircraft was hit by flak which punctured at least one of their petrol tanks and with only ten minutes of fuel remaining, the aircraft was abandoned north-east of Chalons-sur-Marne.[4]

Yves Lavoie landed in a wood, possibly just north of La Cheppe (Champagne-Ardenne), and after hiding his parachute, walked for about two hours in pouring rain before settling down for the rest of the night. In the morning he walked to Tilloy-et-Ballay where he stopped at a house and was given some food. He wasn't allowed to stay because there were Germans in the area so Lavoie carried on to Somme-Vesle where his clothes were dried and he was given a bed for the night – Lavoie's fluent French making communication easier although it also made it harder to convince some of his helpers that he was actually an Allied airman. He left next day at about noon and then rested in a field near Saint Julien before carrying on to a house where he was again taken in for the night. Next day (23 January), he

---

2   Fell's report M.I.9/S/P.G. (-) 1907 in TNA file WO 208/3319. (original note)

3   Extract from the 2009 book 'RAF Evaders' by Oliver Clutton-Brock, published by Grub Street.

4   Two other crew from LK739 also evaded successfully: radio-operator Sgt Thomas W Banner crossed the Pyrenees with Bourgogne at the beginning of March (see earlier) and mid-upper gunner Sgt L R Fryer evaded to Switzerland – only tail-gunner Sgt W Wynveen RCAF was captured.

continued through Saint-Hilaire-le-Grand, Mourmelon and Vaudemange – deliberately avoiding Chalons-sur-Marne – to Ambonnay where he received help. On 4 February, he joined his navigator Alvin Fisher (and the others) at Epernay and their subsequent journey together was arranged.

Alvin Fisher landed somewhere east of Saint Etienne-au-Temple and set off, using his compass, first south and then west for about three hours before stopping to spend the rest of the night in a wood. Next morning, he found that he was about two miles from Chalons-sur-Marne and spent the day drying his clothes and removing the insignia from his uniform. That evening he went to a house on Chemin de Bouy where he was taken in by Mme Maxel and her son Pierre, given food and a bed for the night in a barn. Next morning, a man was brought to see him and Fisher stayed at the house for four days while his journey was arranged.

On 30 January, Fisher was taken by bicycle to a house outside Vraux (just north-west of Chalons) where he joined his flight engineer William Fell then on 2 February, Fisher was taken to stay with their host's brother, Noeillon Henri, in Vraux itself.[5]

William Fell landed about three kilometres south-east of Souain-Perthes-les-Hurlus and after hiding his parachute and flying gear, started walking. He stopped at the first house he found, some five hours later, where he was taken in, given a drink and his wounds were washed. He was told there were Germans nearby and the family could not help him further so after spending the rest of the night in a haystack, Fell carried on walking. He reached Chalons-sur-Marne the following afternoon but on seeing German soldiers parading, turned back to cross some fields where he was intercepted by a girl who recognised him as an evading airman. She (being of Welsh extraction) spoke some English and introduced Fell to a man named Andre who arranged his subsequent journey.

Andre was a railway engineer and Fell stayed overnight with him in his apartment about two miles west of Chalons. Next day, Andre contacted a neighbour named Maurice Rehheiser – who was the chief of police in Chalons – and Maurice took Fell back to his apartment, had Fell's photograph taken and gave him an ID card. While Fell was with Maurice, he was visited by a boy from Veaux named Ronny. Ronny was the step-brother (query) of Noeillon Henri, who was sheltering his navigator, Alvin Fisher.

---

5   For some reason, Fisher doesn't mention Reain in his report who says he joined Fisher at the home of Noeillon Henri (where he stayed for about eight days) while Fell was being sheltered nearby with M Henri's sister.

Fell met Fisher about a week later and a week after that, Fell joined Fisher, their pilot Frederick Reain, Maurice Rehheiser and two other Frenchmen when they left for Epernay. They went to a restaurant where they joined their bomb-aimer Yves Lavoie and Fell was with Lavoie and Fisher from that point.

Frederick Reain landed about 4 kilometres west of Tilloy-et-Bellay (about 15 kms east of Chalons) and after burying his parachute, walked to Somme-Vesle where he hid in a barn. Next morning (21 January), he declared himself to the owners of a nearby farmhouse – M et Mme Paul Arnold and their son Maurice – who contacted a local schoolteacher, who in turn, contacted a local man who spoke perfect English. This man turned out to be less than helpful and advised Reain to give himself up to the Germans. Reain and his helpers left immediately (Reain was later told that the man contacted the Gestapo) and Maurice Arnold took Reain to hide overnight in some nearby woods. The following morning (23 January), Reain approached a woodcutter, who although unable to help very much, did tell him where the local Germans were. Reain then set off for Marson where Joseph and Pierrette Belloiel sheltered him while Joseph contacted the organisation in Chalons and his journey was arranged.

A week later, Joseph Belloiel took Reain to Chalons by bicycle and delivered him to the home of a priest, who in turn took Reain to another house (name and address unknown but his host was thought to be an engineer and his wife spoke good English) where Reain was sheltered for eight days until the chief of police in Chalons, Maurice Rehheiser, took him to his house for the night. Next day, Reain was taken to stay with M et Mme Noeillon Henri in Vraux where he joined his navigator Alvin Fisher and learnt that M Henri's sister was sheltering his engineer William Fell nearby.

About eight days later, Reain, Fisher and Fell (along with three Frenchmen evading the STO – and police chief Maurice Rehheiser) were driven to Epernay where they joined their bomb-aimer Yves Lavoie in a restaurant and they were all taken by train to Paris, arriving there about an hour and a half later.

From the Gare de l'Est they went by Metro to the Gare d'Austerlitz where they took a very crowded overnight train (six of them sharing one seat) to Toulouse, arriving there at eleven o'clock the following morning (5 February). They had a meal in a restaurant before taking a train to Boussens (Haute-Garonne) then a bus to Salies-du-Salat from where they walked south to Mane. They slept in a hotel in Mane and in the morning, Lavoie and Maurice tried to find a guide. They were told to contact a negro veterinary surgeon (Arille Linzau) in Salies-du-Salat and so returned to Salies that afternoon.

The negro, who told them he had been an officer in the French navy at the beginning of the war, said he would send someone to interrogate them, and that evening four men came to their hotel room. The men told them that it was too dangerous for them to try and take the airmen over the mountains but they were prepared to hide them in the woods.

On 6 February, they (it's not clear if the Frenchmen were still with them) took a bus to La Bastide du Salat where they met a maquis man known as the 'chief cook' before winding up with a maquis group near Urau, where Lavoie, Reain, Fisher and Fell stayed for the rest of the month. On about 2 March, the maquis finally deciding they couldn't help after all so the airmen left for Toulouse where they had been told to look out for a man wearing a black hat and brown coat. Having located their contact, he told them that he belonged to an organisation called 'Escaped Prisoners of War' and arranged new ID cards for them. That evening, they left for Murat (query), where the group were split up to spend the night at various addresses before going on to Meillon (south-east of Pau) early the next morning. There was a five kilometre walk to the Chateau Frouard where they were sheltered by Roger and Andree Larromet who had a friend who said he could get them across the mountains. They stayed with the Larromets for about three weeks before being told they couldn't cross the mountains after all because of deep snow.

On about 25 March, the Larromets took Lavoie, Reain, Fisher and Fell to Pau where they stayed overnight with an elderly (sic) lady called Pauline[6] and were questioned by two girls, one English (Joan Moy-Thomas) and one American (Rosemary Maeght). They spent the next four nights at various addresses before returning to Pauline on the fifth night, after which they were put on a bus to Navarennx – where they were told to

---

6   Mme Pauline Helene Lignac (born January 1906) of 28 Blvd Barbanegre, Pau. This was not the first time that Pauline Lignac had helped evaders – she is credited with helping a total of sixteen men (WO208/5459) but the first ones that I know of were 2/Lt Dewey C Brown Jnr and T/Sgt Vern P Long from B-17 42-30147 Flak Dancer. They had been brought to Pau in August 1943 by an English-speaking professor who contacted a local cafe owner named Georges (arrested shortly afterwards following infiltration of his group by a German agent-provocateur) who took them to stay with Mme Lignac. They were sheltered with her for almost four weeks, Mme Lignac selling some of her furniture to raise the money to feed them, before being passed on to Joan Moy-Thomas and Rosemary Maeght who arranged transport to Bielle and their crossing of the Pyrenees in October 1943. Mme Lignac was recommended for a KMS.

go to the Hotel du Commerce (Mme Marthe Camdeborde). That evening, they were collected by a man with a car and driven for about an hour – their party now being nine – to a barn where two more men joined them. They set off at ten o'clock that evening and walked until about half past one in the morning when they stopped at a house for some milk and bread. They then carried on for another half an hour to a barn where they spent the rest of the night. They set off again the following evening, walking to another barn where they stayed for two nights, being joined there by another party of evaders, which included Robert Charters.

On 29 (query) March, they – Yves Lavoie, Alvin Fisher, Frederick Reain, William Fell – plus Robert Charters and his group of six – plus Edward Daly and Hobart Trigg – walked from nine o'clock in the evening until three the following morning then slept until six o'clock in the evening. After another meal, they walked on for several hours to the border, which they crossed in the early hours of 31 March (query), where their guides gave them directions to follow the river Minchate until they reached Ustarroz. The party split up at this point and the evaders found 'carabinieri' waiting for them at Ustarroz.

CHAPTER 58

Felton Luke and another John Carter connection

T/Sgt Felton R Luke was the radio-operator of B-24 42-63973 (389BG/564BS) (Schafer) which was on the way to Ludwigshaven on 30 December 1943. They had just crossed the French coast when they were hit by flak followed by fighters and the aircraft fell out of control and went into a dive. The bale-out order was given but pilot Richard Schafer managed to pull out of the dive and cancelled the order. The aircraft was then flown in circles for half an hour with engines #1 and #2 both running away before the bale-out order was renewed, leaving the aircraft to crash near Cambronne-les-Ribecourt (Oise).[1]

Luke landed about five miles south-east of Soissons and was helped immediately by a farmer who hid him for two days before taking him by bicycle to stay overnight with a M Cochay (nf) in Soissons. He was given civilian clothes and taken next day by train to Paris where he stayed with a gendarme named Jacques Bathiel (query – see below) in his apartment at 262 rue des Pyrenees.[2] On 12 January, a French pilot (5 ft 8 inches, about 160 lbs, black hair, balding at the front) who was apparently head of the local organisation, took Luke to stay with Mlle Paule Vastel at 39 rue Claude Bernard where he met Spitfire pilot F/Lt Hugh Parry.

Parry had been brought to Paris from Arnieres-sur-Iton the day before by an English girl called Nell and a French Secret Service agent known as Jean-Pierre (Jean-Pierre de la Hutiere). Parry understood that the chief of the organisation which was looking after him in Paris was a woman called Madeleine (Grador) and that her boss was an Englishman known as Julian (John Carter) who lived in Lyon. On 24 January, Parry was taken to stay with Jeanne Huet at 48 Avenue du President Wilson and on 7 February, Parry and Mme Huet were arrested.

---

1   Four other crew from 42-63973 also evaded successfully: navigator 2/Lt Morton B Shapiro was evacuated on the first Francois-Shelburn Bonaparte operation in January 1944, bombardier 1/Lt Robert V Krengle crossed the Pyrenees with the Francoise Dissard organisation in February 1944, and pilot 2/Lt Richard F Schafer and waist-gunner S/Sgt Paul F Dicken Snr were helped by the Chauny-Dromas organisation before being evacuated on Operation Bonaparte 4 in March.

2   262 rue des Pyrenees, Paris 20 is the IS9 Helper Awards address given for Brigadier de Police, Jean Bataillard

Luke was told about their arrest that same day by Dr Pierre (query) who was treating his injuries. He was also told (presumably by Paule Vastel) that they had been betrayed (along with Marguerite Schmitz) by a beautiful Russian girl, recently ejected from the organisation for having too many affairs with evaders.[3]

The 'beautiful Russian girl' was Mme Helene Gill (aka Nell aka Mme Antoine) (née Feodossief 12 May 1917 in Petrograd) of 12 rue Le Sueur, Paris XVI. Mme Gill was naturalised as a French citizen in 1936 but then became a British subject by marriage to Englishman James Charles William Gill (who was interned at La Grande Caserne, Saint Denis) and had a young son named Daniel. Nell is described by 2/Lt Sidney Casden as

"a very pretty, striking blonde … a flashy dresser who makes one the centre of attention when walking with her."

Mme Gill first became involved with helping evading airman in July 1943 when she took her young son Daniel (born March 1940) on holiday to Nogent-le-Rotrou (Eure et Loir). She was met on arrival by her friend, local schoolteacher Georges Lemourier, with the news that a British Halifax bomber had crashed nearby and one of the crew was being sheltered on a local farm. It seems that no-one knew what to do with him and it was hoped that Mme Gill (having an English husband) would be able to help. Mme Gill wrote to her husband at La Grande Caserne and eventually received a reply saying that the airman would be collected in a few days time. Meanwhile, Mme Gill met another of her friends at Nogent, Jacqueline Frelat (of 104 rue St Hilaire) who had been looking after the airman, Sgt Ivor Sansum. Mlle Frelat then went to Paris to contact a man she identifies only as Axel (Capt Richard d'Asniere) and returned with the news that a girl would come and collect Sansum and take to him to be sheltered in the little village of Mortree (Orne, Lower Normandy). Mme

---

3   Mme Jeanne Marie Huet (born June 1899 in Aurtenne, Belgium) of 48 Avenue President Wilson. (WO208/5451) Mlle Paule France Vastel (born September 1922 in Bawako, French Soudan) of 39 rue Claude Bernard, Paris V, whose occupation is given as law student, was arrested on the same day as Jeanne Huet. (WO208/5451)

Jeanne Huet and Paule Vastel were helpers with the John Carter organisation until Carter was arrested at Pamiers on 6 January 1944 – and then with reseau Francois-Shelburn. Parry reports seeing Jeanette Huet and Paule Vastel at Fresnes prison and that both women showed signs of extreme ill-treatment. I believe they were both held at Fresnes until liberated by the Allies in August …

Mme Huet's husband, daughter and housekeeper, Irma Manteau (all also credited to Francois-Shelburn) were arrested with her. Mme Irma Manteau (born Oct 1903 in Andenne, Belgium) was deported to Germany until liberated in April 1945. (WO208/5452)

Gill visited Sansum almost every day (she was the first person he had met in France who spoke English) until the girl called Carmen arrived. Mme Gill says that she had been wanting to help evading airmen for some time and took this opportunity to ask Carmen to introduce her to her chief. It then transpired that Carmen didn't speak any English, that this would be her first such trip and she was very nervous about it. It seems that Georges Lemourier and Jacqueline Frelat were not very impressed with Carmen and Mlle Frelat asked Mme Gill to go with Carmen when she took Sansum to Mortree – which she did.

After safely delivering Sansum, Mme Gill returned to continue her holiday at Nogent but in mid-August, Jacqueline Frelat visited Mme Gill at Nogent with the news that Axel (in Paris) had asked her if Mme Gill could take Sansum and two Americans (S/Sgts Willard Freeman and Charles Mankowitz, who were also being sheltered at Mortree) to a man named Julien in Lyon. On 19 August, Mme Gill joined Jacqueline Frelat and the three airmen at Le Mans station and went with them to Lyon via Tours, Bourges, St Florent (where they stayed on Axel's farm before crossing the demarcation line) and Montlucon. In Lyon, they went to Paul Bonnamour's house at 8 Ave Marechal Foch and that afternoon, met Annie (Mlle Anne Sabourault) and Julien (John Carter) in Annie's apartment at 284 rue Vendome – and Mme Gill joined the newly reforming John Carter organisation.

Two days after returning to Paris from her holiday at Nogent, Axel visited Mme Gill's apartment to say he would like to introduce her to a lady named Jeannette Huet. He wanted Mme Gill to be a courier, taking documents from Mme Huet to a M Jacques Dupuis of 5 rue d'Aumale, Paris IX. She was to be the contact between the two as Axel didn't want Mme Huet to meet M Dupuis. At their first meeting, Mme Huet told her that she knew a girl named Paule Vastel who worked for a man called Jean-Pierre Mouline. She said that Jean-Pierre travelled a lot in Normandy and Brittany where he knew a number of farmers who were sheltering evaders but didn't know how to pass them on. Mlle Vastel had spoken to her friend Mme Huet and now Mme Huet was asking on behalf of Jean-Pierre if Mme Gill could help. A meeting between Mme Gill and Jean-Pierre was arranged for the following morning at which he said that he would provide the addresses where airmen were being sheltered if Mme Gill could arrange to have them collected and brought to Paris. As a British subject, Mme Gill was required to report to a police station at regular intervals and her travelling restricted but Jean-Pierre provided her with false identity papers that would (if necessary) enable her to travel throughout the country.

Mme Gill had by then discovered that Jacques Dupuis was also working for Julien so she went to his insurance company office on rue d'Aumale to tell him about Jean-Pierre's offer of addresses. She explained that she couldn't bring them back by herself but Jacques told her that he knew a very suitable girl, energetic and full of courage, named Madeleine Grador.

In October, Mme Gill passed on some addresses for Jacques Dupuis to give to Mme Grador but unfortunately, by the time she got there, the airmen had already left. Mme Gill had one more address (in Normandy) and this time she asked Jacques Dupuis to see that the airman was delivered to Jeanne Huet's apartment. Mme Gill and Axel were waiting with Mme Huet when Madeleine Grador arrived (on 21 November) with T/Sgt Trafford L Curry. Mme Gill visited Curry at the apartment several times, translating between Curry (who hadn't spoken to anyone in English for nearly three months) and Mme Huet who didn't speak any English. This was the only time (and then for only five minutes) that Mme Gill ever saw Madeleine Grador. Mme Gill later delivered Curry (who knew her as Mme Nell) to Paul Bonnamour in Lyon.

On about 10 January, Mme Gill was sent to Evreux by Jean-Pierre de la Hutiere (known to Mme Gill as Jean-Pierre Mouline) to collect a British fighter pilot. F/Lt Hugh Parry had been seriously ill – hovering between life and death for the previous three months according to her account and only kept alive by the skill and dedication of his hostess (Renee Renaudin, whose name Mme Gill never knew). As they had been advised in advance that they would have to almost carry him, Jean-Pierre went with Mme Gill to collect Parry. Mme Gill describes Parry as looking extraordinarily thin, pale and weak and that he could hardly stand.

She says that Jeanne Huet's friend Paule Vastel had been begging to have an airman of her own and despite Jean-Pierre's own misgivings, he had finally agreed that Parry would be delivered to her. The journey to Paris was something of a trial and she describes the final climb to Paule Vastel's fifth-floor apartment as awful, with Parry exhausted and more dead than alive. Mme Gill left instructions that Parry was not to leave the apartment under any circumstances and said she would visit him. Next day (12 January), Jean-Pierre told her that another airman, this one an American, was due to arrive in Paris (with a guide) and since Paule Vastel's apartment at rue Claude Bernard was close to the station, they would take him (Felton

Luke) there. That was the last time that Mme Gill visited Paule Vastel's apartment, and the last time she saw Parry.

On Saturday 5 February, Jeanne Huet telephoned Mme Gill to tell her that Mme Schmitz had been taken to hospital (which she understood to mean arrested) and on the following Monday, Jacques Dupuis told her that Jeanne Huet's apartment had been raided that morning and that she and Hugh Parry (who had been moved there by Paule Vastel) had been captured. Believing that she would be arrested next, Mme Gill destroyed all evidence of her resistance activities and prepared to leave the city.

Nell attracted criticism from various French women, however despite accusations from Paule Vastel that (amongst other things) Nell worked for the Gestapo (and which Mlle Vastel later retracted in full), there is absolutely no evidence to suggest she was in any way responsible for the arrest of Hugh Parry and Jeanne Huet – nor of Mme Schmitz. Jacqueline Frelat declared in November 1944 that "Her conduct never gave any reason for rumours" and Richard d'Asniere confirmed that "Nothing had permitted to give rise to (sic) the slightest suspicions or charges." He concluded that Paule Vastel's accusations were nothing but "the play of feminine rivalry". This rivalry was probably not helped by the fact that Mme Gill, in addition to not being French, was the only one of the women who was fluent in English (as well as French, German and Russian) and so could talk directly to the airmen. Jean-Pierre de la Hutiere says (in an interview dated 11 July 1945) that it was Mlle Nell (Mme Gill) who did the best work while Mme Huet, although patriotic, did not have the least conception of elementary security – his interviewer also notes that he did not appear to have much use (sic) for Paule Vastel either.[4]

Marguerite Schmitz had been involved with helping evaders since July 1943, working with various organisations, including reseau Alsace (Gilbert Thibault) and John Carter, before joining reseau Francois in January 1944. She was arrested on 5 February in an early morning raid on her apartment at 87 rue Rochechouart, along with RAF Typhoon pilot F/Sgt Richard Aitken-Quack and a character known as Olaf (or Fred) who had been passed to her by Marie-Rose Zerling and claimed to be a Norwegian. Mme Schmitz believed that she had been denounced by an associate of her ex-husband Marcel Schnerb – himself arrested on 7 February. It was then the capture of Mary-Rose Zerling (aka Claudette) when she called at Mme Schmitz' apartment later that same day, that led to Jeanne Huet's arrest

---

4   NARA Gill.

after a notebook was found that mentioned the Pension Trocodero and the name Jeannette, as she was generally known.[5]

Because Jeanne Huet had Luke's details, a Dr Pierre (who was attending to Luke's injuries) immediately moved Luke from Paule Vastel's apartment to his own house. Four days later, Claude Charmet took him back to his home at 17 bis Avenue de Bel Air, Paris XII but because 'the Germans were on his trail' moved him next day to stay with a woman (unnamed) whose husband was a pilot in England. On 13 February, Claude Charmet moved Luke again, this time to stay with Joseph Marrocq, caretaker of the famous Hotel Lambert at 2 rue Saint-Louis-en-l'Ile, Paris IV.[6]

On 3 March, Joseph Marrocq took Luke to the railway station and handed him over to Claude Charmet and a woman (5 ft 4 inches tall, 110 lbs, long black hair, glasses) who took Claude and Luke to Bayonne. They were sheltered with friends of the woman guide and after one false start, taken by a relay of seven guides to cross into Spain on the afternoon of 7 March – where Luke was arrested and sent to Lecumberri.[7]

Note that with the break-up of the John Carter organisation following Carter's arrest in January, Luke would probably have been passed on to the Francois-Shelburn organisation for evacuation by MGB from Brittany – along with RAF evaders Hugh Parry and Richard Aitken-Quack. As it was, Luke was lucky to get away when he did.

---

5   Mme Marguerite Schmitz (born July 1888) of 87 rue Rochechouart, Paris IX, is credited with sheltering some twenty Allied personnel as well as helping another thirty. She was recommended for a KMC. (WO208/5453)

6   Luke is also thought to been helped at some stage by English-born Mme Gabrielle Maud Vassal (née Candler in 1880) of 2 Avenue Lamballe, Paris XVI. Mme Vassal was associated with Joseph Marroq, Claude Charmet and the Hotel Lambert.

7   Both Joseph Marrocq and Gabrielle Vassal are associated with ex-racing driver Rene Maurice Biolay of CDLL – and the route sounds like one of those used by the CDLL (*Ceux de la Liberation*) organisation ...

CHAPTER 59

The Girl in the Blue Beret – and two more evaders captured

On 1 April 1944, Sgt Thomas Maxwell, 2/Lt Bernard Rawlings, 2/Lt Dale Kinert, S/Sgt Elres Dowden, T/Sgt Stephen Rodowicz and S/Sgt Herbert Gebers left Paris for Montauban, Toulouse and Pau.

Sgt Thomas J Maxwell was the nineteen-year-old rear-gunner of 622 Sqn Lancaster LL828 (Thomson) which was damaged by flak over Stuttgart then hit again over Paris and the aircraft abandoned in the early hours of 16 March 1944 near Beauvais.[1]

Maxwell landed near Bazancourt, Oise (a few kilometres south from the rest of his crew) and spent the remainder of the night sheltering in a barn. Next day he started walking until approached by a young boy (Maertens) who took Maxwell to his home. That evening he was taken to Menerval where he stayed in a small barn (belonging to the poorest people he had ever encountered) until 22 March when he was collected by car and his journey arranged.[2]

The man in the car was known as 'M Philippe' (Philippe Lechavalier of La Champ de Course, Cuy-Saint-Fiacre – query) and he took Maxwell to a house at 9 rue Croquet du Bosc in Gournay-en-Bray (Seine-Maritime) where Maxwell stayed with an elderly language teacher named Mme Logan and her daughter Yvonne Logan, who was a doctor. On 31 March, M Philippe and a young girl took Maxwell by train to the Gare Saint Lazare in Paris. After a meal in a cafe opposite the station, Maxwell was taken to a priest's home just off the Avenue de l'Opera for the afternoon. Later he was taken to have his photograph taken and then, with two Americans (one of them presumably Clement Mezzanotte – see later) to gendarme Marcelin Villemont's home at 151 Boulevard Davout where Maxwell stayed until the following afternoon. Next day (1 April) Maxwell was taken by Metro

---

1   Three other crew from LL828 also evaded successfully: flight engineer Sgt Frank Harmsworth and wireless operator Sgt Peter Jezzard evaded together and crossed the western Pyrenees in April (meeting Maxwell at Lecumberri in Spain) – and bomb aimer F/Sgt Delbert B Hyde who was sheltered in the MI9 Mission Marathon camp at Freteval until liberated in September 1944.

2   Dominique Lecomte lists Medard Maertens at Bazancourt as helping Maxwell.

to the Gare d'Austerlitz from where two French guides took him and five Americans by train to Montauban, Toulouse and Pau.

2/Lt Bernard W Rawlings was the co-pilot of B-17 42-39786 GI Sheets (303BG/427BS) (Fowler) which was on the way to Frankfurt on 29 January 1944 when #3 engine began to fail and they dropped out of formation. They were attacked by fighters which destroyed the oxygen supply so the aircraft was taken down to low altitude, hiding in cloud cover until it cleared when they were attacked again. With the rudder controls shot away and several of the crew injured (one fatally), the aircraft was crash-landed in south-west Belgium.[3]

Rawlings was confident that they had landed in Belgium (rather than Germany) and local people soon confirmed it. He and his top-turret gunner T/Sgt Curtis Finley set off for the nearest woods where they prepared to stay the night but Finley was poorly clothed and concerned about exposure so he left. Next morning, Rawlings stayed in the wood until noon before setting off and approaching a farmhouse for some food and directions – he was given sandwiches and directed south towards the French border. He spent the night in another farmhouse south of Beaumont (Hainaut) and the following morning, a man showed him how to cross the border. Rawlings came out on a main road and soon found a sign to a town shown on his escape map. Early that afternoon, Rawlings noticed men watching him, smiling and laughing, and he realised that they knew who he was so he might as well declare himself. He was taken in, given food and, more importantly, a proper touring map of the area. After several more days of wandering, Rawlings was taken into a farmhouse where he was sheltered by Henri and Louise Gossiaux and daughter Marianne at their Ferme de Faviere while various plans were made for his return to England before he was finally taken to a place where his journey was arranged.

On 17 February, Rawlings was taken to Sinceny, a small village just south of Chauny, where he was lodged with Marcel Thierry and his wife Simone. That afternoon, he was joined by Dale Kinert.

---

3   The GI Sheets crew scattered and three others also managed to evade successfully: navigator 2/Lt Joseph C Thompson Jnr, waist-gunner S/Sgt Loren E Zimmer – who baled out just before the crash-landing – and ball-turret gunner S/Sgt Richard Arrington, were sheltered in Belgium until liberated. Top-turret gunner T/Sgt Curtis E Finley was helped by the Francoise Dissard organisation but was one of several evaders captured by a German patrol in the Pyrenees near Bagneres-de-Luchon in April 1944. Pilot 2/Lt James F Fowler and radio-operator T/Sgt Donald J Dunwiddie were captured in Lille on 13 May 1944. More details about the last flight of G I Sheets can be found in the 'Fowler's Fate' chapter of the 1999 Special Revised Edition of 'Half a Wing, Three Engines and a Prayer' by Brian D O'Neill, published by McGraw-Hill.

2/Lt Dale W Kinert was the navigator of B-17 42-40032 (92BG/327BS) (Lehner) which was the way to Frankfurt on 8 February 1944 when it was attacked by fighters and abandoned to crash near Vailly-sur-Aisne (Picardy). Kinert was the only one of the crew to evade successfully.

Kinert baled out at about 24,000 feet and whilst he intended to make a delayed jump as advised, was also afraid of blacking out through lack of oxygen. He compromised slightly by counting to twelve before pulling the rip-cord and then spent the next fifteen minutes or so floating down, to land in a tree. Unable to disentangle his parachute from the tree, Kinert left the immediate area as quickly as possible, walking for the rest of the day (still in his heated, one-piece, blue 'bunny' suit) until nightfall when he approached a house where he was welcomed, taken in, fed, given civilian clothes and a bed for the night. Next day, he was taken to a place where his journey was arranged.

Kinnert was taken by train to Soissons, by bus to Compiegne then train to La Ferte and on to St Quentin where he stayed in a small shop for three days (with the family Saillit or Gaillit – query) (Amede Salaunic – query), then with Mlle Paulette Maillet at 55 rue des Patriotes, St Quentin ... Ms Marie Bonny ... school for girls ... until 17 February, when he was taken to Sinceny and joined Barney Rawlings.[4]

Rawlings and Kinert stayed with the Thierry family at Sinceny until the end of March when they were told they would be leaving next day for Spain. Marcel Thierry didn't have any details of their route but he was sure they would go through Paris and his instructions were to take them to Chauny where he was to hand them over to some organisation people at the station. After a short, early morning cycle ride, the two airmen were introduced to a trim, well-dressed man with a small moustache. He was about 45 years old, spoke good English and had two more American evaders with him. The guide explained that they would travel together as a group of deaf mutes from an institution for the handicapped, who had been to Chauny to be assessed for their suitability for war-work. Rawlings never knew the names of the other two Americans but he mentally christened them as Stan and Ollie, after the film comedians. Note that Rawlings makes no mention of Elres Dowden see below.

---

4   The Appendix Cs of Rawlings' and Kinert's reports are almost illegible scribbles by their interviewer (and Kinert's report ends when he joined Rawlings) but fortunately, Barney Rawlings wrote a book about his adventures called 'Off We Went (Into the Wild Blue Yonder)'. The book was printed by Morgan Printers of North Carolina in 1994 and is not easily available but Barney's daughter-in-law Bobbie Ann Mason very kindly sent me copy to use for this story.

They took the train to Paris and at the Gare du Nord, their guide gave them Metro tickets and told them to follow a girl in a blue beret. As soon as the girl saw they were looking at her, she led them to the Metro station and onto a train.[5] She took them to Saint-Mande and they dutifully followed her to the second floor of a large grey stone apartment building. The girl was Michele Moet and inside one of the apartments, they met her parents, Gerard and Genevieve and were later joined by their guide from the train. That evening, Rawlings was taken to another apartment where he shared with an injured RAF gunner and a young organisation member who didn't speak any English. Next morning, Rawlings was returned to the Moet apartment where he rejoined Kinert, Stan and Ollie for breakfast. Later that morning, Michele Moet took all four Americans back into Paris to have their photographs taken for new ID cards. She led them to the Tuileries Gardens and then took them one by one to have their pictures taken at an automated machine in the Louvre before returning them to Saint-Mande. That evening, Rawlings was taken to stay the night with gendarme Gabriel Bouyer at 87 rue Haxo. Next morning, he was taken back to the Moet apartment for the day and that evening, the four Americans were taken to the Gare d'Austerlitz where they met the man who would take them by train to the Pyrenees.

S/Sgt Elres D Dowden was a waist-gunner on B-17 42-3357 Immortal Lady (482BG/813BS) (Gold) and the third member of the crew to evade successfully after the aircraft was abandoned at high altitude to crash near Chevincourt (Oise) on 8 February 1944. Radio-operator T/Sgt Stephen Rodowicz and waist-gunner S/Sgt Herbert Gebers almost made it.

Dowden was helped soon after landing and his journey was arranged. Charles, a Belgian wood-cutter's son, took him to Longueil-Annel (just north-east of Compiegne) where he stayed for nine days with Etienne Demonceaux, his wife and thirteen-year-old daughter. He was helped by Charles Meyer before being taken to Albert's (query) house in Chevincourt and met his co-pilot James Clarendon, who says that Dowden was one of the airmen with him when they were taken to an organisation member named Norbert in Elincourt-Sainte-Marguerite.[6]

---

5   It was Rawlings' recollection of this brief encounter with Michele Moet that inspired his daughter-in-law Bobbie Ann Mason to write her 2012 novel 'The Girl in the Blue Beret' (published by Random House) which is dedicated to Michele Agniel (née Moet).

6   Dowden's report is very hard to read so this part of the story is put together from snippets and other sources. I've not found Charles Meyer in the IS9 Helper List but there is a Paul Meyer of Longueil-Annel. In addition to Etienne Demonceaux of Longueil-Annel, Dominique Lecomte lists Dowden's helpers in Oise as Louis Duchatelet, Andre Lessertisseur and Norbert and Simone Hilger (of rue du Casquet) in Chevincourt, and Marcel Merlier of Crisolles.

On 24 February, Dowden, James Clarendon, their radio-operator Stephen Rodowicz, waist-gunner Herbert Gebers and 2/Lt John Kupsick were taken to Chauny by Albert's son (Clarendon says by Norbert and Martine while Dominique Lecomte says that Marcel Merlier drove them there in his lorry). Dowden was sheltered with Gaston Debrie on his farm at Amigny-Rouy (east of Chauny) for two weeks before being moved to another farm at Champs with Victor Maiger (query spelling) for a further nineteen days. On 29 March, a bald-headed man took Dowden back to Chauny and Albert Logeon took him to Paris, along with Bernard Rawlings, Dale Kinert, Stephen Rodowicz and Herbert Gebers.

They were met by Jean Carbonnet and Michele Moet and the group were split into two parties to be taken to the Moet apartment in Saint-Mande where they met the family – father Gerard, mother Genevieve and young Jean-Marie – and were given new ID cards. Dowden, Rodowicz and Gebers stayed two nights at the Moet apartment – while Rawlings and Kinert stayed elsewhere – before Michele Moet took them to the Gare d'Austerlitz where they were put on a train for Toulouse.[7]

Rawlings says (in his book, page 169 on) that from Paris, they were a group of six Americans (Maxwell was actually from Northern Ireland but Rawlings wasn't to know that) and their guide – a slim, academic man of about 30 – had told him they would change trains at Montauban and that their destination was Oloron (Oloron-Sainte-Marie) at the base of the Pyrenees. He also told Rawlings that if they became separated, they should meet in front of the Church of Saint Croix in Oloron at noon where they would be collected by someone from the Resistance. When they stopped at Montauban (Rawlings doesn't mention Toulouse at all but this was actually at Toulouse), they found their train to Oloron (sic) had been delayed by two hours and so settled down in the station waiting room. Suddenly, a dozen men in civilian clothing 'swarmed' into the station and began demanding to see identification cards. Rawlings was asked his name, age and address and was able to answer in his newly acquired French, which apparently satisfied his questioner (suggesting he may have been German rather than French – or was he only pretending) and Kinert was saved from further scrutiny by a shout from the men questioning two of the other Americans (Stan and Ollie) who found Stan's dog-tags hidden in his shoe. Bizarrely, Stan was then told to put his shoe back on and the agents dispersed, leaving

<hr>

7   Michele Agniel told me (in 2015) that Rodowicz and Gebers were kept at the Moet apartment because they were thought to be particularly indiscreet.

only the man who had questioned Rawlings, sitting reading a newspaper. Rawlings concluded that the agents were more interested in capturing their guide than stray airmen evaders and were hoping that Stan would lead them to him. Sure enough, when the train arrived, the agent followed Stan and Ollie onto the train. Rawlings and Kinert made sure they sat separately from one another and in a different carriage to their guide but Stan soon approached Rawlings in full view of the agent – so he was confirmed as an evader as well – and then Dale Kinert joined Rawlings, again in full view of the enemy agent. Rawlings and Kinert discussed the situation and decided they had to get off the train early rather than lead the agents (whoever they were) to their final destination. Rawlings had a map that suggested the train might stop about ten miles before Oloron, which it did, and then as it was leaving the station, Rawlings and Kinert walked to the end of their carriage and jumped off. They spent the rest of the night walking the final ten miles to Oloron (sic) and after some delay, duly made contact with the organisation there and were passed on to a man they called Paul. Rawlings was told that their guide had arrived safely (and since returned to Paris) but two Americans (Stan and Ollie) had wandered around Pau for some time before being captured.[8]

After a night at Oloron (sic), Rawlings and Kinert were taken by gazogene bus some twelve miles further south where they were passed on to their mountain guide. They were soon joined by another guide and three more people (thought to be civilian refugees) to be taken across the mountains. The journey took three nights and at about three o'clock in the morning of the third night (6 April) they reached the final descent to Spain. Almost needless to say, the group were soon arrested by the Guardia Civil who took them to the village of Ustarroz and next day, to Isaba.

Rawlings says Oloron but he and Kinert were on a train to Pau. It's possible that Rawlings' guide had pointed out Oloron on the map as being on the way to Spain rather than where the train would take them. Tom Maxwell (who spotted some of the other evaders on the train – four or five nervous people in all sorts of weird clothes – but did not travel with them) was told that if anything went wrong, they were to meet at l'Eglise Saint-Jacques [at 8 rue Bernadotte] near by the Palais de Justice in Pau at noon. On leaving Pau station, Maxwell and Dowden avoided the ticket barrier

---

8   Michele Agniel told me that she later saw Rodowicz and Gebers at Fresnes where, despite their earlier indiscretions, she describes them as '*impertubables*' and says they had not spoken a word (about their helpers).

and spent the rest of that night sleeping out. They went to the church the next day and duly made made contact with the local organisation.

Dowden says that they were questioned at Toulouse – which is how Rodowicz and Gebers were caught – and that when they got on the train for Pau, they believed they were being followed and so made sure they avoided any further contact with their guide. Somehow, their guide had got word to Dowden that if they became separated, he was to go to the Hotel (sic) St Jacques.

Maxwell (who says they had two guides from Paris) reports that they were questioned and searched at Toulouse station and followed on the train to Pau after one of the Americans responded to a question put to him in English. Although the rest of the party (Maxwell doesn't mention losing Rawlings and Kinert) managed to shake off their pursuers in Pau, two of the Americans (Rodowicz and Gebers) were captured.

After spending their first night in Pau sleeping in a park, Dowden and Maxwell went to the rendezvous point at l'Eglise Saint-Jacques. Dowden says that their guide took them to a hill where he was collected by a blonde girl who took him (at least) to stay with Leon van de Poele on rue Saint-Jammes. Four days later, Dowden was taken to the bus station by a local guide who passed him and Tom Maxwell (who was helped in Pau by Gerard Hourquet and his family although Maxwell didn't sleep there) over to an auburn-haired woman. They were taken by taxi to a little town where they collected their two mountain guides and joined James Williams, Charles Screws, a Belgian and a Frenchman. Their guides left them about 15 kilometres before Orbaiceta where (on 8 April) the evaders were arrested and two days later, taken to Pamplona – and later Lecumberri, where Maxwell met his crewmates, Sgts Frank Harmsworth and Peter Jezzard.

CHAPTER 60

4 April 1944

On 4 April 1944, F/O Harry Yarwood, F/Sgt Stephen Bulmer, 2/Lt James Williams and 2/Lt Charles Screws left Paris for Toulouse and Pau with their guides, Pierre Le Berre and Genevieve Crosson.

F/O Harry C Yarwood and F/Sgt Stephen T Bulmer were the navigator and rear gunner of 90 Sqn Stirling EH906 (French) which was an SOE mission to France on the night of 4-5 March 1944 when they were hit by flak from Avord aerodrome (near Bourges, Centre) which set fire to the port-outer engine. They were at low altitude when they were hit and the aircraft abandoned and although six of the crew managed to bale out safely, the pilot F/Lt Cyril V French, was killed when the aircraft crashed shortly afterwards.[1]

Yarwood walked until about three o'clock in the morning when he reached the outskirts of Torteron (about 15 kms west of Nevers) where he spent the rest of the night in a barn. In the morning, Yarwood declared himself to a man from a nearby cottage who invited him in and gave him some food – he also called another man (M Pabio) who later took Yarwood to meet a man who could speak English – and Yarwood's journey was arranged.

M Pabio (query) took Yarwood to a house called La Garenne where he met Hubert Pernot, a retired professor of Greek at the Paris (Sorbonne) University, his Dutch wife Nicolette and their daughter Helene (aged 28, 5 ft 3 inches tall, very blonde, aquiline nose) who was a member of a resistance organisation.[2] Helene questioned Yarwood and examined his clothes, accidently destroying three of the photographs he had stitched into the lining of his tunic. He was given civilian clothes and he cut down his escape boots.[3]

---

1   EH906 mid-upper gunner F/Sgt James E G Buchanan also evaded successfully, living and working with the maquis until liberated. Wireless operator F/Sgt Donald A Farrington evaded until captured on 11 June 1944 – both he and Buchanan were amongst the 23 Allied airmen who fought alongside the maquis at the battle of Mont Mouchet in June 1944.

2   Hubert Octave Celestin Pernot (born August 1870) and his daughter Helene Henriette Pernot (aka Lenio) (born Sept 1907 at Fontenay-sous-Bois) were arrested (details unknown) and deported. Helene Pernot died at Ravensbruck in Feb/Mar 1945. Hubert Pernot died in 1946. (IS9 Helper Files & internet)

3   RAF 'escape boots' were black leather walking shoes with discardable, sheepskin-lined leggings attached. There was a small knife concealed inside the right boot to enable the removal of the leggings.

On 5 March, Helene Pernot took Yarwood by bicycle (preceded by the local doctor and chief of police in a car) to Nevers where they stayed for a few hours with a Frenchwoman (married to an American) named Renee Hart in a house opposite the station, at 13 rue Jeanne d'Arc, before Helene took Yarwood to Paris. She led Yarwood to the fourth-floor apartment of M et Mme Francois Vignal (relatives of the Pernots) at 2 rue Dorian, Paris III. Yarwood couldn't stay there because they had young children so he was taken upstairs to stay temporarily with two 'maiden ladies', Mlles Lucille (aged about 70) and Madeleine Pierrard (aged about 55) who lived on the sixth floor. On 7 March, Francois Vignal brought Andre Gilbert (a fifty-year-old Belgian, about 5 ft 4 inches tall with a fresh complexion and thin white hair) to visit and next day Yarwood was taken stay with M Gilbert and his wife at 3 rue Lentonnet, Paris IX. On 12 March, Yarwood was joined by his rear-gunner Stephen Bulmer.

Bulmer landed in a field, buried his Mae West and parachute and set off walking east, using the stars as a guide. After about six kilometres he came to a wood where he hid for the rest of the night and all the following day, living off his aids box. The following evening, Bulmer walked across country for several hours until he found a farm where he spent the rest of the night in a haystack. Next day, he declared himself to a local man who gave him some food and advised Bulmer to head for the little village of Laverdines (about 12 kms west of Torteron). He reached the outskirts of Laverdines that afternoon and declared himself to a farmer who took him in immediately and gave him a meal – he also invited several friends around to meet the airman. Bulmer spent that night and all the next day and night at the farm until being taken (on 8 March) to stay with Jean Sivioreck on his farm near Le Ringard. The following day, M Sivioreck's daughter Christianne contacted a member of an organisation and arranged to meet a man from Nerondes.

On 10 March, the man from Nerondes took Bulmer to a chateau at Nerondes where the owner (a tall, dark man, aged about 40, spoke good English – a big land-owner who said he had served with a British Guards unit earlier in the war – name unknown) (Vicomte Alain de Gourcuff at Chalet de la Niche – query) claimed he had fifteen British Secret Service agents in his house, though Bulmer did not see any of them. Next day, Bulmer was taken by car to Nevers, collecting Mlle Helene Pernot (who had helped and sheltered his navigator Harry Yarwood) on the way and she took Bulmer by train to Paris.

Bulmer spent one night in a block of flats at 2 rue Dorian and next day, was taken to stay with Andre Gilbert at 3 rue Lentonnet where he joined Yarwood – and from here their stories are the same.

Andre Gilbert owned a large printing works and he arranged to have two of his employees come and take photographs of Yarwood and Bulmer for new ID cards. They were also visited by a M Bigaud (about 55 years old, 5 ft 9 inches tall, with white hair, grey moustache, aquiline features) (Pierre Auguste Alfred Bigaud of 12 rue Royer Collard, Paris V – query), a glove manufacturer and organisation member.

On 30 March, Francois Vignal (from rue Dorion) and a young lady took Yarwood and Bulmer to a cafe where they were handed over to a Red Cross nurse. Shortly afterwards, she passed them on to Johnny (about 23 years old, 5 ft 5 inches tall, with long dark, curly hair, spoke English) (Jean-Louis Kervevant). They were joined by a young woman and taken to a flat where they stayed the night. Next day, Johnny took them to a flat on the sixth floor of a large block near the Gare d'Austerlitz where they stayed with Paul and Olga Christol at 4 rue Edouard Quenu. They were visited by Dorothy Tartier and Charles Herring, an Associated Press correspondent who was under strict surveillance by the police, who took their personal details that he said would be sent to London by wireless.

On 4 April, Mme Christol took them to the Gare d'Austerlitz where they met Johnny who handed them over to two guides, Pierre and Jacqueline (Pierre Le Berre and Genevieve Crosson), who took them by train to Pau in a party with James Williams, Charles Screws and two Frenchmen.

2/Lt James Williams was the navigator of B-17 42-37984 (92BG/326BS) (Shevchik) which was on the way to Frankfurt on 8 February 1944 when they were attacked by fighters which set fire to the #2 engine. Shortly after that the bale-out was given and the aircraft abandoned to crash near Catheux (Oise).[4]

Williams landed somewhere south of Poix and walked south-east for four days until 12 February when he asked a young boy to row him across the river Seine. The boy called his mother who called her husband Jacques (who spoke some English) to interrogate Williams. Once he was satisfied that Williams was genuine, Jacques took him to the home of an unemployed butcher where Williams stayed over the weekend. On 15 February, Jacques

---

4   42-37984 bombardier 2/Lt Donald J Periolat was captured (details unknown) but the other eight crew also evaded successfully: six men were evacuated by RN MGB from the beach near Plouha in March by the Francois-Shelburn organisation, radio-operator S/Sgt Robert E Sidders was sheltered in France until liberated at Freteval, and tail-gunner Sgt Francis F Higgins with Bourgogne – see later.

took Williams to Paris and handed him over to a restaurant owner called Jacques de la Lune. Williams stayed two (or six) weeks with Leon Prost at 66 rue de Levis (Paris XVII) eating at Jacque de la Lune's restaurant. During this time Jacques de la Lune took Williams to visit S/Sgt Clement Mezzanotte who was staying with cafe owner and former boxing champion Victor Robert at 31 Chemin des Laitieres, Soissy-sous-Montmorency. He was also visited at the restaurant by Alice Laville who supplied Williams with books and cigarettes. On 29 March, Mezzenotte and Charles Screws were brought to the restaurant and Williams was moved to a fire station where he stayed with the adjutant. On 1 April, Williams, Mezzanotte and Screws were taken to the apartment of a woman doctor (about forty years old, blonde, chain-smoker, spoke English) who lectured them on security before handing them over to a young man (about 25 years old, short, with curly brown hair, spoke English) who took Williams and Screws to gendarme Gabriel Bouyer at 87 rue Haxo – and Mezzanotte to stay with gendarme Marcelin Villemont.

2/Lt Charles B Screws was returning from escorting B-17s and B-24s bound for Frankfurt and approaching the French coast on 29 January 1944 when his P-47 42-75417 (361FG/374FS) was hit by flak. Believing that he wouldn't be able to get across the Channel to England, Screws reversed course and headed inland for about twenty minutes before landing wheels up in a ploughed field roughly half way between the Picardy villages of Etalon and Sept-Fours.

Screws hid in a patch of woods until nightfall before approaching a farmhouse on the outskirts of Curchy. He was soon helped and sheltered in a barn by the d'Hautefeuille family. On 31 January, Elizabeth d'Hautefeuille took Screws by train to Paris where he stayed in an empty apartment near the Opera Metro belonging to one of the d'Hautefeuille's cousins while another cousin tried to contact an organisation. On 8 February, a woman (black hair, slightly freckled face) claiming to be the head of an organisation (since her husband had been arrested) visited and told Screws that the snow was too deep to consider crossing the Pyrenees for the time being. On 8 February, a brunette lady (about 5 ft 6 inches tall, never wore a hat, always wore a kerchief fastened with a broach) moved him to Clichy, stopping off at a cathedral on the way and meeting Christine (head of the another organisation) and her right-hand man (deep set eyes, high forehead, curly hair). Screws was lodged with an elderly man named Andre Bonnard (who worked at an electric wire factory) and his wife Marie at 97 rue Henri

Barbusse, Clichy. Some days later Screws was told that Christine had been arrested – as a de Gaullist rather than for helping evaders.

At the end of March, Screws was taken to stay with Victor Robert in Soissy-sous-Montmorency, who was also sheltering Clement Mezzanotte (not exactly – see Mezzanotte report). After two or three nights, Screws and Mezzanotte went out to meet James Williams – who was with a group of firemen – and then to a cafe where two Englishmen (query) joined them. They were turned over to a short man and a woman doctor who took them the home of gendarme Gabriel Bouyer at 87 rue Haxo where Screws and Williams stayed while Mezzanotte was taken to stay with Marcelin Villemont. On 4 April, the same young man who had brought them to rue Haxo, took Williams and Screws to the Gare d'Austerlitz where he turned them over to a young French couple (the man was about 21 years old, small with black hair and wearing horn-rimmed glasses – the woman was about 19 years old) who took them – along with Yarwood, Bulmer and two Frenchmen – by overnight train to Montauban.

They arrived at Montauban at about one o'clock in the afternoon of 5 April and were taken to a park until it was time to get their connection to Toulouse. From there they went on to Pau where they stayed overnight with Mme Chazal at her Hotel Chazal at 7 rue Henri IV.

The following afternoon, Williams and Screws left Pau, accompanied by a guide. They were taken to a taxi where a blonde woman was waiting with the driver who took them to a village south of Oloron where the two Americans spent the night with a one-armed mountain guide. Next day they were joined by Thomas Maxwell, Elres Dowden, an Irishman, a Belgian and a man who was half French and half English (sic). They set off with their guide at noon and after two hours picked up another guide. They walked all night and the following morning, finally crossing the frontier at two-thirty in the afternoon of the next day (8 April). Their guides left them at the border after giving directions to a certain farmhouse but the party were arrested before they could get there. Next day, they were taken to Orbaiceta for two nights before being transferred to Pamplona.

Shortly after Williams and Screws left, two Frenchmen took Yarwood and Bulmer by bus to Navarennx where they went to the Hotel du Commerce (Mme Marthe Camdeborde) and were joined there by a member of the organisation. At ten o'clock that evening, they left by car with a guide and were driven for about an hour to the foothills. They started walking immediately, continuing until three o'clock in the morning when they stopped at a farm and were given food. Yarwood and Bulmer left the farm again at five, accompanied by the farmer, a guide and a man called Charles (alias Felix Lechat) who travelled all the way with them to Spain and who they saw again in Gibraltar. They eventually reached a barn where they changed guides and then carried on walking until three o'clock the next morning when they were handed over to two more guides. They carried on to another farm where they were fed and slept in another barn. At three o'clock that afternoon they set off with the farmer as guide until the top of the mountain where they were joined by yet another guide – this one with a large moustache and a small white dog. They crossed the frontier at 8 o'clock in the morning of 9 April and shortly afterwards, after pointing out the way, their guides left them and headed back to France. At the foot of the mountain they were arrested by two Spanish policemen who gave them a meal before taking them to Ustarroz where they were searched and their penknives removed.

CHAPTER 61

Balfe to Bourgogne – plus three

By the late spring of 1944, the Bourgogne organisation had a fairly well practised routine so when Joe Balfe and Benjamin Lefebvre brought a group of eleven men from Hornoy (Somme) to Paris on 5 April, they were only sheltered for a week in the capital before being moved on towards the Pyrenees.[1]

The ten of the eleven men from Amiens were airmen: F/Lt Joseph Oliver, F/Sgt Harry Williams, 2/Lt Howard Mays, S/Sgt Milton Mills, T/Sgt Kenneth Morrison, 2/Lt Merlyn Rutherford, T/Sgt John Landers, Sgt Stanley Sokolowski, Sgt Wilson Jones and 2/Lt Frederick Shecter. The eleventh man was believed to be a British Intelligence Officer and was known to the airmen as either Maurice Leslie or Peter Mason.[2]

F/Lt Joseph G Oliver and F/Sgt Harry Williams were the pilot and navigator of 613 Sqn Mosquito LR290 on a raid to a V1 rocket site near Bouttencourt (Somme) on 14 January 1944. They must have been too close to the preceding aircraft because they were brought down by the exploding bombs and had to force-land near Saint-Remy-Boscrocourt (Seine-Maritime).

Oliver and Williams were helped almost immediately and sheltered overnight in a barn near St Remy before being moved south of the village to a farm at Petit Gomard. Next day, four members of a local sabotage group arrived and took them to stay with the leader of their group, Aime Fizelier, in his farmhouse at Baromesnil. It was this group who were in touch with Joe Balfe and on about 22 January, three of the group delivered Oliver and Williams to Joe at the Hotel de France in Hornoy. Joe promptly sent to them to stay with Adrian Thermonir at Linchoux, Hallivillers for about ten days until Joe took them to Amiens, where they

---

1   Benjamin Lefebvre (born August 1900) garage proprietor, is credited with sheltering at least twenty-five evaders in his home at 71 rue de la Demie-Lune, Amiens. He was recommended for a KMC. (WO208/5452)

2   The name Peter Mason is included on the IS9 French Helper List – along with the notation "Paris – no trace". It seems likely that 'Peter Mason' was Pierre Maroger, making his way out of France yet again.

388

(and so many others) were sheltered by Mme Vignon on rue Vulfran-Warme.[3]

2/Lt Howard J Mays Jnr was the co-pilot of B-17 42-3185 Queen Bee (94BG/333BS) (Nienaber) on a mission to Paris on 26 November 1943. Overcast prevented the release of bombs and as they were leaving the target area, they were hit by flak which stopped #1 and #3 engines. As they fell out of formation, they were attacked by fighters and the aircraft was abandoned to crash near Foucarmont (Seine-Maritime).[4]

Mays landed near Villars-sous-Foucarmont and was sheltered a few miles south at Nesle-Hodeng with Roger and Madeleine Cressent[5] until 11 December when he was moved to Hornoy and the Joe Balfe organisation. Mays was sheltered in and around Amiens until 5 April 1944.

S/Sgt Milton J Mills Jnr was the radio-operator of B-17 42-29963 Judy (379BG/527BS) (Camp) which was on the way to Ludwigshaven on 30 December 1943 when they were hit by flak which damaged the #1 engine. Unable to stay in formation they turned back for England and were approaching Paris when they were attacked by fighters and the aircraft was abandoned to crash at Ully-Saint-Georges, south of Beauvais.[6]

Mills landed between Montataire and Gouvieux was sheltered for two days in a farmhouse with the Stoppin (Stopin – query) family in the hamlet of Chateaurouge. While he was there, Dr Charles Andrieu came from Neuilly-en-Thelle and extracted a piece of shrapnel from his thigh. Two days later, an Italian named Innocente Lauro took Mills to his home on rue de Boran in Gouvieux. On 27 January, Edmund Bourge came from Creil to take Mills to Montataire where he stayed with Bourge's mother-in-law,

---

3   Mme Jeanne Vignon-Tellier (born Amiens 5 September 1883) of 137 rue Vulfran-Warme in Amiens, sheltered at least twenty-five evaders at her home, some for several months. Mme Jeanne Vignon was awarded a KMC. (WO208/5452) She is described by Howard Mays as an elderly lady with a son who was MIA fighting the Japanese in Indo-China. Her neighbours, Mme Renee Bochet at 135 rue Vulfran-Warme and M Louis Margage at 138 are also listed in the IS9 Helper files ...

4   Queen Bee ball-turret gunner Sgt Alva S Daniels also evaded successfully, sheltered by Romane de Kimpe on his farm at Coppegueulle par Aumale until liberated on 1 September 1944. Navigator 2/Lt Jacques Keshishian and TTG Sgt Norman M Stephens were captured on 17 December 1943 at l'Eglise de Pantin in Paris (see earlier).

5   Roger Cressent (born March 1911) and his wife Madeleine (born January 1913) are credited with feeding, sheltering and providing clothing for some thirty-five evaders. Both were recommmended for KMCs. (WO208/5454)

6   Three other Judy crew also evaded successfully: bombardier 2/Lt Edward J Donaldson and waist-gunner Sgt Neelan B Parker were evacuated by MGB 503 on the Francois-Shelburn Operation Bonaparte 3 in March – and waist-gunner Sgt Douglas J Farr who was also helped by Bourgogne and crossed the Pyrenees from Pau at the end of January – see earlier.

Mme Marie Dorez on rue de Conde, and joined Kenneth Morrison from Destiny's Tot.[7]

T/Sgt Kenneth A Morrison was the top-turret gunner of B-17 42-30674 Destiny's Tot (95BG/336BS) (Smith) which was approaching Ludwigshaven on 30 December 1943 when they were hit by flak which badly damaged the rudder. As they were leaving, they lost #4 engine and began to drop out of formation. They were hit by more flak over France and then attacked by fighters. The aircraft caught fire and was abandoned to crash at Campeny, near Saint-Just-en-Chaussee (Oise).[8]

Morrison was picked up by the organisation in Saint-Just-en-Chaussee (as were the other six evaders from his crew) and sheltered in Montataire, where he was joined by Milton Mills. On 4 February, Morrison and Mills were passed on to the Joe Balfe organisation who sheltered them at Hornoy and Amiens until 5 April.[9]

2/Lt Merlyn I Rutherford, T/Sgt John R Landers and Sgt Stanley A Sokolowski were the co-pilot, radio-operator and cameraman of B-17 42-29863 Kentucky Babe (351BG/509BS) (Carson) which was damaged by flak over Frankfurt on 11 February 1944, losing two engines. They were hit by more flak over France and then attacked by fighters which shot off their rudder and the aircraft was abandoned to crash west of Amiens.[10]

Rutherford landed near Beaucamps while Landers and Sokolowski landed at nearby Le Quesne. Within a few days all three men were passed to the Joe Balfe organisation and sheltered in Hornoy until 5 April.

Sgt Wilson P Jones and 2/Lt Frederick Shecter were the tail-gunner and bombardier of B-17 42-37932 Ole Bassar (390BG/570BS) (Ferguson) on an operation to Frankfurt on 2 March 1944 that had been frustrated by heavy cloud cover. They were searching for an alternate target when they

---

7   Some additional information from Dominique Lecomte who says that Mills spent two days with the Dorez family before being taken to stay with the Duchateau family the end of the same road until 4 February. He also says that Morrison was sheltered by both Yvonne Fournier and Jean Lacour in Chantilly, and in Gouvieux by Louis Despretz of the Cafe de la Paix (on rue de Creil) and the Lauro family.

8   Six other crew from Destiny's Tot also evaded successfully – all evacuated by MGB from Plouha by the Francois-Shelburn organisation.

9   Dominique Lecomte lists Louis Despretz of rue de Creil, Gouvieux as helping Morrison, and Innocente and Betty Lauro of rue Boran, Gouvieux as helping both Morrison and Mills. In Montataire, they were sheltered with Marie Dorez at 4 rue de Conde.

10   Three other Kentucky Babe crewmen also evaded successfully: bombardier 2/Lt William H Spinning was evacuated by MGB in March on the Francois-Shelburn Operation Bonaparte 3, and navigator 2/Lt Henry Heldman and top-turret gunner T/Sgt Joseph R Heywood crossed the Pyrenees at the end of March with the Marie-Odile organisation.

were hit by flak that struck the ball turret and cut off the tail. I think only five of the crew were able to bale out before the aircraft crashed just east of Oisemont (Somme).

Jones and Shecter landed near Fontaine-le-Sec and were soon taken to Hornoy where they joined other evaders being sheltered by the Joe Balfe organisation until 5 April.

In Paris the evaders were met by two men, one of whom was called Jean (Jean Carbonnet) and a girl (Michele Moet). Milton Mills, Kenneth Morrison and Merlyn Rutherford stayed with Paul and Olga Christol (not leaving the apartment at all during their stay). John Landers, Stanley Sokolowski, Wilson Jones and Frederick Shecter were taken to Juvisy-sur-Orge where Landers and Sokolowski stayed with Andre Lefevre and family at rue Hoche, and Jones and Shecter with the Meilleroux family on rue Pasteur. Howard Mays stayed with Odette Drappier at 11 rue Valentin Hauy, Paris XV – and Joseph Oliver and Harry Williams stayed with Anita Lemonnier at 2 rue Ernest Renan. I don't know where the variously named IO (Maurice Leslie/Peter Mason) stayed.

On 11 April, Genevieve Soulie took Mills, Morrison and Rutherford – and Amelie Meilleroux and Paulette Lefevre (Andre's daughter) took Landers, Sokolowski, Jones and Shecter – to the Gare d'Austerlitz and passed them on to their guides, Pierre Le Berre and Genevieve Crosson. Other helpers brought the rest of the party and they were taken by overnight train to Montauban, arriving at ten-thirty next morning. They waited in a park until it was time to take the two-thirty, afternoon train to Toulouse, where there was another three hour wait for their train to Pau. Oliver reports that their papers were checked twice at Montauban station by men in plain clothes but on each occasion, the party were passed through without comment.

Genevieve Le Berre (née Crosson) (aka Jacqueline) explains in her book that they stopped off at Montauban in order to reduce the time spent at Toulouse station – which was known to be a particularly dangerous place for evaders – whilst waiting for their connection to Pau.[11] Genevieve Crosson and Pierre Le Berre are described by Rutherford as a slender, chataine (auburn-haired) young woman who wore horn-rimmed glasses – and her fiance as a slight, dark, blue-eyed man of 23 who was a cinematographer.

S/Sgt Clement Mezzanotte was a waist-gunner on B-17 42-30362 Wee Bonnie II (388BG/561BS) (Porter) which was on the way to Beaumont-

---

11   See 'Convoyeuse du reseau d'evasion Bourgogne' by Genevieve and Pierre Le Berre (2009).

sur-Oise on 9 September 1943. They were about to start their bomb run when an Me109 attacked the aircraft with heavy-calibre cannon fire. The B-17 began to spin out of control and the pilot gave the bale-out order.

Mezzanotte (who volunteered for the mission at the last moment and didn't know any of the other crew) made a deliberately delayed jump, not opening his parachute until about 2,000 feet. He landed in the garden of a house in Houilles (north-west Paris) where the owner took him into his home. An English neighbour named Dovey (nf) brought Mezzanotte civilian clothes and took him to stay with a refugee family from Alsace, an elderly couple and their thirty-year-old son Albert. On 12 September, a doctor drove Mezzanotte to an apartment in Courbevoie where he stayed with Denise Eisenschmidt (about 25 years old, had been a French army nurse) (the IS9 files have M Henri Eisenschmidt at 224 rue Armand Silvestre). On 2 October, the doctor moved Mezzanotte to stay overnight with Jacques de la Lune (query) and next day, Jean Clarion (nf) (who owned a farm and restaurant) took Mezzanotte back to his home at 37 Chemin des Laitieres, Soissy-sous-Montmorency. Mezzanotte stayed at the Clarion home for nearly six months, taking his meals with Victor Robert (who had owned two garages and a fleet of taxi-cabs before the occupation) at 31 Chemin des Laitieres. Victor Robert contacted Commissioner or Agent No 22 (see below) who hoped to get Mezzanotte out by boat but that idea was abandoned after his current plan failed and (he says) some evaders were machine-gunned as they left Brest.[12] At some time in March 1944, Jacques de la Lune brought 2/Lt James Williams to visit and the two Americans compared notes, concluding that de la Lune was either not able or not willing to send them on to Spain. On 29 March, Victor Robert took Mezzanotte into Paris and Jacques de la Lune's restaurant where he met Williams and 2/Lt Charles B Screws and the three Americans were turned over to a fireman's association. Mezzanotte and Screws stayed two nights with one of the firemen before all three Americans were returned to Jacques de la Lune's restaurant and then led to the apartment of a woman doctor. From there the three Americans were separated (see Williams and Screws

---

12   The planned boat evacuation was probably the Fanfan (Dahlia) operation from Douarnenez (mentioned earlier) at the end of October but may have been a reference to one of Pierre Hentic's operations from Aber-Benoit using RN MGBs. They ended with Operation Felicitate II on Christmas Day 1943 although I've found no mention of any German machine-gun incident. Pierre Hentic was arrested in Paris on 6 January 1944 and deported to Germany – he was liberated from Dachau on 10 May 1945. Major Pierre Hentic (born April 1917) (aka Trellu/Maho) was awarded the MBE as "an outstanding agent, combining escape work with his numerous other activities on behalf of the Allied cause". (WO208/5454)

earlier) and a young man took Mezzanotte to stay with Marcelin Villemont at 151 Boulevard Davout. Two weeks later (on 11 April) the same young man took him to the railway station and turned him over to Peter Mason (a very young, blond-haired man whose picture was at Gibraltar) who had Joseph Oliver and his navigator Harry Williams already on the train. They also joined Howard Mays and Frederick Shecter.

At Toulouse, where they had to change trains for Pau, Peter Mason 'very cleverly' put them on board a Paris train until the control had gone through the train for Pau and then took them over to that train just a minute or two before it was due to depart. At Pau, the French police were supervised by Germans and were checking papers at the station – Harry Williams was first in line and he was detained, Mezzanotte was next and he was passed but Frederick Shecter, despite his perfect French, was also captured.[13]

Outside Pau station they were met by Rosemary Maeght, Joan Moy-Thomas and a young Frenchman who spoke fluent English. Morrison, Mills, Rutherford and Landers were taken to stay with a short, elderly lady who had a 27-year-old (sic) daughter living with her (and another daughter with the French Red Cross in Algiers) in a large house belonging to an artist who lived on the ground floor.[14] Sokolowski and Jones stayed with Alfred Coussies, a professional from the Pau golf club (about 35 years old, lived with his mother, sister and her young son) at 44 rue d'Etigny while Mays stayed with a M Durante (about 5 ft 10 inches, grey hair, moustache), his thin, dark wife and their fifteen-year-old daughter.[15] Mezzanotte, Mays, Oliver, Peter Mason and one of the Frenchmen followed a blonde girl to the villa of Belgian textile broker Leon van de Poele.

On (about) 15 April, Milton Mills, Kenneth Morrison, Merlyn Rutherford, John Landers, Stanley Sokolowski and Wilson Jones were driven for about two and a half hours south-west of Pau to the hills near Oloron-Sainte-Marie where they spent all the following day hiding in a barn.

---

13   After a day in jail at Pau, Williams and Shecter were taken to St Michel prison in Toulouse. They were held there for four weeks until 15 May when they were transferred to Fresnes. On 17 June they were taken to a political prison in Frankfurt-on-Maine where they were interrogated by the Gestapo and held until the end of September before finally being sent to a proper POW camp – Stalag Luft VII (Bankau) for Williams …

14   This was the comtesse Anne de Liedekerke and her daughter Isabelle at Castet de l'Array on Avenue Trespoey.

15   This was probably Georges Durand (born May 1896) and his wife Emilie Durand (born August 1895) who sheltered at least ten Allied evaders at their home, Villa Chantelle on Chemin (Avenue) Beziou. They also arranged their transport using a fleet of cars run on petrol stolen from the Germans. (WO208/5452)

On (about) 17 April, Howard Mays, Clement Mezzanotte, Joseph Oliver and Peter Mason (aka Maurice Leslie) were put on a bus to Navarennx with conductor Robert Piton – and joined Stanley Langcaskey and Frank Mitchell. From Navarennx they were taken by car for half an hour to meet their mountain guide and then walked south to a barn, arriving there at about one-thirty in the morning, where they joined the Milton Mills group, another guide and two Frenchmen.

S/Sgt Stanley G Langcaskey was the ball-turret gunner of B-24 42-7548 Bull O' The Woods (44BG/66BS) (Heskett) which was on the way to Ludwigshaven on 30 December 1944 when two engines failed. The aircraft immediately went into a spin and the bale-out order was given.[16]

Langcaskey landed near Vezaponin (Picardy) north-west of Soissons and was soon helped by a man who took him back to his house in Vezaponin. That afternoon, Langcaskey was taken by bicycle to Soissons where he spent the night before being put on a train to Paris. From the station, Langcasky started walking south and finally declared himself to a man who was whistling 'It's a Long Way to Tipperary' in the third cafe he visited. The man was twenty-six-year-old Rene Paris (nf) and he arranged for Langcaskey to be sheltered for a few days. On 3 January, Rene Paris took Langcaskey and a French escaper called De Fay by train to Vannes where they stayed overnight. Next day they went to Quimper where Paris hoped to meet a contact who was arranging a boat but on the way they saw two gendarmes with his contact under arrest. On 8 January, they went to Les Sables d'Olonne and M Maxim (small, about 50 years old, black hair and a Hitler moustache) (nf) at the Maxim Cafe. Langcaskey was hidden nearby and on 17 January met Emile de Pianelli (aka Piano) (60 years old, 180 lbs, about 5 ft 8 inches tall with balding grey hair) who claimed to be with British Intelligence and promised to help him. Langcaskey was then sheltered and helped by various people – Victor Maurcot (a 31 year-old bachelor), an Italian-looking man named Clotour and his wife, a M Journay, George Schmitt (45 years old), Ed Rasquin (a 72 year-old, grey-haired insurance saleman), Maurice Michoux (a 52 year-old lawyer), 30 year-old Felix Plateur and his wife Marie, and several others (none found).

16　Six other Bull O' The Woods crew evaded successfully: pilot 1/Lt Donald J Heskett, waist-gunner Sgt Charles W Cregger and top-turret gunner T/Sgt Elmer D Risch were evacuated by MGB from Plouha by the Francois-Shelburn organisation, bombardier 1/Lt Adolph Zielenkiewicz and radio-operator T/Sgt Eugene Symons crossed the Pyrenees to Spain in March (Zielenkiewicz with the Marie-Odile organisation) and tail-gunner S/Sgt George R Miller who crossed the Pyrenees with Bourgogne in June 1944 – see later. Navigator 1/Lt William A Rendall evaded (details unknown) until captured on 19 June 1944.

On 9 March, Langcaskey was taken to stay with 19 year-old Aaron Cheminneau (nf) and his widowed mother in La Roche-sur-Yon. On 25 March, he was moved to 44 rue Marechal Petain where he stayed with Firmin Annonier until 13 April, when English-speaking Mme Evelyn Depinay (of 1 bis rue d'Alsace) took him by train to Pau. They stayed overnight in a cafe near the Cafe Royale and then spent the next night with an elderly post-office worker and his family. On 17 April, Joan Moy-Thomas put Langcaskey on a bus to Naverennx with conductor Robert Piton, joining Clement Mezzanotte, Howard Mays, Joseph Oliver, Peter Mason – and 2/Lt Frank Mitchell.

2/Lt Frank Mitchell was the co-pilot of B-17 42-39781 Career Girl (303BG/360BS) (Luke) which was returning from Solingen on 1 December 1943 when #2 engine ran away. Dropping out of formation they were hit by flak which stopped #3 and #4 engines and the aircraft was abandoned to crash just south of Lille. All ten crew are believed to have baled out safely but only Mitchell, who made a deliberately long delayed jump, evaded successfully.

Mitchell was helped immediately on landing but seems to have had a particularly difficult time. Parts of his report are almost illegible but it includes losing touch with the organisation which arranged his – and others, including Edward Daly and Hobart Trigg – travel from Paris to Bordeaux. Mitchell (who was then sheltered with an American bombardier called Jack) reports that

"they had had a lot of trouble before but now men were being picked up right and left … People continued to disappear and we realised that something must be done. We asked to be given train tickets and continue on our own into Spain. Our helper took us to the station and gave us tickets." [17]

Unfortunately, Mitchell's travelling companion was captured at Dax station.

"Everything went alright on the train until the next large town, there a German in civilian clothes came through checking identity papers. Ours were made out for us as deaf and dumb and we were afraid that we might have a

---

17   Information given by Daly and Trigg suggests that Jack was 2/Lt Charles A Bronako, bombardier of B-17 42-29877 Speed Ball which ditched off Guensey on 31 December 1943. If that's correct then I'm guessing he probably baled out over mainland France.

little trouble. The man checked my comrade's identity card, looked at it and at him and exclaimed in English that the identity papers were no good, asking who gave it to you, where are your comrades? You are an English aviator. He then pulled a pistol, backed my comrade to the wall of the car and searched him. He found the road map which we had been given and that gave the situation away. I was standing about ten feet away watching. I figured that there was no need for me to stand around just to be picked up and quietly wormed my way out of the railway car. Germans were standing all around on the platform outside. I went out of the station the wrong way and had to return. I went into an underpass and waited, trying to figure out whether I should risk turning in my ticket which was for another town. While I was wondering what to do, a French woman passed me jabbering about the Gestapo. In my bastard French I told her that I was an American and did not know how to get out of the station. I explained that it was my friend who had just been captured. She exchanged tickets with me and told me to go up and leave the station. I got through on her ticket all right and was convinced that God was leading me around by the hand. While I was walking away from the station the same woman caught up with me and asked what I was going to do now. I said that I was going to Spain. She agreed that that was the best thing to do and left me..." (MIS-X #700 Mitchell)

After walking south for another three days, Mitchell declared himself to the proprietor of a cafe in order to get further assistance – and his subsequent journey was arranged. Mitchell was eventually taken to Pau where he met Howard Mays and Stanley Langcaskey.

As soon as the two groups were brought together, the eleven airmen, Peter Mason and guides set off from the barn, walking until about five o'clock that morning when they reached another barn where they stayed for the rest of the day. They continued walking by night and hiding by day, via Ogeu–les-Bains and south-west of Pic d'Anie, encountering very little snow until just before the border, which they crossed late in the evening of 20 April. At about two o'clock next morning, their guide led them to a cabin where, after giving them further directions, he left them. They started out again at five that morning, following a stream and then a logging road, towards Isaba. On a bridge near Uztarroz (Navarre) they were arrested by Spanish police.

Chapter 62

Earle Carlow and his helper Jean-Paul Cardinal

1/Lt Earle W Carlow was strafing airfields near Bergerac on 20 March 1944 when his P-51 43-6639 (4FG/335FS) was hit by flak and he had to bale out. Carlow landed close to his burning aircraft and was quickly helped by a man who gave him a jacket. By the end of the day, Carlow had found a family to shelter him and help with his subsequent journey.

Rather than wait until an organisation could be contacted, a young man called Jean-Paul Cardinal (nf) opted to go with Carlow to an address in Oloron-Sainte-Marie where someone would help Carlow to cross the mountains. After a long and complicated trip, they missed their planned rendezvous outside a church in Oloron (and there being two large churches to choose from) and having mislaid their guide's address, spent several days trying to find him. Finally, Jean-Paul was able to contact the local resistance group and Carlow's journey across the Pyrenees was arranged.

Carlow's report doesn't specify (although he does mention meeting a girl with an American accent) but contact was made with Rosemary Maeght and Joan Moy-Thomas in Pau.

Further details from his report are almost illegible but Carlow wound up taking a bus to Navarennx ... and crossing into Spain on 24 April. His guide left him part way down and Carlow carried on to Isaba – where he was arrested.

Alice-Leone Moats was an American journalist who had spent twelve months (rather than the intended three) trying to understand the complex social and political situation in Spain before making a brief clandestine visit to France in April 1944. The journey was arranged by a Frenchman from Pau who is only identified as Pierre (a pre-war friend she had bumped into in Madrid) and Alice was taken across the mountains by Basque guides via Oloron-Sainte-Marie to Pau. She was delivered to resistance agents Jean and Yvonne (who she had also met in Madrid) who took her to stay with their English friend, Joan Moy-Thomas.

Alice was with Joan Moy-Thomas (who she describes as being an extremely thin, dark girl with a wax-like face that made her look rather like a mannequin) when Carlow reached Pau. His arrival caused a certain amount of concern amongst the helpers because he hadn't been delivered by anyone known to them and so was suspected of being a German plant. Carlow had actually been sent to a M Dupont who was himself not above suspicion and it was up to Joan and Rosemary Maeght to decide whether Carlow was really an American evader. If genuine, he would be added to a group of eight leaving that afternoon but if not, he would have to be 'disposed of' that evening.

Rosemary told Alice that she had been in France too long to be confident in her ability to detect a genuine American accent and so Alice volunteered to interview Carlow. The interview did not start well – when Rosemary had asked Carlow earlier how many missions he had flown he casually told her 'a hundred or so' which was of course impossible for the bomber crews they were used to dealing with. However, over tea and cakes in Joan's tiny flat, he later revealed that he was a fighter pilot (their very first actual pilot) and had been in England since 1940 flying with an Eagle Squadron (an RAF fighter squadron with volunteer American pilots) before transferring to the USAAF to fly Mustangs. Alice had friends who had been Eagle pilots and when it became clear that Carlow knew some of the same people, he was put on the bus for Navarennx that same afternoon.[1]

---

1   See 'No Passport for Paris' by Alice-Leone Moats (1945) Putnam's Sons, New York. My thanks to Michael Moores LeBlanc for bringing this to my attention.

CHAPTER 63

The Last Balfe group

On 17 April 1944, the Joe Balfe organisation delivered its last group of evaders to Bourgogne when Joe and Benjamin Lefebvre took F/O Kenneth Sim, WO2 Edmund Powell, F/Sgt Edwin Finlay, F/O David Slack, 2/Lt John Avery, Sgt James McGinty, T/Sgt Morris Elisco, S/Sgt Walter Mize, 2/Lt Ernest Lindell and T/Sgt Gaetano Friuli to Paris.

It was Joe's last delivery because on 28 April he lost his contact with the Bourgogne organisation when the Moet family apartment at 22 rue Sacrot in Saint-Mande was raided and the family (except for 12-year-old Jean-Marie) arrested – along with Jean Carbonnet and RAF evaders Edwin Finlay and David Slack.[1]

"We knew the risks – and on 28 April 28, returning from school, I found myself facing three French milice and German feldgendarmes surrounding my mother, my younger brother Jean-Marie, Jean Carbonnet and British airmen David Slack and Eddy Finlay who were sheltered with us. An unfortunate result of circumstances where the milice had discovered that our lodger, Carbonnet, had been looking for equipment for making false identity papers.

My father arrived very late. With a nod, he motioned to us that he had seen the white signal that Mother had the presence of mind to make at the window, while the milice happily appropriated her jewels. A few minutes later the abbe Courcel sounded at the door. He had learned that the milice was on our tracks and came to warn us. It was too late, he was arrested, imprisoned in Fresnes, deported and never returned from Germany. We were all shipped to the Kommandatur of Nogent. All except my brother who they had thought

---

1   Gerard Jacques Jean Moet (born December 1890) was deported to Buchenwald where he died on 6 March 1945. Genevieve Moet (born October 1899) and her daughter Michele (born June 1926) were deported to Ravensbruck then Torgau then Koenigsberg from where they were liberated in February 1945. Gerard Moet was recommended for a posthumous award, Genevieve for a KMC and Michele for an MBE. (WO208-5452) On 28 April 2013, a plaque was unveiled at 22 rue Sacrot in Saint-Mande to honour Gerard Moet and his family.

Jean Carbonnet (born December 1920) was held at Fresnes until deported to Buchenwald on 15 August. He was repatriated to France on 25 May 1945 and recommended for an MBE. (WO208-5453)

too young. Yet before going down, we managed to slip into his trousers a very compromising book. And the last image we had before the black cars took us, was Jean-Marie sitting on the pavement with this bomb on his stomach and in his arms, his old teddy bear that he had recovered before dawn.

Alone, he took refuge with the Hauchecorne family [at 21 rue Sacrot] who were close friends and our telephone relay. M Hauchecorne went out to call the people whose numbers appeared clearly on the book. Fearing the curfew he returned ... with the book. The next morning the milice stopped M et Mme Hauchecorne so my brother, claiming a serious stomach-ache, took the book into the toilet. He was twelve and a half years old. The Hauchecornes were released on 14 July 1944." (Michele Agniel 2013)

Subsequent evaders collected by the Balfe organisation were sheltered, mostly in Amiens, until they were liberated by advancing Allied troops in September.

F/O Kenneth W Sim was the pilot of 245 Sqn Typhoon JR238 on a special mission when his engine failed as he approached the French coast and he crash-landed on mud-flats between Ault (Somme) and Cayeaux-sur-Mer at just after ten-thirty on the morning of 4 January 1944.

Sim was quickly helped and next day taken to nearby Brutelles. The following evening, he was taken by bicycle to Friville-Escarbotin where he was sheltered until 29 January when he was taken by train to Abbeville and then driven to Maison Ponthieu where he stayed overnight. Next day, he was walked to Gueschart where he was sheltered until 11 February when he was moved to nearby Bufflers. The following day, two Frenchmen collected him in a lorry, and after picking up Gaetano Friuli and John Harms from Auxi-le-Chateau, delivered them to Mme Vignon in Amiens where Sim remained until 17 April.

WO2 Edmund A Powell was the bomb-aimer of 425 Sqn Halifax LW390 (Wait) which crashed at Souastre (Nord-Pas-de-Calais) returning from Stuttgart on the morning of 21 February 1944. Two other crew also evaded successfully – gunner Sgt Harley E Gammon evaded with Bourgogne (see earlier) and flight-engineer Sgt William Johnstone who evaded with Powell and stayed on with Mme Vignon in Amiens until the town was liberated on 31 August.

Powell landed near Puchevillers (Somme) and started to walk towards Amiens. He was soon intercepted by a man on a bicycle who took him back to the village and contacted the local organisation. Powell was taken to a cafe where a woman who spoke some English questioned him to establish his identity. An hour later, clothes were brought and Powell was taken to Raincheval where an English-speaking man interrogated Powell again. Powell produced his photographs and ID discs and he was taken back to the man's house for the night. Next morning, Powell was taken by train to Albert where he joined his flight engineer William Johnstone who was being sheltered by M Deflandre and his English wife at 23 rue Jules Ferry. Next day, their host took them to Amiens where they met a crippled Englishman who had served as a Royal Navy gunner in the First War. After more questioning, a man called Michel took them to stay with Mme Vignon where Powell was sheltered until being taken to Amiens station on 17 April.

F/Sgt Edwin Finlay was the air-bomber and only survivor of 625 Sqn Lancaster ND636 (Green) which was returning from an operation to Aulnoye in the early hours of 11 April 1944 when it was shot down and crashed south-west of Amiens.

Finlay had injured his ankle and so hid up in a wood until daybreak when he made his way to a village (name unknown) where he was helped and sheltered. The following night, he was collected by van and driven to Amiens where he stayed with hairdresser Jean (Rene) Lemattre at 3 rue Blin de Bourdon until 17 April when Joe Balfe collected him and took him to the railway station.

F/O David A Slack was returning from a Sweep sortie in 175 Sqn Typhoon JP369 on 5 February 1944 when the engine cut out and he crash-landed in a field south of Amiens. On reaching the nearest road, Slack was picked up by a Frenchman who took him on his bicycle to a small village where he stayed until two in the morning when he was woken up and told that some gendarmes were waiting for him downstairs. One of the gendarmes gave Slack his uniform and the other four took Slack by bicycle to a police station, where they had coffee, before Slack was taken by motorcycle to Saint-Sauflieu to stay with one of the gendarmes and his wife. On 10 February, Slack was driven by truck to Amiens where he was sheltered (like so many others) by Mme Jeanne Vignon.[2]

2/Lt John B Avery and Sgt James W McGinty were the navigator and tail-gunner of B-17 42-3517 Happy Warrior (351BG/508BS) (Caughman) which was had been damaged by flak over Schweinfurt on 24 February

---

2   I met David Slack by chance at a dinner in Yorkshire in 2012. He later put me in touch with Mme Michele Agniel (née Moet) whose family were sheltering him when he was captured, and with whom he remained in contact until he passed away in March 2015.

1944, attacked by fighters and finally abandoned to crash south of Amiens, near Grattepanche.[3]

John Avery landed south of Amiens near Ailly and made his way to Saint-Sauflieu where he was found by a large, burly, good looking gendarme named Edouard Robine who took him back to his house in Amiens.[4] Next day, James McGinty was brought in and the following day their radio-operator John Matilla arrived. On 3 March, the three Americans were taken to stay with Michel Dubois (described as a 48-year-old former Master-Sergeant, slightly bald and with a small moustache) at 45 rue Delpech in Amiens. Later that same day, Richard Caughman, Paul Young, Richard Perkins and Howard Langer from their aircraft also arrived. Avery and McGinty remained with Michel Dubois when the others went to stay with Joe Balfe at Hornoy and about a week later, Matilla, Caughman and Young were returned to Michel Dubois' house while Perkins and Langer went to another address (a grocery shop – query) in Amiens. Perkins and Langer are believed to have left a week later to meet an aircraft for the UK and were not heard from again.

James McGinty was helped soon after landing and taken to Sourdon where the maire passed him on to a blacksmith called Ballenger who fed and sheltered him overnight. Next day, he was taken to Saint-Sauflieu and handed over to gendarme Edouard Robine, where he joined Avery, before they were both passed on to Michel Dubois in Amiens (McGinty adds that Dubois was concierge of a Catholic school for young children).

On 8 April, the Gestapo carried out a series of raids and when they arrived at Michel Dubois' home on rue Delpech, he and the five evaders (Avery, McGinty, Matilla, Caughman and Young) only just managed to escape. They went to Mme Vignon on rue Vulfran-Warme where they joined Kenneth Sim, Edmund Powell, David Slack, Ernest Lindell and Gaetano Friuli.

T/Sgt Morris Elisco was the radio-operator of B-24 41-28649 Little Bryan (453BG/733BS) (Stock) which had turned back with engine trouble from an operation to Friedrichshafen on 18 March 1944 and was running

---

3   Seven of the Happy Warrior crew were sheltered with the Joe Balfe organisation although bombardier 1/Lt Richard E S Perkins and waist-gunner S/Sgt Howard M Langer subsequently left and were later captured. Ball-turret gunner S/Sgt Paul B Young, pilot 1/Lt Richard B Caughman and radio-operator T/Sgt John C Mattila stayed in the Amiens area until it was liberated by the advancing Allies in September. Waist-gunner S/Sgt Eugene A Colburn also evaded successfully – he crossed the Pyrenees to Spain in June.

4   Edouard Louis Robine (born July 1906) of 21 rue Boulet, Amiens is credited with helping at least twenty-four Allied evaders (WO208/5452) and was awarded a Kings Commendation.

out of fuel. The bale-out order was given and although Elisco landed near Hornoy (Somme), the aircraft apparently went on to crash near Vernon-sur-Seine (Yvelines) north-west of Paris. Elisco was the only one of the crew to evade successfully.

Soon after his landing, Elisco was helped by a girl who hid him on the farm of her two elderly parents for four days until a young man took him to Aumale to be interviewed. After two days at Aumale, Elisco was taken by bicycle to a house near Hornoy to meet Jean Fourrage (a frail, light complexioned man, about 5 feet 2 inches tall) who took him to a farm at Liomer owned by a retired French general. The general (aged 80 and 6 feet 2 inches tall) visited Elisco several times and paid for his keep but the farm was run by an elderly caretaker and his 22-year-old nephew, Lucien Belfort. Four days later he was joined by John Landers and Stanley Sokolowski from the Kentucky Babe.

Following the arrest of Jean Fourrage[5] and the rounding up of another twenty or so people (including many not connected to the organisation), the elderly caretaker took Elisco, Landers and Sokolowski to the station on 5 April where guides took them by train to Amiens and Benjamin Lefebvre at 71 rue de la Demi Lune. Twelve evaders were gathered there and (as mentioned earlier) Benjamin and Joe Balfe took ten of them to Paris and the Bourgogne organisation.

Meanwhile, Elisco and Walter Mize were taken to Jean (Rene) Lemattre in Amiens who took them to the home of another man named Jean (5 feet 4 inches tall badly scarred with burns around one eye, about 30 years old, married to a thin, dark woman of the same age and with a young son of about seven) where they stayed for about a week before going back to Jean Lemattre. He took them to stay with Frederick Albert Moore, a wealthy bachelor (52 years old, 5 feet 6 inches tall, grey haired and heavy set, spoke English) at 36 rue Boucher de Pethes, who owned a grocery shop about fifty feet from his house where Edwin Finlay was already living. Three days later (on 17 April), Lemattre took Elisco, Mize and Finlay to the railway station where they met Joe Balfe and Benjamin Lefebvre who had Kenneth Sim, Edmund Powell, David Slack, John Avery, James McGinty, Ernest Lindell and Gaetano Friuli with them.

---

5   24-year-old Jean Fourrage (aka Jacques Vasseur) and his mother Marie Antoinette (43) were arrested on 2 April 1944. Morand Waquez (44) and his 19-year-old son Raymond, Max Edouard Darras (17) and Sigismonde Fourrage (44) were also arrested the same day. Jean Fourrage, Morand and Raymond Waquez were shot at Gentelles the following month. Max Darras died at Bergen-Belsen. Marie Antoinette and Sigismonde Fourrage both survived Ravensbrück.

S/Sgt Walter A Mize Jnr was the tail-gunner of B-17 42-39962 (384BG/547BS) (Widener) which was shot down (details unknown) on 11 February 1944 whilst returning from Frankfurt. The bale-out order was given and the aircraft abandoned to crash south of Dieppe. Mize was the only one of the crew to evade successfully.

Mize landed near Eu (Seine-Maritime) where a farmer sheltered him for three nights until Paulette Marcelin (nf) and Mlle Baubesache (query) took him to Edouard Wandre and his English wife at Touffreville-sur-Eu. He stayed for three weeks at Touffreville before being passed on to Joe Balfe at Hornoy. Joe put him with a man named Henri for one night before taking him to stay on a farm at Hallivillers, 20 kilometres south of Amiens. Mize stayed there for another three weeks before being brought back to Hornoy where he joined Wilson Jones and Frederick Shecter. When Jean Fourrage was arrested, Henri took the three Americans to Amiens where they joined Joseph Oliver, Harry Williams, Merlyn Rutherford and Howard Mays at Benjamin Lefebvre's house on rue de la Demi Lune. Mize stayed on with Morris Elisco in Amiens when the others left on 5 April.

2/Lt Ernest V Lindell was the navigator of B-17 42-31246 (384BG/545BS) (Britt) on a mission to attack rocket sites in the Pas-de-Calais on 14 January 1944 when they were hit by flak which damaged #3 and #4 engines. They dropped out of formation, turned back for the coast and the aircraft was abandoned to crash into a German flak position near St Valery-sur-Somme. Lindell was the only member of the crew to evade successfully, the other nine were captured.

Lindell landed a few miles north of Abbeville and was helped almost immediately. He made his way to Amiens (his report is almost illegible), arriving on 17 January, where he was sheltered by Mme Vignon for three months until 17 April.

T/Sgt Gaetano A Friuli was the top-turret gunner of B-17 42-3427 Canadian Club (390BG/568BS) on a mission to attack rocket sites in the Pas-de-Calais on 21 January 1944 when flak hit #1 and #2 engines and set the aircraft on fire. The bale-out order was given and six of the crew jumped before the pilot, 2/Lt James C Waggoner, returned the aircraft to England.[6]

Friuli landed near Division (Pas-de-Calais) and was helped by Rene Guittard's Bordeaux-Loupiac organisation at Frevent but by early February,

6   Two more of the six men who jumped from Canadian Club also evaded successfully: navigator 2/Lt John G Harms (as mentioned above) was sheltered by Mme Vignon at Amiens until March and then with the Chauny-Dromas organisation, and radio-operator S/Sgt George J Powell who was sheltered in the Pas-de-Calais until liberated.

he and his navigator 2/Lt John G Harms were staying with Mme Vignon in Amiens. Harms left Amiens on 18 March with 2/Lt Alden F Faudie but Friuli stayed on until 17 April.

In Paris, Kenneth Sim, Morris Elisco, Walter Mize, Ernest Lindell and Gaetano Friuli were taken to Gabriel Bouyer at 87 rue Haxo where Sim and Friuli were sheltered while Elisco, Mize and Lindell went to stay with fellow gendarme Marcelin Villemont and his wife Marie at 151 Boulevard Davout. Visitors to the Villemont apartment included George Tissier (of 100 Blvd Davout), Marc Bouchet (of 155 Blvd Davout) and Jules Bernard (an elderly man who lived in the apartment above). After ten days, Elisco, Mize and Lindell were returned to Gabriel Bouyer where they rejoined Sim and Friuli.

Edmund Powell, John Avery and James McGinty were turned over to a tall, clean-cut young man in a pork-pie hat and raincoat who took them to 4 rue Edouard Quenu where Avery and McGinty stayed with Paul and Olga Christol while Powell was taken on to stay with Jacques and Giselle Goux at 160 rue Jeanne d'Arc, Paris XIII.

On (about) 27 April, Sim, Elisco, Mize, Lindell and Friuli were taken to the Gare d'Austerlitz by a short, dark woman of about 22 and two young Frenchmen (who went all the way to Spain with them). They were joined at the station by Edmund Bairstow before taking a train (via Montauban, where they waited in the park) to Toulouse to Pau.

On 1 May, Genevieve Soulie came to interrogate Avery and McGinty at the Christol apartment before taking them (collecting Edmund Powell and Jerome Bajenski on the way) to the Jardin des Plantes where they met Georges Broussine. Avery was told by Broussine that this would be the last group that Bourgogne would be sending through – Genevieve had already told McGinty that his was the last group that Bourgogne had in Paris. Their guides, an anaemic looking young man and an older woman who wore a red bandana, took the four airmen by train to Pau, arriving there late in the evening of 2 May.

T/Sgt Jerome J Bajenski was the radio-operator of B-17 42-31820 (305BG/364BS) (Perry) which was on the way to the Messerschmitt works at Augsburg on 25 February 1944 when they were attacked by a Fw190 which raked the B-17, set the fuels tanks on fire and shot out the intercom. The aircraft went into steep dive and as the pilots pulled out, a wing fell off and the aircraft exploded and crashed near Raucourt–et-Flaba (Champagne-Ardenne). Bajenski, who was thrown from the aircraft, was the only one of the six (query) surviving crew to evade successfully.

Bajenski landed near Stonne (Ardennes) and was helped by a local couple who took him to their home in the village for the night before directing him towards Vouziers. He was sheltered in Vouziers at the home of a French officer (50 years old, 5 feet 5 inches tall, 150 lbs, grey-haired and with a wife of about the same age, a 22-year-old son named Paul and a 25-year-old daughter) and asked to identify 2/Lt Edmund N Bairstow. Next day, Bajenski was introduced to 2/Lt John C Vollmuth and 2/Lt Frank J McNichol who had been shot down on the same mission as him (see later). That afternoon, Bajenski, Bairstow, Vollmuth and McNichol were driven by truck to Ambonnay to stay with Henri Billot (about 23 years old, 5 feet 9 inches tall, worked in a vineyard) and his sister Denise (about 20 years old) and their grand-parents M et Mme Varlot. Bairstow stayed with the Varlots, Bajenski with Jeanot Kinn (between 18 and 20 years old, 5 feet 5 inches tall, black hair) and his father Robert, and Vollmuth and McNichol with Camille Ladurelle at 21 rue Gambetta in Bouzy. On 5 April, Bajenski and Bairstow were taken by bicycle to stay with Henri Beaufort (about 35 years old, married with twin six-year-old daughters) in Trepail. On 10 April, three men came in a car with Vollmuth and McNichol to collect Henri Beaufort, Bajenski and Bairstow and take them to a hotel-cafe on the outskirts of Reims. They were met by a blond, bespectacled doctor (about 30 years old) and a hunchbacked doctor named Michel Poirier (aged about 35, his father was the administrator for the Pomery Winery in Reims) and Dr Poirier took the four Americans by train to Paris where Bajenski and Bairstow stayed with him at 10 (or 18) rue Pierre Leroux (one street away from the Hopital Laennec). On 19 April, Genevieve Soulie moved Bajenski to stay with Odette Drappier at 11 rue Valentin Hauy where he was sheltered until 1 May when Genevieve took him to the Jardin des Plantes. He met the blond (query) and a woman of about 35 (110 lbs) and a young man (20 years old, black hair, glasses, spoke English) (Pierre Le Berre) and Georges Broussine – and joined Powell, Avery and McGinty.

2/Lt Edmund N Bairstow was the bombardier of B-17 42-31820 (305BG/364BS) (Lindstrom) which was hit by flak over Augsburg on 25 February 1944. The bale-out order was given and although some of the crew are thought to have baled out over Germany, six are believed to have waited until they were over France. Bairstow was the only one of the crew to evade successfully.

Bairstow landed near Mouzon (Ardennes) and evaded alone until the evening of the third day when he was taken into a farmhouse from where his journey was arranged and he joined Jerome Bajenski.

While Bajenski was taken to stay with Odette Drappier, Bairstow stayed on with Dr Michel Poirier at 10 rue Pierre Leroux until (about) 27 April when Genevieve Soulie took him to the Gare d'Austerlitz where he joined Kenneth Sim, Walter Mize, Ernest Lindell, Gaetano Friuli and the couple who were to be their guides.

In Pau on (about) 29 April, Sim and Friuli stayed with an elderly man who painted (and were visited there by Rosemary Maeght) while Elisco and Bairstow were sheltered with Belgian textile broker Leon van de Poele. I don't know where Mize and Lindell stayed. Four days later, Isabelle de Liedekerke (the link between various members of the organisation) took Elisco and Bairstow to a church where they followed an auburn-haired American girl in sunglasses to the bus station. They joined Sim, Mize, Lindell and Friuli and took the bus to Naverennx with conductor Robert Piton. They were then driven by car into the mountains and a guide led them to a barn where they spent the night and next day. At eleven o'clock that evening, they were taken to join Edmund Powell, John Avery and James McGinty, Jerome Bajenski and several others.

When Powell, Avery, McGinty and Bajenski had arrived at Toulouse station on 2 May, they noticed they were being watched and so instead of taking the waiting Pau train, they took a bus to the outskirts of town where they caught another train to Pau five hours later. Arriving at Pau late that night, they found one of the same men who had been watching them at Toulouse was at the station exit with a French gendarme and a German policeman, however the group weren't stopped from leaving the station and were even given permits to enter the town after curfew. A local guide took the four evaders to a hotel where they met an American girl (Rosemary Maeght) and an English girl (Joan Moy-Thomas) and spent the rest of the night.

On 5 May, two tall Frenchmen took the four evaders (Powell, Avery, McGinty and Bajenski) by bus to Navarennx where they transferred to a car. They were then driven for about two hours to a place where they found Sim, Elisco, Mize, Bairstow, Lindell and Friuli waiting for them.

The whole party started off walking at once, being joined on the way by a French captain and his wife. They crossed the frontier into Spain at about two o'clock in the morning of 8 May and walked down to Uztarroz where they rested in two cabins. They were arrested there by the Guardia Civil who took them to Isaba. Next day the NCOs were sent to Lecumberri and the officers to Pamplona.

CHAPTER 64

Bressler and Allen

As mentioned (much) earlier, the first name on Georges Broussine's list of evaders is a Sgt Allen and I had thought the only Sgt Allen that seemed likely was S/Sgt Ira R Allen. By the time I realised my mistake, I'd already written this chapter. It should be noted that neither Ira Allen or Walter Bressler is on Geneveive Soulie's list of evaders (which I didn't have access to at the time) and nor are Young, Hard or Watterworth – see later.

S/Sgt Walter Bressler and S/Sgt Ira R Allen were the tail-gunner and right waist-gunner of B-24 42-110087 (448BG/713BS) (Mellor) which was returning from Ludwigshafen on 1 April 1944 and (for various reasons) running out of fuel. With two engines already stopped, the bale-out order was given and the aircraft abandoned to crash near Coulombs-en-Valois (Seine-et-Marne).[1]

Allen made a delayed jump (as per S2 instructions) from about 7,000 to 4,000 feet and landed under a tree. He pulled his parachute down and hid it under bush, changed into GI shoes (which were tied to his parachute harness) and headed south. Soon he came to a small house and after waiting until he saw one man alone, attracted his attention. While they were trying to communicate via Allen's phrase card, another man came over and gave Allen some food. Two hours later Allen reached the outskirts of Bethisy-Saint-Pierre (Oise) where a woman recognised him as an Allied airman and took him into her house.

Bressler (who had attended the same E&E lectures as Allen) also delayed his jump and came down about 3 kilometres north of Bethisy-Saint-Pierre, aiming for a clearing but missing and landing in the top of a tree. When he finally made it to the ground, he changed into his GI shoes

---

1   All ten crew baled out safely and nine of them evaded successfully: LWG S/Sgt Mike Little crossed the Pyrenees in April, bombardier 2/Lt Frank H Jacobson and BTG S/Sgt Nelson A Branch crossed the Pyrenees south of Bayonne in May, radio-operator T/Sgt Francis C Marx crossed the central Pyrenees with the Francois Dissard organisation, also in May, navigator 2/Lt Marvin T Goff was liberated at Freteval in August, pilot 1/Lt Harrison C Mellor evaded with various maquis groups until liberated in August and co-pilot 2/Lt Douglas J Eames was sheltered until liberated in Paris in September. Only TTG T/Sgt William A Warren seems to have been captured.

and starting walking south. After cleaning himself up a bit in a stream, Bressler approached some men working in the fields. They didn't seem to understand but soon a young boy came running up and offered to help. The boy went off to get a girl who brought Bressler some hot bread and wine before calling his father who took Bressler back to a house in Bethisy-Saint-Pierre. Bressler's injuries were treated before he was taken to stay with a neighbour, Mme Carbeau (query), who had a picture of a Mme Smith (query) in Paris who she thought could help Bressler. Two days later, the same young boy moved Bressler to a barn where an English-speaking girl passed him on to a man who had their radio-operator T/Sgt Francis Marx with him and they were both driven about fifteen minutes to a roadhouse (sic) at a cross-roads – they were told that their left waist-gunner, S/Sgt Mike Little (who had been directed there on the first day) had just left for Paris. Their waist-gunner, Ira Allen was brought in that same night and William (query) at the roadhouse took care of them.

The following evening (4 April), Marx left for Paris while Bressler and Allen stayed for another two nights before William took them by local train to Crepy-en-Valois where they stayed overnight with an English-speaking lady who ran a bar-room (sic) about a block from the station. Next day, William and another man took them to Paris where they waited in a bar while William went looking for his contact and then to another bar until a nineteen-year-old boy called James took them to an apartment where they stayed with Perri (Omye – query) who spoke some broken English and had already helped one RAF sergeant evader. After the first night, Bressler and Allen were temporarily separated, James taking Bressler and moving from house to house, never staying in one place for more than two nights, until 19 April – during which time they met a red-haired lady (about 40 years old, spoke good English) and a young girl called Pepe. On 19 April, another young boy took Bressler and Allen by train to Creil and then they walked the 25 kilometres to Grandfresnoy. In Grandfresnoy they met a man named Pinel (assume Paul Pinel) and Rene Pinel (apparently no relation) took them back to his farm at rue de Sacy, Grandfresnoy where they stayed until 3 May, hoping to be picked up by aircraft.[2]

Finally they were told that the aircraft idea was off and a man came from Paris (about 24 years old, hair with middle-parting, had been to University of Georgia in America, lived in Bordeaux – they later saw his picture at Gibraltar) and took them back to the capital. They stayed two nights in Paris

2   Rene Pinel was associated with Patrick Hovelacque's BCRA line Kummel. (MMLB)

in a lady's apartment before she took them to the station where the same man (with the middle-parting) who brought them to Paris, took them to Bordeaux and back to his own house. They stayed overnight in Bordeaux – meeting Dallas Young, Kenneth Hard and Clarence Watterworth – and next day another guide drove Bressler and Allen to the outskirts of the city for the night before driving them 100 miles nearer the border to a farmhouse. Next morning, they were taken into some fields to wait for Young, Hard and Watterworth and then all five were taken in a charcoal-burning lorry towards the border.

2/Lt Dallas F Young, S/Sgt Kenneth E Hard and T/Sgt Clarence Watterworth were the co-pilot, left waist-gunner and radio-operator of B-17 42-97166 (96BG/337BS) which was over Chateaudun aerodrome on the afternoon of 28 March 1944 when they were hit by flak which stopped two engines and set the aircraft on fire. Eight of the crew baled out before pilot 1/Lt William H Young returned the aircraft to the UK – with top-turret gunner S/Sgt R C Hatch still on board.

Young delayed opening his parachute (as per his evasion lectures) until about 2,000 feet, landing in open ground near a river and some woods. He seems to have made a classic landing, somersaulting once and coming up on his feet with his parachute "dead on the ground". Continuing to remember his evasion lectures, rather than making for the obvious wooded area, he rolled up his parachute and headed for the river, following the bank and finding a place to hide his flying equipment and Mae West. Various locals watched his progress and after crossing a bridge to join a farmer who called him over, he was given cigarettes and a drink. While the farmer said he wanted to help Young, his wife was too concerned about the Germans so Young carried on to a small village where three women signalled that he should hide himself as there were Germans approaching. Young hid himself under branches and leaves in a thicket where, apart from waking when the women brought him clothes and food, he slept until dusk. On awakening that evening, he found helpers waiting for him and an English-speaking Frenchman took him to stay overnight in his house. Next morning, a lorry arrived with Kenneth Hard and Clarence Watterworth already on board and their journey was arranged.

Hard also delayed his jump, seeing Young come down but rather than open ground, he managed to land in the tallest tree available. By the time he'd cut himself free and climbed down, a group of local men were waiting for him. They collected all Hard's flying equipment and advised him to hide, which he did in a ditch where he slept for the rest of the day. When he woke up at dusk, he again found his helpers waiting and they took him to a barn where he stayed overnight. Next morning he was picked up by lorry and driven to collect Dallas Young.

Although neither Young or Hard specify their location, they had come down somewhere between their target of Chateaudun and the village of Bonneval, being driven through Bonneval to be sheltered in a house where guns and ammunition were stored under the command of Roland Paul Chauvin (nf). They stayed six nights with M Chauvin, being given new papers and practising writing their new names, before a man and woman took them to Paris and the south-eastern suburb of Alfortville. Young went with Raymond Benoit to his home at 167 Villeneuve (rue de Villeneuve – query) while the two sergeants went with Jean Renier (aka Victor) to 15 rue Victor Hugo. They stayed in and around Alfortville, being moved about several times, for the next month. On 9 May, they were taken by Metro into Paris where they met a new guide who took them by train to Bordeaux.

There was a delay when the car that was due to meet them failed to appear and they were instructed to keep walking around a limited area while their guide located the missing vehicle. Then Young and Watterworth were taken to a wine broker's house and Hard to the home of a police chief (no names given) to stay overnight. Next morning, they were driven in the same car 140 kilometres south on the N132 to a farm where they left the car and walked another three miles, collecting Walter Bressler and Ira Allen along the way.

The five airmen and guide were driven to a place on the Adour river about 21 kilometres from Bayonne, possibly near St Jean de Marsacq, where they crossed the river by boat before a two hour walk to be picked up by another guide and taken to his home, arriving very late that evening. After an hour's rest (and discussion amongst the guides) they set off again at midnight and continued walking until about five in the morning when they reached a hotel. After waiting some time for the owners to wake up, the party were given hot coffee and shelter for the rest of the day. Their French guide paid their new Basque mountain guides 5,000 francs and they set off just as it was getting dark, walking for ten hours, avoiding the town of Cambo-les-Bains, passing east of Mount Idusquimendi, through Bidderay and crossing the frontier on 11 May 1944, just as it was getting light. Shortly before the border, Watterworth was unable to continue and he was left behind.

The remaining four evaders surrendered to a Spanish frontier patrol and were taken to Pamplona where they spent twelve days at the Hotel Pascuelena – then to Alhama for another nine days – before being driven to the British Embassy in Madrid where they were interrogated by the Military Attache.

CHAPTER 65

John Vollmuth and Frank McNichol

2/Lt John C Vollmuth and 2/Lt Frank J McNichol were the bombardier and navigator of B-17 42-31517 (457BG/748BS) (Chinn) which on the way to Augsburg on 25 February 1944 when it was hit by flak over Luxembourg and turned back. Down to two engines, they lost altitude and had just jettisoned their bomb-load when they were attacked by fighters and the aircraft abandoned. Only three of the ten-man crew managed to bale out before the aircraft exploded and crashed near Mont-Saint-Martin (Champagne-Ardenne). The third man, engineer/TTG S/Sgt Vito Peragine, was captured.

Vollmuth and McNichol landed near Marvaux-Vieux (Ardennes), about 12 kilometres south of Vouziers, were quickly helped and taken to the Marvaux home of a middle-aged Frenchman. A Dutch friend of his brought two young men (they later claimed to have helped seventeen evaders before) who asked to see their dog-tags and then took them to Aure where they stayed with a farmer named Robert Decorne. They spent the night there and the following evening two young women visited them, returning the next day with Jeanot Fossier (nf) (about 20 years old, spoke some English), Paul (tall, blond, son of a French officer who had served in Algiers) and a truck driver (in his forties, married, spoke fluent German having been a POW in the first war). The truck driver took them to Jeanot Fossier's house in Terron-sur-Aisne where he lived with his mother, father Francois and sister Mimi. Four days later, Francois Fossier took the two Americans to the home of Paul's father where they met T/Sgt Jerome Bajenski and 2/Lt Edmund Bairstow. Next day, Paul, Jeanot Fossier and Henri Billot took the four Americans to M Billot's house in Ambonny where a man called Rene Hughet (short, about 35 years old, apparently chief of the local organisation) assigned them to different houses and Vollmuth and McNichol stayed with Camille Ladurelle at 21 rue Gambetta in Bouzy (20 kms SSE of Reims) for the next six weeks. During this time, Denise Billot (Henri's sister) heard that Jeanot Fossier and Paul had been arrested. On 8 April, Vollmuth and McNichol were moved to Ambonnay where they stayed with Camille Ladurelle's neighbour, Emile Remy (in his forties, married with a daughter named Jacqueline (18) son Emile (14) and another son POW). Three days later, they were taken by Rene Hughet, a Belgian and two Frenchmen (one of whom had been a steward on the Leviathan) to Rene's house. They dropped Rene off and went on to collect Bajenski and Bairstow before a hunchbacked doctor named Michel Poirier took them all to Paris.

Neither Vollmuth or McNichol spoke any French and John Vollmuth later explained that whilst on the train, they each held a newspaper up as though reading, with their identity card and train ticket between their fingers so they could be checked without the inspector having to disturb them.[1]

In Paris, while Bajenski and Bairstow stayed with Dr Poirier (see earlier), Vollmuth and McNichol followed a man (35-year-old engineer with the Algerian Phosphate Co – had been in the French air force – married with two children) to his apartment in Charenton-le-Pont and stayed with him for two days until Dr Poirier took them to Dr Gaston Bonhomme at 83 Boulevard Auguste-Blanqui where they stayed for a week. Then a young man called Philippe moved them to 5 rue Stephen Pichon where they stayed with Albertine Veron (a portly, red-haired woman in her forties, a nurse whose husband was in Poland, and whose son who was hiding on a farm). About three weeks later (on 9 May), Genevieve Soulie and a young man (about 17, slim with dark hair) visited them. The young man returned and took them to the Jardin des Plantes where they joined Genevieve, a man who was Burgundy's assistant (sic) (and said to be an art dealer) and two guides, Pierre Le Berre and Genevieve Crosson. The two guides took them by evening train from the Gare d'Austerlitz to Montauban, Toulouse and Pau.

At Pau, Vollmuth and McNichol were turned over to a blondish, English-speaking young man who passed them on to Rosemary Maeght. They stayed at the big house of an absent Englishman, looked after by the woman who was taking care of the house. Next day, Rosemary passed them on to Robert Piton, conductor of the bus to Navarennx, with instructions for them to get off at Jasses. There they were met by two Frenchmen and a Spaniard who drove them to a trail that led into the mountains. They walked all that night and lay up the following day in a barn. That evening, another guide arrived and later that night, two more guides took over. They

---

1   John Vollmuth interview with Jane and Joe McNicol in November 2002.

spent one day and night in a Basque family's house before meeting another party (no details) and going on. They finally crossed the border into Spain in the early hours of 15 May. They headed for Isaba but were arrested before they got there.

CHAPTER 66

Charles Hoyes and James Walsh

S/Sgt Charles Hoyes was the radio-operator of B-17 42-31110 Pacific's Dream (94BG/331BS) (Sullivan) which was leaving the target area of Cognac on 31 December 1943 when they were hit by flak. With #2 and #3 engines on fire and #4 engine smoking, pilot 2/Lt Edward J Sullivan told his crew to stand by to abandon the aircraft and as he slipped out of formation, gave the bale-out order.[1]

Hoyes made a delayed jump to about 3,000 feet and landed in a field somewhere between Saintes and Pons (Poitou-Charentes). That evening, a farmer and his two daughters hid Hoyes overnight in their barn. Next day, a young man brought him a note from one of his waist-gunners, S/Sgt John C McLaughlin, and that evening took Hoyes down the road to where the maire of Bougneau (3 kms north-east of Pons) was waiting with McLaughlin in a car. The maire drove them into Pons where he picked up their bombardier, 2/Lt Reuben Fier before taking them back to his chateau at Bougneau. That night they were joined by their ball-turret gunner, S/Sgt Stanley Dymek.

Next morning, the maire drove Hoyes, McLaughlin, Fier and Dymek to a hotel in Cussac (Haute-Vienne) where the owner sent for a young man called Philippe who was head of the local maquis and that afternoon the maire took them to a farmhouse that was the maquis headquarters. That evening, Philippe took them back to the hotel for the night, returning them to the farmhouse again next day. On the second day, their waist-gunner S/Sgt Alvin E Sanderson, and 2/Lt Harold Freeman and S/Sgt Levi H Collins – the navigator and ball-turret gunner of B-17 42-39823 Iron Ass (also FTR 31 December 1943) – were brought in by the maire. That night they were

---

1   Five other Pacific's Dream crewmen also evaded successfully: navigator 2/Lt Harvey B Barr Jnr crossed the Pyrenees to Elizondo in February while top-turret gunner S/Sgt Stanley Dymek, waist-gunners S/Sgt Alvin E Sanderson and S/Sgt John C McLaughlin, and tail-gunner S/Sgt Kenneth Carson crossed the Pyrenees together in March 1944 with a group organised by the Francoise Dissard organisation. Bombardier 2/Lt Reuben Fier and S/Sgt Levi H Collins from B-17 Iron Ass (along with an Australian airman named Rafferty – query) had been with Dymek and the others at Quillan but left with a different group and were captured at Axat (Languedoc-Roussillon) in March.

all taken to a chateau owned by a priest at Grand Mounerie near Cussac and handed over to Jean Pichon/Pichaud (nf) manager of a textile mill in Cussac which was owned by the brother of the same priest.

About two weeks later, a man called Alexandre[2] (Pichaud's superior in Limoges) drove them to Limoges and that night, McLaughlin, Fier, Dymek, Sanderson, Freeman, Collins and Pacific's Dream tail-gunner S/Sgt Kenneth Carson were taken by bus to the maquis at Sussac (12 kms south-west of Eymoutiers) while Hoyes, being ill, stayed behind with Alexandre for some ten weeks – Hoyes spending the first four weeks recovering from an operation performed on him by a doctor from Limoges.

On 29 March, a Spaniard called Petrella (query) took Hoyes to the railway station where he was handed over to a man who was taking two Frenchmen to join a maquis near Perigueux run by a Spanish communist called Carlos. Apart from the two newly delivered Frenchmen, everyone in the maquis were foreigners and the band spent much of their time poaching supplies from the neighbouring Gaullist group who had materiel dropped to them by the RAF. Eventually Hoyes left the maquis along with a disillusioned Russian and a Belgian Jew called Robert Clas and Clas guided them to Montflanquin (Lot-et-Garonne) where the Belgian knew that the maire was the local maquis chief. The maire wanted Hoyes to stay and wait for the invasion but after a week he arranged for a middle-aged Belgian called Floredaire (query) (who said his real name was Collins) to take Hoyes and Clas by truck to a lumber camp at Houeilles. They stayed at Maisonette #86 with a middle-aged couple and their nineteen-year-old daughter for a week before taking a goods train ride to Marmande. Hoyes and Clas stayed for a week just outside Marmande at the Chateau St Jean with Mme Vve Copin and her four daughters before moving back through Houeilles to a small town in the Landes – probably Roquefort – where they stayed overnight in a hotel. Next day, after an encounter with two gendarmes where Hoyes had to admit he was not really a Frenchman, he and Clas took their suggestion to go to a nearby lumber camp from where they were assured they could easily get a ride to Pau. They were duly taken to a cafe about seven kilometres from Pau where they declared themselves to the proprietor whose daughter arranged to have someone from Pau

---

2   Hoyes says that Alexandre was the nom de guerre of Maurice Lacherez (nf) (35 years old, married with one son, very dark complexion, about 6 feet tall, very dapper with a moustache). He was a Parisian who lived with Mme Emma Reix (listed by IS9) on rue Jarjavay (query) on the outskirts of Limoges. He also had a garage that he used as a front for his resistance activities with the FTP (*Francs Tireurs Partisans*). (MIS-X #768 Hoyes)

come and see them. Two days later, a young man took them to his house in Arzacq (north of Pau) but that evening Rosemary Maeght and a man returned them to the cafe for the night and next morning brought them into Pau.

Robert Clas was put into a hotel while Hoyes was taken to a young man who worked with Rosemary until Rosemary and Isabelle de Liedekerke, a blonde Belgian girl who lived with her mother (a sculptress) in a large chateau (Castet de l'Array on Avenue Trespoey) brought Hoyes back to Isabelle's home. After lunch, Isabelle took Hoyes to Belgian textile merchant Leon van de Poele's villa where Hoyes stayed for five days, being joined on the second day by James Walsh.

2/Lt James H Walsh Jnr was the pilot of B-24 42-94999 (44BG/506BS) which was on the way to Epinal-Belfort on 11 May 1944 when they were hit by either flak or fighters – reports vary. With the loss of all four engines, the aircraft was abandoned to crash near Patay (Loiret) a few miles north-west of Orleans.[3]

Walsh landed somewhere near Orleans and made a somewhat haphazard journey across half of France to Dax where he finally found some organised help but his report is almost completely illegible from that point.

He wound up at Pau and stayed at the home of Leon van de Poele where he joined Charles Hoyes. He mentions a Belgian girl (Isabelle de Liedekerke) whose mother was a sculptress, and staying with an American woman (Rosemary Maeght) before going on to Navarennx – and reaching Spain on 26 May.

From the various notes, it seems that Hoyes and Walsh were taken along the same route as so many others – to Navarennx (probably by bus) and then to the mountains and crossing the frontier on 26 May, somewhere north of Isaba, where they were arrested.

---

3   All ten crew baled out of 42-94999 but only two others evaded successfully: top-turret gunner Sgt Lawrence C Richards and waist-gunner S/Sgt Joseph O Peloquin were taken to the MI9 Mission Marathon camp at Freteval and liberated in September.

CHAPTER 67

The Montrejeau Crossing to Les

Towards the end of May 1944, and knowing full well that the Allied invasion was imminent Bourgogne was starting to wind down its operation in Paris. Broussine had already told John Avery at the beginning of the month that his would be the last group that Bourgogne would be sending through but events seem to have overtaken them. In addition to Vollmuth and McNichol – who left on 9 May – another thirty evaders soon arrived in Paris. Broussine planned to take these last thirty men in three groups, in quick succession, to Pau. Due to circumstances beyond their control, this first group never reached Pau – although compared with the experiences of the other two groups (to the first of which yet more evaders were added) this may not have been such a bad thing

On the evening of 23 May 1944, ten evaders – Sgt Gordon Virgo, F/Sgt Jack Hoad, F/Sgt John Wallace, 1/Lt Royston Covington, 1/Lt Charles McClain, S/Sgt Jack Stead, Sgt John Katsaros, Capt Merlin Burgess, 2/Lt Buford Thacker and 1/Lt Raymond Holtz – left Paris by train for Toulouse with their guides Pierre Le Berre and Genevieve Crosson. Thacker also mentions a French Secret Service lieutenant named John Louis LeBranche as travelling to Spain with them and later being held at Lerida.

Sgt Cyril Gordon Virgo was the rear-gunner of 166 Sqn Lancaster ME639 (Jupp) which was returning from Augsberg in the early hours of 26 February 1944 when they were attacked by a night-fighter and the pilot ordered his crew to bale out. Four of the crew were killed and two captured – Virgo was the only successful evader.

Virgo came down in the mountains near Saulxures (Alsace), landing in deep snow, and after burying his parachute and flying gear, hid there until morning. Once it started to get light, he set off in a southerly direction, walking until about five-thirty that afternoon when he met a local man. Using his meagre French, together with his escape kit phrase-card, Virgo was able to tell the man that he was an Allied airman in need of help. The man took Virgo back to his mother's house in Saulxures where he was sheltered for the next eight days, during which time he learned that his pilot had been captured and that an officer and two sergeants from the aircraft had been found dead near the crash-site – from the descriptions given, Virgo was able to identify his navigator, P/O Anthony O Colan. Before he left Saulxures, Virgo was given civilian clothing and some boots. On 5 March, Virgo was taken across the frontier to Saint-Stail in Lorraine where he was handed over to a farmer who sheltered him until 15 March when his journey was arranged.

Robert Veyer, a cafetier at Moussey (Vosges) took Virgo to Paris, changing at Nancy, and arriving early on the morning of 18 April. Virgo was taken to a house in the back streets of Versailles while Veyer tried to contact an organisation. On 20 April, Virgo was interviewed in a cafe in Paris before Veyer took him to a flat belonging to Andre Maitre (apparently a member of the 2ieme Bureau) at 5 rue Louis Dupont, Clamart (Seine). Next day, Virgo was joined by Charles McClain. On 5 May, following a Gestapo round-up, they were both moved to Asnieres-sur-Seine where they stayed with Joseph Claux and his wife Marie Jeanne in their apartment at 103 rue des Bas until 23 May when they were taken into Paris and joined the rest of the group.

F/Sgt Douglas Jack Hoad was the rear-gunner of 44 Sqn Lancaster ND520 (Bartlett) which was on the way to Augsberg on the evening of 25 February 1944 and near Rethel (Ardennes) when, at about eight o'clock, they were attacked by a night-fighter which set the Lancaster on fire. Being unable to control the fire, the pilot gave orders for the crew to bale out.[1]

Hoad landed in a field south-west of Nizy-le-Comte (Aisne), hid his parachute and flying gear, and set off walking south-west for the next eight hours until he reached Saint-Erme-Outre-et-Ramecourt where he rested in a barn. Two hours later, he was found by a man who gave him some bread and advised him to head south to avoid a German post. At about eight o'clock that morning he reached the small village of Saint-Thomas (between Saint-Erme-Outre-et-Ramecourt and Aubigny-en-Laonnois) and a young man named Michel Mascre took him back to his home (IS9 lists a Leon Mascre at Saint-Thomas par Corbeny) where Hoad's journey was arranged.

Hoad was visited by two of Michel's brothers, Jacques and Marcel, who lived in Reims and suggested that Hoad might be taken out by aircraft but

1   ND520 pilot F/O Ernest W Bartlett evaded to Switzerland and wireless operator Sgt Lionel R Scott was sheltered by the Chauny-Dromas organsation until liberated.

on 13 April, their father (Leon – query) took Hoad by train, via Reims to Paris and the home of his other son. Next day, they were summoned by a telegram and a woman from Paris accompanied them back to Reims on 15 April. They went to a cafe where Hoad met various members of the organisation and one of them took Hoad to stay with butcher Marcel Guerin at 130 rue Jean Jaures. On 17 April, owing to Gestapo activities, Hoad was hurriedly moved to another house in the neighbourhood and that afternoon, taken in a police car to the little village of Bourgogne, just north of Reims, where he stayed with Erhard and Eliette Govin at their Cafe de la Gare.[2]

On 8 May, John Katsaros was brought to the cafe and that evening, they were both taken a few kilometres north to a small cottage near Pignicourt (Aisne) where they were joined by Buford Thacker and Raymond Holtz. On 20 May, the four airmen left by car with two guides who took them south of Reims to Epernay and then by train to Paris where Hoad, Thacker and Holtz stayed with gendarme Gabriel Bouyer at 86 rue Haxo. On 23 May, they were taken to a hospital (sic) near the Gare d'Austerlitz where they met Gordon Virgo and John Wallace.

F/Sgt John R Wallace RAAF was the navigator of 466 Sqn Halifax LV956 (Casey) which was returning from Tergnier in the late evening of 18 April 1944 when they were attacked by a night-fighter. The bomber was set alight and abandoned to crash near Forges-les-Eaux.[3]

Wallace landed in a field a few miles north of Argueil (Seine-Maritime), hid his parachute and began walking south. Shortly before dawn, he hid in a wood on the outskirts of Argueil where he stayed for the rest of the day. That evening, he set off to walk around the town but was intercepted by the maire of Argueil who took Wallace back to his home. Two hours later, two men drove Wallace to a farmhouse near La Hallotiere where he stayed until 22 April. That evening, he was taken to the home of a man called Patrice and stayed there for three days until he was moved to another house and then driven to a farmhouse near Bouvray (Beauvoir-en-Lyons – query) called 'Ferme de Guisemiel'. On 1 May, Wallace was taken to another house where a local maquis chief was having a meal and Wallace stayed with the

<hr>

2   Note that the American reports say Gerhard Erhard at the Cafe de Bourgogne. Erhard Govin (born November 1910) is credited with sheltering some twenty-five Allied evaders – including Halifax LV910 crewmen F/O Harold R Weller and W/O Gordon N Johnston before they were moved to Reims where they were captured in August 1944. Erhard Govin was denounced that same month and despite evading initial capture, was later tracked down by the Germans and mortally wounded. (WO208/5453)

3   LV956 engineer Sgt Abbott J Camp also evaded successfully, sheltered in France until liberated.

maquis group until 10 May. Whilst with the maquis, Wallace met Capt Merlin Burgess and his navigator 2/Lt 'Lucky' Hanton who had arrived on 30 April. On 10 May, a Frenchman called Maurice took Wallace, Burgess and Hanton to a house near Lounay (Eure) where they met S/Sgt Ned Daugherty. The four airmen were then taken by car to Forges-le-Eaux where they waited in a cycle shop until their train was due and English-born Mme Eva Aureille (of Cany-Barvile) took them by train to Paris.[4]

They were delivered to Bois-Colombes where they stayed with Gabriel Boulle at 17 Avenue de Saint-Germain (now Avenue Reverend Pere-Corentin-Cloarec) until 19 May when they were taken to a park in Paris. Wallace and Burgess were then taken to a top-floor apartment at 20 Boulevard de Sebastopol, Paris IV where Georges Prevot (often spelt as Prevost) supplied them with ID cards – and they met Sgt John Alexander.

In April 1944, Yves Allain had set up a small 'sub-network' of logeurs, independent of Genevieve Soulie and Jean-Louis Kervevant. He says that Paul Le Baron had given him the address in Paris of a Mlle Jeanette of reseau Bordeaux (Paulette Depesme) who in turn put him in touch with Georges Prevot and Genevieve Rocher at 20 Boulevard de Sebastopol – others in that network included Gabriel Boulle and Camille Schacherer (of 7 bis, rue Geoffroy Marie, Paris IX) and their friends. He says that Jeanette brought airmen from Champagne while Prevot (see later) found evaders in Paris.[5]

On 23 May, Wallace and Burgess were taken to a hospital (sic) where they met Gordon Virgo, Jack Hoad, and six Americans – Royston Covington, Charles McClain, Jack Stead, John Katsaros, Buford Thacker and Raymond Holz – and they followed two guides onto the overnight train to Toulouse.

1/Lt Royston T Covington Jnr was the pilot of B-17 42-39784 Cabin in the Sky (384BG/544BS) which was returning from Frankfurt on 8 February 1944. Already damaged by flak over the target, the aircraft was at low altitude on nearing the French coast and an easy target for the fighters that attacked them and set the left wing on fire. They climbed a little before the aircraft was abandoned to crash south-east of Cherbourg.[6]

Covington was helped almost immediately after landing and seems to

---

4   Mme Eva Marjorie Aureille (born December 1906 in Hanwell, England) (WO208/5451) was awarded a King's Commendation for Brave Conduct. (London Gazette 1 July 1947)

5   NARA Allain.

6   Cabin in the Sky radio-operator T/Sgt Kenneth P C Christian was the only other member of the crew to evade successfully – he was evacuated by RN MGB 502 in March by the Francois-Shelburn organisation on Operation Bonaparte 3.

have been sheltered locally in and around St Lo until being taken to Paris on about 16 March where he stayed with an English-speaking professor named Pierre Hugon at Impasse Guemenee, Paris IV ... unfortunately, the rest of Covington's report is very difficult to decipher.

1/Lt Charles J McClain was the bombardier of B-17 42-5306 (303BG/359BS) (Shoup) which had just turned back from the Pas-de-Calais (with their bombs still on board) on 28 February 1944 when they were hit by flak which took off the right wing. As the aircraft went into a spiral dive, it exploded and crashed near Le Translay (Somme).

McClain was blown from the aircraft and landed about 4 kilometres west of Blangy-sur-Bresle (about 24 kms south-west of Abbeville). He was captured by German troops immediately but for some reason the NCO of the detachment, a man called Horst, apparently decided to arrange for McClain to escape. He provided McClain with civilian clothes and had one of his men buy McClain a train ticket and escort him to St Jean de Luz. For some unexplained reason McClain lost contact with his German escort at Rouen.[7]

McClain was sheltered by a series of helpers, including Doctor Emile and Mme Eva Aureille in Cany-Barville, until 28 March when Mme Aureille took him to Paris. At the Gare St Lazaire, McClain was turned over to Gabriel Boulle (a short, 37-year-old ex-cavalry sergeant) and Roger Lemas (nf) (who worked for Radio Paris) and taken to stay at Boulle's house at 17 Avenue de Saint-Germain, Bois-Colombes. On 21 April, Lucienne Michaut took McClain to Clamart (Seine) where she and her daughter Jacqueline lived with policeman Andre Maitre at 5 rue Louis Dupont and were already sheltering Cyril Virgo. Next day, McClain and Virgo were interrogated by two men and given sweaters and cleated shoes. On 5 May, they were told that a woman in the organisation (a small, thin, artificial blonde, about 35 years old, apparently related to Lucienne or M Andre) had been arrested and McClain and Virgo were immediately taken to stay overnight with two sisters who ran a butchers shop. Next day, they returned to Bois-Colombes but a telephone call sent Andre off to join the maquis (sic) and McClain and Virgo were moved to nearby Asnieres-sur-Seine where they stayed with Joseph Claux (about 35 years old, 5 feet 10 inches tall, heavy-set, ex-French navy) at 103 rue de Bas.

---

7   The only other evader from 42-5306, waist-gunner S/Sgt Nick Asvestos, was also captured by German troops on landing but he escaped the same day and made a particularly determined exit from France, crossing the Pyrenees alone near Fort de Bellegarde, Le Perthus on 14 March 1944.

Meanwhile, Eva Aureille (back in Cany-Barville) had picked up John Wallace, Merlin Burgess, Emil Hanton and Ned Daugherty and brought them to Gabriel Boulle's house in Bois-Colombes and on about 18 May, the four airmen were taken into Paris to stay with fellow gendarme Georges Prevot at 20 Boulevard de Sebastopol.

On 23 May, Gabriel Boulle and Joseph Claux took McClain and Virgo into Paris where they met Boulle's friend Camille Schacherer and a blonde woman (fairly heavy, about 35 years old). They were taken to a park where they met a young man who took McClain and Virgo to a house where they picked up Merlin Burgess and John Wallace, and then to the upper floor of a public building where they met Georges Broussine (aka Burgundy) and joined the rest of the group.

S/Sgt Jack W Stead was the bombardier of B-17 42-31477 (447BG/709BS) (Hofsess) on a No-Ball mission against V1 rocket sites in northern France on 27 April 1944. As they crossed the French coast they were hit by flak and the bale-out order was given, leaving the aircraft to crash near Neufchatel-en-Bray. Stead was the only one of the crew to evade successfully.

Stead landed somewhere south-east of Rouen and walked south for a couple of days until finding someone who arranged his journey. He was taken to Paris where he stayed for three weeks with Marcel Guyon (5 ft 8 inches tall, heavy set, slightly bald – gendarme and local organisation chief) and his wife Paulette, caretakers of a boys school at 11 rue Ferdinand de Lesseps (Neuilly-sur-Seine – query).[8] Around 15-20 May, Stead was told that an English captain (sic) (an airman who had been badly wounded and cared for by the same woman for quite some time) had been caught and made to talk and as a result, sixty people in that branch of the organisation had been arrested. On 23 May, Jean (a gendarme, short with black hair – liaison with Bourgogne) came and took Stead to a house where he met Jack Hoad, John Katsaros, Buford Thacker and Raymond Holtz.

Sgt John Katsaros was a waist-gunner on B-17 42-38033 (401BG/612BS) (Dunaway) which was returning from Frankfurt on 20 March 1944. After taking action to avoid colliding with another B-17, they became separated from their formation, attacked by fighters and the aircraft abandoned.[9]

---

8   Georges Broussine includes Marcel and Paulette Guyon on his list of Bourgogne Helpers and the IS9 French Helper List gives their (post-war) address as 103 rue des Haies, Paris 20 – which is the other side of northern Paris …

9   42-38033 bombardier 2/Lt Theodore J Krol also evaded successfully and was sheltered at Freteval until liberated.

Katsaros, who had a badly injured arm, was helped immediately on landing just south of Fismes by Jean Joly (of 158 Avenue Jean Jaures, Reims) and Pierre Demarchez who, after an incident where the first doctor to treat Katsaros reported his presence to the Germans and he was rescued by two Frenchmen pretending to be German policemen, drove him to a farm belonging to Rene Felix and his wife Madeleine at 187 Route de Witry, Reims. Katsaros' arm still needed treatment before his subsequent journey could be arranged and so he was taken to a clinic in Reims where he was operated on. He stayed there for another two days before being taken to live with baker Pierre Demarchez and his wife Julienne Marie at their home in Chaumuzy for a month to recover.

> *"The doctor soon came and put my arm into a light plaster-cast. He then called up the local Gestapo Hq, reported my case and said that I must be taken to hospital at once as he said he had to amputate my arm. Half an hour later, two men in plain clothes came in, one of them armed with a revolver, and pushing a Frenchman in front of him. While the frightened people of the house watched the man with the gun, the other slipped over and cut the telephone wires. Meanwhile, the Frenchman with the gun in his back and his hands still over his head, tipped me the wink, while his guard told the people that they were Gestapo men come for the American. They hustled me out to a waiting car and we drove off, missing by fifty yards, a detail of four German soldiers who were coming for me. My friends saw to it that I received good care until my arm was well enough for me to travel and then they arranged the rest of my journey." (MIS-X #755 Katsaros)*

On 8 May, the Reims chief of police drove Katsaros to the Cafe de la Gare in the commune of Bourgogne (about 10 kms north of Reims) where he joined Jack Hoad who was being sheltered there by Erhard Govin and his wife. Next day, they heard that Julienne Demarchez had been arrested and Erhard Govin drove them a few kilometres north to a farm where they stayed with a Pole named Bronislaw Korach. In the middle of May, Erhard Govin took them back to Bourgogne to meet a Spanish-looking schoolteacher who was the contact for an organisation that took people across the Pyrenees, before returning them to M Korach. Shortly after that they were joined by Buford Thacker who stayed with Katsaros while Hoad returned to the Cafe de la Gare. Next day Katsaros and Thacker were taken back to the Cafe de la Gare where they met Raymond Holtz.[10]

---

10   John Katsaros wrote his own version of events in his 2008 book 'Code Burgundy, the Long Escape'.

On 20 May, Rene Felix took Katsaros, Thacker, Holtz and Hoad by train from Epernay to Paris where they were met by Genevieve Soulie. Katsaros was taken to stay with Marcelin Villemont and his wife Marie at 151 Boulevard Davout for three days while Thacker, Holt and Hoad stayed with Gabriel Bouyer at 87 rue Haxo. On 23 May, Katsaros joined the other three at rue Haxo and all four were taken by Metro to a school of electrical therapy (a combined hospital and school) where they met several Frenchmen, one being Dr Michel Poirier, a heavy-set hunchbacked man who gave them instructions and handed them over to their guides, Pierre Le Berre and Genevieve Crosson.

Capt Merlin K Burgess was the co-pilot of B-26 42-95845 (391BG/575BS) (Aldridge) which was on the way to bomb some (unidentified) marshalling yards in France on 27 April 1944. As they crossed the coast, they were hit by flak which set fire to the right engine. When the engine fell off and the aircraft started to spin, it was abandoned to crash near Dieppe.[11]

Burgess and his navigator Emil Hanton landed close to one another, just south-east of Dieppe, and were immediately directed to hide in some nearby woods by two Frenchmen. After spending the rest of the evening in the wood, they walked towards Rouen for two nights and on the third day declared themselves to a Frenchman who took them back to his home. He contacted another man who visited them and arranged their journey.

At some stage, they met Australian John Wallace and American Ned Daugherty and were taken to Mme Vau/Voe (Albertine Veron – query) before staying with Gabriel Boulle at 17 Avenue de Saint-Germain, Bois-Colombes. A week later (on 19 May), Burgess and Wallace were taken to stay with Georges Prevot at 20 Boulevard de Sebastopol, where they joined John Alexander, and met George's sister Genevieve and her husband Jean Rocher.

2/Lt Buford H Thacker was flying P-38 42-67522 (474FG/429FS) escorting B-26s to Charleville-Meziers on 7 May 1944. When the bombers were attacked by Me109s near Meziers, Thacker's group attacked the Messerschmitts and Thacker was shot down in the melee, his aircraft crashing in the small village of Petigny in Belgium.

Thacker baled out and landed a few kilometres south-east of Philippeville, Belgium. His report is almost illegible but it mentions Reims

---

11   42-95845 navigator/bombardier 2/Lt Emil M Hanton was the only other member of the six-man crew to evade – he was with Burgess to Paris and crossed the Pyrenees a few days later with another Bourgogne group.

– and Joseph Malherbe (nf) – meeting John Katsaros and Jack Hoad and going to Paris with them ... He describes the school of electric therapy, a combined school and hospital where he joined the rest of the group, and names John Louis LeBranche who he says was a lieutenant in the French Secret Service, last seen at Lerida.

1/Lt Raymond K Holtz was on a fighter sweep in P-47 43-25557 (356FG/359FS) on 27 April 1944 when he was shot down in a dog-fight near Passy-sur-Marne.

Holtz landed on the bank of the Marne, close to his burning aircraft, and was helped immediately by local people who disposed of his flying equipment and gave him a civilian coat. That night he was taken to a nearby house in Trelou-sur-Marne where he was sheltered overnight by a baker named Long and his journey arranged. Next day, Holtz was visited by a M Lombard (nf) and taken the following day to stay with miller Charles Cochois at Verneuil. Eight days later, Holtz was returned to M Long at Trelou-sur-Marne. On (about) 18 May, he was moved to Reims where he stayed with an unnamed barber and the following day, was visited by Rene Felix (from Reims – not to be confused with Rene Felix of Chauny), a short little man with a lot of pep, who was to be their guide to Paris. The day after that, Erhard Govin drove Holtz and Jack Hoad to collect John Katsaros and Buford Thacker from Bronislaw Korach and take them all back to his Cafe de la Gare in Bourgogne.

Their guides were intending to take the evaders on to Pau but at Toulouse station they were intercepted by members of the organisation with news that express trains to Pau were being checked by German inspectors and they should take the slower train instead. Unfortunately a bridge near Saint-Gaudens had been destroyed by saboteurs and the passengers were obliged to leave the train early. Their guides from Toulouse walked them to Montrejeau (Midi-Pyrenees) and after waiting a day, they set off across the mountains in the late evening of 25 May.

After being asked by Georges Broussine in Paris to tell the British authorities they had come from Burgundy, the ten evaders caught the eight o'clock evening train to Toulouse and according to Virgo, the journey was without incident. The party was split into two groups and they had two guides. They arrived at Toulouse the following day and were met at the station by some more members of the organisation. They were taken to a house near the station where they had a meal and were given a packet of food for their journey. Katsaros says that the party was broken up and that an English-speaking

Frenchman with a wooden leg took him, Holtz and Stead to an apartment house in a back street. At about six o'clock that afternoon, they were passed on their mountain guides (a short man with glasses who did not look the part at all, and another man) and took a train for Pau but could get no further than Montrejeau. Their guides took them on foot for about half an hour and they spent that night (24 May) and the next day on the top of a mountain.

Virgo may have thought the journey without incident but that wasn't the case for Charles McClain.

On arrival at Toulouse station, the evaders were scattered about while they waited for the train to Pau and McClain noticed that a man had walked past him several times, giving him odd looks. He also noticed that some of the other evaders had also been approached by other men in civilian clothes (Katsaros says they were recognised by their shoes) and saw Virgo give him a covert sign. McClain took this to mean they were being rounded up by police or Gestapo and quickly left the station. After walking south a few miles to Castenet-Tolosan and staying the night with a farmer, McClain returned to Toulouse station the following morning where he encountered the same man who had looked at him the previous day. McClain left the station immediately but the man followed him, telling McClain in English, that he was the one that had been left behind and finally persuading McClain to follow him to a house. Two more men and a woman gave McClain a meal whilst a local florist, who could speak English, was called. The florist explained that the men at the station had been trying to warn the group that the express trains to Pau were now too dangerous and that they should take a slow train instead. McClain was told he would have to wait for the next group but that evening he was taken back to the station where a guide took him by train to Montrejeau.

At about eleven o'clock in the evening of 25 May, the nine evaders from Paris were joined by another French guide who brought a group of Frenchmen – and McClain – and they started out immediately – Covington says the Frenchmen were elderly and that the airmen wound up carrying their luggage for them. For the next two days they didn't stop to sleep for more than three hours at a stretch. Their guides left them just before reaching the border and the following night (28 May), they arrived at Les (south of Canejan and not to be confused with Lez) in Spain – all that is, except for 1/Lt Raymond Holtz.

On the second night of the crossing the group were taken to a barn to rest after having to run for it when they were "spotted by Germans who lit

428

up the mountains with searchlights". Holtz was the last man into the barn and apparently mistook the rustling of rats for the noise of his companions settling into the straw, and so went to sleep. When he woke up at about six o'clock, he found that the others had left without him. After waiting for a while in the hope that one of the guides would come back, Holtz set off along the only trail that he could find, generally heading south and spending the next night in another barn. The following morning he carried on walking south. Once he knew that he was in Spain, Holtz stayed in the hills in order to try and get through the dangerous border area and catch a train to Barcelona. He was lucky enough to be driven the last few kilometres into Vielha by a helpful Spaniard but as he walked through the town, he heard his name being called and found it was Merlin Burgess who, along with the rest of the group, was already under arrest.

John Wallace recounts that in the evening of 25 May, McClain rejoined them, along with six (sic) Frenchmen who wanted to cross with them. At midnight, they walked south along the railway near Estanos (Carbonne) and then south-west over the mountains almost into Cier-de-Luchon, where they hid in a barn from mid-day until dark on 26 May. As night fell, they walked east and at dawn on 27 May, discovered that Holz was missing. They continued walking and crossed the frontier, where their guides left them. They went on and spent the night of 27 May in a barn. On the morning of 28 May, Burgess, Stead, Thacker and McClain set off together while the remainder walked to Les where they had a meal in a hotel. McClain and Stead arrived later and said they had lost Burgess and Thacker. The Spanish police arrived and took them to a police station where they were searched and questioned before being returned to the hotel. On 30 May, they were taken by bus to Vielha where they were searched again and put into a hotel, where they met Burgess, Thacker and Holz.

CHAPTER 68

Alexander and McPhee's group

On 24 May 1944, the second group of ten evaders – Sgt John Alexander, WO2 Archibald McPhee, P/O Harry Fisher, F/Sgt Harry Bossick, P/O Donald Courtenay, S/Sgt Ned Daugherty, 2/Lt Emil Hanton, Sgt Francis Higgins, T/Sgt Anthony Paladino and S/Sgt George Miller – and two women guides (Dr Alice Willm and Mlle David) (assume Catherine David) who took five men each – left the Gare d'Austerlitz in Paris by train for Toulouse and Pau.

Sgt John MacKenzie Alexander was tail-gunner of 101 Sqn Lancaster DV288 (Nimmo) which was shot down returning from Aulnoye in the early hours of 11 April 1944.[1]

Alexander landed near Willencourt (Nord-Pas-de-Calais) and was sheltered locally for five days before walking south towards Amiens. He was sheltered overnight in Amiens where he was helped by railway workers to take a train for Paris. Alexander arrived in Paris on 16 April and after wandering about for a while finally went to a police station near Notre Dame. He declared himself as an English airman and after searching him, a senior officer discretely passed him a piece of paper with an address.

The address was a hotel at 3 rue Bude, Ile Saint-Louis (Mme Louise Landroit) but because hotel registers were likely to be checked, he spent the first night in a house in a neighbouring street. Next day, he was moved to 11 rue Bude where the English-speaking concierge, Mme Crabbe, sheltered him while Mme Landroit provided his meals. He stayed with Mme Crabbe until 24 April when he was moved to Sainte-Genevieve-des-Bois to stay with Mme Crabbe's mother. Alexander returned to Mme Crabbe at rue Bude on 26 April and was taken that evening by Georges Prevot back to 20 Boulevard de Sebastopol where he was sheltered until 23 May. While Alexander was there, two more evaders arrived, John Wallace and Merlin Burgess, and on 22 May, Harry Fisher was brought in to have

---

1   Three other crew from DV288 also evaded successfully: pilot F/Lt Neil D Nimmo was liberated in Paris in August while navigator P/O Ernest J Burchell and bomb aimer F/O R N Johnson were sheltered with Mme Vignon in Amiens until liberated in September.

his identity checked. Wallace and Burgess left that same day (see later) and the following morning (query), Alexander was taken to a house where he joined Harry Fisher, Harry Bossick, Donald Courtenay and one other. They were taken to a clinic (sic) where they joined another five British and American evaders, including Ned Daugherty.

WO2 Archibald J McPhee, P/O Harry H J Fisher and F/Sgt Harry Bossick were the bomb-aimer, wireless operator and engineer of 218 Sqn Stirling EH942 (Poulton) which was returning from Laon on the night of 22-23 April 1944 when they were attacked by a night-fighter. The aircraft was abandoned and crashed about 20 kms WSW of Soissons.[2]

McPhee landed near Ressons-le-Long where Lucien Crepin at the Ferme du Chatelet, Montigny-Lengrain helped him, and next day brought in his wireless operator Harry Fisher.

Fisher also landed near Ressons-le-Long and had knocked on the door of Andre Lajoie and his wife. He was taken in and the following day, taken to join McPhee at the Ferme du Chatelet. The two evaders were then moved to a quarry where they were hidden in a mushroom cave for about a week, visiting the farm every second day for food. On about 4 May, Lucien Crepin took them by cart into nearby Vic-sur-Aisne where they stayed overnight with local resistance chief Gabriel Cochet before being taken on motorcycles to Morsain to stay with the Preux family.

On about 10 May, a young girl took McPhee and Fisher to Paris. They went to her mother's apartment (Mme Germaine Guinet – query) where they met Donald Courtenay and then all three airmen were taken to stay with nurse Therese Bailleul (nf) at 113 rue de l'Abbe Groult, Paris XV – where their various injuries were tended by two more nurses (Mme Germaine Renoncourt (of 135 Boulevard Brune) and Denise). In Paris they also met George Miller. Whilst staying with Mme Bailleul they were interrogated by a man claiming to be Canadian (probably French traitor and German infiltration agent Guy Marcheret) and were soon given ID cards. On 23 May, they were joined by their engineer Harry Bossick and next day the three crewmen were taken to a top floor apartment (apparently owned by a senior police officer) where they joined several American evaders.

Harry Bossick was helped almost immediately on landing near Vic-sur-Aisne, sheltered and fed until 27 April, when he was taken to Ressons-le-Long. On 21 May, he was moved to Morsain, where he stayed for another two days

---

2   Two of the crew from EH942 were killed but navigator F/O Hugh D Thomas (who crossed the Pyrenees in June) and rear-gunner F/Sgt Lawrence N Clay also evaded successfully.

(assume with Marie-Louise Preux) until being taken to Paris. In Paris, he joined McPhee and Fisher from his own aircraft and P/O Donald Courtnay.[3]

P/O Donald H Courtenay was the pilot of 635 Sqn Lancaster ND508 which was returning from Laon on the night of 22-23 April 1944.

> *"When ND508 was hit by a night-fighter, it exploded before anyone had the chance to bale out. Blown into the dark night sky he (Courtenay) was able to open his parachute before making a heavy landing near Vic-sur-Aisne. Unable to move, he was found by a farm labourer, and on 24 April, taken by train to Paris, where he received medical attention."[4]*

Courtenay was helped by Eugene Sive from Autrêches (just north of Vic-sur-Aisne) before being taken to Mme Marie-Louise Preux at Morsain and on to Paris.[5]

Whilst hidden in Paris, Courtenay says he met Archibald McPhee, Harry Fisher, Harry Bossick and S/Sgt George Miller – false papers were provided and they were put in touch with an escape organisation called the Burgundy line.

S/Sgt Ned A Daugherty was a waist-gunner on B-24 41-28666 (445BG/703BS) (Parker) which had turned back from a mission to Friedrichshafen on 18 March 1944. They were returning over France when they were attacked by fighters. Several of the crew, including both pilots, were killed before the aircraft was abandoned to crash near Saint-Lucien (Seine-Maritime). Daugherty landed about 4 kilometres north of Nolleval and was the only one of the crew to evade successfully.

Daugherty's report is almost illegible but on about 18 May (see Hanton and others reports), Mme Eva Aureille brought him from Cany-Barville to Paris where he stayed firstly with Mme Vau/Voe (Albertine Veron – query) and then with Gabriel Boulle at 17 Avenue de Saint-Germain, Bois-Colombes before moving to stay briefly with Georges Prevot at 20 Boulevard de Sebastopol.[6]

---

3   Some additional information on helpers in and around Ressons-le-Long is taken from the French website http://mairieressonslelong.free.fr/ressons_le_long.htm, and from the Scottish Saltire Aircrew Association Library Ref: 143 'Bailing Out' & 148 'Addendum to Bailing Out' – both written by Harry Fisher and published in 2009.

4   Extract from the 2009 book 'RAF Evaders' by Oliver Clutton-Brock, published by Grub Street.

5   Research by Dominique Lecomte.

6   Daugherty is also claimed as sheltered by Marie Allain at 4 Avenue de la Porte Brancion, Paris XV. (NARA Allain)

2/Lt Emil M Hanton was navigator/bombardier of B-26 42-95845 (Aldridge) which was on the way to bomb some (unidentified) marshalling yards in France on 27 April 1944 when they were hit by flak and the aircraft was abandoned to crash near Dieppe.

Hanton evaded with his co-pilot Merlin Burgess as far as Paris (see earlier) where he left Burgess with Mme Vau/Voe (query) and was taken to stay with Jean Camp, a professor of Spanish at the University of Paris, who lived near the university at 7 Place Paul Painleve.[7] Three days later, Hanton was moved to 11 rue Valentin Hauy where he stayed with Odette Drappier (who worked at the Ministry of Agriculture) for two days before he was taken to a public building (school/hospital) where he joined a group of evaders which included Ned Daugherty.

Sgt Francis F Higgins was the tail-gunner of B-17 42-37984 (92BG/326BS) (Shevchik) which was on the way to Frankfurt on 8 February 1944 when they were attacked by fighters which set fire to the #2 engine. Shortly after that the bale-out was given and the aircraft abandoned to crash near Catheux (Oise).[8]

"Eight (sic) out of ten back from this crew. Sgt Higgins was in the party that had to make the Pyrenean crossing with a train of refugees (see E&E Report #773 Berglind). In this dangerous passage, Sgt Higgins carried a baby the whole way. In Spain, he and several others mistakenly gave their civilian occupation to the Spanish authorities instead of maintaining that they were escapers. As a consequence, they were interned for some time in the civilian concentration camp at Miranda del Ebro. Besides the great discomfort of the camp, they were exposed to the attention of a man said to be a colonel in the German Secret Intelligence." (MIS-X #825 Higgins)

In his typed basic statement, Higgins simply says he sprained his ankle on landing and was knocked out. A crew-member (S/Sgt Robert Sidders) landed close by, ran over and brought him to his senses before some French children told them both to go and hide in some woods. They were brought

---

7   Jean Camp (born Salles d'Aude, Narbonne in February 1891) was, along with his wife and son Andre, one of the earliest members of Bourgogne and is described by Broussine as one of 'the main pillars' of his network. His home at 7 Place Paul Painleve was used as the organisation's headquarters, and radio sets and other materiel were hidden there. Hanton is one of only two evaders to be sheltered at his home. (WO208/5451) Jean Camp, who was awarded a KMS, was also an acclaimed writer, playwright and poet – he died in Paris in 1968.

8   42-37984 bombardier 2/Lt Donald J Periolat was captured (details unknown) but the other eight crew also evaded successfully – see 2/Lt James Williams earlier.

cognac and raw eggs and that evening, Higgins was taken by horse to a village, then to a place where he saw some of his crewmates and his journey was arranged. Unfortunately, the rest of his story is contained in scribbled notes that are almost impossible to decipher.[9]

Higgins and Sidders are reported by other crewmates as being sheltered with them in and around Crevecoeur-le-Grand (Oise) where their identities were checked by Gilbert Thibault and Jacky du Pac (of reseau Francois) before they were passed on to the Francois-Shelburn organisation in Paris. Higgins and Sidders seem to have lost contact with the rest of their crew soon after but like them, were sheltered by the Francois organisation at 5 rue Baudin, Levallois-Perret, with Marguerite (Margot) Di Giacomo.

After two weeks with Margot, her next door neighbour Yvonne Latrace moved Sidders to stay with Anita Lemonnier at 2 rue Ernest Renan for another seven weeks until Rene Loiseau took him to Chateaudun in early June and the Mission Marathon camp at Freteval.

I don't know why Higgins didn't go with the other six men from his crew when they left for St Brieuc in March. He mentions Marcel Cola (Yvon of reseau Francois) – and Rene Loiseau taking him to stay with Jean Charles Pradal and his dog Tout Suite at 6 Villa Auguste Blanqui, 44 rue Jeanne d'Arc. On 25 May, M Pradal took Higgins and Anthony Paladino to the third floor of a large hospital building where they joined a group of more airmen evaders.

Note that Sgt Charles W Creggor had stayed with M Pradal for ten weeks from 3 January until 14 March, when he and Sgt Dennis Brown were taken to St Brieuc and Plouha (for operation Bonaparte 3) and since neither mention meeting Higgins, he and Paladino probably arrived after they left. Paladino says they stayed about three weeks with M Pradal before leaving Paris on (about) 25 May, which suggests that Higgins probably stayed on at Levallois-Perret for several weeks after the others left.

T/Sgt Anthony R Paladino was the top-turret gunner of B-24 42-100345 (93BG/409BS) (Mankin) which was on the way to Frankfurt on 2 March 1944 when they were hit by flak over Abbeville. They carried on for some time before the aircraft was finally abandoned to crash north-east of Lille.[10]

---

9   Dominique Lecomte reports Higgins being helped by Rene and Eva Moreau (and son Jean) at rue Pierre Budin in Chaumont-en-Vexin and (along with Sidders) by Marcel and Helene Dumont at Montjavoult.

10   Three other crew from 42-100345 also evaded successfully: radio-operator T/Sgt Robert J Rujawitz with Francois-Shelburn and evacuated by MGB at the end of March, and bombardier 2/Lt Roy W Carpenter Jnr and co-pilot 2/Lt Melvin L Heinke who crossed the Pyrenees from Aquitaine in April and May respectively.

Paladino landed near Brunvillars-la-Motte (Oise) and with the aid of his escape kit compass, walked south through the snow. He passed though (or bypassed) Plainval, Saint-Just-en-Chausee, Le Plessier-sur-Bulles, La Rue-Saint-Pierre, La Neuville-en-Hez, Angy, Mouy, Cavigny and Sainte-Genevieve, getting occasional help, sleeping in haystacks where possible but generally living off his escape kit rations until finally reaching a farm at Laboussiere-en-Thellelate four days later where he was taken in. After having to almost boil the socks from his battered feet, Paladino was given a meal while an organisation was contacted. Some time later, Paladino was taken to Paris.

The scribbled notes of Paladino's report are very hard to decipher but there is mention of Gilbert (Thibault) and meeting various other evaders – Francis Higgins in particular – and Robert Sidders (both from 42-37984) at some stage. He also mentions Yvonne (Latrace) and Rene (Loiseau) at Levallois-Perret, and a woman doctor (probably Bertranne d'Hespel). Note that these helpers were all associated with Paul Campinchi's reseau Francois and that six other crewmen from 42-37984 were helped by reseau Francois and evacuated by MGB from Brittany in March on various Shelburn Bonaparte operations.

At some stage, Marcel Cola (Yvon of Francois-Shelburn) took Paladino and Higgins to stay with Jean Charles Pradal at 44 rue Jeanne d'Arc for three weeks and since Higgins says that it was M Pradal who took him and Paladino to join the other evaders on 25 May, that was presumably the last place he was sheltered in Paris.

S/Sgt George R Miller was the tail-gunner of B-24 42-7548 Bull O' The Woods (44BG/66BS) (Heskett) which was on the way to Ludwigshaven on 30 December 1943 when two engines failed. The aircraft immediately went into a spin and the bale-out order was given. Six other crew also evaded successfully – see Lancaskey earlier.

Miller was badly injured in the aircraft before he baled out, landing in the front garden of a deserted house but so close to the road that he was quickly spotted by children from a neighbouring farm. Later that day, two men took him by cart to another farm before a third man took Miller by train to Paris and a house where a doctor gave him morphine and arranged to have him admitted to a hospital. In the months that Miller was in the hospital he had four operations and five blood transfusions before his journey was arranged. Unfortunately Miller's report is so faded as to be almost completely illegible – however ...

In addition to providing some details about Miller's ordeal, these lightly edited extracts from a draft of *"Hopeful Monster: Guy Marcheret's Passage Through the Violent First Half of the Twentieth Century"* by John S Hill (and used with the author's kind permission) illustrate some of the complications experienced by those wishing to help evading airmen, and the dangers to which they were exposed.

"Mme Marie-Louise Preux worked a farm at Morsain, near Vic-sur-Aisne, about sixty miles north-east of Paris. Her husband belonged to a Resistance group and had gone into hiding. Madame Preux's mother, Madame Benoite Nicot, lived at 7 rue de Berger in Montreuil-sous-Bois. Madame Preux rented the land from Mme Berthe Lion of 19 rue Jean Beausire in Paris. One day, Madame Preux and a neighbouring farmer, Robert Mouton, found and hid a badly wounded American flyer named George Miller ... Madame Preux brought the wounded flyer to her mother, Madame Nicot who called in her physician, a Doctor Goujard. The doctor recommended that she have Miller treated at a clinic run by a Doctor Guillemin in the Rue Leon Delhomme in Paris. Madame Nicot gave Miller her grandson's ration-card and got him into Doctor Guillemin's clinic where the doctor operated on him. From the clinic, Miller went to the home of a nurse at the clinic, a Madame Yon. Then Madame Nicot, took in another evader, a man named Donald Cameron [query]. Madame Preux also continued to collect evaders. She passed them to Madame Yon for a time; she passed them to Madame Therese Hugon; she passed them to a Madame Briand, the wife of a policeman. Madame Preux played a vital role in these operations by providing food from her farm as well as the flyers who consumed it. However, they had no contact with an evasion line by which to send the evaders home, so a pool of flyers just piled up ...

Efforts to resolve the problem inevitably extended the circle of people who knew that Madame Preux was sheltering evaders. Monsieur Mouton, the neighboring farmer at Morsain, wrote to Madame Lion in Paris, their common land-lord, to inform her that Madame Preux had a downed Allied flyer. Madame Preux herself then went to visit Madame Lion. Her daughter, Odette Lion, who taught English in a lycee, then visited Madame Nicot several times to talk to Cameron. After several days, on a Sunday, Odette Lion brought her mother to visit Madame Nicot as well. M and Mme Yon were present at this visit. Soon afterward, Madame Lion told her nephew, Doctor Bauchard, about the flyers being hidden by Madame Nicot. Bauchard tried to help her make useful contacts, although he himself was not a member of any Resistance group. The doctor visited Madame Nicot, bringing with him a M Lebeleguic. Bauchard's friend was about fifty, spoke perfect "American", and claimed to have a Canadian pension for the loss of his left leg during the First World War. Madame Preux, who was present, instantly distrusted Lebeleguic and refused to turn over the evaders to him. Seeking to reassure the family, Lebeleguic returned later with a young man who claimed to be the son of a general and in possession of false identity documents, but he seemed too badly dressed to be the son of a general. Both parties were stymied by this refusal.

The pressure on the Nicot-Preux group suddenly mounted to a terrifying level when Doctor Guillemin received an anonymous letter stating that he was harbouring an evader and demanding that 100,000 francs be paid into a post office box at the Avenue d'Orleans. The letter was signed "La Rose". Knowledge of the evader's presence and of the operations performed on him (Miller) was relatively restricted, so the blackmailer had to belong to a small group of people. Mme Hugon and Mme Yon were both nurses at the clinic where the operation had been performed and had assisted in the operation. Mme Hugon had a sister, Mme Germaine Renoncourt (of 135 Boulevard Brune, Paris XIV), who had shared in nursing Miller while he was at the Yon's home. Mme Yon and Mme Briand were known to be close friends. Madame Yon had introduced Madame Preux to the Briands. Edmond Coattrieux (of 25 rue du Commandeur, Paris XIV), another policeman and Resistance member, had taken some of the evaders off the hands of the Briands. At the same time as the attempt to blackmail Dr Guillemin, Mme Briand reported to Coattrieux that Mme Renoncourt had told her that she would denounce the policeman to the Gestapo for having helped evaders. Then a fellow policeman named Saintier introduced Coattrieux to Georges Prevost (sic) …

Georges Prevost and his brother-in-law, Jean Rocher, lived with their partners, Jean's wife Genevieve (Georges' sister) and Raymonde Garin. The two men were also policemen and Mme Rocher worked as a cashier at a bank. The four shared an apartment on the top floor at 20 Boulevard de Sebastopol, within walking distance of the Prefecture de Police building, where Georges worked. They had begun by hiding "refractaires" fleeing the STO. From this they had moved naturally into producing false identity papers for the Resistance. Prevost did the forging work, essentially doing the same thing for the Resistance that he did for the police: filling out identity documents, attaching photographs, and stamping them with official seals. At the end of 1943 the group to which they belonged, the "Front National de Police" decided to try its hand at helping evaders. The Prevost household became the center of this effort.[11]

Prevost had a connection to a functioning evasion line and was looking for evaders; Coattrieux knew of some people with evaders, but no link to an evasion line; Coattrieux closed the circuit between the two groups. Coattrieux got in touch with Madame Yon to say that he had found a link to an evasion line. Madame Yon introduced Coattrieux to Madame Nicot. Through Madame Yon again, Coattrieux introduced Madame Nicot to Georges Prevost. Coattrieux also took Mme Preux to meet Prevost so she could judge for herself. After Preux had been reassured that Prevost seemed legitimate, Coattrieux and Yon escorted four or five evaders being hidden by Nicot, Preux and Briand to the Prevost apartment. One of these was George Miller, passed to the Rocher-Prevost group on 24 May 1944. As improvised, insecure, and rickety as this system may appear, it worked well – between January 1944 and May 1944 the Prevost-Rocher group sent 28 evaders out through the "Burgundy" line ..."

It's not clear where the ten airmen were assembled on 25 May prior to being taken to the Gare d'Austerlitz but it seems likely they went to the same combined hospital and school of electrical therapy (probably part of *l'Hopital de la Pitie-Salpêtriere*) that Georges Broussine had used the previous night to bring Royston Covington and his group together.

The evaders were taken in two groups of five by two guides (a man and woman) and joined by a third guide who led them to another apartment. The party was split again and they followed two girls to the station where they took the ten o'clock evening train to Toulouse. They reached Toulouse the following morning, where they were joined by another girl. While waiting for their connection to Pau some French prisoners on another platform escaped and their German guards opened fire with machine-guns, spraying the station with bullets.

Genevieve Crosson (who must have come straight from Montrejeau) says in her book that while she was waiting for the group to arrive in Pau, she was questioned by a German policeman who asked why she was at

---

11   Georges Michel Prevot (born April 1911), Jean Rocher (born June 1905) and his wife Genevieve (born Feb 1910) were arrested on 11 August 1944. All three were deported to Germany – George Prevot and Jean Rocher to Buchenwald where Jean Rocher died two months later and Georges Prevot, a few days before the liberation. Genevieve Rocher was repatriated to France in the summer of 1945. (WO208/5453)

the station without luggage. She told him that she was waiting for a group of friends who were coming to attend her engagement party. She was particularly concerned that the evaders' ID papers might not be up to the standards set by Jean Carbonnet, who had been arrested less than a month earlier. She apparently convinced the German that both she and her friends were 'good' French and when the group finally arrived (and she saw Alice Willm leading them) she was able to point them out and he let the ten evaders pass without further inspection.

They reached Pau late in the evening of 26 May. Outside Pau station, their guides handed them over to a group of well dressed girls (including Rosemary Maeght) and they were taken off in couples to various houses (Fisher at least to stay with Leon van de Poele) where they spent the night. On the following evening, the party reassembled at a house in Pau where it was decided that only eight could be taken and so the two youngest, nineteen-year-olds John Alexander and Ned Daugherty, were left behind.

Alexander and Daugherty stayed in Pau until 30 May when they joined a group of ten more evaders, which included John Pittwood and Charles Clonts and the rest of their journey was with Pittwood – see later.

The remaining eight airmen were put into two waiting cars and driven into the foothills. McPhee's group of four had an armed guard and when the second car failed to arrive, they began walking. They stopped at a barn that night where they waited for four days, being joined on the second day by the rest of their party. A tall guide called Jean collected money from them and moved them to another barn where they were joined by S/Sgt Lester Knopp and a group of Jewish refugees (12 men, 12 women and some children) guided by four Frenchmen with Sten guns – and by 2/Lt Elmo H Berglind.

CHAPTER 69

Clonts Group

On 25 May 1944, the third group of ten evaders – F/O Maurice Steel, F/O William Alliston, S/Ldr Ernest Sparks, F/Sgt John Pittwood, Sgt John Pearce, Sgt Wilfred Greene, Sgt Patrick Evans, Capt Maurice Thomas, 1/Lt Charles Clonts and T/Sgt Kenneth Nice – and guides Charlie and Henri – left Paris for Toulouse and Pau.

F/O Maurice S Steel was the navigator and F/O William Alliston the mid-upper gunner of 10 Sqn Halifax LV858 (Barnes) which was nearing Tergnier (Aisne) on the night of 10-11 April 1944 when it was attacked by a night-fighter. The two starboard engines caught fire and the aircraft was abandoned. The pilot and rear-gunner were killed and three crew captured – wireless operator F/Lt John H Coller (see below) was the only other successful evader – he was liberated in Paris in August.

Steel and Alliston both landed near Berzy-le-Sec (Picardy) and were soon sheltered there, along with their wireless operator John Coller. However, rather then endanger their helpers any more than necessary, the three airmen decided to make their own way, leaving Berzy early next morning (12 April) and walking south. They found more help the following day and were driven to Armentieres-sur-Ourcq, where they stayed at various places until 2 May, when they were taken to a farm just outside Armentieres while arrangements were made by a veterinary surgeon from Couchy-le-Chateau to take them to Soissons.

On 4 May, they were taken by lorry to stay with Maurice Dupuis (influential man, ex-Major in the French army) on rue Montague.[1] On 24 May, Steel and Alliston were driven to Paris in a lorry owned by a M Blossard (nf), accompanied by him and Maurice Dupuis while Coller stayed behind with the maquis as a radio-operator. They were introduced to a young man who took them to a flat (no address) for the night and next day a young man and woman (no names) took them to another house (no address) where Steel stayed overnight while Alliston went to meet a party

---

1   The IS9 Helper List give an address for Maurice Dupuis as Vauxrot-la-Montagne, par Soissons – I think this is Crouy, just north-east of Soissons.

of about a dozen evaders and guides in the room of large hospital. After the meeting, Yves Allain (aka Gregoire) took Alliston back to his flat at 4 Avenue de la Porte Brancion, Paris XV for the night where he met Yves' wife Mimi (Marie Francoise).

Next day, Steel and Alliston were taken to the hospital where they met the other airmen evaders in their party before setting out for the station with guides Henri (a radio-telegraphist) and Charles.

S/Ldr Ernest N M Sparks was the pilot of 83 Sqn Lancaster JB402 which was returning from Mailly-le-Camp in the early hours of 4 May 1944 when they were attacked by a night-fighter. The aircraft caught fire and was abandoned to crash near Orbais-l'Abbaye (Champagne-Ardenne).[2]

Sparks landed somewhere near Margny (Champagne-Ardenne) which he reached that evening and where he was given food and clothes before he set off again at midnight. Over the following three days Sparks made his way to Courtenay (Loiret) from where his journey was arranged and he was sheltered with a blacksmith. On 8 May, Marcel Raffard took Sparks back to his house 'Idle Hour' at Ervauville, where he stayed until 15 May when Raffard took him by bicycle to La Chappelle-Saint-Sepulcre. He was passed on to a youth named Bernard who took Sparks (still on his bike) to Montargis where they took a train to Paris. They went straight through Paris to Lagny where an important looking man checked Sparks' identity then went with Sparks and Bernard to Dampmart where Sparks joined John Pearce, who was lodged with a baker named Michel Place at 7 rue du Chateau.

On 24 May, a youth and a girl came to tell Sparks and Pearce they would be leaving the following day. The youth duly returned next day and took them to Paris where they picked up John Pittwood and all three airmen were handed over to a girl on a street corner. Sparks, Pearce and Pittwood were immediately passed on to a man who took him to his flat at the top of a building (address unknown) where he lived with his sister – both about thirty-five to forty years old and of Jewish appearance. There they met Gregoire (Yves Allain) (apparently a well known agent). At six o'clock that afternoon, they were taken to the first floor of a building where they met Maurice Steel, William Alliston and the other evaders.

F/Sgt John Pittwood was the navigator of 207 Sqn Lancaster ND556 (Lissett) which was shot down by fighters returning from Mailly-le-Camp

---

2   Six other members of the eight-man JB402 crew also evaded successfully: engineer Sgt Cyril Steele, rear-gunner W/O Walter G Teague, mid-upper gunner F/Sgt Kenneth Hunter, wireless operator W/O D A Woodland, bomb aimer F/Lt L G Foley and bomb aimer (Special) F/Lt Tindall – Hunter and Woodland evading together until liberated in August.

on the night of 3-4 May 1944 and abandoned to crash near Chaintreaux (Seine-et-Marne).[3]

Pittwood came down near Rosieres (Seine-et-Marne) and was soon joined by his mid-upper gunner Ronald Emeny. They walked south and were sheltered near Griselles where their journeys were arranged. On 5 May, Pittwood and Emeny were sent to La Selle-en-Hormoy where a doctor tended to Emeny's burn injuries before they were taken to a farm near Louzouer. On 10 May, the two men separated and Emeny was moved to Chateau-Renard. Two days later, a man called Sebastian took Pittwood via Paris to Lagny (Seine-et-Marne) where he stayed with Henri Hebert Cane and his wife at 13 rue de la Paix. On 25 May, Sebastian took Pittwood back to Lagny station where he met Ernest Sparks and John Pearce and the rest of his journey was with them.

Sgt John G Pearce was the top-turret gunner of 550 Sqn Lancaster ND733 (Lloyd) which was returning from Mailly-le-Camp in the early hours of 4 May 1944 when they were attacked by a night-fighter.[4]

Pearce landed near Dampierre-en-Yvelines (south-west of Paris) and was heading towards Rambouillet when he approached a man and his journey was arranged. Pearce was taken by horse and cart to Monfor-l'Amaury where he was given a meal at the home of the cart-driver before being sheltered overnight with a neighbour. Next day, a young man came to take Pearce to Rambouillet, where they had lunch with the (unnamed) owner of an artificial manure manufacturing business, before taking a train to Paris. They went on through Paris to Lagny where Pearce was taken to a man called 'the Chief' who seemed to an important member of the local organisation.[5] After an interrogation, Pearce was taken to stay with Henri Hebert Cane at 13 rue de la Paix, Lagny. On 7 May, Pearce was moved across the river to Dampmart and sheltered by Michel Place in his bakery at 7 rue du Chateau, where he

---

3   Three other crew also evaded successfully: mid-upper gunner Sgt Ronald T Emeny crossed the Pyrenees with Comete (the last man to do so) in June, engineer Sgt Nicholas J Stockford crossed the Pyrenees to Irun, also in June, while wireless operator Sgt Phillip N King was sheltered in France until liberated. Bomb aimer W/O Laurie Wesley was captured in Paris on 4 July 1944 by the Belgian traitor and German infiltration agent Prosper Dezitter (aka the Captain) and his Spanish associate, Florentina Dings.

4   Pearce says that the pilot (F/Sgt T Lloyd) gave the order to abandon the aircraft and Pearce (along with bomb aimer P/O Yaternick and rear gunner Sgt A C Crilly) baled out before the aircraft returned to the UK.

5   F/Lt James H Foy, who was sheltered by Michel Place at Dampmart in January 1944, says the head of the local organisation was a man named Octave Boutellier who lived in Lagny. (WO208/5583-1868) The IS9 Helper List has Henri Bouttellier of 23 rue du Colonel Durand, Lagny.

was joined by Ernest Sparks about a week later – and the rest of his journey was with him.

Sgt Wilfred A Greene was the mid-upper gunner of 419 Sqn Halifax HX189 (Thomas) which was attacked by a night-fighter over Laon late in the evening of 22 April 1944. The Halifax was so badly damaged in the attack that it was abandoned.[6]

Greene landed in the northern suburbs of Laon, about 100 yards from the wreckage of the Ju88 that his tail-gunner (Sgt Victor A Knox RCAF – KIA) had just shot down. With Germans from the local garrison rushing to the burning Junkers, Greene quickly shed his parachute harness before escaping into the night. He ran several kilometres north to some woods near Chery-les-Pouilly where he rested through the following day. That evening, he carried on northwards but found he couldn't cross the river Serre and so turned south-west, reaching Crepy-en-Laonnois by morning. He was soon spotted by two local men and identified himself to them as a British airman, whereupon one of them gave Greene some bread and a civilian set of overalls. Greene continued south to Chivy-les-Etouvelles where he approached a small house where he was given food, and then late that evening, carried on, reaching Chevregny the following morning (26 April) where he rested in a barn. Later that day he walked on to Conde-sur-Aisne where he was helped and his journey arranged.

Greene was sheltered in Conde-sur-Aisne by Berton Ridgundy (query) until 28 April when Leo Nathie took him back to his house at Cuffies, just north of Soissons – Greene says at 37 Avaxrot (sic). About a fortnight later, Greene was taken to Paris where he met Maurice Steel and William Alliston.

Sgt Patrick J Evans was the wireless operator of 625 Sqn Lancaster ME697 (Grey) which was attacked by a night-fighter over Mailly-le-Camp in the early hours of 4 May 1944. The aircraft exploded, blowing Evans and S/Ldr Robert W H Grey (the only other survivor) from the aircraft.[7]

Evans landed in some woods about three kilometres north of Villethierry (Yonne) and after burying his parachute, began walking. In his dazed state, Evans soon found he was going in circles and so lay down to sleep for a

---

6   HX189 pilot F/O Charles A Thomas (an American serving with the RCAF) crossed the Pyrenees to Elizondo in June, while navigator F/Sgt Robert P Lindsay and bomb aimer P/O John A Neal were sheltered by the Chauny-Dromas organisation until liberated.

7   Robert Grey almost made it – he evaded alone for five days, taking a series of trains to Perpignan and then walking to the Spanish border at Le Perthus on 9 May 1944, only to be captured by a lone German soldier.

couple of hours. He rested all the next day before setting off, meeting a man named Saussey early on the morning of 5 May who took Evans back to his house where Evans journey was arranged.

Aristide Saussey was a baker in Villethierry where Evans met his wife, child (Pierre) and his assistant, Charles. At about nine o'clock that morning, the maire, Robert Hure, visited and later that day, returned with his wife Gilberte who spoke enough English to explain that they didn't know of any escape organisations but would contact the local Roman Catholic priest. M Hure returned again that evening to tell Evans that he should stay with M Saussey for another week. Meanwhile, M Hure contacted the maire of Pont-sur-Yonne and on 11 May, took Evans to Pont-sur-Yonne where he was lodged with Henri Goldvin and his married sister at 9 bis rue Paul Bert. On 18 May, the maire and an English-speaking woman came to tell Evans that he would be taking a train to Paris and that evening, M Goldvin took him to the station where they met two women, both doctors – one named Dr Ville (query spelling) – who took him to Paris.

They went by Metro to a friend of Dr Ville's who lived on rue Louis Philippe, where Evans stayed three days until being taken to Dr Ville's apartment, where he was questioned about his aircraft by a male doctor, before a young girl took him to stay with Paul and Olga Christol.

On 22 May, Evans met a tall blonde American woman named Mme Tartiere (aka Drue Leyton) and in the evening, Maurice Thomas and Kenneth Nice arrived. That night, the same girl who'd taken him to Dr Ville's apartment took the three of them to a clinic where they joined the doctor who'd asked about Evans' aircraft and some 13 (sic) more British and American airmen.

Capt Maurice S Thomas was the pilot of B-17 42-97077 (305BG/366BS) which was hit by flak over Saarbrucken on 11 May 1944 and lost three engines. The bale-out order was given and the aircraft abandoned.[8]

Thomas landed about 30 miles north of Hirson (Aisne) and headed south, evading alone (although with regular assistance) for seven days until being taken to l'Esperance Ferme, just south of Auberive, where he was sheltered overnight. The following afternoon, two men in a car collected him and drove him to a 'tavern' near Reims. He was interrogated by an English-speaking Belgian (6ft 3 inches tall, 230 lbs, dark hair and

8   Command pilot Capt Magnus G Bolken and radio-operator T/Sgt Joseph K Regan also evaded successfully – Bolken was sheltered until liberated in Paris in August and Regan was sheltered in Petigny, Belgium until liberated in September. 42-97077 waist-gunner S/Sgt Francis P Sanford was injured and captured – he was liberated at Reims hospital in August.

moustache) before being taken to the home of one of the men who had collected him (another Belgian, 6 ft tall, married to a Frenchwoman, with five children) where Thomas stayed for five days. Then a short, English-speaking Frenchman took him by car, collecting Elmo Berglind, Kenneth Nice and three (query) other Americans (Berglind says one was S/Sgt Lester W Knopp and another an Indian) on the way, to the railway station at Epernay where they took a train to Paris.[9]

In Paris, they were taken to an office building where they met a blonde, English-speaking girl (Genevieve Soulie) who took Thomas and Nice to the apartment of a man (about 5 ft 5 inches tall, 150 lbs, half bald, about 45 years old) and his wife (about 5 ft 11 inches, very conspicuously dressed) where Patrick Evans was already staying with Paul and Olga Christol. The following night, Genevieve returned with a man called Charlie (5 ft 10 inches, about 21 years old, brownish hair, spoke English) and they led Thomas, Nice and Evans back to the office building. Here they joined about a dozen evaders and several guides, including the man who had brought Thomas to Paris. Georges Broussine gave them their instructions (and asked them to say they were sent by Burgundy) and then Charlie (and Henri – who went to Spain with them) took them by train to Pau.

1/Lt Charles R Clonts Jnr was flying P-47 42-75173 (404FBG/506FBS) at the back of a group of ten fighters on a Sweep mission on 8 May 1944 when he was shot down. Clonts baled out just north of Soissons and landed in a field before running to hide in a nearby wood where he stayed overnight. He started walking the following day and in the afternoon, approached a house where he was taken in and his journey arranged.

Clonts was sheltered at Pasly, just north-west of Soissons, with Cecile Lengele and her mother (query) Mme Le Blanc. He was visited next day by Professor Obner (nf) a professor of English from Soissons who was the organisation contact man and who assured Clonts that he was in good hands. One day the professor took Clonts to meet Maurice Steel, William Alliston and John Coller who were being sheltered nearby with Maurice Dupuis. On Tuesday 23 May, two men took Clonts to M Dupuis' house where he met Wilfred Greene and they, Steel and Alliston were taken into Soissons. The four evaders were then driven to Paris, the railway between Soissons and Paris being closed to civilian traffic.[10]

---

9   Pierre Jacob describes taking a (second) group of evaders from Epernay to Paris in May 1944, which included *"un superbe Hindou au visage pain brûle tout tatoue de bleu"*. (NARA Jacob)

10   Note that Greene, in his very brief report (WO208/5583-1990) simply says he was taken to Paris where he met Steel and Alliston – and they don't mention travelling with Clonts either.

Clonts and Greene followed a woman in a red hat to the seventh-floor apartment of an elderly couple, he was a judge and she was a nurse. On 25 May, a young man took Clonts and Greene to a hospital (sic) where they joined Steel and Alliston and met Maurice Thomas, Kenneth Nice, Ernest Sparks, Patrick Evans and another RAF sergeant. They were given instructions by a man (about 30 years old, stout, heavy, fleshy face, big stomach and round shoulders, spoke fair English) and a girl (medium build with a roll of light brown hair) (Genevieve Soulie) who told them to say that they came from Burgundy. They also met Henri and Charlie (about 22 years old, who went through to Spain with them) their guides to Toulouse.

T/Sgt Kenneth H Nice was the radio-operator of B-17 42-3348 Dottie J III (96BG/337BS) (Bye) which was returning from Schweinfurt on 14 October 1943. Flak over the target had damaged #2 and #4 engines and as they dropped out of formation, they were attacked by fighters. The badly damaged aircraft (described by the navigator as a sieve) was crash-landed between Metz and Nancy.

All ten crew survived the landing although several of them were injured. They split into groups to evade, but only three other Dottie J crew did so successfully, all being picked up by RN MGBs from Brittany – navigator 2/Lt Merle E Woodside (Op Envious IIb), pilot 2/Lt Raymond F Bye (Op Felicitate II) and waist-gunner S/Sgt Mike Olynik (Op Bonaparte 2).

Nice started off with Woodside and Bye and they walked to Richecourt (Lorraine) where they spent the night and following day in a deserted hayloft. During the following night they walked to Saint-Mihiel where their journeys were arranged.

Nice's Appendix C is almost illegible but his report does include a typed statement that suggests he was sheltered locally for several months until the house was raided by the Germans. Nice – and S/Sgt Lester Knopp – were able to hide in the roof and heard the Germans abusing the husband and wife who had sheltered them – and were told later by their daughter that they had both been shot. Nice and Knopp then left the area and walked for five days before finding more help and having their journey arranged.

Nice and Knopp were sheltered by Maurice and Jeanne Dezothez on rue de la Gare in Fismes for six weeks from mid-November, escaping on 31 December when Maurice Dezothez was arrested. 2/Lt Everett Lynn Childs reports Nice and Knopp as staying with a farmer in the Fismes area in late November/early December, and following the arrest of a local resistance man on 29 December, Childs went to see them just before the Gestapo arrived to search the place. The three airmen set off walking south-west, reaching somewhere near Montmirail (Marne) on the third day, where a chance resistance contact sheltered them overnight, and two days later (via Les Essarts-les-Sezanne) somewhere near Fere-Champenoise where they were sheltered on a Polish farm. On 31 January, they were all moved – Nice and Knopp to a farm near Champigneul, at which point they seem to have lost contact with Childs.

It isn't clear from either report exactly what happened (or when) but Knopp says they were sheltered at Mailly-Champagne (which is just south of Reims) (possibly with Mme Lea Chandelot on rue Gambetta – but that's just a guess). Nice and Knopp were still together on 25 May when they joined Maurice Thomas and Elmo Berglind on the train from Epernay to Paris.

Steele and Alliston say they took the eight-thirty evening train for Toulouse but were delayed outside Paris for four hours and didn't reach Toulouse until six o'clock the following afternoon. They waited three hours at Toulouse station before taking a train to Tarbes where they spent the rest of the night in the waiting room and went on to Pau next morning. Clonts reports a mix-up of trains at Toulouse, they were delayed through bomb damage and missed their connection to Pau, wound up at Tarbes and then when they got to Pau there was no-one to meet them.[11]

> "Etienne [Etienne Lalou], the guide who should have met us at Pau was not there since we were a day late in arriving, so we were forced to spend the day in a park while our guides tried to find somewhere for us to stay. We were eventually taken to a derelict farm 5 kms out of Pau and stayed here until 30 May. That day we walked back into Pau and caught a bus to Navarennx. From here were taken by taxi to a small village 1 km west of Barcus." (TNA Files WO208/5583 1980/1981 Steele & Alliston)

In Pau, Maurice Thomas, Kenneth Nice and Ernest Sparks stayed in a vacant house on a hill outside of town. The elderly couple who owned the house (and their 25-year-old daughter-in-law) supplied their food. Their guide Charlie returned to Paris and Rosemary Maeght and an English-speaking Frenchman took the three airmen into town and turned them over to Leon van de Poele who took them to his villa where he lived with his wife and children. The following afternoon (28 May), Leon van de

---

11 See also *'Convoyeuse du reseau d'evasion Bourgogne'* by Genevieve and Pierre Le Berre (2009).

Poele took them to the bus station and the whole party – the ten who had left Paris on 25 May plus Ned Daugherty and John Alexander – were taken to Navarennx where a car was waiting. They were driven into the foothills where they met a mountain guide and a group of sixteen Jewish refugees, mostly middle-aged, including three women. The party took five days to cross the mountains, crossing the border north of Isaba at six-thirty in the morning of 3 June. They were picked up by Spanish police on the approach to Isaba and next day were taken to Pamplona.[12]

"We set off from here for the Pyrenees at 0100hrs on 31 May with a party of Jewish refugees. We walked until 0500hrs when we reached a shepherd's hut, where we stayed for the rest of the day. We changed guides and set out again late that night but after about an hour and half, our guide said that due to the slowness of the refugees, we could not to reach our next stopping place before daybreak. We found another shepherd's hut and remained there for the rest of the night and the whole of the next day. We started out again at 2000hrs and walked until 0535hrs (2 Jun) when we reached a hut near Sainte-Engrace. We stayed here until 1600hrs when another guide led us to a place in the forest where we were fed. We set off again at 1700hrs and walked to the border at 0600 hrs (3 Jun). Our guide took us to a hut beyond the border and after giving us directions to Ustarroz he left us. We continued on our way but shortly afterwards were arrested by Carabineros. We were taken into Ustarroz, where we were searched and given a brief interrogation. That evening we were taken to Isaba, where we were again interrogated as to our personal details, and placed in a barn for the night. Next day (4 Jun) we were taken by bus to the police station at Pamplona, where we were given identity cards and then taken to a hotel in the town. On 6 Jun the British Consul's representative came to see us." (TNA Files WO208/5583 1980/1981 Steele & Alliston)

"When we started walking over the mountains we were joined by a band of Jewish refugees. Our mountain guide had made a financial arrangement to take them across, unknown to the patriots who had been helping the Allied airmen in the party. There was a girl of eighteen, two women over forty and two old men amongst their group. It was suggested that we carry the luggage of these five people as we were travelling light. We did, which was a mistake, for we had little food, and the guide only gave us one meal during the three day

---

12   MIS-X #760 Thomas.

trip through the clouds. The luggage added to the strain, and while the refugees had plenty of food, they would not share it. The guide had to spend most of his time keeping order in this mob and had particular difficulty making them be quiet when we passed through danger areas. We finally reached Spain and were glad to be arrested. It was another thirteen hours however before the police treated us to a meal of boiled potatoes." (MIS-X #761 Clonts)

The interviewer notes Clonts bad luck in being 'stuck with a group of refugees' but says this is not general enough to justify special attention.

CHAPTER 70

L'affaire Saint-Engrace

On 29 May 1944, three evaders – 2/Lt Elmo Berglind, S/Sgt Lester Knopp and an unnamed Indian – left Paris by train for Pau with guide Genevieve Crosson.[1]

2/Lt Elmo H Berglind was flying P-51 43-6711 (363FG/381FS) on 18 March 1944 and had just made a rendezvous (he doesn't say who with or where) when the aircraft caught fire. Berglind baled out at about 24,000 feet but delayed pulling the ripcord until about 3,000 feet, landing close to his burning Mustang.

Berglind quickly left the area, setting off in the opposite direction to a crowd of people running towards the crash-site. An hour and a half later, he met a man, woman and boy out on their bicycles and on declaring himself to them, was told they would return at midnight with some civilian clothes. That night, having exchanged his uniform for civilian attire, Berglind was taken back to their home on rue Pasteur in Le Mesnil-sur-Oger (Champagne-Ardenne) where Maurice Lamiraux, his mistress and their friends sheltered Berglind for the next two days – Berglind being moved from house to house in a wheelbarrow and covered with straw. On 20 March, Berglind was taken a few kilometres south to Bergeres-les-Vertus to meet an American S/Sgt called Bill (apparently the radio-operator of a B-17 shot down on 4 March 44) who was living with an elderly schoolteacher. Berglind stayed there for five days until being told that he should join the maquis but Berglind preferred to be returned to the Lamiraux house where he stayed until 18 April. A man came and took Berglind's photograph and promised him ID papers before taking Berglind to Champigneul-Champagne. Berglind stayed at the only cafe in Champigneul and a man came from Epernay with his papers and a promise of an aircraft. However, this plan fell through when the aircraft Berglind was hoping to steal, turned out

---

1   Mme Le Berre says (in May 2013 in answer to a question from me via Dave Minett) there were just the three of them and that the third man not only was a North American Indian but he walked like a North American Indian.

to be a Fieseler Storch (a small liaison aircraft with insufficient range to get to England) and on 1 May, Berglind returned to M Lamireux in Le Mesnil once more. Shortly after this, a bragging contest between Maurice and a group of Germans led to Berglind getting into a fist-fight with some drunken German soldiers which put Berglind in bed for ten days – but on the plus side, during that time, arrangements were made for the rest of his journey.

Berglind was taken to Chouilly, just outside Epernay, where he stayed with an English 'maquis chief' until 25 May when he joined Maurice Thomas, Kenneth Nice, Lester Knopp and an Indian to be driven by truck to Epernay where they met an English-speaking guide who took them by train to Paris.

They were met at the railway station by two men, one of whom led Berglind, Knopp and the Indian to 117 rue de la Tour, Paris XVI where they stayed with Mme Jeanne Bera (described by Berglind as a wealthy woman who lived in a large, three-story house full of antiques – one floor Japanese with inlaid ivory) until the afternoon of 29 May.

S/Sgt Lester W Knopp was a waist-gunner on B-17 42-30040 Wabbit Twacks III (96BG/337BS) (Harmeson) which had aborted from a mission to Schweinfurt on 14 October 1943 due to an engine failure. A second fighter attack set the aircraft on fire and it was abandoned to crash near Bar-le-Duc (Lorraine).[2]

Knopp made a delayed jump, landing near Lisle-en-Barrois (Lorraine) and spraining his ankle. He was taken into the forest to hide and that evening taken into Lisle where he met his ball-turret gunner S/Sgt Jay B Jolly, whose ankle was broken. Four days later, a local farmer took them to a hotel in Bar-le-Duc where they met a postman who seemed to be the chief of the local organisation. Knopp and Jolly separated at this point and Knopp was taken to a house in Bar-le-Duc where he met 2/Lt Merle Woodside, 2/Lt Raymond Bye and T/Sgt Kenneth Nice from B-17 42-3348 Dottie J III – and Knopp stayed with Nice for a couple of weeks until the postman took them both to Mailly-Champagne. The interrogator notes that Knopp and Nice then evaded together for an awfully long time – they were still together when they joined Maurice Thomas and Elmo Berglind on the train from Epernay to Paris on 25 May – and only separated on arrival at

---

2   Wabbit Twacks III navigator 2/Lt Vernon E Clark, bombardier 2/Lt Charles P Bronner and top-turret gunner T/Sgt William B Dunning Jnr also evaded successfully, all three being evacuated from Brittany at Christmas 1943 by MGB 318 on Operation Felicitate II.

the capital when Knopp was taken with Berglind to be sheltered by Mme Jeanne Bera at 117 rue de la Tour.

On 29 May, the two men who had met them at the railway station took Berglind, Knopp and the Indian to the Jardin des Plantes where they joined their guide from Epernay. However, something went wrong.

"This time there were only six (sic) men [Berglind, Knopp and the Indian]. But it was just after the big bombing of the marshalling yards at Juvisy [in April] and everything was disorganised. We had to leave Paris by the underground on the Sceaux line from the Denfert-Rochereau station and get off at Massy-Palaiseau and from there, take a train to Juvisy. After that we had to cover more than a kilometre on foot along demolished railway tracks to at last catch the express for Toulouse ... and all this, still being followed by our chaps, who understood nothing of these complications and who had tickets for Pau in their pockets."[3]

On the train to Toulouse, Berglind was the only one with an ID card and he says that the 'train conductor' put all three of them on one ticket and gave it to him. Berglind worried about the Indian who seemed to trust all Frenchmen equally – Berglind saw him pointing out the evaders and their guide to other passengers on the train until Berglind spoke to him 'quite severely'. There was a two hour wait at Toulouse before they went on to Pau and then half way there, the train was stopped because of train wreckage. They had to walk around and catch another train, arriving at Pau at midnight. They were met by Rosemary Maeght and an English-speaking French girl (who had spent time in South America) and taken to the home of an elderly woman for the night.

On 31 May, Berglind and Knopp (and the Indian – query) were taken to a little park and where two Frenchmen who had been with them on the train, picked them up in a car with a Red Cross and drove twenty-odd miles into the foothills of Pyrenees. They then walked about half a mile to wait for their mountain guide.

Berglind's Crossing

Of the several groups of evaders being sent out from Pau around this time, it would seem that Berglind and his group – who set off on 1 June and

---

3   Translation from 'Convoyeuse du reseau d'evasion Bourgogne' by Genevieve and Pierre Le Berre (2009).

crossed into Spain near Isaba on 5 June 1944 – really got the short straw when it came to local guides.

"Soon after our group of evaders was turned over to the mountain guide we were told to throw away all our excess equipment. To our surprise however, we were soon joined by a man, his wife and three children, all under nine years old. They had big packs which they were not told to abandon and while we helped them, we realised that a good twelve hours had been added to the crossing. We reached a barn in which we found another group of evaders [Archibald McPhee and his group of eight], and 35 Jewish refugees. The guide left us for the night and the evaders got together to discuss the situation. Most of us were in bad physical condition and we had all been short of food for some time. We had been given no food for the crossing as the guide was [supposed] to provide it. The refugees had a great deal of baggage which they and the guide expected us to carry. We evaders did not feel that we could in our weakened condition but it was obvious that the refugees could not carry the stuff either for there were only 9 men in their group, 3 of whom were elderly. A boy of seventeen, 7 children under the age of twelve and 18 women completed the group. There was no help for it and when the guide said it was time to go, we loaded up and set off.

We travelled with the guide for four days, walking twelve hours and resting four hours. We were carrying 60lb packs with a child on the top of each and pushing a woman ahead. Each morning the guide gave us a three inch square of bread covered in bacon fat. He and the refugees ate well but they would never share their food with us. Towards the end we could hardly drag ourselves, and many packs had to be thrown over the cliffs. Occasionally the guide would offer to help a woman with her small pack and then he would slip off and empty out any money.

One evening the guide told us that we had reached the border. He pointed to the valley below and said it would lead us to a town. We checked with our compasses and pointed out that the valley ran north-west. He said that he was sorry and had forgotten to mention that when we were a half mile down the mountain, we should take a valley south. We did not trust him but there was nothing we could do about it. We [and the four Frenchmen] left the refugees and told them we would send help as soon as possible.

After four or five hours we had still to find a valley south. My feet were so bad that I had been travelling barefoot for the last three hours. We camped in mud at midnight and as there was no water available, licked the grass for

453

dew. As we thought we were safely in Spain, we built a big fire. The next morning we approached a shepherd who told us that Spain was still fifteen minutes due south. He gave us milk and told us that German patrols were due at the border in two hours but that we had plenty of time to get there. He described the border as a saddle-back between two peaks.

It took us two hours and forty-five minutes to get to the saddle-back but we crossed it safely and saw in the distance, the Spanish town described to me in France. A half a mile beyond the border we were surprised by two German soldiers who stepped out of a small wood twenty-five feet to the side of us. Eight of us were in two ranks of four. The four in front [Berglind, Hanton, Higgins and Paladino] started to run. The Germans fired a shot and then turned their attention to guarding the other four [Fisher, Courtenay, Bossick and Knopp] who had stopped and thrown up their hands. There were no Spanish guards about. When we were later taken into custody [by the Spanish] they asked us not to mention the fact that they had been in town and not at their posts. Several days later we were joined by a French evader who had remained with the refugees. He told us that the night we left they were surrounded by 20 Germans armed with machine guns. He was the only one to escape. We strongly suspected that our guide had betrayed us to the Germans." (MIS-X #773 Berglind)

The four men captured – Harry Fisher, Donald Courtenay, Harry Bossick and Lester Knopp – were taken back to Pau and then to Saint Michel prison in Toulouse where they stayed until liberated on 19 August 1944 when the FFI (*Forces francaises de l'interieur*) took over the city.

Shortly after crossing the border, George Miller, who had spent so long in hospital in Paris, dropped out and McPhee, who was also very tired, stayed with him. While the rest of the group carried on, McPhee and Miller spent the night in a shepherd's cottage. Setting off again next morning, they saw Fisher, Courtenay, Bossick, the five Americans and four Frenchmen coming towards them, apparently lost. This group continued, leaving McPhee and Miller to make their own way. A little while later, while resting in another shepherd's hut, they heard a rifle shot. McPhee and Miller continued to make their way south (on a different route to the others) before stopping at a Spanish farmhouse. That evening (5 June), the farmer took them by cart to Isaba and handed them over to the frontier police – where they joined Berglind, Hanton, Higgins and Paladino.

In his book, Georges Broussine refers to this incident as "*l'affaire Saint-Engrace*".

CHAPTER 71

The Final Few

On 22 June 1944, Genevieve Crosson (but not Georges Broussine, Genevieve Soulie or Pierre Jacob) left Paris from the Gare de Lyon for Toulouse and Pau. She left with Yves Allain and his friend Lucien Stervinoou, Jacques Duceau, Pierre Le Berre, Pierre Le Mogne, Charles Ploncard and his wife Georgette, Xavier Poincet and Jean-Louis Kervevant. Etienne Lalou took them from Pau by bus to Oloron-Sainte-Marie where they joined two Spanish guides (one of them Tino San Roman) who led them on a two-day walk, crossing the frontier at the Col de Pau (south of Lescun) to give themselves up to Spanish guards.[1]

Yves Allain says that after the Normandy landings, no trains were running and it became impossible to evacuate airmen to the Pyrenees. However, it was possible for a group of French people, using 'tortuous means' to get there – his group's journey to Pau (not described) taking three days.

2/Lt Alfred H Richter and Sgt Robert W Peterson were navigator and waist-gunner of B-24 41-29468 Peg O My Heart (487BG/838BS) (Vratny) which was en route for the marshalling yards at Chaumont on 11 May 1944 when it was hit by flak. With the loss of all four engines, the aircraft was abandoned to crash near Nogent-le-Retrou (Lower Normandy).[2]

Richter landed south-east of Nogent-le-Rotrou and was soon helped by a farmer who fed him and gave him civilian clothes. The following afternoon, he was found by two French boys who took him to join his co-pilot Capt Donald E Wilson and waist-gunner S/Sgt Arthur J Pelletier who were hiding in a wood and being supplied with food by a local farmer. The following afternoon, they were visited by a French officer who had pictures of waist-gunner Robert Peterson, top-turret gunner S/Sgt John P Watson

---

1   See '*Convoyeuse du reseau d'evasion Bourgogne*' by Genevieve and Pierre Le Berre (2009). Yves Allain says that he (and I assume the others) arrived in England on 22 July, while Jean-Louis Kervevant says they reached Gibraltar on 27 July and were in England two days later.

2   Air Leader Lt/Col Beirne Lay Jnr and Peg O My Heart observer 2/Lt Walter A Duer also evaded successfully – both men being liberated at Freteval in August.

and ball-turret gunner S/Sgt Lawrence Heimerman. This same officer supplied them with ID cards and arranged to have two men take them to Paris, arriving at Versailles at eleven-thirty in the evening where they slept for the rest of the night in a railway carriage. Next morning, they were taken to a jewellery shop in eastern Paris (owned by one of their guides) for breakfast then on to a school in Lagny-sur-Marne for refugee children, run by an elderly lady, her daughter and son-in-law, where they joined Peterson, Watson and Heimerman. A couple of days later, the son-in-law took all six evaders to another part of Paris where they met a Frenchman who had been in the Royal Navy in the First War, and several armed men who took them to a caretaker's house in a cemetery where they were interrogated.

That night the evaders were separated and Richter was taken to stay with M Dupres (sic) (a submariner in previous war) and his wife at their small general store. Two days later, a French detective (Canadian born, 35 years old, well educated, tall, slender with curly, wavy hair) moved Richter to his father's house a block away for a meal before taking him by bike to another part of town where he joined another five evaders and Frenchmen. Then on to another organisation house (five men had just been caught and shot) and after a couple of hours, Richter, Peterson and Wilson were taken to a French policeman's house. Richter and Wilson moved two days later to stay with a French girl who had been in America for seven years, and two days after that, were taken to a small house where they rejoined Watson and Heimeman and told that plans to move them had been changed. Richter and Peterson were taken to stay overnight with an English-speaking Frenchman before a young man with a hare-lip took them to stay with Olga Christol in her sixth-floor apartment at 4 rue Edouard Quenu.

A few days later (on 30 May) they were visited by Dorothy Tartiere (the American actress Drew Leyton) and Genevieve Soulie who said they would be leaving soon but that they were unable to find the other four members of their crew (Wilson, Pelletier, Watson and Heimeman – all of whom were captured – no details). On 6 June, Genevieve told them they probably couldn't get them out of Paris (due to the invasion) and on 11 June, she took them to meet Typhoon pilot James Stewart, who was being sheltered by Georges Prevot at 20 Boulevard de Sebastopol.[3]

Next day, Albert Mahuzier took the three airmen to the Trocodero

3   F/O James A Stewart – 609 Sqn Typhoon MN414 – FTR 13 May 44 – was captured (with others) on 8 July by Guy Marcheret. Stewart was sent to Buchenwald then Stalag Luft III – see 2002 book "We that are left – Remember" published by 250 RCAF (Saint John) Wing Association of Canada. (Thank you MMLB for that connection)

and photographed them walking along the river (see later) and on 27 June, Genevieve Soulie told Richter that Mahuzier was going to the south of France and could take one man with him.[4] Genevieve took Richter to the Jardin des Plantes where they met Mahuzier who took Richter across the river to the Gare de Lyon (trains no longer ran from the Gare d'Austerlitz) where they caught a train via Clermont and Nimes to Montpellier. They stayed overnight in a hotel before going on to Toulouse, where they again stayed overnight in a hotel, and then on to Tarbes and Pau where they stayed in yet another hotel.

Next day, Richter and Mahuzier were met in Pau by a Frenchman and a girl and the following day, Richter met Rosemary Maeght who told him that he would have to stay a second night in the hotel. Next day, Rosemary explained that the local mountain guides had all left Pau to join the maquis and she took him to Leon van de Poele's villa on rue Saint-Jammes, where Richter stayed for three weeks. It seems that M van de Poele decided to make his own arrangements and on 22 July, he took Richter (and son Jacques) on an eighty kilometre cycle ride to Saint-Palais (Aquitaine). There they joined a Belgian, his French wife and a French officer and they all cycled to a farm near Saint-Jean-Pied-de-Port. A Basque guide then took Richter, the Belgian and his wife across the Pyrenees on the night of 23-24 July to Roncesvalles where they were met by a car and driven to the American Consul in San Sebastian. For some reason, the Consul seems to have taken Richter to Irun and handed him over to the Spanish authorities – Richter was held at Alhama until 13 August before being driven to Madrid and Gibraltar, leaving Gibraltar by air for England on 16 August 1944.

Robert Peterson also landed south-east of Nogent-le-Rotrou and was soon joined by his top-turret gunner S/Sgt John P Watson and ball-turret gunner S/Sgt Lawrence Heimerman. They walked to Conde-sur-Huisne where the caretaker of Conde cemetery hid them in a cave for three days, bringing them food which had been donated by local families. They were then taken to Paris and sheltered in a children's refugee school in the eastern suburbs at Lagny-sur-Marne for six days. Peterson was moved around to several addresses (not given) until 30 May when he was taken to stay with Olga Christol at 4 rue Edouard Quenu. He shared with his navigator Alfred Richter until Richter left on about 7 July (Richter says 27 June) with the organisation chief (sic) and Peterson was then joined by John Wood, who doesn't mention travelling with Peterson at all.

---

4   Albert Mahuzier (born 1907) (and Janine) of 62 rue Tiquitonne, Paris 2 – this is the same address as Genevieve Schneegans and Olympe Strouken of reseau Francois-Shelburn ...

2/Lt John R Wood Jnr was the navigator of B-24 42-94858 Northern Star (489BG/847BS) (Cross) which was shot down on 2 June 1944. With two engines hit and the aircraft on fire, it was abandoned to crash about 20 miles south-east of Paris.[5]

Wood landed near Serris (Seine-et-Marne) and hid until the following day when he approached Bertin Benard who sheltered him. About two weeks later, a thin Frenchman (about 35) took Wood to Paris and, through a cut-out, passed him to Paul and Olga Christol at 4 rue Edouard Quenu. He stayed with the Christols for three days during which time he met Alfred Richter and Robert Peterson before being taken to stay with Gabriel Bouyer at 87 rue Haxo. He was later joined there by Marvin Long and George McKewin before Genevieve Soulie took him back to the Christol apartment where he stayed until 7 August, during which time John Bonnin and John Meade were brought in.

On 7 August, a one-eyed Frenchman took Peterson and Wood on a six-day train journey to Toulouse by way of Dijon. Four other men were supposed to be on the train (see Long and McKewin) but did not turn up. They spent a day in a hotel in Toulouse before going on to Foix and then on foot across the Pyrenees. They spent one night in a house above Ferriers-sur-Ariege (a few kilometres north of Tarascon) owned by an elderly couple whose son then guided them to Andorra. After a brief rest, they went on to Alp in Spain (arriving 22 August) and Barcelona.

Peterson and Wood were the last of the Bourgogne evaders to be taken across the Pyrenees.

1/Lt John J Meade and 2/Lt John D Bonnin were the pilot and bombardier of B-24 Carpetbagger 42-95317 (801BG/850BS) which was attacked by a night-fighter in the early hours of 5 July 1944. With two engines and the bomb-bay on fire, the aircraft was abandoned over Mereville (Essonne) to crash near Autruy-sur-Joine (Loiret).[6]

---

5   Northern Star co-pilot F/O Paul E Bartlett, ball-turret gunner Sgt Dominick M Dentino, top-turret gunner Sgt Eugene Kieffer, tail-gunner Sgt Joseph A LeBlanc and waist-gunner Sgt Bruce C Reeverts also evaded successfully, sheltered together in Lagny-sur-Marne until early July when they were taken into Paris and sheltered by Jean Mehuest at 190 rue de la Convention until liberated.

6   42-95317 top-turret gunner T/Sgt Frank E Hines, waist-gunner S/Sgt William R DuBois and radio-operator T/Sgt Edward J Jones also evaded successfully, sheltered until liberated in August: Hines in Le Mans, Dubois (and William Laverty) in the Paris suburb of Livry-Gargan, and Jones with Clovis and Marie Bigot at 46 Boulevard Sebastopol, Paris III. Carpetbagger squadrons were the American version of the RAF Special Duties squadrons, dropping agents and materiel to resistance groups in Occupied Europe.

Meade landed in a field and quickly made his way to the nearest village and then hid in some nearby woods until about ten o'clock the following morning when he declared himself to a man on a cart. The man soon returned with civilian clothes and food and took Meade to a nearby house where he was sheltered for five days. On 10 July, Meade was taken to Merreville where he joined his bombardier John Bonnin, dispatcher S/Sgt William R DuBois and radio-operator T/Sgt Edward J Jones – and B-17 pilot 2/Lt William H Lafferty. On 12 July, the two sergeants and Lafferty left together and Meade and Bonnin were moved to various addresses for the next week – and shown the graves of their co-pilot 2/Lt James L Lovelace and tail-gunner S/Sgt Ellis H Syra, which were covered in flowers. On 20 July, a M Poirier (Dr Michel Poirier – query) took Meade and Bonnin to Paris where they stayed with Paul and Olga Christol.[7]

It was planned to take them to Spain but two attempts (on 2 and 9 August) went wrong. On 11 August, Meade and Bonnin took a train to Versailles and started walking towards Chartres, hoping to join American forces. They stayed in Chartres 'with friends' until 16 August when the Americans arrived.

1/Lt Marvin R Long and 1/Lt George I McKewin were the pilot and navigator of B-17 42-107163 (92BG/407BS) which was hit by flak over Le Bourget on 14 June 1944 and abandoned to crash south of Paris, near Bretigny-sur-Orge.[8]

Long landed in a small lake and was taken to Corbeil-Essonnes where he was sheltered with a butcher's widow named Mme Hoye (nf). McKewin landed near Mennecy, south of Corbeil, and that afternoon approached some women who took him home and gave him civilian clothes. The following morning a gendarme took him by bicycle to stay with Philippe Drouet (nf) (maker of dental appliances) where he stayed until 19 June when he was taken to join Long in Corbeil-Essonnes.

On 20 June, a woman took Long and McKewin into Paris where they spent three days with an elderly man who had been a motor mechanic, in his fifth-floor apartment on the corner of rue Broca and rue St Hippolyte (this was Paul Christol at 4 rue Edouard Quenu) where they met Alfred Richter and Robert Peterson and were visited by Genevieve Soulie. On 23 or 24 June, Long and McKewin were moved to 87 rue Haxo where

---

7   Meade and Bonnin were also sheltered by Marie Allain at 4 Avenue de la Porte Brancion, Paris XV. (NARA Allain)

8   42-107163 waist-gunner S/Sgt John L Hewitt also evaded successfully – he was liberated in Paris on 25 August 1944.

they joined John Wood who being sheltered by gendarme Gabriel Bouyer. They also met a number of other gendarmes, detectives, a mortician and a shoemaker. At some point (no date given), a dead German was found on Gaby's beat and a young man (about twenty years old, thought to be Genevieve's brother) took Long and McKewin to stay with Genevieve in her fourth-floor apartment on the NW corner of rue Vesale[9] while Genevieve took Wood to join Peterson at 4 rue Edouard Quenu. On 9 July, a doctor (tall, well built, going bald, spoke better German than English) took Long and McKewin to his home on nearby rue du Fer a Moulin until 12 July when he took them one at a time on his motorcycle to stay with Louis Laille at 8 rue Louis Ganne, Bagrolet, Paris XX. On 7 August, they were taken to the Gare de Lyon where they were meant to take a train to Pau (sic) with Wood and Peterson (and possibly others) but were taken off the train at the last moment for no known reason. At the station they met a blond man called Pierre (Pierre Maroger) who was with Genevieve. They were taken back to the Gare de Lyon two days later but there were no trains. On 24 August, they were taken to FFI HQ and next day reported to O-286360 Colonel Charles S Vanderbilt of the US Signal Corps who 'whisked them away before they could even say goodbye to Genevieve and thank her'.

F/O Patrick Moorhead (the last man on Genevieve Soulie's list) was the bombardier of 35 Sqn Lancaster ND731 (Lambert) which was returning from an operation to the marshalling yards at Villeneuve-Saint-Georges in the early hours of 5 July 1944 when it was shot down by fighters. His navigator, F/O Frank Salt almost made it, he joined F/Sgt E J Davis from 83 Sqn Lancaster ND966 but they (and five other airmen) were captured in a German trap in Paris on 7 August and sent to Buchenwald.

The thirty-year-old ex-police officer from Exeter, who was on his twenty-first operation, was knocked out in the aircraft and when he regained consciousness, found himself staggering through a wheat field.

Moorhead had landed just south of Rambouillet and that afternoon met a man who directed him to Prunay-sous-Ablis (Prunay-en-Yveline) (Seine et Oise) where he stayed with Maurice and Simone Dupeyroux. After two nights with the Dupeyroux family, Maurice took him to St Symphorien-le-Chateau where they caught a bus to Paris. They went to La Chapelle (Paris X/XVIII) to find Maurice's son before spending the night in a house

---

9   Rue Vesale (Paris V) runs between rue de la Collegiate and rue Sapion – but I query that as being Genevieve Soulie's apartment as I think she was still living at 3 rue de l'Aude, Paris XIV.

on Avenue de Choisy (Place d'Italie) while Maurice's son contacted an organisation. Next day, Moorhead was taken to Draveil where he stayed with the chief of the local resistance before being taken to the home of Dr Maurice Blondeau at the Sanatorium Joffre in Champrosay (now part of the commune of Draveil). After ten days at the sanatorium, one of the nurses took Moorhead to Antony (Seine) where he stayed with M et Mme Albert Ribier at 60 rue de la Mutualite.

On 29 July, Moorhead was taken back to Paris where he met Dr Blondeau and the nurse and they took him to stay with Mme Paulette Soucher at 62 Blvd de Bercy, Paris XII. Moorhead stayed with Mme Soucher until 27 August when he was taken to the Hotel Pont Royal – from where he was directed to IS9 at the Hotel Windsor.

CHAPTER 72

Extras

In his book, Broussine mentions a film being made showing three American (sic) airmen walking around Paris. It was shot by professional cameraman Gaston Madru on 12 June 1944 and directed by Albert Mahuzier. Following an interview in Jean Jay's apartment at Place Vauban, the film shows Mahuzier leading the three evaders from the Trocodero and under the Eiffel Tower. It includes a scene near the Quai d'Orsay where the three airmen visit a *pissoir* on which there was a notice warning Parisians of the perils and penalties for helping Allied airmen, which each man makes a point of studying. They then walk on to Notre Dame, mingling with French and Germans alike before finishing at the Place Saint-Michel.

The film was released at the 1946 Cannes Film Festival as 'Reseau X' and the three airmen were (of course) 2/Lt Alfred H Richter, Sgt Robert W Peterson and F/O James A Stewart RAF – see earlier.

Broussine had been asked by BCRA about the possibility of creating what he describes as camps for 'airmen maquis' where evaders could be gathered to await the arrival of Allied troops – similar to the MI9 camps at Freteval and the Belgian Ardennes. Broussine didn't think this was a very good idea but he had to explore the possibilities and so shortly after the filming episode, he set off with Rene Tourriel and Jacques Cahen by car for Tours. After several adventures, they finally arrived at Roger Bodineau's farm at Larcay.

Broussine realised that any such camp would have to be supported (probably by air drops) and he needed to confer with his bosses in London as quickly as possible. Having (for various reasons) lost all radio contact, he decided he would have to go to London himself. He also thought that since the Allies had by then gained a foot-hold in Normandy, the quickest way to England might be through the battle lines – and at the same time, perhaps he could establish a new escape route.

Broussine returned to Paris where he put Genevieve Soulie in charge of the remaining evaders in their care, including the three heroes of the film, and at the end of June, set off on his attempt to cross the lines. That attempt failed when he was apprehended by German soldiers, almost within sight of the Allies. Broussine was being driven back to Paris to establish his somewhat complicated and unlikely cover story, and had reached the outskirts of the city, when he finally managed to escape. He returned to his house on rue Raffet and re-established contact with his remaining Bourgogne agents. Broussine finally left France for England on board an RAF Hudson (Operation Machete) from a field near Macon the night of 7-8 August.

Broussine spent three weeks in London, where he was subjected to the political machinations between various security departments. He was also refused leave to return to France as it was felt that he had completed his mission. It was only after the liberation of Paris that Broussine managed to get a ride on a Royal Navy vessel that landed him at Isigny-sur-Mer on about 29 August from where he hitch-hiked his way to Paris.

Sadly, *"The joy of liberation and my return* home *were spoilt by two pieces of bad news."* Broussine learned that Pierre Maroger had been killed in the liberation of Paris, and in Larcay, Robert and Marcelle Bodineau had been arrested, along with radio-operator Michel Bourgeois.[1]

There is still much more to be written about the Bourgogne organisation – the many helpers whose details I don't yet have, the links to other organisations, the radio-operators, and the parachute drops in May and June 1944 to Brittany for example …

---

1   Roger Pierre Bodineau (born February 1900) his wife Marcelle (born Jan 1905) and son Raoul, sheltered a number of Allied evaders (and radio-operators) on their farm 'la Salle Girault'. They (along with radio-operator Michel Bourgeois aka Maxime) were arrested on 24 July 1944 following the capture of an agent from another organisation who had letters in his possession, including one from F/O James M Clement RCAF, who was being sheltered on the Bodineau farm. Roger Bodineau was executed (WO208/5451) – shot at Saint Symphorien, Tours (along with James Clement) on 9 August 1944 – and Marcelle Bodineau deported to Ravensbruck – she was repatriated by the Swedish Red Cross as a semi-permanent invalid on 29 June 1945. (WO208/5455)

Michel Bourgeois (born December 1921) was landed by MGB near Plouha on 28 (query) February 1944. He spent the next several weeks locating landing grounds, accomodation for evaders and centres for radio transmissions. He was held at Tours before being deported to Neuengamme where he became seriously ill. He was transferred to Bergen-Belsen in April 1945 and liberated two months later. Michel Bourgeois was recommended for a KMC. (WO208/5455)

Comments, Acknowledgements and Thanks

I mentioned at the beginning of this work that Bourgogne is the least well known of all the major evasion lines. Georges Broussine himself makes a similar point in the introduction to his book, which was published in 2000, shortly before his death the following year. He cites the French National Archive as having only three references to the BCRA files and only the American archives having a file of any significance to indicate Bourgogne's scale and success. He says he had the feeling that the 'adventure' risked falling into a forgotten tale of history, or worse still, being subject to inaccurate accounts and it was for those reasons that he finally wrote his own account, mostly from his memories of those days but also with what reports he could find, and with the help of those of his comrades still alive at the time.

Most books published in English about WW2 escape and evasion only mention Bourgogne in passing, if at all and I can only suggest this was partly due to it being an exclusively French network (unlike the much more widely recognised Pat, Comete and Shelburn organisations), partly because there were relatively few dramas (infiltrations, arrests and betrayals) involving Bourgogne – an indication of their inherent security – and partly because there were few (if any) post-war gatherings of evader veterans to raise Bourgogne's profile. Airey Neave's 1969 book 'Saturday at MI9' for instance, only mentions Broussine and Bourgogne on two pages, and although extremely flattering, gives few details. I hope this study (based around contemporary military escape and evasion reports that weren't available to either Neave or Broussine at the time) adds some useful knowledge to the subject, and some recognition for the Bourgogne line and its helpers who deserve so much more than to be just another short page of forgotten history.

I've been researching World War Two escape and evasion (on a purely amateur and part-time basis) since 1999, shortly after discovering the story of my late father's experience as an escaper in the Pas-de-Calais in 1940. I began by trying to confirm and explain various events mentioned in his diaries and that quite naturally led to learning more about the

Pat O'Leary line (PAO) which arranged his journey to the Pyrenees in September 1941.

It soon became obvious that the heroes of the stories were not the evaders themselves (as they would be the first to admit) but the countless thousands of helpers who made such evasions possible. Very few evaders got far without outside help and yet in the majority of cases, those helpers are largely unknown, or at least unrecognised or acknowledged today. During my investigations I met several of the French families who helped and sheltered my father and over the years, have met many more helpers from France, Belgium and Holland. What they all have in common is their quiet, almost embarrassed, modesty – "It's what we did" would be a typical reply – and that's what inspired me to write about the subject. I have tried to name as many helpers as possible in this study but there are many more still to be identified.

I also found a select group of others with interests and aims similar to my own and it is because of those two groups of people, the inspiration of the former and the generosity when it comes to sharing knowledge of the latter, that I have continued to study and try to learn as much as possible about the subject. There are far too many individuals to name but they know who they are – so thank you all.

For this particular study, I offer my grateful thanks to (in alphabetical order) Michele Agniel, Beatrice Belz, Claude Benet, Bruce Bollinger, Jean-Claude Bourgeon, Oliver Clutton-Brock, Philippe Connart, Mary d'Hoop, Daniel Droniou, Terry duSoleil, John Howes, John Hill, Michael Moores LeBlanc, Dominique Lecomte, Rene Lesage, Christopher Long, Bobbie Ann Mason, Marguerite Miller, Dave and Gisele Minett, Keith Morley, Edouard Reniere, Lee Richards (at Arcre.com), Norman Schroeder Jnr, Franck Signorile, David Slack, Heather Steele, Anne Ploux Vourc'h and Geoff Warren … for providing some of the information used in this story that otherwise would not have been found.

Thanks also to everyone at evasioncomete.org – Philippe Connart, Michet Dricot, Edouard Reniere and Victor Schutters.

Additional and extra special thanks to Dave and Gisele Minett for all the French to English translations, to Michael Moores LeBlanc for the many documents he shared, and to Edouard Reniere (again) for the endless extra research hours he put in for me.

Bibliography

Benet, Claude (2010) *Passeurs, Fugitifs et Espions*. Le Pas d'oiseau, Toulouse

Bennett, George (1992) *Shot Down! Escape and Evasion*. MediaWorks, West Virginia

Broussine, Georges (2000) *L'evade de la France libre*. Tallandier, Paris

Chorley, W R (various) *RAF Bomber Command Losses*. Midland Publishing

Clark, Freddie (1999) *Agents by Moonlight*. Tempus, Stroud

Clutton-Brock, Oliver (2003) *Footprints on the Sands of Time*. Grub Street, London

Clutton-Brock, Oliver (2009) *RAF Evaders*. Grub Street, London

Foot, M R D (1966) *SOE in France*. HM Stationery Office

Fraser, Marguerite (2002) *The War Years of Marguerite*. Regis University, Denver

Huguen, Roger (1976) *Par les nuits les plus longues*. Les Presses Bretonnes, Saint-Brieuc

Katsaros, John (2008) *Code Burgundy, the Long Escape*. published by the author

Lasseter, Don (2002) *Their Deeds of Valour*. Xlibris

Le Berre, Genevieve & Pierre (2009) *Convoyeuse du reseau d'evasion Bourgogne*. CDDP de l'Oise

Le Blanc, Philippe (2015) *Comete, le reseau derriere la ligne*. Memogrames

Luccesi, Roland (1984) *De l'interieur vers la force*. Clement

Maigret, Henri (1994) *Un reseau d'evasion dans l'Oise a Auneuil*. Association des Sauveteurs d'Aviateurs Allies

Mavre, Marcel (2009) *La Guerre 39-45 Dans le Ciel de l'Oise*. Delattre, Grandvilliers

Millar, George (1957) *Horned Pigeon*. Pan Books

Moats, Alice-Leone (1945) *No Passport for Paris*. Putnum's Sons, New York

O'Neill, Brian D (1999) *Half a Wing, Three Engines and a Prayer*. McGraw-Hill, New York

Poullenot, Louis (2008) *Basses Pyrenees Occupation Liberation 1940-1945*. Editions Atlantica

Prosser, David (1945) *Journey Underground*. E P Dutton & Company, New York

Rawlings, Barney (1994) *Off We Went (Into the Wild Blue Yonder)*. Morgan Printers, North Carolina

Richards, Brooks (1996) *Secret Flotillas*. HMSO

Rougeyron, Andre (1996) *Agents for Escape*. Louisiana State University Press

Tartier, Drue (1946) *The House Near Paris*. Simon & Schuster, New York

Index of the Allied servicemen included in this study

Numbers in brackets refer to report numbers: MI9, IS9 or Liberation reports for the British and Commonwealth servicemen, and MIS-X reports for the Americans.

471

472

McMath, 2/Lt James G (#183) Pg 118, 128 (f/n), 129

McMillan, Sgt David B RCAF (1457) Pg 54, 65-68, 72-73, 76, 83

McNemar, T/Sgt Charles H (#110) Pg 62 (f/n), 65, 70-71, 84

McNichol, 2/Lt Frank J (#767) Pg 406, 413-414, 419

McPhee, WO2 Archibald J (2019) Pg 430-432, 439, 453-454

McQueen, 2/Lt Sabron A (#249) Pg 178 (f/n)

McTrach, WO2 J (2/420/1072) Pg 345 (f/n)

Meade, 1/Lt John J (#1093) Pg 458-459

Mellor, 1/Lt Harrison C (#1100) Pg 408 (f/n)

Merlin, Sgt Harold E R (2432) Pg 155

Mezynski, S/Sgt Thomas R (#374) Pg 209, 215, 217, 220-221, 270-273

Mezzanotte, S/Sgt Clement (#688) Pg 230, 375, 385-386, 391-395

Milasius, S/Sgt Peter P (#73) Pg 37, 51-52, 54

Mildren, F/O William E (captured) Pg 234-235, 237, 239-240

Millar, Captain George (1716) Pg 223, 230-231, 269

Miller, 2/Lt Karl D (#446) Pg 233, 240, 243-244, 250-254

Miller, S/Sgt Rosswell (#582) Pg 223, 226 (f/n), 228-232

Miller, T/Sgt William J (#636) Pg 218, 219 (f/n), 234, 237, 246-251, 254-256, 276, 320-321, 338

Miller, 2/Lt Edward C (#693) Pg 333 (f/n)

Miller, S/Sgt George R (#847) Pg 394 (f/n), 430-432, 435-438, 454

Mills, S/Sgt Milton J Jnr (#689) Pg 315 (f/n), 388-391, 393-394

Milne, Sgt Joseph R (1360) Pg 38, 40-42, 44

Minor, Sgt Walter R (#43) Pg 14, 17, 19

Minor, S/Sgt Harry L (#421) Pg 219 (f/n), 276, 286 (f/n), 288-290, 320-321, 337-338

Mitchell, 2/Lt Frank (#700) Pg 362, 394-396

Mize, S/Sgt Walter A Jnr (#716) Pg 399, 403-405, 407

Monser, S/Sgt George S (#169) Pg 109-110, 112, 115

Moore, Sgt Stanley J (1253) Pg 8-10

Moore, Sgt Kenneth R (#214) Pg 110 (f/n), 139

Moore, T/Sgt Thomas R (#332) Pg 223-224, 261, 267-269, 273, 279, 313

Moorhead, F/O Patrick (7/139/1267) Pg 460-461

Morris, F/O Harry D G (KIA) Pg 345

Morrison, T/Sgt Kenneth A (#690) Pg 388, 390-391, 393

Motheral, P/O Clarence O RCAF (1592) Pg 171-175

Muir, S/Sgt Robert D (#217) Pg 178 (f/n)

Mulholland, 2/Lt Eugene V (#397) Pg 62 (f/n), 223, 226 (f/n), 227-232

Munday, 1/Lt James S (#104) Pg 63, 70, 76, 79-80, 87

Murphy, F/Lt Wilfred L (LIB/37) Pg 9

Murray, Sgt Gordon H (1272) Pg 14-15, 17, 19

Murray, 2/Lt Keith W (#196) Pg 140-145, 361

Myers, T/Sgt Edwin R (#135) Pg 161-162, 164, 168, 209 (f/n)

Neal, P/O John A (MB/1490) Pg 443 (f/n)

Neil, S/Sgt Robert G (#268) Pg 178, 181

Newton, Dvr George (3027) Pg 9 (f/n)

Nice, T/Sgt Kenneth H (#772) Pg 440, 444-447, 451

Nichols, 2/Lt Donald L (#75) Pg 14, 42-43, 51-52

Nielsen, Sgt Harold L (1649) Pg 164-166

Nimmo, F/Lt Neil D (8/192/-) Pg 430 (f/n)

Nolan, F/Sgt Douglas K RCAF (1348) Pg 18, 20-23

Normile, 2/Lt Joseph (#58) Pg 59-60

Nutting, 2/Lt Raymond J (#313) Pg 215 (f/n), 223, 224 (f/n) 313

O'Brart, Sgt David F R (1411) Pg 72, 81-84

Oliver, F/Lt Joseph G (1924) Pg 388, 391, 393-395, 404

Olson, 2/Lt Robert L (captured) Pg 79

Olynik, S/Sgt Mike (#431) Pg 446

Owen, Sgt D H (captured) Pg 102

Owens, Sgt Francis E (died) Pg 140, 142-145, 361

Padgett, 2/Lt George C (captured) Pg 203 (f/n), 275-276, 289-290, 295-296, 322-323, 337-341

Page, F/Sgt Frederick J (1876) Pg 233, 241-242, 246, 249-250, 252-254, 256

Paladino, T/Sgt Anthony R (#826) Pg 430, 434-435, 454

Parker, Sgt Neelan B (#461) Pg 315 (f/n), 389 (f/n)

Parkinson, Sgt Robert (1410) Pg 259

Parks, S/Sgt Donald C (captured) Pg 15 (f/n), 42-44, 52

Parry, F/Lt Hugh L (LIB/1057) Pg 206, 308, 369-370, 372-374

Pascal, 1/Lt Paul (#278) Pg 206-208

Patterson, 2/Lt Omar M Jnr (#648) Pg 350

(f/n)

Peacock, T/Sgt Charles B (died) Pg 114, 134, 137-139

Pearce, Sgt Merlin (1505) Pg 112-113, 115, 185

Pearce, Sgt John G (1989) Pg 440-442

Pearce, F/Lt F J (captured) Pg 342

Pelletier, S/Sgt Arthur J (captured) Pg 455-456

Peloquin, S/Sgt Joseph O (#1054) Pg 418 (f/n)

Periolat, 2/Lt Donald J (captured) Pg 384 (f/n), 433 (f/n)

Perkins, T/Sgt Asbury L (#221) Pg 148, 150, 152-153, (180 (f/n)

Perkins, 1/Lt Richard E S (captured) Pg 402

Perrica, 2/Lt Frank R (#64) Pg 35, 37-39, 44, 46, 51

Peterson, 1/Lt Theodore M (#69) Pg 45-46, 49, 51-52, 54, 322

Peterson, Sgt Robert W (#1511) Pg 455-460, 462

Philippe, 1/Lt Hilbert W (captured) Pg 220, 270, 301, 303-304

Phillips, Sgt W Edward (1268) Pg 17-19

Pierre, F/Lt Moire A J (1171) Pg 16, 31

Pilkington, F/Lt John G (LIB/1372) Pg 281, 283

Pitner, 2/Lt Jean B (#375) Pg 220 (f/n), 298, 301-304

Pittwood, F/Sgt John (1988) Pg 439-442

Plasket, T/Sgt William B Jnr (died) Pg 108 (f/n), 109-110, 115, 140, 143-145, 361

Poirier, Sgt Andre (LIB/1499) Pg 161-162, 234, 255, 294, 295 (f/n)

Polk, S/Sgt Jefferson D (#109) Pg 62 (f/n), 65, 70-71, 84

Potvin, T/Sgt Samuel E (#101) Pg 63, 77-79

Powell, F/Sgt Edmund A (1952) Pg 358 (f/n), 399-403, 405-407

Powell, S/Sgt George J (#1934) Pg 404 (f/n)

Plischke, 2/Lt Arno E (#376) Pg 220 (f/n), 298, 301-304

Prickett, F/Lt Leslie (LIB/1561) Pg 234, 295 (f/n)

Priebe, T/Sgt Allen J (#295) Pg 158-160, 164, 166, 201 (f/n)

Prosser, F/O David G (#269) Pg 176-182

Quinn, Sgt William N (#385) Pg 209-210, 213-217, 221, 224, 278, 312-313

Rader, 2/Lt Wayne S (#137) Pg 162-164, 168

Raginis, Sgt Witold (1589) Pg 95

Ransom, 2/Lt Glen F (#163) Pg 112-115, 119, 185

Raoul-Duval, Lt Claude (1471) Pg 42, 46, 51, 53-54, 77, 79

Rashley, Sgt Colin E (KIA) Pg 81, 82 (f/n)

Rawlings, 2/Lt Bernard W (#671) Pg 375-381

Reain, F/Sgt Frederick F E (1897) Pg 325 (f/n), 359, 363-368

Reeverts, Sgt Bruce C (#1257) Pg 458 (f/n)

Reeves, Sgt Bernard C (1506) Pg 118

Regan, T/Sgt Joseph K (#1488) Pg 444 (f/n)

Resseguie, 2/Lt Franklin B (#228) Pg 171-174, 204

Reynolds, Sgt Anthony J A (1835) Pg 213, 216, 263, 265-267, 278, 310-313, 315-316, 318

Rice, S/Sgt William W (#297) Pg 153, 155-156, 160, 167-169

Richards, Sgt Lawrence C (#996) Pg 418 (f/n)

Richardson, S/Sgt Herschell L (#176) Pg 158-160, 168-169, 199 (f/n)

Richter, 2/Lt Alfred H (#1036) Pg 455-459, 462

Riley, Sgt Henry (1359) Pg 32, 35-38, 44, 45

Rimer, Sgt Kenneth M (captured) Pg 234-235, 239-240

Risch, T/Sgt Elmer D (#498) Pg 394 (f/n)

Riseley, F/O Arthur H (1496) Pg 154, 156, 160, 164, 167-169

Ritt, 2/Lt Louis E (captured) Pg 74, 207

Robinson, S/Sgt Allen N (#103) Pg 42-43, 73-76

Rodowicz, T/Sgt Stephen (captured) Pg 347, 375, 378-381

Rosio, 1/Lt Joseph (#54) Pg 34, 44, 60, 212

Ross, P/O Donald G (1255) Pg 18-19

Rowland, 2/Lt Henry C (#243) Pg 229

Roznetinsky, 1/Lt Andrew (#1493) Pg 350 (f/n)

Ruby, T/Sgt Edward C (#108) Pg 63, 65, 70, 79, 84

Rujawitz, T/Sgt Robert J (#534) Pg 434 (f/n)

Rutherford, 2/Lt Merlyn I (#695) Pg 388, 390-391, 393, 404

Ryan, 2/Lt Jack E (#136) Pg 162-164, 167-169

Salt, F/O Frank (captured) Pg 460

Salter, F/Sgt Hubert (1748) Pg 284 (f/n)

Sanderson, S/Sgt Alvin E (#579) Pg 416-417

Sandvik, 2/Lt Sigmund J M RNAF (1661) Pg 173, 198-199, 205

Sanford, S/Sgt Francis P (#1336) Pg 444 (f/n)

Sankey, Sgt Joseph (1324) Pg 15-19

476

Williamson, Dvr Frederick G (died) Pg 153

Wilschke, 2/Lt James S (#267) Pg 178, 181

Wilson, T/Sgt Claiborne (#46) Pg 53

Wilson, S/Sgt James G (#289) Pg 154-156, 160, 168-169

Wilson, Capt Donald E (captured) Pg 455-456

Winkelman, 2/Lt Charles B (#468) Pg 316 (f/n)

Winter, T/Sgt Leroy R (#177) Pg 109 (f/n)

Winters, 1/Lt August (#179) Pg 106, 108-112, 115, 118-119, 149

Witheridge, Sgt Clarence H (1665) Pg 121, 206

Wood, 2/Lt John R Jnr (#1510) Pg 457-458, 460

Woodland, W/O D A (2934) Pg 441 (f/n)

Woodside, 2/Lt Merle E (#244) Pg 446, 451

Woodstock, S/Sgt Joseph S (#96) Pg 49, 61-63

Woollard, Sgt Leslie C (1718) Pg 213-214, 261-263, 265-266, 268, 278-280

Wornson, 2/Lt Arnold (#435) Pg 275, 290, 292, 295-297

Wright, S/Sgt Douglas G (#262) Pg 108 (f/n)

Wynveen, Sgt W RCAF (captured) Pg 325 (f/n), 364 (f/n)

Yarwood, F/O Harry C (1926) Pg 382-384, 386-387

Yaternick, P/O (captured) Pg 442 (f/n)

Young, Sgt Daniel C (LIB/1290) Pg 28

Young, 2/Lt Dallas F (#722) Pg 408, 410-411

Young, S/Sgt Paul B (#1531) Pg 402

Zaborowski, Sgt Leszek (LIB/1006) Pg 32 (f/n)

Zelanak, S/Sgt Michael G Jnr (#107) Pg 110 (f/n)

Zeman, 2/Lt Jack R (#417) Pg 316-318

Zeoli, S/Sgt Alfred J (#259) Pg 115, 183-186, 188

Zielenkiewicz, 1/Lt Adolph (#552) Pg 394 (f/n)

Zimmer, S/Sgt Loren E (#1722) Pg 376 (f/n)

Zioance, S/Sgt John (#122) Pg 123-125

Zum, 2/Lt Benjamin J (captured) Pg 108 (f/n), 121 (f/n), 209 (f/n)

Index of Helpers included in this study

Berthe, Paul (of Bruyeres-et-Montberault) Pg 120

Berthe-Cottereau, Maurice – see Cottereau

Berthou, Louis (of Bonsmoulins) Pg 102

Bertran, Roger (of Chatelus-Malvaleix) Pg 184

Bertrand, Paul (of Loches) Pg 327, 332

Bertrand-Fontaine, Dr Pg 6

Besson, Simone Pg 203, 217, 289, 340, 361

Betbeder-Matibet, Marie Pg 75, 108 (f/n), 121 (f/n), 193, 209

Bichelot, Rene Pg 287

Bidaud, Maurice & Marie (of Juvisy-sur-Orge) Pg 46, 71, 72, 113, 115, 185, 357

Biernaux, Florent & Olympe (of Hasselt) Pg 215, 216

Bietrix, Pierre Pg 340

Bigaud, Pierre Pg 384

Billot, Henri & Denise (of Ambonnay) Pg 406, 413

Bimbault, Jean Pg 202

Biscuit (query) Mons (of Toulouse) Pg 88

Blanc, Clothilde (of Poitiers) Pg 124 (f/n)

Blanchard, Louis & Pierre (of La Chapelle-Thouarault) Pg 341

Blary, Abel (of Chauvigny) Pg 124

Blateyron, Andre Pg 129, 135, 144, 179, 229

Blondeau, Felix & Marthe (of Poitiers) Pg 124

Blondeau, Roland (of Nevers) Pg 178

Blondeau, Dr Maurice (of Champrosay) Pg 461

Bochet, Renee (of Amiens) Pg 389 (f/n)

Bodin, Christiane (aka Marie-Christine) Pg 73-76, 91-92, 108 (f/n), 120-121, 193

Bodineau, Roger and wife Marcelle (of Larcay) Pg 2-3, 6, 462-463

Bohn, Drs Andre and Marguerite Pg 14, 15 (f/n), 17-18, 44

Bollelandt, Andre and Madeleine (or Bornel) Pg 129 (f/n)

Bonafos, Mons (of Rivesaltes) Pg 84, 99

Bonhomme, Dr Gaston Pg 414

Bonnard, abbe Jean (of Clerey) Pg 218

Bonnard, Mary Louise Pg 218

Bonnard, Andre (of Monein) Pg 317-318

Bonnard, Andre & Marie (of Clichy) Pg 385

Bonnemour, Paul (of Lyon) Pg 304, 371, 372

Bonneron, Jacques Pg 46 (f/n), 53

Bonnet, Dr Roger (of Escobille) Pg 103

Boran, Andre (of Saint-Herblain) Pg 82

Borde, Henri (of Lourdes) Pg 190

Borossi, Jean Pg 98, 195

Boschet, Mme (of Flers) Pg 144

Bosniere, Suzanne Pg 54-55, 60, 74, 91-92, 108 (f/n), 120-121, 193

Boucher, Jacques (of Saint-Cloud) Pg 5, 21

Boucher, Gaston Pg 112

Bouchet, Marc Pg 405

Boudot, Lucien (of Bleury) Pg 165

Bougeard, Bernard (of Guipry) Pg 322

Boulcour, Mons Pg 358

Boulet, Henri (of Taupont) Pg 219, 247

Boulle, Gabriel Pg 422-424, 426, 432

Boulvais, Louis (of Saint-Servant) Pg 275-276

Bourge, Edmund (of Creil) Pg 389

Bourgeois, Michel (aka Maxime) Pg 196, 462

Bourgeois, Mlle (sic) Pg 209-210, 213-217, 264, 267, 312

Bourgeois, Rene (of Livry-Gargan) Pg 249, 254-256

Bourges, Emile (of Chalons) Pg 363

Bourgoin, Emmanuel & Lucienne (of Champsecret) Pg 143, 224

Boursain, Marthe Pg 77

Boury, Mlles Yvonne Renee and Solange Pg 177, 202, 210, 214

Boussard, M & Mme Clement (of Lourdes) Pg 343

Bouttellier, Henri (of Lagny) Pg 442 (f/n)

Bouyer, Gabriel Pg 234, 350, 378, 385-386, 405, 421, 426, 458, 460

Boy, Marthe Pg 221, 273

Brancart, Marcel Pg 308

Branchoux, Maturin Pg 98

Braquet, Gilbert Pg 313

Bree, Henri (of Guipry) Pg 287

Brezillon, Andre and son Max (of Noyon) Pg 347-349

Brice, Etienne (of Charleville) Pg 31

Brice, Stefan (of Charleville) Pg 31

Bringuet, Pauline (of Saint-Quay-Portrieux) Pg 51

Bronne, Rene (of Chalons) Pg 363

Brouard, Alice Pg 32-33, 52, 69, 77, 129, 135, 184, 192 (f/n), 229, 327

Broussine, Georges Pg 1-7, 8, 10, 19, 21, 26, 32, 34, 35, 40, 54, 56, 59, 63, 69, 76, 85, 90, 91, 93, 97-98, 100-101, 121, 123, 191, 193-194, 195-196, 199, 258-260, 287, 297, 298, 308, 320, 339, 350, 354, 355 (f/n), 359, 405-406, 408, 419, 424, 427, 433 (f/n), 438, 445, 454, 455, 462-463

Brun, M et Mme (of Chassy par Aillant-sur-Tholon) Pg 157

Bruxelle, Jean (of Flavy-le-Martel) Pg 244

Buffet, Elisabeth Pg 192

Buisson, Marcel (of Dammarie-les-Lys) Pg 344

Buitne, Rene (of Troyes) Pg 158

Bush, Major Pg 20

Cahen-Delabre, Dr Jacques Pg 3-4, 195, 462

Caillard, Dr Edmond (of Saint-Just-en-Chaussee) Pg 203

Caillaux, Hubert (of Pont l'Eveque) Pg 166

Calmet, Jean (of Lyon) Pg 13, 220 (f/n), 298, 301-304

Calonne, Albert Pg 32, 118 (f/n)

Camard, Jerome (of Etables) Pg 36, 46, 75

Camard, Jean Pg 46, 52, 53 (f/n), 75

Camdeborde, Marthe (of Navarennx) Pg 368, 386

Cameau, Maurice (of Joigny) Pg 361

Camors, Jean-Claude Pg 2, 56-58, 154, 156-157, 160, 162-165, 167, 200 (f/n), 258, 259, 280, 288, 295 (f/n)

Camp, Dr Jean Pg 2, 4-5, 433

Camp, Andre Pg 2, 195

Campinchi, Paul Francois Pg 21, 29-30, 32, 38 (f/n), 39, 79 (f/n), 180 (f/n), 258, 352, 434

Canal, Marcel (of Toulouse) Pg 83

Canal, Louis & Lucienne (of Mercus-Garrabet) Pg 87

Cane, Henry Hebert (of Lagny) Pg 442

Carabelli, Dominique & Odette Pg 52

Caralp, Marcel (of Foix) Pg 207

Carbonnet, Jean Pg 99, 101, 111, 186, 193, 195, 241, 276-277, 289, 323, 338-339, 346, 349-351, 379, 391, 399, 439

Cardinal, Jean-Paul Pg 397

Carel, Mons (of Saint-Mande) Pg 110

Carmalt, Elisabeth Pg 43, 75

Carmoin, Joseph & Antoinette Pg 36 (f/n)

Carraz, Henriette (of Caluir-et-Cuire) Pg 343

Carre, Maxine (of Saint-Aubin-Chateau-Neuf) Pg 165

Cartelet, Pierre (or Louis) (of Perpignan) Pg 231

Carter, John (aka Jules/Julien) Pg 13, 19, 71, 77 (f/n), 120, 220 (f/n), 277, 292, 298-299, 300-304, 369-371, 373-374

Casenave, Robert (of Pau) Pg 120

Castanie, Andree Pg 341

Castelaine, Georges (of Pont l'Eveque) Pg 166

Cauet, Marcel & Marcelle (of Noyon) Pg 349

Cazeneuve, Jean (of Toulouse) Pg 87

Cellarier, Emilie (of Treveneuc) Pg 31, 36

Celton, Mme (of Ergue-Armel) Pg 166

Chaintre, Giselle Pg 7, 355-356

Challemel du Rosiers, M (of Chateau du Petit-Jard) Pg 225, 226

Chandelot, Lea (of Mailly-Champagne) Pg 447

Chanez, Pierre and son Rene (of Gagny) Pg 203

Chanfreau, Rene and daughter Marthe Pg 217

Chapelet, Julien and son Daniel (of Saint-Erme-Outre-et-Ramecourt) Pg 114-115

Chapelle, Dr (of Scaer) Pg 177

Charie, Pierre (of Egry) Pg 331-332

Charise, Suzanne (of Courbevoie) Pg 227

Charles, Marcel (of Vannes) Pg 165

Charmet, Claude Pg 374

Charneau, Marie (of Saint-Quay-Portrieux) Pg 46, 54

Charnier, Pierre Pg 156-160, 162-163, 165, 167, 200 (f/n), 275, 294, 322

Charpentier, Rene (of Fromentieres) Pg 284

Chauvin, Roland (of Bonneval) Pg 411

Chazal, Mme (of Pau) Pg 353, 386

Chede, Mons (of Frieres-Faillouel) Pg 243

Cheminneau, Aaron (of La Roche-sur-Yon) Pg 395

Cheron, Germaine (of Rouen) Pg 294

Cintrat, Jacqueline (of Pau) Pg 343, 353

Claquin, Pierre (of Douarnenez) Pg 279

Clarion, Jean (of Soissy-sous-Montmorency) Pg 392

Claux, Joseph & Marie (of Asnieres-sur-Seine) Pg 420, 423-424

Claverie, Georges (of Pau) Pg 353

Clement, Georges (of Mondrepuis) Pg 31

Cloarec, Gabriel (of Douarnenez) Pg, 260, 279-280

Clotour, M et Mme (of Les Sables d'Olonne) Pg 394

Cochery, Pierre Pg 4

Cochet, Gabriel (of Vic-sur-Aisne) Pg 431

Cochois, Charles (of Verneuil) Pg 427

Coffin, Dr Pierre (of Ault) Pg 132

Cola, Marcel (aka Yvon) Pg 434, 435

Collaine, Mme (of Toulouse) Pg 282

Coltel, Dr Marguerite Pg 98

Copin, Mme Vve (of Marmande) Pg 417

Cornet, Pierre Pg 166

Cornu-Thenard, Pauline Pg 49

Cottereau, Maurice Pg 103 (f/n), 210, 212, 213 (f/n), 226, 277

Coupaisse, Robert & Marguerite (of Tours) Pg 317

Courcel, abbe Jean Pg 100, 111, 193, 323, 399

Courmontagne, Odette (née Sellier) Pg 74

Coussies, Alfred (of Pau) Pg 393

Couve, Maud Pg 32-33, 52, 69, 77, 129, 134, 135, 142 (f/n), 184, 191, 229, 327

Crabbe, Mme Pg 430

Crepin, Lucien (of Montigny-Lengrain) Pg 431

395

Gaultier, Georges & son Robert (of Orgeval) Pg 110

Geniaux, Mons (of Rouen) Pg 74

Gentille, Marie Therese Pg 74

Geoffroy-Dechaume, Marie-France Pg 313, 315, 316 (f/n)

Gerard, Suzanne Pg 29, 57 (f/n)

Gerard, Rene Pg 56-57

Gerard, Mons (of Messac) Pg 288

Gerardot, Marcel & Renee (of Creil) Pg 116, 180

Geslin, Andre (of Saint-Opportune) Pg 143

Gilard, Georges (of Domfront) Pg 143, 226

Gilbert, M et Mme Andre Pg 383, 384

Gilbert, Mary-Rose (of Troyes) Pg 200, 201, 218

Gill, Helene Pg 206 (f/n), 300 (f/n), 302, 370-373

Gillet, Edwige Pg 26

Gimpel, Germaine Pg 77

Girard, Roland Pg 113

Girard, M et Mme Roger (of Livry-Gargan) Pg 249, 253

Goetschel, Fernande Pg 256

Goldvin, Henri (of Pont-sur-Yonne) Pg 444

Goret, Alice and her son Francis Pg 195 (f/n)

Gossart, Emile (of Chauny) Pg 347

Gossiaux, Henri & Louise and daughter Marianne Pg 376

Gouineau, Yvette Pg 98, 99, 100, 101, 195

Gouriou, Mons (of Morgat) Pg 168

Goux, Jacques & Giselle Pg 334, 352, 405

Govin, Erhard & Eliette (of Bourgogne) Pg 421, 425, 427

Grador, Madeleine (aka Colette) Pg 13, 300-304, 369, 372

Gransard, Raymond Pg 67

Grassot, Ulysse & Germaine (of Fontenay-sous-Bois) Pg 179, 181

Gravier, Leon (of Grand-Fougeray) Pg 337

Grecourt, Jean & Frances (of Noyon) Pg 348

Grenier, Marcel (of Rouvrel) Pg 300

Gruz, Felix Pg 207, 218, 220

Guelat, Olivier & Suzanne Pg 38, 46, 51, 200, 218

Guerin, Marcel (of Reims) Pg 421

Gueulette, Charles (aka Felix) Pg 215, 216, 262, 311, 314

Guidet, Abel (of Bapaume) Pg 66, 172, 173

Guillard, Raymond Pg 247, 288

Guillaume, Marie Francoise Pg 63, 70, 79

Guillaume, Albert Pg 77

Guillaume, Jean Pg 101

Guillemin, Georges (aka Gilles) Pg 5, 67 (f/n), 97, 100, 106, 109, 110, 111, 115, 132, 134, 192-194, 195

Guillet, Robert (aka Max) Pg 33, 177, 204, 228

Guillo, Mme (of Josselin) Pg 289

Guillouet, Roger (of Saint-Servan-sur-Mer) Pg 338

Guimard, Emile Pg 219, 220 (f/n), 248, 276, 286, 288-290, 320-321, 338

Guinet, Germaine Pg 431

Guittard, Rene Pg 154, 204, 358 (f/n), 404

Guyon, Marcel & Paulette Pg 424

Hagues, Pauline (of Asnieres-sur-Seine) Pg 138

Hairaux, Germaine Pg 273

Hannigan, Elisabeth (of Poigny-la-Foret) Pg 212

Hart, Renee (of Nevers) Pg 383

Hauchecorne, M et Mme (of Saint-Mande) Pg 193, 400

Hauser, Dr Francois & wife Linette (of Narbonne) Pg 3, 4

Hedin, Gabriel (of Guiscard) Pg 300-301

Helbling, Jeanne Pg 83

Henri, M et Mme Noeillon (of Vraux) Pg 365, 366

Henron, Louis (of Oloron) Pg 343

Henry, Anna (of Vincennes) Pg 324

Hentic, Pierre (aka Trellu/Maho) Pg 103 (f/n), 169 (f/n), 392 (f/n)

Herisse, Auguste (of Chigne) Pg 317

Herment, Jean (of Metz) Pg 207-208

Herring, Charles Pg 339, 384

Herry, Henri (of Chalons) Pg 363

Hilger, Norbert & Simone (of Chevincourt) Pg 347 (f/n), 378 (f/n)

Hollender, Denis (of Chalons) Pg 363

Horn, Emil (of Belfort) Pg 131

Houcke, Jules & Marcel (of Pont-de-Nieppe) Pg 171

Houdet, Mons & son (query) Jacques (of Corbeil-Essonnes) Pg 162

Hucleux, Fernande Pg 109

Huet, Dr Suzanne (of Evreux) Pg 206 (f/n)

Huet, Jeanne Pg 300-302, 305, 369, 370 (f/n), 371-374

Hughet, Rene (of Ambonny) Pg 413-414

Hugon, Pierre Pg 423

Hugonnier, M (of Chantilly) Pg 78 (f/n)

Hure, Robert & Gilberte (of Villethierry) Pg 443

Huyton, Jackie Pg 323

Jacob, Pierre (aka Daniel) Pg 5, 99, 100, 195, 199, 263, 277, 324, 445 (f/n), 450 (f/n), 455

Jacquelin, Louis Pg 234-235, 239

Jagu family (of La Chapelle-Thouartault)

Pg 291

Jagu Antoine (of Rennes) Pg 292 (f/n), 341

Jameson, Liliane Pg 290, 358

Janet, Maurice Pg 74

Janssoone, Lucien & Yvonne (of Caudry) Pg 73

Jauquet, Jeanne (of Soissons) Pg 41

Jean-Jean, Celestin Pg 312

Jolivot, Felix (of Saint-Maur-des-Fosses) Pg 52, 69

Joly, Jean (of Reims) Pg 425

Jones, Mme Jeanne & daughter Helen (of Montfermeil) Pg 253

Josso, Dr Alain (of Aubenton) Pg 41, 177

Jost, Mederic (of Saint-Leu-la-Foret) Pg 148, 150, 151

Jouan, Felix (of Bedee) Pg 291-292, 296

Jouanjean, Georges Pg 28 (f/n), 29, 42, 43, 46 (f/n)

Joubaud, Alex (of Taupont) Pg 219, 247

Jouve, Jeannine (of Livry-Gargan) Pg 235-240, 248, 249

Jouve, Jean (of Livry-Gargan) Pg 235, 249, 252-253, 255

Juillard, Camille (of Livry-Gargan) Pg 249, 253-254

Justeau, Eugene & Maria (of Pipriac) Pg 288, 320

Kahn, Georges (aka Geo) Pg 101, 233, 234-237, 239, 240, 244, 246, 249, 251, 255

Kaiser, Albert Pg 159

Kemsnviz, Mme Albert Pg 177

Kervarec, Desiree (of Douarnenez) Pg 279

Kervevant, Jean-Louis Pg 5, 99, 100, 183-184, 186, 195, 199, 325, 327, 328, 333, 334, 384, 422, 455

Kinn, Robert and son Jeanot (of Ambonnay) Pg 406

Kister, Robert (of Chalons) Pg 363

Klinkers, Marie (of Diepenbeek) Pg 215

Kocera-Massenet, Jeanne Pg 111, 326

Kocera-Massenet, Jean Pg 326 (f/n)

Kocher, Andre (of Courbevoie) Pg 228

Kolman, Maurice (of Gournay-en-Bray) Pg 135

Korach, Bronislaw Pg 425, 427

Kremer, Charles & Celestine (of Liege) Pg 223-224, 269, 310, 313

L'Hoir-Sivry, Olga Pg 30

Lacherez, Maurice Pg 417 (f/n)

Lacour, Jean (of Chantilly) Pg 78 (f/n)

Lacroix, Camille Pg 189

Ladurelle, Camille (of Bouzy) Pg 406, 413

Laghos, M et Mme Haralampos Pg 216-217, 312

Laille, Louis Pg 460

Lajoie, Andre (of Lessons-le-Long) Pg 431

Lajon, Robert (of Saint-Germaine par Saint Savin) Pg 227

Lallot, M et Mme Leon (of Boutencourt) Pg 74

Lalou, Rene Pg 4, 193, 195

Lalou, Etienne Pg 4, 195, 353, 447, 455

Lami, Vassilli & Mariette Pg 351 (f/n)

Lamiraux, Maurice (of Le Mesnil-sur-Oger) Pg 450-451

Lamort, Lucienne (of Le Vesinet) Pg 144

Lamquin, Simone (of Hasselt) Pg 16

Landron, Jean (of Grand-Fougeray) Pg 337

Landroit, Louise Pg 430

Landry, Michel & Renee (of Malesherbes) Pg 331, 332

Lanlo, Jean & Virginia (of Saint-Quay-Portrieux) Pg 36-37, 43, 51

Lanos, Edouard & Clara (of Ouilly-de-Houley) Pg 166

Laporte, Maurice Pg 38

Lapotre, Jean & daughter Francoise (of Thorigny-sur-Oreuse) Pg 24

Lapouge, Gaston Pg 196

Larre-Brieux, Jacques Pg 341

Larromet, Roger & Andree (of Chateau Frouard) Pg 367

Lascombes, Alain Pg 165

Lassialle, Andre (of Livry-Gargan) Pg 237, 244-246

Lassouquere, Julienne Pg 28

Latouquette, Julien (of Billere) Pg 317

Latrace, Yvonne (of Levallois-Perret) Pg 434, 435

Laurencet, Helene Pg 323

Laurent, Marcel (of Douarnenez) Pg 166

Laurentie, Lucienne Pg 11 (f/n), 16

Lauro, Innocente & Betty (of Gouvieux) Pg 389, 390 (f/n)

Lautier, Mons (of Ante) Pg 47-48

Laville, Alice Pg 384

Le Baron, Paul (of Brest) Pg 100, 164, 166, 168, 195, 422

Lebeau, Mme Alphonse (Marie-Louise) (of Concremiers) Pg 328, 332

le Bec, Jean (aka Job) (of Moulin de la Pie) Pg 29, 42

Lebegue, Andree Pg 142, 144, 228, 361

Le Berre, Pierre Pg 5, 259, 353, 358, 382, 384, 391, 406, 414, 419, 426, 455

Le Bigaignon, Louis (of Saint-Brieuc) Pg 339

Leblanc, Jean Gilbert & Marie Louise (of Foix) Pg 64

Leboeuf, Henri (of Clamart) Pg 323, 340

Le Bris, Mlle (of 1 Quai des Fleurs) Pg 306

Marechal, Rene (of Noyon) Pg 348-349

Marechaux, Henri, Emilienne & son Jacques 160, 161, 162, 234

Margage, Louis (of Amiens) Pg 389 (f/n)

Marmousez, Mlle (of Roubaix) Pg 241

Maroger, Pierre Pg 26, Pg 388 (f/n), 460, 463

Marrocq, Joseph Pg 374

Martin, Marie (of Chatelus-Malvaleix) Pg 183

Martin, Pierre (of Montmorrillon) Pg 227

Mary, Martin Pg 196-197

Mme Mary (query) Pg 228, 229

Mascre, Michel (of Saint-Thomas par Corbeny) Pg 420

Masse, M et Mme Georges (of Fontenay-sous-Bois) Pg 68, 108, 130, 177, 179

Massiot, Albert, Clementine and son Robert (of Saint-Ganton) Pg 226

Mathieu, David (of Bouillancourt-en-Sery) Pg 74

Maurcot, Victor (of Les Sables d'Olonne) Pg 394

Maury, Louis & Yvette (of Evreux) Pg 238, 240

May, Dr Michel (of Puiceaux) Pg 331, 332

Maynard family (near Vannes) Pg 160

Mayor, Frederic (of Dole) Pg 356

Mazeline, Andre (of Sainte-Opportune) Pg 143

McCarthy, Elsa Janine Pg 73, 75

McDonnel, Mme Pg 281

Medlicott, Marie (of Bapaume) Pg 67-68

Meha, Yvonne (of Sermaize) Pg 349

Mehudin, Maurice and Marguerite Pg 9

Mehuest, Jean Pg 458 (f/n)

Meilleroux, Leon & Amelie (of Juvisy-sur-Orge) Pg 201, 227 (f/n), 319-320, 333, 351, 357, 391

Mellon, M et Mme (of Soilly) Pg 150 (f/n)

Melot, Madeleine Pg 6-7, 32, 35, 37, 42, 54, 55 (f/n), 62, 69, 98, 101, 103, 104, 110, 115, 117, 133, 136, 137, 143, 145, 174, 176, 181, 184, 191, 192-194, 195, 199, 203, 212, 221, 229, 246, 273, 355 (f/n)

Menou, Joseph (of Chalons) Pg 363

Merel, M & Mme Germaine (of Thiron-Gardais) Pg 283

Merlier, Marcel (of Crisolles) Pg 347 (f/n), 378 (f/n), 379

Merovitz, Reine Pg 27

Merrien, Pierre (of Camaret) Pg 164

Meyer, Maurice (of Billere) Pg 317

Meyer, Charles (of Longueil-Annel) Pg 378

Meyer, Paul (of Longueil-Annel) Pg 378 (f/n)

Mhaeveski, Stanislav (of Montieramey) Pg 201

Michaut, Simone Pg 216, 312

Michaut, Lucienne (of Clamart) Pg 423

Michoux, Maurice (of Les Sables d'Olonne) Pg 394

Mignon, Ellie Pg 142

Milleret, Jean Pg 256

Miquel, Georges (of Les Cabannes) Pg 138

Mistler, Carlos (of Perpignan) Pg 100

Moet, Michele Pg 99, 101, 185, 195, 276, 289, 323, 338, 346, 349-350, 351, 378-379, 391, 399-400

Moet, Gerard & Genevieve (of Saint-Mande) Pg 110, 128, 174, 185, 241, 276, 323, 340, 350-351, 378-379, 399-400

Moeul, Mme Malard (of Saint-Aubin par Plomb) Pg 296

Molin, Simone Pg 143, 144, 204, 327

Montalibet, Dominique & Germaine (of Mauleon-Licharre) 126-127, 343

Montchausse, Raymond (of Orbais l'Abbaye) Pg 284

Moore, Frederick (of Amiens) Pg 403

Moquet, Marie (of Langon) Pg 337

Mora, Roger (of Gondreville) Pg 323-324

Moreau, Pierre (of Saint-Quay-Portrieux) Pg 51 (f/n)

Moreau, Rene & Eva (of Chaumont-en-Vexin) Pg 434 f/n)

Morelle, M et Mme (of Laon) Pg 120

Morin, Georges, Denise & daughter Yvette Pg 34, 69, 70, 102

Morvan, Jean Pg 20

Morvan, Jeanette Pg 20

Mottay, Renee (aka Francoise) (of Rennes) Pg 295-296

Moureau, Julien (of Ploermel) Pg 288

Mourlet, Jacques (of Quimper) Pg 277

Mourot, Andre & Andree (of Livry-Gargan) Pg 235-237, 239, 240, 249, 256

Mourot, Charles & Claire (of Montfermeil) Pg 236, 249, 251

Moy-Thomas, Joan (of Pau) Pg 126-127, 343, 354, 367 (f/n), 397-398, 407

Mueler/Muller, M et Mme (of Amifontaie) Pg 114, 137

Muffat, Jean & brother Roland (of Orvillers-Sorel) Pg 315

Mullot, Marcel (of Troyes – query) Pg 218

Murillo, Father George (of Stanislas College) Pg 22

Nantier, Henriette (of La Vacherie) Pg 68

Nathie, Leo (of Cuffies) Pg 443

Nelle, M et Mme Leon (of Torvilliers) Pg 218

Neville, M et Mme Georges (of Pau) Pg 317

Nicolas, Camille (of Livry-Gargan) Pg 220, 233, 235-237, 239-246, 248-256, 289
Nicolas, Marcel (of Tergnier – query) Pg 350
Niepceron, Jacques Pg 5, 18, 34, 40, 98, 99
Niox, Ghislaine (of Brest) Pg 164, 166-167
Normand, M et Mme Lucien Pg 144, 212
Nouet, Franz (of Rennes) Pg 294
Nouveau, Louis Henri Pg 29, 57 (f/n)

Obner, Professor (of Soissons) Pg 445
Olders, Maurice & Yvonne (of Brussels) Pg 262
Olibo, Jean (of Perpignan) Pg 4, 90, 98-99, 259
Orsini, Colette Pg 104 (f/n), 117
Ouzilleau, Colonel & family (of Anteuil) Pg 113
Owen, Renee (of Saint-Florent-le-Jeune) Pg 91-92

Page, Andre (aka Antonio) Pg 99, 100
Pansart, Roger & family (of Parame) Pg 219, 275, 276, 320, 321, 338
Papoint, Suzanne (of Corbeil-Essonnes) Pg 163
Parant, Georges (of Wattrelos) Pg 189
Pasco, Alphonse (of Brosville) Pg 238-240, 242
Pasque, Simone (of Perpignan) Pg 336
Patenotte, Raymond Pg 22
Paul, Mme (of Colombes) Pg 243
Pauli, Isabelle & daughter Dominique (of Ixelles) Pg 9, 15
Payen, M et Mme Pg 301
Pensec, Mme Alberte (of Douarnenez) Pg 279
Percival, Henri Pg 22
Perez, Francisco (of Andorra la Vieja) Pg 12
Pernot, Hubert, Nicolette & daughter Helene (of Tortoron) Pg 382-383
Peroy, Gaston & son Lucien (of Wicquinghem) Pg 161
Perseval, Georgette pg 55 (f/n), 62
Perus, Estelle (of Bapaume) Pg 66
Pesch, Roger (of Le Blanc) Pg 332, 333
Peschrey, Louise (of Brosville) Pg 240
Pezard, Helene Pg 121
Pfahl, Mme Pg 44
Philippon, Pierre (of Quimper) Pg 164, 167, 169, 280
Philippon, Rene (of Noyon) Pg 348
Picourt, Raymond & Elzevir (of Chartres) Pg 104
Pierrard, Lucille & Madeleine Pg 382
Pierrot, Rene (of Ymonville) Pg 117
Pilard, Edouard (of Andilly) Pg 148

Pillin, Marcel (of Bonnard) Pg 362
Pinel, Paul (of Grandfresnoy) Pg 409
Pinel, Rene (of Grandfresnoy) Pg 409
Piot, Jean Jacques Pg 298
Piton, Robert (of Pau) Pg 316, 353, 394, 395, 407, 414
Place, Michel (of Dampmart) Pg 441, 442
Planquart, Stephanie (of Armentieres) Pg 171-172
Plateur, Felix & Marie (of Les Sables d'Olonne) Pg 394
Ploncard, Charles (aka Michel Lefevre) Pg 99, 100, 128, 129, 131, 195-196, 455
Poincet, Xavier Pg 196-197, 455
Point, Alfred (of Epernay) Pg 284
Poirier, Dr Michel Pg 406-407, 414, 426, 459
Poitier, Lt Paul Pg 83
Pollac, Andre (aka Sherry) Pg 83 (f/n), 84, 119, 125
Pommery, Andre (of Breuil-le-Sec) Pg 136
Ponchon, Edouard (of Beaumont-en-Beine) Pg 355
Pons, M et Mme Gabriel (of Bobigny) Pg 212, 226
Pontremoli, Olga Pg 75
Potty, Dr Claude (of Valenciennes) Pg 204
Pouchet, Dr Auguste (of Ham) Pg 346
Powell, Marthe Pg 244
Pradal, Jean Charles Pg 434, 435
Preux, Marie-Louise (of Morsain) Pg 431-432, 436-438
Prevot, Georges Pg 422, 424, 426, 430, 432, 437-438

Quenot, Theodrine (of Bobigny) Pg 210, 213 (f/n), 277, 283, 284
Quentel, Louis (of Scaer) Pg 337
Quespigne, Robert (of Charleville) Pg 31

Rabache, Georges Pg 110
Radelet, Fernando Pg 9
Raffard, Marcel (of Ervauville) Pg 441
Ramsey, Charles & Jeanne Pg 281
Raoul-Duval, Josette
Raoul-Duval, M et Mme (of Le Vaudreuil) Pg 42
Raquin, Andre & Madeleine (of La Ferte-Alais) Pg 185, 188
Rasquin, Ed (of Les Sables d'Olonne) Pg 394
Rassiniers, Paul (of Belfort) Pg 100, 131
Rault, Albert Pg 34
Raut, Georges Pg 71
Recipon, Andree (of Chateau de Laille) Pg 275, 288, 295
Regeaux, Lucien (of Bailleul) Pg 171